Policies and Practices for Supporting Workers With Intellectual Disabilities

Udeme Samuel Jacob
https://orcid.org/0000-0002-3234-8226
University of South Africa, South Africa

Mbulaheni Maguvhe
University of South Africa, South Africa

Sri Nurhayati
https://orcid.org/0000-0002-2273-9143
IKIP Siliwangi, Indonesia

IGI Global
Scientific Publishing
Publishing Tomorrow's Research Today

Vice President of Editorial Melissa Wagner
Director of Acquisitions Mikaela Felty
Director of Book Development Jocelynn Hessler
Production Manager Mike Brehm
Cover Design Jose Rosado

Published in the United States of America by
IGI Global Scientific Publishing
701 East Chocolate Avenue
Hershey, PA, 17033, USA
Tel: 717-533-8845 | Fax: 717-533-7115
Website: https://www.igi-global.com E-mail: cust@igi-global.com

Library of Congress Cataloging-in-Publication Data

Names: Jacob, Udeme Samuel, 1979- author. | Maguvhe, Mbulaheni Obert author. | Nurhayati, Sri, 1984- author.
Title: Policies and practices for supporting workers with intellectual disabilities / Udeme Samuel Jacob, Mbulaheni Maguvhe, Sri Nurhayati.
Description: Hershey, PA : IGI Global Scientific Publishing, [2027] | Includes bibliographical references and index. | Summary: "This book emerges at a critical juncture in the evolution of work, society, and our collective understanding of human potential. For too long, the narrative surrounding individuals with intellectual disabilities has been one of limitation, defined by what they cannot do rather than illuminated by what they uniquely can. In the workplace, this has translated into systemic exclusion, where a vast reservoir of talent, dedication, and perspective has been overlooked, relegated to the margins of our economy and, by extension, our communities. Policies and Practices for Supporting Workers with Intellectual Disabilities is a direct response to this oversight. It is a pragmatic blueprint, a call to action, and a foundational text designed to transform workplaces by harnessing the power of true inclusion. Our core premise is both simple and profound: creating pathways to meaningful employment for individuals with intellectual disabilities is not merely a charitable act or a compliance obligation; it is a strategic imperative that strengthens businesses, enriches workplaces, and builds a more equitable and productive economy. This belief is the thread that runs through every chapter of this book. We move beyond theoretical advocacy to provide the concrete "how-to" that has been missing. We bridge the gap between well-intentioned policy and effective, sustainable practice, recognising that intention without implementation is meaningless"-- Provided by publisher.
Identifiers: LCCN 2026020548 (print) | LCCN 2026020549 (ebook) | ISBN 9798337391854 hardcover | ISBN 9798337391861 paperback | ISBN 9798337391878 ebook
Subjects: LCSH: People with mental disabilities--Employment. | People with mental disabilities--Services for. | Diversity in the workplace.
Classification: LCC HV3005 .J33 2026 (print) | LCC HV3005 (ebook)
LC record available at https://lccn.loc.gov/2026020548
LC ebook record available at https://lccn.loc.gov/2026020549

British Cataloguing in Publication Data
A Cataloguing in Publication record for this book is available from the British Library.

Table of Contents

Preface

FROM MARGINALISATION TO MEANINGFUL CONTRIBUTION: BUILDING AN INCLUSIVE FUTURE OF WORK

This book emerges at a critical juncture in the evolution of work, society, and our collective understanding of human potential. For too long, the narrative surrounding individuals with intellectual disabilities has been one of limitation, defined by what they cannot do rather than illuminated by what they uniquely can. In the workplace, this has translated into systemic exclusion, where a vast reservoir of talent, dedication, and perspective has been overlooked, relegated to the margins of our economy and, by extension, our communities. *Policies and Practices for Supporting Workers with Intellectual Disabilities* is a direct response to this oversight. It is a pragmatic blueprint, a call to action, and a foundational text designed to transform workplaces by harnessing the power of true inclusion.

Our core premise is both simple and profound: creating pathways to meaningful employment for individuals with intellectual disabilities is not merely a charitable act or a compliance obligation; it is a strategic imperative that strengthens businesses, enriches workplaces, and builds a more equitable and productive economy. This belief is the thread that runs through every chapter of this book. We move beyond theoretical advocacy to provide the concrete "how-to" that has been missing. We bridge the gap between well-intentioned policy and effective, sustainable practice, recognising that intention without implementation is meaningless.

WHERE OUR TOPIC FITS IN THE WORLD TODAY

The landscape of work is undergoing a seismic transformation. We face acute talent shortages, a reevaluation of corporate purpose, and a growing demand from consumers and employees alike for businesses to demonstrate authentic social responsibility. Simultaneously, the disability rights movement, powerfully championed by self-advocates, has cemented a new paradigm: "Nothing About Us Without Us." This principle demands that inclusion be made *with* individuals with disabilities, not *for* them. Our topic sits squarely at the convergence of these powerful trends.

Today, supporting workers with intellectual disabilities is no longer a niche consideration but a mainstream component of smart business strategy and ethical leadership. Landmark legislation, such as the Americans with Disabilities Act, laid the legal groundwork, but contemporary frameworks, including the United Nations Convention on the Rights of Persons with Disabilities and the Sustainable Development Goals (specifically, Goal 8: Decent Work for All), have elevated inclusion to a global priority. Furthermore, the growing embrace of Diversity, Equity, and Inclusion (DEI) initiatives has created an opening demand for expertise on how to operationalise these principles for the neurodiverse workforce, which includes individuals with intellectual disabilities.

Although a persistent gap remains between this evolving context and on-the-ground reality. Employers often express willingness but cite a lack of knowledge or fear of complexity. Service providers navigate fragmented systems. Families and individuals confront the daunting "benefits cliff" and low societal expectations. This book is designed to close that gap. It provides the missing manual, translating rights into routines, obligations into opportunities, and support needs into strategic successes.

A GUIDE TO ARCHITECTS OF INCLUSION

We have written this book with a collaborative ecosystem of change-makers in mind, recognising that no single actor can build an inclusive workplace alone.

- **To Human Resource Managers, Employers, and Business Owners:** This is your playbook. We address your core concerns: risk, ROI, and operational integration. You will find strategies to tap into a loyal and motivated talent pool, reduce turnover costs, and foster a more innovative and cohesive company culture. The chapters on recruitment, job customisation, supervision, and the step-by-step implementation framework are designed for direct application in your organisation.
- **To Job Coaches and Vocational Rehabilitation Specialists:** You are the essential bridges between talent and opportunity. This book aims to be a resource that deepens your practice, offering frameworks for effective job analysis, training using Universal Design for Learning principles, and fostering natural supports. It also provides the broader context of policy and business

strategy, empowering you to be more effective partners and advocates within the organisations you support.

- **To Policymakers and Government Officials:** Effective policy is informed by practical reality. We provide an analysis of how existing laws function in practice and identify areas where policy can be strengthened to better incentivise hiring, streamline support, and promote economic self-sufficiency. Our hope is that the evidence and models presented here inform more effective and collaborative public-private partnerships.
- **To Disability Advocates and Organisations:** This book arms you with the data, case studies, and practical arguments needed to advance your mission. It validates your lived experience and professional expertise, providing a comprehensive resource to cite in your work to educate employers, shape policy, and empower individuals and families.
- **To Educators and Researchers:** We offer a synthesised, interdisciplinary framework that connects special education, vocational rehabilitation, business management, and disability studies. This book outlines a robust agenda for applied research, highlighting where further study on outcomes, effective interventions, and systemic barriers is critically needed.

The journey we outline is not about lowering standards, but about rethinking processes. It is about building workplaces where success is accessible to all, where communication is clear, and where every employee has the tools and support they need to contribute their best. The stories of success are already there in the employee whose meticulous attention to detail ensures flawless inventory, in the greeter whose authentic warmth defines a company's customer experience, and in the packaging specialist whose reliability is the linchpin of a production line.

This book is an invitation to multiply those stories. It is a testament to the belief that a truly inclusive workplace is not just a more moral one, but a more robust, creative, and resilient one. We appreciate your involvement in this project. By turning these pages and applying their lessons, you become an active architect of a future where the world of work truly works for everyone.

A GUIDE FOR ARCHITECTS OF INCLUSION: ENGAGING OUR TARGET AUDIENCE

This book is intentionally crafted not as a monolithic academic text, but as a collaborative toolkit for the interconnected ecosystem of professionals who, together, build inclusive pathways to employment. We address each key stakeholder with respect for their unique role and challenges, providing relevant insights to catalyse coordinated action.

- **Human Resource Managers, Employers, and Business Owners:** You are the ultimate gatekeepers of opportunity and the stewards of organisational culture. This book addresses your operational and strategic imperatives directly. We translate the principles of inclusion into actionable HR processes—from recruitment and onboarding to performance management and retention. The frameworks provided here are designed to mitigate perceived risk, demonstrate clear return on investment, and integrate seamlessly with your existing talent management systems, empowering you to lead with both competence and compassion.
- **Job Coaches and Vocational Rehabilitation Specialists:** You are the essential engineers on the ground, turning possibility into practice. This book serves as both a validation and an extension of your critical expertise. It offers advanced strategies for task analysis, fostering natural support, and navigating complex workplace dynamics. Furthermore, it provides a broader business and policy context, equipping you to communicate more effectively with employer partners and advocate more powerfully for the individuals you serve, moving from a model of support to one of strategic partnership.
- **Policymakers and Government Officials:** You create the scaffolding within which inclusion either flourishes or falters. For you, this book provides a ground-level view of how policies are implemented in practice. It highlights where legislation, such as the Workforce Innovation and Opportunity Act (WIOA), catalyses success and where regulatory complexities create unintended barriers. Our analysis aims to inform more effective, streamlined, and incentive-based policies that promote public-private collaboration and move beyond compliance toward genuine economic participation.
- **Disability Advocates and Organisations (including Self-Advocates):** You are the conscience and the driving force of this movement. This book serves as a resource to strengthen your advocacy with evidence, case studies, and practical business logic. It articulates the "why" in the language of boardrooms and legislative chambers, providing you with powerful tools to challenge stereotypes, negotiate for better services, and demand equitable treatment. It centres on the principle of "nothing about us without us" by providing a common reference point for collaborative dialogue.
- **Educators and Researchers:** You are the builders of foundational knowledge and the assessors of impact. This book provides a synthesised, interdisciplinary framework spanning disability studies, vocational rehabilitation, organisational psychology, and business ethics. It identifies critical gaps in

literature, particularly regarding long-term career advancement, the economics of inclusion, and the efficacy of specific interventions, thereby charting a course for future applied research that can deepen and expand the field's evidence base.

THE ARCHITECTURAL BLUEPRINT: IMPORTANCE OF EACH CHAPTER

The following 16 chapters form a cohesive architectural blueprint, each a critical load-bearing wall in the structure of inclusive employment.

Part I: Foundations and Frameworks

1. **Redefining Ability: The Business Case for Inclusion** establishes the entire project's credibility. It moves the conversation from altruism to strategy, providing readers with empirical evidence and persuasive arguments to secure organisational buy-in, making inclusion a priority rather than an afterthought.
2. **Understanding Intellectual Disability: Spectrum, Strengths, and Support Needs** is the essential vocabulary lesson. It dispels clinical abstraction and fosters a human-centred, strengths-based understanding, ensuring all subsequent practices are built on a foundation of respect for neurodiversity and individual potential.
3. **The Legal Landscape: Rights, Obligations, and Incentives** provide the rulebook and the playbook. It demystifies complex legislation, empowering employers to confidently meet their obligations while proactively leveraging available incentives, thereby transforming legal compliance from a source of fear into a framework for action.
4. **Ethical Foundations: Dignity, Autonomy, and the Right to Work** grounds the entire endeavour in moral conviction. This chapter ensures that our pursuit of efficiency and profit remains anchored in the inviolable principles of human dignity and self-determination, serving as a crucial touchstone when practical challenges arise.

Part II: The Employment Pathway

5. **Inclusive Recruitment and Accessible Hiring** dismantles the first and most common barrier. It provides concrete tools to widen the talent pipeline, ensuring that capable individuals are not filtered out by archaic, inaccessible processes before they even have a chance to demonstrate their abilities.

6. **Job Analysis, Customisation, and Competitive Integrated Employment** is the heart of sustainable inclusion. It offers a methodology for aligning business needs with human talent, proving that valued roles can be crafted or adapted, which is fundamental to achieving the core goal of competitive, integrated employment.
7. **Onboarding for Success: Structured Support from Day One** addresses the critical transition where many well-intentioned hires falter. This chapter ensures the first days and weeks build confidence and competence, setting a trajectory for long-term retention and success.

Part III: Sustaining Success in the Workplace

8. **The Art of Effective Training: Universal Design for Learning at Work** equips managers and coaches with proven pedagogical tools. It shifts training from a one-size-fits-all lecture to a customizable process, ensuring every employee can acquire the skills needed to excel in their role.
9. **Natural Supports and the Role of Co-Workers as Allies** tackles the social ecosystem of work. This chapter provides a blueprint for creating an organically supportive culture, reducing dependency on formal coaching and fostering a sense of belonging that benefits the entire team.
10. **Supervision Reimagined: Communication, Feedback, and Growth** transforms management from a top-down directive to a collaborative partnership. It provides specific techniques for clear, growth-oriented communication, which is essential for employee development, engagement, and performance management.
11. **Reasonable Accommodations and Assistive Technology in Action** demystifies an often-intimidating concept. By presenting accommodations as a standard tool of talent optimisation akin to providing a computer, this chapter encourages proactive and creative problem-solving to unlock employee potential.

Part IV: The Supporting Ecosystem

12. **The Vital Role of Vocational Rehabilitation and Employment Services** maps the external support network. It teaches employers how to effectively partner with these agencies and guides providers on how to better align their services with business needs, ensuring these partnerships are seamless and productive.
13. **Families, Guardians, and Self-Advocates:** Partners in Employment navigates a sensitive but crucial relationship. It provides a framework for respectful, appropriate collaboration that honours the employee's autonomy while leveraging family insight, a balance critical for holistic support.

14. **Financial Literacy and Benefits Navigation** confronts one of the most pernicious systemic barriers to economic advancement. This chapter provides essential knowledge for navigating complex benefit systems, empowering individuals to pursue career growth without fear of incurring catastrophic financial loss.

Part V: Systemic and Sectoral Approaches

15. **Implementing Inclusion: A Step-by-Step Framework for Organisations** is the strategic culmination. It synthesises the preceding chapters into a master plan, offering leaders a clear, phased process to assess, plan, execute, and sustain a comprehensive inclusion initiative, moving from ad-hoc practices to embedded organisational change.

CONCLUSION: OUR CONTRIBUTION TO THE FIELD

Policies and Practices for Supporting Workers with Intellectual Disabilities aims to make a definitive and multifaceted contribution to the field. First, it **synthesises and translates** knowledge from disparate domains law, business, education, rehabilitation, and disability studies into a single, coherent, and actionable guide. It breaks down silos, providing a common language and framework for the entire ecosystem of stakeholders to collaborate effectively.

Second, it **shifts the paradigm from theory to implementation**. While much literature eloquently argues *why* inclusion is needed, this book provides the details of *how*. It is designed to live not only on bookshelves but on the desks of HR professionals, in the meeting rooms of managers, and in the toolkits of job coaches, bearing the coffee stains and notes that mark a frequently used resource.

Finally, this book seeks to **reframe the narrative** from one of charity and compliance to one of talent, strategy, and mutual benefit. It contributes to the subject matter by asserting that supporting workers with intellectual disabilities is a hallmark of sophisticated, forward-thinking, and resilient business practice and social policy. Our ultimate impact will be measured not in citations alone, but in the proliferation of inclusive workplaces, the advancement of supportive policies, and the expanded life opportunities for individuals who, given the right environment and support, are fully prepared to contribute, excel, and redefine what is possible in the world of work. This book is our invitation to you to join in that essential work.

The Authors

Introduction

The pursuit of talent, dedication, and innovation fundamentally shapes the modern workplace. Despite this, a significant segment of the potential workforce remains systematically overlooked. This exclusion stems not from a lack of ability but from a persistent deficit of understanding, accessible pathways, and actionable frameworks. Individuals with intellectual disabilities constitute this vast and underutilised reservoir of talent. Although societal attitudes have evolved from institutionalisation toward inclusion, a profound chasm persists between the promise of equitable employment and the daily reality for millions of job seekers and organisations that could benefit from their skills. We designed this book, Policies and Practices for Supporting Workers with Intellectual Disabilities, to serve as the definitive bridge across that divide.

The challenge we address represents both a pressing economic issue and a profound social imperative. Employers confront persistent talent shortages while striving to build resilient and innovative teams and to meet calls for authentic corporate social responsibility. At the same time, adults with intellectual disabilities have much higher rates of unemployment and underemployment than the general population. This circumstance does not reflect an inherent lack of capacity to contribute. Rather, it reveals that traditional hiring practices, workplace structures, and management styles frequently fail to align with their strengths. Between these two realities lies a landscape of well-intentioned but fragmented policies, under-resourced support systems, and a self-perpetuating cycle of low expectations that stifles human potential.

This book originates from a straightforward, evidence-based conviction: this gap signifies a solvable problem, not an intractable one. Effective solutions require a rethinking of processes, not a lowering of standards. They demand authentic collaboration, not charitable sympathy. Our purpose is to move beyond establishing why inclusion is necessary, a case already solidly grounded in law, ethics, and business logic, to providing the crucial knowledge of how to achieve it. We aim to demystify the process, transforming what may appear to be a complex and specialised endeavour into a structured, manageable, and rewarding component of standard professional practice.

The architecture of this book follows a deliberate journey from conceptual foundation to practical implementation. We begin by establishing core frameworks, articulating the compelling business case and clarifying the governing legal and ethical foundations. The text then proceeds systematically through the employment pathway, commencing with the first touchpoint of accessible recruitment and advancing to the crafting of roles that align individual strengths with organisational needs. The central portion focuses on sustaining success, offering proven strategies for training, supervision, fostering natural support, and implementing accommodations that foster independence and growth. Recognising that no employer operates in isolation, we provide essential guidance on engaging the broader ecosystem, including vocational rehabilitation specialists, job coaches, and family networks. Finally, we expand the perspective to present a strategic implementation framework for organisations and a forward-looking analysis of technology and policy.

Our approach is relentlessly practical. Each chapter is designed to furnish concrete tools, adaptable checklists, and applicable models. We draw upon the latest research, illustrative case studies, and the collective wisdom of practitioners, advocates, and self-advocates who have pioneered this work. While informed by theory, this is fundamentally a book of practice.

This introduction serves as your entry point to a reconceived vision of the workplace. It is a vision where the principle of "nothing about us without us" is realised through meaningful partnership, where a focus on ability reframes disability, and where appropriate supports unlock productivity and pride for both employees and employers. Whether you are a human resources leader developing a sustainable talent strategy, a job coach refining support techniques, a policymaker shaping effective programs, or an advocate demanding change, the pages that follow are intended to equip, inspire, and challenge you.

The task of building genuinely inclusive workplaces constitutes both professional responsibility and a historic opportunity. It is a necessary step toward a more equitable economy and a more just society. Let us begin the work.

Chapter 1
Redefining Ability:
The Business Case for Inclusion

ABSTRACT

This chapter examines how workers with intellectual disabilities continue to be excluded from employment through narrow assumptions about competence, productivity, and independence. It argues for a shift from deficit-based thinking to a contextual and relational understanding of ability, showing that work performance is shaped by job design, support, communication, and workplace culture. The chapter explores historical constructions of disability in labour markets, key theoretical frameworks for redefining ability, and the ethical, legal, and economic reasons inclusion matters. It also addresses common organisational myths and outlines the conditions required for an inclusive employment culture. The chapter concludes that employing workers with intellectual disabilities is both a matter of justice and a sound organisational strategy.

1.1 INTRODUCTION

Across many labour markets, workers with intellectual disabilities continue to be excluded from meaningful employment, not because they lack the capacity to contribute, but because organisations often remain structured around narrow and outdated assumptions about competence, speed, communication, and productivity. For too long, disability in the workplace has been interpreted through a deficit lens that emphasises what people cannot do rather than the strengths, supports, and environmental adjustments that enable them to thrive. This chapter begins from a different premise. It argues that employing workers with intellectual disabilities is both a matter of social justice and a sound organisational strategy. In this sense, inclusion is not a charitable concession extended to a marginalised group. It is a deliberate, sustainable, and evidence-informed workplace practice that expands op-

DOI: 10.4018/979-8-3373-9185-4.ch001

portunities, strengthens organisations, and affirms the dignity and rights of workers with intellectual disabilities.

Employment occupies a central place in adult life. It shapes economic security, social participation, identity, self-worth, and a sense of belonging to a community. For individuals with intellectual disabilities, access to employment can support autonomy, improve quality of life, and foster social inclusion beyond the workplace. Research has shown that workers with intellectual disabilities often view employment not only as a source of income, but also as a pathway to purpose, recognition, and interpersonal connection (Pereira-Silva et al., 2018). Workplace participation can therefore serve as a vital mechanism for personal development and broader citizenship, especially when workers are supported in ways that respect their agency and preferences. From this standpoint, exclusion from employment is not simply an economic issue. It is a denial of full participation in one of the most socially valued domains of adult life.

The social justice case for inclusive employment is closely tied to a rights-based understanding of disability. Contemporary disability scholarship and international policy frameworks increasingly affirm that persons with intellectual disabilities have the right to work on an equal basis with others, in environments that are open, inclusive, accessible, and supportive. Yet legal recognition alone does not guarantee participation. Workers with intellectual disabilities still face substantial barriers in recruitment, job matching, workplace relationships, advancement, and retention. These barriers are frequently rooted in low employer expectations, inaccessible employment systems, and the persistence of stereotypes that equate intellectual disability with incompetence or dependency. Employers may assume that workers with intellectual disabilities will be less productive, require excessive supervision, or struggle to integrate into organisational culture. Such assumptions continue to limit opportunities even where evidence suggests that many of these concerns are exaggerated, misinformed, or based on a poor understanding of support needs (Lysaght et al., 2012).

To redefine ability, therefore, is to question the very standards by which organisations judge who is employable and who is not. Ability is not a fixed and purely individual trait. It is shaped by the interaction between a worker's strengths and the workplace's design. When work tasks are clearly structured, support is available, supervisors are responsive, and co-workers act as allies, workers with intellectual disabilities can perform successfully and contribute meaningfully to organisational life. Recent studies have emphasised that inclusive workplaces are often characterised by flexibility, cognitive diversity, collaborative cultures, and a willingness to recognise diverse forms of competence rather than privileging a single performance norm (Sigstad et al., 2025; Joyce et al., 2025). In this sense, the problem is not disability alone. It is frequently the failure of institutions to imagine, design, and support inclusive work.

This shift from a deficit-based to an asset-based perspective is crucial. Asset-based thinking recognises that workers with intellectual disabilities bring valuable qualities to the workplace, including reliability, commitment, consistency, honesty, and task focus. These strengths are often overlooked because traditional employment systems tend to privilege conventional credentials, rapid communication, or narrow ideas of independence. However, evidence from supported and competitive employment contexts shows that, with appropriate natural support, coaching, and inclusive supervision, workers with intellectual disabilities can experience high levels of job satisfaction and workplace participation, while employers benefit from stronger team cultures and improved staff engagement (Akkerman et al., 2018). Asset-based thinking does not romanticise disability or ignore support needs. Rather, it acknowledges that contribution is relational and context dependent, and that workplaces can be designed to bring out the best in a wider range of employees.

Alongside the social justice argument, there is also a compelling business case for inclusion. Organisations are increasingly expected to demonstrate responsible employment practices, align with diversity and inclusion goals, and respond to broader calls for equitable participation in the workforce. Employers who hire workers with intellectual disabilities may strengthen their corporate social responsibility profile, improve public reputation, and signal commitment to fairness and community engagement (Dean et al., 2022). Beyond reputational gains, inclusive employment can positively influence workplace culture by promoting empathy, team cohesion, and respect for difference. Studies have also indicated that customers often respond positively to inclusive service environments, and such visibility may enhance trust and loyalty when organisations are perceived as genuinely committed to social inclusion (Osorio & del Castillo, 2025). Inclusion, then, should not be viewed as an external obligation detached from organisational priorities. It is increasingly part of what defines sustainable and socially responsive business practice.

Importantly, the business case should not be framed in opposition to the rights-based case, as though workers with intellectual disabilities must prove their worth in purely economic terms before they are granted access to employment. Rather, the two perspectives are mutually reinforcing. A just workplace is often a stronger workplace. Organisations that learn to recruit, support, and retain workers with intellectual disabilities frequently become more adaptable, humane, and effective overall. Inclusive practices such as clearer communication, structured onboarding, task redesign, mentoring, and supportive supervision tend to improve work environments not only for employees with disabilities but for all staff. Thus, disability inclusion can function as a catalyst for broader organisational improvement.

This chapter sets the foundation for the rest of the book by advancing a central argument: workers with intellectual disabilities, particularly those whose functional abilities permit participation in vocational and employment activities, should be understood not as burdens to be managed, but as contributors whose participation can enrich organisations and challenge conventional ideas of workplace value. Although the nature and extent of workplace participation vary across mild, moderate, severe, and profound levels of intellectual disability, meaningful contributions can be made when workplace expectations align with individual abilities and appropriate supports are provided.

1.2 UNDERSTANDING INTELLECTUAL DISABILITY IN EMPLOYMENT CONTEXTS

In workplace settings, the central issue is how cognitive and adaptive differences interact with job design, communication patterns, supervision, and organisational culture. Many barriers arise not from impairment alone but from the mismatch between worker needs and workplace arrangements (Ellenkamp et al., 2016; Dearing, 2020). A worker with an intellectual disability may perform well in one organisation and struggle in another because the demands, support, and expectations are different.

In practical terms, intellectual disability may affect learning pace, memory, problem-solving, communication, abstract reasoning, and adaptive functioning. At work, these differences can influence how quickly a person understands instructions, adjusts to new routines, manages multi-step tasks, interprets social expectations, or responds to change. These features should not be treated as proof of inability. Instead, they point to the need for appropriate support. Employment outcomes improve when workplace supports match individual needs (Readhead & Owen, 2020), and vocational preparation can strengthen participation and work performance (Gomes-Machado et al., 2016). Clear instruction, repetition, visual guidance, structured routines, and extra time to learn can make a substantial difference.

A workplace-relevant view of intellectual disability begins with the idea that employment is relational. Performance depends not only on the worker but also on how work is organised. Problems often emerge when employers assume that all staff members learn in the same way, communicate similarly, and adapt at the same pace. Such assumptions create barriers that remain hidden until a worker is judged against them. Complex verbal instructions, inconsistent routines, and vague expectations may disadvantage workers with intellectual disabilities, even when they are fully capable of completing the essential duties of the role. The issue, therefore, often lies in workplace design rather than in the person alone.

Several practical issues shape how intellectual disability is experienced at work:

1. **Task structure matters:** Workers with intellectual disabilities often do well when tasks are clearly defined, sequenced, and consistently reinforced. Structured work reduces ambiguity and builds confidence.
2. **Learning style matters:** Demonstration, repetition, modelling, shadowing, and hands-on practice are often more effective than one-time verbal explanations.
3. **Routine matters:** Predictable schedules and stable processes can reduce anxiety and support successful task completion.
4. **Support matters:** Access to co-worker assistance, patient supervision, and job coaching strengthens both performance and retention.
5. **Belonging matters:** Workers are more likely to thrive when they are respected, included, and recognised as legitimate members of the team (Fillary & Pernice, 2006).

These factors show that intellectual disability should not be understood only as an individual condition. It is also a workplace issue because organisational systems can either reduce barriers or intensify them. Workplace structures and culture strongly influence the well-being of people with intellectual disability (Joyce et al., 2024). A supportive environment treats difference as a cue for adaptation, whereas an unsupportive one treats it as evidence of failure.

Job expectations are especially important in this regard. Many organisations still define a good worker through narrow standards such as speed, multitasking, rapid communication, independent problem-solving, and instant adaptation to change. These expectations may exclude workers with intellectual disabilities even when the essential duties of the job can be completed successfully with small adjustments. Reframing expectations requires employers to distinguish between what is truly essential and what reflects routine practice or bias. Environments that embrace cognitive diversity enable workers to contribute their strengths, including consistency, reliability, attention to routine, and commitment (Sigstad et al., 2025). Roles can therefore be designed or modified to draw on these strengths.

Communication is another major consideration. Many workplaces depend on rapid, layered, and sometimes ambiguous communication. Instructions may be informal, policies may be difficult to read, and expectations may rest on unwritten rules. For workers with intellectual disabilities, such systems can create confusion and increase the likelihood of mistakes that are then interpreted unfairly. In inclusive workplaces, communication is more likely to be:

- clear and direct
- supported by visual or written prompts
- repeated when necessary, without stigma
- broken into manageable steps

- checked for understanding rather than assumed

These approaches are not exceptional accommodations. They are sound management practices that improve clarity for all workers. Communication, supervision, and guidance influence whether paid work is obtained and maintained (Ellenkamp et al., 2016).

Organisational culture also shapes employment outcomes. A workplace may be physically accessible and still remain socially excluding if supervisors hold low expectations, co-workers are dismissive, or disability is treated as a burden. By contrast, workers with intellectual disabilities are more likely to succeed where respect, patience, collaboration, and inclusion guide everyday interactions. Culture affects whether workers feel safe asking questions, whether mistakes are treated as learning opportunities, and whether support is offered constructively. Workplace participation is linked to job satisfaction (Akkerman et al., 2018), and competence, autonomy, and relatedness are important to well-being (Fajardo-Castro et al., 2024). Inclusive workplace conditions are associated with stronger well-being and greater job satisfaction among employees with intellectual disability (Joyce et al., 2025).

This understanding has several implications for employers:

i. Inclusive recruitment is insufficient if the workplace culture remains exclusive
ii. Productivity must be judged in context rather than through stereotypes
iii. Support should be treated as part of effective supervision
iv. Co-worker attitudes can strengthen or weaken retention (Kumar et al., 2019)
v. inclusion depends on systems and practices, not goodwill alone

A practical understanding of intellectual disability in employment requires considering both adaptive and environmental factors. Some workers may need more time to learn, more explicit communication, or more stable support, but these needs do not diminish their status as workers. Many organisations overlook the potential of workers with intellectual disabilities; however, workplaces already accommodate differences through training and support.

Attention must also be given to transitions into work and the maintenance of employment. Difficulties may arise during induction, due to changes in supervision, workplace restructuring, or the assumption of unfamiliar responsibilities. Employment is more likely to be sustained when organisations plan ahead, communicate clearly, and respond early to emerging challenges. Peer mentoring, routine feedback, and coordinated support systems can therefore reduce preventable job loss.

Workers with intellectual disabilities are shaped not only by cognitive difference but also by whether workplaces communicate clearly, organise tasks effectively, build respectful relationships, and value more than one form of competence. The question is not simply whether workers can fit existing workplaces. The more important question is whether workplaces are willing to become places where different workers can succeed.

1.3 HISTORICAL AND SOCIAL CONSTRUCTION OF DISABILITY IN THE WORKPLACE

Across much of modern labour history, workers with intellectual disabilities were pushed to the margins of economic life. Their exclusion reflected not only impairment but also social beliefs about worth, dependence, normality, and productivity. In many countries, labour systems assumed they could not meet the demands of paid work and therefore placed them outside mainstream employment. British labour categories attached moral and economic judgements to perceived slowness, reinforcing the idea that some workers were less valuable (Delap, 2024). This framing legitimised exclusion and segregation. People with intellectual disabilities were often directed into institutions, welfare systems, or restricted occupational roles. Where work existed, it was treated less as a right than as an occupation, a discipline, or a form of care. Swedish vocational initiatives often positioned them as socially useful only within tightly controlled systems, preserving ableist assumptions rather than transforming labour markets for inclusion (Barow, 2025).

Sheltered workshops emerged from this tradition and became one of the most influential employment models associated with intellectual disability. These settings were presented as protective, therapeutic, or transitional, but they often reproduced segregation and restricted mobility. Historically, sheltered and parallel employment models offered few pathways into open labour markets, even when framed as supportive alternatives (Babikian & Hamdani, 2023). Workers were often paid below-standard wages, assigned repetitive, low-status tasks, and denied the standing associated with ordinary employment. Expectations within disability employment systems became disconnected from aspirations for autonomy, progression, and equal participation (Bigby et al., 2011). What appeared to be support often functioned as containment.

Several assumptions sustained these models:

- People with intellectual disabilities were viewed as permanently dependent
- Productivity was judged through narrow norms that excluded diverse forms of competence
- Employers were assumed to bear excessive risk if they hired disabled workers
- Segregation was framed as protection rather than exclusion
- Support was treated as incompatible with ordinary employment

These assumptions shaped policy, training systems, and employer decision-making. They also normalised the belief that disability belonged outside the competitive economy. In relation to American disability policy, legal and welfare frameworks sometimes produced contradictory outcomes by promoting inclusion rhetorically while preserving labour market marginality (Ruppel, 2025). Policies intended to protect disabled citizens could therefore coexist with arrangements that kept them in precarious or secondary labour positions.

A gradual shift emerged as disability activism, rights-based advocacy, and changing social policy challenged these models. The movement away from charity and custodial care toward citizenship and participation reframed the debate. Instead of asking whether people with intellectual disabilities were fit for work, attention increasingly turned to whether labour markets were themselves exclusionary. Inclusion, when examined through lived experience, is not secured by policy language alone (Meneley et al., 2021). What matters is whether people can enter, remain in, and shape ordinary working environments. Formal access by itself does not dismantle inherited inequalities.

In recent decades, inclusive employment approaches have gained greater visibility. Supported employment, supported internships, customised employment, and social enterprise models have emerged as alternatives to segregated work. Supported internships are important vocational bridges that strengthen labour inclusion for students with intellectual and developmental disabilities (Folguera Bellmunt, 2026). These approaches differ from older sheltered models by emphasising participation in ordinary work settings, skill development, and long-term integration. Moving from exclusion to inclusion requires more than relocation from one setting to another (Lysaght et al., 2024). It requires rethinking assumptions, support, and workplace expectations.

The legacy of earlier constructions, however, remains strong. Contemporary hiring patterns are still shaped by stereotypes about productivity, dependence, and capability. Employers may assume that workers with intellectual disabilities will be slower, less reliable, or too costly to support. Employer hesitation often reflects concerns about work competence and social functioning rather than direct knowledge of actual performance (Mihić & Kiš-Glavaš, 2010). Recruitment and retention barriers are rooted in employers' perceptions of costs, risks, and adjustment burdens (Jupille et al., 2025). These judgements reflect long-standing cultural narratives that equate disability with deficiency. Such stereotypes shape workplaces in several ways:

1. They narrow who is considered employable before recruitment begins
2. They justify restrictive job matching and limited advancement opportunities
3. They reinforce low expectations among supervisors and co-workers
4. They shape policies that prioritise conformity over flexibility

5. They make support appear exceptional rather than routine

Exclusion, in this sense, is socially produced. Barriers to obtaining and maintaining open employment in Australia are often tied to structural conditions and employer responses rather than to disability alone (Meltzer et al., 2020). Employer decisions about inclusive hiring are strongly influenced by organisational attitudes, knowledge, and willingness to adapt (Nagtegaal et al., 2025). The issue is not simply access to jobs, but access to workplaces prepared to recognise more than one form of competence.

Public attitudes play an important role in sustaining or challenging exclusion. Support for the employment of people with intellectual disabilities often coexists with doubts about competence and workplace integration (Burge et al., 2007). This ambivalence matters because labour markets reflect broader social values. Where disability is associated with dependence, workers are more likely to be confined to marginal roles. At the same time, attitudes can shift through meaningful contact and shared experience, indicating that stereotypes are socially learned rather than fixed (Huber & Pochstein, 2025).

At the workplace level, stigma remains one of the clearest expressions of this legacy. Stigma toward employees with intellectual disabilities continues to shape perceptions of competence and belonging (Gormley, 2015). These patterns carry both visible and hidden costs, including identity threat, emotional strain, and restricted participation (Van Laar et al., 2019). Drawing on intergroup contact theory, prejudice can be reduced when workplace contact is structured, meaningful, and supported (Novak et al., 2011).

Progress toward inclusion has therefore been uneven. Even where rights-based frameworks exist, major barriers remain, including negative social attitudes and structural constraints (Rachanioti et al., 2021). Employers' willingness to hire is shaped by prior exposure, assumptions, and confidence in available support systems (Milanović-Dobrota et al., 2025). Inclusion is strongest when policy commitment is matched with practical hiring and retention strategies (Strauser et al., 2026).

This history changes how barriers are interpreted. Workers with intellectual disabilities associate inclusion with recognition, participation, and respect (Pereira-Silva et al., 2018). The implication is clear: exclusion is not inevitable. Labour markets have actively shaped disability through labels, stereotypes, institutions, and policy choices, and a more inclusive future depends on reshaping those structures.

1.4 THEORETICAL PERSPECTIVES FOR REDEFINING ABILITY

Inclusive employment depends not only on goodwill but also on the conceptual frameworks that shape how disability, competence, and workplace adaptation are understood. When employers rely on narrow assumptions about normal productivity, independence, or communication style, they often assess workers with intellectual disabilities against standards that ignore context. Theoretical perspectives challenge this pattern by showing that ability is shaped not only by individual characteristics but also by workplace structures, social arrangements, legal protections, and opportunities for participation. Redefining ability, therefore, requires movement away from impairment-centred interpretations of work performance toward contextual and relational understandings of employee potential.

1.4.1 Foundational models of disability and inclusion

Disability models shape how employment inclusion is understood and addressed. This section outlines key perspectives on disability and their implications for creating inclusive employment opportunities for individuals with intellectual disabilities.

1.4.1.1 Medical model

The medical model has traditionally framed disability as a deficit located within the person. In employment contexts, this perspective often encourages employers to focus on what an individual cannot do, what needs correction, or what intervention might make the worker fit existing job structures. This view reduces inclusion to a prosthetic or corrective logic rather than addressing the work environment itself (Grijseels et al., 2023). In practice, it can lead to hiring decisions based on diagnosis, perceived limitations, or assumed support costs, rather than considering job redesign or organisational change.

1.4.1.2 Social mode

The social model offers a contrasting perspective by locating disability in the barriers created by environments, institutions, and attitudes. From this standpoint, exclusion from employment arises when workplaces are rigid, inaccessible, or shaped by low expectations. Inclusive job design is central to this approach because roles can be tailored to actual strengths and conditions for success rather than forcing workers to conform to narrow norms (Bredgaard, 2025). This model links to broader debates about justice, participation, and equal treatment (Casadei, 2018). The social model shifts attention from individual deficit to structural responsibility.

1.4.1.3 Human rights model

The human rights model extends this shift by grounding access to employment in dignity, equality, legal recognition, and non-discrimination. The CRPD has been especially important in establishing that people with disabilities are rights holders entitled to work on an equal basis with others (Morrissey, 2012). Legal reforms related to supported decision-making and legal capacity can strengthen autonomy and participation (Encalada, 2021). In employment contexts, this model challenges paternalistic practices and requires organisations to treat accommodation, accessibility, and inclusion as obligations rather than optional gestures.

1.4.1.4 Capability approach

The capability approach broadens the discussion by asking not only whether a person has formal access to work, but whether they have genuine opportunities to achieve valued ways of living. Capabilities depend on both personal resources and enabling environments (Sourbati, 2012). In employment, this means that success depends on whether workplaces expand or restrict a worker's freedom to participate, contribute, and flourish. This perspective connects to agency and quality of life (Croes et al., 2025), and sustainable inclusion depends on pathways that strengthen participation and belonging rather than mere placement (Wided & Abdulaziz, 2024).

1.4.1.5 Strengths-based approaches

Strengths-based approaches reject deficit thinking by focusing on talents, preferences, and contributions. Rather than beginning with limitations, they ask what conditions enable success and what value a person can bring to an organisation. The importance of lived experience in designing accessible employment journeys has been emphasised (Lovegrove et al., 2025), and open employment outcomes improve when inclusion is organised around opportunity and contribution (Smith et al., 2018). For workers with intellectual disabilities, this approach encourages employers to recognise reliability, commitment, task consistency, and other strengths that conventional assessments often overlook.

1.4.1.6 Ecological and intersectional extensions

Employment should be understood through interactions among individual, organisational, and societal factors (Karanikolas & Qian-Khoo, 2025). This ecological view avoids locating success or failure solely in the worker and allows for an intersectional analysis of how disability may interact with poverty, gender, education, and social exclusion. Technology and AI can support inclusion when combined with participatory design and attention to social context (Kiettikunwong et al., 2025).

1.4.2 From impairment to context in defining competence

These frameworks reshape how competence is interpreted. Traditional workplace thinking often treats competence as a fixed trait measured against standardised expectations. Career alignment improves when interests and skills are considered in relation to opportunity rather than generic norms (Ravindranathan et al., 2024). Broader competence frameworks that include intrapersonal, interpersonal, and societal capacities are needed (Lecours et al., 2025). This matters because workers with intellectual disabilities are often judged through narrow criteria that privilege speed, abstract reasoning, or dominant communication styles.

A contextual view of competence also aligns with earlier findings in this chapter. Workplace performance is strongly shaped by environmental conditions (Ellenkamp et al., 2016), and workplaces that embrace cognitive diversity enable workers to contribute their strengths (Sigstad et al., 2025). Competence, therefore, should be understood as relational, emerging through the fit among the worker, the task, the available support, and workplace culture.

1.4.3 Workplace adaptation as a theoretical and practical obligation

These theories also shape employers' understanding of adaptation. Under deficit-oriented thinking, adaptation is often treated as an exception or special favour. Inclusive frameworks, in contrast, present it as part of responsible organisational practice. Using the COM-B lens, inclusive companies differ from non-inclusive ones in knowledge, motivation, and organisational opportunity structures (Breit et al., 2025). Employer behaviour and workplace climate shape employees' experiences of inclusion (Hujerat, 2024).

Adaptation may involve:

- redesigning tasks to align with strengths
- using multiple communication formats
- building supportive supervision and co-worker relationships
- allowing gradual learning and structured feedback
- embedding inclusion in routine HR practice

This view reflects earlier findings that stigma and exclusion are socially produced rather than natural consequences of disability (Novak et al., 2011; Gormley, 2015).

1.4.4 Redefining employee potential in inclusive employment

Another contribution of these perspectives lies in their recasting of employee potential. Employers often confuse potential with conformity to conventional workplace norms. Disability-inclusive and neurodivergent frameworks can reveal forms of human capital that remain hidden in non-inclusive settings (Maria Szulc et al., 2021). Employment systems become more effective when families and other actors are recognised as part of a broader support ecology (Smith, 2026). This reinforces that workers with intellectual disabilities associate inclusion with recognition, participation, and respect (Pereira-Silva et al., 2018).

These frameworks make clear that redefining ability does not mean lowering standards. It means changing the lens through which work, competence, and contribution are understood. When employers move beyond impairment-focused assumptions and adopt contextual, relational, and rights-based perspectives, they are better positioned to recognise the potential of workers with intellectual disabilities and to create workplaces in which that potential can be realised.

1.5 WHY INCLUSION MATTERS: ETHICAL, LEGAL, AND ECONOMIC IMPERATIVES

Supporting workers with intellectual disabilities is not merely a charitable act. It is an ethical responsibility, a legal obligation, and an economic decision with practical organisational benefits. These imperatives matter because they shape how organisations define fairness, respond to regulatory duties, and build sustainable workforces. Together, they provide a clear rationale for embedding inclusion within employment systems rather than treating it as a peripheral initiative.

1.5.1 Ethical imperatives

The ethical case begins with human dignity. Work offers more than wages. It can provide social recognition, routine, identity, and a sense of contribution. Workers with intellectual disabilities associate employment with a sense of belonging and personal value (Pereira-Silva et al., 2018). Inclusion in the workplace is closely connected to recognition in the labour market (Hafsteinsdóttir & Hardonk, 2023).

Ethics also requires fairness in access to opportunity. Exclusion often occurs not because workers lack value, but because organisations define merit too narrowly.

Workplace contexts that support autonomy, competence, and relatedness are important sources of well-being (Fajardo-Castro et al., 2024). Job satisfaction among workers with intellectual disabilities is linked to participation and the fulfilment of basic psychological needs (Akkerman et al., 2018). These findings suggest that ethical employment involves more than hiring. It also requires conditions that enable workers to participate meaningfully and develop with dignity.

A further ethical concern is social responsibility. Labour market inclusion is central to improving the life chances of people with intellectual disability and borderline intellectual ability (Argüeso, 2025). When organisations create accessible pathways into employment, they contribute to a fairer society by reducing exclusion from one of the most important domains of adult life.

1.5.2 Legal imperatives

The legal case for inclusion rests on disability rights legislation, anti-discrimination norms, and employment equity obligations. In many contexts, employers must provide equal access to employment, prevent discrimination, and make reasonable accommodations. The inclusion of people with disabilities in workplaces is shaped by both legal standards and practical organisational responses (Ortiz-Marcos et al., 2024).

Legal obligations are especially important because they move inclusion from voluntary intention to enforceable duty. Supported employment and integrated workplace approaches have become important within Nordic policy contexts, reflecting efforts to align employment systems with disability rights (Garrels & Sigstad, 2021). In Greece, supported employment services can help workers with disabilities access and retain jobs, although service quality and policy support remain essential (Vlachou et al., 2021).

Law, however, does not remove barriers on its own. Employment strategies may fail when they do not produce genuine access to the open labour market (May-Simera, 2018). Continuing barriers in Australia include stigma and weak structural support (Meltzer et al., 2020). For organisations, the legal imperative therefore extends beyond minimum compliance. It requires active review of recruitment practices, workplace procedures, and support systems to ensure that inclusion is substantive rather than symbolic.

1.5.3 Economic imperatives

The economic rationale for inclusion is increasingly clear. Inclusive organisations can widen access to talent, strengthen participation, and improve retention. Employers who embrace cognitive diversity often recognise the value that standard recruitment systems overlook (Sigstad et al., 2025). This matters in labour markets where many organisations face labour shortages, intense competition for workers, and pressure to diversify talent pipelines.

Inclusion can also reduce turnover-related costs. Disability inclusion initiatives can create a competitive advantage, partly because employees with disabilities are often regarded as dependable and committed (Kalargyrou, 2014). Organisational inclusion is associated with lower turnover intentions among employees with disabilities (Chordiya, 2022). Stable retention reduces the financial and operational costs associated with repeated recruitment, onboarding, and workforce disruption.

Reputation is another economic consideration. Positive customer attitudes toward frontline employees with intellectual disabilities suggest that visible inclusion can strengthen public trust (Osorio & del Castillo, 2025). People with disabilities can influence sustained improvements in employment systems and organisational practice (Gendera et al., 2025). Inclusion, therefore, contributes not only to internal workforce outcomes but also to the organisation's external standing.

1.5.4 Business case implications for organisations

The business case becomes stronger when these gains are considered together. Inclusion can support organisations in several practical ways.

1.5.4.1 Strengthening workforce participation

Accessible employment expands participation by bringing more people into productive roles. This can increase workforce capacity and reduce the exclusion of available talent.

1.5.4.2 Reducing turnover

Supportive and inclusive workplaces are more likely to retain employees. Lower turnover reduces replacement and retraining costs.

1.5.4.3 Widening talent pipelines

Conventional recruitment systems often overlook workers with valuable skills and perspectives. Recognising different learning profiles in workforce development is important (Riviez, 2019), and diversity can strengthen organisational intelligence (Casalino et al., 2024).

1.5.4.4 Improving organisational reputation

Inclusion can signal fairness, responsibility, and modern leadership. Strategic planning for disability inclusion strengthens credibility with regulators, communities, and partner institutions (Moore & Huberty, 2020). Inclusive pathways can open broader opportunities for participation (Howlett & Harvey, 2012).

For these reasons, inclusion matters not only because it is ethically right or legally required, but also because it supports stronger organisations. It provides a foundation for the broader business case developed later in the chapter by showing that workers with intellectual disabilities are not peripheral to organisational success. They are part of a more equitable, lawful, and sustainable vision of work.

1.6 BUSINESS CASE FOR INCLUSION

The business case for employing workers with intellectual disabilities lies in the organisational value that inclusive employment can generate when carefully planned and consistently supported. The central issue is not whether inclusion appears morally desirable, but whether it contributes to stronger performance, healthier workplaces, and long-term organisational benefit. When organisations move beyond stereotypes and design roles thoughtfully, inclusive employment can improve reliability, strengthen staff retention, support customer confidence, and enrich workplace culture. These gains are both measurable and intangible, making inclusion relevant not only to human resource practice but also to wider organisational strategy.

1.6.1 Operational and performance gains

One of the clearest business benefits is dependable work performance in appropriately matched roles. Workers with intellectual disabilities often perform well when duties are structured, expectations are clear, and support is available. Job satisfaction is influenced by employment settings and support conditions, suggesting that well-organised roles can sustain stronger engagement and consistency (Akkerman et al., 2016). For employers, this has practical value in positions that require repetition, stability, and careful task completion.

Another advantage relates to continuity of staffing. Organisations incur costs when positions are repeatedly vacated, refilled, and retrained. Employment barriers can be reduced when organisations strengthen communication, understanding, and support for people with intellectual disability (Christianson-Barker et al., 2025). When workers receive appropriate support, employment is more likely to be sustained, thereby improving workforce continuity and reducing disruption.

Work continuity is also shaped by organisational climate. Workplace structures and culture influence the well-being of people with intellectual disability (Joyce et al., 2024). This matters because participation and stability rarely result from individual effort alone. Where systems are predictable and support is embedded, organisations are better placed to maintain dependable performance over time.

1.6.2 Staff loyalty, attendance, and retention value

A strong business case also emerges through loyalty and retention. Employees who feel respected and adequately supported are more likely to remain committed to their roles. This is especially important in sectors where high turnover creates financial strain and weakens service quality. Although some organisations frame inclusion as administratively demanding, it may, in fact, reduce losses associated with unstable staffing.

Retention has both relational and practical dimensions. Removing barriers that undermine participation is essential (Christianson-Barker et al., 2025), and employers' experiences and perceptions of work influence their willingness to hire (Dean et al., 2022). These findings suggest that organisations able to build confidence in inclusive employment may benefit from stronger long-term staff commitment.

Attendance is often discussed through deficit-based assumptions, but a support quality lens is more useful. When job roles are clear and workers experience stability, participation becomes easier to sustain. For organisations, this means inclusion should not be viewed as an inevitable source of disruption, but as an area where design influences attendance, motivation, and continuity.

1.6.3 Culture, morale, and organisational learning

Some important returns from inclusion are not captured in payroll figures or quarterly reports. Inclusive employment can strengthen workplace culture by encouraging clearer communication, mutual support, and more thoughtful supervision. Worker attitudes toward the employment of people with intellectual disabilities are shaped by knowledge and experience (Elahdi & Alnahdi, 2022). This suggests that inclusion can influence how teams understand cooperation, fairness, and social responsibility.

Workplace culture affects the well-being of employees with intellectual disability (Joyce et al., 2024). In practical terms, workplaces that support inclusion often become more deliberate in how they organise tasks, communicate expectations, and build team relationships. These adjustments can improve the quality of the work environment for other employees as well.

Inclusion may also contribute to organisational learning. Employment opportunities for people with intellectual disability are shaped by wider workplace trends, including technological change and restructuring (Moore et al., 2018). Organisations that learn to adapt to human diversity may become more flexible and reflective in other areas of management. Inclusion, therefore, can strengthen institutional learning rather than complicate it.

1.6.4 Brand identity and market advantage

The business case is also evident in how inclusion shapes reputation. Employing workers with intellectual disabilities can strengthen public perceptions of fairness, responsibility, and authenticity. In customer-facing roles, these effects may be especially important. Customers have positive attitudes toward frontline employees with intellectual disabilities, indicating that inclusive staffing can support favourable brand associations (Osorio & del Castillo, 2025). Several practical advantages emerge in this area.

1.6.4.1 Positive brand identity

Visible inclusion can reinforce organisational values and distinguish employers in competitive markets. It shows that inclusion is part of everyday practice rather than a symbolic gesture.

.6.4.2 Customer trust

Inclusive staffing can strengthen public confidence when customers see fairness and social responsibility in action. This helps build trust and signals that the organisation values people as well as performance.

1.6.4.3 CSR alignment

Social responsibility can influence employer willingness to hire, linking inclusion to wider CSR goals (Dean et al., 2022). Employing workers with intellectual disabilities makes CSR commitments visible in the workplace.

1.6.4.4 Stakeholder legitimacy

Strategic planning for disability inclusion strengthens credibility with regulators, communities, and partner institutions (Moore & Huberty, 2020). Inclusion can therefore improve legitimacy across key stakeholder groups.

These benefits are not merely symbolic. They shape how organisations are perceived, how they distinguish themselves, and how they align practice with stated commitments.

1.6.5 Long-term value beyond cost assumptions

A persistent misconception is that inclusive employment is mainly costly or burdensome. This view reduces organisational value to immediate expense and ignores longer-term returns. Some HR managers increasingly understand inclusive employment as a normal investment rather than an exceptional burden (Antonova et al., 2021). This marks an important shift because all employment systems require training, supervision, and adaptation. Inclusion is not unusual and often requires support. What matters is whether organisations recognise the value such support can produce.

That value may include staff stability, improved morale, wider recruitment possibilities, and stronger brand positioning. Diversity and social equity can strengthen organisational intelligence (Casalino et al., 2024). Support and legal practice can be integrated in ways that make inclusion workable rather than disruptive (Arpangi et al., 2025). Person-centred supported employment can build confidence and sustain participation (Malekinezhad & Courtney, 2026).

The business case for inclusion, therefore, does not depend on a sentimental argument. It rests on organisational outcomes. Workers with intellectual disabilities can contribute to dependable performance, a healthier culture, a stronger reputation, and more adaptive institutional practice. When organisations strategically support inclusion, they position themselves to create lasting value. The next section turns from these broad organisational benefits to the practical conditions that enable inclusive employment to succeed in everyday workplace settings.

1.7 ORGANISATIONAL MYTHS AND MISCONCEPTIONS ABOUT WORKERS WITH INTELLECTUAL DISABILITIES

These myths often appear in managerial concerns about efficiency, risk, cost, or team fit. Although presented as practical judgments, they are often shaped by low expectations, limited exposure, and a weak understanding of intellectual disability.

Employer willingness to hire may be influenced by attitudinal and regulatory concerns (Duvdevany et al., 2016), and disability bias often operates implicitly (Antonopoulos et al., 2023). Challenging these misconceptions is necessary if inclusion is to move beyond policy language into everyday workplace practice.

1.7.1 Common myths and why they endure

Several misconceptions remain embedded in organisational thinking because they place workplace difficulties on workers rather than on management systems or employer beliefs. Attitudes toward people with intellectual disabilities can be improved through knowledge-based interventions, suggesting that many assumptions are socially learned rather than evidence-based (Seewooruttun & Scior, 2014). Employer perceptions can themselves become barriers to employment (Milanović-Dobrota, 2018).

1.7.1.1 Myth: They are less productive

This assumption is sustained by narrow conceptions of productivity that privilege speed, independence, and rapid task-switching, while undervaluing consistency, concentration, punctuality, and commitment. Evidence indicates that performance is closely linked to workplace conditions and support structures rather than fixed individual traits (Joyce et al., 2025). Participation in work has also been shown to be meaningful and contributory, challenging the perception that such roles lack substantive value (Alves & da Silva, 2020).

1.7.1.2 Myth: They cannot learn new or complex tasks

This belief often reflects limitations in instructional design rather than actual learning capacity. Where training relies on brief verbal instruction or assumes immediate adaptation, difficulties may arise that are incorrectly attributed to inability. Meaningful participation in work depends on opportunities for learning and development (Riches, 2023). Differences in learning pace or style should therefore not be interpreted as incapacity, but as a need for more accessible and responsive training approaches.

1.7.1.3 Myth: They are unsafe to employ

Concerns about safety are frequently based on assumptions rather than evidence. Workplace safety is determined by clear procedures, effective induction, accessible communication, and appropriate supervision. Structured interactions and support contribute to safer, more inclusive work environments (Novak et al., 2011). Safety should therefore be understood as a function of organisational practice rather than as an attribute of individual characteristics.

1.7.1.4 Myth: They are too costly to support

Perceptions of high cost often arise from exaggerated assumptions about accommodation needs. In practice, many adjustments involve low-cost strategies such as structured feedback, task clarification, and peer support. Strategic planning embeds inclusion within standard organisational processes (Moore & Huberty, 2020). The issue is therefore not the cost itself, but the tendency to treat adaptation as exceptional rather than integral to effective workforce management.

1.7.2 Reframing workplace assumptions through evidence

Evidence shows that workplace misconceptions are less prevalent when employers have knowledge, familiarity, and direct experience (Seewooruttun & Scior, 2014; Antonopoulos et al., 2023). Attitudes toward employing persons with intellectual disabilities are associated with contact and prior exposure, which suggests that negative assumptions often thrive where experience is limited (Elahdi & Alnahdi, 2022). Social inclusion is also frequently misunderstood. Equal opportunity is closely tied to being treated as a legitimate participant, meaning that belonging depends on workplace relationships, supervisory practices, and team culture rather than mere presence in the organisation (Li, 2004).

Another wrong assumption is that segregated settings are naturally more suitable than open employment. Employment setting influences job satisfaction (Akkerman et al., 2016), and exclusion from mainstream work leaves substantial potential unused (Lysaght et al., 2012). Misconceptions also shape how difficulties are interpreted. The importance of resilience and support has been highlighted (Grant et al., 2003), and person-centred supported employment can strengthen confidence and ongoing participation (Malekinezhad & Courtney, 2026). Workplace difficulties should therefore prompt organisational adjustment rather than fixed judgements about incapacity.

1.7.3 Organisational responses for challenging myths

1.7.3.1 Build disability knowledge into staff development

Training can help employers and co-workers examine stereotypes and replace assumptions with evidence. Targeted interventions can improve knowledge and attitudes (Seewooruttun & Scior, 2014), and implicit bias may persist unless it is actively addressed (Antonopoulos et al., 2023).

1.7.3.2 Create opportunities for meaningful workplace contact

Direct, respectful contact between workers with and without intellectual disabilities can reduce prejudice and strengthen inclusion. Supported interaction matters, especially when equality and shared purpose are present (Novak et al., 2011).

1.7.3.3 Normalise support as part of good management

Support should not be framed as unusual or burdensome. Well-being and job satisfaction are shaped by work conditions, underscoring the importance of structured feedback, mentoring, and accessible supervision for sustaining participation (Joyce et al., 2025).

1.7.3.4 Review policy and practice for hidden assumptions

Recruitment procedures, training systems, and performance expectations may reproduce myths even when organisations endorse inclusion rhetorically. Disability is also a legal and justice issue, which means organisations must examine whether their own systems exclude through routine design (Casadei, 2018).

Misconceptions about workers with intellectual disabilities persist because they are embedded in everyday assumptions about value, competence, and risk. Evidence shows that these beliefs are unreliable guides for employment practice. They can be challenged through knowledge, experience, and organisational reflection.

1.8 TOWARD AN INCLUSIVE EMPLOYMENT CULTURE

An inclusive employment culture is built through repeated organisational choices about how people are led, informed, supported, and retained. Formal commitment matters, but culture is shaped more decisively by everyday practice. Disability-inclusive employment remains shallow when organisations stop at visible commitment without changing how work is structured (Shaw et al., 2022). For this reason, inclusion must be treated as an operating principle that influences decisions across the employment cycle.

Leadership is one of the strongest signals of whether inclusion is real. Organisational commitment to diversity, equity, inclusion, and justice requires visible direction and accountability (Moreno et al., 2024). In practical terms, leaders influence whether managers regard inclusion as central or optional, whether support is resourced, and whether exclusionary behaviour is challenged. Inclusive leadership depends on intentional practice, especially during organisational change (Simmons & Yawson, 2022).

Where leaders frame inclusion as part of institutional quality, it is more likely to shape ordinary management behaviour. Leadership commitment is often reflected through:

- Explicit expectations for inclusive management
- Resource allocation for support and adjustment
- Routine review of recruitment, retention, and progression patterns
- Prompt response to exclusionary conduct or inaccessible practice

Policy is another important layer, but it must be workable rather than symbolic. Many organisations adopt equality statements that mention disability without setting out how participation will be supported in practice. Inclusive employment becomes more sustainable when employers understand it as a normal feature of organisational life (Antonova et al., 2021). This means policies should address how jobs are advertised, how induction is handled, how adjustments are arranged, and how concerns are resolved. Inclusive pathways depend on practical conditions that support continued participation (Wided & Abdulaziz, 2024).

a. Useful policy areas include:
b. accessible recruitment and onboarding procedures
c. clear channels for identifying support needs
d. structured review of workplace barriers
e. consistent supervisory guidance on inclusive practice

Communication is equally important because many workplace difficulties begin with ambiguity rather than conflict. Open communication strengthens equity within organisations (Abravan et al., 2023). Inclusive communication requires more than courtesy. It demands clarity, consistency, and a willingness to make expectations explicit. Workers should not be expected to infer hidden norms or rely on informal guesswork to understand role requirements. Communication systems shape whether inclusion is experienced as predictable and fair or as confusing and unstable.

1. Organisations can strengthen communication by:
2. using direct and accessible language
3. combining verbal guidance with written or visual prompts where useful
4. checking understanding during instruction and feedback

5. making workplace routines and expectations explicit
6. allowing questions without penalty or embarrassment

Staff awareness also matters because organisational culture is reinforced by colleagues' behaviour, not just by policy documents. Capacity-building is essential for fostering a sense of belonging in institutions (Samuel et al., 2024). Awareness work should therefore address common assumptions, practical interaction, and the everyday responsibilities of co-workers and supervisors. Inclusion is strengthened when employees practise it regularly rather than encounter it only through abstract training sessions (Steele, 2024). A workforce that understands how inclusion operates in daily work is better prepared to respond constructively when support, flexibility, or adaptation is needed. Awareness efforts are stronger when they:

a. address bias and misconception directly
b. use examples drawn from real workplace situations
c. connect inclusion to professional responsibility
d. build confidence in respectful interaction and problem-solving
e. continue over time instead of being treated as a single event

Supervision is another point where culture becomes visible. Building a skilled and inclusive workforce is essential (Banihammad et al., 2023), and an inclusive work climate shapes the employee experience (Major & Morganson, 2008). Supervisors influence whether support is experienced as respectful, whether performance concerns are handled fairly, and whether workers feel able to raise difficulties early. Collaborative supervision does not weaken accountability. It improves it by making communication clearer and support more responsive. In practice, collaborative supervision often involves:

- regular check-ins rather than reactive correction
- shared review of what is working and what is difficult
- clear, timely, and specific feedback
- co-ordination with mentors, peers, or support staff where relevant

Early accommodation planning is also necessary. Waiting until difficulties intensify can turn manageable issues into avoidable setbacks. Inclusive work environments can be strengthened through thoughtful integration of supportive technologies (George et al., 2025). Organisational monitoring can help identify where inclusive systems are succeeding or failing (Agasti et al., 2026). Early planning makes adjustment part of ordinary workplace design rather than an improvised response to a crisis. This may involve:

i. identifying likely support needs at entry stage
ii. preparing supervisors before challenges emerge
iii. reviewing adjustments as tasks or roles change
iv. integrating accommodation into workforce planning processes

Inclusion is strongest when systems and relationships reinforce one another. Policies without leadership attention lose force. Training without supervisory follow-through fades quickly. Communication without trust does not produce belonging. Inclusion should be understood systemically (Ferdman, 2013), and workplace inclusion is also shaped through social relationships and network patterns (Butler et al., 2025). These insights matter because employment culture is not created by one intervention. It is produced through the alignment of structures, expectations, and interaction.

For organisations, the central task is to move from declaration to routine practice. Inclusion becomes cultural when it is visible in how people are recruited, guided, corrected, supported, and valued across ordinary work processes. It is sustained not by isolated gestures but by systems that make fair participation easier to achieve and maintain. The next section considers how these cultural conditions support continuity, retention, and growth at work.

CONCLUSION

This chapter has argued that redefining ability is essential to building workplaces in which workers with intellectual disabilities can participate meaningfully, and organisations can function more effectively. It challenged deficit-based assumptions that define employability through narrow ideas of speed, independence, and productivity, and replaced them with a contextual view in which competence is shaped by job design, support, communication, supervision, and workplace culture.

The chapter showed that exclusion is not inevitable. It is often produced by inaccessible structures, historical segregation, low expectations, and persistent misconceptions about cost, safety, and performance. Through historical, theoretical, ethical, legal, and economic analysis, the chapter demonstrated that inclusion is both a rights issue and a strategic organisational concern. Workers with intellectual disabilities are entitled to dignity, fairness, and meaningful participation, while organisations benefit through stronger retention, broader talent access, healthier workplace culture, and improved reputation.

A further contribution of the chapter has been to show that inclusion cannot remain a statement of intent. It must be embedded in leadership practice, disability-confident policies, accessible communication, staff awareness, collaborative supervision, and early accommodation planning. Organisational culture changes when inclusive principles shape ordinary workplace decisions rather than symbolic commitments alone.

This chapter, therefore, provides the foundation for the rest of the book. It positions workers with intellectual disabilities not as burdens to be managed, but as contributors whose participation can enrich organisational life and reshape conventional ideas of workplace value. The chapters that follow build on this foundation by turning to the practical policies and workplace strategies needed to recruit, support, retain, and advance workers with intellectual disabilities.

REFERENCES

Abravan, A., Correia, D., Gasnier, A., Shakhverdian, S., van der Stok, T., Bertholet, J., Dubois, L. J., Jereczek-Fossa, B. A., Eng, M. P., Spalek, M., Petit, S. F., Franco, P., & Petit-Steeghs, V. (2023). Qualitative study on diversity, equity, and inclusion within radiation oncology in Europe. *International Journal of Radiation Oncology, Biology, Physics*, *116*(2), 246–256. DOI: 10.1016/j.ijrobp.2023.02.009 PMID: 36792016

Agasti, N. R., Martha, S. S., & Mohanty, I. (2026). HR analytics & inclusive growth: Driving sustainable development for Generation Z and beyond. In *Navigating digital disruption: Strategies for sustainable business management* (pp. 326–332). Routledge., DOI: 10.4324/9781003716617-58

Akkerman, A., Janssen, C. G. C., Kef, S., & Meininger, H. P. (2016). Job satisfaction of people with intellectual disabilities in integrated and sheltered employment: An exploration of literature. *Journal of Policy and Practice in Intellectual Disabilities*, *13*(3), 205–216. DOI: 10.1111/jppi.12168

Akkerman, A., Kef, S., & Meininger, H. P. (2018). Job satisfaction of people with intellectual disabilities: The role of basic psychological need fulfilment and workplace participation. *Disability and Rehabilitation*, *40*(10), 1192–1199. DOI: 10.1080/09638288.2017.1294205 PMID: 28288522

Alves, A. P. R., & da Silva, N. R. (2020). What the people with intellectual disability think about their participation in the work from two case studies. *Revista Brasileira de Educação Especial*, *26*(1), 109–124. DOI: 10.1590/s1413-65382620000100007

Antonopoulos, C. R., Sugden, N., & Saliba, A. (2023). Implicit bias toward people with disabilities: A systematic review and meta-analysis. *Rehabilitation Psychology*, *68*(2), 121–134. DOI: 10.1037/rep0000493 PMID: 37079819

Antonova, V., Prisyazhniuk, D., & Ryabichenko, T. (2021). Investment and inclusion as a norm of life: Attitudes of Russian HR-managers to inclusive employment. *Zhurnal Issledovanii Sotsial'noi Politiki*, *19*(3), 373–388. DOI: 10.17323/727-0634-2021-19-3-373-388

Argüeso, M. S. (2025). Intellectual disability and borderline intellectual ability: Keys for a better labour market insertion. *Oñati Socio-Legal Series*, *15*(3), 790–817. DOI: 10.35295/osls.iisl.2170

Arpangi, S., Suwondo, D., Laksana, A. W., & Yassine, C. (2025). Integrating Australian employment law practice in support of people with disabilities in Indonesia. *Khazanah Hukum*, *7*(2), 236–254. DOI: 10.15575/kh.v7i2.44946

Babikian, V. A., & Hamdani, Y. (2023). Social enterprises and transition to employment for people labelled with intellectual and developmental disabilities. *Current Developmental Disorders Reports, 10*(1), 40–46. DOI: 10.1007/s40474-023-00267-7

Banihammad, B. A., Al Mirza, J. J., Ashraf, A. A., & Kumaresan, R. S. (2023). Creating an inclusive and skilled workforce. Society of Petroleum Engineers - ADIPEC. *ADIP, 2023*. Advance online publication. DOI: 10.2118/215968-MS

Barow, T. (2025). "Needed and valuable instead of just being employed": Vocational training, work and social usefulness regarding people with intellectual disability in Sweden, 1945–1989. *Nordic Journal of Educational History, 12*(2), 63–87. DOI: 10.36368/njedh.v12i2.1314

Bigby, C., Wilson, N. J., Balandin, S., & Stancliffe, R. J. (2011). Disconnected expectations: Staff, family, and supported employee perspectives about retirement. *Journal of Intellectual & Developmental Disability, 36*(3), 167–174. DOI: 10.3109/13668250.2011.598852 PMID: 21843031

Bredgaard, T. (2025). Inclusive job design. In *Shaping inclusive workplaces for persons with disabilities: A management and HRM practitioner perspective* (pp. 85–95). Springer., DOI: 10.1007/978-3-031-96315-5_7

Breit, E., Bråthen, M., & Sadeghi, T. (2025). Distinctions between inclusive and non-inclusive companies for persons with disability: Exploring the impact of COM-B and HRM practices. *Work (Reading, Mass.), 81*(2), 2651–2661. DOI: 10.1177/10519815251320275 PMID: 40421555

Burge, P., Ouellette-Kuntz, H., & Lysaght, R. (2007). Public views on employment of people with intellectual disabilities. *Journal of Vocational Rehabilitation, 26*(1), 29–37. DOI: 10.3233/JVR-2007-00360

Butler, T., Falk, E., & Kleinbaum, A. M. (2025). Workplace inclusion: A social network perspective. *Research in Organizational Behavior, 45*, 100221. Advance online publication. DOI: 10.1016/j.riob.2025.100221

Casadei, T. (2018). Disability and law. *Rivista di Filosofia del Diritto, 7*(2), 273–279. DOI: 10.4477/91675

Casalino, N., Żuchowski, I., Veglianti, E., Borin, B., & Skrodzki, I. (2024). Improving managerial approaches and human resources strategies in the banking sector regarding inclusion, diversity, social equity and organisational intelligence. *Law and Economics Yearly Review, 13*, 281–312.

Chordiya, R. (2022). Organizational inclusion and turnover intentions of federal employees with disabilities. *Review of Public Personnel Administration, 42*(1), 60–87. DOI: 10.1177/0734371X20942305

Christianson-Barker, J., Morris, R., Stainton, T., Cox, J., Rowley, C., Schroeder, M., Mills, R., & Hole, R. (2025). Addressing barriers to employment for workers with an intellectual disability in Canada: A focus group study. *Research and Practice in Intellectual and Developmental Disabilities, 12*(2), 195–210. DOI: 10.1080/23297018.2025.2501261

Croes, R., Lee, S. H., Renduchintala, C., Badu-Baiden, F., & Tavares, K. (2025). Tourism, quality of life, and disability: An agency perspective. *Journal of Hospitality & Tourism Research (Washington, D.C.)*. Advance online publication. DOI: 10.1177/10963480251361952

Dean, E. E., Garrels, V., Sigstad, H. M. H., & Wendelborg, C. (2022). Employer willingness to hire people with intellectual disability: The influence of employer experience, perception of work, and social responsibility. *Journal of Vocational Rehabilitation, 57*(1), 85–95. DOI: 10.3233/JVR-221201

Dearing, K. (2020). 'Not worth the minimum wage?' Unpacking the complexities of intellectual disability and its intersection with employment structures. *Scandinavian Journal of Disability Research, 22*(1), 360–370. DOI: 10.16993/sjdr.729

Delap, L. (2024). Slow workers: Labelling and labouring in Britain, c. 1909–1955. *Social History of Medicine, 37*(1), 160–182. DOI: 10.1093/shm/hkad043 PMID: 38947272

Duvdevany, I., Or-Chen, K., & Fine, M. (2016). Employers' willingness to hire a person with intellectual disability in light of the regulations for adjusted minimum wages. *Journal of Vocational Rehabilitation, 44*(1), 33–41. DOI: 10.3233/JVR-150778

Elahdi, A., & Alnahdi, G. H. (2022). Factors associated with workers' attitudes towards employment of persons with intellectual disabilities in Saudi Arabia. *Journal of Applied Research in Intellectual Disabilities, 35*(3), 856–866. DOI: 10.1111/jar.12990 PMID: 35174588

Ellenkamp, J. J. H., Brouwers, E. P. M., Embregts, P. J. C. M., Joosen, M. C. W., & van Weeghel, J. (2016). Work environment-related factors in obtaining and maintaining work in a competitive employment setting for employees with intellectual disabilities: A systematic review. *Journal of Occupational Rehabilitation, 26*(1), 56–69. DOI: 10.1007/s10926-015-9586-1 PMID: 26112400

Encalada, A. V. (2021). The potential of the legal capacity law reform in Peru to transform mental health provision. In *Mental health, legal capacity, and human rights* (pp. 124–139). Cambridge University Press., DOI: 10.1017/9781108979016.011

Fajardo-Castro, L. V., Martínez-Tur, V., Moliner, C., Plavsic, A., & Arbués, J. (2024). Organizational context and satisfaction of basic needs of workers with intellectual disability as sources of well-being. *Social Sciences (Basel, Switzerland), 13*(10), 523. Advance online publication. DOI: 10.3390/socsci13100523

Ferdman, B. M. (2013). The practice of inclusion in diverse organizations: Toward a systemic and inclusive framework. In *Diversity at work: The practice of inclusion* (pp. 3–54). Wiley., DOI: 10.1002/9781118764282.ch1

Fillary, R., & Pernice, R. (2006). Social inclusion in workplaces where people with intellectual disabilities are employed: Implications for supported employment professionals. *International Journal of Rehabilitation Research. Internationale Zeitschrift fur Rehabilitationsforschung. Revue Internationale de Recherches de Readaptation, 29*(1), 31–36. DOI: 10.1097/01.mrr.0000185952.87304.63 PMID: 16432387

Folguera Bellmunt, C. (2026). Supported internships: Vocational training and labor inclusion for students with intellectual and developmental disabilities. *Equality, Diversity and Inclusion, 45*(1), 86–100. DOI: 10.1108/EDI-05-2024-0218

Garrels, V., & Sigstad, H. M. H. (2021). Employment for persons with intellectual disability in the Nordic countries: A scoping review. *Journal of Applied Research in Intellectual Disabilities, 34*(4), 993–1007. DOI: 10.1111/jar.12880 PMID: 33709541

Gendera, S., Alexander, J., Burton, J., Fisher, K. R., & Robinson, S. (2025). People with disability influencing sustained improvements to employment. *Social Policy and Administration.* Advance online publication. DOI: 10.1111/spol.70022

George, G., Kulkarni, M., & Varghese, B. (2025). AI in creating inclusive work environments for neurodiverse employees. *Advances in Autism.* Advance online publication. DOI: 10.1108/AIA-05-2025-0046

Gomes-Machado, M. L., Santos, F. H., Schoen, T., & Chiari, B. (2016). Effects of vocational training on a group of people with intellectual disabilities. *Journal of Policy and Practice in Intellectual Disabilities, 13*(1), 33–40. DOI: 10.1111/jppi.12144

Gormley, M. E. (2015). Workplace stigma toward employees with intellectual disability: A descriptive study. *Journal of Vocational Rehabilitation, 43*(3), 249–258. DOI: 10.3233/JVR-150773

Grant, G., Ramcharan, P., & Goward, P. (2003). Resilience, family care, and people with intellectual disabilities. *International Review of Research in Mental Retardation, 26*, 135–173. DOI: 10.1016/S0074-7750(03)01004-8

Grijseels, M., Zuiderent-Jerak, T., & Regeer, B. J. (2023). Technologies for inclusive employment: Beyond the prosthetic fix—social transformation axis. *Disability & Society, 38*(9), 1534–1557. DOI: 10.1080/09687599.2021.1997720

Hafsteinsdóttir, Á., & Hardonk, S. C. (2023). Understanding work inclusion: Analysis of the perspectives of people with intellectual disabilities on employment in the Icelandic labor market. *Work (Reading, Mass.), 75*(2), 433–445. DOI: 10.3233/WOR-211219 PMID: 36641711

Howlett, S., & Harvey, R. (2012). Rachel's story: A bridge to inclusion. *JANZSSA. Journal of the Australian and New Zealand Student Services Association*, (39), 42–48.

Huber, M., & Pochstein, F. (2025). Attitudes towards individuals with intellectual disabilities: Comparison between Special Olympic partners and non-partners during the Special Olympics World Summer Games 2023. *Journal of Intellectual & Developmental Disability, 50*(2), 211–220. DOI: 10.3109/13668250.2024.2405972 PMID: 40390320

Hujerat, E. (2024). Managing employees with disabilities: The impact of employer behavior and workplace climate from an employee perspective in Israel. In *Springer Proceedings in Business and Economics* (pp. 817–839). Springer., DOI: 10.1007/978-981-97-0996-0_50

Joyce, A., Campbell, P., Crosbie, J., & Wilson, E. (2024). Workplace structures and culture that support the wellbeing of people with an intellectual disability. *International Journal of Environmental Research and Public Health, 21*(11), 1453. Advance online publication. DOI: 10.3390/ijerph21111453 PMID: 39595719

Joyce, A., Campbell, P., Crosbie, J., & Wilson, E. (2025). Wellbeing and job satisfaction among employees with intellectual disability. *Frontiers in Public Health, 13*, 1503932. Advance online publication. DOI: 10.3389/fpubh.2025.1503932 PMID: 40124410

Jupille, J., Deloffre, S., Leguay, D., & Chirio-Espitalier, M. (2025). Disability, recruitment and job retention: Identifying barriers and facilitators from the employers' point of view. *Work (Reading, Mass.), 80*(1), 202–211. DOI: 10.3233/WOR-230444 PMID: 39121145

Kalargyrou, V. (2014). Gaining a competitive advantage with disability inclusion initiatives. *Journal of Human Resources in Hospitality & Tourism, 13*(2), 120–145. DOI: 10.1080/15332845.2014.847300

Karanikolas, P., & Qian-Khoo, J. X. (2025). Enablers and barriers to youth employment: An employment ecosystem approach. *Encyclopedia, 5*(2), 73. Advance online publication. DOI: 10.3390/encyclopedia5020073

Kiettikunwong, N., Narot, P., & Deeod, P. (2025). Advancing disability inclusion in Thailand through AI for sustainable development. *International Journal of Developmental Disabilities, 71*(6), 919–928. DOI: 10.1080/20473869.2025.2521666

Kumar, A., Srivastava, S. K., & Singh, K. K. (2019). Study on attitude of coworkers towards employees with intellectual disabilities. *Indian Journal of Public Health Research & Development, 10*(12), 720–724. DOI: 10.37506/v10/i12/2019/ijphrd/192049

Lecours, A., Laribi, S., Laliberté, M., & Kiki, G. M. (2025). Mapping transversal competences for vocational education learners in response to transformations in the world of work: A scoping review. *Education + Training*, •••, 1–18. Advance online publication. DOI: 10.1108/ET-08-2025-0678

Li, E. P. Y. (2004). Self-perceived equal opportunities for people with intellectual disability. *International Journal of Rehabilitation Research. Internationale Zeitschrift fur Rehabilitationsforschung. Revue Internationale de Recherches de Readaptation, 27*(3), 241–245. DOI: 10.1097/00004356-200409000-00011 PMID: 15319696

Lovegrove, E., Bertilone, D., Brown, J., & Beaumont-Bilsby, E. (2025). Harnessing lived experience to promote accessible employment journeys. In W4A 2025 - Proceedings of the 22nd International Web for All Conference (pp. 18–21). ACM. DOI: 10.1145/3744257.3744264

Lysaght, R., Krupa, T., & Packalen, K. (2024). From exclusion to inclusion. In *The Routledge companion to disability and work* (pp. 67–83). Routledge., DOI: 10.4324/9781003350781-7

Lysaght, R., Ouellette-Kuntz, H., & Lin, C.-J. (2012). Untapped potential: Perspectives on the employment of people with intellectual disability. *Work (Reading, Mass.), 41*(4), 409–422. DOI: 10.3233/WOR-2012-1318 PMID: 22495411

Major, D. A., & Morganson, V. L. (2008). An inclusive IS&T work climate. In *Encyclopedia of information science and technology* (2nd ed., pp. 1899–1905). IGI Global., DOI: 10.4018/978-1-60566-026-4.ch299

Malekinezhad, F., & Courtney, P. (2026). Framing the shift to supported employment: Exploring the impacts of a person-centred programme evaluation approach through peer led participatory research. *Evaluation and Program Planning, 114*, 102723. Advance online publication. DOI: 10.1016/j.evalprogplan.2025.102723 PMID: 41151422

Maria Szulc, J., Davies, J., Tomczak, M. T., & McGregor, F.-L. (2021). AMO perspectives on the well-being of neurodivergent human capital. *Employee Relations, 43*(4), 858–872. DOI: 10.1108/ER-09-2020-0446

May-Simera, C. (2018). Is the Irish (Republic of) Comprehensive Employment Strategy fit for purpose in promoting the employment of people with intellectual disabilities in the open labor market? *Journal of Policy and Practice in Intellectual Disabilities, 15*(4), 284–294. DOI: 10.1111/jppi.12259

Meltzer, A., Robinson, S., & Fisher, K. R. (2020). Barriers to finding and maintaining open employment for people with intellectual disability in Australia. *Social Policy and Administration, 54*(1), 88–101. DOI: 10.1111/spol.12523

Meneley, T., Crawford, L., & Huddleston, G. (2021). Sherry: "Inclusion" interpreted through a life-story lens. *International Journal of Developmental Disabilities, 67*(1), 67–78. DOI: 10.1080/20473869.2019.1613849 PMID: 34141400

Mihić, S. S., & Kiš-Glavaš, L. (2010). Work and social competence of people with intellectual disabilities: Barriers for employers in their employment. *Revija za Socijalnu Politiku, 17*(3), 387–399. DOI: 10.3935/rsp.v17i3.912

Milanović-Dobrota, B. (2018). Barriers to employing persons with intellectual disability - Employers' perception. *Specijalna Edukacija i Rehabilitacija, 17*(3), 189–212. DOI: 10.5937/specedreh17-16987

Milanović-Dobrota, B., Jelić, S., Buha, N., & Japundža-Milisavljević, M. (2025). Employer perspectives on hiring individuals with intellectual disabilities: A case study from Serbia. *Journal of Applied Research in Intellectual Disabilities, 38*(2), e70045. Advance online publication. DOI: 10.1111/jar.70045 PMID: 40156224

Moore, K., McDonald, P., & Bartlett, J. (2018). Emerging trends affecting future employment opportunities for people with intellectual disability: The case of a large retail organisation. *Journal of Intellectual & Developmental Disability, 43*(3), 328–338. DOI: 10.3109/13668250.2017.1379250

Moore, M. E., & Huberty, L. L. (2020). Strategic planning for the inclusion of people with disabilities into work organizations. In *The Palgrave handbook of disability at work* (pp. 187–202). Palgrave Macmillan., DOI: 10.1007/978-3-030-42966-9_11

Moreno, J. V., Marshall, D. R., Girard, A., Mitchell, N. M. B., Minissian, M. B., & Coleman, B. (2024). An organizational commitment to diversity, equity, inclusion, and justice. *Nursing Administration Quarterly*, *48*(1), 33–48. DOI: 10.1097/NAQ.0000000000000611 PMID: 38051208

Morrissey, F. (2012). The United Nations Convention on the Rights of Persons with Disabilities: A new approach to decision-making in mental health law. *European Journal of Health Law*, *19*(5), 423–440. DOI: 10.1163/15718093-12341237 PMID: 23198484

Nagtegaal, R., de Boer, N., van Berkel, R., & Tummers, L. (2025). Unlocking inclusive hiring: Understanding employers' decisions about hiring people with disabilities. *International Journal of Human Resource Management*, *36*(20), 3717–3756. DOI: 10.1080/09585192.2025.2607539

Novak, J., Feyes, K. J., & Christensen, K. A. (2011). Application of intergroup contact theory to the integrated workplace: Setting the stage for inclusion. *Journal of Vocational Rehabilitation*, *35*(3), 211–226. DOI: 10.3233/JVR-2011-0573

Ortiz-Marcos, J. M., Invernón-Gómez, A. I., Medina-García, M., & Higueras-Rodríguez, L. (2024). Workplace inclusion of people with disabilities: Legislative challenges and practical solutions. *Revista Espanola de Orientacion y Psicopedagogia*, *35*(3), 105–122. DOI: 10.5944/reop.vol.35.num.3.2024.40820

Osorio, M. L., & del Castillo, E. (2025). Customers' attitudes toward frontline employees with intellectual disabilities: Scale development and validation. *Journal of Service Research*. Advance online publication. DOI: 10.1177/10946705251391145

Pereira-Silva, N. L., Furtado, A. V., & Andrade, J. F. C. D. M. (2018). Workplace inclusion from the standpoint of individuals with intellectual disabilities. *Temas em Psicologia*, *26*(2), 1017–1030. DOI: 10.9788/TP2018.2-17En

Rachanioti, E., Giaouri, S., Laskaraki, E., & Alevriadou, A. (2021). "Can I work here?": Employment barriers for individuals with intellectual disabilities in Greece. Journal of Intellectual Disability - Diagnosis and Treatment, 9(4), 354–362. DOI: 10.6000/2292-2598.2021.09.04.1

Ravindranathan, R., Usha, S., Tommy, R., & George, S. R. (2024). Interest and skill correlation model for career aligning of young persons with disabilities. Journal of Intellectual Disability - Diagnosis and Treatment, 12(4), 228–239. DOI: 10.6000/2292-2598.2024.12.04.5

Readhead, A., & Owen, F. (2020). Employment supports and outcomes for persons with intellectual and/or developmental disabilities: A review of recent findings. *Current Developmental Disorders Reports*, *7*(3), 155–162. DOI: 10.1007/s40474-020-00202-0

Riches, V. C. (2023). The importance of economic participation for quality of life. In *Disability practice: Safeguarding quality service delivery* (pp. 79–99). Springer., DOI: 10.1007/978-981-99-6143-6_5

Riviez, D. A. (2019). Employee learning disabilities and workforce learning. In *The Wiley handbook of global workplace learning* (pp. 215–240). Wiley., DOI: 10.1002/9781119227793.ch13

Ruppel, E. H. (2025). The making of a reserve army of labor: Paradoxes of American disability policy. *Critical Sociology*, *51*(3), 451–469. DOI: 10.1177/08969205241246446

Samuel, H. S., Etim, E. E., Nweke-Maraizu, U., & Shinggu, J. P. (2024). Promoting diversity, equity, and inclusion: Strategies for building capacity and fostering belonging. In *Building organizational capacity and strategic management in academia* (pp. 445–462). IGI Global., DOI: 10.4018/979-8-3693-6967-8.ch016

Seewooruttun, L., & Scior, K. (2014). Interventions aimed at increasing knowledge and improving attitudes towards people with intellectual disabilities among lay people. *Research in Developmental Disabilities*, *35*(12), 3482–3495. DOI: 10.1016/j.ridd.2014.07.028 PMID: 25213473

Shaw, J., Wickenden, M., Thompson, S., & Mader, P. (2022). Achieving disability inclusive employment – Are the current approaches deep enough? *Journal of International Development*, *34*(5), 942–963. DOI: 10.1002/jid.3692

Sigstad, H. M. H., Garrels, V., Dean, E. E., & Wendelborg, C. (2025). Characteristics of workplaces and employers that embrace cognitive diversity on the work floor. *Intellectual and Developmental Disabilities*, *63*(2), 105–119. DOI: 10.1352/1934-9556-63.2.105 PMID: 40139232

Simmons, S. V., & Yawson, R. M. (2022). Developing leaders for disruptive change: An inclusive leadership approach. *Advances in Developing Human Resources*, *24*(4), 242–262. DOI: 10.1177/15234223221114359

Smith, P. (2026). Families as system actors in discovery embedding co-production within the equilibrium systems model of employment. *Journal of Health and Rehabilitation Sciences*, *5*(1), 1–8. DOI: 10.33700/jhrs.5.1.202

Smith, P., McVilly, K. R., McGillivray, J., & Chan, J. (2018). Developing open employment outcomes for people with an intellectual disability utilising a social enterprise framework. *Journal of Vocational Rehabilitation*, *48*(1), 59–77. DOI: 10.3233/JVR-170916

Sourbati, M. (2012). Disabling communications? A capabilities perspective on media access, social inclusion and communication policy. *Media Culture & Society*, *34*(5), 571–587. DOI: 10.1177/0163443712442702

Steele, Y. (2024). *Impactful inclusion toolkit: 52 activities to help you learn and practice inclusion every day in the workplace*. Wiley.

Strauser, D. G., Price, R. A., Brehmer, C. E., & Strauser, D. R. (2026). Exploring employer's successful hiring and retention practices of individuals with disabilities. *Rehabilitation Counseling Bulletin*, *69*(2), 109–119. DOI: 10.1177/00343552241265319

Van Laar, C., Meeussen, L., Veldman, J., Van Grootel, S., Sterk, N., & Jacobs, C. (2019). Coping with stigma in the workplace: Understanding the role of threat regulation, supportive factors, and potential hidden costs. *Frontiers in Psychology*, *10*, 1879. Advance online publication. DOI: 10.3389/fpsyg.2019.01879 PMID: 31507478

Vlachou, A., Roka, O., & Stavroussi, P. (2021). Experiences of workers with disabilities receiving supported employment services in Greece. *Journal of Intellectual Disabilities*, *25*(2), 151–167. DOI: 10.1177/1744629519871172 PMID: 31476953

Wided, R., & Abdulaziz, A. (2024). Facilitating sustainable employment for people with physical disabilities: A pathway to inclusion: An ISM-MICMAC approach. *Journal of Disability Research*, *3*(6), e20240070. Advance online publication. DOI: 10.57197/JDR-2024-0070

Chapter 2
Understanding Intellectual Disability:
Spectrum, Strengths, and Support Needs

ABSTRACT

This chapter examines intellectual disability in employment through a strengths-based, inclusion-focused lens. It argues that intellectual disability should be understood as a spectrum marked by differences in communication, learning pace, social interaction, adaptive functioning, and support needs rather than as a fixed limitation. The chapter highlights the strengths many workers bring to the workplace, including reliability, adherence to routine, honesty, and practical engagement. It also outlines common workplace supports such as clear instructions, visual prompts, predictable routines, communication adjustments, assistive tools, and supportive supervision. Attention is given to job matching as a proactive strategy for aligning workplace demands with individual support profiles. The chapter concludes that informed employer understanding is essential for equitable, respectful, and sustainable inclusive practice.

2.1 INTRODUCTION

Reframing intellectual disability in employment contexts requires a decisive shift away from deficit-oriented assumptions toward a strengths-based and rights-conscious understanding of workers as capable contributors within diverse organisational environments. Historically, employment systems have too often interpreted intellectual disability through the language of limitation, dependency, and risk, thereby narrowing expectations and shaping exclusionary decisions in recruitment,

DOI: 10.4018/979-8-3373-9185-4.ch002

supervision, and advancement (Meltzer et al., 2020; Li, 2004). Such assumptions do not merely distort employer perceptions; they also shape workplace cultures that deny individuals meaningful participation and recognition.

A more constructive framing understands intellectual disability as part of human diversity and recognises that inclusion is not achieved solely through physical placement, but by ensuring that workers are respected, supported, and positioned to contribute in valued ways (Hafsteinsdóttir & Hardonk, 2023). From this standpoint, the workplace becomes a social and relational space in which dignity, trust, reciprocity, and belonging matter alongside productivity. This perspective challenges employers to reconsider taken-for-granted ideas about competence and to appreciate that performance is often shaped by environment, support, and opportunity rather than by diagnosis alone (Francescutti et al., 2022).

Stigma and low expectations remain major barriers to equitable employment for persons with intellectual disabilities. Employers and co-workers may incorrectly assume that such individuals are unable to learn, adapt, or sustain productive roles, even when evidence suggests otherwise (Morris et al., 2024; Burge et al., 2007). These misconceptions can translate into restricted job roles, limited progression, and dismissive workplace interactions. In contrast, when organisations cultivate informed understanding, they are better positioned to identify strengths, tailor support, and create environments in which workers can flourish (Carlson et al., 2020).

Accurate and respectful knowledge is therefore essential. Employers need more than compliance-based awareness; they require practical understanding of how intellectual disability may affect communication, task learning, confidence, and workplace adjustment, while also recognising the varied abilities, aspirations, and contributions of each person (Hennessy et al., 2026; Cavanagh et al., 2017). Training and disability awareness initiatives have been shown to improve attitudes, reduce bias, and support more positive interactions among colleagues and supervisors (Ben-Amram & Shapira-Lishchinsky, 2025; Antonopoulos et al., 2023). This matters because inclusive employment depends not only on policy, but also on the everyday judgments made by those who hire, manage, and work alongside employees with disabilities.

Importantly, workers with intellectual disabilities often describe employment as a source of identity, autonomy, social connection, and self-worth, not merely income (Voermans et al., 2021; Pereira-Silva et al., 2018). Their inclusion can also enrich workplace culture by broadening understandings of diversity and prompting more relational, cooperative forms of work (Efeoğlu & Kılınçarslan, 2024; Gendera et al., 2025). Thus, reframing intellectual disability is not an abstract conceptual task; it is a practical foundation for fairer employment systems. By moving beyond stereotypes and uncertainty, organisations can adopt more equitable, informed, and supportive practices that recognise both the rights and the potential of workers with intellectual disabilities (Suresh & Dyaram, 2022; Novak et al., 2011).

2.2 INTELLECTUAL DISABILITY AS A SPECTRUM

Employers need a nuanced understanding of intellectual disability to create workplaces that are genuinely inclusive, responsive, and fair. Deredzai et al. (2024) and Carroll et al. (2025) show that intellectual and developmental disabilities do not constitute a single, uniform condition with predictable traits or fixed limitations. Rather, they encompass a broad range of experiences, abilities, strengths, and support needs that vary considerably from one person to another. This variation appears in communication, learning pace, problem-solving, social interaction, emotional regulation, and independent functioning. For this reason, employers should avoid one-size-fits-all assumptions and instead treat workers with intellectual disability as individuals whose workplace success depends on the alignment of personal strengths, job demands, and available support.

A spectrum-based understanding is especially important because intellectual disability is often misrepresented in simplistic ways. Terras et al. (2021) emphasise the importance of accessible information and communication support, while Copeland et al. (2014) demonstrate that people with intellectual disability differ in how they express views, understand services, and communicate satisfaction with support. In practice, some individuals may communicate fluently and perform familiar tasks independently, whereas others may require structured guidance, visual support, or repeated demonstration before mastering a role. Some may manage workplace routines effectively but need assistance with unfamiliar changes, while others may excel in repetitive-task environments but struggle with rapid transitions or abstract instructions. These differences are central to understanding intellectual disability in employment contexts. Recognising such diversity allows employers to move beyond rigid stereotypes and create environments where workers are supported based on actual needs rather than presumed limitations.

Figure 1. Strengths-based model for inclusive employment

Figure 1 presents a strengths-based model for inclusive employment. It shows that successful inclusion is shaped by the interaction of four elements: employee strengths and talents, personalised job matches, support and accommodations, and an inclusive workplace culture. The figure emphasises that workers with intellectual disability contribute most effectively when employers align job roles with individual abilities, provide appropriate support, and foster respectful, enabling environments. Rather than focusing on deficits, the model highlights capacity, fit, and organisational responsibility as the basis for meaningful participation, job retention, and positive workplace outcomes.

2.2.1 Cognitive, Adaptive, and Communication Diversity

The spectrum of intellectual disability is most clearly reflected in the wide variation in cognitive and adaptive functioning. Intellectual and developmental disabilities affect individuals differently, meaning the level and type of support required can vary across workers, even when they share the same diagnostic label (Deredzai et al., 2024; Carroll et al., 2025). Some workers may need additional time to process instructions, while others may learn best through practical demonstration or repetition. Adaptive functioning also varies and may include differences in self-care, time management, decision-making, travel confidence, and task organisation.

Communication represents another major area of diversity. Workers with intellectual disability may differ in speech clarity, vocabulary, comprehension, expressive confidence, and ability to interpret workplace language. Some may understand concrete instructions well but find abstract or multi-step explanations confusing. Others may struggle to ask questions or communicate dissatisfaction, particularly in unfamiliar or intimidating settings. Accessible communication, therefore, becomes a core condition for inclusion rather than a peripheral adjustment (Terras et al., 2021). Research also indicates that people with intellectual disability can express their views and evaluate services more effectively when communication is adapted to their needs, confirming the value of plain language, visual cues, and responsive interaction (Copeland et al., 2014).

Employers should therefore recognise that cognitive and communication diversity carries practical implications for supervision and task allocation. Useful responses include:

1. breaking tasks into smaller steps
2. using visual aids or demonstrations
3. checking understanding without judgment
4. allowing additional time for learning
5. offering predictable routines and feedback

These strategies do not lower standards; rather, they strengthen access to successful performance.

Table 1. Common Strengths and Support Needs of Workers with Intellectual Disability

Area	Examples of Strengths	Possible Support Needs	Workplace Implications
Communication	May communicate clearly in familiar contexts; may respond well to plain language, visual prompts, or demonstrations	Simplified instructions, repetition, visual aids, and extra time to process information	Employers should use accessible communication methods to improve understanding, reduce errors, and support confidence
Learning and Task Performance	Often learn effectively through repetition, modelling, and hands-on practice; may show strong task focus	Step-by-step guidance, task demonstration, practice opportunities, and regular feedback	Training should be practical, structured, and paced to match individual learning styles
Routine and Consistency	May perform strongly in predictable environments and show commitment to repeated tasks	Clear schedules, stable routines, and advance notice of changes	Jobs with defined routines may enhance productivity, reduce anxiety, and support retention
Reliability and Work Commitment	May demonstrate punctuality, loyalty, dedication, and commitment to assigned responsibilities	Support with task clarification, encouragement, and consistent supervision	Employers may benefit from dependable performance when roles are clearly defined and expectations are supported

continued on following page

Table 1. Continued

Area	Examples of Strengths	Possible Support Needs	Workplace Implications
Social Interaction	May contribute positively to team spirit, friendliness, and workplace morale	Peer mentoring, social guidance, and help with workplace norms and communication	Inclusive teams and supportive colleagues can strengthen belonging and improve collaboration
Problem-Solving and Decision-Making	May solve practical problems effectively in familiar situations and routine settings	Extra time, guided choices, simplified options, coaching for unfamiliar tasks	Supervisors should avoid assumptions and provide decision support where needed
Emotional and Behavioural Regulation	May remain engaged and cooperative when work environments are supportive and predictable	Calm supervision, clear expectations, reassurance, structured responses to stress	Supportive management can reduce distress, improve adjustment, and encourage stable performance
Independence in Work Tasks	May complete assigned duties independently once trained and familiar with expectations	Initial coaching, reminders, checklists, periodic monitoring	Employers should balance autonomy with appropriate support to promote confidence and competence
Honesty and Integrity	May be perceived as trustworthy, sincere, and committed to doing tasks correctly	Respectful guidance, fair treatment, opportunities to build confidence	These qualities can strengthen workplace trust and contribute to a positive organisational culture
Motivation and Practical Engagement	May show enthusiasm and strong engagement when tasks match interests and abilities	Role matching, encouragement, recognition, opportunities for skill development	Aligning tasks with strengths can improve job satisfaction, performance, and long-term inclusion

[Author, 2026]

Table 2.1 summarises common areas of strength, possible support needs, and their workplace implications for workers with intellectual disability. It shows that support needs do not negate strengths; rather, both must be understood together to promote effective job matching and inclusive practice.

2.2.2 Behavioural, Emotional, and Social Variability

Intellectual disability also varies in emotional, behavioural, and social presentation. Some individuals may display confidence and sociability in the workplace, while others may experience anxiety, frustration, or withdrawal, particularly when expectations are unclear or support is inconsistent. Behavioural difficulties should not be interpreted simply as personal deficits. In many cases, they arise from environmental mismatch, communication barriers, sensory stress, or limited opportunities for self-expression (Inoue, 2019; Carroll et al., 2025).

This variability has significant implications for employers. Workers who appear resistant, slow, or disengaged may in fact be responding to inaccessible instructions, unfamiliar expectations, or the absence of supportive relationships. Similarly, differences in social interaction may affect teamwork, customer engagement, or help-seeking behaviour, but these challenges can often be reduced through orientation, mentoring, and structured inclusion. A spectrum approach requires employers to examine the context in which difficulties arise rather than placing sole blame on the individual. To support behavioural and social diversity, employers may consider:

1. Providing clear expectations and routine
2. Assigning supportive supervisors or peer mentors
3. Reducing unnecessary complexity in communication
4. Responding calmly to distress or confusion
5. Creating psychologically safe environments for questions and clarification

Such practices can improve confidence, reduce misunderstanding, and strengthen workplace participation.

2.2.3 Implications for Employment Design and Employer Practice

Viewing intellectual disability as a spectrum has direct implications for employment outcomes and workplace design. Research shows that employment rates for people with intellectual disability remain low and that successful participation is shaped by a range of factors, including adaptive behaviour, emotional stability, prior work experience, and quality of support (Siperstein et al., 2014; Butterworth et al., 2024). This means that inclusion cannot rest on broad assumptions about what all workers with intellectual disability can or cannot do. Instead, employers must assess each worker in relation to actual job tasks, learning style, and support profile.

Further evidence suggests that employment attainment is influenced by individual capabilities, daily living skills, family support, and environmental opportunities, reinforcing the need for tailored pathways into work (Lee et al., 2026). Many workers also continue to encounter narrow employer expectations, inaccessible recruitment systems, and insufficient workplace support, all of which restrict access to open employment opportunities (Meltzer et al., 2020). A spectrum-based perspective helps address these barriers by encouraging differentiation and individualisation in workplace practice rather than forcing all workers into standardised systems that may not fit them (Wiesel et al., 2024). For employers, this means moving toward practices such as:

1. role matching based on strengths and support needs
2. flexible onboarding and training methods
3. individualised accommodations
4. inclusive performance support
5. regular review of workplace fit and expectations

A careful appreciation of this diversity enables organisations to design more responsive roles, more effective supports, and fairer pathways to participation. When employers recognise that workers with intellectual disability are not a homogeneous group, they are better positioned to foster meaningful inclusion, stronger retention, and workplace practices that reflect equity in action.

2.3 STRENGTHS, TALENTS, AND WORKPLACE CONTRIBUTIONS

A strengths-based understanding of workers with intellectual disability is central to inclusive employment. Too often, workplace discussions emphasise limitations, dependency, or the burden of accommodation rather than the capacities individuals bring to their roles. This imbalance can obscure the practical, social, and organisational value of inclusive hiring. Workers with intellectual disability contribute in many ways when tasks are aligned with their abilities, interests, and support needs. These contributions include dependability, commitment to routine, honesty, practical engagement, and a positive influence on workplace relationships (Kåhlin & Haglund, 2009; Nota et al., 2014).

Meaningful work also serves as an important source of identity, satisfaction, and participation for many people with intellectual disability. When workers are given roles that are well-matched, well-supported, and socially valued, they often demonstrate commitment, motivation, and sustained engagement. Akkerman et al. (2016) and Akkerman et al. (2018) link this alignment to stronger workplace participation and job satisfaction. This section, therefore, shifts attention from deficits to capacities by showing that workers with intellectual disability are active contributors whose strengths can enrich teams, strengthen workplace culture, and advance organisational goals when inclusive conditions are in place.

2.3.1 Personal Strengths and Work-Related Talents

Workers with intellectual disability often demonstrate valuable personal strengths that make them effective contributors in structured employment environments. These strengths are not always recognised within conventional recruitment systems, especially when employers rely on narrow definitions of competence. A strengths-based lens, in contrast, highlights qualities that support job performance, stability, and positive engagement at work.

2.3.1.1 Reliability and Commitment to Work: Work is often regarded by people with intellectual disability as an important part of adult life, identity, and social participation. Kåhlin and Haglund (2009) describe work-related psychosocial strengths, including commitment and a sense of purpose, while Akkerman et al. (2016) associate positive job experiences with meaningful participation. When expectations are clear and support is available, many workers show dependability, punctuality, and consistency in carrying out assigned tasks.

2.3.1.2 Adherence to Routine and Structured Practice: Many workers with intellectual disability perform particularly well in environments where tasks are predictable and routines are clearly organised. Such a structure can reduce uncertainty, support confidence, and improve performance in everyday work activities. Gasset and Ero (2016) show that competence is strengthened when supported employment aligns tasks with individual capacity and offers consistent practice. This makes many workers especially effective in roles that depend on repetition, sequence, and procedural stability.

2.3.1.3 Honesty, Trustworthiness, and Integrity: Honesty and trustworthiness are qualities often associated with workers with intellectual disability in discussions of workplace inclusion and well-being. These qualities contribute to interpersonal confidence and can improve everyday working relationships. Fajardo-Castro et al. (2024) connect supportive organisational contexts with workers' satisfaction with basic needs, while Cavanagh et al. (2021) highlight the importance of fair treatment in enabling workers to thrive. Such qualities can strengthen team cohesion and reinforce a respectful organisational culture.

2.3.1.4 Practical Engagement and Task Motivation: Workers with intellectual disability often show strong practical engagement when job tasks are aligned with their skills and interests. Motivation tends to increase when individuals experience competence, participation, and recognition in the workplace (Akkerman et al., 2018; Gasset & Ero, 2016). In such contexts, work becomes more than a routine obligation; it becomes a space for contribution, confidence, and achievement. This practical engagement can be especially valuable in roles that require focus, repetition, and steady application.

2.3.2 Workplace Contributions Beyond Task Performance

The value of workers with intellectual disability extends beyond the completion of assigned duties. Their presence and participation can shape workplace culture, strengthen relationships, and influence how teams understand inclusion. Inclusive employment, therefore, benefits not only the individual worker but also the wider organisation.

2.3.2.1 Positive Influence on Workplace Culture: Including workers with intellectual disability can challenge stereotypes and foster a more inclusive organisational ethos. Gormley (2015) illustrates how workplace stigma operates and how contact and participation can alter assumptions about capacity and contribution. As colleagues interact more closely with workers with intellectual disability, attitudes may shift from doubt to appreciation. This cultural shift can foster a more respectful and open environment for everyone.

2.3.2.2 Contribution to Organisational Goals: Workers with intellectual disability can contribute meaningfully to organisational objectives when training, supervision, and task design are tailored appropriately. Their effectiveness is often enhanced when employers provide clear guidance, realistic expectations, and accessible forms of support. Joyce et al. (2024) emphasise workplace structures and cultures that sustain well-being, while Gasset and Ero (2016) highlight the importance of matching competencies to role demands. Contribution should therefore be understood in relation to enabling workplace conditions, not solely to diagnosis.

2.3.2.3 Strengthening Team Dynamics and Social Cohesion: Inclusive workplaces often encourage patience, cooperation, and collective responsibility among team members. Environments that support workers with intellectual disability may also strengthen a sense of belonging and interpersonal respect across the organisation. Fajardo-Castro et al. (2024) emphasise the organisational context, and Joyce et al. (2025) connect this environment to well-being and job satisfaction. In this way, inclusion can enrich team dynamics and reinforce shared values.

2.3.3 Conditions That Strengthen Workplace Contribution

The strengths of workers with intellectual disability become more visible when workplaces are organised to support participation, development, and fair recognition. Talent does not emerge in isolation. It is shaped by job design, supervisory attitudes, organisational culture, and access to practical support. Employers, therefore, play a decisive role in creating the conditions under which these strengths can be expressed and sustained.

2.3.3.1 Supportive Work Environments: Flexible arrangements, mentoring, clear supervision, and accessible communication can improve workplace participation and confidence among employees with intellectual disability. Joyce et al. (2024) and Joyce et al. (2025) associate these features with well-being and stronger engagement at work. Such support does not merely respond to difficulty; it enables strengths to translate into effective performance.

2.3.3.2 Strengths-Based Framing and Employer Attitudes: Employer attitudes influence whether workers are viewed through the lens of capability or limitation. When disability is framed in terms of strengths, competencies, and contribution, employers may be more willing to support inclusion and equitable role design. Nota et al. (2014) link employer attitudes to work inclusion, showing the importance of how workers are perceived from the outset. A strengths-based framing helps reduce stigma and opens space for more balanced expectations.

2.3.3.3 Opportunities for Development and Advancement: Workers with intellectual disability should not be confined to narrow or static roles. Access to skill development, role expansion, and meaningful participation can improve workplace contribution and personal well-being. Cavanagh et al. (2021) identify barriers to thriving, while Carr-Kirby et al. (2025) highlight hope and possibility within strengths-based employment services. Inclusive employment becomes more sustainable when it includes pathways for learning, recognition, and growth.

Workers with intellectual disability bring more than symbolic value to the workplace. They offer qualities and contributions that can support routine operations, enrich team culture, and strengthen inclusive organisational practice. Reliability, honesty, practical engagement, and commitment are workplace assets that deserve recognition. Employers who identify and nurture these strengths are better positioned to build environments that are productive, respectful, and socially responsive (Kåhlin & Haglund, 2009; Joyce et al., 2024).

2.4 COMMON SUPPORT NEEDS IN THE WORKPLACE

Successful workplace inclusion depends on recognising the practical supports that enable workers with intellectual disability to perform their roles with confidence and consistency. This support should not be viewed as an exceptional demand. Rather, they form part of effective management because they improve clarity, reduce uncertainty, and strengthen participation. Garrels and Sigstad (2021) link sustained employment to practical and individualised support that responds to both workplace demands and worker needs.

Many effective supports are low-cost, relational, and easy to incorporate into everyday practice. These include clear communication, task breakdown, predictable routines, visual prompts, and responsive supervision. When employers integrate such supports into routine management, they can improve performance, confidence, and retention while strengthening inclusion across the workplace.

2.4.1 Practical Supports That Enable Workplace Success

Workers with intellectual disability may require different forms of support depending on the role, work setting, and individual learning and communication profiles. The most effective forms of support are usually simple, consistent, and closely connected to everyday tasks. These include clear instructions, visual prompts, predictable routines, communication adjustments, supportive supervision, and natural supports.

2.4.1.1 Clear Instructions and Task Breakdown: Clear instructions are among the most important supports in workplace settings. Tasks are easier to complete when supervisors use simple language and divide duties into manageable steps. Garrels and Sigstad (2021) emphasise individualised support as a means of helping workers meet workplace expectations. This approach improves understanding, reduces avoidable errors, and supports gradual skill development.

2.4.1.2 Visual Prompts and Assistive Tools: Visual prompts, checklists, picture cues, and assistive technologies can strengthen task completion and independent functioning. Morash-Macneil et al. (2018) describe assistive technology as effective in improving productivity and work performance for people with intellectual disability. Marelle et al. (2023) also highlight the usefulness of wireless and wearable tools for navigation, time management, and task monitoring. These supports are particularly useful for workers who respond well to visual or hands-on learning.

2.4.1.3 Predictable Routines: Stable routines can foster confidence, consistency, and emotional security at work. Workers with intellectual disability may perform more effectively when expectations are predictable, and changes are introduced clearly. Nijhof et al. (2024) note the importance of consistent support practices, while Bigby (2023) links structured support with stronger engagement in everyday activities. Predictability can therefore reduce anxiety and support sustained participation.

2.4.1.4 Communication Adjustments: Workplace communication often requires adjustment to ensure understanding and participation. This may involve plain language, slower pacing, repetition, demonstrations, or supported ways of expressing needs and concerns. Pouliot et al. (2017) discuss tools that support communication in workplace settings, including resources that help employees describe preferences and advocate for themselves. Communication adjustments also require supervisors and co-workers to clearly convey tasks and respond thoughtfully to questions.

2.4.1.5 Supportive Supervision: Supervisory support is a major factor in workplace inclusion. Workers are more likely to thrive when supervisors provide guidance respectfully, offer reassurance, and create opportunities for learning. Cavanagh et al.

(2021) highlight subtle workplace discrimination that can limit thriving and underscore the importance of responsive, inclusive supervision. Supportive management affirms competence while allowing space for clarification and improvement.

2.4.1.6 Natural Supports: Support does not come only from supervisors or external professionals. Co-workers can provide natural supports through reminders, modelling, informal guidance, and everyday inclusion in team routines. Athamanah et al. (2024) describe natural supports as valuable for vocational and social outcomes in competitive integrated employment. Li (2004) also points to the importance of equal opportunity and social inclusion in shaping participation. These supports help normalise assistance and strengthen a sense of belonging.

2.4.2 Organisational Practices That Strengthen Support: Practical supports become more effective when reinforced by organisational systems and culture. Support should not depend solely on individual goodwill. Employers need structures that make responsive practice consistent across departments and roles. Assistive technology, inclusive workplace practices, and holistic transitional support are especially important in this regard.

2.4.2.1 Assistive Technology as a Workplace Enabler: Assistive technology can help workers manage tasks more independently and with greater confidence. This may include reminders, scheduling apps, digital prompts, wearable supports, or navigation tools. Bryant (2012) highlights the broader role of assistive technology in support provision, while Marelle et al. (2023) show how wireless technology can reduce barriers in workplace contexts. When selected appropriately, these tools can enhance autonomy without replacing human support.

2.4.2.2 Inclusive Workplace Practices: Support is stronger when organisations adopt inclusive policies and build awareness among supervisors and co-workers. Cavanagh et al. (2021) show that workplace cultures can either enable or inhibit thriving, depending on how difference is understood and managed. Inclusive practices may include team orientation, flexible training approaches, anti-discrimination awareness, and procedures that promote fair treatment. These measures make support part of organisational culture rather than an isolated adjustment.

2.4.2.3 Holistic and Transitional Support: Workplace success is often stronger when practical, emotional, and technological supports are combined. Piccolo et al. (2023) discuss digital support for people entering the labour market and emphasise the importance of coordinated assistance during transition. Holistic support recognises that job adjustment involves more than task competence. Confidence, communication, routine, and social connection also shape successful participation in employment.

2.4.3 Support as Good Management Practice

Support for workers with intellectual disability should be understood as part of effective management rather than as a special concession. Many of the adjustments discussed in this section, including clarity, structure, feedback, and supportive supervision, are features of good workplace practice more broadly. Their value in inclusive employment lies in their capacity to help workers understand expectations, demonstrate ability, and contribute meaningfully. This perspective includes normalising support within supervision, balancing support with autonomy, and building inclusive organisational capacity.

2.4.3.1 Normalising Support Within Supervision: When support is integrated into routine supervision, it becomes easier to sustain and less likely to be treated as exceptional. This approach helps reduce stigma and promotes fairness in workplace relationships.

2.4.3.2 Balancing Support and Autonomy: Effective support should strengthen independence rather than create overreliance. Workers benefit when assistance matches need and is adjusted as competence develops.

2.4.3.3 Building Inclusive Capacity: Supportive workplaces require accessible systems, informed supervision, and a culture that treats responsiveness as a professional responsibility.

In this way, support becomes a practical expression of inclusion. It enables workers with intellectual disability to perform successfully while helping organisations become more equitable and effective.

2.5 MATCHING JOB DEMANDS WITH INDIVIDUAL SUPPORT PROFILES

Aligning workplace demands with individual support profiles is a practical step toward sustainable inclusive employment. For workers with intellectual disability, workplace success depends not only on personal capability but also on the extent to which role expectations, task demands, and available supports are aligned. Poor alignment can create avoidable difficulties, including stress, underperformance, and premature exit from employment. Careful alignment, by contrast, increases the likelihood that workers will contribute effectively in roles that are realistic, meaningful, and manageable.

This approach requires employers to examine the nature of the job itself. Tasks vary in pace, complexity, communication demands, degree of supervision, and social expectations. Workers also differ in interests, stamina, preferred ways of learning, and forms of support required. Job matching therefore involves comparing these two sets of factors to identify the most suitable fit. Morgan (2008) emphasises the assessment of employment preferences, while Kukla and Bond (2012) associate stronger job match with longer job tenure. These insights support the view that sound placement decisions begin with fit rather than assumption.

2.5.1 Core Elements of Job Matching

Effective role alignment begins with careful attention to the relationship between the individual and the role. It requires more than identifying whether a vacancy exists. Employers must consider the specific demands of the job and the particular qualities of the worker before making placement decisions.

2.5.1.1 Abilities, Interests, and Preferences: A suitable role should reflect not only what a worker can do, but also what the worker enjoys, values, or finds motivating. Morgan (2008) highlights the importance of assessing the degree of match between employment preferences and available roles. Kukla and Bond (2012) also show that interest and enjoyment are closely linked to job tenure. When roles align with personal preferences, workers are often more committed and more likely to remain employed.

2.5.1.2 Customised Employment: Tailored role design provides a useful option where standard job descriptions do not adequately reflect individual strengths. Christianson-Barker et al. (2025) describe this approach as one that adapts roles to fit both worker capability and employer need. Plotner and Oertle (2021) also highlight the contribution of job coaches and support facilitators in shaping duties and supporting implementation. This process can open employment opportunities that might otherwise be overlooked within rigid staffing structures.

2.5.2 Job Matching as a Structured and Ongoing Process

Successful placement should be treated as a structured process rather than as a single decision made at the point of recruitment. Initial placement may require later adjustment as workers gain experience, as supervisors develop a better understanding of support requirements, or as the nature of the job changes.

2.5.2.1 Job Analysis and Ability Profiling: Suresh and Dyaram (2023) describe job matching as involving job analysis, ability profiling, and the identification of gaps between work demands and worker capacity. This process helps employers determine whether changes are needed in task allocation, scheduling, supervision, or work methods. It also improves the precision of role design by grounding decisions in actual job content rather than in general impressions.

2.5.2.2 Planning for Accommodation: Accommodation planning strengthens job matching by identifying, in advance, the adjustments needed for effective participation.

Gignac et al. (2025) present the Job Demands and Accommodation Planning Tool as a useful mechanism for improving self-efficacy and reducing absenteeism among workers with disabilities. Planning tools of this kind help employers anticipate barriers and organise support more systematically. This approach makes the placement process more intentional and reduces the likelihood of reactive problem-solving.

2.5.2.3 Collaborative Decision-Making: Effective job matching often depends on collaboration among the worker, the employer, and relevant support personnel. Persch et al. (2015) highlights the value of coordinated practice in transition and placement processes. Collaboration allows different perspectives to inform the match, including operational needs, worker goals, and practical support considerations. It also helps ensure that employment decisions are not made solely from the employer's viewpoint.

2.5.3 Organisational Value of Thoughtful Job Matching

Thoughtful job matching benefits both workers and organisations. It enables employers to use talent more effectively, reduce avoidable placement difficulties, and establish clearer pathways for inclusion within ordinary workplace systems.

2.5.3.1 Stronger Retention: Retention is more likely when the demands of the role are compatible with the worker's abilities and preferences. Kukla and Bond (2012) associate a stronger job match with longer tenure, and Morgan (2008) emphasises the compatibility between worker preferences and job characteristics. Workers are more likely to remain in positions that feel manageable and worthwhile.

2.5.3.2 Better Work Performance: Performance improves when workers are placed in roles that fit their profile and when anticipated barriers are addressed in advance. Christianson-Barker et al. (2025) emphasise strength-based employment practices, while Gignac et al. (2025) show the value of accommodation planning in supporting work functioning. In this sense, better performance reflects effective alignment rather than simple compliance.

2.5.3.3 More Sustainable Inclusion Job matching also supports inclusion at the organisational level by encouraging employers to carefully consider role design, workplace flexibility, and long-term participation. Johnsen et al. (2022) describe inclusive leadership responses that support participation across diverse employee groups. When employers approach placement with this mindset, inclusion becomes part of workforce planning rather than a response to difficulty after hiring.

Employers should therefore treat job matching as a forward-looking strategy that improves both equity and effectiveness. By aligning job demands with individual support profiles, organisations can create employment arrangements that are more stable, productive, and responsive to difference.

2.6 CONCLUSION

Building employer understanding is central to the success of inclusive employment. Knowledge about intellectual disability does more than improve awareness; it influences how employers design roles, communicate expectations, supervise workers, and respond to differences in everyday workplace interactions. Where understanding is weak, stereotypes, low expectations, and poor decisions can shape recruitment, training, and performance management. Where understanding is informed and respectful, employers are better able to create environments in which workers with intellectual disability are recognised as capable contributors and supported in ways that promote participation and dignity.

This chapter has shown that intellectual disability should be understood as a spectrum rather than a fixed or uniform condition. Workers bring varied strengths, preferences, and support needs, which means that inclusive practice depends on flexibility, responsiveness, and attention to individual fit. Employers who understand this are more likely to avoid one-size-fits-all approaches and instead adopt strategies that strengthen job match, communication, supervision, and workplace belonging. Such understanding also influences peer relations, because attitudes within teams are often shaped by leadership signals, organisational culture, and everyday management practice.

In this sense, employer understanding is not an abstract ideal but a practical foundation for equitable and sustainable employment. It supports better decision-making at every stage of the employment process, from recruitment and onboarding to workplace support and retention. It also creates the conditions under which accommodations and support systems can function effectively rather than superficially. The chapters that follow build on this foundation by examining how inclusive recruitment, tailored support, and workplace structures can translate informed understanding into practice. Respectful and knowledgeable employer engagement remains essential to achieving meaningful inclusion for workers with intellectual disability.

REFERENCES

Akkerman, A., Janssen, C. G. C., Kef, S., & Meininger, H. P. (2016). Job satisfaction of people with intellectual disabilities in integrated and sheltered employment: An exploration of the literature. *Journal of Policy and Practice in Intellectual Disabilities*, *13*(3), 205–216. DOI: 10.1111/jppi.12168

Akkerman, A., Kef, S., & Meininger, H. P. (2018). Job satisfaction of people with intellectual disabilities: The role of basic psychological need fulfilment and workplace participation. *Disability and Rehabilitation*, *40*(10), 1192–1199. DOI: 10.1080/09638288.2017.1294205 PMID: 28288522

Antonopoulos, C. R., Sugden, N., & Saliba, A. (2023). Implicit bias toward people with disabilities: A systematic review and meta-analysis. *Rehabilitation Psychology*, *68*(2), 121–134. DOI: 10.1037/rep0000493 PMID: 37079819

Athamanah, L. S., Cushing, L. S., Fastzkie, E. M., & Brown, E. R. (2024). Natural supports in competitive integrated employment: A scoping review. *Journal of Vocational Rehabilitation*, *60*(3), 327–339. DOI: 10.3233/JVR-240017

Ben-Amram, M., & Shapira-Lishchinsky, O. (2025). Employer training interventions in supported employment workplaces and their impact on hiring attitudes. *International Journal of Training and Development*. Advance online publication. DOI: 10.1111/ijtd.70015

Bigby, C. (2023). Supporting engagement in everyday life at home and in the community: Active support. In *Disability practice: Safeguarding quality service delivery* (pp. 121–142). Springer., DOI: 10.1007/978-981-99-6143-6_7

Bryant, B. R. (2012). Assistive technology and support provision for individuals with intellectual and developmental disabilities: Introduction to the topical issue. *Journal of Special Education Technology*, *27*(2), 1–2. DOI: 10.1177/016264341202700201

Burge, P., Ouellette-Kuntz, H., & Lysaght, R. (2007). Public views on employment of people with intellectual disabilities. *Journal of Vocational Rehabilitation*, *26*(1), 29–37. DOI: 10.3233/JVR-2007-00360

Butterworth, J., Winsor, J. E., Kamau, E., Migliore, A., & Mahoehney, D. (2024). The state of employment for people with IDD: Implications for practice, policy, and equity. *Intellectual and Developmental Disabilities*, *62*(3), 225–240. DOI: 10.1352/1934-9556-62.3.225 PMID: 38802097

Carlson, S. R., Morningstar, M. E., & Munandar, V. (2020). Workplace supports for employees with intellectual disability: A systematic review of the intervention literature. *Journal of Vocational Rehabilitation, 52*(3), 251–265. DOI: 10.3233/JVR-201075

Carr-Kirby, K., Horton, S., Sutherland, C. A., Paraschak, V., & Weir, P. (2025). 'I don't think they've ever seen people like me do jobs like this': Exploring hope within strengths-based employment services for people with disability. *Journal of Applied Research in Intellectual Disabilities, 38*(6), e70147. DOI: 10.1111/jar.70147 PMID: 41177549

Carroll, R. A., Halbur, M., & Preas, E. J. (2025). Autism spectrum disorder and other developmental disabilities. In *Applied behavior analysis for clinical, educational, and training applications* (pp. 305–326). Elsevier., DOI: 10.1016/B978-0-443-22361-7.00011-3

Cavanagh, J., Bartram, T., Meacham, H., Bigby, C., Oakman, J., & Fossey, E. (2017). Supporting workers with disabilities: A scoping review of the role of human resource management in contemporary organisations. *Asia Pacific Journal of Human Resources, 55*(1), 6–43. DOI: 10.1111/1744-7941.12111

Cavanagh, J., Meacham, H., Pariona-Cabrera, P., & Bartram, T. (2021). Subtle workplace discrimination inhibiting workers with intellectual disability from thriving at the workplace. *Personnel Review, 50*(7/8), 1739–1756. DOI: 10.1108/PR-10-2021-0723

Christianson-Barker, J., Franzius, A., Mills, R., Lomness, A., & Hole, R. (2025). Employing strength: A scoping review of customized employment practices to support inclusive employment for people with intellectual disabilities. *Journal of Vocational Rehabilitation, 63*(2), 119–140. DOI: 10.1177/10522263251356445

Copeland, S. R., Luckasson, R., & Shauger, R. (2014). Eliciting perceptions of satisfaction with services and supports from persons with intellectual disability and developmental disabilities: A review of the literature. *Journal of Intellectual Disability Research, 58*(12), 1141–1155. DOI: 10.1111/jir.12114 PMID: 24433252

Deredzai, M., Maupa, B., & Mashiri, W. (2024). Social inclusion tactics for people with intellectual and developmental disabilities: Support for families of people with intellectual and developmental disabilities in Zimbabwe. In *Social inclusion tactics for people with intellectual and developmental disabilities* (pp. 367–388). IGI Global., DOI: 10.4018/979-8-3693-3176-7.ch016

Efeoğlu, İ. E., & Kılınçarslan, Ö. (2024). How do individuals with autism participate in work life? A study on inclusive employability. *Equality, Diversity and Inclusion, 43*(2), 173–187. DOI: 10.1108/EDI-09-2022-0254

Fajardo-Castro, L. V., Martínez-Tur, V., Moliner, C., Plavsic, A., & Arbués, J. (2024). Organizational context and satisfaction of basic needs of workers with intellectual disability as sources of well-being. *Social Sciences (Basel, Switzerland), 13*(10), 523. DOI: 10.3390/socsci13100523

Francescutti, C., Diminutto, M., & Zorzi, S. (2022). Work and occupation. In *Textbook of psychiatry for intellectual disability and autism spectrum disorder* (pp. 941–968). Springer., DOI: 10.1007/978-3-319-95720-3_38

Garrels, V., & Sigstad, H. M. H. (2021). Employment for persons with intellectual disability in the Nordic countries: A scoping review. *Journal of Applied Research in Intellectual Disabilities, 34*(4), 993–1007. DOI: 10.1111/jar.12880 PMID: 33709541

Gasset, D. I., & Ero, P. R. H. (2016). Evaluation of the methodology supported employment in promentor program (UAM-PRODIS). Competence setting [Evaluación de la metodología empleo con apoyo (ECA) en el programa promentor (UAM-PRODIS). El ajuste competencial]. *Siglo Cero, 47*(1), 37–54. DOI: 10.14201/scero201613754

Gendera, S., Alexander, J., Burton, J., Fisher, K. R., & Robinson, S. (2025). People with disability influencing sustained improvements to employment. *Social Policy and Administration*. Advance online publication. DOI: 10.1111/spol.70022

Gignac, M. A. M., Bowring, J., Navaratnerajah, L., Saunders, R., Jetha, A., Thompson, A., Shaw, W. S., Franche, R.-L., Van Eerd, D., Irvin, E., Tompa, E., Macdermid, J. C., & Smith, P. M. (2025). The Job Demands and Accommodation Planning Tool (JDAPT): A nine-month evaluation of use, changes in self-efficacy, presenteeism, and absenteeism in workers with chronic and episodic disabilities. *Journal of Occupational Rehabilitation, 35*(3), 625–640. DOI: 10.1007/s10926-024-10231-w PMID: 39120861

Gormley, M. E. (2015). Workplace stigma toward employees with intellectual disability: A descriptive study. *Journal of Vocational Rehabilitation, 43*(3), 249–258. DOI: 10.3233/JVR-150773

Hafsteinsdóttir, Á., & Hardonk, S. C. (2023). Understanding work inclusion: Analysis of the perspectives of people with intellectual disabilities on employment in the Icelandic labor market. *Work (Reading, Mass.), 75*(2), 433–445. DOI: 10.3233/WOR-211219 PMID: 36641711

Hennessy, T., McMahon, J., & Doody, O. (2026). Informing the design of inclusive post-secondary education: A qualitative exploration of the perspectives of individuals with intellectual disabilities. *British Journal of Learning Disabilities, 54*(2), 263–275. Advance online publication. DOI: 10.1111/bld.70033

Inoue, M. (2019). Assessments and interventions to address challenging behavior in individuals with intellectual disability and autism spectrum disorder in Japan: A consolidated review. *Yonago Acta Medica, 62*(2), 169–181. DOI: 10.33160/yam.2019.06.001 PMID: 31320821

Johnsen, T. L., Fyhn, T., Jordbru, A., Torp, S., Tveito, T. H., & Øyeflaten, I. (2022). Workplace inclusion of people with health issues, immigrants, and unemployed youths—A qualitative study of Norwegian leaders' experiences. *Frontiers in Psychology, 13*, 687384. DOI: 10.3389/fpsyg.2022.687384 PMID: 35783778

Joyce, A., Campbell, P., Crosbie, J., & Wilson, E. (2024). Workplace structures and culture that support the wellbeing of people with an intellectual disability. *International Journal of Environmental Research and Public Health, 21*(11), 1453. DOI: 10.3390/ijerph21111453 PMID: 39595719

Joyce, A., Campbell, P., Crosbie, J., & Wilson, E. (2025). Wellbeing and job satisfaction among employees with intellectual disability. *Frontiers in Public Health, 13*, 1503932. DOI: 10.3389/fpubh.2025.1503932 PMID: 40124410

Kåhlin, I., & Haglund, L. (2009). Psychosocial strengths and challenges related to work among persons with intellectual disabilities. *Occupational Therapy in Mental Health, 25*(2), 151–163. DOI: 10.1080/01642120902859055

Kukla, M., & Bond, G. (2012). Job match and job tenure in persons with severe mental illness. *Journal of Rehabilitation, 78*(1), 11–15.

Lee, C. E., Koo, J., & Li, C. (2026). Application of machine learning to predict employment attainment among individuals with intellectual and developmental disabilities. *Research in Developmental Disabilities, 168*, 105181. DOI: 10.1016/j.ridd.2025.105181 PMID: 41386177

Li, E. P. Y. (2004). Self-perceived equal opportunities for people with intellectual disability. *International Journal of Rehabilitation Research. Internationale Zeitschrift fur Rehabilitationsforschung. Revue Internationale de Recherches de Readaptation, 27*(3), 241–245. DOI: 10.1097/00004356-200409000-00011 PMID: 15319696

Marelle, C., Vinoski Thomas, E., & Donehower Paul, C. (2023). A survey of wireless technology supporting individuals with intellectual and developmental disabilities in the workplace. *Journal of Special Education Technology, 38*(4), 434–444. DOI: 10.1177/01626434221131463

Meltzer, A., Robinson, S., & Fisher, K. R. (2020). Barriers to finding and maintaining open employment for people with intellectual disability in Australia. *Social Policy and Administration, 54*(1), 88–101. DOI: 10.1111/spol.12523

Morash-Macneil, V., Johnson, F., & Ryan, J. B. (2018). A systematic review of assistive technology for individuals with intellectual disability in the workplace. *Journal of Special Education Technology, 33*(1), 15–26. DOI: 10.1177/0162643417729166

Morgan, R. L. (2008). Job matching: Development and evaluation of a web-based instrument to assess degree of match among employment preferences. *Journal of Vocational Rehabilitation, 29*(1), 29–38. DOI: 10.3233/JVR-2008-00424

Morris, R., Christianson-Barker, J., Stainton, T., Mills, R., Rowley, C., Cox, J., Schroeder, M., & Hole, R. (2024). 'They don't think I can do it': Experiences of self-advocates, employment specialists, and employers on employment of adults with intellectual disability. *Journal of Applied Research in Intellectual Disabilities, 37*(3), e13231. DOI: 10.1111/jar.13231 PMID: 38561915

Nijhof, K., Boot, F. H., Naaldenberg, J., Leusink, G. L., & Bevelander, K. E. (2024). Health support of people with intellectual disability and the crucial role of support workers. *BMC Health Services Research, 24*(1), 4. DOI: 10.1186/s12913-023-10206-2 PMID: 38167137

Nota, L., Santilli, S., Ginevra, M. C., & Soresi, S. (2014). Employer attitudes towards the work inclusion of people with disability. *Journal of Applied Research in Intellectual Disabilities, 27*(6), 511–520. DOI: 10.1111/jar.12081 PMID: 24288164

Novak, J., Feyes, K. J., & Christensen, K. A. (2011). Application of intergroup contact theory to the integrated workplace: Setting the stage for inclusion. *Journal of Vocational Rehabilitation, 35*(3), 211–226. DOI: 10.3233/JVR-2011-0573

Pereira-Silva, N. L., Furtado, A. V., & Andrade, J. F. C. D. M. (2018). Workplace inclusion from the standpoint of individuals with intellectual disabilities. *Temas em Psicologia, 26*(2), 1017–1030. DOI: 10.9788/TP2018.2-17En

Persch, A. C., Cleary, D. S., Rutkowski, S., Malone, H. I., Darragh, A. R., & Case-Smith, J. D. (2015). Current practices in job matching: A Project SEARCH perspective on transition. *Journal of Vocational Rehabilitation, 43*(3), 259–273. DOI: 10.3233/JVR-150774

Piccolo, L., Gruber, B. C., Knobel, M., & Stähler, L. (2023). A digital support for people with disabilities entering the labour market: Ideation process and design requirements. In *ACM International Conference Proceeding Series* (pp. 265–270). https://doi.org/DOI: 10.1145/3582515.3609543

Plotner, A. J., & Oertle, K. M. (2021). Employment support facilitator (job coach). In *Collaboration: A multidisciplinary approach to educating students with disabilities* (pp. 339–351). Routledge., DOI: 10.4324/9781003233688-28

Pouliot, D. M., Müller, E., Frasché, N. F., Kern, A. S., & Resti, I. H. (2017). A tool for supporting communication in the workplace for individuals with intellectual disabilities and/or autism. *Career Development and Transition for Exceptional Individuals*, *40*(4), 244–249. DOI: 10.1177/2165143416683927

Siperstein, G. N., Heyman, M., & Stokes, J. E. (2014). Pathways to employment: A national survey of adults with intellectual disabilities. *Journal of Vocational Rehabilitation*, *41*(3), 165–178. DOI: 10.3233/JVR-140711

Suresh, V., & Dyaram, L. (2022). Diversity in disability: Leaders' accounts on inclusive employment in the Indian context. *Equality, Diversity and Inclusion*, *41*(3), 454–473. DOI: 10.1108/EDI-05-2020-0133

Suresh, V., & Dyaram, L. (2023). Job matching for persons with disabilities: An exploratory study. *Employee Responsibilities and Rights Journal*, *35*(4), 475–492. DOI: 10.1007/s10672-022-09421-6

Terras, M. M., Jarrett, D., & McGregor, S. A. (2021). The importance of accessible information in promoting the inclusion of people with an intellectual disability. *Disabilities*, *1*(3), 132–150. DOI: 10.3390/disabilities1030011

Voermans, M. A. C., Taminiau, E. F., Giesbers, S. A. H., & Embregts, P. J. C. M. (2021). The value of competitive employment: In-depth accounts of people with intellectual disabilities. *Journal of Applied Research in Intellectual Disabilities*, *34*(1), 239–249. DOI: 10.1111/jar.12802 PMID: 32945056

Wiesel, I., Bigby, C., van Holstein, E., & Gleeson, B. (2024). Three modes of inclusion of people with intellectual disability in mainstream services: Mainstreaming, differentiation and individualisation. *Disability & Society*, *39*(1), 40–61. DOI: 10.1080/09687599.2022.2060803

Chapter 3
The Legal Landscape:
Rights, Obligations, and Incentives

ABSTRACT

An analysis of the legal landscape shaping the employment of workers with intellectual disabilities is presented with particular attention to the Americans with Disabilities Act, the Individuals with Disabilities Education Act, and the Workforce Innovation and Opportunity Act. It considers how these laws support rights protections, employer obligations, workplace accommodations, transition planning, and labour market participation. The discussion also addresses implementation barriers, such as weak employer knowledge, fragmented transition systems, and symbolic compliance. The discussion argues that inclusive employment depends not only on legal protection but also on coordinated governance, practical support, and institutional accountability across education and employment systems.

3.1 INTRODUCTION

The employment of workers with intellectual disability is shaped not only by employer attitudes, organisational culture, and workplace design, but also by a legal framework that defines rights, duties, and accountability. For employers, understanding this framework is no longer optional. It is a practical necessity for lawful decision-making across recruitment, selection, onboarding, supervision, performance management, accommodation, and retention. Moreover, many organisations still approach disability law narrowly, treating it as a matter of avoiding complaints rather than as a guide for building fair and sustainable employment systems. This chapter begins from a different premise. It argues that the legal landscape should be understood not merely as a set of restrictions on employer action, but as an enabling

DOI: 10.4018/979-8-3373-9185-4.ch003

structure that clarifies how inclusion can be implemented in ways that are both just and operationally sound.

In the employment of workers with intellectual disability, legal knowledge matters because misunderstanding the law often reproduces exclusion. Employers may incorrectly assume that intellectual disability automatically prevents effective job performance, that accommodation is always costly, or that legal compliance is limited to reacting when a problem arises. Such assumptions can influence hiring decisions, shape performance expectations, and discourage the development of inclusive workplace systems. Anti-discrimination law was developed precisely to challenge these forms of exclusion by requiring that individuals be assessed on their ability to perform essential job functions with or without reasonable accommodation, rather than on stereotypes or generalised assumptions about disability (Rabenu & Tziner, 2016; Bennett & Randolph, 2010). In this sense, the law does more than prohibit unfair treatment. It requires employers to rethink long-standing assumptions about merit, productivity, and workplace participation.

A practical understanding of disability law is especially important in relation to intellectual disability because barriers often emerge through routine employment practices rather than overt discrimination. Job advertisements may use unnecessarily complex language. Interview formats may privilege fast verbal responses over demonstrable ability. Orientation procedures may assume that all new employees learn in the same way. Supervisors may interpret communication differences or slower task acquisition as a lack of competence rather than as indicators that better instructional support is needed. These problems are not always driven by hostility; often, they arise from limited legal and procedural awareness. Disability law, therefore, provides an essential framework for recognising when apparently neutral practices produce exclusion and when employers are required to modify such practices to ensure equal opportunity (Cox, 2009; Towns & Moore, 2005).

The legal landscape also matters because it addresses the question of reasonable accommodation, which sits at the centre of fair employment practice. Employers are not only prohibited from discrimination; they are often required to make adjustments that enable a worker with a disability to perform essential aspects of a role. Such adjustments may include modified instructions, structured supervision, altered communication methods, environmental changes, assistive tools, or revised training arrangements. While some employers continue to regard accommodation as burdensome, scholarship shows that many adjustments are modest, practical, and beneficial beyond the individual case, especially when they improve clarity, accessibility, and workflow across the wider organisation (Bentley & Clarke, 2005; Rabenu & Tziner, 2016). Thus, the law functions not simply as a compliance mechanism but as a practical prompt toward better organisational design.

Effective communication is a critical but often overlooked component of disability inclusion. Workers with intellectual disability may encounter barriers when workplace information is communicated through complex language, abstract instructions, rapid verbal exchanges, or inaccessible organisational procedures. Such barriers can affect recruitment, onboarding, performance evaluation, accommodation requests, and everyday workplace participation. Employers may misinterpret communication difficulties as indicators of low competence rather than as differences in information processing, comprehension, or expression. Communication challenges may also reduce workers' willingness to disclose support needs or seek clarification when difficulties arise. Consequently, accessible communication practices such as plain language, visual supports, structured feedback, task demonstrations, and opportunities for clarification should be viewed as essential components of equitable employment. Effective communication not only improves understanding and performance but also strengthens trust, participation, and access to workplace accommodations.

Another important legal issue is disclosure. Workers with intellectual disability may need accommodation, but disclosure remains a personal and sometimes difficult decision because of the risk of stigma, bias, or reduced expectations. Research on disability disclosure shows that employer practices and workplace climate strongly influence whether employees feel safe identifying support needs (von Schrader et al., 2014). This means that legal compliance cannot be reduced to policy documents alone. Employers must also cultivate workplace environments in which disclosure is treated respectfully, confidentially, and constructively. A lawful workplace is therefore not only one that has the right written procedures, but one that aligns those procedures with trust, fairness, and supportive management.

At the same time, law should not be interpreted only in defensive terms. Legal frameworks also interact with broader policy incentives and structural reforms that encourage the employment of people with disabilities. Inclusive employment is associated with economic participation, enhanced quality of life, and access to meaningful social roles for workers with intellectual disability (Ahmad et al., 2026; Riches, 2023). Employers themselves may benefit through improved workplace culture, stronger inclusion practices, and access to external support systems that strengthen hiring and onboarding processes (Brooke et al., 2025; Glade et al., 2020). However, these benefits do not emerge automatically. They depend on whether employers understand the law well enough to translate rights and obligations into everyday workplace practice.

This chapter, therefore, examines the legal foundations that shape the employment of workers with intellectual disability and explains why employers need a practical understanding of disability law. It frames law as both a compliance requirement and a tool for advancing inclusion. In doing so, it sets the stage for a deeper analysis of anti-discrimination protections, reasonable accommodation duties, disclosure issues, employer obligations, and policy incentives that can support more equitable and sustainable employment systems.

3.2 METHODOLOGY

This chapter adopts a conceptual and integrative methodology to examine the relationship among legal scholarship, disability policy, employment law, and workplace inclusion. Rather than relying on primary empirical data, it draws on a critical review and synthesis of scholarly, legal, and policy literature. This approach is appropriate because disability inclusion in employment is multidisciplinary and must be understood through legal principles, policy frameworks, and organisational practices.

The methodology is grounded in an integrative review, which combines evidence from conceptual studies, legal analyses, policy documents, and workplace inclusion research. This approach is useful where knowledge is dispersed across fields and where the aim is to develop a coherent interpretation rather than statistical generalisation. In disability employment research, integrative methods help connect debates on rights, accommodations, employer responsibilities, and institutional barriers. Bezyak et al. (2024) show that synthesising the disability-employment literature can yield practical lessons for inclusive employment and demonstrate how organisational actors can shift from gatekeeping roles to enabling participation.

The chapter also employs systematic thematic analysis as its principal analytical strategy. Relevant literature was reviewed to identify recurring themes, including workplace accommodation, equality of opportunity, accessibility, organisational responsibility, and barriers to implementation. Thematic analysis is suitable because it allows diverse forms of literature to be coded, organised, and interpreted in a structured manner. Sundar (2017) shows how workplace accommodation literature can be thematically organised to clarify fragmented evidence and reveal conceptual and practical gaps.

In addition, the study uses comparative synthesis to examine the assumptions, priorities, and implications of disability inclusion frameworks across legal, policy, and workplace contexts. This is important because formal legislation often differs from workplace realities. Vedeler and Anvik (2023) illustrate how workplace accommodation has been framed differently over time, while Baker and Moon (2008) highlight the barriers and opportunities that shape implementation in practice. Overall, this methodology provides a critical and interdisciplinary foundation for examining the promises and limitations of workplace inclusion frameworks.

3.3 CONCEPTUAL AND THEORETICAL FOUNDATIONS

This section examines the conceptual and theoretical foundations of disability law in employment by situating the Americans with Disabilities Act (ADA), the Individuals with Disabilities Education Act (IDEA), and the Workforce Innovation and Opportunity Act (WIOA) within broader rights-based and governance traditions. Disability law in employment is not merely a technical matter of complying with statutory rules. It reflects a stronger commitment to equality, non-discrimination, participation, reasonable accommodation, and transition support as core conditions for inclusive labour market participation. These legal frameworks emerged in response to enduring patterns of exclusion in education, training, recruitment, workplace access, and career advancement. They should therefore be understood not only as regulatory instruments but also as normative and institutional mechanisms for expanding opportunity and promoting justice in employment systems.

Historically, disability was viewed through medical and charitable lenses that emphasised deficit, incapacity, and welfare dependence. This perspective shaped exclusionary workplace practices by treating people with disabilities as objects of care rather than as rights-bearing citizens capable of meaningful participation in work and public life. Contemporary disability law departs from this narrow view and aligns more closely with the social and human rights model, which locates disadvantages not only in impairment but also in disabling environments, institutions, and attitudes. Lord et al. (2015) note that modern disability law increasingly reflects human rights norms centred on dignity, equal citizenship, participation, and the removal of systemic barriers. This shift reframes employment as a right that must be supported through fair legal and organisational arrangements.

Within this changing framework, the ADA occupies a central place because it prohibits discrimination and requires employers to provide reasonable accommodations unless doing so would create an undue hardship. The ADA shows that formal equality alone is insufficient. Treating everyone the same in workplaces structured around narrow assumptions about productivity, mobility, or communication may reproduce exclusion. Reasonable accommodation addresses this problem by recognising that equitable participation often requires structural and procedural adjustments. Bender et al. (2005) and Isetti and Eadie (2016) reinforce the legislative and practical value of the ADA as a framework that translates anti-discrimination principles into workplace obligations.

3.3.1 Rights-Based Foundations of Disability Law

The rights-based foundation of disability law in employment rests on the recognition that persons with disabilities are entitled to equal protection, equal opportunity, and full participation in social and economic life. This perspective challenges discriminatory assumptions that historically justified exclusion from mainstream education, training, and employment. Quinn (2007) notes that disability discrimination law is grounded in the broader equality project, which seeks not only to prohibit overt discrimination but also to dismantle systemic structures that limit participation. From this standpoint, the role of law is both protective and transformative. It protects individuals from unfair treatment while also compelling institutions to redesign environments, policies, and procedures to promote accessibility and inclusion.

Several principles define this rights-based orientation:

1. **Equality and non-discrimination:** Disability law affirms that exclusion based on disability violates equal citizenship and equal opportunity.
2. **Reasonable accommodation:** Inclusion requires practical adjustments that address environmental and organisational barriers.
3. **Participation:** Persons with disabilities must be included in decisions affecting their education, work preparation, and employment conditions.
4. **Accessibility:** Legal equality remains incomplete without access to the physical, informational, social, and procedural dimensions of work.
5. **Dignity and autonomy:** Disability law recognises the agency of persons with disabilities and rejects paternalistic approaches that undermine self-determination.

These principles also explain why IDEA and WIOA are relevant to employment law. IDEA establishes a rights-based framework for education and transition planning, ensuring that learners with disabilities receive support that prepares them for adulthood, further training, and employment. WIOA extends this trajectory by promoting competitive integrated employment, career pathways, vocational rehabilitation, and informed choice. Moore and Friedman (2017) emphasise that informed choice is central to advancing competitive integrated employment because it strengthens autonomy and meaningful participation in career decision-making. ADA, IDEA, and WIOA therefore form a continuum of rights protection and opportunity building that links school preparation, transition services, workplace entry, and employment retention.

3.3.2 Governance, Accountability, and Inclusive Workforce Design

In addition to their rights-based foundations, disability laws in employment must be understood through the lens of governance. Governance here refers to the systems, processes, institutional responsibilities, and accountability mechanisms through which inclusion is pursued and sustained. Legal compliance is therefore not only a matter of avoiding sanctions or satisfying procedural requirements. It also reflects responsible governance and inclusive workforce design. Employers, educational institutions, vocational systems, and public agencies are expected to create structures that enable equal participation and prevent exclusion before it occurs.

A governance perspective highlights that effective disability inclusion depends on coordination across multiple levels:

1. **Macro level:** Legislation, national disability policy, labour regulations, and public accountability frameworks.
2. **Meso level:** Organisational culture, recruitment policies, workplace accommodation procedures, supervision, and performance systems.
3. **Micro level:** The lived experiences, choices, rights awareness, and support needs of individual workers with disabilities.

This multilevel perspective is useful because disability inclusion often breaks down when policy intent is not translated into organisational practice. Ferri et al. (2025) argue that disability rights governance is increasingly complex, involving multiple actors, participatory mechanisms, and intersecting legal obligations. Novikov (2025) similarly suggests that business inclusion of persons with disabilities should extend beyond token representation and be tied to deeper organisational transformation. This interpretation shifts disability law from a reactive compliance model to a proactive governance model in which inclusion is embedded in workforce planning, job design, performance management, and institutional accountability.

Responsible governance also connects disability law with broader debates on corporate social responsibility and ethical business conduct. Ghose et al. (2024) show that integrating disability rights into inclusive business practices strengthens both equity and sustainability. Compliance with the ADA, IDEA, and WIOA should therefore not be viewed as a narrow administrative burden. These laws support a broader model of organisational stewardship in which equity, accessibility, and participation are recognised as central dimensions of legitimate and effective governance.

3.3.3 Reasonable Accommodation, Transition Support, and Practical Inclusion

A third conceptual foundation lies in the relationship among reasonable accommodation, transition support, and practical inclusion. While rights and governance establish the legal and institutional basis for inclusion, accommodation and transition support provide the practical means through which inclusion becomes meaningful in everyday employment settings. Reasonable accommodation may include modified duties, flexible scheduling, assistive technologies, accessible communication systems, adapted supervision, or physical workplace adjustments. These measures are not discretionary favours; they are mechanisms for ensuring equitable access to work and meaningful participation in workplace activities.

Workplace accommodation has evolved over time as a policy issue, revealing tensions concerning who bears responsibility for adjustment, how barriers are defined, and whether disability is framed as an individual limitation or a structural concern (Vedeler & Anvik, 2023). This indicates that accommodation is not simply a technical response to impairment, but part of a broader governance and fairness question in employment. Gutierrez (2025) further argues that inclusive performance management systems must recognise hidden disabilities and adjust workplace expectations in ways that prevent employees from being disadvantaged by differences that responsive support structures could address.

Transition support is equally significant. IDEA and WIOA recognise that inclusion in employment begins well before recruitment or hiring. Young people with disabilities need coordinated support that connects schooling, vocational preparation, career exploration, and entry into competitive integrated employment. Without such continuity, the legal promise of workplace equality remains weak. Transition services, therefore, function as a bridge between educational and employment rights. They help ensure that participation in work is deliberately prepared through guidance, training, informed choice, and interagency collaboration.

ADA, IDEA, and WIOA are therefore more than separate statutes. They reflect a shared normative vision grounded in human rights, equality, participation, governance, and practical support. Their importance lies in promoting a model of inclusion in which legal compliance becomes part of responsible institutional design and in which employment systems are restructured to accommodate diversity rather than perpetuate exclusion.

3.4 LITERATURE REVIEW

This section reviews scholarship on disability rights, employer compliance, transition policy, workplace accommodation, and labour market inclusion. Existing scholarship suggests that legal protections have improved access to employment for persons with disabilities, although significant implementation gaps remain (Modise et al., 2014; Vedeler & Anvik, 2023). Across different contexts, scholars have highlighted tensions between formal rights and workplace realities, particularly in recruitment, accommodation, retention, and school-to-work transition for persons with intellectual disability (Burke et al., 2013; McCollin & Obiakor, 2009). Scholarship in this area also indicates that labour market inclusion is shaped not only by legislation, but also by employer attitudes, organisational systems, and the availability of coordinated support across education, vocational rehabilitation, and employment sectors (Cavanagh et al., 2017; Yaeda, 2009).

3.4.1 Disability Rights and Labour Market Inclusion

Scholarship on disability rights and labour market inclusion has examined how anti-discrimination law and related policy frameworks have strengthened recognition of the employment rights of people with disabilities. Legal protections such as the ADA have contributed to a shift in employment policy from charity-based thinking toward a rights-based model of participation. Modise et al. (2014) argue that reasonable accommodation is central to labour market access because it translates legal rights into practical measures that enable employment. Vedeler and Anvik (2023) likewise show that accommodation has become a central issue in disability policy, although its meaning and application remain contested across workplaces and policy systems. These contributions suggest that legal rights are important, but their practical value depends on how employers and institutions interpret and implement them.

Authors have also argued that rights alone do not guarantee inclusion. Towns and Moore (2005) note that employer compliance becomes more difficult where disability is less visible or where support needs are viewed as complex. This concern has relevance for persons with intellectual disability, who may face assumptions about limited competence, productivity, or adaptability. In such cases, the protective value of disability law may be weakened when employers adopt narrow views of compliance or when organisational systems do not support inclusive practice. This body of work points to the need for institutional commitment, employer awareness, and workplace redesign alongside legal recognition.

3.4.2 Workplace Accommodation and Employer Compliance

A major strand of scholarship focuses on workplace accommodation as a mechanism for hiring, retaining, and supporting employees with disabilities. Accommodation is commonly described as including modified duties, flexible scheduling, technical aids, accessible communication systems, transportation support, and physical workplace adjustments. Anand and Sevak (2017) found that workplace accommodations are associated with improved employment outcomes by reducing barriers to job performance and participation. Dall and Madsen (2025) also position accommodation as a central element of inclusive workplace management rather than an optional addition to employment practice.

Even so, implementation remains inconsistent. Dong et al. (2023) found that access to accommodations is shaped not only by policy, but also by psychosocial factors such as employee confidence, workplace relationships, and organisational climate. This suggests that legal entitlement does not automatically lead to practical access. Emens (2008) argues that accommodation should be integrated into mainstream institutional design rather than treated as an exceptional response to individual need. This position is particularly relevant for people with intellectual disability, whose support needs may be misunderstood or minimised by employers.

The COVID-19 period added another dimension to this discussion. Fuentes and Lindsay (2022) show that the pandemic increased the visibility of flexible work arrangements and remote accommodations, illustrating that many adjustments once considered burdensome were achievable. At the same time, they note that new barriers emerged, including digital exclusion and inconsistent access to support. These findings frame accommodation as both a legal requirement and an indicator of organisational willingness to adapt work structures to diverse needs.

3.4.2.1 Barriers to Effective Accommodation

This section identifies recurring barriers to effective accommodation and employer compliance:

1. Limited employer knowledge of disability rights and accommodation duties.
2. Negative assumptions about productivity, supervision, or cost.
3. Weak organisational procedures for requesting and implementing accommodation.
4. Inconsistent managerial support across departments and workplaces.
5. Poor integration of HR systems with disability inclusion strategies.

Cavanagh et al. (2017) stress that human resource management plays a central role in determining whether disability inclusion becomes part of everyday organisational practice. Where this integration is absent, compliance may remain reactive and fragmented.

3.4.3 Transition Policy, Recruitment, and Retention Challenges

Another major theme concerns the transition from school to work and the continuing difficulties people with intellectual disability face in recruitment and retention. Transition scholarship suggests that labour market exclusion often begins before labour market entry. Wittenburg and Loprest (2007) found that many young people with disabilities experience uneven transition pathways characterised by limited preparation, fragmented service delivery, and weak employment outcomes. Yaeda (2009) similarly highlights the importance of coordinated systems linking schools, families, vocational agencies, and employers. Without such coordination, the move from education to employment may become uncertain and exclusionary.

For people with intellectual disability, the challenge may be greater because transition is often shaped by low expectations, segregated training pathways, and weak employer engagement. McCollin and Obiakor (2009) argue that successful transition requires structured planning, self-determination, and practical development linked to meaningful employment opportunities. Vlachos (2024) adds that transition programmes are more effective when they are person-centred and extend beyond academic preparation to include daily living, social participation, and vocational readiness. These contributions suggest that transition policy should be treated as part of labour market inclusion rather than as a separate educational issue.

Recruitment and retention scholarship reveals similar tensions between policy and practice. Shamshiri-Petersen and Krogh (2020) found that disability can negatively affect employers' hiring intentions even where legal protections are in place. Burke et al. (2013) likewise report that employer attitudes remain a significant factor in hiring and retention outcomes. Although some employers endorse inclusion in principle, this support does not always translate into recruitment decisions or sustained workplace investment.

Supported employment scholarship offers a more encouraging perspective. Gustafsson et al. (2018) found that supported employment can improve both work participation and social inclusion through job matching, workplace relationships, and natural supports. Rashid et al. (2020), however, note that employment support professionals often encounter tensions when trying to secure meaningful work for persons with developmental disabilities in labour markets that continue to undervalue them. Bacon and Hoque (2022) further demonstrate that firm size alone does not determine inclusion outcomes.

3.4.3.1 Recurring Tensions in the Literature

The scholarship reviewed points to several recurring tensions:

1. Formal legal rights versus weak implementation in practice.
2. Employer support in principle versus discrimination in recruitment and retention.
3. Accommodation as entitlement versus accommodation as discretion.
4. Transition policy goals versus fragmented service delivery.
5. Inclusive rhetoric versus exclusionary workplace cultures.

Jaffrès and Guével (2017) show that quota and non-discrimination systems may still fail where employer practices are not aligned with policy goals. Hujerat (2024) similarly demonstrates that inclusion depends heavily on workplace climate and employer behaviour.

This review suggests that disability rights frameworks have strengthened the legal basis for inclusion, but movement from rights to practice remains uneven (Modise et al., 2014; Jaffrès & Guével, 2017). Recruitment, accommodation, retention, and transition continue to expose gaps between legislative commitment and institutional reality (Burke et al., 2013; Vedeler & Anvik, 2023). For people with intellectual disability, these challenges may be intensified by low expectations, limited workplace flexibility, and fragmented support systems (McCollin & Obiakor, 2009; Rashid et al., 2020).

3.5 ANALYTICAL FRAMEWORK: RIGHTS–OBLIGATIONS–INCENTIVES MODEL

This section presents the analytical framework for interpreting the legal landscape of disability inclusion in employment. The Rights–Obligations–Incentives Model provides a structured framework for understanding how disability law operates across multiple levels of policy and practice. Rather than treating inclusion as the outcome of a single legal mandate, the model explains it through three linked dimensions. Rights establish the legal protections available to workers with disabilities. Obligations define the duties placed on employers and institutions. Incentives create supportive conditions that encourage inclusive hiring, accommodation, and retention. Examining these dimensions together enables us to understand both the strengths and the limits of disability law in practice.

3.5.1 Rights as the Basis of Protection

The first dimension of the framework is rights. Legal rights provide the normative basis for protecting workers with disabilities from discrimination and exclusion in employment. Rights-based approaches move disability law beyond older assumptions of charity or welfare and instead position persons with disabilities as full rights-bearing citizens entitled to equal opportunity, participation, and dignity. Hadush and Mekonen (2020) note that rights-based employment frameworks support inclusion by affirming access to work, non-discrimination, and reasonable accommodation. In a similar way, Sayers (2017) argues for a shift from needs-based to rights-based legal models, emphasising empowerment rather than dependence.

Within this framework, rights serve two functions. They protect individuals from direct and indirect discrimination and establish the legal basis for claims for accommodation, accessibility, and fair treatment. Rights are therefore not merely symbolic declarations. They shape how institutions define equality and how workers challenge exclusionary practices. In the context of disability employment, rights also connect education, transition, and labour market participation by affirming that access to work is part of broader social citizenship.

3.5.2 Rights and Inclusive Participation

Rights become meaningful only when they support participation in real settings. This means that legal recognition must be linked to practical access in recruitment, workplace adjustment, promotion, and retention. The significance of rights lies not only in formal legal protection but also in their capacity to reshape institutional expectations about who belongs in the workforce and under what conditions.

3.5.3 Obligations as the Structure of Compliance

The second dimension of the framework is obligations. If rights identify what workers are entitled to, obligations determine what employers, institutions, and public bodies must do in response. Employer obligation's structure compliance by translating broad equality principles into practical duties. These duties may include nondiscriminatory hiring, providing reasonable accommodations, job reassignment where appropriate, and maintaining fair workplace procedures. Paluszkiewicz (2025) explains that employer obligations are central to contemporary standards of equal treatment in disability employment because they define the operational steps required to give effect to legal rights.

This dimension also helps explain why implementation often varies across contexts. In some systems, employer obligations are reinforced through mandatory quotas, reporting structures, or penalties for non-compliance. Polishko and Zelinskyi (2025) note that inclusive labour market regulation in Europe reflects both opportunities and normative barriers, especially where enforcement mechanisms are uneven. Agovino et al. (2019) similarly show that quota-based systems may not always produce meaningful inclusion if employers comply only formally or prefer sanctions to substantive workplace change. Obligations are therefore essential, but their effectiveness depends on enforcement, monitoring, and organisational commitment.

3.5.4 Obligations and Institutional Responsibility

Obligations are not limited to legal compliance in a narrow sense. They also reflect institutional responsibility for designing workplaces that do not exclude people by default. In this way, obligations connect anti-discrimination law with broader questions of organisational governance, accountability, and inclusive design.

3.5.5 Incentives as Drivers of Inclusive Practice

The third dimension of the framework is incentives. While rights and obligations establish the legal foundation for inclusion, incentives help create practical motivation for employers to adopt inclusive hiring and retention practices. Incentives may be financial, administrative, or policy-based. They can include tax relief, wage subsidies, cost-sharing arrangements for workplace adaptations, or public programmes that reduce the compliance burden. Hadush and Mekonen (2020) show that tax incentive mechanisms can encourage employers to recruit and retain people with disabilities by offsetting the costs of adaptation and support. Van der Ploeg (2018) similarly argues that employers play a decisive role in transforming disability into ability when supportive policy arrangements reduce perceived risks and increase confidence in inclusive employment.

At the same time, incentive systems are not automatically effective. Hao and Li (2020) found that legal frameworks may be weakened when incentive and enforcement systems fail to align with employer behaviour. An (2024) also suggests that inflexible legal and policy arrangements can discourage participation, particularly among smaller enterprises with limited resources. This means that incentives should be understood as complementary rather than secondary. They do not replace rights or obligations, but they strengthen the conditions under which compliance becomes feasible and sustainable.

3.5.6 Interaction of Rights, Obligations, and Incentives

The analytical value of this model lies in the interaction among its three dimensions. Rights without obligations may remain abstract. Obligations without incentives may generate weak or reluctant compliance. Incentives without rights may encourage participation but fail to guarantee justice or accountability. The framework, therefore, provides a balanced approach to understanding how disability law can protect workers, shape employer behaviour, and encourage inclusive workforce participation. The interaction of rights, obligations, and incentives in shaping inclusive employment practice is illustrated in Figure 1.

Figure 1.

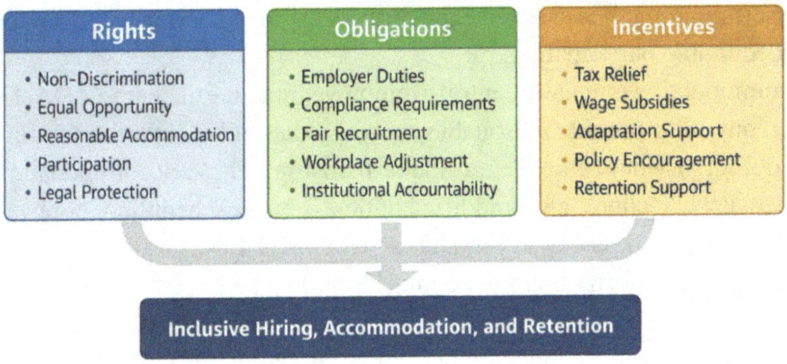

Figure 1 shows that inclusive employment depends on the interaction of three elements. Rights protect workers through non-discrimination, equal opportunity, accommodation, participation, and legal safeguards. Obligations define employer and institutional responsibilities for fair recruitment, workplace adjustment, and accountability. Incentives encourage implementation through tax relief, subsidies, adaptation support, and retention measures. These elements support inclusive hiring, accommodation, and long-term retention.

3.6 PRACTICAL IMPLICATIONS FOR EMPLOYERS

This section translates legal principles into workplace practice by showing how the ADA, IDEA, and WIOA shape employer action in recruitment, interviewing, accommodation, confidentiality, onboarding, supervision, and retention. Legal awareness supports not only compliance and risk reduction but also stronger inclusion outcomes.

3.6.1 Recruitment, Accommodation, and Workplace Management

Employers must ensure that recruitment and interviewing processes are accessible and non-discriminatory. This includes using fair selection procedures, avoiding disability-based assumptions, and providing reasonable accommodation during interviews where necessary. Goodman et al. (2024) show that employer perceptions and bias remain significant barriers to the employment of persons with disabilities, while Kaye et al. (2011) identify persistent misconceptions about cost, productivity, and supervision as major reasons employers fail to hire and retain disabled workers. These findings suggest that compliance in recruitment requires more than avoiding overt discrimination; it also requires intentional efforts to design hiring systems that support equitable participation.

Accommodation is equally central to employer practice under the ADA. Employers are required to provide reasonable accommodation for essential job functions, unless doing so would impose an undue hardship. These accommodations may include assistive technologies, modified duties, flexible scheduling, or physical adjustments to the workplace (Geyer, 2021; Niccolini & Basu, 2009). Confidentiality is also essential. Information concerning disability and accommodation must be handled carefully and disclosed only for legitimate workplace purposes. Strauser et al. (2026) further indicate that employers who adopt universal design and proactive inclusion strategies are often better positioned to consistently and effectively meet accommodation needs.

3.6.1.1 Onboarding, Supervision, and Retention

Onboarding and supervision are crucial in determining whether inclusive hiring leads to sustained employment. Brooke et al. (2025) found that employers value early relationship-building, role clarity, and practical support during the initial adjustment period for employees with disabilities. Effective supervision therefore requires communication, flexibility, and a willingness to respond to support needs without stigma. Ochrach et al. (2022) further show that a disability-inclusive mindset can strengthen workplace culture and improve managerial responsiveness.

Retention depends on whether employees with disabilities receive fair opportunities for support, growth, and advancement. Hartnett et al. (2011) note that employers often recognise the organisational benefits of accommodation and retention, including reduced turnover, stronger morale, and improved workplace commitment. Employers should therefore treat disability inclusion as an ongoing workforce development issue rather than a one-time compliance exercise.

3.6.2 Transition, Collaboration, and Legal Risk Reduction

IDEA and WIOA extend these implications by shaping how young people with disabilities move from school to employment. WIOA's pre-employment transition services encourage employers to collaborate with vocational rehabilitation agencies, schools, and community partners to support career exploration, work-based learning, and entry into competitive integrated employment (Taylor et al., 2022; Whittenburg et al., 2024). Carlson (2022) also emphasises that transition planning is more effective when schools and employers share responsibility for preparing youth with disabilities for work.

Legal awareness reduces risk by helping employers understand their obligations before disputes arise. Employers that adopt proactive policies, disability-informed training, and access to specialist guidance are better placed to meet legal requirements and improve inclusion outcomes. By aligning recruitment, accommodation, onboarding, and retention with the ADA, IDEA, and WIOA, employers can create workplaces that are both legally compliant and genuinely inclusive.

3.7 POLICY AND GOVERNANCE IMPLICATIONS

Disability law has important implications for institutional policy and governance because compliance is most effective when embedded in organisational systems rather than treated as an isolated legal or human resource function. Anti-discrimination obligations require organisations to establish clear internal procedures that guide recruitment, interviewing, accommodation, performance management, confidentiality, and dispute resolution. When these procedures are absent or poorly coordinated, implementation often becomes inconsistent and reactive, thereby weakening both legal compliance and inclusion outcomes.

Governance-oriented compliance also requires organisations to adopt formal accommodation policies that specify request processes, decision pathways, timelines, confidentiality standards, and the responsibilities of managers and supervisors. Such policies help translate statutory duties into predictable workplace practice and reduce ambiguity for both employers and employees. Accommodation is more effective where institutional processes are supported by management commitment, structured communication, and inclusive organisational design.

A further governance implication concerns transition partnerships. IDEA and WIOA indicate that workforce inclusion begins before recruitment and depends on collaboration among employers, schools, vocational rehabilitation agencies, and community partners. Organisations that engage in structured transition partnerships are better positioned to support school-to-work entry, work-based learning, and early career adjustment for persons with disabilities. This makes disability inclusion a cross-sector governance matter rather than a workplace issue alone.

Staff training is also central to governance reform. Employers need training not only on legal duties, but also on disability-responsive supervision, inclusive communication, confidentiality, and the practical management of accommodations. Workplace attitudes, managerial assumptions, and limited disability knowledge can undermine implementation even where legal frameworks are in place. Documentation systems and accountability mechanisms are equally necessary. Accurate records of accommodation requests, responses, transition supports, and retention practices create an institutional basis for monitoring compliance and identifying gaps. Organisational accountability is further strengthened when disability inclusion is linked to leadership responsibility, workplace culture, and performance review systems.

These considerations suggest that disability law should be integrated into institutional governance through strategic planning, operational policy, and workforce development. When organisations treat disability compliance as a narrow HR or legal matter, they risk fragmented implementation and limited inclusion. A governance approach encourages coordinated policy, clearer responsibility, and stronger accountability for equitable employment practice.

3.7.1 Factors That Enhance Effective Accommodation and Employer Compliance

Effective accommodation depends on more than legal requirements. It requires organisational commitment, clear procedures, and a workplace culture that values accessibility and inclusion. Several factors can strengthen accommodation practices and support employer compliance.

Leadership commitment is particularly important because organisational priorities are often shaped by senior management's actions and expectations. When leaders actively support disability inclusion, accommodation becomes part of everyday workplace practice rather than an isolated administrative process. Disability awareness and training programmes also strengthen implementation by helping supervisors, managers, and co-workers understand accommodation responsibilities and inclusive workplace practices.

Clear accommodation policies provide guidance on how requests should be made, assessed, implemented, and reviewed. Effective communication systems encourage collaboration among employees, supervisors, human resource personnel, and external support providers where necessary. Regular monitoring of accommodation arrangements allows organisations to identify challenges early and make appropriate adjustments. Collaboration with vocational rehabilitation agencies, disability organisations, and transition service providers can also provide valuable guidance and practical support. These factors strengthen organisational capacity, support legal compliance, and contribute to more accessible and inclusive employment environments.

3.7.2 Tools for Advancing Workplace Inclusivity

Legal frameworks establish rights and responsibilities, but practical tools help organisations implement inclusion in everyday workplace settings. A range of tools can support accommodation, accessibility, and workforce participation.

Accommodation assessment checklists can help employers identify workplace barriers and determine appropriate supports. Plain-language workplace documents can improve accessibility by making policies, procedures, and instructions easier to understand. Disability awareness training modules can help build organisational knowledge and reduce misconceptions about disability. Inclusive recruitment toolkits can support accessible job advertisements, interview procedures, and selection processes.

Additional tools include job coaching programmes, mentoring systems, workplace accessibility audits, accommodation tracking systems, and employee feedback mechanisms. Assistive technologies, visual task supports, digital scheduling tools, and communication aids can further improve participation and independence within workplace environments. Inclusion climate surveys may also help organisations evaluate workplace culture and identify areas requiring additional attention. The use of these tools enables organisations to move beyond basic compliance and develop workplace systems that support accessibility, participation, retention, and long-term inclusion.

3.8 CHALLENGES, RISKS, AND IMPLEMENTATION BARRIERS

Effective implementation of disability law in employment continues to face multiple barriers despite the existence of legal protections and policy frameworks. One major challenge is employers' limited knowledge of disability rights, accommodation obligations, and lawful workplace procedures. Where employers lack understanding of their responsibilities, compliance may become inconsistent, delayed, or reactive rather than embedded in organisational practice (Cavanagh et al., 2017). This challenge is often reinforced by persistent misconceptions about the costs of accommodation, productivity, supervision, and the perceived complexity of employing people with disabilities. Kaye et al. (2011) found that such assumptions remain a significant reason why employers hesitate to hire or retain disabled workers, even where legal obligations are clear.

Another barrier concerns uncertainty around disclosure and confidentiality. Employees may be reluctant to disclose disability where they anticipate stigma, misunderstanding, or negative treatment, while employers may be unsure about how to respond appropriately to disclosure without violating privacy or mishandling accommodation processes (Niccolini & Basu, 2009). This uncertainty can weaken access to support because accommodation often depends on effective communication and trust between employees and employers. Geyer (2021) similarly suggests that access to accommodation may become difficult where management support is inconsistent or where workers are left to negotiate support without clear institutional procedures.

Transition systems also present major implementation difficulties. IDEA and WIOA emphasise the importance of coordinated school-to-work planning, but fragmented transition structures often limit effective movement from education into employment. Taylor et al. (2022) show that pre-employment transition services vary significantly in implementation across systems, while Whittenburg et al. (2024) note that the use of research-based transition recommendations is uneven in workforce planning. Where coordination between schools, employers, and vocational rehabilitation agencies is weak, young people with disabilities may experience disrupted or exclusionary pathways into work.

A further risk is symbolic compliance. This occurs when organisations satisfy minimum legal requirements without creating genuinely accessible and supportive workplaces. Vedeler and Anvik (2023) show that accommodation policy may be shaped more by formal compliance logic than by substantive inclusion, while Jaffrès and Guével (2017) demonstrate that legal mandates can fall short where employer practices are not aligned with broader equality goals. In such contexts, organisations may adopt policies on paper yet fail to change workplace culture, supervision practices, or retention structures. Goodman et al. (2024) further indicate that employer bias continues to influence disability employment decisions, suggesting that legal compliance alone is insufficient unless accompanied by bigger institutional change.

3.9 CONCLUSION

The legal landscape provides an essential foundation for the inclusive employment of workers with intellectual disability. The Americans with Disabilities Act, the Individuals with Disabilities Education Act, and the Workforce Innovation and Opportunity Act together create a framework that supports equality, participation, transition, and workplace access. These laws do more than establish legal standards. They shape how employers, educators, service providers, and institutions understand their responsibilities in promoting access to employment and sustaining inclusion in practice.

The chapter has shown that these statutes should not be treated as separate legal instruments operating in isolation. Instead, they function as interconnected tools for advancing rights, clarifying employer duties, and supporting coordinated transition from education into employment. The ADA addresses workplace discrimination and accommodation; IDEA provides support for educational preparation and transition planning; and WIOA strengthens the movement toward competitive integrated employment through workforce and rehabilitation systems. Their value lies in the way they connect protection, preparation, and participation within a broader inclusion framework.

The discussion has also shown that legal protection alone is not enough. Inclusive employment depends on how effectively these laws are translated into workplace policy, staff awareness, transition planning, institutional accountability, and practical support. Legal knowledge is therefore important not only for compliance, but also for improving organisational responsiveness and inclusion outcomes.

This chapter provides the legal and conceptual base for the chapters that follow. It prepares the ground for further discussion of recruitment, workplace support, accommodation, supervision, retention, and the wider factors that influence long-term success and meaningful participation for workers with intellectual disability.

REFERENCES

Agovino, M., Marchesano, K., & Garofalo, A. (2019). Policies based on mandatory employment quotas for disabled workers: The case of Italy. *Modern Italy*, *24*(3), 295–315. DOI: 10.1017/mit.2019.14

Ahmad, M., Raziq, M. M., & Akhtar, M. N. (2026). Inclusive leadership and employee well-being: A study of the mediating role of psychological safety. *Leadership & Organisation Development Journal, 47*(1), 1–18.

An, N. B. (2024). A global lens: Comparing international and Vietnamese laws on work for persons with disabilities. In *Sustainable Legacies: A Legal Inquiry into PwDs' Rights in Vietnam's Development* (pp. 19–45). Springer., DOI: 10.1007/978-981-97-9566-6_2

Anand, P., & Sevak, P. (2017). The role of workplace accommodations in the employment of people with disabilities. *IZA Journal of Labor Policy*, *6*(1), 12. Advance online publication. DOI: 10.1186/s40173-017-0090-4

Bacon, N., & Hoque, K. (2022). The treatment of disabled individuals in small, medium-sized, and large firms. *Human Resource Management*, *61*(2), 137–156. DOI: 10.1002/hrm.22084

Baker, P. M. A., & Moon, N. W.Baker Paul M.A.Moon Nathan W. (2008). Policy change and the accommodating workplace: Issues, barriers, and opportunities. *Assistive Technology Research Series*, *22*, 161–174. DOI: 10.3233/978-1-58603-902-8-161

Bender, D. E., Overman, B., & Arnold, M. S. (2005). The Americans With Disabilities Act: Explaining legislative intent through experiential learning. *The Journal of Health Administration Education*, *22*(4), 435–458.

Bennett, T., & Randolph, D. S. (2010). Employment and disability: The role of the Americans with Disabilities Act. *Journal of Employment Counseling, 47*(2), 50–58.

Bentley, T., & Clarke, J. (2005). Workplace accommodation for employees with disabilities: A review of the literature. *Journal of Occupational Rehabilitation, 15*(3), 329–342.

Bezyak, J., Chan, F., Tansey, T. N., Wu, J.-R., Iwanaga, K., & Lee, D. (2024). Changing human resource professionals from gatekeepers to enablers of disability employment: Lessons learned from disability-employment research. *Journal of Vocational Rehabilitation. Article, 10522263241300813*. Advance online publication. DOI: 10.1177/10522263241300813

Brooke, A. M., Taylor, J. P., Inge, K., Wright, T., Wehman, P., McDonough, J., & Brooke, V. (2025). Employer perceptions of hiring and initial support of employees with disabilities. *Rehabilitation Counseling Bulletin, 68*(4), 249–261. DOI: 10.1177/00343552241265317

Burke, J., Bezyak, J., Fraser, R. T., Pete, J., Ditchman, N., & Chan, F. (2013). Employers' attitudes towards hiring and retaining people with disabilities: A review of the literature. *Australian Journal of Rehabilitation Counselling, 19*(1), 21–38. DOI: 10.1017/jrc.2013.2

Carlson, S. R. (2022). Pre-employment transition services: What secondary special education teachers need to know. *Intervention in School and Clinic, 57*(5), 338–342. DOI: 10.1177/10534512211032631

Cavanagh, J., Bartram, T., Meacham, H., Bigby, C., Oakman, J., & Fossey, E. (2017). Supporting workers with disabilities: A scoping review of the role of human resource management in contemporary organisations. *Asia Pacific Journal of Human Resources, 55*(1), 6–43. DOI: 10.1111/1744-7941.12111

Cox, J. S. (2009). Redefining disability. *Paper360, 4*(1), 32.

Dall, T., & Madsen, M. B. (2025). Workplace accommodations. In *Shaping Inclusive Workplaces for Persons with Disabilities: A Management and HRM Practitioner Perspective* (pp. 71–84). Springer., DOI: 10.1007/978-3-031-96315-5_6

Dong, S., Eto, O., Liu, L., & Villaquiran, A. (2023). Examining psychosocial factors associated with receiving workplace accommodations among people with disabilities. *Work (Reading, Mass.), 75*(3), 799–811. DOI: 10.3233/WOR-220230

Emens, E. F. (2008). Integrating accommodation. *University of Pennsylvania Law Review, 156*(4), 839–922.

Ferri, D., Broderick, A., & Leahy, A. (2025). The global governance of disability rights: Complexities, participatory trends and intersections. In *Research Handbook on Global Governance* (pp. 299–329). Edward Elgar Publishing., DOI: 10.4337/9781789906332.00025

Fuentes, K., & Lindsay, S. (2022). Workplace accommodations during the COVID-19 pandemic: A scoping review of the impacts and implications for people with disabilities. *Work (Reading, Mass.), 74*(2), 381–406. DOI: 10.3233/WOR-220129

Geyer, P. D. (2021). Acquiring workplace accommodations when management support is voluntary: Crafting jobs and accommodations. *Journal of Rehabilitation, 87*(3), 31–35.

Ghose, A., Kochher, H. S., & Ali, S. M. A. (2024). Towards equity and inclusion: Legal exploration for inclusive business practices integrating CSR and disability rights in India. In *Bridging Human Rights and Corporate Social Responsibility: Pathways to a Sustainable Global Society* (pp. 127–154). IGI Global. DOI: 10.4018/979-8-3693-2325-0.ch006

Glade, R., Koch, L. C., & Rumrill, P. D. (2020). Employer practices and the employment of people with disabilities: A review of the literature. *Journal of Vocational Rehabilitation, 52*(3), 221–234.

Goodman, N., Deane, S., Hyseni, F., Soffer, M., Shaheen, G., & Blanck, P. (2024). Perceptions and bias of small business leaders in employing people with different types of disabilities. *Journal of Occupational Rehabilitation, 34*(2), 359–372. DOI: 10.1007/s10926-024-10201-2

Gustafsson, J., Peralta, J., & Danermark, B. (2018). Supported employment and social inclusion - experiences of workers with disabilities in wage subsidised employment in Sweden. *Scandinavian Journal of Disability Research, 20*(1), 26–36. DOI: 10.16993/sjdr.36

Gutierrez, B. D. (2025). Developing a performance management system for employees with hidden disabilities. In *New Horizons in Leadership: Inclusive Explorations in Health, Technology, and Education* (pp. 221–237). IGI Global. DOI: 10.4018/979-8-3693-6437-6.ch010

Hadush, G., & Mekonen, B. (2020). Exploring tax incentive mechanisms to strengthen the inclusion of persons with disabilities in the private workforce in Ethiopia. *International Studies in Human Rights, 131*, 241–260. DOI: 10.1163/9789004415966_012

Hao, Y., & Li, P. (2020). Employment legal framework for persons with disabilities in China: Effectiveness and reasons. *International Journal of Environmental Research and Public Health, 17*(14). *International Journal of Environmental Research and Public Health, 4976*(14), 1–20. DOI: 10.3390/ijerph17144976

Hartnett, H. P., Stuart, H., Thurman, H., Loy, B., & Batiste, L. C. (2011). Employers' perceptions of the benefits of workplace accommodations: Reasons to hire, retain and promote people with disabilities. *Journal of Vocational Rehabilitation, 34*(1), 17–23. DOI: 10.3233/JVR-2010-0530

Hujerat, E. (2024). Managing employees with disabilities: The impact of employer behavior and workplace climate from an employee perspective in Israel. *Springer Proceedings in Business and Economics*, 817–839. DOI: 10.1007/978-981-97-0996-0_50

Isetti, D., & Eadie, T. (2016). The Americans with Disabilities Act and voice disorders: Practical guidelines for voice clinicians. *Journal of Voice*, *30*(3), 293–300. DOI: 10.1016/j.jvoice.2015.04.006

Jaffrès, F., & Guével, M.-R. (2017). Quota and non-discrimination approach on employment of persons with disabilities in the French public service: What are the employers' practices? [L'emploi des personnes handicapées dans la fonction publique: Entre quota et non-discrimination, quelles pratiques des employeurs?]. *Travail et Emploi*, (152), 33–57. DOI: 10.4000/travailemploi.7759

Kaye, H. S., Jans, L. H., & Jones, E. C. (2011). Why don't employers hire and retain workers with disabilities? *Journal of Occupational Rehabilitation*, *21*(4), 526–536. DOI: 10.1007/s10926-011-9302-8

Lord, J. E., Raja, D. S., & Blanck, P. (2015). Law and people with disabilities. In *International Encyclopedia of the Social & Behavioral Sciences* (2nd ed., pp. 497–503). Elsevier., DOI: 10.1016/B978-0-08-097086-8.86053-5

McCollin, M. J., & Obiakor, F. E. (2009). Transition from school to adult life. In *International Encyclopedia of Education* (3rd ed., pp. 876–879). Elsevier., DOI: 10.1016/B978-0-08-044894-7.01121-0

Modise, J. R., Olivier, M. P., & Miruka, O. (2014). Reasonable accommodation for people with disabilities in the labour market. *Mediterranean Journal of Social Sciences*, *5*(4), 578–588. DOI: 10.5901/mjss.2014.v5n4p578

Moore, R., & Friedman, M. (2017). The role of informed choice in advancing competitive integrated employment. *Journal of Vocational Rehabilitation*, *46*(2), 245–264. DOI: 10.3233/JVR-160860

Niccolini, R. R., & Basu, N. (2009). Disability and accommodation in the healthcare workplace. *Journal of Health & Life Sciences Law*, *2*(3), 93–120.

Novikov, I. (2025). Beyond inclusion: How people with disabilities are involved in business [ЗА ПРЕДЕЛАМИ ИНКЛЮЗИИ: КАК ВОВЛЕКАЕТСЯ ТРУД ЛЮДЕЙ С ИНВАЛИДНОСТЬЮ В БИЗНЕС]. *Zhurnal Issledovanii Sotsial'noi Politiki*, *23*(2), 289–308. DOI: 10.17323/727-0634-2025-23-2-289-308

Ochrach, C., Thomas, K., Phillips, B., Mpofu, N., Tansey, T., & Castillo, S. (2022). Case study on the effects of a disability inclusive mindset in a large biotechnology company. *Journal of Work-Applied Management, 14*(1), 113–125. DOI: 10.1108/JWAM-06-2021-0045

Paluszkiewicz, M. (2025). A few comments on the employer's obligations towards an employee unable to perform his current job or position in the light of the latest international standards of equal treatment regardless of disability in employment *Acta Universitatis Lodziensis. Folia Iuridica, 112*, 137–156. DOI: 10.18778/0208-6069.112.09

Polishko, N., & Zelinskyi, D. (2025). Inclusive labour market: Normative barriers and opportunities for persons with disabilities in Europe [Інклюзивний ринок праці: нормативні бар'єри та можливості людей з інвалідністю в Європі]. *Law. Human. Environment, 16*(3), 92–112. DOI: 10.31548/law/3.2025.92

Quinn, G. (2007). Disability discrimination law in the European Union. In *Equality Law in an Enlarged European Union: Understanding the Article 13 Directives* (pp. 231–277). Cambridge University Press. DOI: 10.1017/CBO9780511493898.009

Rabenu, E., & Tziner, A. (2016). The role of the law in the employment of people with disabilities. *Journal of Organisational Behaviour, 37*(4), 537–553.

Rashid, M., Thompson-Hodgetts, S., & Nicholas, D. (2020). Tensions experienced by employment support professionals when seeking meaningful employment for persons with developmental disabilities. *Research in Developmental Disabilities, 99*, 103603. Advance online publication. DOI: 10.1016/j.ridd.2020.103603

Riches, V. C. (2023). Employment and intellectual disability: A review of the literature. *Journal of Intellectual & Developmental Disability, 48*(2), 123–136.

Sayers, D. (2017). Rights not needs: Changing the legal model for special educational needs (SEN). In *The Palgrave Handbook of Disabled Children's Childhood Studies* (pp. 617–642). Palgrave Macmillan. DOI: 10.1057/978-1-137-54446-9_37

Shamshiri-Petersen, D., & Krogh, C. (2020). Disability disqualifies: A vignette experiment on Danish employers' intentions to hire applicants with physical disabilities. *Scandinavian Journal of Disability Research, 22*(1), 198–209. DOI: 10.16993/sjdr.661

Strauser, D. G., Price, R. A., Brehmer, C. E., & Strauser, D. R. (2026). Exploring employer's successful hiring and retention practices of individuals with disabilities. *Rehabilitation Counseling Bulletin, 69*(2), 109–119. DOI: 10.1177/00343552241265319

Sundar, V. (2017). Operationalizing workplace accommodations for individuals with disabilities: A scoping review. *Work (Reading, Mass.), 56*(1), 135–155. DOI: 10.3233/WOR-162472

Taylor, J. P., Whittenburg, H. N., Rooney-Kron, M., Gokita, T., Lau, S. J., Thoma, C. A., & Scott, L. A. (2022). Implementation of pre-employment transition services: A content analysis of Workforce Innovation and Opportunity Act state plans. *Career Development and Transition for Exceptional Individuals, 45*(2), 60–70. DOI: 10.1177/2165143421993027

Towns, D. M., & Moore, J. E. (2005). Who is running the asylum? A practical approach to managing mental disabilities under the ADA. *Employee Relations Law Journal, 30*(4), 27–41.

Van der Ploeg, R. (2018). Role of employers in transforming disability into ability: Learning from Dutch mistakes. In *Transforming Disability Welfare Policies: Towards Work and Equal Opportunities* (pp. 341–347). Routledge. DOI: 10.4324/9781315235769-41

Vedeler, J. S., & Anvik, C. H. (2023). What's the 'problem' with workplace accommodation? A disability policy journey over time. *Scandinavian Journal of Disability Research, 25*(1), 119–131. DOI: 10.16993/sjdr.918

Vlachos, E. (2024). The transition from school to adult life and independent living for individuals with disabilities: Development tools and programs. In *Tools for Promoting Independent Living Skills in Individuals with Disabilities* (pp. 235–260). IGI Global., DOI: 10.4018/979-8-3693-6026-2.ch011

Von Schrader, S., Malzer, V., & Bruyère, S. M. (2014). Perspectives on disability disclosure: The importance of employer practices and workplace climate. *Employee Responsibilities and Rights Journal, 26*(4), 251–269.

Whittenburg, H. N., Rooney-Kron, M., Carlson, S. R., Malouf, E. T., & Taylor, J. P. (2024). Use of research-based transition recommendations for youth with disabilities in Workforce Innovation and Opportunity Act plans. *Rehabilitation Counseling Bulletin, 67*(4), 283–294. DOI: 10.1177/00343552231155218

Wittenburg, D. C., & Loprest, P. J. (2007). Early transition experiences of transition-age child SSI recipients: New evidence from the national survey of children and families. *Journal of Disability Policy Studies, 18*(3), 176–187. DOI: 10.1177/10442073070180030601

Yaeda, J. (2009). Transition from secondary school to employment in Japan for students with disabilities. In *Educational Transitions: Moving Stories from Around the World* (pp. 205–220). Routledge. DOI: 10.4324/9780203859124-22

Chapter 4
Ethical Foundations:
Dignity, Autonomy, and the Right to Work

ABSTRACT

This chapter explores the ethical foundations of inclusive employment for persons with intellectual disabilities, grounded in the principles of dignity, autonomy, justice, and the right to work. Employment is presented as a matter of human worth, fair participation, and social membership rather than charity or organisational goodwill. The chapter shows how ethical principles shape workplace language, supervision, decision-making, access, and progression. It also addresses tensions between support and autonomy, protection and freedom, and productivity and fairness, concluding that inclusive employment systems are most effective when policy compliance is strengthened by moral clarity.

4.1 INTRODUCTION

Ethical reflection is essential to any serious discussion of inclusive employment for people with intellectual disabilities. This chapter examines the moral principles that should guide workplace policy and practice by treating employment as a matter of dignity, autonomy, justice, and social recognition. Work is not only a means of earning income. It is also connected to identity, belonging, contribution, and participation in shared social life. Jahoda et al. (2009) show that beginning employment carries strong social and emotional meaning for people with intellectual disabilities, while Dehuri and Mukund (2020) place vocational participation within broader rights-

DOI: 10.4018/979-8-3373-9185-4.ch004

based and rehabilitative concerns. These perspectives make clear that employment must be understood within an ethical framework as well as an economic one.

At the centre of this framework is the idea of equal human worth. People with intellectual disabilities are not to be viewed as objects of sympathy or as dependents whose access to work rests on goodwill. They are rights-bearing individuals whose presence in the workplace must be grounded in respect and fairness. Menke (2025) presents recognition as a key element of equality and liberation, while Rössler (2007) connects work with recognition and emancipation beyond narrow measures of productivity. Arruda (2016) similarly highlights the significance of recognition in collective human activity. Within employment contexts, these ideas challenge assumptions that people with intellectual disabilities are peripheral to economic and organisational life. Several principles shape the ethical foundations of this chapter:

1. **Dignity:** work affirms personhood, worth, and social value
2. **Autonomy:** employment can support choice, voice, and self-direction
3. **Justice:** fair access requires the removal of structural and attitudinal barriers
4. **Recognition:** workers must be acknowledged as contributors with equal moral standing
5. **Equity:** inclusion may require differentiated support to achieve fair participation

Employment also has ethical importance because it creates opportunities for contribution and self-determination. Mikołajczyk-Lerman and Potoczna (2019) associate supported employment with enhanced autonomy among adults with intellectual disabilities. Doussard et al. (2024) further argue that workplace inclusion raises ethical questions about how organisations are designed and whose participation is assumed to matter. In this sense, employment is one of the settings in which citizenship, belonging, and social adulthood are expressed. Exclusion from work, therefore, represents more than economic disadvantage; it signals a failure to recognise people as full participants in society.

Persistent barriers make this ethical discussion necessary. Rachanioti et al. (2021), Mihić and Kiš-Glavaš (2010), and Li (2004) point to employer bias, unequal opportunity, and exclusionary assumptions that continue to shape access to work. Jacob and Pillay (2023) and May-Simera (2018) also show that policy commitments do not always produce meaningful labour market inclusion. Against this background, this chapter explores the ethical foundations of inclusive employment by focusing on dignity, autonomy, justice, recognition, and the right to work. It argues that employment practices become more equitable and humane when these principles are treated as central rather than optional.

4.2 DIGNITY AS A FOUNDATION FOR EMPLOYMENT PRACTICE

Dignity is a central ethical principle in inclusive employment because it affirms that workers with intellectual disabilities are people of inherent worth whose presence, choices, and contributions deserve respect. In employment settings, dignity requires more than courteous treatment. It calls for workplace practices that recognise workers as full participants rather than passive recipients of support or charity. Chicoine and Kirschner (2022) connect dignity with the right to make choices and take reasonable risks, while Gallo and Melé (2025) associate work with personal growth, recognition, and human flourishing. In this chapter, dignity is understood as a guiding principle that should shape organisational language, everyday supervision, social interaction, and broader expectations about work and contribution.

Work has ethical significance because it can affirm identity, competence, and a sense of belonging. When workers with intellectual disabilities have genuine opportunities to participate, make decisions, and contribute to organisational life, employment becomes a context in which dignity is enacted in practice. This perspective challenges approaches that define workers solely by impairment, support needs, or perceived limitation. Instead, it emphasises that respect must be evident in how work is structured, how people are addressed, and how their contributions are evaluated. Dignity in employment is not an abstract moral ideal. It is reflected in ordinary decisions about whose voice matters, who is trusted, and how fairness is expressed in workplace relationships.

4.2.1 Core Ethical Dimensions of Dignity

Dignity in employment rests on several interconnected ethical ideas. These include respect for autonomy, recognition of work as a source of meaning, and a humanistic understanding of the worker as more than a unit of labour. Together, these ideas provide a strong ethical basis for inclusive practice.

4.2.1.1 Respect for Autonomy and Decision-Making: Workers with intellectual disabilities should be supported in expressing preferences, making decisions, and actively participating in shaping their work experiences. Chicoine and Kirschner (2022) discuss the dignity of risk as a principle that enables people with intellectual disabilities to make choices and learn from experience, even in the face of some uncertainty. Morgan and Keys (2026) similarly connect dignity with opportunities for participation and self-direction in inclusive educational and transitional settings. In workplace practice, this means that support should not displace decision-making. Instead, it should strengthen the worker's ability to exercise choice regarding tasks, routines, and aspirations.

4.2.1.2 Work as a Source of Meaning and Growth: Work is not only a means of earning income. It can also provide self-respect, purpose, routine, social value, and opportunities for development. Ortiz-Marcos et al. (2024) frame workplace inclusion as both a legislative and practical concern, while Gallo and Melé (2025) present work integration as a process that can support empowerment and personal development. For workers with intellectual disabilities, employment may affirm identity and expand opportunities for participation in community and organisational life. When work is approached in this way, dignity is reinforced through meaningful engagement rather than reduced to mere job presence.

4.2.1.3 A Humanistic View of the Worker: A dignity-based approach also requires employers to adopt a humanistic view of the worker. This means seeing workers with intellectual disabilities as people with aspirations, relationships, strengths, and the capacity for development. Work can serve as a vehicle for integration, personal development, and human flourishing within a humanistic-personalist framework (Gallo & Melé, 2025). Such a view resists reductionist assumptions that measure worker value only by speed, output, or independence. Dignity requires recognition of the whole person and attention to the broader human meaning of participation in work.

4.2.2 How Dignity Should Shape Employment Practice

The principle of dignity must be translated into concrete workplace practice. This translation occurs through everyday language, supervisory relationships, organisational culture, role design, and access to support. Respect for dignity becomes visible when workers are treated as valued participants rather than tolerated exceptions.

4.2.2.1 Language and Workplace Relationships: Workplace language communicates value. Inclusive language avoids labels, pity, and infantilising expressions and instead reflects respect, competence, and personhood. Employees with disabilities have identified respectful interactions, recognition, and a sense of belonging as important factors for creating inclusive workplaces (Glade et al., 2020). Subtle forms of discrimination can also undermine the workplace experiences of employees with intellectual disabilities, often through everyday attitudes and interpersonal interactions rather than overt exclusion (Cavanagh et al., 2021). Dignity is therefore protected when language affirms adulthood, capability, and equal standing within workplace relationships.

4.2.2.2 Supervision and Organisational Culture: Supervisors play an important role in either supporting or undermining dignity. Respectful supervision involves clear guidance, patient communication, fair expectations, and feedback that affirms learning rather than humiliation. Organisational culture also matters because workers are influenced not only by managers but also by peer behaviour, team norms, and institutional attitudes. Inclusive workplace environments play a critical role in supporting the participation, well-being, and success of employees with disabilities (Glade et al., 2020), whereas subtle discriminatory practices can undermine inclusion and workplace well-being (Cavanagh et al., 2021). A workplace committed to dignity will therefore invest in informed supervision and respectful social norms.

4.2.2.3 Role Design and Tailored Opportunity: Dignity is also shaped by whether work opportunities align with worker strengths and whether roles allow meaningful contribution. Christianson-Barker et al. (2025) describe customised employment as a strength-based approach that can support better inclusion for people with intellectual disabilities. A tailored opportunity should not be confused with lowered expectations. Rather, it reflects the idea that fair and respectful employment involves designing or adapting work so that workers can participate fully and demonstrate competence.

4.2.2.4 Structural and Educational Supports: A dignity-based workplace also depends on broader structural support. Ortiz-Marcos et al. (2024) point to the importance of anti-discrimination measures and practical inclusion strategies, while Olsson and Gustafsson (2020) emphasise the value of education and knowledge in intellectual disability practice. Job coaching, structured induction, accessible training, and informed workplace policy can all support workers' dignity by reducing avoidable barriers and strengthening participation.

4.2.3 Barriers to Dignity and Directions for Change: Although dignity is widely recognised as an ethical principle, many workplace conditions continue to compromise it. These barriers often arise through employer assumptions, organisational design, and broader labour market conditions.

4.2.3.1 Common Barriers to Dignified Employment: Workers with intellectual disabilities may encounter several obstacles that undermine dignity in employment, including:

1. Low expectations about competence and potential
2. Infantilising language or behaviour
3. exclusion from workplace decisions
4. Centralised recruitment processes that overlook individual fit
5. Productivity pressures that prioritise speed over inclusion
6. limited access to training or advancement
7. Subtle forms of discrimination from supervisors or co-workers

Future employment challenges are further compounded by changing workplace demands and labour market expectations (Moore et al., 2018). Additional barriers have been identified among self-advocates and families in low- and middle-income countries, where limited support systems and structural constraints continue to restrict access to meaningful employment opportunities (Bialik & Mhiri, 2022).

4.2.3.2 Directions for More Dignified Practice: A stronger ethical commitment to dignity requires practical change at organisational and systemic levels. Useful directions include:

1. embedding respect and inclusion in workplace training and policy
2. creating role pathways that support participation, growth, and recognition
3. strengthening supported employment systems and collaborative workplace support

Workers with intellectual disabilities possess considerable skills and capabilities that often remain underutilised within many employment settings (Lysaght et al., 2012). Supported employment programmes can enhance autonomy, independence, and social participation by facilitating meaningful occupational engagement among individuals with intellectual disabilities (Mikołajczyk-Lerman & Potoczna, 2019).

Dignity should therefore be treated as a foundational principle for employment practice rather than as a secondary value added after placement. When workplaces are organised around respect, recognition, and meaningful opportunity, workers with intellectual disabilities are more likely to experience employment as a site of contribution, self-direction, and belonging. This approach strengthens both ethical integrity and inclusive practice.

Figure 1 provides a conceptual representation of how dignity and respect underpin the ethical principles and workplace practices that support inclusive employment.

Figure 1. Ethical foundations of inclusive employment model

Figure 1 illustrates dignity as the central ethical foundation of inclusive employment. It shows that dignity and respect shape three core principles: autonomy and decision-making, meaningful work and growth, and recognition of the whole person. These principles, in turn, support inclusive practices and a supportive work environment. At the operational level, the model highlights inclusive language, respectful supervision, and accessible resources as practical expressions of dignity in the workplace. The diagram, therefore, presents dignity not as an abstract value, but as a principle that should guide daily interactions, organisational culture, and workplace structures that enable equitable participation for workers with intellectual disabilities.

A concise version (about 145 words) that avoids unsupported emphatic claims:

4.2.3.3 Workplace Illustrations of Dignity, Justice, and Social Recognition

Dignity, justice, and social recognition can be reflected in everyday workplace interactions and organisational practices. In relation to dignity, a supervisor may discuss workplace accommodations directly with an employee, seek their views on support needs, and provide feedback respectfully. Such practices acknowledge the individual as an active participant in workplace decisions.

Justice may be reflected through equitable access to training opportunities, career development programmes, workplace benefits, and organisational resources. These practices support fair participation and reduce the likelihood that decisions are influenced by assumptions about disability.

Social recognition may occur when workers with intellectual disabilities are included in team discussions, workplace activities, collaborative projects, and recognition programmes. Such opportunities acknowledge their presence and contribution within the workplace community.

Conversely, exclusion from decision-making, unequal opportunities, or limited recognition may create barriers to participation and inclusion. These examples illustrate how ethical principles can be expressed through everyday workplace practice.

4.3 AUTONOMY, CHOICE, AND SELF-DETERMINATION

Autonomy concerns the ability to express preferences, influence decisions, and exercise control over matters that affect one's work. For workers with intellectual disabilities, this includes having a say in tasks, routines, supports, communication methods, and future development. Engagement should occur in ways that reflect the lives people want to live, while self-determination is closely connected to the quality of relationships and professional practices that shape everyday experiences. As a result, autonomy is not a peripheral concern in employment but a central factor in determining whether work is experienced as participatory or imposed (Dew et al., 2019; Vaucher et al., 2021).

This issue becomes particularly important because employment settings can easily drift toward over-direction. Decisions may be made quickly for operational convenience, and workers may be excluded from discussions based on assumptions that others know what is best. Decision-making environments can therefore encourage external control rather than genuine choice, while highly regulated settings may further constrain opportunities for autonomy (Carey, 2021; Clark et al., 2004). These conditions highlight the need for employers to create deliberate opportunities for workers to influence decisions affecting their work experience and career development

4.3.1 Autonomy in Workplace Decision-Making

Autonomy in employment extends beyond formal consent. It involves ongoing participation in ordinary workplace decisions and recognition of the worker's perspective as relevant to planning, adjustment, and progression.

4.3.1.1 Voice, Preference, and Participation: Workers with intellectual disabilities should be able to communicate what they prefer, what they find difficult, and what kinds of support are useful. Dew et al. (2019) emphasise the importance of planning that reflects individual priorities, and Vaucher et al. (2021) show that self-determination is shaped by the quality of relationships surrounding the person. This means that participation depends not only on willingness to ask but also on whether the workplace enables such participation.

4.3.1.2 Constraints on Choice: Choice can be limited by rigid routines, inaccessible communication, protective attitudes, or workplace cultures that favour compliance over participation. Carey (2021) illustrates how people may align themselves with prevailing systems of control rather than exercise independent agency. Ryan et al. (2025) similarly note that support for autonomy depends on how seriously staff take the person's wishes and identity. Where workers are routinely spoken for, choice becomes nominal rather than substantive.

4.3.1.3 Supported Choice: Workers may require assistance in considering options, understanding consequences, or communicating decisions. This does not diminish autonomy. Morgan and Keys (2026) discuss the dignity of risk as a principle that allows people to make decisions and learn from experience, even in the face of uncertainty. In practice, supported choice means making room for decision-making while providing the information, time, and guidance needed for informed participation.

4.3.2 Organisational Supports for Self-Determination

Self-determination is strengthened when workplace systems and practices enable participation. Employers do not support autonomy merely by stating that workers are free to choose. They support it by creating conditions in which choice can be meaningfully exercised.

4.3.2.1 Involvement in Everyday Work Decisions: Participation should be embedded in daily work rather than reserved for major reviews or formal meetings. Workers can be involved in discussions about task sequencing, preferred routines, breaks, support arrangements, and changes in responsibilities. Ryan et al. (2025) highlight the importance of attending to who people are and what they want, while Morgan and Keys (2026) reinforce the value of allowing people to make decisions in settings that do not eliminate all risk. These practices help establish choice as a normal part of working life.

4.3.2.2 Self-Directed Career Planning: Career planning can also be organised in ways that increase worker control. Wehmeyer et al. (2009) describe self-directed employment planning as a way of helping individuals define goals and shape their own pathways. Dean et al. (2017) likewise show that the Self-Determined Career Development Model can promote integrated employment through active goal setting and self-direction. This approach shifts attention from placement alone to longer-term participation in employment development.

4.3.2.3 Skills and Tools That Enable Agency: Agency is easier to exercise when workers have opportunities to develop self-advocacy, decision-making, and problem-solving skills. Di Maggio et al. (2019) associate self-determination and psychological empowerment with job satisfaction. Ahmad et al. (2026) also point to transition practices that support movement from school to work. Reinersmann et al. (2025) add that digital assistive technologies can strengthen participation and task performance in the open labour market. Together, these supports make autonomy more workable in practice.

4.3.3 Why Autonomy Matters in Inclusive Employment

Supporting autonomy has implications beyond decision-making itself. It affects how workers experience their roles, how they engage with their tasks, and how employment contributes to wider well-being.

4.3.3.1 Greater Job Satisfaction: A sense of influence overwork can strengthen satisfaction and commitment. Di Maggio et al. (2019) show that self-determination and psychological empowerment are positively associated with job satisfaction among persons with intellectual disability. Where workers feel heard and involved, employment is more likely to be experienced as worthwhile and sustaining.

4.3.3.2 Stronger Participation and Independence: Participation in choice can also strengthen confidence, responsibility, and everyday independence. Pereira-Silva et al. (2018) discuss workplace inclusion from the standpoint of individuals with intellectual disabilities and highlight the value of belonging and participation. Chandrasekaran et al. (2022) further show that supported employment can strengthen independence when organised in ways that respect the individual's role in decision-making.

4.3.3.3 More Responsive Employment Practice: Attention to autonomy encourages employers to listen more carefully, adapt more thoughtfully, and plan with workers rather than around them. This produces employment arrangements that are more responsive to individual goals and less dependent on assumptions made by others.

Autonomy, choice, and self-determination should therefore be treated as practical features of inclusive employment. Employers who make room for workers to influence tasks, support, routines, and career direction help create employment that is more participatory and more just.

4.4 EQUITY, JUSTICE, AND FAIR ACCESS TO WORK

Equity and justice in employment concern the fair distribution of opportunity, support, and recognition across the full employment pathway. For people with intellectual disabilities, access to work is often shaped by patterned disadvantage rather than by neutral competition. Exclusion does not begin only at the point of hiring. It is embedded in how opportunities are advertised, how suitability is judged, which forms of communication are assumed, and which kinds of support are considered legitimate. Unequal opportunities experienced by people with intellectual disabilities continue to influence their participation in the labour market (Li, 2004). Barriers to open employment also extend across recruitment, retention, and workplace participation (Meltzer et al., 2020). Fair access to work must therefore be understood as a matter of justice rather than mere availability.

A justice-based approach also requires attention to the distinction between formal equality and substantive fairness. Formal equality assumes that everyone should be treated equally. However, people do not enter employment from equal social positions, nor do they face identical institutional conditions. Workers with intellectual disabilities often encounter structures designed around speed, abstraction, self-promotion, and unspoken workplace norms. Employment practices are experienced differently by workers, employers, and employment specialists, suggesting that fairness cannot be measured solely by whether the same procedures are applied to all (Morris et al., 2024). Justice may instead require accommodation, accessible procedures, and differentiated forms of support to make participation genuinely possible.

4.4.1 Patterned Disadvantage Across Employment Stages

Exclusion from work rarely results from a single barrier. More often, it is produced through repeated disadvantages that operate at entry, during participation, and in opportunities for progression. A justice lens helps identify these patterns and clarify why equitable access requires more than encouragement or goodwill.

4.4.1.1 Barriers at Entry: Access to employment is often restricted by inaccessible recruitment systems, negative assumptions about capability, and narrow definitions of employability. Meltzer et al. (2020) describe barriers to finding and maintaining open employment for people with intellectual disability, and Lawrence et al. (2026) identify policy and practice factors that shape workforce participation. Entry barriers may include application procedures that rely heavily on complex written communication, interviews that privilege verbal fluency, and screening practices that overlook potential when support needs are visible.

4.4.1.2 Unequal Conditions During Participation: Fairness also remains important after entering the workforce. Workers with intellectual disabilities may face exclusion from informal communication, limited access to training, inconsistent support, or workplace expectations that disregard different ways of learning and performing. Morris et al. (2024) show that employment practices are experienced unevenly among workplace actors, underscoring the importance of examining the quality of participation rather than assuming that hiring alone signals inclusion. Justice requires attention to whether workers can participate on fair terms once employed.

4.4.1.3 Restricted Progression and Advancement: Patterned disadvantages also appear in promotion, role expansion, and career development. Workers with intellectual disabilities are often channelled into narrow roles with limited opportunities for growth. May-Simera (2018) questions whether existing employment strategies adequately promote open labour market participation, while Migliore et al. (2008) show how institutional arrangements can keep adults with intellectual disabilities in sheltered settings. Justice in employment must therefore include fair access to advancement, not only to initial placement.

4.4.2 Sources of Structural Inequality

The disadvantages described above do not arise solely from individual prejudice. They are embedded in broader systems, assumptions, and institutional arrangements that shape who is seen as employable and under what conditions.

4.4.2.1 Stigma and Attitudinal Bias: Negative assumptions about competence, reliability, and workplace suitability continue to shape employment access for people with intellectual disabilities. Perceived inequalities in employment opportunities remain a significant concern for this population (Li, 2004). Stigma and employer assumptions further constrain access to open employment opportunities (Meltzer et al., 2020). These perceptions influence how workers are evaluated, trusted, supported, and integrated within workplace environments. Consequently, promoting justice in employment requires direct attention to the role of attitudinal bias and discriminatory perceptions that contribute to labour market exclusion.

4.4.2.2 Segregated and Inflexible Systems: Structural inequality is reinforced when employment systems continue to direct people toward segregated or restricted pathways. Concerns remain regarding the effectiveness of policies in promoting access to the open labour market for people with intellectual disabilities (May-Simera, 2018). Adults with intellectual disabilities also continue to be disproportionately represented in sheltered workshops rather than competitive employment settings (Migliore et al., 2008). Such systems often reflect institutional convenience rather than fair opportunity. Equity requires movement away from arrangements that normalise separation and low expectations.

4.4.2.3 Intersectional Disadvantage: Justice must also account for the fact that some workers face multiple forms of marginalisation at once. Lindsay et al. (2024) show that young adults with multiple minoritised identities face layered challenges related to race and disability, while Whitaker (2019) underscores the persistent role of racial discrimination in the workplace. Equitable employment practice, therefore, cannot assume that disability is experienced in isolation from other structures of disadvantage.

4.4.3 Toward Fairer Employment Practice

Correcting structural inequality requires more than statements of inclusion. It requires practical reform in policy, procedure, and organisational evaluation so that access to work is shaped by fairness rather than inherited disadvantages.

4.4.3.1 Accessible and Fair Procedures: Recruitment, induction, and performance evaluation should be designed in ways that do not exclude workers through avoidable complexity. Examining employment practices from multiple stakeholder perspectives can help identify barriers and improve fairness in workplace processes (Morris et al., 2024). Employment systems should also be redesigned to promote equity, access, and inclusion for all workers (Godden & Hoessler, 2024). Fair evaluation standards should recognise competence in accessible and context-sensitive ways rather than relying exclusively on conventional measures that privilege narrow performance norms.

4.4.3.2 Supported and Sustained Participation: Fair access also depends on support systems that enable workers to enter and remain in employment on just terms. The experiences of school leavers with intellectual disabilities demonstrate the importance of sustained support during transitions into employment (Scanlon & Doyle, 2021). Supported employment has also been conceptualised as an issue of occupational justice for young people with intellectual disabilities (Engelbrecht et al., 2023). These perspectives suggest that support should be treated as an integral component of fair labour market participation rather than as an optional add-on.

4.4.3.3 Reforming Opportunity Structures: A justice-based approach requires employers and policymakers to address the deeper structures that organise opportunity. This includes revising segregated pathways, improving support funding, strengthening transition mechanisms, and challenging assumptions that equate fairness with sameness. Equity becomes meaningful when institutions are willing to adjust the conditions under which work is accessed, experienced, and evaluated.

Fairness in employment extends beyond access to work. It also shapes employee engagement, workplace relationships, and organisational culture. When workers perceive employment processes as fair, they are more likely to participate actively, collaborate with colleagues, and contribute to organisational goals. Equitable access to training, advancement, and workplace participation can strengthen commitment and trust, whereas persistent inequities may contribute to disengagement, reduced morale, and weaker team cohesion. Justice, therefore, supports both ethical employment practice and organisational effectiveness.

Equity, justice, and fair access to work, therefore, require a shift from formal inclusion to corrective fairness. Workers with intellectual disabilities do not simply need entry points into employment. They need employment systems that recognise structural disadvantages, remove avoidable barriers, and distribute opportunities in ways that support genuine participation and progression.

4.5 THE RIGHT TO WORK AS A MORAL AND SOCIAL COMMITMENT

The right to work should be understood not only as a legal entitlement but also as a moral and social commitment. For persons with intellectual disabilities, access to meaningful work is closely linked to recognition, participation, economic inclusion, and social belonging. Work creates opportunities to contribute, occupy valued social roles, and participate in community life. When disability restricts access to work, exclusion extends beyond loss of income. It affects identity, public participation, and the ability to be recognised as a full member of society. For this reason, the right to work belongs at the centre of ethical discussion in inclusive employment.

International human rights frameworks have reinforced this position by treating employment as a matter of equality, accessibility, and non-discrimination. General Comment No. 8 (2022) states that its purpose is to clarify the obligations of States parties regarding the right to work and employment under Article 27 of the Convention. Article 27 of the Convention on the Rights of Persons with Disabilities (CRPD) provides an important foundation for inclusive employment by affirming the right of people with disabilities to work on an equal basis with others (Fasciglione, 2015). Disability has also been positioned within broader discussions of decent work and the Sustainable Development Goals, highlighting the importance of employment in achieving social inclusion and sustainable development (Welti, 2025). These perspectives demonstrate that work is not a privilege granted selectively. Rather, it is a fundamental condition for equal citizenship and social justice.

4.5.1 The Right to Work as a Human Rights and Ethical Principle

The right to work carries legal, moral, and social significance. It requires recognition that persons with intellectual disability are entitled to participate in labour markets on equal terms and that exclusion from work represents a broader ethical failure.

4.5.1.1 Work as a Human Right: International and national frameworks recognise work as a right that should be protected through non-discrimination, accessibility, and reasonable accommodation. General Comment No. 8 (2022) gives detailed attention to the obligations attached to the right to work for people with disabilities. Welti (2025) further connects disability rights with the broader agenda of decent work. These frameworks matter because they reject the notion that access to employment should depend on employer generosity or social sympathy.

4.5.1.2 Work as Social Participation: The right to work also has social significance because employment is one of the principal ways in which people participate in public life. Employer practices play an important role in shaping employment outcomes within broader regulatory settings (Saleh & Bruyère, 2018). The right to work is also experienced through everyday participation and continuity in working life (Jakobsen, 2009). For people with intellectual disability, meaningful work may support identity, routine, visibility, and contribution in ways that extend beyond wages alone.

4.5.1.3 Work as an Ethical Obligation of Inclusion: The right to work also imposes an ethical obligation on societies and institutions to organise employment in inclusive ways. Excluding people from work based on disability is not simply a technical failure of policy implementation. It reflects a moral failure to treat people as full participants in social and economic life. Inclusive employment forms part of the obligations arising from Article 27 of the CRPD (Fasciglione, 2015). Legal protection across jurisdictions, however, remains uneven (Nardodkar et al., 2016). Ethical commitment is therefore needed alongside law if the right to work is to be realised in practice.

4.5.2 What Is Lost When Access to Work Is Denied

The denial of work has consequences that extend far beyond employment status. It affects justice, democratic participation, and the distribution of social and economic opportunities.

4.5.2.1 Loss of Social Justice: When people with intellectual disabilities are excluded from employment, they are denied access to one of the central institutions of adult social life. Saleh and Bruyère (2018) show that employer practices shape outcomes for people with disabilities, and Polishko and Zelinskyi (2025) discuss normative barriers within the labour market. Exclusion from work, therefore, sustains inequality and weakens claims to fairness and inclusion.

4.5.2.2 Weakening of Democratic and Inclusive Society: A democratic society depends on the principle that all citizens should have the opportunity to participate in social and economic life. General Comment No. 8 (2022) and Fasciglione (2015) both position inclusive employment within this broader framework of equal participation. When disability-based exclusion persists, societies signal that some people are less entitled to public contribution and less visible within shared institutions. This weakens the moral basis of democracy itself.

4.5.2.3 Economic and Social Consequences: The denial of work also has material consequences. It may increase dependence, reinforce poverty, and waste human capability that could contribute to organisational and social life. McEwin (2017) discusses technology as a foundation for improving employment outcomes for people with disability, showing that practical means of inclusion already exist. Continued exclusion is therefore not only unjust but also socially and economically costly.

The consequences of exclusion extend beyond the individual worker. Organisations may lose valuable perspectives, skills, and experiences when opportunities are restricted. Teams may become less diverse in their problem-solving and collaboration approaches, while workplaces may miss opportunities to build cultures characterised by inclusion, respect, and mutual support. Inclusive employment, therefore, benefits not only workers with intellectual disabilities but also the wider organisational environment.

4.5.3 Realising the Right to Work in Practice

Recognising the right to work requires action at policy, organisational, and societal levels. Legal recognition alone is not enough if employment systems remain inaccessible or exclusionary in practice.

4.5.3.1 Stronger Legal and Policy Protection: States and institutions should strengthen anti-discrimination protections, enforce accessibility requirements, and ensure that reasonable accommodation is consistently available. Laflamme (2017) discusses the potential of legal accommodation frameworks in the workplace, and Nardodkar et al. (2016) show the uneven nature of protection across different legal contexts. A right without enforcement remains fragile.

4.5.3.2 Employer Responsibility for Inclusion: Employers also play a direct role in realising the right to work. Saleh and Bruyère (2018) emphasise the importance of employer practices, while Welti (2025) links disability inclusion to decent work principles. Inclusive hiring, accessible work design, support provision, and fair progression pathways are all part of translating the right to work into daily organisational practice.

4.5.3.3 Shared Commitment to Inclusive Labour Markets: The right to work should also be treated as a shared commitment across governments, institutions, and workplaces. Polishko and Zelinskyi (2025) identify both barriers and opportunities in inclusive labour markets, suggesting that structural reform is possible when inclusion is treated as a normative priority. The task is not only to admit people into work but to create labour markets in which participation is sustained and valued.

The right to work is therefore both a human rights principle and a moral commitment that speaks to the kind of institutions we seek to build. For people with intellectual disabilities, meaningful work supports participation, recognition, and economic inclusion. Denying that opportunity undermines justice and weakens commitments to democratic and inclusive social life. See Figure 2 for a visual pathway showing how ethical principles are translated into policy, organisational action, and inclusive employment practice.

Figure 2. Pathway from ethical principles to inclusive employment practice

Figure 2 shows that inclusive employment practice develops through a logical, ethical pathway. Ethical foundations establish the moral base, commitment to equity and justice shapes institutional intent, and strategic policy and action translate these commitments into concrete measures. The outcome is inclusive employment practice. The figure, therefore, presents inclusion as the result of ethical principles being carried through policy and workplace action.

4.6 ETHICAL TENSIONS IN WORKPLACE DECISION-MAKING

Inclusive employment often involves decisions in which legitimate values pull in different directions. Employers may need to decide how much support is appropriate without becoming controlling, how to respond to risk without becoming overprotective, and how to maintain performance expectations without allowing efficiency to override fairness. These tensions do not necessarily indicate poor leadership. They are part of the ethical complexity of workplace life. What matters is whether such decisions are approached reflectively, transparently, and with attention to the rights and interests of workers with intellectual disabilities.

Ethical tensions become especially significant when one value is treated as automatically superior to another. A workplace may, for example, prioritise productivity to the point that support is viewed as a disruption, or it may emphasise protection so strongly that workers are denied opportunities to exercise judgment and grow through experience. Durocher et al. (2016) discuss ethical tensions arising from systemic constraints, while Juujärvi et al. (2023) show that ethical conflicts affect work-related well-being when professionals are unable to act in line with their values. In inclusive employment, ethical reflection is therefore not optional. It is part of responsible leadership and fair decision-making.

4.6.1 Recurring Ethical Tensions in Inclusive Employment

Ethical tensions in the workplace often emerge through everyday decisions rather than exceptional crises. They appear in supervision, task assignment, accommodation, evaluation, and risk and responsibility management.

4.6.1.1 Support and Autonomy

One of the most common tensions concerns the relationship between assistance and self-direction. Workers with intellectual disabilities may require structured support, but support becomes ethically problematic when it displaces voice, choice, or control. Durocher et al. (2016) show how systemic conditions can limit ethically responsive practice, and Juujärvi et al. (2023) point to the strain created when workplace arrangements conflict with professional judgment. In employment contexts, this tension appears when supervisors make decisions for workers in the name of helping them, rather than with them. Responsible practice requires support that enables participation rather than replacing it.

4.6.1.2 Protection and Freedom

A second tension concerns the balance between safeguarding and allowing freedom. Employers may feel pressure to reduce risk, avoid mistakes, or shield workers from situations that appear demanding. Yet excessive protection can restrict learning, confidence, and participation. Bushby et al. (2015) identify ethical tensions around safety and choice in practice settings, while Durocher et al. (2016) show how institutional pressures can narrow the scope for ethical action. In inclusive employment, the challenge is to respond to risk proportionately. Workers should be protected from harm, but they should not be denied ordinary opportunities to try, decide, and develop simply because disability is present.

4.6.1.3 Productivity and Fairness

A third tension arises when organisational demands for speed, output, or standardisation conflict with fairness in treatment and evaluation. Employers may rely on uniform expectations in the name of efficiency, even when those expectations fail to account for different support needs or learning styles. Gingerich (2021) addresses legal and ethical safeguards in relation to workplace inclusion, and McAuliffe and Greenslade (2025) argue for ethical decision-making models that attend to interdependence and fairness. In this context, fairness does not mean lowering standards without justification. It means ensuring that performance expectations, assessment methods, and opportunities are structured in ways that do not reproduce exclusion.

4.6.2 Ethical Reflection as a Leadership Responsibility

Because ethical tensions cannot be eliminated entirely, leaders must develop thoughtful ways to address them. Reflection is necessary not only to resolve difficult situations but also to prevent routine decisions from becoming ethically careless.

4.6.2.1 Critical Dialogue and Shared Deliberation: Ethical workplace cultures are strengthened when decisions can be discussed openly. Lamontagne (2015) shows that behavioural and cultural influences shape ethical dilemmas in organisations, while Mishra and Ray (2024) connect ethical decision-making with diversity, inclusion, and shared values. In inclusive employment, critical dialogue allows supervisors, co-workers, and support personnel to consider competing values before decisions are finalised. It also helps identify whether a proposed action prioritises organisational convenience over worker participation.

4.6.2.2 Use of Ethical Frameworks: Structured frameworks can help leaders think more clearly about difficult decisions. An updated inclusive model of ethical decision-making provides guidance for navigating complex workplace situations (McAuliffe & Greenslade, 2025). Universal moral competencies such as prudence and justice also support ethical leadership and decision-making (Morales-Sánchez & Cabello-Medina, 2013). These approaches encourage leaders to move beyond instinct or habit by asking whose interests are affected, what values are in conflict, and whether a decision can be justified in ethical rather than merely procedural terms.

4.6.2.3 Organisational Justice and Transparency: Reflection must also be supported by systems that promote fairness and transparency. Juujärvi et al. (2023) show that unresolved ethical conflict can affect well-being, while Valentine et al. (2019) indicate that organisational ethics structures influence judgment and behaviour. In inclusive employment, ethical leadership requires clear reasoning, consistent procedures, and openness about how decisions are made. Transparency helps reduce arbitrariness and makes it easier to challenge decisions that unfairly disadvantage workers.

4.6.3 Implications for Inclusive Workplace Leadership

Ethical tensions reveal that leadership in inclusive employment is not simply about compliance or operational management. It is also about moral judgment. Leaders must ask not only what is efficient or permissible, but also what is fair, respectful, and consistent with inclusion.

4.6.3.1 Attending to Prioritised Interests: Ethical reflection requires leaders to examine whose interests carry the most weight in decision-making. A decision may appear neutral while in practice favouring speed, convenience, or institutional comfort over worker dignity and opportunity. Mishra and Ray (2024) emphasise the importance of aligning ethical decision-making with shared values, and Wang et al. (2025) show that ethical conflict can produce mixed reactions among observers in the workplace. Leaders must therefore be attentive to the values embedded in their choices.

4.6.3.2 Encouraging Ethical Voice: Inclusive workplaces should encourage staff to raise concerns when decisions appear unfair or exclusionary. Ethical silence can allow problematic practices to continue unchecked. Wang et al. (2025) show that workplace conflict may reveal opportunities for improvement when people respond rather than withdraw. Leadership should therefore create conditions in which questioning, reflection, and respectful challenge are possible.

Ethical tensions in workplace decision-making are unavoidable in inclusive employment, but they can be approached responsibly. When employers reflect critically on support, protection, fairness, and freedom, they are better positioned to make decisions that respect workers with intellectual disabilities as full participants in organisational life. Ethical reflection is therefore not a peripheral activity. It is part of what responsible workplace leadership requires.

4.7 CONCLUSION: BUILDING ETHICALLY GROUNDED EMPLOYMENT SYSTEMS

Ethically grounded employment systems emerge when organisations translate dignity, autonomy, justice, and the right to work into the arrangements that shape daily workplace life. These principles should operate not only as stated values but also as practical guides for recruitment, role allocation, communication, support, supervision, performance review, and advancement. When ethics are embedded in organisational systems, inclusive employment becomes more coherent, accountable, and sustainable.

This chapter has shown that inclusive employment is as much a moral concern as it is a legal or administrative one. Dignity calls for respect in workplace language, relationships, and expectations. Autonomy calls for participation in decision-making and support that strengthens agency rather than replacing it. Justice calls for attention to structural disadvantage, fair procedures, and equitable access to opportunity. The right to work calls for employment to be treated as a matter of social membership and human worth rather than as a matter of selective permission.

The chapters that follow extend this foundation by examining recruitment, support, supervision, and progression in more applied terms. Their practical value depends on the ethical commitments established here. Inclusive employment is strongest when organisational systems are guided by moral clarity alongside policy compliance, and when everyday practice reflects both rights and respect.

REFERENCES

Ahmad, W., Shokeen, R., Raj, R., Ramkumar, B. V., Singh, R. R., & Mohammad, S. (2026). Transition of Persons with Intellectual and Developmental Disabilities from School to Work: Evidence-Based Practices. In *Vocational Rehabilitation for Students with Developmental Disabilities: Transition from Education to Employment* (pp. 79-132). IGI Global Scientific Publishing. https://doi.org/DOI: 10.4018/979-8-3693-9541-7.ch003

Arruda, C. T. (2016). What we can intend: Recognition and collective intentionality. *The Southern Journal of Philosophy*, *54*(1), 5–26. DOI: 10.1111/sjp.12162

Bialik, K., & Mhiri, M. (2022). Barriers to employment for people with intellectual disabilities in low- and middle-income countries: Self-advocate and family perspectives. *Journal of International Development*, *34*(5), 988–1001. DOI: 10.1002/jid.3659

Bushby, K., Chan, J., Druif, S., Ho, K., & Kinsella, E. A. (2015). Ethical tensions in occupational therapy practice: A scoping review. *British Journal of Occupational Therapy*, *78*(4), 212–221. DOI: 10.1177/0308022614564770

Carey, E. (2021). Aligning with the flow of control: A grounded theory study of choice and autonomy in decision-making practices of people with intellectual disabilities. *International Journal of Qualitative Studies on Health and Well-Being, 16*(1), Article 1857053. https://doi.org/DOI: 10.1080/17482631.2020.1857053

Cavanagh, J., Meacham, H., Pariona-Cabrera, P., & Bartram, T. (2021). Subtle workplace discrimination inhibiting workers with intellectual disability from thriving at the workplace. *Personnel Review*, *50*(7–8), 1739–1756. DOI: 10.1108/PR-10-2021-0723

Chandrasekaran, P., Thekkumkara, S. N., Jothibalan, A., Jagannathan, A., Jayarajan, D., & Reddy, S. K. (2022). Hybrid supported employment approach for persons with intellectual disabilities in India: Evidence based case studies. *Journal of Psychosocial Rehabilitation and Mental Health*, *9*(3), 317–323. DOI: 10.1007/s40737-021-00241-9 PMID: 34642615

Chicoine, B., & Kirschner, K. L. (2022). Considering dignity of risk in the care of people with intellectual disabilities: A clinical perspective. *Perspectives in Biology and Medicine*, *65*(2), 189–198. DOI: 10.1353/pbm.2022.0014 PMID: 35938426

Christianson-Barker, J., Franzius, A., Mills, R., Lomness, A., & Hole, R. (2025). Employing strength: A scoping review of customized employment practices to support inclusive employment for people with intellectual disabilities. *Journal of Vocational Rehabilitation*, *63*(2), 119–140. DOI: 10.1177/10522263251356445

Clark, E., Olympia, D. E., Jensen, J., Heathfield, L. T., & Jenson, W. R. (2004). Striving for autonomy in a contingency-governed world: Another challenge for individuals with developmental disabilities. *Psychology in the Schools*, *41*(1), 143–153. DOI: 10.1002/pits.10146

Dean, E. E., Burke, K. M., Shogren, K. A., & Wehmeyer, M. L. (2017). Promoting self-determination and integrated employment through the self-determined career development model. *Advances in Neurodevelopmental Disorders*, *1*(2), 55–62. DOI: 10.1007/s41252-017-0011-y

Dehuri, B. K., & Mukund, B. (2020). Recent trends and issues in vocational rehabilitation of people with ID. In *Research anthology on rehabilitation practices and therapy* (pp. 1202–1228). IGI Global., DOI: 10.4018/978-1-7998-3432-8.ch059

Dew, A., Collings, S., Dillon Savage, I., Gentle, E., & Dowse, L. (2019). "Living the life I want": A framework for planning engagement with people with intellectual disability and complex support needs. *Journal of Applied Research in Intellectual Disabilities*, *32*(2), 401–412. DOI: 10.1111/jar.12538 PMID: 30358022

Di Maggio, I., Santilli, S., Nota, L., & Ginevra, M. C. (2019). The predictive role of self-determination and psychological empowerment on job satisfaction in persons with intellectual disability. *Advances in Neurodevelopmental Disorders*, *3*(2), 197–203. DOI: 10.1007/s41252-019-00110-4

Doussard, C., Garbe, E., Morales, J., & Billion, J. (2024). Universal design for the workplace: Ethical considerations regarding the inclusion of workers with disabilities. *Journal of Business Ethics*, *194*(2), 285–296. DOI: 10.1007/s10551-023-05582-y

Durocher, E., Kinsella, E. A., McCorquodale, L., & Phelan, S. (2016). Ethical tensions related to systemic constraints: Occupational alienation in occupational therapy practice. *OTJR (Thorofare, N.J.)*, *36*(4), 216–226. DOI: 10.1177/1539449216665117 PMID: 27591435

Engelbrecht, M., van Niekerk, L., & Shaw, L. (2023). Supported employment for youth with intellectual disability: Promoting occupational justice. *Journal of Occupational Science*, *30*(3), 403–419. DOI: 10.1080/14427591.2022.2146159

Fasciglione, M. (2015). Article 27 of the CRPD and the right of inclusive employment of people with autism. In *Protecting the rights of people with autism in the fields of education and employment: International, European and national perspectives* (pp. 145–170). Springer., DOI: 10.1007/978-3-319-13791-9_6

Gallo, I., & Melé, D. (2025). Work integration of people with mental disorders through social enterprise: A humanistic-personalist framework and case study. *Journal of Business Ethics*, *199*(4), 693–713. DOI: 10.1007/s10551-024-05853-2

General Comment No. 8 (2022) on the right of persons with disabilities to work and employment. (. (2022). International. *Human Rights Law Review*, *11*(2), 273–303. DOI: 10.1163/22131035-11020004

Gingerich, E. F. R. (2021). Working for inclusion: Addressing legal and ethical safeguards for LGBTQ employees. In *The Palgrave handbook of workplace well-being* (pp. 1379–1403). Palgrave Macmillan., DOI: 10.1007/978-3-030-30025-8_65

Glade, R., Koch, L. C., Zaandam, A., Simon, L. S., Manno, C. M., Rumril, P. D., & Rosen, C. C. (2020). Recommendations from employees with disabilities for creating inclusive workplaces: Results from a grounded theory investigation. *Journal of Vocational Rehabilitation*, *53*(1), 77–88. DOI: 10.3233/JVR-201087

Godden, L., & Hoessler, C. (2024). (Re)designing for equity, access and inclusion in work-integrated learning. *. *International Journal of Work-Integrated Learning*, *25*(1), 37–50.

Jacob, U. S., & Pillay, J. (2023). Studies related to employment of persons with intellectual disability: A systematic review. *Journal of Vocational Rehabilitation*, *59*(2), 169–181. DOI: 10.3233/JVR-230035

Jahoda, A., Banks, P., Dagnan, D., Kemp, J., Kerr, W., & Williams, V. (2009). Starting a new job: The social and emotional experience of people with intellectual disabilities. *Journal of Applied Research in Intellectual Disabilities*, *22*(5), 421–425. DOI: 10.1111/j.1468-3148.2009.00497.x

Jakobsen, K. (2009). The right to work: Experiences of employees with rheumatism. *Journal of Occupational Science*, *16*(2), 120–127. DOI: 10.1080/14427591.2009.9686651

Juujärvi, S., Nummela, O., & Sinervo, T. (2023). Aspects of ethical conflicts and their implications for work-related well-being: A cross-sectional study among health and social care professionals. *Scandinavian Journal of Work and Organisational Psychology*, *8*(1). *Article*, *1*(1), 1–15. DOI: 10.16993/sjwop.176

Laflamme, A.-M. (2017). Mental disorders and reasonable accommodation at work: The potential of Quebec law. *Sante Mentale au Quebec*, *42*(2), 39–56. DOI: 10.7202/1041913ar PMID: 29267412

Lamontagne, R. M. (2015). Ethical dilemmas in the workplace: HR managers' perceptions of behavioural influences with implications for building an ethical culture in organisations. *International Journal of Knowledge. Culture and Change Management, 15*, 1–21.

Lawrence, K., Mellifont, D., & Bulkeley, K. (2026). Disability employment policy in Australia: Barriers and facilitators to workforce participation. *Social Policy and Administration, 60*(1), 112–123. DOI: 10.1111/spol.13147

Li, E. P. Y. (2004). Self-perceived equal opportunities for people with intellectual disability. *International Journal of Rehabilitation Research. Internationale Zeitschrift fur Rehabilitationsforschung. Revue Internationale de Recherches de Readaptation, 27*(3), 241–245. DOI: 10.1097/00004356-200409000-00011 PMID: 15319696

Lindsay, S., Dain, N., & Hsu, S. (2024). Exploring the employment experiences of young adults with multiple minoritised identities: A qualitative study focusing on race and non-apparent disabilities. *PLoS One, 19*(11), e0313295. Advance online publication. DOI: 10.1371/journal.pone.0313295 PMID: 39485781

Lysaght, R., Ouellette-Kuntz, H., & Lin, C.-J. (2012). Untapped potential: Perspectives on the employment of people with intellectual disability. *Work (Reading, Mass.), 41*(4), 409–422. DOI: 10.3233/WOR-2012-1318 PMID: 22495411

May-Simera, C. (2018). Is the Irish (Republic of) Comprehensive Employment Strategy fit for purpose in promoting the employment of people with intellectual disabilities in the open labor market? A discussion using evidence from the National Intellectual Disability Database. *Journal of Policy and Practice in Intellectual Disabilities, 15*(4), 284–294. DOI: 10.1111/jppi.12259

McAuliffe, D., & Greenslade, L. (2025). Turn it and turn it again: The updated inclusive model of ethical decision making. *Ethics & Social Welfare, 19*(2), 161–173. DOI: 10.1080/17496535.2025.2483668

McEwin, A. (2017). Working together: Technology as the foundation for better employment outcomes for people with disability. In *Proceedings of the 14th Web for All Conference, W4A 2017*, Article a1. https://doi.org/DOI: 10.1145/3058555.3058556

Meltzer, A., Robinson, S., & Fisher, K. R. (2020). Barriers to finding and maintaining open employment for people with intellectual disability in Australia. *Social Policy and Administration, 54*(1), 88–101. DOI: 10.1111/spol.12523

Menke, C. (2025). Equality, interpellation, liberation: Three vectors of recognition. In *Recognition: Historical and philosophical perspectives* (pp. 422–436). Routledge., DOI: 10.4324/9781003686521-33

Migliore, A., Grossi, T., Mank, D., & Rogan, P. (2008). Why do adults with intellectual disabilities work in sheltered workshops? *Journal of Vocational Rehabilitation, 28*(1), 29–40. DOI: 10.3233/JVR-2008-00402

Mihić, S. S., & Kiš-Glavaš, L. (2010). Work and social competence of people with intellectual disabilities: Barriers for employers in their employment. *Revija za Socijalnu Politiku, 17*(3), 387–399. DOI: 10.3935/rsp.v17i3.912

Mikołajczyk-Lerman, G., & Potoczna, M. (2019). Enhancing autonomy through the occupational engagement of adults with intellectual disabilities: Supported employment model applied by the Polish Association for Persons with Intellectual Disabilities (Branch in Zgierz). *Przegląd Socjologii Jakościowej, 15*(4), 184–203. DOI: 10.18778/1733-8069.15.4.09

Mishra, A., & Ray, A. K. (2024). Ethical decision-making, diversity, and inclusion: Building the foundation for sustainable business success through shared values. In *Organization, purpose and values: Integrating diversity, equity and inclusion* (pp. 3–20). Routledge., DOI: 10.4324/9781003501374-2

Moore, K., McDonald, P., & Bartlett, J. (2018). Emerging trends affecting future employment opportunities for people with intellectual disability: The case of a large retail organisation. *Journal of Intellectual & Developmental Disability, 43*(3), 328–338. DOI: 10.3109/13668250.2017.1379250

Morales-Sánchez, R., & Cabello-Medina, C. (2013). The role of four universal moral competencies in ethical decision-making. *Journal of Business Ethics, 116*(4), 717–734. DOI: 10.1007/s10551-013-1817-9

Morgan, C. L., & Keys, B. (2026). Dignity of risk in inclusive postsecondary education programs. In *Implementing inclusive postsecondary programs for students with intellectual disabilities* (pp. 413–460). IGI Global., DOI: 10.4018/979-8-3373-2767-9.ch015

Morris, R., Christianson-Barker, J., Stainton, T., Mills, R., Schroeder, M., Cox, J., Rowley, C., & Hole, R. (2024). Employment practices as experienced by persons with intellectual disability, employers, and employment specialists across Canada. *Journal of Vocational Rehabilitation, 61*(1), 55–66. DOI: 10.3233/JVR-240019

Nardodkar, R., Pathare, S., Ventriglio, A., Castaldelli-Maia, J., Javate, K. R., Torales, J., & Bhugra, D. (2016). Legal protection of the right to work and employment for persons with mental health problems: A review of legislation across the world. *International Review of Psychiatry (Abingdon, England), 28*(4), 375–384. DOI: 10.1080/09540261.2016.1210575 PMID: 27499197

Olsson, S., & Gustafsson, C. (2020). Employees' experiences of education and knowledge in intellectual disability practice. *Journal of Policy and Practice in Intellectual Disabilities*, *17*(3), 219–231. DOI: 10.1111/jppi.12338

Ortiz-Marcos, J. M., Invernón-Gómez, A. I., Medina-García, M., & Higueras-Rodríguez, L. (2024). Workplace inclusion of people with disabilities: Legislative challenges and practical solutions. *Revista Española de Orientación y Psicopedagogía*, *35*(3), 105–122. DOI: 10.5944/reop.vol.35.num.3.2024.40820

Pereira-Silva, N. L., Furtado, A. V., & Andrade, J. F. C. D. M. (2018). Workplace inclusion from the standpoint of individuals with intellectual disabilities. *Temas em Psicologia*, *26*(2), 1017–1030. DOI: 10.9788/TP2018.2-17En

Polishko, N., & Zelinskyi, D. (2025). Inclusive labour market: Normative barriers and opportunities for persons with disabilities in Europe. *Law. Human. Environment*, *16*(3), 92–112. DOI: 10.31548/law/3.2025.92

Rachanioti, E., Giaouri, S., Laskaraki, E., & Alevriadou, A. (2021). "Can I work here?": Employment barriers for individuals with intellectual disabilities in Greece. *Journal of Intellectual Disability—Diagnosis and Treatment, 9*(4), 354–362. https://doi.org/DOI: 10.6000/2292-2598.2021.09.04.1

Reinersmann, A., Heinz-Jakobs, M., Bicker, E., & Röcker, C. (2025). Examples of implementing digital assistive technologies in the open labor market. *Communications in Computer and Information Science*, *2524*, 161–171. DOI: 10.1007/978-3-031-94156-6_17

Rössler, B. (2007). Work, recognition, emancipation. In *Recognition and power: Axel Honneth and the tradition of critical social theory* (pp. 135–163). Cambridge University Press., DOI: 10.1017/CBO9780511498732.006

Ryan, J., Brown, H. M., Borden, A., Devlin, C., Kedmy, A., Lee, A., Nicholas, D. B., & Thompson-Hodgetts, S. (2025). "It's really who they are and what they want": Staff perspectives on supporting autonomy for autistic adults with intellectual disabilities. *Journal of Applied Research in Intellectual Disabilities*, *38*(4), e70106. Advance online publication. DOI: 10.1111/jar.70106 PMID: 40731376

Saleh, M. C., & Bruyère, S. M. (2018). Leveraging employer practices in global regulatory frameworks to improve employment outcomes for people with disabilities. *Social Inclusion (Lisboa)*, *6*(1), 18–28. DOI: 10.17645/si.v6i1.1201

Scanlon, G., & Doyle, A. (2021). Transition stories: Voices of school leavers with intellectual disabilities. *British Journal of Learning Disabilities*, *49*(4), 456–466. DOI: 10.1111/bld.12433

Valentine, S. R., Hanson, S. K., & Fleischman, G. M. (2019). The presence of ethics codes and employees' internal locus of control, social aversion/malevolence, and ethical judgment of incivility: A study of smaller organizations. *Journal of Business Ethics, 160*(3), 657–674. DOI: 10.1007/s10551-018-3880-8

Vaucher, C., Cudré-Mauroux, A., & Piérart, G. (2021). Perceptions and understandings of self-determination in the context of relationships between people with intellectual disabilities and social care professionals. *International Journal of Developmental Disabilities, 67*(2), 121–130. DOI: 10.1080/20473869.2019.1623595 PMID: 34141405

Wang, Y., Luo, J., Guo, L., & Zhao, H. (2025). Seeing opportunities from conflicts: Exploring third parties' mixed reactions to ethical conflict in the workplace. *Journal of Business Ethics*. Advance online publication. DOI: 10.1007/s10551-025-06213-4

Wehmeyer, M. L., Parent, W., Lattimore, J., Obremski, S., Poston, D., & Rousso, H. (2009). Promoting self-determination and self-directed employment planning for young women with disabilities. *Journal of Social Work in Disability & Rehabilitation, 8*(3–4), 117–131. DOI: 10.1080/15367100903200429 PMID: 20183627

Welti, F. (2025). People with disabilities. In *The Elgar companion to decent work and the sustainable development goals* (pp. 236–246). Edward Elgar Publishing., DOI: 10.4337/9781035300907.00026

Whitaker, T. R. (2019). Banging on a locked door: The persistent role of racial discrimination in the workplace. *Social Work in Public Health, 34*(1), 22–27. DOI: 10.1080/19371918.2019.1572564 PMID: 30700222

Chapter 5
Inclusive Recruitment and Accessible Hiring

ABSTRACT

Inclusive recruitment for individuals with intellectual disabilities requires coordinated efforts across systems, practices, and ethical considerations. This chapter examines how organisations can design accessible hiring processes through inclusive job descriptions, flexible application pathways, and equitable interview practices. It highlights the role of support systems, organisational readiness, and policy frameworks in shaping recruitment outcomes. Key challenges, including employer stigma, resource concerns, tokenistic hiring, and ethical issues such as fairness, autonomy, and disclosure, are critically discussed. The chapter also explores emerging digital and AI-driven recruitment trends, emphasising the need for transparency and inclusivity in technological adoption. It argues that effective inclusive recruitment depends on aligning organisational strategy, culture, and practice to create equitable and sustainable employment opportunities.

5.1 INTRODUCTION

Inclusive recruitment requires deliberately restructuring hiring systems to ensure that individuals with intellectual disability can access, navigate, and succeed in recruitment processes on equitable terms. This approach shifts attention from exclusionary selection practices toward systems that recognise diverse abilities, accommodate different ways of demonstrating competence, and remove structural and procedural barriers embedded in conventional hiring models (Scholz, 2020; Chen et al., 2023). Recruitment is not a neutral administrative process; it reflects

DOI: 10.4018/979-8-3373-9185-4.ch005

organisational values, assumptions about productivity, and broader social attitudes toward disability (McKinney & Swartz, 2021).

Within the employment pathway, recruitment functions as a decisive point at which access to work is either enabled or constrained. For many individuals with intellectual disability, the hiring stage determines whether participation in the labour market becomes a realistic possibility or remains unattainable. When organisations design recruitment systems that are flexible, accessible, and responsive to diverse needs, they expand opportunities for entry into meaningful employment. Evidence indicates that inclusive recruitment practices contribute to improved workforce diversity and create conditions that support innovation, adaptability, and overall organisational performance (Chen et al., 2023; Ochrach et al., 2022). Recruitment, therefore, serves not only as an operational function but also as a strategic mechanism for advancing equity in employment systems.

Persistent barriers continue to shape recruitment experiences for individuals with intellectual disability. Accessibility challenges remain prominent, particularly in digital recruitment environments, where application platforms, instructions, and assessment procedures are often complex and difficult to navigate. These barriers are compounded by the limited availability of alternative formats, insufficient communication support, and inflexible timelines that disadvantage candidates who require additional processing time (Scholz, 2020; McKinney & Swartz, 2021). Physical interview environments and standardised testing formats further restrict participation when reasonable adjustments are not incorporated into recruitment design.

Normative assumptions embedded in hiring practices also contribute to exclusion. Conventional recruitment models frequently prioritise speed, verbal fluency, and abstract reasoning, which may not accurately reflect job performance for many roles. These expectations reinforce ableist norms by equating competence with narrow indicators of productivity and independence, thereby excluding candidates who demonstrate capability in different ways (Scholz, 2020; Cortéséro et al., 2013). Attitudinal biases among recruiters further influence decision-making processes. Research indicates that perceptions of reduced competence, increased supervision needs, or perceived risk can affect candidate evaluation, even when such assumptions lack empirical support (Leasher et al., 2009).

Technological developments in recruitment introduce both opportunities and risks. Digital platforms and artificial intelligence tools can enhance efficiency and expand outreach; however, they may also replicate historical biases if inclusivity is not embedded in their design. Algorithms trained on existing hiring data may inadvertently disadvantage candidates with disabilities when prior patterns of exclusion are reflected in the data used for decision-making (Rigotti & Fosch-Villaronga, 2024; Bano et al., 2025). These developments require critical oversight to ensure that technological innovation does not undermine equitable access to employment.

Inclusive recruitment is guided by principles that inform the design and implementation of hiring systems. Fairness requires that all candidates are assessed using criteria relevant to job performance and applied consistently across applicants (Cortéséro et al., 2013). Accessibility involves ensuring that recruitment processes are usable by individuals with diverse cognitive, communication, and functional needs through adjustments such as simplified language, flexible formats, and supportive technologies (Craven-Staines & Finch, 2025). A capability-oriented perspective emphasises strengths, skills, and potential contributions rather than perceived limitations, thereby aligning assessment practices with actual job requirements (Ochrach et al., 2022; Yang, 2026). Equity requires recognising that equal treatment alone is insufficient and that differentiated supports may be necessary to achieve comparable outcomes for candidates with intellectual disability (Lindsay et al., 2017).

The implications of inclusive recruitment extend beyond individual hiring decisions to broader labour participation patterns. Increased access to employment contributes to economic inclusion, reduces dependency, and supports social participation for individuals with intellectual disability. Organisations that implement inclusive hiring practices report improved employee engagement, stronger team cohesion, and enhanced organisational reputation (Ochrach et al., 2022; Lindsay et al., 2017). These outcomes demonstrate the relationship between inclusive recruitment and sustainable organisational performance.

Inclusive recruitment operates within wider employment systems shaped by social, economic, and institutional factors. These systems recognise that disability intersects with other dimensions of inequality, including gender, education, and socioeconomic status, which influence access to employment opportunities (Varga, 2025; Lindstrom et al., 2020). Embedding inclusive recruitment within such systems requires coordinated efforts across policy, organisational practice, and support services to ensure that hiring processes align with broader inclusion goals.

Individuals with intellectual disability do not constitute a homogeneous group. Differences in intellectual functioning, adaptive behaviour, and support needs influence how individuals participate in employment. Intellectual disability is commonly categorised as mild, moderate, severe, and profound. Individuals with mild intellectual disability are often able to perform a wide range of employment tasks with limited support and appropriate workplace accommodations. Those with moderate intellectual disability may require structured supervision, task modification, and ongoing guidance. Individuals with severe intellectual disability generally benefit from substantial support and highly structured work environments, while persons with profound intellectual disability may require extensive assistance and specialised support systems.

These differences highlight the importance of recognising individual strengths, preferences, and support needs during recruitment. Inclusive hiring systems should therefore avoid broad assumptions about capability and instead focus on matching job requirements with the abilities and potential contributions of everyone. The purpose of this chapter is to provide a structured analysis of inclusive recruitment practices, focusing on how organisations can design accessible hiring systems that reduce barriers, promote equity, and improve employment outcomes for workers with intellectual disability.

5.2 LEGAL AND POLICY FRAMEWORKS GUIDING INCLUSIVE HIRING (900 WORDS)

Employment systems operate within regulatory environments that define acceptable conduct, establish rights, and assign responsibilities to organisations. In recruitment, these frameworks shape how fairness, accessibility, and non-discrimination are interpreted and applied in practice. For individuals with intellectual disability, legal and policy provisions influence whether hiring processes enable participation or reinforce exclusion. These frameworks, therefore, function as both protective instruments and operational guides that direct how inclusive recruitment is designed and implemented.

5.2.1 Disability Rights and Anti-Discrimination

Disability rights and anti-discrimination laws provide the legal foundation for inclusive hiring across national and international contexts. These frameworks establish the principle that individuals with disabilities are entitled to equal access to employment opportunities and must not be excluded from recruitment processes on the basis of disability. One of the most influential legislative instruments is the Americans with Disabilities Act (ADA), which mandates reasonable accommodation and prohibits discrimination in all aspects of employment, including recruitment (Donald & Ralston, 2005; Shinall, 2020). The ADA requires employers to review hiring practices and ensure that candidates with disabilities can participate in recruitment processes without disadvantage.

Complementing this framework, Section 504 of the Rehabilitation Act extends similar protections by prohibiting disability-based discrimination in federally funded programmes. This provision places responsibility on institutions receiving public funding to ensure that recruitment systems are accessible and equitable (Crawford, 2005). Together, these laws reinforce the expectation that accessibility is an integral component of fair hiring practices rather than an optional consideration.

At the international level, the United Nations Convention on the Rights of Persons with Disabilities (CRPD) provides a comprehensive rights-based framework for workplace inclusion. The Convention defines reasonable accommodation as a legal obligation linked to equality and non-discrimination, thereby strengthening global standards for inclusive hiring (Mégret & Msipa, 2014). It emphasises the removal of barriers across all stages of employment and promotes equal participation in labour markets.

In addition to rights-based approaches, some countries adopt quota systems to address structural inequalities in employment. For example, Germany and Brazil require employers to meet specified targets for hiring individuals with disabilities, with penalties imposed for non-compliance (Welti, 2018; Dos Santos Rodrigues et al., 2013). These measures aim to increase representation by introducing enforceable expectations within labour systems. Collectively, these legal and policy frameworks establish the normative basis for inclusive hiring and shape how organisations interpret and implement equitable recruitment practices. Together, these legal instruments provide the foundation for employer obligations, inclusive hiring to be derived and operationalised.

5.2.2 Employer Obligations in Hiring

Employers are required to align recruitment practices with legal standards that promote fairness, accessibility, and inclusion.

5.2.2.1 Provision of Reasonable Accommodation: Employers are required to provide reasonable accommodation to qualified candidates with disabilities. This includes modifying recruitment procedures, adapting communication methods, and providing assistive technologies where necessary (Shinall, 2020; Taylor & Wituk, 2025). These adjustments enable candidates to participate meaningfully in hiring processes and demonstrate their abilities without disadvantage.

5.2.2.2 Non-Discrimination in Recruitment: Employers must avoid both direct and indirect discrimination during recruitment. This involves ensuring that job advertisements, selection criteria, and assessment methods do not exclude candidates with disabilities (Crawford, 2005; Making it Work, 2011). Recruitment decisions must be grounded in job-relevant competencies rather than assumptions about capability.

5.2.2.3 Accessibility Across Recruitment Stages: Accessibility must be integrated across all stages of recruitment, including job postings, application systems, and interviews. Employers are expected to design both digital and physical recruitment environments that accommodate diverse needs (Taylor & Wituk, 2025). This ensures that candidates can engage fully in the hiring process.

5.2.2.4 Compliance with Quota Requirements: In jurisdictions that implement quota systems, employers are required to meet specified employment targets for individuals with disabilities. Failure to meet these targets may result in financial penalties or regulatory consequences (Welti, 2018; Dos Santos Rodrigues et al.,

2013). These obligations reinforce the expectation that inclusive hiring is an integral component of organisational practice. Within this framework, the practical expression of these obligations becomes most evident in the provision of reasonable accommodation during recruitment.

5.2.3 Reasonable Accommodation at the Recruitment Stage

Reasonable accommodation plays a central role in enabling equitable access to recruitment processes.

5.2.3.1 Adjustments to Recruitment Processes: At the recruitment stage, accommodations may include adapting interview formats, providing additional time, simplifying instructions, or using alternative communication methods. Assistive technologies and support personnel may also facilitate candidate participation (Taylor & Wituk, 2025; Yatheesha et al., 2024). These adjustments ensure that candidates can engage effectively with recruitment activities.

5.2.3.2 Adaptation of Job Requirements: Accommodation may extend to the design of job descriptions and selection criteria. Employers are expected to focus on essential job functions and remove unnecessary requirements that may exclude candidates with intellectual disability (Shinall, 2020; Legarreta, 2025). This approach supports fair assessment and aligns recruitment practices with actual job demands.

5.2.3.3 Implementation Challenges: Despite legal requirements, challenges persist in implementing accommodation. Employers often express uncertainty regarding appropriate adjustments or perceive accommodation as costly and burdensome (Vedeler & Anvik, 2023). These perceptions can limit the consistent application of inclusive practices. However, the application of these accommodations in practice frequently exposes underlying gaps in policy implementation.

5.2.4 Policy Implementation Gaps

Although legislative and policy frameworks provide important protections for individuals with intellectual disabilities, their effectiveness depends largely on implementation. In many contexts, gaps emerge between policy intentions and workplace realities. These gaps are reflected in unclear legal provisions, inadequate data systems, persistent employer bias, and contextual challenges that limit enforcement. As a result, the consistent application of inclusive employment policies is undermined, weakening efforts to promote equitable labour market participation. The presence of legal frameworks does not guarantee effective implementation.

5.2.4.1 Ambiguity in Legal Provisions: Ambiguity in policy language can create uncertainty among employers, particularly regarding the definitions of reasonable accommodation and undue burden (Mégret & Msipa, 2014; Hameed et al., 2024). This often results in inconsistent interpretation and application across organisations.

5.2.4.2 Data Limitations: Limited availability of reliable data on disability employment outcomes constrains monitoring and evaluation efforts. Without accurate data, it becomes difficult to assess compliance or measure the effectiveness of inclusive hiring policies (Hameed et al., 2024).

5.2.4.3 Employer Attitudes and Bias: Attitudinal barriers remain a significant challenge. Misconceptions about the capabilities of individuals with intellectual disability continue to influence hiring decisions and reduce the impact of legal protections (Making it Work, 2011; Strauser et al., 2026).

5.2.4.4 Contextual Constraints in LMICs: In low- and middle-income countries, implementation challenges are intensified by broader labour market constraints, including high unemployment and limited enforcement capacity (Akyeampong et al., 2025). These factors restrict the effectiveness of policy interventions.

These gaps, in turn, reveal systemic challenges associated with enforcement and compliance across employment systems.

5.2.5 Enforcement and Compliance Challenges

Enforcing inclusive employment policies remains difficult despite legal protections. Compliance often varies across organisations due to weak enforcement, limited accountability, and inadequate monitoring. These issues reduce policy effectiveness and may limit employment opportunities for individuals with intellectual disabilities.

5.2.5.1 Monitoring and Accountability Limitations: Weak monitoring systems limit regulatory bodies' ability to track compliance and enforce legal provisions effectively (Vedeler & Anvik, 2023; Hameed et al., 2024). This reduces the practical impact of existing policies.

5.2.5.2 Cost Concerns and Resource Constraints: Employers frequently cite financial constraints as barriers to providing accommodations, particularly during recruitment (Shinall, 2020; Vedeler & Anvik, 2023). These concerns can discourage the adoption of inclusive practices.

5.2.5.3 Symbolic Inclusion: There is a risk of symbolic compliance, where organisations meet formal requirements without achieving substantive improvements in employment outcomes. In such cases, inclusion remains procedural rather than meaningful (Kohli & Vedeler, 2023; Maclean et al., 2024). Responding to these challenges requires robust governance structures and accountability mechanisms.

5.2.6 Role of Governance and Accountability Systems

Advancing inclusive employment requires collaboration among policymakers, employers, educators, and advocates. Priorities include improving accessibility, applying evidence-based practices, strengthening leadership commitment, and supporting ongoing evaluation. These efforts can promote more inclusive and equitable labour markets.

5.2.6.1 Government Role: Governments play a central role by providing financial incentives, such as tax benefits and subsidies, to encourage inclusive hiring (Welti, 2018; Dos Santos Rodrigues et al., 2013). They also coordinate across agencies to ensure that recruitment efforts are supported by broader institutional systems (Vedeler & Anvik, 2023).

5.2.6.2 Employer Engagement: Employer engagement is critical for sustaining inclusive hiring practices. Collaboration with disability organisations and vocational services provides expertise and support for implementing inclusive recruitment strategies (Iwanaga et al., 2024; Lindsay et al., 2017). Training programmes further strengthen organisational capacity and reduce bias.

5.2.6.3 Accountability Mechanisms: Accountability mechanisms, including transparent reporting and evaluation systems, enable organisations to monitor progress and ensure compliance with legal requirements (Vedeler & Anvik, 2023; Hameed et al., 2024). These mechanisms support continuous improvement and reinforce commitment to inclusive hiring practices. Accessible recruitment systems are justified not only by legal obligations but also by the need to reduce barriers that may prevent qualified candidates from demonstrating their abilities. Recruitment processes that rely exclusively on conventional application formats, standardised assessments, or inflexible communication methods may unintentionally limit participation for some individuals with intellectual disability. Flexible and accessible recruitment practices create opportunities for candidates to demonstrate their skills through different pathways and support a fairer assessment of their potential contributions.

Designing recruitment systems in this manner promotes equitable participation while expanding access to employment opportunities. Such mechanisms consolidate the role of legal and policy frameworks in sustaining inclusive hiring practices within organisational contexts.

5.3 DESIGNING ACCESSIBLE JOB DESCRIPTIONS AND ADVERTISEMENTS (≤850 WORDS)

Job descriptions and advertisements shape how potential applicants interpret opportunities and whether they perceive themselves as capable of applying. The structure, wording, and presentation of recruitment information influence access at the earliest stage of the employment pathway. When job information is ambiguous, overly technical, or rigidly framed, individuals with intellectual disability may disengage before submitting an application. Designing accessible job descriptions, therefore, requires deliberate attention to language, structure, format, and dissemination, ensuring that recruitment communication functions as an enabling rather than exclusionary mechanism.

Accessible job communication is grounded in principles of usability, clarity, and inclusivity. It recognises that candidates differ in how they process information and demonstrate competence. Embedding accessibility into job descriptions and advertisements expands participation and aligns recruitment practices with equity-oriented employment systems.

5.3.1 Plain Language Job Descriptions

Clarity in communication is central to accessibility. Many job descriptions rely on dense text, technical terminology, and abstract phrasing that limit comprehension. Plain language ensures that information is presented in a clear, direct, and structured manner, enabling broader understanding across diverse audiences (Huang, 2024; Javahery et al., 2011).

1. Use clear and concise sentences that communicate one idea at a time.
2. Replace technical jargon with familiar and accessible vocabulary.
3. Organise content using headings and short paragraphs to improve readability.

Plain language should also describe tasks in concrete terms rather than abstract competencies. For example, specifying "serving customers at the front desk" provides greater clarity than generalised references to communication skills. This approach reduces cognitive load, minimises misinterpretation, and supports informed decision-making by applicants.

5.3.2 Focus on Essential Job Functions

Job descriptions often present long lists of duties that extend beyond the role's core requirements. This can create confusion and discourage applicants who may interpret all listed tasks as mandatory. A focus on essential job functions ensures that descriptions reflect actual job demands and support realistic self-assessment.

1. Identify and prioritise core tasks required for successful performance.
2. Distinguish clearly between essential and non-essential duties.

3. Provide examples of how tasks are performed in practice.

Providing context through examples helps candidates visualise the role and assess their capabilities more accurately. This approach aligns recruitment criteria with genuine job requirements rather than inflated expectations (Javahery et al., 2011). It also reduces unnecessary barriers at the entry stage.

5.3.3 Avoid Unnecessary Qualifications

Rigid qualification requirements can unintentionally exclude capable candidates. Employers often include criteria such as advanced academic credentials or extensive experience that are not directly related to job performance. These expectations may deter individuals with intellectual disability who possess relevant skills but lack formal qualifications.

Inclusive design requires a critical reassessment of such criteria. Organisations should ensure that requirements are directly linked to job tasks and allow flexibility in how competence is demonstrated.

1. Limit qualifications to those essential for performing the role.
2. Use inclusive wording that encourages applications from diverse candidates.

Reducing unnecessary qualifications broadens access and challenges narrow definitions of competence. It supports equity by recognising multiple pathways through which individuals acquire skills and experience.

5.3.4 Multiple Formats: Visual, Digital, Audio

Accessibility extends beyond content to how information is delivered. Candidates differ in their preferred modes of engagement, and reliance on text-only formats can create barriers. Providing job descriptions in multiple formats enhances accessibility and supports inclusive participation (Yeung et al., 2024; Gahane et al., 2026).

1. Offer job information in text, audio, and visual formats.
2. Ensure compatibility with assistive technologies such as screen readers.
3. Use visual aids, including icons or diagrams, to support understanding.
4. Provide alternative application options where feasible.

Multimodal communication reduces dependence on a single format and improves engagement. Accessibility standards such as WCAG offer useful guidance for designing inclusive digital job advertisements.

5.3.5 Universal Design in Job Communication

Universal design emphasises creating systems that are usable by the widest range of individuals without requiring adaptation. In recruitment, this approach ensures that accessibility is embedded from the outset rather than added retrospectively (Pierson et al., 2026).

1. Use consistent layouts and clear visual structure.
2. Apply readable fonts and appropriate contrast for visibility.
3. Structure content into logical sections for easy navigation.
4. Ensure digital platforms are responsive across devices.
5. Minimise unnecessary complexity in both content and design.

Information should be organised logically, allowing candidates to easily locate key details such as responsibilities, requirements, and application procedures. Simplifying design reduces cognitive demand and supports independent access. Universal design strengthens inclusivity by integrating accessibility into standard organisational practice.

5.3.6 Inclusive Outreach Strategies

The accessibility of job descriptions is closely linked to how opportunities are communicated. Outreach strategies determine who becomes aware of vacancies and who feels encouraged to apply. Inclusive outreach requires extending recruitment efforts beyond traditional channels.

1. Use inclusive language that reflects openness to diverse applicants.
2. Highlight organisational commitments to accessibility and inclusion.

Partnerships with disability organisations, vocational services, and community networks can expand reach. Advertising across multiple platforms, including those targeting underrepresented groups, increases visibility. Providing clear information about available accommodations also reassures candidates that support will be available throughout the recruitment process.

5.3.7 Employment Opportunities and Job Matching

People with mild intellectual disability may participate in roles within retail services, hospitality, customer service, administration support, manufacturing, and agriculture. Individuals with moderate intellectual disability may engage successfully in structured positions involving packaging, stock management, housekeeping, food preparation, grounds maintenance, and routine clerical tasks. Supported employment, customised employment, and task-specific roles may provide opportunities for individuals requiring higher levels of support. Effective recruitment, therefore, involves identifying job demands, recognising individual strengths, and providing reasonable accommodations that support successful workplace participation.

Designing accessible job descriptions and advertisements requires an integrated approach that combines clarity, relevance, flexibility, and inclusive dissemination. These practices reduce barriers at the entry stage and create pathways for broader participation. Prioritising accessibility in recruitment communication supports individuals with intellectual disability while enhancing the overall effectiveness and inclusivity of hiring systems.

5.4 INCLUSIVE APPLICATION PROCESSES AND ALTERNATIVE ENTRY PATHWAYS

Application processes serve as a critical gateway between interest in employment and actual participation in hiring systems. When these processes are rigid, complex, or inaccessible, they can exclude individuals with intellectual disability before their abilities are assessed. Traditional recruitment systems often prioritise standardised formats, written communication, and time-bound procedures that do not accommodate diverse ways of demonstrating competence. Inclusive application processes, therefore, require a reconfiguration of how candidates enter recruitment systems, ensuring that pathways are flexible, accessible, and responsive to varied needs.

Inclusive approaches to application design emphasise simplicity, support, and alternative modes of engagement. They recognise that fairness in recruitment is not achieved through uniform procedures but through equitable systems that allow candidates to participate meaningfully. By introducing alternative entry pathways, organisations can reduce systemic barriers and expand access to employment opportunities.

5.4.1 Barriers in Traditional Application Systems

Conventional application systems often embed structural barriers that disadvantage individuals with intellectual disability. These barriers are not always explicit but arise from assumptions about how candidates should communicate, present information, and demonstrate competence.

5.4.1.1 Systemic Exclusion: Traditional recruitment methods, including standardised interviews and rigid application forms, frequently rely on verbal fluency, written articulation, and rapid response. These expectations can disadvantage individuals who process information differently or require alternative communication formats (Sachse & Melzer, 2025; Yan, 2026; Novak, 2017). As a result, capable candidates may be excluded before their skills are recognised.

5.4.1.2 Bias and Discrimination: Application materials such as résumés often contain personal identifiers that can trigger unconscious bias. Names, educational backgrounds, and demographic indicators may influence decision-making, leading to unequal outcomes. While anonymised applications have been introduced to reduce bias, their effectiveness depends on their consistent implementation (Lacroux & Martin-Lacroux, 2020; Büttner et al., 2026; Risavy et al., 2022).

5.4.1.3 Accessibility Challenges: Digital application platforms can pose significant barriers when not designed with accessibility in mind. Complex navigation, inaccessible interfaces, and a lack of assistive features can prevent individuals with disabilities from completing applications (Novak, 2017; Sarto et al., 2026). These challenges highlight the need for systems that accommodate diverse user needs from the outset.

These limitations highlight the need to redesign application structures to reduce complexity and improve accessibility, particularly by adopting simplified, more inclusive application formats.

5.4.2 Simplified Application Forms

Simplified application forms provide a practical approach to reducing barriers and improving accessibility. By focusing on essential information and reducing unnecessary complexity, these forms enable candidates to engage more effectively with the application process.

5.4.2.1 Streamlined Processes: Simplified forms prioritise job-relevant competencies rather than extensive personal or background information. This reduces cognitive load and allows candidates to focus on demonstrating their suitability for the role (Büttner et al., 2026; Risavy et al., 2022). Standardised formats can also promote fairness by ensuring that all applicants are assessed using consistent criteria.

5.4.2.2 Enhanced Accuracy: Customised application forms designed to minimise ambiguity and reduce opportunities for misrepresentation can improve the accuracy of candidate information. Structured formats guide applicants in providing relevant details and reduce reliance on self-presentation skills that may disadvantage some individuals (Srour & Py, 2023).

While simplified forms reduce structural barriers, effective participation often depends on the availability of targeted support throughout the application process.

5.4.3 Supported Application Processes: Support mechanisms play a crucial role in enabling equitable participation in recruitment. Individuals with intellectual disability may require additional guidance to navigate application systems, interpret requirements, and present their abilities effectively. Supported application processes include:

1. Personalised assistance through digital platforms that integrate accessibility features such as voice input and visual guidance (Sarto et al., 2026; Norzin et al., 2025).
2. One-on-one support through employment programmes that provide coaching, confidence-building, and practical assistance during application stages (Malekinezhad & Courtney, 2026; Shatil et al., 2024).

These approaches enhance applicant confidence and reduce the likelihood of disengagement. They also recognise that support is not an advantage but a necessary adjustment to ensure equitable participation. Beyond support mechanisms, expanding the ways candidates can present their abilities further enhances inclusivity in recruitment systems.

5.4.4 Use of Video or Practical Submissions

Alternative submission formats offer candidates opportunities to demonstrate their skills beyond written applications. Video and practical submissions allow for more dynamic and authentic representations of competence. Key approaches include:

1. Video-based applications that enable candidates to present their skills, experiences, and communication abilities in a more flexible format (Liao, 2007; Raju et al., 2015; Azambuja et al., 2010).
2. Interactive and segmented assessments that evaluate practical competencies through demonstration rather than description (Hamzah et al., 2025; Ertelt et al., 2006).

These methods reduce reliance on written communication and provide a more inclusive basis for assessment. They also allow employers to evaluate candidates in contexts that more closely resemble real work situations. These alternative submission approaches create opportunities to extend assessment beyond simulated formats into real-world performance contexts.

5.4.5 Work Trials as an Alternative Entry:

Work trials provide an alternative pathway that shifts assessment from hypothetical evaluation to practical demonstration. This approach enables candidates to showcase their abilities within real or simulated work environments.

5.4.5.1 Practical Demonstrations: Work trials allow candidates to demonstrate job-related skills directly, reducing dependence on formal qualifications or written applications. This is particularly beneficial for individuals with intellectual disability, whose competencies may not be fully captured through traditional assessment methods (Shatil et al., 2024; Dyer et al., 2006).

5.4.5.2 Employer Engagement: Successful work trials depend on the employer's commitment to inclusive practices. Programmes such as STAR+ highlight the importance of selecting supportive employers and providing structured assistance to ensure positive outcomes (Shatil et al., 2024). These initiatives strengthen collaboration between employers and support services.

Building on these practical pathways, broader flexibility in assessment design becomes essential for ensuring fairness across diverse applicant groups.

5.4.6 Flexibility and Fairness in Assessment Pathways

Flexible assessment pathways are essential for ensuring that recruitment systems accommodate diverse abilities. Traditional assessments often prioritise speed, standardisation, and narrow measures of competence, which can disadvantage individuals with intellectual disability.

5.4.6.1 Gamified and AI-Driven Assessments: Gamification and AI-based tools offer alternative methods for evaluating skills in less stressful and more engaging environments. These approaches can reduce anxiety and provide more objective performance measures (Sachse & Melzer, 2025; Iftikhar et al., 2025).

5.4.6.2 Anonymised and Competency-Based Models: Anonymised application processes and competency-based interviews focus on skills rather than demographic characteristics. These models reduce bias and promote fairness by ensuring that candidates are evaluated based on relevant abilities (Büttner et al., 2026; Risavy et al., 2022).

5.4.6.3 Inclusive Policies: Strengths-based hiring approaches and intersectional inclusion frameworks address systemic barriers by recognising diverse experiences and capabilities. These models promote equity by aligning recruitment practices with broader inclusion goals (Yan, 2026; Gonzalez & Karimy, 2025). Such flexible and inclusive assessment pathways reinforce the role of application systems in promoting equitable access to employment opportunities.

5.5 ACCESSIBLE INTERVIEWING AND CANDIDATE ASSESSMENT PRACTICES

Equitable hiring decisions depend on assessment processes that accurately capture candidates' abilities rather than their conformity to conventional communication or evaluation norms. Many interview systems privilege rapid verbal responses, abstract reasoning, and socially constructed expectations of competence, which may not reflect the capabilities of individuals with intellectual disability. When assessment practices rely narrowly on these indicators, they risk excluding qualified candidates whose strengths are better demonstrated through practical performance or alternative forms of expression. Creating accessible interviewing systems, therefore, requires intentional redesign, ensuring that evaluation methods are transparent, flexible, and aligned with diverse ways of demonstrating competence.

5.5.1 Structured and Inclusive Interview Formats

Structured approaches to interviewing enhance consistency and fairness by ensuring that all candidates are assessed using comparable criteria. In structured interviews, candidates respond to the same set of job-relevant questions, and responses are evaluated using predefined rating scales. This approach improves reliability and reduces subjectivity, thereby strengthening the validity of hiring decisions (Bartels et al., 2006; Gerritsen, 2022; Brecher et al., 2006). Standardisation also limits the influence of personal bias, ensuring that evaluation focuses on evidence of competence rather than subjective impressions (Pogrebtsova et al., 2020).

5.5.1.1 Structured Interviews: Structured interviews require all candidates to respond to identical questions, with scoring guided by consistent criteria. This approach reduces bias and enhances comparability, particularly in relation to disability and gender (Brecher et al., 2006; Pogrebtsova et al., 2020).

5.5.1.2 Interviewer Training: Training interviewers to apply structured techniques improves interrater agreement and reduces inconsistencies in scoring. Evidence indicates that trained interviewers demonstrate greater accuracy and consistency in evaluating candidate responses (Gardner et al., 2022).

5.5.1.3 Multiple Interview Formats: Incorporating multiple formats, such as situational or scenario-based interviews, allows candidates to demonstrate competence across varied contexts. These approaches are often perceived as fairer because they emphasise practical reasoning and problem-solving (Gardner, 2014).

These structured and standardised approaches provide a stable foundation for expanding assessment beyond uniform questioning toward methods that recognise and evaluate individual strengths.

5.5.2 Practical and Strength-Based Assessment Approaches

A shift toward strength-based and practical evaluation broadens the scope of assessment by focusing on what candidates can do rather than what they lack. Strength-based assessment emphasises competencies, potential, and contextual performance, and has been widely used in educational and clinical settings to support individualised development (Rashid, 2015; Nickerson & Fishman, 2013; Bozic, 2013).

Within recruitment, these principles can be applied through practical demonstrations, behavioural tasks, and simulated work activities that allow candidates to exhibit their abilities in realistic contexts. For example, candidates may be asked to complete tasks that mirror job requirements, enabling employers to observe performance directly rather than relying solely on verbal explanations. Such approaches provide a more accurate representation of job readiness and allow for the identification of strengths across personal, interpersonal, and situational dimensions (Bozic et al., 2018; Climie & Henley, 2016).

Focusing on strengths also supports more inclusive decision-making by recognising diverse pathways through which competence is developed. It challenges deficit-oriented perspectives and aligns assessment practices with actual job demands. While these approaches enhance the relevance of evaluation, their effectiveness depends on how well communication processes are adapted to support diverse candidates.

5.5.3 Communication Adjustments and Candidate Support

Differences in communication styles and processing significantly influence interview performance. Standard interview formats often assume uniform communication abilities, which can disadvantage candidates who require alternative methods of expression or additional time to respond. Adapting communication practices is therefore essential for ensuring that candidates can participate fully in assessment processes.

Technological innovations provide valuable tools for enhancing accessibility. Real-time text conversion, speech recognition systems, and sign language translation technologies can support clearer communication during interviews, enabling candidates to express their ideas more effectively (Jaiswal et al., 2025). Virtual interviews can also improve access by reducing logistical barriers such as travel. However, they may introduce new challenges, including unequal access to technology and biases related to candidates' physical environments (Marbin et al., 2021). Addressing these issues requires thoughtful design and standardisation.

Supportive practices further enhance accessibility. Allowing additional time, simplifying questions, and providing prompts can reduce cognitive demands and improve understanding. In some cases, the involvement of a support person or job coach can facilitate communication and reduce anxiety. These adjustments acknowledge that equitable assessment requires flexibility in how candidates engage with interview processes.

These communication adjustments, however, must be complemented by deliberate efforts to address bias and strengthen interviewer capacity within assessment systems.

5.5.4 Bias Reduction and Interviewer Capacity Development

Bias reduction and interviewer capacity development improve the fairness, consistency, and inclusiveness of candidate assessment. Bias may influence evaluations through subjective perceptions, inconsistent assessment practices, and limited awareness of diversity issues. Key strategies include raising awareness of unconscious bias, providing ongoing interviewer training, and incorporating cultural sensitivity into interview processes. These measures support more equitable and consistent hiring decisions.

5.5.4.1 Bias Awareness Tools: Tools such as implicit association tests and targeted training programmes can increase awareness of unconscious biases related to disability, gender, and other characteristics (Mudiayi et al., 2024). Structured interview methods also contribute to bias reduction by standardising evaluation criteria (Brecher et al., 2006; Pogrebtsova et al., 2020).

5.5.4.2 Ongoing Training: Continuous professional development is necessary to maintain consistency and ensure that inclusive practices are applied effectively. Ongoing training improves evaluation accuracy and reduces scoring variability (Gardner et al., 2022; Mudiayi et al., 2024).

5.5.4.3 Cultural Considerations: Incorporating cultural sensitivity into interview design helps address broader forms of bias and ensures that assessment processes are respectful of diverse backgrounds. Structured approaches can support this by balancing consistency with contextual awareness (Zink et al., 2014). These practices reinforce the development of inclusive interviewing systems that support fair, accessible, and equitable candidate assessment.

The differences between traditional and inclusive interview practices become more apparent when examined across key dimensions of assessment, communication, evaluation, and candidate support. Table 1 presents a comparative overview of these approaches, illustrating how inclusive interviewing practices enhance accessibility, reduce bias, and improve the identification of job-relevant competencies among diverse candidates.

Table 1. Comparison of traditional vs inclusive interview practices

Dimension	Traditional Interview Practices	Inclusive Interview Practices
Interview Structure	Unstructured or loosely structured questions vary across candidates	Structured and standardised questions applied consistently to all candidates
Evaluation Criteria	Subjective judgments based on the interviewer's impressions	Predefined, job-related criteria with standardised scoring systems
Assessment Focus	Emphasis on verbal fluency, confidence, and abstract reasoning	Emphasis on practical skills, strengths, and job-relevant competencies
Communication Style	Assumes uniform communication abilities and rapid responses	Allows flexible communication methods, simplified language, and additional time
Use of Technology	Limited or not designed for accessibility	Incorporates assistive technologies (e.g., speech-to-text, sign language tools)
Candidate Support	Minimal support; candidates expected to navigate independently	Provides accommodations, prompts, and optional support persons where appropriate
Bias Management	Limited awareness of implicit bias; inconsistent evaluation	Use of structured formats, bias awareness tools, and interviewer training
Assessment Methods	Reliance on verbal responses and hypothetical questions	Integration of practical demonstrations, simulations, and task-based assessments
Flexibility	Rigid processes with little adaptation	Flexible processes tailored to diverse candidate needs
Outcome Orientation	Focus on selecting candidates who fit traditional norms	Focus on identifying capability, potential, and inclusive job fit

Source: Author's construct (2026).

Table 1 compares traditional and inclusive interview practices across key dimensions, including structure, assessment focus, communication, and bias management. It demonstrates how inclusive approaches emphasise accessibility, flexibility, and capability-based evaluation, whereas traditional methods rely on rigid, subjective criteria. The table highlights the importance of redesigning interview systems to enhance fairness, reduce barriers, and improve the accuracy of candidate assessment in diverse recruitment contexts.

5.6 ROLE OF SUPPORT SYSTEMS IN RECRUITMENT

Access to employment is shaped not only by organisational practices but also by the systems of support that enable individuals to prepare for, engage with, and navigate recruitment processes. For individuals with intellectual disability, these support systems are particularly significant, as they mediate the relationship between individual capabilities and institutional expectations. Effective support structures enhance readiness, reduce barriers, and facilitate meaningful participation in hiring processes. By integrating professional, social, and systemic support mechanisms, recruitment can be transformed into a coordinated pathway that promotes equitable access and sustainable employment outcomes.

5.6.1 Professional and Institutional Support Mechanisms

Professional and institutional support mechanisms provide structured pathways through which individuals can develop competencies, access opportunities, and engage effectively in recruitment processes. These systems operate within organisational, educational, and technological environments, shaping both candidate preparation and employer engagement.

5.6.1.1 Institutional Support: Institutional mechanisms such as professional development programmes, administrative assistance, and work-life balance initiatives contribute to improved recruitment and retention outcomes by enhancing job satisfaction and productivity (Aswathy & Jayalakshmi, 2024; Uslu, 2017). These supports create stable environments that enable individuals to build confidence and demonstrate their capabilities during recruitment processes.

5.6.1.2 Educational Support: Educational interventions, including support groups, mentoring programmes, and co-curricular activities, play a critical role in preparing individuals for employment. These initiatives provide opportunities for skill development, networking, and exposure to workplace expectations, thereby strengthening recruitment readiness and long-term engagement (Shahhosseini et al., 2020; Jenson et al., 2006).

5.6.1.3 Technological Integration: Technological systems, particularly those based on artificial intelligence, are increasingly used to streamline recruitment processes and match candidate skills with organisational needs. When designed inclusively, these tools enhance efficiency and accessibility while reducing bias in selection processes (Saxena et al., 2025; Jayasekara et al., 2023).

These institutional mechanisms provide a structured foundation for recruitment participation, but their effectiveness is influenced by the broader social networks that shape individual engagement with employment opportunities.

5.6.2 Family, Advocacy, and Social Support Networks

Family, advocacy, and social networks function as critical enablers of recruitment participation, shaping how individuals access opportunities, interpret employment pathways, and make career decisions. Their influence is multifaceted, reflecting both supportive and constraining dynamics.

Family and Social Networks:

1. Provide emotional encouragement and motivation to engage in recruitment processes.
2. Offer practical support such as assistance with applications and interview preparation.
3. Influence decision-making through expectations and perceived job suitability.
4. May restrict participation due to protective attitudes or limited awareness of opportunities.
5. Shape confidence and self-perception in relation to employment readiness (Tueme, 2021; Napier et al., 2023).

Social Media and Online Networks:

1. Expand access to job information and recruitment opportunities.
2. Enable organisations to reach diverse candidate pools beyond traditional channels.
3. Allow recruiters to assess candidates' social capital and professional networks.
4. Influence hiring decisions through perceptions of credibility and connectedness (Golovko & Schumann, 2019; Hedenus et al., 2021; Ollington et al., 2013).

Peer Influence:

1. Shapes perceptions of organisational fit and job attractiveness.
2. Reinforces attitudes toward specific employers or career paths.
3. Encourages or discourages application behaviour based on shared experiences.
4. Strengthens decision-making through social validation.
5. Amplifies influence where strong interpersonal connections exist.
6. Facilitates social learning about recruitment processes and expectations (Sullivan & Swider, 2025).

While these networks enhance access and engagement, their effectiveness depends on how well they are aligned with formal recruitment systems and institutional support structures.

5.6.3 Transition and Coordination in Recruitment Systems

Recruitment processes are most effective when integrated into broader systems that support transition into employment. This requires coordinated efforts among multiple stakeholders, including employers, support agencies, families, and policy institutions. Coordination ensures that recruitment is not treated as an isolated event but as part of a continuous pathway leading to workplace integration.

Coordination mechanisms are essential for managing interdependencies within recruitment systems. Approaches such as mutual adjustment, direct supervision, and standardisation enable stakeholders to align their efforts and achieve shared objectives. Effective coordination enhances communication, reduces fragmentation, and improves the overall efficiency of recruitment processes (Wagner, 2024).

Transition processes, however, often present challenges that can disrupt recruitment outcomes. Organisational restructuring, the introduction of new recruitment models, and resistance to change may create uncertainty for both candidates and employers. Addressing these challenges requires adaptive strategies, including flexible planning and continuous system evaluation.

1. Transition processes may be disrupted by organisational change and restructuring.
2. Resistance to new recruitment models can limit effective implementation.
3. Lack of coordination among stakeholders may create inefficiencies.
4. Insufficient planning can hinder smooth movement from recruitment to employment.
5. Adaptive and flexible strategies are required to support successful transitions (Steur & Wittek, 2005; Ambrose, 2018).

Efforts to standardise recruitment practices further contribute to coordination and transparency. Initiatives aimed at harmonising recruitment systems across institutions promote consistency and fairness but may also introduce ethical and procedural challenges.

1. Standardisation promotes consistency across recruitment systems.
2. It enhances transparency in selection processes.
3. It may limit the flexibility required for inclusive practices.
4. Ethical concerns may arise in balancing uniformity and equity.
5. E-recruitment systems provide adaptive solutions to these challenges (Pollifroni et al., 2025; Fumasoli & Goastellec, 2015).

Effective recruitment systems, therefore, depend on integrating transition and coordination mechanisms that align institutional, social, and organisational efforts. When these systems function cohesively, they support not only access to employment but also sustained participation and long-term inclusion.

5.7 ORGANISATIONAL READINESS AND CAPACITY FOR INCLUSIVE HIRING

The effectiveness of inclusive hiring depends on the extent to which organisations are prepared to design, implement, and sustain equitable recruitment systems. Organisational readiness reflects the alignment of leadership commitment, institutional policies, workforce capacity, and cultural orientation toward inclusion. Without such readiness, inclusive hiring efforts often remain symbolic, lacking the structural and operational depth required to produce meaningful outcomes. Capacity for inclusive hiring therefore involves not only compliance with diversity expectations but also the integration of inclusive principles into organisational strategy, decision-making processes, and everyday practices.

5.7.1 Leadership, Policy, and Strategic Alignment

Leadership commitment is a central determinant of organisational readiness for inclusive hiring. Leaders shape organisational priorities, allocate resources, and establish norms that influence how inclusion is enacted across recruitment systems. When leadership actively promotes diversity, equity, and inclusion, it fosters ethical work climates characterised by fairness, trust, and accountability (Tjimuku et al., 2025; Ferdman, 2020). This commitment functions as a catalyst for translating inclusive values into operational practices, ensuring that inclusion is embedded across all levels of the organisation.

Strategic alignment further strengthens this process by integrating inclusive hiring within broader organisational goals. Aligning human, informational, and organisational resources with inclusion objectives enhances adaptability and responsiveness to changing workforce needs (James, 2018). Organisations that demonstrate strategic readiness are better positioned to address structural barriers and implement inclusive recruitment practices effectively.

Five key elements underpin leadership, policy, and strategic alignment in inclusive hiring. First, leadership commitment must be visible and sustained, signalling that inclusion is a core organisational priority rather than a peripheral initiative. Second, human resource policies should reflect inclusive hiring practices, including accessible recruitment procedures and equitable selection criteria. Third, organisations must move beyond compliance-driven diversity initiatives toward justice-oriented and intersectional approaches that address systemic inequalities (Asrifan et al., 2026). Fourth, alignment with diversity and inclusion goals ensures that recruitment practices contribute to broader organisational outcomes such as innovation, employee engagement, and performance (Rusilowati et al., 2025). Fifth, accountability mechanisms, including performance metrics and monitoring systems, are necessary to track progress and ensure that inclusive hiring commitments are implemented consistently.

These leadership and policy frameworks establish a strategic foundation for inclusive hiring, but their effectiveness depends on how they are translated into organisational culture and operational capacity.

5.7.2 Organisational Culture, Capacity, and Readiness Systems

Organisational culture and capacity play a critical role in determining whether inclusive hiring practices are effectively implemented and sustained. Culture influences how employees perceive diversity, interact with colleagues, and respond to organisational initiatives. A supportive and inclusive culture fosters trust, openness, and collaboration, creating an environment in which diverse individuals can participate fully and contribute meaningfully (Perez-Uribe et al., 2022; Wichinsky et al., 2012).

Capacity for inclusive hiring is shaped by the availability of resources, skills, and systems that enable organisations to operationalise inclusive practices. Large organisations often implement formal structures, such as accessibility frameworks, diversity-tracking systems, and structured career development pathways. In contrast, smaller organisations may rely on informal practices and interpersonal relationships, which can either support or constrain inclusive hiring depending on the organisational context (Antonova et al., 2022).

Four key dimensions define organisational culture, capacity, and readiness systems. First, staff training and awareness are essential to equip employees with the knowledge and skills needed to implement inclusive practices effectively. Training programmes that address unconscious bias, disability awareness, and inclusive communication enhance organisational capacity and improve recruitment outcomes. Second, workplace culture and attitudes significantly influence the success of inclusive hiring. Positive attitudes toward diversity promote acceptance and collaboration, while negative perceptions can create barriers to inclusion. Third, organisational readiness systems, including tools for assessing culture, climate, and capacity, enable organisations to evaluate their preparedness for inclusive hiring and identify areas for improvement (Najm & Ali, 2024). Fourth, accountability and monitoring mechanisms, such as performance metrics and inclusion benchmarks, ensure that inclusive practices are sustained over time and aligned with organisational goals (Adjo et al., 2021).

These cultural and capacity-related factors interact with leadership and policy frameworks to shape the overall effectiveness of inclusive hiring systems. When organisational culture supports inclusion and capacity is adequately developed, recruitment processes become more accessible, equitable, and responsive to diverse candidate needs. The key dimensions of organisational readiness for inclusive hiring can be systematically understood through the indicators outlined in Table 2.

Table 2. Organisational readiness indicators for inclusive recruitment

Dimension	Key Indicators	Description of Practice
Leadership Commitment	Vision, accountability, resource allocation	Leadership demonstrates visible commitment to inclusion through strategic priorities, allocation of resources, and accountability mechanisms for inclusive hiring outcomes
Policy Frameworks	Inclusive HR policies, non-discrimination, accessibility guidelines	Recruitment policies reflect inclusive principles, ensuring equitable access, reasonable accommodations, and transparent selection criteria
Strategic Alignment	Integration with DEI goals, organisational objectives	Inclusive hiring practices are aligned with broader diversity, equity, and inclusion goals and contribute to innovation and performance outcomes
Staff Capacity	Training programmes, awareness initiatives	Staff are trained in inclusive recruitment practices, including bias reduction, disability awareness, and accessible communication
Workplace Culture	Attitudes toward diversity, inclusion climate	Organisational culture supports inclusion through positive attitudes, openness, and collaborative practices among employees
Technological Readiness	Accessible recruitment systems, AI tools	Recruitment technologies are designed to be inclusive, accessible, and free from bias, supporting diverse candidate participation
Readiness Assessment Systems	Evaluation tools, organisational diagnostics	Tools are used to assess organisational readiness, identify gaps, and guide improvements in inclusive hiring practices
Accountability Mechanisms	Monitoring systems, performance metrics	Organisations track inclusive hiring outcomes and use data-driven approaches to ensure continuous improvement

Table 2 outlines key indicators of organisational readiness for inclusive recruitment across leadership, policy, culture, and operational systems. It highlights that inclusive hiring effectiveness depends on aligned strategies, trained staff, accessible technologies, and accountability mechanisms. The table emphasises that readiness is multidimensional, requiring coordinated efforts to create equitable recruitment processes that support diverse candidates and sustain inclusive employment outcomes.

5.8 CHALLENGES, ETHICAL CONSIDERATIONS, AND FUTURE DIRECTIONS

Inclusive recruitment for individuals with intellectual disability is shaped by persistent structural, attitudinal, and ethical challenges. Employer stigma and misconceptions remain a major barrier, as assumptions about reduced productivity or increased supervision needs often influence hiring decisions, limiting opportunities before candidates can demonstrate their capabilities. Addressing these perceptions requires awareness, exposure to inclusive practices, and leadership that challenges deficit-based views.

Resource and cost concerns further affect organisational engagement. Employers may perceive accommodation and support systems as burdensome, despite evidence that many adjustments are low-cost and yield long-term benefits such as improved retention and workplace performance. Without reframing inclusion as an investment, organisations may remain hesitant to adopt inclusive hiring practices.

The risk of tokenistic hiring also undermines meaningful inclusion. In such cases, recruitment is driven by compliance or image rather than genuine integration, limiting opportunities for development and participation. Preventing tokenism requires accountability, alignment with organisational goals, and a focus on sustained employment outcomes.

Ethical considerations are central to inclusive recruitment. Ensuring fairness involves balancing standardised assessment with flexibility to accommodate diverse abilities. Autonomy must be respected by supporting individuals to make informed decisions without undue influence. Disclosure and consent present additional complexities, as candidates may face risks in revealing disabilities while also needing access to accommodations. Recruitment systems must therefore ensure confidentiality, voluntary disclosure, and informed participation.

Digital and AI-driven recruitment introduces both opportunities and risks. While these technologies can improve efficiency and reduce bias, they may also reproduce inequalities if not designed inclusively. Transparent, accessible, and accountable systems are essential to ensure that technological innovation supports rather than undermines equitable recruitment.

REFERENCES

Adjo, J., Maybank, A., & Prakash, V. (2021). Building inclusive work environments. *Pediatrics, 148*, Article e2021051440E. https://doi.org/DOI: 10.1542/peds.2021-051440E

Akyeampong, G. B.-D., Ajonbadi, H. A., & Mordi, C. (2025). International laws and framework on disability and employment: The Ghanaian context. In *Careers in Africa: Trends, opportunities and challenges* (pp. 111–133). Springer., DOI: 10.1007/978-3-031-68214-8_6

Ambrose, A. (2018). An introduction to transitional thinking. In *The transitional approach to change* (pp. 1–28). Routledge., DOI: 10.4324/9780429483523-1

Antonova, V. K., Aleksandrova, M. Y., Prisyazhniuk, D. I., & Ryabichenko, T. A. (2022). Inclusive organizational culture as an anomaly: The impact of company size on the manifestation of inclusive norms and practices [Инклюзивная организационная культура как аномалия: Взаимосвязь размера компании и проявления в ней инклюзивных норм и практик]. *Monitoring Obshchestvennogo Mneniya: Ekonomicheskie i Sotsial'nye Peremeny, 4*, 172–198. DOI: 10.14515/monitoring.2022.4.2223

Asrifan, A., Sudirman, R., Supriadi, S., & Utiarahman, N. (2026). The intersection of political economy and workplace equity: Implications for talent acquisition. In *Developing diversity, equity, and inclusion policies for talent acquisition and retention* (pp. 59–90). IGI Global., DOI: 10.4018/979-8-3373-2312-1.ch003

Aswathy, S. A., & Jayalakshmi, G. (2024). Role of institutional support in enhancing faculty job satisfaction and performance. In *Public sector and workforce management in the digital age* (pp. 197–217). IGI Global., DOI: 10.4018/979-8-3373-1137-1.ch010

Azambuja, M., Pereira, R., Breitman, K., & Endler, M. (2010). An architecture for public and open submission systems in the cloud. *Proceedings of the 2010 IEEE 3rd International Conference on Cloud Computing*, 513–517. https://doi.org/DOI: 10.1109/CLOUD.2010.77

Bano, M., Zowghi, D., Mourao, F., Kaur, S., & Zhang, T. (2025). Requirements for inclusive AI-driven recruitment: Lessons learned from an industry workshop. *Proceedings of the IEEE International Conference on Requirements Engineering*, 292–302. https://doi.org/DOI: 10.1109/RE63999.2025.00035

Bartels, L. K., Nordstrom, C. R., & Koski, J. A. (2006). A structured interview demonstration. *Teaching of Psychology, 33*(1), 55–57. DOI: 10.1207/s15328023top3301_12

Bozic, N. (2013). Developing a strength-based approach to educational psychology practice: A multiple case study. *Educational and Child Psychology*, *30*(4), 18–29. DOI: 10.53841/bpsecp.2013.30.4.18

Bozic, N., Lawthom, R., & Murray, J. (2018). Exploring the context of strengths–A new approach to strength-based assessment. *Educational Psychology in Practice*, *34*(1), 26–40. DOI: 10.1080/02667363.2017.1367917

Brecher, E., Bragger, J., & Kutcher, E. (2006). The structured interview: Reducing biases toward job applicants with physical disabilities. *Employee Responsibilities and Rights Journal*, *18*(3), 155–170. DOI: 10.1007/s10672-006-9014-y

Büttner, J. C., Degenbeck, V. K., Schütz, V. G., & Melchers, K. G. (2026). More than bias reduction? How applicants view anonymous application procedures. *International Journal of Selection and Assessment*, *34*(2), e70054. Advance online publication. DOI: 10.1111/ijsa.70054

Chen, A., O'Neill, J., Phillips, K. G., Houtenville, A. J., & Katz, E. (2023). Relationship of business practices and characteristics to supervisors' perceived effectiveness of disability recruitment. *Journal of Vocational Rehabilitation*, *59*(3), 301–310. DOI: 10.3233/JVR-230047

Climie, E., & Henley, L. (2016). A renewed focus on strengths-based assessment in schools. *British Journal of Special Education*, *43*(2), 108–121. DOI: 10.1111/1467-8578.12131

Cortéséro, R., Kerbourc'H, S., Mélo, D., & Poli, A. (2013). Recruiters under pressure. Discrimination and diversity through the prism of interwoven discursive registers [Recruteurs sous tensions. Discrimination et diversité au prisme de registres argumentaires enchevêtrés]. *Sociologie du Travail*, *55*(4). Advance online publication. DOI: 10.4000/sdt.6474

Craven-Staines, S., & Finch, J. (2025). Equality, diversity and inclusion at Teesside doctorate in clinical psychology: Working towards inclusive interview processes. *Clinical Psychology Forum*, *1*(385), 22–27. DOI: 10.53841/bpscpf.2025.1.385.22

Crawford, R. H. (2005). Equity in testing deaf and hard of hearing individuals-legal considerations. In *Assessing deaf adults: Critical issues in testing and evaluation* (pp. 93–108). Gallaudet University Press.

Donald, C. G., & Ralston, J. D. (2005). Supremacy or subordination? Is the issue of ADA and CBA conflicts resolved? *Employee Relations Law Journal*, *31*(2), 55–78.

Dos Santos Rodrigues, P., Luecking, R. G., Glat, R., & Daquera, A. F. C. (2013). Improving workforce outcomes among persons with disabilities in Brazil through youth apprenticeships and customized employment. *Journal of Vocational Rehabilitation, 38*(3), 185–194. DOI: 10.3233/JVR-130633

Dyer, J. L., Twillman, N., & Sequeira, N. (2006). Determining the barriers to employment of HIV+ clients. *Journal of Social Work in Disability & Rehabilitation, 5*(1), 21–43. DOI: 10.1300/J198v05n01_02

Ertelt, A., Renkl, A., & Spada, H. (2006). Making a difference - Exploiting the full potential of instructionally designed on-screen videos. *ICLS 2006 - International Conference of the Learning Sciences, Proceedings, 1*, 154–160.

Ferdman, B. M. (2020). Inclusive leadership: The fulcrum of inclusion. In *Inclusive leadership: Transforming diverse lives, workplaces, and societies* (pp. 3–24). Routledge., DOI: 10.4324/9780429449673-1

Fumasoli, T., & Goastellec, G. (2015). Global models, disciplinary and local patterns in academic recruitment processes. In *Academic work and careers in Europe: Trends, challenges, perspectives* (pp. 69–93). Springer., DOI: 10.1007/978-3-319-10720-2_4

Gahane, S., Khode, P., Kapse, A., Sharma, D., & Anawade, P. (2026). Techniques and best practices for creating accessible websites and applications. *Lecture Notes in Networks and Systems, 1457 LNNS*, 523–531. https://doi.org/DOI: 10.1007/978-981-96-7496-1_42

Gardner, A. K., Costa, P., & Willis, R. E. (2022). Getting on the same page: The impact of interviewer education and structured interviews on interrater agreement in residency interviews. *Journal of Surgical Education, 79*(6), e12–e16. DOI: 10.1016/j.jsurg.2022.05.013 PMID: 35803882

Gardner, K. M. (2014). Developing a customized multiple interview for dental school admissions. *Journal of Dental Education, 78*(4), 597–604. DOI: 10.1002/j.0022-0337.2014.78.4.tb05711.x PMID: 24706690

Gerritsen, C. (2022). Structured diagnostic interview schedules. In *Comprehensive clinical psychology* (2nd ed., Vol. 4, pp. 72–85). Elsevier., DOI: 10.1016/B978-0-12-818697-8.00112-6

Golovko, D., & Schumann, J. H. (2019). Influence of company Facebook activities on recruitment success. *Journal of Business Research, 104*, 161–169. DOI: 10.1016/j.jbusres.2019.06.029

Gonzalez, P. A., & Karimy, P. (2025). Breaking barriers: Retention strategies for underrepresented groups in the IT workforce. *Americas Conference on Information Systems, AMCIS 2025, 7*, 4352–4356.

Hameed, S., Huq, L., Musendo, D. J. N., Banks, L. M., Olenja, J., & Shakespeare, T. (2024). "I don't know whether it's priority, or capacity, or both": Implementation gaps in employment policies targeting people with disabilities in Kenya and Bangladesh. *Disabilities*, *4*(4), 781–800. DOI: 10.3390/disabilities4040048

Hamzah, N. R., Hanid, M. F. A., & Zakaria, M. I. (2025). The effect of segmented-interactive video demonstration on student performance in procedural skills among healthcare students. *Advances in Health Sciences Education : Theory and Practice*. Advance online publication. DOI: 10.1007/s10459-025-10471-2 PMID: 40889025

Hedenus, A., Backman, C., & Håkansson, P. (2021). Whom do you know? Recruiters' motives for assessing jobseekers' online networks. *International Journal of Human Resource Management*, *32*(8), 1754–1777. DOI: 10.1080/09585192.2019.1579245

Huang, W.-T. (2024). Designing effective career websites: A study on user experience and job seeker engagement. *Communications in Computer and Information Science, 2314 CCIS*, 144–155. https://doi.org/DOI: 10.1007/978-981-97-9910-7_12

Iftikhar, A., Mohammad, S. I., Alqudah, M. N., Al-Adwan, A. S., Vasudevan, A., Ali, I., & Farhan, M. (2025). Evaluating inclusivity and fairness of AI recruitment tools for hiring people with disabilities in the United Arab Emirates (UAE) [Evaluación de la Inclusividad y la Equidad de las Herramientas de Reclutamiento de IA para la Contratación de Personas con Discapacidad en los Emiratos Árabes Unidos (EAU)]. *Data and Metadata*, *4*, 487. Advance online publication. DOI: 10.56294/dm2025487

Iwanaga, K., Chan, F., Bezyak, J., Wu, J. R., Lee, D., Rumrill, P., West, A. E., Zapata, P., Ho, H., Tansey, T. N., & Wehman, P. (2024). Fortune 500 companies and employment of people with disabilities: The intermediary role of disability inclusion policies and practices. *Journal of Vocational Rehabilitation*, *61*(1), 17–24. DOI: 10.3233/JVR-240026

Jaiswal, A., Gangwani, A., Rakesh, N., Oberoi, M., Chauhan, P., & Dewangan, B. K. (2025). Interview assistance system for deaf and mute candidates using real-time sign language translation and speech recognition. *2025 4th OPJU International Technology Conference on Smart Computing for Innovation and Advancement in Industry 5.0*. https://doi.org/DOI: 10.1109/OTCON65728.2025.11070383

James, M. (2018). Strategic readiness. In *The international encyclopedia of strategic communication* (pp. 1–5). Wiley., DOI: 10.1002/9781119010722.iesc0178

Javahery, H., Gower, M., Sinnig, D., & Forbrig, P. (2011). Patterns for usable accessible design. *Lecture Notes in Computer Science*, *6761*(Part 1), 248–257. DOI: 10.1007/978-3-642-21602-2_28

Jayasekara, C., Senarathne, I., Wickramasinghe, A., Jayathilaka, N., Thelijjagoda, S., De Silva, H., Giguruwa, N., & Abeysinghe, N. (2023). Artificial intelligence agent to identify the correct human resources. *ICAC 2023 - 5th International Conference on Advancements in Computing*, 424–429. https://doi.org/DOI: 10.1109/ICAC60630.2023.10417197

Jenson, C. M., Hutchins, A. J., & Rowlands, G. (2006). Is small-group education the key to retention of sessional GPs? *Education for Primary Care*, *17*(3), 218–226. DOI: 10.1080/14739879.2006.11864065 PMID: 28240104

Kohli, J., & Vedeler, J. S. (2023). Social exclusion and disability: Exploring the role of ingroup/outgroup dynamics in employment. In *Citizenship and social exclusion at the margins of the welfare state* (pp. 78–91). Routledge., DOI: 10.4324/9781003347279-7

Lacroux, A., & Martin-Lacroux, C. (2020). Anonymous résumés: An effective preselection method? *International Journal of Selection and Assessment*, *28*(1), 98–111. DOI: 10.1111/ijsa.12275

Leasher, M. K., Miller, C. E., & Gooden, M. P. (2009). Rater effects and attitudinal barriers affecting people with disabilities in personnel selection. *Journal of Applied Social Psychology*, *39*(9), 2236–2274. DOI: 10.1111/j.1559-1816.2009.00523.x

Legarreta, R. E. (2025). The reform of termination of contract of employment due to permanent invalidity and its connection to the implementation of reasonable accommodations [La reforma de la extinción del contrato de trabajo por incapacidad permanente y su vinculación con la implementación de adaptaciones razonables]. *Trabajo y Derecho*, *129*, 1–26. DOI: 10.32029/2386-8112.02.129.2025

Liao, C. L. (2007). Collaboration and dialogue: Video as an agent in extending and enriching learning and writing. *ACM SIGGRAPH 2007: Educators Program. Article*, *5*, 5. Advance online publication. DOI: 10.1145/1282040.1282046

Lindsay, S., Goodfellow, A., Stergiou-Kita, M., Kirsh, B., & Lero, D. (2017). Inclusionary business practices for recruiting and retaining people with disabilities: A scoping review. In *Physical disabilities: Perspectives, risk factors and quality of life* (pp. 17–45). Nova Science Publishers.

Lindstrom, L., Hirano, K., & Ingram, A. (2020). Finding our voices: Employment and career development for women with disabilities. In *The Palgrave handbook of disability at work* (pp. 387–402). Palgrave Macmillan., DOI: 10.1007/978-3-030-42966-9_22

Maclean, N., Geiger, M., & Ned, L. (2024). Employment equity targets: How a state-owned enterprise recruits people with disabilities. *SA Journal of Human Resource Management*, *22*(0), a2355. Advance online publication. DOI: 10.4102/SAJHRM.v22i0.2355

Making it work: Employment of people with disabilities. (2011). Recruitment and retention of people with disabilities employment issue brief #1. In *Making it work: Employment of people with disabilities* (pp. 49–58). Disability and Business Technical Assistance Centers.

Malekinezhad, F., & Courtney, P. (2026). Framing the shift to supported employment: Exploring the impacts of a person-centred programme evaluation approach through peer led participatory research. *Evaluation and Program Planning*, *114*, 102723. Advance online publication. DOI: 10.1016/j.evalprogplan.2025.102723 PMID: 41151422

Marbin, J., Hutchinson, Y.-V., & Schaeffer, S. (2021). Avoiding the virtual pitfall: Identifying and mitigating biases in graduate medical education videoconference interviews. *Academic Medicine*, *96*(8), 1120–1124. DOI: 10.1097/ACM.0000000000003914 PMID: 33464743

McKinney, E. L., & Swartz, L. (2021). Employment integration barriers: Experiences of people with disabilities. *International Journal of Human Resource Management*, *32*(10), 2298–2320. DOI: 10.1080/09585192.2019.1579749

Mégret, F., & Msipa, D. (2014). Global reasonable accommodation: How the convention on the rights of persons with disabilities changes the way we think about equality. *South African Journal on Human Rights*, *30*(2), 252–274. DOI: 10.1080/19962126.2014.11865109

Mudiayi, D., Shariff, F., Bridgland, L., Mathura, P., & Ringrose, J. (2024). Elevating equity: Advancing diversity and inclusivity through trialing bias reduction tools in the general internal medicine program resident application process. *BMC Medical Education*, *24*(1), 1265. Advance online publication. DOI: 10.1186/s12909-024-06244-x PMID: 39501300

Najm, N. A., & Ali, W. W. (2024). Organizational readiness and innovation in the Jordanian telecommunication companies. *International Journal of Productivity and Performance Management*, *73*(1), 242–269. DOI: 10.1108/IJPPM-01-2022-0051

Napier, T. R., Howell, K. H., Scheid, C. R., & Miller-Graff, L. E. (2023). Empirically derived patterns of adverse childhood experiences and associations with prenatal social networks. *Psychology of Violence*, *13*(3), 219–228. DOI: 10.1037/vio0000453

Nickerson, A. B., & Fishman, C. E. (2013). Promoting mental health and resilience through strength-based assessment in US schools. *Educational and Child Psychology*, *30*(4), 7–17. DOI: 10.53841/bpsecp.2013.30.4.7

Norzin, T., Mehta, D., Sarwat, E., Basha, M. J., Dhrupadha, D. L., & Ramesh, S. (2025). Adaptive job portal for specially abled students. *2025 World Skills Conference on Universal Data Analytics and Sciences*. https://doi.org/DOI: 10.1109/WorldSUAS66815.2025.11199216

Novak, J. (2017). Making the cut when applying for jobs online. *Journal of Vocational Rehabilitation*, *46*(3), 293–299. DOI: 10.3233/JVR-170864

Ochrach, C., Thomas, K., Phillips, B., Mpofu, N., Tansey, T., & Castillo, S. (2022). Case study on the effects of a disability inclusive mindset in a large biotechnology company. *Journal of Work-Applied Management, 14*(1), 113–125. https://doi.org/DOI: 10.1108/JWAM-06-2021-0045

Ollington, N., Gibb, J., & Harcourt, M. (2013). Online social networks: An emergent recruiter tool for attracting and screening. *Personnel Review*, *42*(3), 248–265. DOI: 10.1108/00483481311320390

Perez-Uribe, R. I., Ocampo-Guzman, D., & Moreno-Monsalve, N. (2022). *Handbook of research on promoting an inclusive organizational culture for entrepreneurial sustainability*. IGI Global., DOI: 10.4018/978-1-6684-5216-5

Pierson, K., Oshodi, R., & Borowsky, I. (2026). Applying accessibility theory by implementing gradual, sustainable change in daily practice. *Academic Pediatrics*, *26*(3), 103205. Advance online publication. DOI: 10.1016/j.acap.2025.103205 PMID: 41490875

Pogrebtsova, E., Luta, D., & Hausdorf, P. A. (2020). Selection of gender-incongruent applicants: No gender bias with structured interviews. *International Journal of Selection and Assessment*, *28*(1), 117–121. DOI: 10.1111/ijsa.12270

Pollifroni, M., Ioana, A., Canuta, I. L., & Pollifroni, F. (2025). AI-driven e-recruitment in education and science: Moving towards good governance, prevention of corruption, administrative transparency, and bias-free decision-making. *Business Ethics and Leadership*, *9*(2), 225–237. DOI: 10.61093/bel.9(2).225-237.2025

Raju, U. S. N., Kadambari, K. V., & Venkata Subba Reddy, P. (2015). A new method of assessing the students using video assignments. *IEEE Global Engineering Education Conference*, 771–773. https://doi.org/DOI: 10.1109/EDUCON.2015.7096058

Rashid, T. (2015). Strength-based assessment. In *Positive psychology in practice: Promoting human flourishing in work, health, education, and everyday life* (2nd ed., pp. 519–542). Wiley., DOI: 10.1002/9781118996874.ch31

Rigotti, C., & Fosch-Villaronga, E. (2024). Fairness, AI & recruitment. *Computer Law & Security Review, 53*, 105966. Advance online publication. DOI: 10.1016/j.clsr.2024.105966

Risavy, S. D., Robie, C., Fisher, P. A., & Rasheed, S. (2022). Resumes vs. application forms: Why the stubborn reliance on resumes? *Frontiers in Psychology, 13*, 884205. Advance online publication. DOI: 10.3389/fpsyg.2022.884205 PMID: 35967708

Rusilowati, U., Muti, R. N., Mudrika, F., Kamil, M. F., Lutfiani, N., & Immanuel, A. J. (2025). Data-driven inclusive HR and leadership strategies for enhancing innovation and employee engagement. Proceeding - 2025 4th International Conference on Creative Communication and Innovative Technology. https://doi.org/DOI: 10.1109/ICCIT65724.2025.11167031

Sachse, M., & Melzer, J. (2025). Breaking barriers: Gamification in recruiting to overcome communication challenges - Psychological, social and cultural differences in perception and participation. *Proceedings of the International Conferences on Interfaces and Human Computer Interaction 2025; Game and Entertainment Technologies 2025; and Computer Graphics, Visualization, Computer Vision and Image Processing 2025*, 172–176.

Sarto, P. A., Lorzano, E. R., Artes, A., Bobis, H. M., Intal, G. L., Moreno, D. E., & Tan, M. E. (2026). A strategic approach to developing AbiliNet: Leveraging the business model canvas for an inclusive AI-driven job-matching platform. ICBIM 2025 - The 9th International Conference on Business and Information Management, 28–35. https://doi.org/DOI: 10.1145/3785171.3785188

Saxena, P., Agrawal, V., & Pradhan, I. P. (2025). AI-powered talent acquisition and recruitment. In *Human resource management and artificial intelligence: Automating and optimizing processes* (pp. 25–43). Routledge., DOI: 10.4324/9781003474265-2

Scholz, F. (2020). Taken for granted: Ableist norms embedded in the design of online recruitment practices. In *The Palgrave handbook of disability at work* (pp. 451–469). Palgrave Macmillan., DOI: 10.1007/978-3-030-42966-9_26

Shahhosseini, A. M., Moayed, F. A., & McLeod, A. (2020). Strategies for increasing enrollment, retention, and graduation in two baccalaureate degree STEM programs: Mechanical Engineering Technology (MET) and Safety Management (SM). *ASEE Annual Conference and Exposition, Conference Proceedings*, Article 1253. DOI: 10.18260/1-2--35209

Shatil, T., Carew, M. T., Chowdhury, S., Biswas, D., Adiba, A., Banks, L. M., Shakespeare, T., & Das, N. (2024). Process evaluation of a disability-inclusive employment programme: Examining the design and implementation of STAR+. *Oxford Development Studies*, *52*(2), 146–159. DOI: 10.1080/13600818.2024.2371125

Shinall, J. B. (2020). Anticipating accommodation. *Iowa Law Review*, *105*(2), 621–686.

Srour, C., & Py, J. (2023). Making job candidates more honest with a theory-based form: A field study. *Journal of Personnel Psychology*, *22*(2), 89–98. DOI: 10.1027/1866-5888/a000313

Steur, J., & Wittek, R. (2005). The governance of transition processes in an organization: A cognitive mapping approach. *Academy of Management Annual Meeting Proceedings*. https://doi.org/DOI: 10.5465/ambpp.2005.18781706

Strauser, D. G., Price, R. A., Brehmer, C. E., & Strauser, D. R. (2026). Exploring employer's successful hiring and retention practices of individuals with disabilities. *Rehabilitation Counseling Bulletin*, *69*(2), 109–119. DOI: 10.1177/00343552241265319

Sullivan, D. W., & Swider, B. W. (2025). The influence of friends' person-organization fit during recruitment. *The Journal of Applied Psychology*, *110*(2), 238–255. DOI: 10.1037/apl0001226 PMID: 39115896

Taylor, M. A., & Wituk, E. (2025). Reasonable accommodation for neurodiversity: Legal, organizational and managerial considerations. *Employee Responsibilities and Rights Journal*. Advance online publication. DOI: 10.1007/s10672-025-09546-4

Tjimuku, M., Atiku, S. O., & Villet, H. J. (2025). Inclusive leadership: A catalyst for ethical work climate and enhanced employee performance in diverse workforce. In *Advances in ethical work climate and employee well-being* (pp. 331–354). IGI Global., DOI: 10.4018/979-8-3693-8819-8.ch016

Tueme, N. (2021). All in the family: The role of family networks, collective action frames, and identity in Latino movement participation. *Sociology Compass*, *15*(4), e12866. Advance online publication. DOI: 10.1111/soc4.12866

Uslu, B. (2017). The influence of organisational features in high-ranked universities: The case of Australia. *Journal of Higher Education Policy and Management, 39*(5), 471–486. DOI: 10.1080/1360080X.2017.1354755

Varga, A. (2025). Equality of opportunity, sustainable development, and the role of civil society in higher education ethical and socio-philosophical approaches in international and Hungarian contexts [Esélyegyenlőség, fenntartható fejlődés és a civil társadalom szerepe a felsőoktatásban: Etikai és társadalomfilozófiai megközelítés nemzetközi és magyarországi kontextusban]. *Civil Szemle, 9*(Special Issue), 41–55. DOI: 10.62560/CSZ.2025.05.3

Vedeler, J. S., & Anvik, C. H. (2023). What's the 'problem' with workplace accommodation? A disability policy journey over time. *Scandinavian Journal of Disability Research, 25*(1), 119–131. DOI: 10.16993/sjdr.918

Wagner, J. A.III. (2024). Inter-team coordination in multiteam systems: Mechanisms, transitions, and precipitants. *Organizational Psychology Review, 14*(3), 425–448. DOI: 10.1177/20413866231153537

Welti, F. (2018). Work disability policy in Germany: Experiences of collective and individual participation and cooperation. In *The science and politics of work disability prevention* (pp. 171–188). Routledge., DOI: 10.4324/9780429443398-11

Wichinsky, L., Thomlison, B., & Pennell, J. (2012). Exploring organizational culture and climate in community coalitions. *Community Development (Columbus, Ohio), 43*(2), 133–146. DOI: 10.1080/15575330.2011.567418

Yan, C. O. (2026). Redesigning employment systems for neurodivergent inclusion: A structural, intersectional, and theoretical inquiry. In *Vocational rehabilitation for students with developmental disabilities: Transition from education to employment* (pp. 339–376). IGI Global., DOI: 10.4018/979-8-3693-9541-7.ch011

Yang, M. M. (2026). Mitigating disability bias in hiring: The role of inclusion-focused generative AI in complex HR decisions. *Human Resource Management Journal, 36*(3), 553–565. Advance online publication. DOI: 10.1111/1748-8583.70044

Yatheesha, V. H., Reddy, S. K., Angothu, H., Vranda, M. N., Raju, K. T., & Pallerla, S. (2024). Caregivers' perspectives on reasonable accommodation for persons with severe mental disorders at the workplace. *Indian Journal of Occupational and Environmental Medicine, 28*(3), 177–181. DOI: 10.4103/ijoem.ijoem_195_23 PMID: 39618901

Yeung, C., Kohno, T., & Roesner, F. (2024). Analyzing the (in)accessibility of online advertisements. *Proceedings of the ACM SIGCOMM Internet Measurement Conference*, 92–106. https://doi.org/DOI: 10.1145/3646547.3688427

Zink, D., Lee, B., & Allen, D. (2014). Structured and semistructured clinical interviews available for use among African American clients: Cultural considerations in the diagnostic interview process. In *Guide to psychological assessment with African Americans* (pp. 19–42). Springer., DOI: 10.1007/978-1-4939-1004-5_3

Chapter 6
Job Analysis and Inclusive Employment

ABSTRACT

This chapter presents a structured pathway for advancing inclusive employment through job analysis, role customisation, strengths alignment, and workplace supports. It examines the conceptual foundations of Competitive Integrated Employment and integrates theoretical, methodological, and practical perspectives to guide implementation. The chapter also addresses organisational benefits, implementation challenges, and system-level considerations, culminating in an integrated framework for practice that supports sustainable, equitable, and productive employment outcomes for individuals with intellectual disabilities.

6.1 INTRODUCTION

Job analysis and inclusive employment are foundational to the development of equitable labour systems that recognise diverse capabilities while maintaining organisational effectiveness. Job analysis is commonly defined as a systematic process for identifying job tasks, responsibilities, and the knowledge, skills, and abilities required for effective performance (Brannick et al., 2012; Ellington et al., 2015). Beyond its traditional human resource function, it serves as a critical mechanism for structuring work to promote fairness, transparency, and accessibility (Caughron et al., 2013; Strah & Rupp, 2022). When applied within inclusive employment systems, job analysis supports the design of roles that enable individuals with intellectual disabilities to participate in meaningful and productive work.

At its core, job analysis involves breaking work into its component tasks and identifying the competencies required to perform them. This process allows organisations to distinguish between essential and non-essential job functions, which is particularly important in inclusive employment contexts (Wilson, 2012). By

DOI: 10.4018/979-8-3373-9185-4.ch006

identifying which tasks are fundamental and which can be modified or reassigned, employers can create flexible job roles that align with the abilities of individuals with intellectual disabilities without compromising productivity. Such an approach strengthens job matching processes, ensuring that individuals are placed in roles that reflect their strengths, interests, and support needs (Suresh & Dyaram, 2023; Dall, 2026).

Inclusive employment systems extend beyond job design to encompass organisational practices that support equitable participation. These systems emphasise the removal of structural and attitudinal barriers that limit marginalised groups' access to employment. Individuals with intellectual disabilities often encounter challenges such as discrimination, limited access to training, and inadequate workplace support (Finstad et al., 2022; Rachanioti et al., 2021). Addressing these challenges requires a shift from deficit-oriented perspectives toward strengths-based approaches that recognise the capabilities and contributions of all workers. Within this framework, job analysis serves as an enabling tool to support the restructuring of work environments to enhance inclusion and participation.

Workplace accessibility is a central component of inclusive employment and operates across multiple dimensions. Physical accessibility involves designing work environments that are safe and navigable, while digital accessibility ensures that information and communication systems are usable by all employees (Persson et al., 2015). Procedural accessibility focuses on organisational processes such as recruitment, onboarding, and performance evaluation, ensuring they do not inadvertently exclude individuals with disabilities. Job analysis contributes to these dimensions by providing detailed insights into work processes, enabling organisations to implement targeted accommodations and adjustments that support diverse employee needs.

Despite growing recognition of the importance of inclusive employment, individuals with intellectual disabilities remain underrepresented in the labour market. Barriers such as employer misconceptions, limited opportunities for skill development, and inadequate support systems continue to restrict access to employment (Soeker et al., 2021). However, research demonstrates that structured support mechanisms, including job coaching and supported employment programmes, can significantly improve employment outcomes for this population (Quintana et al., 2022). These findings highlight the importance of integrating job analysis with inclusive employment strategies to create sustainable pathways into the workforce.

Equity in hiring practices is another critical dimension of inclusive employment systems. Equity requires that organisations recognise differences in individual needs and provide appropriate support to ensure fair outcomes. Job analysis plays a central role in promoting equity by ensuring that job requirements are clearly defined and aligned with actual work demands, thereby reducing the risk of unnecessary exclusion.

Clear role definitions also enhance transparency in recruitment and performance evaluation, contributing to improved job satisfaction and organisational trust.

Organisational inclusion frameworks provide the structural and cultural foundation for sustaining inclusive employment practices. These frameworks integrate diversity, equity, and inclusion principles into organisational policies, leadership practices, and human resource systems. Effective implementation requires leadership commitment, ongoing training, and mechanisms for monitoring inclusion outcomes. Within such frameworks, job analysis functions as a practical tool that translates inclusive values into everyday workplace practices, ensuring that inclusion is embedded in organisational operations rather than treated as an add-on.

Persistent challenges, including limited employer awareness and resource constraints, continue to affect the implementation of inclusive employment practices (Finstad et al., 2022). Nevertheless, these challenges also create opportunities for innovation through evidence-based approaches such as universal design, participatory job design, and collaborative employment models. Strengthening the integration of job analysis and inclusive employment systems provides a pathway to improve labour market participation, enhance organisational performance, and support the long-term inclusion of individuals with intellectual disabilities.

6.2 CONCEPTUAL FOUNDATIONS OF COMPETITIVE INTEGRATED EMPLOYMENT

This section examines the conceptual foundations of Competitive Integrated Employment (CIE) to clarify its principles, structures, and relevance in advancing inclusive labour market participation for individuals with intellectual and developmental disabilities.

6.2.1 Core Principles of Competitive Integrated Employment

Competitive Integrated Employment (CIE) represents a rights-based framework that promotes access to meaningful work for individuals with disabilities, including those with intellectual and developmental disabilities (IDD). Central to this framework is the principle that individuals should work in typical community settings and earn wages comparable to those of their non-disabled peers (Taylor et al., 2022; Mostafa & Wang, 2023). This emphasis on fair wages and mainstream workplaces distinguishes CIE from segregated employment models and reinforces dignity, participation, and equality in labour systems. The CIE is grounded in broader equality frameworks that prioritise integration rather than separation.

It aligns with policy and practice efforts aimed at dismantling segregated employment structures such as sheltered workshops, which have historically restricted opportunities and limited career progression for individuals with intellectual disabilities (Sulewski et al., 2017; Migliore et al., 2008). By promoting participation within standard workplace environments, CIE enhances both economic inclusion and social engagement.

Another key principle is person-centred planning, which ensures that employment pathways are tailored to individual strengths, preferences, and long-term goals. Evidence shows that individuals with clearly defined employment objectives are more likely to secure and sustain competitive employment (DuBois et al., 2025). In addition, informed choice is central to this process, as individuals are supported to participate actively in employment decisions, thereby reinforcing autonomy and self-determination (Moore & Friedman, 2017).

6.2.2 Key Components of Competitive Integrated Employment

The implementation of CIE is supported by several interrelated components that enable the transition from segregated to integrated employment systems. Policy reform remains a major driver, particularly through initiatives such as the Workforce Innovation and Opportunity Act (WIOA) and Employment First policies, which position competitive employment as the preferred outcome for individuals with disabilities (Wehman et al., 2018; Taylor et al., 2022). These shifts reflect a broader movement toward community-based participation and long-term labour market inclusion. Supported and customised employment pathways further strengthen implementation. Supported employment provides structured assistance, including job coaching, workplace accommodations, and ongoing support, enabling individuals to obtain and retain employment (Cheng et al., 2015).

Customised employment aligns job roles with individual capabilities and employer needs, thereby enhancing productivity and job satisfaction while supporting organisational efficiency. Early transition interventions also play a critical role. Programmes such as Pre-Employment Transition Services (Pre-ETS) offer opportunities for career exploration, work-based learning, and skill development, thereby improving employment-readiness among young people with disabilities (Taylor et al., 2022). Collectively, these components contribute to the development of inclusive and sustainable employment pathways.

6.2.3 Barriers and Challenges to Competitive Integrated Employment

Despite growing policy support, multiple structural and workplace-related constraints continue to limit the effective implementation and expansion of Competitive Integrated Employment.

6.2.3.1 Systemic Barriers: Systemic challenges, including disparities in funding allocation and policy implementation, often favour traditional sheltered employment models over integrated alternatives (Jordán de Urríes & Verdugo, 2012). These structural constraints reduce the effectiveness of inclusive employment initiatives and hinder large-scale transformation toward integrated labour systems.

6.2.3.2 Workplace Challenges: Workplace-level barriers also persist. Employers may lack awareness of inclusive employment practices or hold misconceptions about the productivity and capabilities of individuals with disabilities, which can affect hiring decisions and retention (Vijayakumar et al., 2023). Additionally, insufficient workplace accommodations and limited access to support services can create barriers to successful job integration, particularly for individuals with higher support needs (Tomás & Fluixá, 2020).

6.2.3.3 Low Participation Rates: Low participation rates further illustrate the gap between policy aspirations and real-world outcomes. A significant proportion of individuals with intellectual and developmental disabilities remain unemployed or underemployed, highlighting the need for improved implementation strategies and stronger collaboration across systems (Tomaszewski et al., 2024).

6.2.4 Benefits of Competitive Integrated Employment

Competitive Integrated Employment offers a range of economic, psychological, and social advantages that enhance individual well-being while contributing to more inclusive and productive labour systems.

6.2.4.1 Economic and Psychological Gains: Individuals engaged in competitive employment often experience improved financial independence, increased self-esteem, and enhanced overall well-being (Taylor et al., 2022). Employment also supports skill development, career progression, and long-term stability.

6.2.4.2 Social Inclusion: Integrated employment environments promote social inclusion by enabling individuals with disabilities to interact with diverse colleagues and participate actively in community life. This reduces social isolation and fosters a sense of belonging, which is essential for holistic development and quality of life (Novak, 2015).

6.2.5 Policy and Practice Recommendations

Advancing CIE requires sustained commitment from policymakers, employers, and service providers. Interagency collaboration is essential to align education, vocational rehabilitation, and employment systems to support seamless workforce transitions (Tucker et al., 2017). Such collaboration ensures that individuals receive coordinated and continuous support throughout their employment journey. Strengthening transition-focused programmes remains critical. Initiatives such as Pre-ETS equip young people with the skills and experiences necessary for successful labour market participation (Taylor et al., 2022). Long-term systems change is necessary to sustain inclusive employment practices. Addressing structural barriers, increasing investment in support services, and promoting employer engagement are essential steps toward building labour markets that are accessible, equitable, and responsive to the needs of individuals with intellectual disabilities.

6.3 THEORETICAL PERSPECTIVES SUPPORTING JOB CUSTOMISATION

Job customisation is a theoretically grounded process that involves restructuring work to align with diverse human capabilities while maintaining organisational effectiveness. These perspectives collectively explain how flexible roles, adaptive task structures, and supportive environments enable meaningful participation for workers with intellectual disabilities.

6.3.1 Universal Design for Learning and Inclusive Job Design: Designing work systems that anticipate human variability provides a strong foundation for inclusive employment. Principles derived from Universal Design for Learning support the development of flexible roles that accommodate diverse abilities from the outset. In workplace contexts, this aligns with inclusive job design, where tasks, tools, and expectations are structured to enhance accessibility and reduce the need for reactive adjustments (Bredgaard, 2025).

6.3.2 Social Model of Disability and Environmental Adaptation: Attention to environmental and organisational barriers shifts the focus from individual limitations to structural constraints. The biopsychosocial perspective further underscores how capability is shaped by interactions with contextual conditions (Carus & Messina, 2025). Within employment settings, this orientation supports the redesign of workflows, communication systems, and supervisory practices to enable participation.

6.3.3 Strengths-Based Approach and Capability Alignment: Focusing on what individuals can do rather than what they cannot do enables more effective job alignment. Evidence on job matching shows that linking tasks to individual strengths enhances both performance and job satisfaction (Suresh & Dyaram, 2023). This approach supports the development of roles that maximise contribution while challenging deficit-oriented assumptions about workers with intellectual disabilities.

6.3.4 Capability Theory and Meaningful Work: Expanding opportunities for individuals to achieve valued outcomes strengthens the quality of employment experiences. Capability theory emphasises access to resources, autonomy, and opportunities for development as central to meaningful participation. In employment contexts, this includes career progression and the formation of professional identity (Meacham et al., 2020). Job customisation creates conditions that support growth rather than mere job placement.

6.3.5 Ecological Systems Theory and Multilevel Influence: Understanding employment outcomes requires attention to multiple layers of influence. Interactions between individual, organisational, and policy-level factors shape the effectiveness of inclusive practices (Novikov, 2025). Job customisation, therefore, operates within a broader system that includes workplace culture, institutional policies, and socio-economic conditions, all of which must align to support inclusion.

6.3.6 Person–Environment Fit and Job Matching: Alignment between individual capabilities and job demands remains central to sustainable employment. Research on person–environment fit highlights the importance of tailoring tasks, schedules, and supports to individual needs (Suresh & Dyaram, 2023). This perspective reinforces the idea that job customisation is an ongoing process requiring continuous adjustment as both workers and organisational contexts evolve.

6.3.7 Disability Inclusion Theory and Organisational Practice: Workplace participation is shaped not only by job design but also by organisational culture and practices. Inclusive leadership, equitable human resource systems, and supportive workplace environments play a critical role in enabling participation (Suresh & Dyaram, 2020). At the same time, subtle forms of discrimination can limit inclusion, indicating the need for both structural and cultural change (Cavanagh et al., 2021).

6.3.8 Adaptive Work Systems and Continuous Redesign: Sustaining inclusive employment requires flexibility and responsiveness to change. Adaptive work systems emphasise continuous evaluation and modification of tasks, processes, and supports to meet evolving needs (Suresh & Dyaram, 2023).

6.4 METHODS AND TOOLS FOR CONDUCTING JOB ANALYSIS

A rigorous approach to job analysis is essential for designing inclusive and adaptable work roles that align with organisational objectives and individual capabilities. This section outlines key methods and tools for examining job tasks, competencies, workflows, and environmental conditions. These approaches provide the empirical basis for job customisation by ensuring that decisions about task restructuring, role allocation, and workplace adjustments are grounded in systematic evidence rather than intuition.

6.4.1 Task Analysis: Breaking work into its core components remains a central method in job analysis. Task analysis identifies specific duties, subtasks, and sequences of activities required to perform a role effectively. This method helps organisations determine task complexity and distinguish between essential and non-essential functions (Kittinger & Bender, 2015; Ulrich et al., 2019). In inclusive employment contexts, task analysis supports the simplification, modification, or redistribution of duties to match individual abilities. Data-driven approaches, including semi-automated models, can further enhance accuracy by identifying patterns in work processes (Lin & Lehto, 2007).

6.4.2 Functional Job Analysis: Functional job analysis extends beyond task identification to examine how job roles contribute to organisational goals. It focuses on the relationships among tasks, worker characteristics, and expected outcomes, thereby producing structured job descriptions and specifications (Brannick et al., 2012; Dunckel, 2015). This method is valuable for aligning roles with organisational performance while also supporting inclusion. A clear understanding of required competencies enables workplace adjustments that balance employee needs with organisational performance requirements.

6.4.3 Workplace Observation: Direct observation provides insight into how work is actually performed. Techniques such as time-and-motion studies and video-based observation capture real-time behaviours, interactions, and environmental influences (Hanvey, 2018). Observation is particularly useful for identifying discrepancies between formal job descriptions and actual work practices. In inclusive settings, it helps reveal barriers, inefficiencies, and contextual factors that may affect workers with intellectual disabilities.

6.4.4 Structured Interviews: Structured interviews are widely used to collect detailed qualitative information about job roles, responsibilities, and required competencies. These interviews often involve supervisors, employees, and subject-matter experts, ensuring a comprehensive understanding of job performance (Verma & Singh, 2024). Behavioural event interviews focus on specific instances of performance, enabling the identification of critical skills and decision-making processes. This method contributes to the development of competency frameworks that inform recruitment, training, and job redesign.

6.4.5 Skills Assessment Tools: Standardised assessment tools provide a systematic way to identify abilities required for specific roles. Instruments such as the Fleishman Job Analysis Survey evaluate cognitive, psychomotor, and sensory-perceptual skills, offering detailed insight into job demands (Ghanbari et al., 2024; Shabani et al., 2025). These tools are particularly useful in inclusive employment contexts, where accurate identification of skill requirements supports effective job matching and the design of targeted support strategies.

6.4.6 Job Component Breakdown and Competency Mapping: Breaking jobs into components such as tasks, knowledge, skills, and abilities (KSAs) provides a structured understanding of work roles. This process supports competency mapping, which identifies key competencies required for effective performance (Brannick et al., 2012; Andre et al., 2015). Competency mapping is important for aligning job roles with training and development initiatives. It also highlights areas where adjustments or additional support may be required to enhance inclusion.

6.4.7 Workflow Analysis: This examines how tasks are connected within work processes. It identifies inefficiencies, redundancies, and bottlenecks that may affect performance and productivity (Ulrich et al., 2019; Robinson, 2010). In job customisation, this method supports redesigning processes to improve flexibility and efficiency. It also enables the redistribution of tasks to create roles that better match individual capabilities.

6.4.8 Environmental Assessment: Evaluating the physical and organisational environment is critical for understanding the conditions under which work is performed. Environmental assessment considers workspace design, safety conditions, and organisational practices that influence job performance (Dunckel, 2015; Hanvey, 2018). This approach is especially relevant in inclusive employment, as it identifies barriers that may limit accessibility. Addressing these factors through environmental adjustments enhances participation and effectiveness.

6.4.9 Evidence-Based Job Evaluation Methods: Evidence-based job evaluation combines analytical and non-analytical approaches to assess the value and requirements of job roles. These methods inform decisions about job classification, remuneration, and organisational structure (Verma & Singh, 2024). Cognitive Task Analysis (CTA) provides deeper insight into decision-making processes and situational awareness, particularly in complex roles (Roberts & Flin, 2016). Such approaches improve the accuracy and reliability of job analysis outcomes. These methods and tools provide a structured approach to understanding job roles and designing inclusive work environments. By integrating multiple techniques, organisations can align job requirements with both performance expectations and the diverse capabilities of workers with intellectual disabilities.

6.5 JOB CARVING, JOB CRAFTING, AND ROLE CUSTOMISATION

Achieving inclusive employment requires deliberate restructuring of work to reflect both organisational demands and individual capabilities. Strategies such as job carving, job crafting, and role customisation provide practical mechanisms for aligning tasks, responsibilities, and work environments with the diverse needs of workers. These approaches extend beyond static job descriptions, allowing roles to evolve in response to changing performance expectations, workplace dynamics, and individual strengths.

6.5.1 Concepts and Strategies

Inclusive job design is shaped by both organisational decisions and employees' active involvement in tailoring their work experiences. The following strategies illustrate how tasks and roles can be adapted to support inclusion while maintaining productivity.

6.5.1.1 Job Crafting: A proactive orientation to work design enables employees to reshape aspects of their roles to better reflect their skills, interests, and preferences (De Gennaro, 2019; Tims & Twemlow, 2024). Job crafting can occur across several dimensions, including task modification, workplace relationships, and the way individuals perceive their work. Adjusting task responsibilities enables employees to focus on activities that better match their skills and strengths. Changes in workplace interactions can strengthen collaboration, social support, and professional relationships. In addition, reshaping perceptions of work can enhance meaning, purpose, and overall engagement in job roles. These processes are associated with improved well-being, motivation, and performance outcomes (Menachery, 2018; Demerouti et al., 2025).

6.5.1.2 Job Carving and Task Redistribution: Restructuring roles through selective task reallocation creates opportunities to align work demands with individual capabilities. This approach involves identifying components of existing jobs that can be grouped or reassigned to form new, more accessible roles. Redistributing tasks across employees ensures that responsibilities are matched with appropriate skill levels, thereby enhancing efficiency and inclusion. In practice, routine or clearly defined tasks can be organised into roles that support workers with intellectual disabilities while maintaining overall organisational productivity.

6.5.1.3 Role Redesign and Customised Employment: Expanding beyond task-level adjustments, broader changes to job structures allow roles to be tailored to both organisational objectives and individual capacities. Customised employment builds on this principle by integrating employer needs with personal strengths to create flexible and meaningful work opportunities. This approach encourages continuous adaptation, enabling roles to evolve as job demands, technologies, and individual performance levels change. Such flexibility supports long-term participation and reduces the rigidity associated with traditional job design.

6.5.1.4 Workplace Flexibility and Task Negotiation: Creating space for adaptation within work arrangements enhances the effectiveness of job customisation strategies. Flexible schedules, hybrid work models, and adjustable workflows offer opportunities to align responsibilities with individual capacities (Lazauskaite-Zabielske et al., 2021). Negotiation between employees and employers plays a central role in this process, allowing tasks and expectations to be refined to balance organisational goals with individual needs. In digitally mediated work environments, these practices are increasingly relevant as workers navigate shifting demands and resources (Zeshan et al., 2025; Lin et al., 2026).

6.5.1.5 Inclusive Job Design and Productivity Alignment: Ensuring that accessibility and efficiency coexist requires careful alignment between task allocation and performance expectations. Integrating principles of job carving and job crafting supports the development of roles that are both inclusive and productive. Matching tasks to individual strengths enhances output while reducing inefficiencies associated with poor job fitness. Continuous monitoring and adjustment remain essential to maintain this balance as organisational priorities and workforce capabilities evolve.

6.5.2 Practical Implications

Translating these strategies into practice requires coordinated efforts across multiple stakeholders. The following implications highlight how job customisation can be effectively implemented in organisational settings.

6.5.2.1 Implications for Managers: Leadership practices play a critical role in enabling adaptive work design. Creating environments that support autonomy, flexibility, and collaboration encourages employees to actively shape their roles (Demerouti et al., 2025). Attention to interpersonal dynamics is equally important, as workplace relationships influence how individuals engage with job crafting processes (Harju et al., 2023). Providing training and guidance equips supervisors to facilitate task negotiation and support inclusive employment practices (Mansour & Mohanna, 2024).

6.5.2.2 Implications for Organisations: Embedding flexibility within organisational systems enhances the capacity to respond to diverse workforce needs. Structured interventions aimed at supporting job crafting have been shown to improve engagement, resilience, and adaptability in dynamic work environments (Roczniewska et al., 2023). Adopting inclusive design approaches and flexible work models also strengthens retention and supports organisational performance by aligning roles with employee capabilities.

6.5.2.3 Implications for Employees: Active participation in shaping work roles enables individuals to improve both performance and job satisfaction. Adjusting tasks, strengthening workplace relationships, and redefining work meaning contribute to more positive employment experiences (Tims & Twemlow, 2024). For workers with intellectual disabilities, access to supportive environments and flexible role structures enhances independence and participation. Engaging in task negotiation further aligns individual strengths with job responsibilities, supporting long-term employment outcomes.

6.6 ALIGNING INDIVIDUAL STRENGTHS WITH WORKPLACE DEMANDS

Effective workplace inclusion depends on the extent to which individual capabilities align with job demands and organisational expectations. Aligning strengths with workplace requirements involves recognising employees' unique skills, interests, and attributes, and systematically integrating these into job roles. This approach shifts attention from standardised job requirements to flexible role design, ensuring that individuals are positioned to contribute meaningfully while maintaining performance standards.

6.6.1 Strategies for Aligning Individual Strengths with Workplace Demands

Achieving alignment requires deliberate strategies that connect individual capabilities with organisational needs while supporting sustained engagement and performance.

6.6.1.1 Strength-Based Deployment: Positioning employees in roles that reflect their strengths enhances both performance and long-term engagement. Strength-based deployment involves continuously matching individual abilities, interests, and attributes with job requirements, rather than relying on static job placements (Troger, 2022). This dynamic approach ensures that employees remain motivated and capable of performing effectively over time. It is particularly relevant for workers with intellectual disabilities, as it enables organisations to build roles around existing competencies rather than imposing rigid expectations.

6.6.1.2 Strengths Use and Job Engagement: Encouraging employees to apply their strengths in daily work activities contribute significantly to engagement, well-being, and productivity. The Job Demands–Resources (JD-R) framework explains that strengths use enhances motivation by fostering feelings of purpose, energy, and meaningfulness (Ilies et al., 2024; Bakker & Van Woerkom, 2018). Empirical evidence also shows that employees who actively use their strengths achieve higher performance and satisfaction (Zhang et al., 2025). In addition, strengths use supports broader outcomes such as improved work–life balance and reflective work practices, which further reinforce sustainable employment.

6.6.1.3 Person-Centred and Individualised Support Planning

Aligning strengths with workplace demands requires structured planning that considers both individual goals and support needs. Person-centred approaches, including Individual Support Plans (ISPs), provide a framework for identifying strengths, setting clear objectives, and outlining tailored support strategies (Shurack & Roling, 2014). These plans ensure that employees receive the resources and accommodation they need to perform effectively. In inclusive employment contexts, such planning is essential for creating pathways that support both productivity and well-being.

6.6.1.4 Job Crafting and Vocational Profiling: Allowing employees to shape aspects of their roles strengthens alignment between personal capabilities and job requirements. Job crafting enables individuals to adjust tasks, interactions, and perceptions of work in ways that reflect their strengths and interests (He, 2021). Complementing this, vocational profiling and interest inventories provide systematic methods for identifying individual strengths and matching them with suitable roles. These approaches enhance job fit by ensuring that role expectations align with individuals' abilities and aspirations.

6.6.1.5 Organisational Support and Leadership: Supportive organisational environments are critical for sustaining strengths alignment. Leadership practices that encourage autonomy, provide developmental opportunities, and recognise individual contributions create conditions in which employees can apply their strengths effectively (Bakker & Van Woerkom, 2018). Organisational support also includes access to training, mentoring, and resources that enable employees to develop and utilise their capabilities. Without such support, efforts to align strengths with job demands may remain limited in impact.

6.6.2 Benefits of Strengths Alignment

The alignment of personal strengths with job demands contributes to improved outcomes for employees, organisations, and employment systems.

6.6.2.1 Enhanced Employee Engagement and Well-Being: When employees can use their strengths, they experience greater authenticity, energy, and psychological well-being. Strengths use contributes to a sense of purpose and engagement, which are essential for sustained participation in the workplace (Bakker & Van Woerkom, 2018). These outcomes are particularly important for workers with intellectual disabilities, as they support confidence and independence.

6.6.2.2 Improved Performance and Productivity: Matching job demands with individual strengths leads to more efficient task performance and improved organisational outcomes. Employees are likely to perform better when their roles align with their skills and capabilities, resulting in greater productivity and fewer errors (Zhang et al., 2025). Such alignment also strengthens adaptability, enabling employees to respond more effectively to changing workplace demands and challenges.

6.6.2.3 Sustainability in Employment: Sustained alignment between strengths and job demands supports long-term employment outcomes. Strength-based approaches reduce physical and mental strain, improve job satisfaction, and increase organisational commitment (Troger, 2022; Hodges & Asplund, 2009). This contributes to lower turnover rates and more stable workforce participation. For individuals with intellectual disabilities, such sustainability is critical for achieving long-term inclusion and economic independence.

Aligning individual strengths with workplace demands, therefore, represents a central strategy in inclusive employment systems. By integrating strength-based deployment, supportive organisational practices, and continuous role adjustment, organisations can create work environments that support both performance and meaningful participation.

6.7 WORKPLACE SUPPORTS AND REASONABLE ACCOMMODATIONS

Workplace support and reasonable accommodation play a central role in enabling employees with disabilities to perform effectively and participate fully in organisational life. These supports involve structured adjustments to tasks, environments, tools, and organisational processes, ensuring that employees can meet job expectations while maintaining well-being and productivity. The provision of accommodation reflects a commitment to equality, recognising that individuals may require different forms of support to achieve comparable outcomes in the workplace.

6.7.1 Types of Workplace Accommodations

Providing appropriate accommodation requires a clear understanding of the range of supports available within workplace settings.

6.7.1.1 Assistive Technology: Enhancing accessibility and task performance often involves the use of assistive technologies, including tools that support communication, information access, and task efficiency. These technologies enable employees to work more independently while improving accuracy and productivity (Stoddard & Kraus, 2006).

6.7.1.2 Flexible Work Arrangements: Adjustments to work schedules and structures create opportunities for employees to manage job demands effectively. Flexible hours, teleworking, reduced workloads, and modified job duties support sustained participation and improved work outcomes (McDowell & Fossey, 2015; Urrejola-Contreras et al., 2025).

6.7.1.3 Environmental Modifications: Addressing physical and organisational barriers enhances accessibility in the workplace. Modifications such as accessible facilities, adapted equipment, and improved workspace layouts support mobility, safety, and effective task performance.

6.7.1.4 Job Coaching and Support Services: Structured support through job coaching and employment services facilitates workplace integration. These supports help employees understand job expectations, develop skills, and navigate workplace interactions (Ortiz-Marcos et al., 2024).

6.7.1.5 Personal Assistance Services: Providing direct support for specific tasks can be essential in certain contexts. Personal assistance services enable employees to perform job-related activities that may otherwise be difficult to manage independently.

6.7.2 Barriers to Accessing Accommodations

A range of social, organisational, and structural factors influences access to workplace supports.

6.7.2.1 Stigma and Disclosure Challenges: Concerns about stigma influence decisions to request accommodations. Fear of negative perceptions or potential career consequences often discourages employees from disclosing their needs (Sanrey et al., 2026; Gonzalez et al., 2020).

6.7.2.2 Organisational and Managerial Gaps: The absence of clear policies, inconsistent procedures, and limited managerial awareness can restrict access to accommodations. In some cases, managers lack the knowledge or resources required to respond effectively (Thomson et al., 2026; Taylor & Wituk, 2025).

6.7.2.3 Cost Concerns: Perceptions of high costs can discourage the implementation of accommodation, even though many adjustments require minimal financial investment (de Jonge & Gibson, 2009).

6.7.2.4 Occupational Segregation: Concentration of workers with disabilities in specific roles can limit access to flexible accommodations, particularly in jobs with rigid structures (Shinall, 2022).

6.7.3 Facilitators of Effective Accommodations:

Effective implementation of workplace supports is strengthened by enabling organisational conditions.

6.7.3.1 Supportive Workplace Culture: Inclusive supervision, collaborative leadership, and positive co-worker relationships enhance the success of accommodations by creating environments that value diversity (Dong et al., 2022; Hyseni et al., 2023).

6.7.3.2 Centralised Accommodation Budgets: Allocating resources at an organisational level reduces financial barriers and encourages departments to provide necessary accommodations without budget constraints (Stoddard & Kraus, 2006).

6.7.3.3 Education and Awareness: Training programmes that increase understanding of accommodation needs and legal obligations improve communication and implementation processes (Taylor & Wituk, 2025).

6.7.3.4 Communities of Practice: Collaborative learning networks support knowledge sharing and continuous improvement in inclusive workplace practices (Gendera et al., 2025).

6.7.4 Benefits of Workplace Supports and Accommodations

Providing accommodations generates positive outcomes for individuals and organisations.

6.7.4.1 Improved Job Retention and Performance: Access to appropriate supports enhances job satisfaction, productivity, and long-term retention (Gold et al., 2012; Rumrill et al., 2023).

6.7.4.2 Cost-Effectiveness: Many accommodations involve minimal cost while contributing to financial benefits such as reduced turnover and training expenses (de Jonge & Gibson, 2009).

6.7.4.3 Cultural Transformation: Inclusive practices foster diversity, improve workplace culture, and enhance overall organisational well-being.

6.7.5 Recommendations for Improvement

Strengthening workplace supports requires coordinated action across policy and practice.

6.7.5.1 Streamlined Policies: Clear and accessible procedures for requesting and implementing accommodations improve consistency and reduce uncertainty (Thomson et al., 2026).

6.7.5.2 Legislative Enhancements: Strengthening legal frameworks addresses gaps in access and enforcement, supporting more effective implementation (Cuervo-Botero et al., 2025).

6.7.5.3 Focus on Inclusion: Promoting inclusive workplace cultures and addressing attitudinal barriers enhances psychological safety and encourages employees to seek support (Gonzalez et al., 2020; Hyseni et al., 2023).

6.8 ORGANISATIONAL BENEFITS AND BUSINESS CASE FOR JOB CUSTOMISATION

Positioning job customisation within organisational strategy requires a clear articulation of its value, particularly when considered alongside job analysis processes, role redesign strategies, strengths alignment, and workplace supports discussed in preceding sections. Aligning roles with individual capabilities creates conditions in which organisations can optimise human capital while responding to evolving labour market demands. This section examines how job customisation strengthens organisational outcomes through diversity, productivity, retention, and strategic investment decisions.

6.8.1 Business Case for Inclusion and Workforce Diversity

Integrating diverse talent into organisational systems introduces a broader range of perspectives, experiences, and problem-solving approaches. Diversity initiatives framed around competitive advantage often generate stronger employee engagement and more positive workplace attitudes (Kulik & Roberson, 2008). Varied viewpoints contribute to improved decision-making processes and enable organisations to respond more effectively to diverse customer needs. Embedding job customisation within diversity strategies strengthens these outcomes by ensuring that individuals are positioned in roles where their capabilities can be fully utilised. This alignment reflects earlier discussions on structuring roles through job carving and crafting processes, which create opportunities for meaningful participation across diverse workforce groups. In inclusive employment contexts, such practices reinforce organisational legitimacy while expanding access to talent that might otherwise remain underutilised.

6.8.2 Productivity Outcomes

Tailoring roles to align with individual strengths and preferences creates measurable gains in productivity. Adjustments to workload, task structure, and pace allow employees to perform more efficiently while maintaining quality standards (Straub et al., 2020). These gains are reinforced when job analysis methods are used to identify task requirements and when job customisation strategies redistribute tasks in ways that reflect individual capability profiles.

Technological and organisational customisation initiatives further demonstrate productivity improvements. Evidence from digital transformation contexts indicates reductions in training costs and shorter timeframes for achieving competency (Hoske, 2023a; Hoske, 2023b). These outcomes illustrate how aligning work processes with user capabilities enhances operational efficiency. When combined with strength-based alignment practices, such as those outlined in earlier sections, organisations can achieve more consistent and sustainable performance outcomes.

6.8.3 Employee Retention and Organisational Performance

Sustaining a stable and engaged workforce requires alignment between employee expectations and organisational structures. Customised career pathways provide individuals with opportunities to adjust their workloads, schedules, and responsibilities to reflect changing personal and professional priorities (Straub et al., 2020). These adjustments resonate with earlier discussions on strengths alignment, where roles are shaped to reflect individual preferences and capabilities. Work environments that reflect individual identities and preferences also contribute to stronger organisational commitment. Personalised workspaces and flexible role arrangements have been associated with improved morale and reduced turnover (Wells et al., 2007). Retention gains are further strengthened when workplace support and accommodation are integrated into organisational systems, enabling employees to sustain performance over time. These combined practices contribute to improved organisational performance by reducing recruitment costs and enhancing continuity.

6.8.4 Inclusive Human Resource Practices and Workplace Culture

Embedding job customisation within human resource practices supports the development of inclusive organisational cultures. Approaches such as Mass Career Customisation (MCC) create structured pathways for accommodating diverse employee needs, including variations in career progression and work intensity (Straub et al., 2020). These practices extend earlier discussions on workplace flexibility and task negotiation, reinforcing the role of adaptable work structures in promoting inclusion. At the same time, implementation requires attention to organisational norms and perceptions. Flexibility stigma may arise when employees who utilise customised arrangements are viewed as deviating from standard expectations. Addressing such perceptions through inclusive leadership and supportive organisational policies strengthens the effectiveness of job customisation and complements the role of workplace supports in fostering equitable participation.

6.8.5 Cost–Benefit Considerations

Implementing job customisation involves both direct and indirect costs, including investment in systems development, training, and organisational restructuring. Evaluating these costs alongside potential gains in performance, retention, and employee satisfaction is essential for informed decision-making. Evidence from organisational systems customisation indicates that value is realised when adjustments are strategically aligned with organisational goals (Aslam et al., 2012; Balint, 2015; Balint, 2020). This reinforces earlier arguments on the importance of systematic job analysis and structured role design, where alignment between tasks and capabilities enhances efficiency. Poorly targeted customisation can increase complexity, while carefully designed interventions strengthen organisational effectiveness.

Balancing flexibility with standardisation ensures that individual adjustments contribute to broader organisational objectives. When job customisation is implemented alongside strengths alignment and workplace support, organisations can create a coherent system in which inclusion and performance mutually reinforce one another. Aligning job customisation with organisational strategy strengthens the capacity to integrate diverse talent, enhance productivity, and sustain workforce engagement. Through coordinated application of job analysis, role redesign, strengths alignment, and workplace support, organisations can create adaptive systems that support both performance and inclusion while maintaining long-term effectiveness.

6.9 CHALLENGES, RISKS, AND IMPLEMENTATION BARRIERS

Advancing inclusive employment through job analysis, customisation, strengths alignment, and workplace support requires coordinated implementation across organisational systems. While the preceding sections have outlined structured pathways to achieving inclusion, translating these approaches into practice is often constrained by interrelated challenges. These constraints operate at organisational, individual, and systemic levels, influencing the extent to which inclusive employment initiatives can be sustained and scaled.

6.9.1 Cost Concerns and Financial Constraints

Financial considerations remain a central concern in implementing job customisation and inclusive workplace practices. Investment is required for assistive technologies, training programmes, job coaching, and organisational restructuring. For smaller organisations and those operating within resource-constrained environments, these costs can limit the adoption of inclusive practices (Dahooie et al., 2022; Zsifkovits et al., 2021). These constraints are particularly evident when implementing the workplace support discussed in Section 6.7, where initial investment may be perceived as disproportionate to expected returns. Although long-term organisational benefits have been established in Section 6.8, short-term financial pressures often influence decision-making, leading to delayed or partial implementation of inclusive strategies.

6.9.2 Training Gaps and Capacity Limitations

Effective implementation of job customisation relies on organisational capacity, including the availability of skilled personnel and structured training systems. Gaps in training frameworks can limit managers' and employees' ability to engage with job analysis methods (Section 6.4) and role redesign strategies (Section 6.5). A lack of clarity in identifying required competencies, insufficient documentation practices, and limited understanding of inclusive employment processes contribute to weak implementation outcomes (Sigle & Hertweck, 2026). In addition, shortages of skilled professionals capable of supporting inclusive workplace technologies and adaptive work systems further constrain progress (Macurová et al., 2017). These challenges highlight the importance of continuous learning systems and knowledge-sharing practices within organisations.

6.9.3 Policy Limitations and Institutional Gaps

Policy frameworks play a critical role in shaping inclusive employment systems; however, limitations in policy design and implementation can hinder progress. Rapid changes in labour markets, including digitalisation and the expansion of non-standard employment arrangements, place pressure on existing regulatory systems (Niederfranke & Drewes, 2017). These institutional gaps affect the implementation of Competitive Integrated Employment principles discussed in Section 6.2, particularly in contexts where policy enforcement is inconsistent or fragmented. Without strong alignment between policy, organisational practice, and support systems, inclusive employment initiatives may remain aspirational rather than operational.

6.9.4 Workplace Bias, Stigma, and Inclusion Risks

Attitudinal barriers continue to influence the effectiveness of inclusive employment practices. Employer misconceptions about the capabilities and productivity of individuals with intellectual disabilities can affect recruitment, role allocation, and performance evaluation. Such biases undermine the strength-based alignment strategies outlined in Section 6.6 and limit opportunities for meaningful participation. In addition, the risk of tokenistic hiring arises when inclusion is treated as a symbolic activity rather than a substantive organisational commitment. In such cases, employees may be placed in roles without adequate alignment, support, or opportunities for progression. Workplace bias also affects the implementation of accommodations, as limited awareness of inclusive practices and ergonomic considerations can restrict access to necessary supports (Tompa et al., 2025).

6.9.5 Resource Constraints and Organisational Readiness

Organisational readiness plays a critical role in determining the success of inclusive employment initiatives. Limited financial, human, and technological resources can restrict the implementation of job customisation strategies, particularly in smaller organisations (Dahooie et al., 2022). These constraints affect multiple stages of the inclusive employment pathway, including job analysis, role redesign, and the provision of workplace supports. Without adequate resources, organisations may struggle to sustain the continuous adjustment processes required for effective person–environment alignment. This limitation underscores the need for scalable, context-sensitive implementation approaches.

6.9.6 Systemic Barriers and Resistance to Change

Broader systemic factors also shape the implementation of inclusive employment practices. Competitive pressures, volatile demand, and cost-driven operational models can limit an organisation's willingness to adopt flexible and inclusive approaches (Macurová et al., 2017). Resistance to change further complicates implementation. Employees and managers accustomed to traditional job structures may be reluctant to adopt new practices such as job carving, task redistribution, and adaptive work systems introduced in Section 6.5. These mental and cultural barriers can slow the transition toward inclusive organisational models, even when structural conditions are favourable. Systemic barriers also interact with organisational and individual factors, creating complex challenges that require coordinated responses across multiple levels of the employment system.

6.9.7 Navigating Implementation Risks

Addressing implementation challenges requires a coordinated approach that integrates policy, organisational practice, leadership commitment, and continuous evaluation. Organisations should strengthen internal capacity through staff training, managerial development, and investment in inclusive workplace systems. Promoting awareness and reducing stigma can improve acceptance of workplace accommodations and strengthen the effectiveness of strengths-based employment practices. Collaboration among employers, policymakers, educational institutions, and support service providers can further enhance implementation by improving access to resources and expertise, and by coordinating support. Continuous monitoring and feedback mechanisms are also important for identifying emerging barriers and refining inclusive employment strategies. Although financial, organisational, and systemic challenges remain, proactive planning and sustained commitment can support the successful implementation of job analysis, role customisation, workplace accommodations, and inclusive employment practices.

6.10 INTEGRATED FRAMEWORK FOR PRACTICE AND CONCLUSION

Translating inclusive employment into sustained organisational practice requires a coherent framework that integrates job analysis, role customisation, strengths alignment, and workplace support into a unified system. The preceding sections have established a sequential pathway; this section consolidates these elements into an applied framework that guides implementation, coordination, and long-term sustainability. The emphasis shifts from isolated strategies to system-level integration, where organisational structures, policies, and practices align.

6.10.1 Integrated Framework for Practice: Operationalising inclusive employment begins with systematic job analysis, which provides the evidence base for identifying task structures, competency requirements, and opportunities for adaptation. These insights inform job carving, job crafting, and role redesign strategies, ensuring that work is configured to reflect both organisational objectives and individual capabilities. The framework progresses through alignment of individual strengths with workplace demands. Strength-based deployment and person-centred planning ensure that employees are positioned in roles where they can contribute effectively.

This alignment is reinforced by workplace supports and accommodations that address environmental and organisational barriers to performance. Policy integration strengthens consistency and accountability by aligning organisational practices with broader regulatory frameworks. Recruitment, training, performance management, and accessibility policies must support inclusive employment outcomes rather than function as isolated compliance measures. Organisational strategy plays a central role in sustaining these practices. Leadership commitment, resource allocation, and performance metrics must reflect the importance of inclusive employment as a strategic priority. Embedding inclusion within organisational planning ensures continuity and long-term impact.

6.10.2 Multi-Stakeholder Collaboration and Implementation Systems: Effective implementation requires collaboration across multiple stakeholders, including employers, employees, policymakers, educators, and support service providers. Each stakeholder contributes expertise and resources that strengthen inclusive employment systems.

Partnerships with external service providers enhance access to specialised support, such as vocational assessment, job coaching, and assistive technologies. Collaboration with educational institutions supports transition pathways into employment, while policymakers establish frameworks that promote inclusion and accountability. Within organisations, cross-functional coordination aligns human resource practices, operational processes, and leadership strategies. This integration ensures that inclusive employment practices are embedded across departments. Implementation systems must also include feedback mechanisms that support adaptation. Continuous communication among stakeholders enables organisations to identify challenges, refine strategies, and remain responsive to changing conditions.

6.10.3 Monitoring, Evaluation, and Continuous Improvement: Sustaining inclusive employment requires systematic monitoring and evaluation processes. Performance indicators should capture outcomes such as employee engagement, productivity, retention, and workplace inclusion. Data from job analysis, performance assessments, and workplace evaluations provide insight into the effectiveness of job customisation and support strategies. Regular review of these data enables organisations to identify gaps and improve practices. Qualitative measures, including employee experiences and organisational culture, provide additional depth to the evaluation of inclusion. Continuous improvement is achieved through iterative cycles of assessment, reflection, and adaptation, ensuring that practices remain effective over time.

6.10.4 Best Practices, Scalable Systems, and Conclusion: Establishing effective practice requires integrating job analysis with role customisation, aligning tasks with individual strengths, and embedding workplace supports within organisational systems. These elements form the foundation of scalable inclusion systems that can be adapted across different organisational contexts. Scalability is achieved through flexible frameworks and clear practice guidelines that maintain core principles while allowing contextual adaptation. Investment in training, leadership development, and organisational capacity strengthens the sustainability of these systems.

Clear practice guidelines should prioritise comprehensive job analysis, structured role redesign, strength-based alignment, and integrated workplace supports. Policy alignment and leadership commitment ensure that these practices are embedded within organisational strategy, while stakeholder collaboration and monitoring systems support continuous refinement.

This integrated framework positions inclusive employment as a coordinated system of practices rather than a discrete intervention. By aligning analysis, design, and support within organisational strategy, workplaces can achieve both performance outcomes and meaningful inclusion, demonstrating that productivity and equity can be advanced in parallel.

CONCLUSION

Creating meaningful employment opportunities for individuals with intellectual and developmental disabilities requires more than access to jobs; it requires workplaces that intentionally align organisational needs with individual strengths, abilities, and support requirements. This chapter examined the role of job analysis, role redesign, strengths-based alignment, and workplace accommodations in promoting inclusive employment practices. Attention was given to how these approaches can support job performance, workplace participation, and long-term employment sustainability.

The discussion highlighted that inclusive employment is strengthened when organisations adopt flexible approaches to job design and recognise the diversity of abilities that workers bring to the workplace. Effective workplace accommodations, supportive organisational cultures, and collaborative implementation processes can contribute to more accessible employment environments. The chapter also considered implementation challenges, including organisational, financial, and systemic barriers that may affect the adoption of inclusive employment practices.

As organisations continue to pursue workforce diversity and inclusion, the principles discussed in this chapter provide practical guidance for developing employment systems that support participation, contribution, and workplace success among individuals with intellectual and developmental disabilities. By integrating inclusive job design, strengths-based approaches, and appropriate workplace supports, employers can create environments that facilitate meaningful and sustainable employment opportunities.

REFERENCES

Andre, T., Meyer, R., Chik, K., & Lofgren, E. (2015). Experience Map: A tool to help training managers develop learning experiences. *Procedia Manufacturing*, *3*, 1511–1518. DOI: 10.1016/j.promfg.2015.07.405

Aslam, U., Coombs, C., & Doherty, N. F. (2012). Benefits realisation from ERP systems: The role of customisation. In ECIS 2012 - Proceedings of the 20th European Conference on Information Systems.

Bakker, A. B., & Van Woerkom, M. (2018). Strengths used in organisations: A positive approach to occupational health. *Canadian Psychology*, *59*(1), 38–46. DOI: 10.1037/cap0000120

Balint, B. (2015). Obtaining value from the customisation of packaged business software: A model and simulation. *International Journal of Enterprise Information Systems*, *11*(1), 33–49. DOI: 10.4018/ijeis.2015010103

Balint, B. (2020). To code or not to code: Obtaining value from the customisation of packaged application software. In *Research Anthology on Recent Trends, Tools, and Implications of Computer Programming* (pp. 1426–1445). IGI Global. DOI: 10.4018/978-1-7998-3016-0.ch065

Brannick, M. T., Cadle, A., & Levine, E. L. (2012). Job analysis for knowledge, skills, abilities, and other characteristics, predictor measures, and performance outcomes. In *The Oxford Handbook of Personnel Assessment and Selection*. Oxford University Press., DOI: 10.1093/oxfordhb/9780199732579.013.0007

Bredgaard, T. (2025). Inclusive job design. In *Shaping Inclusive Workplaces for Persons with Disabilities: A Management and HRM Practitioner Perspective* (pp. 85–95). Springer., DOI: 10.1007/978-3-031-96315-5_7

Carus, I., & Messina, M. (2025). Skills for life, skills for careers, skills for inclusion. *European Public and Social Innovation Review, 10*. Advance online publication. DOI: 10.31637/epsir-2025-1721

Caughron, J. J., Peterson, D. K., & Mumford, T. V. (2013). Job analysis. In *The Encyclopedia of Human Resource Management*. Wiley.

Cavanagh, J., Meacham, H., Pariona-Cabrera, P., & Bartram, T. (2021). Subtle workplace discrimination inhibiting workers with intellectual disability from thriving at the workplace. *Personnel Review*, *50*(7–8), 1739–1756. DOI: 10.1108/PR-10-2021-0723

Cheng, C., Oakman, J., & Bigby, C. (2015). Supported employment for people with intellectual disability: A systematic review. *Journal of Intellectual Disability Research*, *59*(12), 1109–1122.

Cuervo-Botero, G.-R., Zuñiga-Bolívar, S.-M., Abella-León, C., & Betancur-Agudelo, J.-E. (2025). Reasonable accommodations for the social and productive inclusion of persons with disabilities in Colombia: Progress and implementation challenges. *Prisma Social*, (50), 189–219. DOI: 10.65598/rps.5859

Dahooie, J. H., Habibollahi, H., & Qorbani, A. R. (2022). Identifying and prioritizing barriers of Industry 4.0 adoption, using fuzzy Delphi and group ZBWM: A case study in an emerging economy. In *Lecture Notes in Operations Research* (pp. 209–227). Springer., DOI: 10.1007/978-3-030-89795-6_15

Dall, M. (2026). Job matching for people with disabilities: A systematic review. *Journal of Vocational Rehabilitation*, *64*(2), 145–160.

De Gennaro, D. (2019). *Job crafting: The art of redesigning a job*. FrancoAngeli. DOI: 10.1108/9781838672195

de Jonge, D., & Gibson, L. (2009). Effective utilization of assistive devices in the workplace. In *Ergonomics for Rehabilitation Professionals* (pp. 477–506). CRC Press. DOI: 10.1201/9780849382697.ch14

Demerouti, E., Peeters, M., & Van den Heuvel, M. (2025). Job crafting interventions. In *Transformative Work Design: Synthesis and New Directions* (pp. 439–464). Oxford University Press. DOI: 10.1093/oso/9780197692554.003.0017

Dong, S., Hespe, P., & Monagas, K. (2022). Requesting workplace accommodation among individuals with mobility disabilities: A qualitative investigation on barriers and facilitators. *Journal of Applied Rehabilitation Counseling*, *53*(3), 193–209. DOI: 10.1891/JARC-D-21-00005

DuBois, D. L.. (2025). Person-centered planning and employment outcomes for adults with intellectual disabilities. *Intellectual and Developmental Disabilities*, *63*(1), 22–35.

Dunckel, H. (2015). Job analysis and work roles, psychology of. In *International Encyclopedia of the Social & Behavioral Sciences* (2nd ed., pp. 811–815). Elsevier., DOI: 10.1016/B978-0-08-097086-8.22009-6

Ellington, J. K., Rehwaldt, R., & Knapp, S. (2015). Job analysis in human resource management. *The Journal of Applied Psychology*, *100*(3), 789–802.

Finstad, G. L.. (2022). Barriers to employment for individuals with intellectual disabilities: A systematic review. *Journal of Vocational Rehabilitation*, *56*(3), 245–260.

Gendera, S., Alexander, J., Burton, J., Fisher, K. R., & Robinson, S. (2025). People with disability influencing sustained improvements to employment. *Social Policy and Administration*. Advance online publication. DOI: 10.1111/spol.70022

Ghanbari, Z., Abouee-Mehrizi, A., Rasoulzadeh, Y., & Hokmabadi, R. (2024). Psychometric properties of the Persian version of the Fleishman Job Analysis Survey (FJAS). *Work (Reading, Mass.)*, *77*(1), 113–121. DOI: 10.3233/WOR-220004 PMID: 37483042

Gold, P. B., Oire, S. N., Fabian, E. S., & Wewiorski, N. J. (2012). Negotiating reasonable workplace accommodations: Perspectives of employers, employees with disabilities, and rehabilitation service providers. *Journal of Vocational Rehabilitation*, *37*(1), 25–37. DOI: 10.3233/JVR-2012-0597

Gonzalez, K., Tillman, C. J., & Holmes, J. J. (2020). Coming home: Why veterans with disabilities withhold workplace accommodation requests. *Human Relations*, *73*(10), 1439–1466. DOI: 10.1177/0018726719875810

Hanvey, C. (2018). Data collection methods. In *Wage and Hour Law: Guide to Methods and Analysis* (pp. 19–46). Springer. DOI: 10.1007/978-3-319-74612-8_2

Harju, L. K., Tims, M., Hakanen, J. J., & Khapova, S. N. (2023). Crafting for oneself while considering others: How the relational design of work shapes job crafting. *International Journal of Human Resource Management*, *35*(1), 67–97. DOI: 10.1080/09585192.2023.2211711

He, Y. (2021). Research on job crafting based on the theory of strength perspective. *IOP Conference Series. Earth and Environmental Science*, *632*(4), 042034. Advance online publication. DOI: 10.1088/1755-1315/632/4/042034

Hodges, T. D., & Asplund, J. (2009). Strengths development in the workplace. In *Oxford Handbook of Positive Psychology and Work*. Oxford University Press., DOI: 10.1093/oxfordhb/9780195335446.013.0017

Hoske, M. T. (2023a). How control-system integration advances competitiveness. *Control Engineering*, *70*(3), 29.

Hoske, M. T. (2023b). How to determine ROI and get buy-in for workforce digital transformation. *Control Engineering*, *70*(3), 27.

Hyseni, F., Kruse, D., Schur, L., & Blanck, P. (2023). Disability, workplace inclusion and organizational citizenship behaviour: An exploratory study of the legal profession. *Journal of Participation and Employee Ownership*, *6*(1), 31–50. DOI: 10.1108/JPEO-10-2022-0017 PMID: 38528853

Ilies, R., Liu, Y., Aw, S., Heras, M. L., & Rofcanin, Y. (2024). Why does using personal strengths at work increase employee engagement? Who makes the most out of it, and how? *Journal of Occupational Health Psychology*, *29*(2), 113–129. DOI: 10.1037/ocp0000374 PMID: 38647463

Jordán de Urríes, F. B., & Verdugo, M. Á. (2012). Sheltered employment versus supported employment: A review of the literature. *Journal of Vocational Rehabilitation*, *37*(2), 85–95.

Kittinger, R., & Bender, J. (2015). Methods for determining the role of fatigue and cognitive load on behaviour detection officers' (BDOs) performance in the field. *Lecture Notes in Computer Science*, *9183*, 36–43. DOI: 10.1007/978-3-319-20816-9_4

Kulik, C. T., & Roberson, L. (2008). Diversity initiative effectiveness: What organisations can (and cannot) expect from diversity recruitment, diversity training, and formal mentoring programs. In *Diversity at Work* (pp. 265–317). Cambridge University Press., DOI: 10.1017/CBO9780511753725.010

Lazauskaite-Zabielske, J., Ziedelis, A., & Urbanaviciute, I. (2021). Who benefits from time-spatial job crafting? The role of boundary characteristics in the relationship between time-spatial job crafting, engagement and performance. *Baltic Journal of Management*, *16*(1), 1–19. DOI: 10.1108/BJM-07-2020-0236

Lin, Q., Sun, R., & Zhu, Q. (2026). Adaptive job recrafting of gig workers: Concept, measurement, and validation of its impact on job satisfaction. *Acta Psychologica*, *262*, 106034. Advance online publication. DOI: 10.1016/j.actpsy.2025.106034 PMID: 41351970

Lin, S.-C., & Lehto, M. R. (2007). A Bayesian methodology for semi-automated task analysis. *Lecture Notes in Computer Science*, *4557*(1), 697–704. DOI: 10.1007/978-3-540-73345-4_79

Macurová, P., Ludvík, L., & Žwaková, M. (2017). The driving factors, risks and barriers of the Industry 4.0 concept. *Journal of Applied Economic Sciences*, *12*(7), 2003–2011.

Mansour, S., & Mohanna, D. (2024). How does organisational support for innovation influence job crafting and knowledge sharing behaviours? A comparison between teleworkers and office workers. *International Journal of Manpower*, *45*(9), 1673–1700. DOI: 10.1108/IJM-02-2024-0106

McDowell, C., & Fossey, E. (2015). Workplace accommodations for people with mental illness: A scoping review. *Journal of Occupational Rehabilitation*, *25*(1), 197–206. DOI: 10.1007/s10926-014-9512-y PMID: 24841728

Meacham, H., Bartram, T., & Cavanagh, J. (2020). Career management: The transition process for workers with disabilities. In *The Palgrave Handbook of Disability at Work* (pp. 99–114). Palgrave Macmillan., DOI: 10.1007/978-3-030-42966-9_6

Menachery, T. J. (2018). Employees shaping their own jobs: How to enable job crafting? *Human Resource Management International Digest*, *26*(5), 27–29. DOI: 10.1108/HRMID-05-2018-0106

Migliore, A., Mank, D., Grossi, T., & Rogan, P. (2008). Integrated employment or sheltered workshops: Preferences of adults with intellectual disabilities. *Journal of Vocational Rehabilitation*, *29*(1), 23–32.

Moore, C., & Friedman, M. (2017). Informed choice in employment for people with intellectual disabilities. *Journal of Policy and Practice in Intellectual Disabilities*, *14*(2), 123–130.

Mostafa, A., & Wang, W. (2023). Competitive integrated employment for people with disabilities: A systematic review of policy and practice. *Disability and Rehabilitation*, *45*(12), 1945–1958.

Niederfranke, A., & Drewes, M. (2017). Non-standard forms of employment in a globalised world: Risk of undermining labour standards and social security provisions? *Sozialer Fortschritt*, *66*(12), 919–934. DOI: 10.3790/sfo.66.12.919

Novak, J. (2015). Social inclusion and employment for people with intellectual disabilities. *Journal of Intellectual Disability Research*, *59*(8), 765–774.

Novikov, I. (2025). Beyond inclusion: How people with disabilities are involved in business. *Zhurnal Issledovanii Sotsial'noi Politiki*, *23*(2), 289–308. DOI: 10.17323/727-0634-2025-23-2-289-308

Ortiz-Marcos, J. M., Invernón-Gómez, A. I., Medina-García, M., & Higueras-Rodríguez, L. (2024). Workplace inclusion of people with disabilities: Legislative challenges and practical solutions. *Revista Española de Orientación y Psicopedagogía*, *35*(3), 105–122. DOI: 10.5944/reop.vol.35.num.3.2024.40820

Persson, H., Åhman, H., Yngling, A. A., & Gulliksen, J. (2015). Universal design, inclusive design, accessible design, design for all: Different concepts—one goal? On the concept of accessibility—historical, methodological and philosophical aspects. *Universal Access in the Information Society*, *14*(4), 505–526. DOI: 10.1007/s10209-014-0358-z

Quintana, M.. (2022). Job coaching and supported employment for individuals with intellectual disabilities: A meta-analysis. *Journal of Applied Research in Intellectual Disabilities*, *35*(3), 631–644.

Rachanioti, E.. (2021). Barriers to employment for people with intellectual disabilities: A systematic review. *Journal of Vocational Rehabilitation*, *54*(2), 117–130.

Roberts, R. C., & Flin, R. (2016). Behavioural rating of drillers' cognitive skills. In *SPE International Conference and Exhibition on Health, Safety, Security, Environment, and Social Responsibility*. Society of Petroleum Engineers. DOI: 10.2118/179270-MS

Robinson, M. A. (2010). Work sampling: Methodological advances and new applications. *Human Factors and Ergonomics in Manufacturing*, *20*(1), 42–60. DOI: 10.1002/hfm.20186

Roczniewska, M., Rogala, A., Marszałek, M., Hasson, H., Bakker, A. B., & von Thiele Schwarz, U. (2023). Job crafting interventions: What works, for whom, why, and in which contexts? Research protocol for a systematic review with coincidence analysis. *Systematic Reviews*, *12*(1), 10. Advance online publication. DOI: 10.1186/s13643-023-02170-z PMID: 36670492

Rumrill, P. D., Rumrill, S. P., Wickert, K., Sheppard-Jones, K., Baumunk, M., & Roessler, R. T. (2023). A 'win-win' perspective on workplace accommodations: RETAIN Kentucky's self-advocacy guide to promote successful return to work and stay at work outcomes for workers with disabilities. *Work (Reading, Mass.)*, *74*(1), 3–10. DOI: 10.3233/WOR-223651 PMID: 36463483

Sanrey, C., Conguista, T., Beyer, H., & Rohmer, O. (2026). Determinants of legal disclosure intentions in academia. *Disability & Society*, *41*(6), 1445–1469. Advance online publication. DOI: 10.1080/09687599.2026.2640939

Shabani, M., Heidarimoghadam, R., Faradmal, J., & Babamiri, M. (2025). Identify the cognitive, psychomotor and sensory-perceptual abilities required for the role of pre-hospital emergency medical personnel. *Work (Reading, Mass.)*, *80*(4), 1607–1616. DOI: 10.1177/10519815241295907 PMID: 40337819

Shinall, J. B. (2022). Without accommodation. *Industrial Law Journal, 97*(4), 1147–1201.

Shurack, N. Y., & Roling, C. (2014). Incorporating the concept of quality of life in individual support plans. In *Quality of Life and Intellectual Disability: Knowledge Application to Other Social and Educational Challenges* (pp. 265–283). Nova Science Publishers.

Sigle, N., & Hertweck, D. (2026). Identification of barriers that lead to problems in the further training of employees. *Communications in Computer and Information Science, 2787*, 265–276. DOI: 10.1007/978-3-032-15463-7_22

Soeker, S.. (2021). Employer attitudes towards hiring people with intellectual disabilities: A systematic review. *Journal of Vocational Rehabilitation, 55*(1), 45–58.

Stoddard, S., & Kraus, L. (2006). Arranging for personal assistance services and assistive technology at work. A report of the rehabilitation research and training centre on personal assistance services. *Disability and Rehabilitation. Assistive Technology, 1*(1–2), 89–95. DOI: 10.1080/09638280500167365 PMID: 19256171

Strah, N., & Rupp, D. E. (2022). The role of job analysis in promoting workplace inclusion. *Journal of Business and Psychology, 37*(4), 789–805.

Straub, C., Vinkenburg, C. J., & van Kleef, M. (2020). Career customisation: Putting an organisational practice to facilitate sustainable careers to the test. *Journal of Vocational Behavior, 117*, 103320. Advance online publication. DOI: 10.1016/j.jvb.2019.103320

Sulewski, J. S.. (2017). From sheltered workshops to integrated employment: A review of the literature. *Journal of Vocational Rehabilitation, 46*(3), 273–284.

Suresh, V., & Dyaram, L. (2020). Workplace disability inclusion in India: Review and directions. *Management Research Review, 43*(12), 1545–1562. DOI: 10.1108/MRR-11-2019-0479

Suresh, V., & Dyaram, L. (2023). Job matching for persons with disabilities: An exploratory study. *Employee Responsibilities and Rights Journal, 35*(4), 475–492. DOI: 10.1007/s10672-022-09421-6

Taylor, M.. (2022). Competitive integrated employment for individuals with intellectual and developmental disabilities: A systematic review of outcomes. *Journal of Vocational Rehabilitation, 56*(2), 123–140.

Taylor, M. A., & Wituk, E. (2025). Reasonable accommodation for neurodiversity: Legal, organizational, and managerial considerations. *Employee Responsibilities and Rights Journal*. Advance online publication. DOI: 10.1007/s10672-025-09546-4

Thomson, A. E., Van Mulligen, L., Winsor Murray, J., Adair, J., Schira, H. R., Ramage, M., & Torres-Salbach, S. (2026). Workplace accommodations for nurses who experience disabilities: A scoping review. *Canadian Journal of Nursing Research*, 08445621261430964. Advance online publication. DOI: 10.1177/08445621261430964 PMID: 41787870

Tims, M., & Twemlow, M. (2024). A contemporary view on job crafting. In *Elgar Encyclopedia of Occupational Health Psychology* (pp. 4–6). Edward Elgar Publishing., DOI: 10.4337/9781035313389.ch02

Tomás, J., & Fluixá, C. (2020). Workplace accommodations for people with intellectual disabilities: A systematic review. *Journal of Intellectual Disability Research*, *64*(10), 789–802.

Tomaszewski, B.. (2024). Employment outcomes for adults with intellectual and developmental disabilities: A 20-year review. *Intellectual and Developmental Disabilities*, *62*(1), 12–25.

Tompa, J., Buchmeister, B., & Vujica Herzog, N. (2025). Inclusive workplace design using MOCAP technology. *International Journal of Simulation Modelling*, *24*(4), 577–588. DOI: 10.2507/IJSIMM24-4-737

Troger, H. (2022). Strength-based deployment. In *Management for Professionals* (pp. 85–98). Springer., DOI: 10.1007/978-3-031-06166-0_4

Tucker, M.. (2017). Interagency collaboration for employment of people with disabilities: A systematic review. *Journal of Vocational Rehabilitation*, *47*(1), 1–14.

Ulrich, T. A., Boring, R. L., McJunkin, T., & Rege, A. (2019). A visualisation approach to performing task analysis of time series event log data from a microworld simulation. *Proceedings of the Human Factors and Ergonomics Society Annual Meeting*, *63*(1), 1867–1871. DOI: 10.1177/1071181319631534

Urrejola-Contreras, G. P., Pérez, M. A., Herrera-Miranda, F., López, B., Gary Zambra, B., & Hernández Pérez, K. (2025). Adaptations in the workplace as a labour inclusion strategy for people with physical disabilities: An integrative review. *Work (Reading, Mass.)*, *80*(3), 962–973. DOI: 10.1177/10519815241289677 PMID: 40297889

Verma, A., & Singh, S. (2024). Job analysis and job evaluation. In *Clinical Laboratory Management* (pp. 23–28). Springer., DOI: 10.1007/978-3-031-46420-1_5

Vijayakumar, P.. (2023). Employer attitudes toward hiring people with disabilities: A systematic review. *Journal of Vocational Rehabilitation*, *58*(2), 145–160.

Wehman, P.. (2018). Competitive integrated employment for people with disabilities: The role of policy and practice. *Journal of Vocational Rehabilitation*, *49*(1), 1–12.

Wells, M. M., Thelen, L., & Ruark, J. (2007). Workspace personalization and organizational culture: Does your workspace reflect you or your company? *Environment and Behavior*, *39*(5), 616–634. DOI: 10.1177/0013916506295602

Wilson, M. G. (2012). Essential job functions and reasonable accommodation. *Journal of Applied Rehabilitation Counseling*, *43*(4), 3–10.

Zeshan, M., Khalid, H., Rasool, S., Centobelli, P., Cerchione, R., & Morelli, M. (2025). Digitalisation for sustainable working environments: The role of job crafting and job resources on employee engagement. *Business Strategy and the Environment*, *34*(8), 10296–10312. DOI: 10.1002/bse.70103

Zhang, C., Zhang, J., Zhan, X., Zheng, Y., & Yang, G. (2025). Strengths use in the workplace and its effects on individual work outcomes: A meta-analysis. *Applied Psychology*, *74*(5), e70036. Advance online publication. DOI: 10.1111/apps.70036

Zsifkovits, H., Woschank, M., & Pacher, C. (2021). A case study: Industry 4.0 and human factors in SMEs. In *Implementing Industry 4.0 in SMEs: Concepts, Examples and Applications* (pp. 233–261). Springer. DOI: 10.1007/978-3-030-70516-9_8

Chapter 7
Onboarding for Success: Structured Support From Day One

ABSTRACT

Onboarding is positioned as a structured and adaptive process that supports the transition from recruitment to sustained workplace participation, particularly for employees with intellectual disabilities. The chapter examines how clarity, predictability, and accessibility enhance role understanding, reduce anxiety, and promote integration. It presents structured frameworks, visual communication support, and socialisation strategies that strengthen engagement and competence. Emphasis is placed on coaching, continuous support, and participatory evaluation as mechanisms for sustaining performance. The chapter advances onboarding as a dynamic system that evolves through monitoring and refinement to support long-term inclusion.

7.1 INTRODUCTION

Inclusive recruitment is an important step in creating more diverse and equitable workplaces; however, hiring individuals with intellectual disabilities does not automatically result in meaningful inclusion. The success of disability-inclusive employment depends significantly on what happens after a candidate joins the organisation. Onboarding should therefore be viewed not merely as a short orientation process but as a structured inclusion strategy that intentionally supports the integration of workers with intellectual disabilities into the organisation's operational, social, and cultural life (Szeluga-Romańska, 2025). A structured onboarding process introduces employees to workplace expectations, organisational culture, job responsibilities, and available support systems. By reducing uncertainty during the early stages of employment and helping employees understand workplace routines and procedures, effective onboarding promotes confidence, engagement, and a sense of belonging. It also establishes the foundation for long-term participation by ensuring that em-

DOI: 10.4018/979-8-3373-9185-4.ch007

ployees receive the information, guidance, and support necessary to navigate their new work environment successfully.

Traditional onboarding approaches often focus heavily on administrative requirements while giving less attention to the social and psychological aspects of workplace integration. Research indicates that structured onboarding can improve job satisfaction, enhance performance, and reduce turnover intentions (Lourenço & Rodrigues, 2025; Mosquera & Soares, 2025). Organisations that invest in intentional onboarding programmes also report stronger employee commitment and sustained engagement over time (Costa & Rodrigues, 2025). In addition, onboarding supports the development of workplace relationships by creating opportunities for interaction with supervisors, colleagues, mentors, and support personnel. For workers with intellectual disabilities, clearly communicated expectations, predictable routines, accessible learning methods, and explicit explanations of workplace norms are particularly valuable in reducing anxiety and supporting successful adjustment to employment.

Psychological safety is another essential element of effective onboarding. It allows employees to ask questions, seek clarification, and learn through experience without fear of embarrassment or negative consequences. Studies consistently link psychologically safe workplaces with improved learning, engagement, collaboration, and productivity (Atiku et al., 2023; Patil et al., 2023). Psychological safety also contributes to stronger job performance by encouraging work engagement and adaptive job crafting behaviours (Petrov et al., 2023). Establishing such an environment during onboarding is especially important for workers with intellectual disabilities, many of whom may have experienced exclusion, limited opportunities, or negative assumptions about their abilities in educational or employment settings. Access to clear guidance, structured orientation activities, and supportive workplace interactions can strengthen confidence, encourage active participation, and improve understanding of job responsibilities and workplace expectations.

Inclusive onboarding is also rooted in ethical and legal obligations. Employers are responsible not only for meeting compliance requirements but also for fulfilling the psychological contract established during recruitment (Caldwell & Peters, 2018). Onboarding practices that demonstrate fairness, respect, and genuine consideration contribute to higher levels of employee engagement and organisational trust (Al Zmammi & Ateeq, 2025). For workers with intellectual disabilities, early onboarding experiences often shape perceptions of whether an organisation's commitment to accessibility, equity, and inclusion is authentic and meaningful.

Furthermore, onboarding should be aligned with broader organisational diversity and disability inclusion strategies. Historically, organisational socialisation processes have often overlooked the experiences of marginalised groups, including women and minority employees (Rogers, 2020). Workers with intellectual disabilities frequently encounter similar forms of exclusion within employment settings. As a result, inclusive onboarding requires thoughtful adaptation rather than a one-size-fits-all approach. The application of principles such as Universal Design for Learning can help ensure that communication methods, training materials, and workplace expectations are accessible to employees with diverse cognitive and learning needs (Hoeh & Bonat, 2020). Practical supports such as visual schedules, step-by-step task instructions, peer mentoring, and regular feedback mechanisms can enhance understanding, increase confidence, and promote equitable participation in the workplace.

From an organisational perspective, effective onboarding contributes to smoother workplace integration, stronger communication, and better alignment between employee strengths and job requirements. When onboarding processes are accessible and responsive to individual support needs, they create a strong foundation for workplace participation, employee retention, and long-term employment success. Effective onboarding also benefits organisations by fostering inclusion, strengthening workplace culture, and supporting productivity through clearer communication and role understanding.

This chapter examines onboarding as a critical bridge between recruitment and sustained workplace participation for workers with intellectual disabilities. It begins by discussing the principles of clarity, predictability, accessibility, and psychological safety that underpin effective onboarding systems. The chapter then explores structured, visually supported onboarding practices, workplace orientation processes, and strategies for fostering social inclusion and relationship-building. Attention is also given to the role of training, coaching, mentoring, and ongoing support in facilitating early employment success. The discussion further considers approaches for monitoring, evaluating, and continuously improving onboarding systems to promote long-term inclusion, retention, and career development. By examining these interconnected elements, the chapter highlights how organisations can design onboarding processes that move beyond compliance and actively support meaningful, sustainable, and inclusive employment outcomes for workers with intellectual disabilities.

7.2 DESIGNING CLEAR AND PREDICTABLE ONBOARDING PATHWAYS

This is central to inclusive employment practices for workers with intellectual disabilities. Recruitment may open the organisational door, but structured onboarding determines whether new employees develop the confidence and competence required for sustained contribution. For workers with intellectual disabilities, predictability and structure are not optional enhancements; they are essential conditions for equitable participation in competitive and integrated employment settings. Importantly, the principles discussed in this section benefit all employees by reducing ambiguity, strengthening engagement, and accelerating professional adjustment.

7.2.1 The Strategic Importance of Structured Onboarding: Structured onboarding provides the foundation for successful workplace integration. Research demonstrates that well-designed onboarding programmes improve adaptation, job satisfaction, and perceptions of workplace safety among newly hired employees (Muñoz et al., 2025). Within disability-inclusive workplaces, structured onboarding offers cognitive scaffolding that supports learning, task sequencing, and adjustment to organisational routines. Beyond facilitating adaptation, structured onboarding reflects organisational preparedness, fairness, and commitment to inclusion.

7.2.2 Routine, Structure, and Clarity as Foundations for Inclusion: Routine and clarity reduce uncertainty and provide stability during the transition into employment. Role clarity, defined as a clear understanding of responsibilities, expectations, and performance standards, positively influences organisational commitment and creativity (W.-J. Lee & Lee, 2017). Employees who understand how their work contributes to organisational objectives are more likely to engage fully in their roles. Conversely, ambiguity can generate anxiety, confusion, and disengagement. For workers with intellectual disabilities, explicit expectations and clearly communicated responsibilities foster confidence, independence, and a positive professional identity. Role clarity also contributes to psychological safety and encourages initiative by establishing clear decision-making boundaries (Zinnah et al., 2025).

7.2.3 Developing Accessible and Sequential Onboarding Roadmaps: Predictable onboarding requires deliberate sequencing and clear progression. Effective onboarding roadmaps guide employees from initial orientation to independent performance through manageable stages of learning and skill development. Research on organisational change highlights the value of phased implementation for sustaining improvement efforts (De Feo & Barnard, 2005). In inclusive employment settings, onboarding roadmaps may include pre-boarding preparation, structured orientation, guided practice, supported performance, and consolidation phases. Expectation-alignment tools further strengthen these pathways by clarifying responsibilities, timelines, and performance indicators (Leung et al., 2024). Presenting onboarding information through plain language guides, visual schedules, competency checklists, and workflow diagrams enhances accessibility and reduces cognitive overload.

7.2.4 Strengthening Role Clarity and Task Expectations: Role clarity and task clarity are essential for effective performance and workplace well-being. Role ambiguity has been shown to undermine both individual effectiveness and team functioning (Kauppila, 2014). Similarly, organisational stability and supervisory support enhance the positive effects of role clarity on performance outcomes (Fried et al., 2003). Task clarity complements these benefits by providing explicit instructions, timelines, and quality standards. Evidence suggests that clearly defined tasks improve engagement and output quality (Yang & Zhao, 2025). For workers with intellectual disabilities, visual demonstrations, step-by-step instructions, modelling, and guided practice can make complex responsibilities more manageable while maintaining high performance expectations. Clarity should therefore be viewed as a mechanism for supporting excellence rather than lowering standards.

7.2.5 Communicating Workplace Norms and Expectations Transparently: Successful onboarding extends beyond formal job responsibilities to include communicating informal workplace norms. Employees benefit from understanding communication protocols, feedback processes, meeting expectations, and organisational values. Transparent communication strengthens trust and contributes to employee voice, loyalty, and positive workplace behaviours (Kim & Uysal, 2025). Strong employee–organisation relationships are also associated with authentic leadership and effective internal communication practices (Men & Stacks, 2014). For workers with intellectual disabilities, transparency reduces reliance on social inference and promotes understanding of behavioural expectations. Written guides, communication procedures, grievance mechanisms, and clearly articulated performance timelines help establish a more inclusive and predictable work environment.

7.2.6 Reducing Anxiety and Supporting Early Adjustment: Beginning employment often involves uncertainty and adjustment challenges. Predictable onboarding processes reduce stress by providing consistent routines, accessible information, and reliable support structures. Research indicates that structured onboarding strengthens professional confidence and reduces workplace stress (Girshausen et al., 2025). Mentorship-based onboarding models further improve adjustment and integration outcomes (Ross et al., 2014). Within disability-inclusive workplaces, scheduled feedback meetings, consistent supervision, and structured mentoring relationships enhance security, self-efficacy, and readiness for independent performance. Knowing when support will be available and how progress will be evaluated helps reduce anxiety and encourages active participation.

7.2.7 Balancing Structure, Flexibility, and Continuous Improvement: Although structure is essential, effective onboarding must also remain responsive to individual needs. Inclusive onboarding systems combine consistency with flexibility by allowing adjustments based on employee progress, feedback, and accommodation requirements. Regular review checkpoints enable supervisors to assess development, identify emerging needs, and refine support strategies. Reflective discussions encourage shared understanding and continuous improvement while maintaining accountability. When organisations balance predictability with adaptability, they create onboarding systems that support both inclusion and performance. Such systems establish a durable foundation for long-term engagement, retention, advancement, and inclusive workplace excellence.

7.3 VISUAL SUPPORTS AND ACCESSIBLE COMMUNICATION TOOLS

Accessible onboarding depends on communication systems that employees can interpret accurately and use independently. For workers with intellectual disabilities, accessible communication is not a supplementary feature but a foundational condition for equitable participation. Visual supports and adaptive communication tools translate organisational expectations into formats that enhance comprehension and application. These tools promote autonomy, minimise cognitive strain, and strengthen task execution while maintaining professional standards.

7.3.1 Visual Schedules and Workflow Charts: Visual schedules organise activities into structured sequences that employees can follow without constant verbal prompting. By presenting information through images, symbols, or simplified text, these tools strengthen task initiation and completion. For workers with intellectual disabilities who benefit from explicit sequencing and visual reinforcement, structured scheduling enhances independence and behavioural regulation (Liang, 2025). Clear sequencing reduces uncertainty and supports sustained engagement.

Workflow charts extend this principle to broader organisational processes. They illustrate task interdependencies, reporting lines, and procedural steps. Digital mapping tools such as Lucidchart improve knowledge retention and decision-making by clarifying process flow (Faulkner, 2018). When applied to inclusive onboarding, workflow charts help workers with intellectual disabilities understand how their responsibilities connect to team objectives and organisational goals. This system's clarity enhances accountability and situational awareness.

7.3.2 Checklists and Task Decomposition: Checklists remain among the most reliable tools for enhancing accuracy and consistency in complex environments. The aviation and healthcare sectors use them to standardise procedures and reduce errors (Auvinen & Arminen, 2013; Bernstein et al., 2017; Elmezzi & Deering, 2019). Their effectiveness lies in structured sequencing and explicit articulation of essential steps. Within disability-inclusive workplaces, structured checklists provide cognitive scaffolding for workers with intellectual disabilities. They ensure that supervisors communicate expectations consistently and allow employees to track progress visibly(Flynn et al., 2025). Task decomposition further strengthens performance by breaking complex responsibilities into manageable components. Visual demonstrations, step-by-step written guides, and opportunities for guided repetition support mastery while preserving performance standards. Properly designed checklists function as performance support tools rather than control mechanisms. They enhance independence and reduce reliance on memory recall, particularly for individuals who benefit from externalised task guidance.

7.3.3 Plain Language as Inclusive Practice: Language accessibility directly influences comprehension and inclusion. For workers with intellectual disabilities, plain language communication reduces ambiguity and strengthens confidence. Plain language eliminates unnecessary jargon, shortens complex constructions, and foregrounds essential information. Clarity in written and verbal communication promotes fairness and professional equity(Dreher & Willerton, 2025).

Interactive systems research demonstrates that simplified language structures improve usability across diverse populations (Oliveira et al., 2026). In onboarding contexts, concise instructions, defined terminology, and logically sequenced information enhance interpretability. Plain language does not dilute complexity or lower expectations. It enhances precision and ensures that workers with intellectual disabilities can equitably access organisational knowledge. Organisations should therefore audit onboarding documents to remove unexplained acronyms, idiomatic expressions, and culturally implicit assumptions.

7.3.4 Assistive and Digital Technologies: Assistive technologies expand workplace participation by removing functional barriers. Communication devices, cognitive support applications, adaptive software, and environmental control systems enhance independence and accessibility (Mahmoudi-Dehaki et al., 2025). For workers with intellectual disabilities, these tools may support task sequencing, memory prompts, time management, and communication clarity. Collaborative selection of assistive tools ensures alignment with individual preferences and role requirements (Haase et al., 2020).

Inclusive onboarding should introduce such technologies as performance enhancers rather than remedial devices. Accessible digital platforms, guided tutorials, and structured visual onboarding interfaces further support comprehension and retention (Stoiber et al., 2021, 2024). Digital guidance systems that balance instructional structure with user autonomy strengthen independence (Pohl et al., 2025). Practical applications include captioned instructional videos, speech-to-text tools, interactive simulations, and visual dashboards that allow workers to revisit training materials as needed.

7.3.5 Multimodal Instruction and Inclusive Design: Workers with intellectual disabilities process information through diverse modalities. Multimodal instruction integrates visual, auditory, and experiential learning approaches to strengthen retention and application. Augmented reality–based onboarding systems illustrate how interactive scenarios enhance engagement and transfer of learning (Sharma et al., 2024).

Inclusive design principles emphasise adaptable interfaces and accessible instructional formats (Dar & Dar, 2024). Effective onboarding may therefore combine written guides, live demonstrations, recorded modules, and supervised practice.

Exposure to information through multiple channels reduces cognitive overload and reinforces understanding.

7.3.6 Institutionalising Accessible Communication: Accessible communication should be part of the organisational infrastructure rather than provided as an accommodation upon request. Embedding visual tools, plain-language practices, assistive technologies, and multimodal instruction into onboarding reflects a commitment to workers with intellectual disabilities as integral members of the workforce.

Clear visual systems reduce errors. Structured language enhances comprehension. Adaptive technologies expand independence. Multimodal learning strengthens mastery. When organisations intentionally design onboarding materials that workers with intellectual disabilities can readily interpret and apply, they reinforce dignity, competence, and equitable opportunity. Accessible communication does not modify expectations; it equips workers with intellectual disabilities with the tools necessary to meet established professional standards confidently and consistently.

7.4 EARLY ACCOMMODATION PLANNING AND ENVIRONMENTAL PREPARATION

Inclusive onboarding is most effective when organisations anticipate support requirements before challenges emerge. Early accommodation planning and environmental preparation help ensure that workers with intellectual disabilities enter workplaces that are intentionally structured to support performance, participation, and long-term success. Rather than addressing barriers only after they affect productivity or employee well-being, proactive planning integrates accommodation into routine organisational practices from the outset. This approach reflects not only legal and ethical responsibilities but also a strategic commitment to fostering disability-inclusive employment.

7.4.1 Proactive Accommodation Planning and Individualised Adjustments

Effective accommodation planning begins with open, respectful, and structured communication among workers with intellectual disabilities, human resource professionals, and line managers. Early discussions provide opportunities to clarify job expectations, identify potential workplace barriers, and determine reasonable accommodations that align with both employee needs and organisational requirements. Accommodation is most successful when it is developed collaboratively rather than imposed through unilateral decisions and when support measures are established before employees assume full job responsibilities.

Managers should focus on the essential requirements of the role and the strengths of the employee rather than relying on assumptions about disability-related limitations. Since workers with intellectual disabilities vary considerably in their learning styles, communication preferences, and support needs, accommodation planning should incorporate individualised onboarding strategies. These may include adjusted training schedules, simplified or alternative instructional materials, assistive technologies, structured opportunities for practice, and enhanced supervisory guidance. Such adjustments promote equitable access to workplace opportunities by ensuring that employees have the resources necessary to perform effectively while maintaining consistent performance standards.

7.4.2 Environmental Accessibility and Sensory-Friendly Workspaces

The physical work environment significantly influences employee comfort, concentration, and overall productivity. Elements such as lighting, noise levels, workspace design, and patterns of movement within the workplace can affect cognitive functioning, attention, and emotional well-being. For workers with intellectual disabilities who may experience sensory sensitivities, environmental modifications can reduce distractions and create conditions that support effective job performance.

Practical measures may include adjustable lighting systems, noise-reduction strategies, clearly organised workstations, structured storage arrangements, and designated quiet areas for focused work or brief breaks. Workplace accessibility can also be enhanced through assistive technologies that support communication, scheduling, task management, and information processing. By proactively addressing environmental factors, organisations create workplaces that encourage independence, reduce unnecessary stress, and support employee success.

7.4.3 Flexible Scheduling and Structured Task Progression

The transition into a new role often requires time, support, and opportunities for gradual adjustment. Flexible scheduling and phased task progression can help workers with intellectual disabilities build competence and confidence while becoming familiar with workplace expectations. Introducing responsibilities incrementally allows employees to develop skills systematically and reduces the likelihood of becoming overwhelmed during the onboarding process.

Managers can support this transition by providing regular coaching, constructive feedback, and opportunities for reinforcement of newly acquired skills. Flexible arrangements may include modified start times, shorter shifts during the initial stages of employment, or the gradual expansion of job responsibilities as competence develops. However, flexibility should be implemented within a structured framework that includes clear objectives, defined timelines, and regular progress evaluations to ensure accountability and continuous development.

7.4.4 Collaborative Leadership and Ongoing Accommodation Review

Maintaining effective accommodations requires ongoing collaboration and shared responsibility among organisational stakeholders. Human resource professionals play a key role in ensuring policy compliance, documentation, and procedural consistency, while line managers provide day-to-day supervision and operational support. Working together, these stakeholders can ensure that accommodations remain practical, effective, and aligned with organisational goals.

Regular review meetings during the onboarding period provide valuable opportunities to assess the effectiveness of accommodations, address emerging concerns, clarify expectations, and make necessary adjustments. As employees gain experience and job responsibilities evolve, support strategies may need to be refined to remain relevant and beneficial. Continuous evaluation not only supports individual employee success but also contributes to organisational learning and the development of more inclusive workplace practices.

7.4.5 Embedding Preparedness as an Organisational Standard

Early accommodation planning and environmental preparation demonstrate a genuine organisational commitment to inclusion and accessibility. Through proactive communication, personalised support, accessible workplace design, structured flexibility, and collaborative leadership, organisations can create conditions that enable workers with intellectual disabilities to focus on developing their skills and contributing effectively rather than overcoming preventable barriers.

These practices support positive outcomes for both employees and organisations by enhancing productivity, job satisfaction, retention, and workplace participation while maintaining high performance expectations. When accommodation planning is embedded within standard onboarding procedures, accessibility becomes an integral component of organisational culture rather than an exceptional response to individual circumstances. This proactive approach strengthens the transition from recruitment to long-term employment success and reinforces the organisation's commitment to equitable and inclusive employment practices.

7.5 MENTORSHIP, PEER SUPPORT, AND SOCIAL INTEGRATION

Professional success requires more than technical competence. New employees must interpret communication patterns, build collegial relationships, and understand informal workplace expectations that shape daily interactions. Mentorship and peer support systems provide structured relational frameworks that strengthen adjustment, confidence, and sustained participation. For workers with intellectual disabilities, these supports are particularly significant in fostering belonging, visibility, and professional development.

7.5.1 Structured Peer Buddy Systems: A structured peer buddy system assigns a trained colleague to guide a new employee during the initial phase of employment. Unlike informal assistance, this model clearly defines responsibilities, timeframes, and interaction expectations. The buddy introduces workplace routines, explains informal norms, and serves as a reliable contact for practical questions. Clearly organised peer mentoring initiatives reduce transition anxiety and strengthen engagement (Bleasby et al., 2025; Lefera & Swart, 2020). In workplace settings, buddy systems create accessible channels for seeking clarification without the pressure of formal reporting structures. This accessibility builds confidence and mitigates feelings of isolation.

Effective implementation requires preparation. Organisations should train buddies in respectful communication, boundary awareness, and strengths-based engagement. Scheduled check-ins during the first weeks establish consistency, while brief documentation allows supervisors to monitor progress without formalising the relationship excessively. A well-designed buddy system benefits all participants. New employees gain orientation and reassurance. Buddies refine leadership and interpersonal skills. The organisation strengthens a culture of shared responsibility and collaborative support.

7.5.2 Supervisors as Models of Inclusive Practice

Supervisors shape workplace climate through everyday behaviour. Their conduct influences how teams respond to diversity and how secure employees feel when seeking support. Leaders who demonstrate fairness, openness, and developmental commitment cultivate environments in which individuals perform with confidence. Inclusive supervisory practice involves providing constructive feedback, recognising incremental progress, and addressing concerns promptly. Developmental feedback connects effort to improvement and reinforces growth. Consistency in communication conveys reliability and investment in employee advancement.

Supervisors also establish relational norms. When leaders model respectful dialogue and equitable treatment, they affirm that inclusion is integral to organisational identity. Inconsistent behaviour or disengagement weakens supportive structures. Authority must therefore operate alongside empathy and accountability. Intentional relationship-building strengthens supervisory influence. Regular one-to-one meetings, clear performance discussions, and visible encouragement during team interactions reinforce psychological security. Supervisors should remain actively involved in integration efforts rather than delegating relational responsibility entirely to peers.

7.5.3 Facilitating Informal Social Participation: Workplace integration develops through informal interaction. Shared conversations, collaborative exchanges, and voluntary social activities allow employees to build familiarity and trust beyond formal roles. Social connection contributes to well-being and job satisfaction (Mittal et al., 2025). Organisations can promote inclusive participation by organising accessible team events, cross-functional collaborations, and structured networking opportunities. Managers should explicitly communicate invitations and ensure activities remain welcoming and voluntary. Active listening strengthens informal engagement.

Environments characterised by attentive and respectful dialogue reduce misunderstanding and exclusion (Belgasm et al., 2025). Encouraging team members to listen carefully and respond thoughtfully fosters mutual respect. Peer support can extend into informal contexts by inviting new employees to meetings, professional development sessions, or collaborative projects. Participation in shared activities increases familiarity and reduces marginal positioning within teams.

7.5.4 Building Confidence and Professional Identity: Mentorship contributes significantly to the development of professional identity. Beyond procedural instruction, mentors provide encouragement, perspective, and affirmation of capability. Professional advancement frameworks highlight the role of mentorship in transforming potential into sustained proficiency (Seotsanyana, 2025). For workers with intellectual disabilities, recognition of strengths and progress reinforces self-efficacy. Feedback that emphasises development rather than deficiency strengthens resilience and persistence. Over time, employees internalise a sense of competence and contribution.

Peer mentoring also fosters leadership capacity and a sense of belonging (Sunderman & Adebayo, 2025). Engagement in collaborative dialogue and shared problem-solving broadens professional perspective. Identity solidifies when employees perceive that their contributions align with organisational goals and values. Confidence deepens when individuals recognise that the organisation values their development. Structured mentorship ensures that this recognition remains intentional rather than incidental.

7.5.5 Monitoring Social Belonging Indicators: Belonging influences engagement, retention, and workplace stability. Employees who experience connection demonstrate stronger participation and commitment. Organisations should therefore monitor indicators that reflect social integration. Relevant indicators include participation in collaborative activities, frequency of peer interaction, comfort during meetings, and self-reported satisfaction. Structured feedback tools and periodic supervisory check-ins provide insight into relational adjustment. Peer-based initiatives have demonstrated positive effects on social participation and continuity (Struchen et al., 2011). Supervisors and HR personnel should review social integration indicators alongside performance measures. Early identification of isolation enables timely intervention. Ongoing evaluation ensures that mentorship structures remain purposeful and responsive.

7.5.6 Sustaining Relational Inclusion: Mentorship and peer support represent sustained organisational commitments rather than temporary onboarding measures. Structured buddy systems, inclusive supervision, and facilitated social participation establish durable networks of trust. When organisations invest in relational infrastructure, they strengthen collaboration and resilience. Workers with intellectual disabilities develop both technical competence and meaningful connections. Inclusive employment flourishes when individuals experience recognition, respect, and shared purpose within their professional community.

7.6 PERFORMANCE SUPPORT, FEEDBACK, AND SKILL DEVELOPMENT

Sustained inclusion in the workplace requires more than initial orientation and relational integration. Workers with intellectual disabilities must receive ongoing performance support that strengthens competence, clarifies expectations, and promotes professional advancement. When structured thoughtfully, performance management becomes a developmental tool rather than a compliance exercise. This section examines how structured feedback, coaching, recognition, and long-term development planning can support high performance while ensuring equitable access to workplace success.

7.6.1 Structured Feedback and Performance Monitoring

Performance support should operate as a continuous process rather than a one-time evaluation. Structured feedback loops create predictable opportunities for reviewing progress, identifying areas for improvement, and establishing future goals. Effective feedback systems align individual responsibilities with organisational objectives while reinforcing learning and performance improvement (Mayfield & Mayfield, 2011). Integrating feedback into daily work activities, rather than relying solely on annual appraisals, helps employees view guidance as a normal aspect of professional development. Dynamic performance management systems emphasise clarity, timeliness, and responsiveness (Pathirana, 2024).

For workers with intellectual disabilities, regular feedback sessions reduce ambiguity and help prevent minor misunderstandings from becoming significant performance concerns. Feedback is most effective when focused on specific behaviours and observable outcomes. Concrete examples improve understanding and minimise reliance on abstract interpretation. Evidence from skills-based training environments demonstrates that consistent instructor feedback enhances competency development (Elemam & Abdelaal, 2025). Similar principles can be applied in workplace settings by breaking performance expectations into measurable indicators and reviewing them systematically. Written summaries, visual checklists, and progress-tracking tools may further strengthen understanding and retention.

7.6.2 Strength-Based Coaching and Recognition Practices

Effective performance support should build upon existing strengths while creating opportunities for growth. Strength-based coaching focuses on identifying successful practices and using those competencies as foundations for further development. Transformational leadership approaches emphasise goal clarity, encouragement, and meaningful performance dialogue (Leggat, 2009). Consequently, coaching conversations should acknowledge effective performance before addressing areas requiring improvement.

Recognition of strengths is particularly important for workers with intellectual disabilities because it reinforces confidence, competence, and intrinsic motivation. Coaching should involve collaborative goal-setting processes that allow employees to participate actively in defining realistic development objectives. This participatory approach encourages ownership, engagement, and accountability.

Constructive feedback remains essential but should be delivered within a developmental framework. Effective workplace feedback balances affirmation with guidance, helping employees understand both performance expectations and pathways for improvement (Rogito & Makabe, 2023). Supervisors should provide actionable recommendations rather than general criticism. Recognition also plays a vital role in sustaining motivation and reinforcing positive workplace behaviours. Verbal affirmation, written acknowledgement, expanded responsibilities, and formal commendations can all contribute to employee engagement. Timely and authentic recognition signals that effort, achievement, and continuous improvement are valued within the organisation.

7.6.3 Maintaining High Standards Through Equitable Support

Inclusive performance management requires a careful balance between accommodation and accountability. While adjustments may be necessary to ensure accessibility and understanding, organisational performance standards should remain consistent. Supervisors must distinguish between modifying support mechanisms and lowering performance expectations. Structured feedback systems based on observable behaviours help maintain this balance (Mayfield & Mayfield, 2011; Rogito & Makabe, 2023).

Clearly communicated expectations enable employees to understand the criteria for success and the steps required to achieve performance goals. Adjustments may include additional training time, alternative instructional methods, visual support, or increased opportunities for guided practice. However, these modifications should facilitate the achievement of established standards rather than replace them.

For workers with intellectual disabilities, gradual skill development often strengthens long-term competence and confidence. Evidence from structured learning environments indicates that sustained reinforcement contributes to durable skill acquisition (Nigam et al., 2025). Patience in pacing should therefore be viewed as a strategy for mastery rather than an indication of reduced expectations. Supervisors must avoid assumptions that equate disability with limited capability. High standards, combined with equitable support, communicate professional respect and reinforce the organisation's commitment to inclusion.

7.6.4 Career Development and Continuous Growth

The completion of formal onboarding should mark the beginning of long-term professional development rather than the end of organisational support. Performance systems should extend beyond initial adjustment and focus on sustained learning, career progression, and continuous improvement. Clear performance criteria, documented competencies, and progressive goal-setting provide direction for ongoing growth (Pathirana, 2024). Competency-based development approaches emphasise continuous assessment and feedback as mechanisms for supporting lifelong learning and professional advancement (Baboolal & Singaram, 2024; Kinnear et al., 2023).

Practical workplace applications may include periodic skills reviews, cross-training opportunities, mentoring programmes, and structured advancement pathways. Workers with intellectual disabilities should have equal access to career development discussions, leadership opportunities, and professional learning resources. Long-term growth also depends on monitoring engagement, motivation, and evolving career aspirations. Supervisors should regularly review individual development plans to ensure alignment between employee goals and organisational needs.

Organisations that integrate structured feedback, strength-based coaching, equitable performance expectations, and career development opportunities transform performance management into a tool for empowerment rather than solely for evaluation. Such approaches promote competence, confidence, workplace participation, and sustained contribution, ensuring that workers with intellectual disabilities have meaningful opportunities to grow and succeed throughout their careers.

7.7 CONCLUSION

Effective onboarding for workers with intellectual disabilities must extend beyond initial adjustment to influence long-term retention and career progression. Organisations should therefore evaluate onboarding effectiveness through measurable indicators such as job satisfaction, role clarity, early performance outcomes, supervisor feedback, and retention rates within the first year of employment. Regular evaluation allows leaders to determine whether structured supports, accommodations, and relational strategies are achieving their intended impact. Feedback from workers with intellectual disabilities themselves remains central to this process, as lived experience offers direct insight into accessibility and workplace inclusion.

Preventing early turnover requires deliberate monitoring during the first six to twelve months of employment. Workers with intellectual disabilities may face challenges related to task complexity, social integration, or communication barriers if support structures weaken after initial orientation. Proactive follow-up meetings, structured performance reviews, and mentorship continuity help identify emerging concerns before they result in disengagement. Stability during the early employment period strengthens confidence, reinforces competence, and reduces avoidable attrition.

Onboarding should also connect explicitly to career progression pathways. Workers with intellectual disabilities must have access to advancement opportunities, skills development programs, and transparent promotion criteria. Clear articulation of growth pathways communicates that employment is not limited to entry-level roles but also offers opportunities for increased responsibility and professional recognition. Structured development plans, cross-training opportunities, and incremental skill certification can reinforce upward mobility.

Institutional learning remains essential. Organisations should analyse onboarding data, retention patterns, and advancement outcomes to continuously refine inclusive practices. This iterative approach strengthens organisational responsiveness and accountability.

This chapter has positioned onboarding as a strategic foundation for sustainable inclusion. Chapter 8 builds upon this foundation by examining workplace integration and support systems that maintain performance, engagement, and long-term success for workers with intellectual disabilities.

REFERENCES

Al Zmammi, R. A., & Ateeq, A. (2025). The Impact of an Ethical Onboarding Program on Employee Engagement. In *Studies in Systems* (Vol. 584, pp. 677–685). Decision and Control., DOI: 10.1007/978-3-031-85898-7_58

Atiku, S. O., Soneye, F. A., & Anane-Simon, R. (2023). Fostering psychological safety for team effectiveness in family businesses: Insights from Royal Savoy Hotel. In *Cases on the Interplay Between Family* (pp. 84–121). Society, and Entrepreneurship., DOI: 10.4018/978-1-6684-8748-8.ch004

Auvinen, P., & Arminen, I. (2013). An airline checklist use as a sociomaterial practice. *Proceedings of the Annual Hawaii International Conference on System Sciences*, 1590–1599. DOI: 10.1109/HICSS.2013.80

Baboolal, S. O., & Singaram, V. S. (2024). Implementation and Impact of an Adapted Digital Perioperative Competency-Building Tool to Enhance Teaching, Learning And Feedback in Postgraduate Competency-Based Medical Education. *Journal of Surgical Education*, *81*(5), 722–740. DOI: 10.1016/j.jsurg.2024.01.015 PMID: 38492984

Belgasm, H., Alzubi, A., Iyiola, K., & Khadem, A. (2025). Interpersonal Conflict and Employee Behavior in the Public Sector: Investigating the Role of Workplace Ostracism and Supervisors' Active Empathic Listening. *Behavioral Sciences (Basel, Switzerland)*, *15*(2), 194. Advance online publication. DOI: 10.3390/bs15020194 PMID: 40001825

Bernstein, P. S., Combs, C. A., Shields, L. E., Clark, S. L., & Eppes, C. S. (2017). The development and implementation of checklists in obstetrics. *American Journal of Obstetrics and Gynecology*, *217*(2), B2–B6. DOI: 10.1016/j.ajog.2017.05.032 PMID: 28549984

Bleasby, C., Coffey, L.-A., Sweeney, H., & Thompson, J. (2025). Developing social worker student belonging, engagement and confidence through peer mentoring: a case study exploration. In *Building Student Belonging in Higher Education* (pp. 195–214). Perspectives on Driving and Developing Change., DOI: 10.1108/978-1-80592-242-120251025

Caldwell, C., & Peters, R. (2018). New employee onboarding – psychological contracts and ethical perspectives. *Journal of Management Development*, *37*(1), 27–39. DOI: 10.1108/JMD-10-2016-0202

Costa, B., & Rodrigues, R. I. (2025). The Invisible Bond: Exploring the Sequential Mediation of Interpersonal Connections and Engagement in the Relationship Between the Onboarding Process and Talent Retention. *Administrative Sciences*, *15*(7), 281. Advance online publication. DOI: 10.3390/admsci15070281

Dar, H., & Dar, M. A. (2024). Redefining Success of the Tourism Sector Through Technological Advancements. In *AI Technologies for Personalized and Sustainable Tourism* (pp. 201–214). DOI: 10.4018/979-8-3693-5678-4.ch008

De Feo, J. A., & Barnard, W. W. (2005). A roadmap for change. *Quality Progress*, *38*(1), 24–30. https://www.scopus.com/inward/record.uri?eid=2-s2.0-12344312247&partnerID=40&md5=7ee1533c75c9a71de5c50ace75fd9102

Dreher, K., & Willerton, R. (2025). ETHICS AND PLAIN LANGUAGE. In *The Routledge Handbook of Ethics in Technical and Professional Communication* (pp. 282–297). DOI: 10.4324/9781003434375-33

Elemam, R. F., & Abdelaal, H. M. (2025). The impact of structured assessment attempts and instructor feedback on clinical competency development in dental assistant training. *BMC Medical Education*, *25*(1), 1412. Advance online publication. DOI: 10.1186/s12909-025-07842-z PMID: 41088169

Elmezzi, K., & Deering, S. (2019). Checklists in emergencies. *Seminars in Perinatology*, *43*(1), 18–21. DOI: 10.1053/j.semperi.2018.11.004 PMID: 30473312

Faulkner, A. (2018). Lucidchart for Easy Workflow Mapping. *Serials Review*, *44*(2), 157–162. DOI: 10.1080/00987913.2018.1472468

Flynn, R., Brez, J., & Fritz, E. (2025). Standardizing Orientation Checklists. *Journal for Nurses in Professional Development*. Advance online publication. DOI: 10.1097/NND.0000000000001196 PMID: 40996164

Fried, Y., Slowik, L. H., Shperling, Z., Franz, C., Ben-David, H. A., Avital, N., & Yeverechyahu, U. (2003). The moderating effect of job security on the relation between role clarity and job performance: A longitudinal field study. *Human Relations*, *56*(7), 787–805. DOI: 10.1177/00187267030567002

Girshausen, R., Graf, S., Holz, T., Lorenz, J., Masson, T., Wolff, J., & Azad, N. (2025). Einarbeitung in der Notfallmedizin. *Medizinische Klinik, Intensivmedizin und Notfallmedizin*, *120*(6), 473–480. DOI: 10.1007/s00063-025-01281-w PMID: 40293484

Haase, T., Termath, W., Berndt, D., & Dick, M. (2020). Assistive technologies: Companion or controller? Appropriation instead of instruction. *WMSCI 2020 - 24th World Multi-Conference on Systemics, Cybernetics and Informatics. Proceedings, 3*, 150–155. https://www.scopus.com/inward/record.uri?eid=2-s2.0-85096598538&partnerID=40&md5=97269c23e7550175259327de80ca3adf

Hoeh, E., & Bonat, M. L. (2020). Higher education faculty addressing the diverse learning needs of students with disabilities within the universal design for learning framework. In *Ethics in Higher Education* (pp. 97–126). https://www.scopus.com/inward/record.uri?eid=2-s2.0-85125611492&partnerID=40&md5=57caac83e681dad9f368e3efa153f866

Kauppila, O.-P. (2014). So, What am i supposed to do? A multilevel examination of role clarity. *Journal of Management Studies, 51*(5), 737–763. DOI: 10.1111/joms.12042

Kim, Y., & Uysal, N. (2025). Transparent Communication and Employee Outcomes: The Mediating Role of Workplace Sense of Community in Enhancing Voice, Loyalty, and Positive Work Behaviors. *International Journal of Business Communication*, 23294884251349496. Advance online publication. DOI: 10.1177/23294884251349496

Kinnear, B., Santen, S. A., Kelleher, M., Martini, A., Ferris, S., Edje, L., Warm, E. J., & Schumacher, D. J. (2023). How Does TIMELESS Training Impact Resident Motivation for Learning, Assessment, and Feedback? Evaluating a Competency-Based Time-Variable Training Pilot. *Academic Medicine, 98*(7), 828–835. DOI: 10.1097/ACM.0000000000005147 PMID: 36656286

Lee, W.-J., & Lee, J.-K. (2017). Role clarity and organizational commitment in food manufacturing and distribution firms: The mediating role of creativity. *Journal of Distribution Science, 15*(1), 115–121. DOI: 10.15722/jds.15.1.201701.115

Lefera, M., & Swart, A. J. (2020). Reflecting on the success of a Peer Mentorship Programme - A scholarly personal narrative. *2020 IFEES World Engineering Education Forum - Global Engineering Deans Council, WEEF-GEDC 2020.* DOI: 10.1109/WEEF-GEDC49885.2020.9293640

Leggat, S. G. (2009). A guide to performance management for the health information manager. *The HIM Journal, 38*(3), 11–17. DOI: 10.1177/183335830903800303 PMID: 19875850

Leung, K., Clement, L., Lewis, J., & Saul, N. (2024). A tool for clarifying expectations in undergraduate research experiences. *Journal of Microbiology & Biology Education*, *25*(2), e00204-23. Advance online publication. DOI: 10.1128/jmbe.00204-23 PMID: 38842314

Liang, Z. (2025). CHECK Visual Schedules to Support Individuals on the Autism Spectrum. *Intervention in School and Clinic*, *60*(4), 228–235. DOI: 10.1177/10534512241300157

Lourenço, B., & Rodrigues, R. (2025). Organisational onboarding and talent retention: The mediating role of workplace attachment and supervisor support. *Social Sciences & Humanities Open*, *12*, 101909. Advance online publication. DOI: 10.1016/j.ssaho.2025.101909

Mahmoudi-Dehaki, M., Nasr-Esfahani, N., & Vasan, S. (2025). The Transformative Role of Assistive Technology in Enhancing Quality of Life for Individuals With Disabilities. In *Assistive Technology Solutions for Aging Adults and Individuals with Disabilities* (pp. 45–72). https://doi.org/DOI: 10.4018/9798369363089.ch003

Mayfield, M., & Mayfield, J. (2011). Effective performance feedback for learning in organizations and organizational learning. *Development and Learning in Organizations*, *26*(1), 15–18. DOI: 10.1108/14777281211189128

Men, L. R., & Stacks, D. (2014). The Effects of Authentic Leadership on Strategic Internal Communication and Employee-Organization Relationships. *Journal of Public Relations Research*, *26*(4), 301–324. DOI: 10.1080/1062726X.2014.908720

Mittal, S., Kanwal, P., & Dang, T. T. (2025). Impact of Workplace Social Connections on Employee Wellbeing and Happiness. In *Insights on Wellbeing and Happiness in the Workplace* (pp. 109–129). DOI: 10.4018/979-8-3693-2939-9.ch006

Mosquera, P., & Soares, M. E. (2025). Onboarding: A key to employee retention and workplace well-being. *Review of Managerial Science*, *19*(12), 3687–3711. DOI: 10.1007/s11846-025-00864-3

Muñoz, P. M., Cardinal-Fernández, P., Morales Rodríguez, Á., Ruiz-Zaldibar, C., & de la Cuerda López, A. (2025). The Impact of an Onboarding Plan for Newly Hired Nurses and Nursing Assistants: Results of a Quasi-Experimental Study. *Nursing Reports*, *15*(11), 398. Advance online publication. DOI: 10.3390/nursrep15110398 PMID: 41295822

Nigam, A., Kellam, J. F., Ambrose, C. G., & Tai, B. L. (2025). Impact of Quantitative Feedback on Motor Skill Acquisition in Bone Drilling: A Pilot Study Using Radar Plots. *Journal of Orthopaedic Trauma, 39*(10S), S21–S26. DOI: 10.1097/BOT.0000000000003033

Oliveira, R., De Castro Salgado, L. C., Seixas, F., & Cappelli, C. (2026). How Is Plain Language Applied in Interactive Systems Design? A Systematic Mapping Study. *Lecture Notes in Computer Science, 16111 LNCS*, 260–264. DOI: 10.1007/978-3-032-05008-3_49

Pathirana, G. (2024). Beyond metrics: Crafting a dynamic performance evaluation system. In *Employee Performance Management for Improved Workplace Motivation* (pp. 145–171). DOI: 10.4018/979-8-3693-4387-6.ch006

Patil, R., Raheja, D. K., Nair, L., Deshpande, A., & Mittal, A. (2023). The Power of Psychological Safety: Investigating its Impact on Team Learning, Team Efficacy, and Team Productivity. *The Open Psychology Journal, 16*(1), e187435012307090. Advance online publication. DOI: 10.2174/18743501-v16-230727-2023-36

Petrov, S., Oprea, B., & Opariuc-Dan, C. (2023). Psychological Safety and Job Performance: The Mediating Role of Work Engagement and Job Crafting. *Psihologia Resurselor Umane, 21*(2), 89–99. DOI: 10.24837/pru.v21i2.536

Pohl, M., Potzmann, B., Stoiber, C., & Aigner, W. (2025). Inconspicuous Guides: A Qualitative Study to Understand the Degree of Intrusiveness in Visualization Onboarding. *Proceedings of the International Joint Conference on Computer Vision, Imaging and Computer Graphics Theory and Applications, 1*, 706–717. DOI: 10.5220/0013135900003912

Rogers, A. M. (2020). Avoiding the issue: A critique of organizational socialization research from feminist and minority perspectives. *Organization Development Journal, 38*(1), 75–88. https://www.scopus.com/inward/record.uri?eid=2-s2.0-85089549634&partnerID=40&md5=e23e06cd3b99f40fc7c7a4e834fcc86e

Rogito, J., & Makabe, M. (2023). The Art and Act of Providing Feedback at the Workplace: Effective Feedback for Positive Results. *Pan-African Journal of Education and Social Sciences, 4*(1), 49–56. https://www.scopus.com/inward/record.uri?eid=2-s2.0-105004581237&partnerID=40&md5=2142362703ec1934c29f9596f6f01b3f

Ross, W. E., Huang, K. H. C., & Jones, G. H. (2014). Executive onboarding: Ensuring the success of the newly hired department chair. *Academic Medicine, 89*(5), 728–733. DOI: 10.1097/ACM.0000000000000214 PMID: 24667516

Seotsanyana, M. B. (2025). Transforming Potential into Proficiency: Mentorship as a Catalyst for Professional Advancement in the Workplace. In *Fostering Lifelong Learning Through Mentoring in Adult Education* (pp. 283–320). DOI: 10.4018/979-8-3373-3516-2.ch011

Sharma, V., Rani, S., & Chauhan, D. (2024). Enhancing New Hire Onboarding Through Immersive Augmented Reality Training: A Comparative Study. *Proceedings of International Conference on Communication, Computer Sciences and Engineering, IC3SE 2024*, 1737–1740. DOI: 10.1109/IC3SE62002.2024.10593605

Stoiber, C., Moitzi, D., Stitz, H., Grassinger, F., Prakash, A. S. G., Girardi, D., Streit, M., & Aigner, W. (2024). VisAhoi: Towards a library to generate and integrate visualisation onboarding using high-level visualisation grammars. *Visual Informatics*, *8*(3), 1–17. DOI: 10.1016/j.visinf.2024.06.001

Stoiber, C., Walchshofer, C., Grassinger, F., Stitz, H., Streit, M., & Aigner, W. (2021). Design and Comparative Evaluation of Visualisation Onboarding Methods. *ACM International Conference Proceeding Series*. DOI: 10.1145/3481549.3481558

Struchen, M. A., Davis, L. C., Bogaards, J. A., Hudler-Hull, T., Clark, A. N., Mazzei, D. M., Sander, A. M., & Caroselli, J. S. (2011). Making connections after brain injury: Development and evaluation of a social peer-mentoring program for persons with traumatic brain injury. *The Journal of Head Trauma Rehabilitation*, *26*(1), 4–19. DOI: 10.1097/HTR.0b013e3182048e98 PMID: 21209559

Sunderman, H. M., & Adebayo, B. (2025). Peer mentoring for leader development. In *Moving the Needle: What We Know (and Don't Know) About Developing Leaders* (pp. 283–296). https://www.scopus.com/inward/record.uri?eid=2-s2.0-105012207489&partnerID=40&md5=26baa48055850f4c2b2c51d90aa24b93

Szeluga-Romańska, M. (2025). Barriers to Knowledge Sharing During the Onboarding Process. *Proceedings of the European Conference on Knowledge Management, ECKM, 2*, 981–986. DOI: 10.34190/eckm.26.2.4092

Yang, X., & Zhao, Q. (2025). Making crowdsourcing contests better: The power of task clarity. *Management Decision*. Advance online publication. DOI: 10.1108/MD-09-2024-2153

Zinnah, C. A., Xue, X. F., & Ali, A. (2025). It's The Details That Matter: Role Clarity and Creative Service Performance; The Moderation Role of Supervisor Bottom-Line Mentality. *Basic and Applied Social Psychology*, *47*(6), 361–376. DOI: 10.1080/01973533.2025.2528837

Chapter 8
The Art of Effective Training:
Universal Design for Learning at Work

ABSTRACT

This chapter examines how effective workplace training can support sustainable employment outcomes for workers with intellectual disabilities. It discusses practical strategies for designing inclusive training systems that prioritise accessible instruction, supportive learning environments, and performance-based evaluation. The chapter highlights the importance of assistive technologies, psychologically safe learning spaces, and capacity building among supervisors and human resource professionals. Attention is also given to monitoring skill transfer, retention, and workplace integration to ensure that training leads to meaningful participation and productivity. Emphasis is placed on aligning training practices with Universal Design for Learning principles, inclusive leadership, and organisational policies. Collectively, these strategies strengthen pathways for continuous learning, long-term career development, and sustainable workplace inclusion for workers with intellectual disabilities.

8.1 INTRODUCTION

Workplace training is a critical component of organisational effectiveness because it equips employees with the competencies needed to perform tasks efficiently, adapt to evolving job demands, and contribute to overall organisational productivity. Despite its importance, conventional corporate training models have historically been designed around standardised assumptions about how employees

DOI: 10.4018/979-8-3373-9185-4.ch008

learn. These assumptions often fail to recognise the diverse cognitive and learning needs of workers with intellectual disabilities (ID). As organisations increasingly prioritise inclusive employment and equitable participation in the workforce, there is growing recognition that workplace training systems must be redesigned to ensure accessibility, flexibility, and effectiveness for all employees. This chapter examines how organisations can reconceptualise workplace training by applying the principles of Universal Design for Learning (UDL) in workplace contexts, thereby enabling workers with intellectual disabilities to acquire relevant skills, sustain employment, and pursue career advancement.

Traditional workplace training often relies on instructional approaches that assume uniform learning styles, including lecture-based instruction, text-heavy manuals, and verbal explanations. Although such methods may work for some employees, they frequently create barriers for workers with intellectual disabilities who benefit from structured guidance, visual supports, and experiential learning opportunities. Evidence indicates that training methods based solely on verbal instruction are less effective than approaches that incorporate visual and graphic supports. These supports improve comprehension and task performance among workers with intellectual disabilities (Becerra et al., 2018). Furthermore, many organisations lack the infrastructure, pedagogical expertise, or inclusive training frameworks needed to design learning environments that effectively support neurodiverse employees (Alexander et al., 2018; Satpathy et al., 2018). These limitations highlight the need to move beyond traditional corporate training models toward approaches that recognise diverse learning needs within the workplace.

Practitioners increasingly advocate a shift from deficit-oriented perspectives to strengths-based approaches in workplace capability development. Historically, training programmes for individuals with intellectual disabilities often focused on remediating perceived limitations rather than developing existing strengths and competencies. Contemporary approaches recognise that individuals with intellectual disabilities possess valuable abilities, including adaptability and practical problem-solving skills, which can be strengthened through supportive training environments. For example, web-based learning platforms that incorporate visual supports and interactive instructional strategies have been shown to enhance autonomy and improve work performance among individuals with intellectual disabilities (Benda et al., 2019). Similarly, supported employment models emphasise personalised job coaching, workplace accommodations, and task-specific instruction that enable employees with intellectual disabilities to succeed in competitive employment environments (Ahmad et al., 2026; Kearney et al., 2026).

Inclusive workplace training also provides important organisational benefits beyond individual skill development. Training systems designed with inclusive principles strengthen diversity, equity, and inclusion (DEI) initiatives by ensuring that all employees have opportunities to develop their skills and participate fully in organisational processes. When organisations invest in inclusive learning environments, employees experience a stronger sense of belonging and motivation, which enhances productivity and organisational commitment (McCabe, 2023; Panda et al., 2018). In addition, organisations that implement inclusive training practices align more closely with global frameworks, such as the Sustainable Development Goals, particularly those that promote inclusive economic growth and decent work for all (Collett-Schmitt et al., 2025).

Effective training also plays a crucial role in job retention and career progression for workers with intellectual disabilities. Programmes that incorporate extended job coaching, mentorship, and practical skill development improve long-term employment outcomes. (Carlson et al., 2020) found that workplace support interventions, including structured coaching and tailored training, enhance job stability and increase advancement opportunities for workers with intellectual disabilities. Likewise, initiatives such as Integrated Practical Placement programmes, which combine work placements with structured learning experiences, have demonstrated significant success in promoting employment and continued education opportunities for individuals with intellectual disabilities (Burgin et al., 2026).

In this context, learning accessibility should be regarded not merely as accommodation but as a central organisational responsibility. Creating accessible training environments requires deliberate strategies, including integrating assistive technologies, adopting flexible instructional methods, and fostering workplace cultures that value diversity. According to Yang et al. (2021) and Chattopadhyay (2025), emerging technologies such as virtual reality simulations and adaptive digital learning platforms offer new opportunities to enhance engagement and skill acquisition among workers with intellectual disabilities. In the opinion of Joyce et al. (2024), organisational structures that prioritise inclusive culture and employee wellbeing play a vital role in sustaining inclusive workplace practices.

This chapter, therefore, discusses effective workplace training through the lens of Universal Design for Learning applied to employment contexts. It argues that inclusive training systems should not be viewed as specialised interventions for a small group of employees but as strategic organisational practices that enhance learning accessibility for the entire workforce. By integrating UDL principles with strengths-based employment practices, organisations can develop training environments that empower workers with intellectual disabilities while strengthening organisational performance and workforce diversity.

8.2 TRANSLATING EDUCATIONAL THEORY INTO WORKPLACE PRACTICE

Universal Design for Learning (UDL) is a framework that creates inclusive learning environments by anticipating and accommodating learners' natural variability. Instead of reacting to challenges, UDL promotes proactive design to facilitate diverse access to and processing of information. In workplace training, especially for employees with intellectual disabilities, UDL is vital as it addresses different cognitive styles, learning speeds, and communication preferences. By adopting UDL-informed strategies, organisations can enhance training effectiveness for all employees while supporting those with unique needs.

Origins and Principles of Universal Design for Learning

Universal Design for Learning (UDL) originated from the concept of Universal Design in architecture, which sought to create environments accessible to individuals with diverse abilities. Educational researchers later adapted these principles to learning environments, recognising that learners vary in how they access, process, and engage with information. Consequently, instructional systems increasingly emphasised flexibility, accessibility, and learner-centred design in educational and training contexts (Leung et al. 2023; Beckman (2009). UDL promotes proactive instructional planning that anticipates learner variability rather than relying solely on accommodations after barriers emerge (Bryant et al., 2015). The framework is organised around three interconnected principles that guide inclusive learning design.

1. **Multiple Means of Representation:** This principle focuses on how information is presented to learners. Because individuals vary in perceptual and cognitive processing abilities, presenting information through a single format can limit accessibility. Providing information through visual, textual, and multimedia formats broadens access to learning materials (Courtad, 2019) In workplace training environments involving workers with intellectual disabilities, this may include combining written instructions with visual task guides, demonstrations, or simplified digital tutorials to improve comprehension (Mohamad & Pozzi, 2023).
2. **Multiple Means of Engagement:** This principle addresses how learners become motivated and remain involved in learning activities. Opportunities for collaboration, choice, and meaningful participation can strengthen engagement (Frolli et al., 2022). Linking training activities to practical workplace contexts also increases motivation (Mohamad & Pozzi, 2023). For workers with intellectual

disabilities, engagement improves when training reflects real job activities and includes structured guidance and supportive feedback.

3. **Multiple Means of Action and Expression:** This principle focuses on how learners demonstrate knowledge and skills. Flexible assessment strategies allow individuals to demonstrate competence through demonstrations or applied tasks rather than written tests (Courtad, 2019). Providing multiple ways for employees to show competence enables training systems to evaluate actual workplace performance (Taylor et al., 2026).

Adapting UDL from Classroom Settings to Employment Environments

Although Universal Design for Learning (UDL) originated in educational settings, its principles can inform the design of inclusive workplace training systems. Organisations commonly use structured training programmes to teach operational procedures, technical skills, and workplace protocols. Applying UDL principles encourages the development of training systems that accommodate diverse learning needs while maintaining organisational efficiency.

One important application involves presenting information through multiple forms of representation. Combining visual demonstrations with written instructions improves comprehension among diverse learners (Beckman, 2009). Consequently, organisations may provide written manuals alongside visual task guides, instructional videos, and digital simulations to support understanding of job procedures.

Engagement strategies can also be adapted to workplace learning environments. Flexible training systems that acknowledge individual motivations and learning preferences enhance employee participation (Doussard et al., 2024). Practical approaches include collaborative learning activities, mentoring opportunities, and flexible training schedules that allow employees to progress at appropriate rates. Such strategies are particularly beneficial for workers with intellectual disabilities who may require guided practice and structured feedback during skill development.

The principle of action and expression further supports inclusive training. Flexible performance pathways allow learners to demonstrate competence using different methods and tools (Novembli et al., 2024). In workplace settings, this may involve practical task demonstrations, assistive technologies, or digital records of completed work. These approaches enable organisations to assess competence based on actual job performance rather than relying exclusively on written assessments.

Effective application of UDL also requires proactive design. Inclusive principles should be integrated during programme development rather than introduced only after barriers emerge. Proactive accessibility design reduces the need for individual accommodations and supports inclusive learning environments for all employees, including workers with intellectual disability (Doussard et al., 2024).

Aligning UDL with Disability-Inclusive Workplace Policies

1. **Integration of UDL within Disability-Inclusive Employment Frameworks**: Universal Design for Learning (UDL) aligns with disability-inclusive workplace policies that prioritise accessibility, participation, and equity for employees with disabilities. Inclusive employment frameworks encourage organisations to examine how organisational systems, workplace policies, and training programmes influence opportunities for workers with disabilities. When UDL principles are incorporated into organisational structures, learning and participation become more accessible for employees with diverse abilities. This alignment ensures that workplace learning systems support inclusion while enabling workers with intellectual disabilities to engage meaningfully in training and professional development activities.
2. **Embedding UDL in Workplace Training and Learning Systems**: Embedding UDL within workplace training systems allows organisations to design learning environments that accommodate diverse learning preferences, cognitive abilities, and communication needs. Flexible instructional methods, varied learning materials, and accessible training resources make it easier for employees with intellectual disabilities to understand workplace expectations and develop relevant skills. When training programmes incorporate multiple ways to present information and engage learners, employees are more likely to participate actively and build confidence in their abilities. Integrating UDL into workplace learning, therefore, strengthens the effectiveness of training while supporting inclusive participation in professional development.
3. **Strengthening Inclusive Organisational Culture through UDL**: Training systems that recognise diverse learning needs can contribute to the development of inclusive organisational cultures. When learning environments encourage collaboration and mutual support, employees become more willing to share knowledge and assist one another in completing workplace tasks. Inclusive workplace design allows individuals to leverage their strengths while contributing to collective learning processes within teams (Doussard et al., 2024). Such environments reinforce shared responsibility for learning and encourage employees to view inclusion as an everyday organisational practice rather than a specialised intervention.
4. **Ethical and Equity Considerations in UDL Implementation:** Implementing UDL within workplace training also involves addressing ethical responsibilities related to equity and accessibility. Organisations that adopt inclusive training

practices recognise the need to remove systemic barriers that restrict participation for workers with disabilities. Embedding flexibility and accessibility within workplace learning structures helps ensure that all employees have equitable opportunities to develop their skills and advance professionally. These practices support the sustained participation and long-term professional development of workers with intellectual disabilities while reinforcing organisational commitments to fairness and inclusion.

8.3 STRUCTURED LEARNING AND COGNITIVE SCAFFOLDING

Breaking job tasks into structured learning sequences is essential for helping workers with intellectual disabilities acquire workplace competencies. This section examines practical strategies such as task analysis, chunking, visual sequencing, and the gradual release of responsibility. These approaches simplify complex job processes and support cognitive functioning during skill development.

Task Analysis and Job Deconstruction Techniques

These approaches provide structured methods for breaking complex workplace tasks into manageable learning steps, enabling workers with intellectual disabilities to understand, practise, and master job routines more effectively. This can be achieved through the following strategies:

1. **Deconstructing tasks into procedural components:** Systematically breaking tasks into smaller procedural steps helps trainers and supervisors clarify the sequence of actions necessary for effective job performance.
2. **Identifying prerequisite skills and instructional steps:** Task analysis enables trainers to determine the skills and instructional stages required for vocational learning goals (Yasak & Alias, 2016).
3. **Use of cognitive task analysis to understand professional processes:** Cognitive task analysis can inform training protocols by identifying the detailed processes involved in professional tasks (Read & Baillie, 2013).
4. **Providing structured learning pathways for workers with intellectual disabilities:** Task analysis offers a clear and structured pathway for learning job routines, allowing employees to learn tasks progressively rather than all at once.
5. **Step-by-step instruction to reduce ambiguity:** Trainers introduce tasks gradually with targeted guidance, enabling employees to master one component before progressing to the next stage.

6. **Improving predictability and manageability in workplace training:** Applying task analysis makes workplace training more predictable and manageable, particularly for employees who may struggle with complex or multi-step activities.
7. **Technological support for task analysis:** Digital systems can assist in identifying task components and workflow dependencies in dynamic work environments (Lin & Lehto, 2008).
8. **Enhancing understanding of organisational workflows:** Analytical tools help organisations identify subtasks and relationships within workflows, complementing traditional task analysis methods.

Chunking Complex Processes into Manageable Steps

This instructional strategy groups related steps within a task into smaller, manageable units. It reduces cognitive overload by allowing learners to focus on key components rather than processing an entire procedure at once.

Benefits of chunking are:

1. **Reducing cognitive overload and supporting problem-solving:** Dividing procedures into smaller units allows learners to focus on key components rather than trying to process an entire procedure at once. By narrowing the amount of information considered at each stage of a task, learners can concentrate on solving immediate problems and completing each step effectively. This structured approach improves comprehension and task accuracy during learning activities Ho and Liausvia (2013).
2. **Organising information into meaningful units for effective learning:** Presenting information in smaller, organised units helps individuals structure and interpret workplace instructions more effectively. When information is grouped into meaningful segments, learners can recognise relationships between steps and understand how tasks are organised within a broader process. This method strengthens information processing and helps individuals retain task-related knowledge during training (Ramkumar et al., 2016).
3. **Simplifying workplace training for workers with intellectual disabilities:** Complex job routines can be presented as structured sequences of smaller steps, making training activities more accessible for workers with intellectual disabilities. Trainers can divide multi-stage processes into shorter routines that employees practise individually before combining them into the complete workflow. This structured approach allows workers to develop competence gradually while reducing cognitive strain during skill acquisition.
4. **Supporting progressive knowledge and skill development in vocational settings:** Hierarchical instructional models allow learners to build knowledge

progressively from smaller units toward more complex task structures. Such approaches are particularly valuable in vocational environments where employees must learn multiple procedures within a single job role. Structured sequencing supports gradual competence development and strengthens employees' ability to perform workplace tasks effectively (Wu et al., 2022).

Potential Challenges

1. **Risk of excessive segmentation:** When tasks are divided into too many small units, important contextual cues that help learners understand and recall task sequences may be lost. Excessive fragmentation can therefore disrupt learners' ability to connect individual steps into a coherent workflow (Cohen & Sekuler, 2010).
2. **Mismatch with task complexity and learner needs:** This approach may become ineffective if it is not carefully aligned with the complexity of the task and the learning needs of employees. If instructional segmentation does not reflect learners' cognitive abilities and prior experience, it may create confusion rather than support understanding (O'Shea & Clegg, 2006).

Visual Sequencing and Workflow Mapping

Visual sequencing strategies offer another effective way to support structured learning in workplace environments. Visual tools represent task sequences to clarify workflows and highlight relationships across different stages of a process. Workflow mapping, for example, visually illustrates how tasks progress from one step to another. Perrotta et al. (2020) report that workflow mapping can reveal inefficiencies and clarify operational processes.

Visual workflow tools also help training designers represent task dependencies and priorities. In Faulkner (2018), digital workflow mapping tools enable organisations to visualise complex processes and identify opportunities to streamline tasks. In workplace training for workers with intellectual disabilities, visual representations can help employees understand the order of actions required to complete tasks.

Additional tools, such as Directed Acyclic Graphs, can also represent relationships between tasks within organisational systems. Amalarethinam and Muthulakshmi (2012) demonstrate how visual modelling tools illustrate connections among workflow components, while Yuan et al. (2024) emphasise that visual task representations support decision-making and task prioritisation. For workers with intellectual disabilities, these visual supports provide clear cues that assist memory, organisation, and task completion.

Gradual Release of Responsibility (GRR)

The Gradual Release of Responsibility (GRR) model is a structured approach that progressively transfers responsibility for learning from trainers to learners. Initially, trainers model tasks and demonstrate correct procedures before learners engage in guided practice and eventually perform tasks independently. Scaffolded approaches such as GRR support the development of independence while maintaining structured assistance during skill acquisition (Hall et al., 2021) The model typically involves modelling, guided practice, collaborative learning, and independent performance (Ortlieb & Schatz, 2019). Gradual transfer of responsibility also helps learners build confidence while receiving support during early learning stages (Lin & Cheng, 2010).

For workers with intellectual disabilities, GRR provides a balance between support and autonomy. Trainers demonstrate tasks, provide feedback during guided practice, and gradually reduce assistance as competence develops. The approach is particularly beneficial for individuals with executive functioning challenges because it promotes self-regulation, strategic learning, and independent performance (Alstete et al., 2024; Salehomoum, 2019). By reducing cognitive demands during initial learning and progressively increasing responsibility, GRR helps workers with intellectual disabilities acquire workplace skills, build confidence, and achieve greater independence in job performance.

Supporting Executive Functioning and Working Memory

Executive functioning and working memory play an important role in how individuals organise information, follow instructions, and complete multi-step workplace tasks. These cognitive processes enable employees to plan actions, remember instructions, and sequence activities correctly during job performance.

Workers with intellectual disabilities may experience difficulties with sequencing tasks, planning actions, and retaining the information required to complete job routines. Such challenges can affect their ability to follow instructions accurately and perform multi-step tasks efficiently in workplace environments.

Importance of structured training strategies

Structured training strategies can therefore support cognitive functioning during workplace learning. According to Precin (2010), visual imagery techniques can enhance task sequencing for individuals experiencing executive functioning difficulties. In workplace settings, visual prompts, diagrams, and step-by-step guides help employees remember task sequences and perform routines more independently.

Reducing cognitive load is another important strategy in workplace training. Fry (2018) notes that information-reduction techniques simplify learning environments by directing attention to essential information. Dividing instructional content into smaller learning segments improves retention (Munyofu et al., 2007). These approaches create learning environments that strengthen comprehension, memory, and effective job performance.

8.4 MULTI-MODAL TRAINING APPROACHES

Multi-modal training combines different instructional methods to support diverse learning needs in workplace environments. By providing multiple pathways for understanding information, practising tasks, and demonstrating competence, organisations can strengthen workplace participation while accommodating varied cognitive processing strengths.

8.4.1 Visual supports in workplace training: It plays a critical role in making workplace training accessible for workers with intellectual disabilities. Diagrams, pictorial instructions, infographics, and structured visual guides simplify complex information and clarify workplace procedures. Predictable visual formats improve access to learning environments and help employees follow task sequences more effectively (Foster-Cohen & Mirfin-Veitch, 2017). In practice, workflow charts, labelled photographs, pictorial checklists, colour-coded prompts, and workstation reminders help employees recognise equipment and complete tasks accurately. Such supports can increase engagement and reduce anxiety associated with unfamiliar routines (Rutherford et al., 2020). Emerging technologies, including augmented reality, further enhance visual learning by providing step-by-step guidance within workplace settings (Bryant & Hemsley, 2024).

8.4.2 Demonstration-based instruction: It is another important multi-modal strategy. Trainers model task procedures while employees observe and subsequently perform the activity themselves. Observational learning helps employees understand processes and recognise the sequence of actions required for successful task completion. Demonstrations often improve performance more effectively than written instructions alone (Can & Cengiz, 2026). Their effectiveness increases when combined with guided practice and immediate feedback. Through repeated observation and supervised practice, workers with intellectual disabilities can refine skills, improve accuracy, and build confidence

8.4.3 Role-play and simulation activities: They provide opportunities to practise workplace skills in structured and realistic settings. These approaches allow employees to rehearse communication, decision-making, and problem-solving skills before applying them in actual work environments. Experiential learning environments that replicate workplace conditions support the development of practical competencies (Maqbool et al., 2021). Examples include customer-service scenarios, teamwork exercises, and workplace safety simulations. Game-based learning can also strengthen collaboration, communication, and problem-solving skills while increasing engagement (Marchiori & Song, 2024),

8.4.4 Experiential and hands-on learning: Hands-on learning is central to effective workplace training, particularly for employees who learn best through direct experience. Experiential approaches emphasise active participation rather than passive observation. Through guided practice, employees gain practical understanding of workplace processes and strengthen connections between theory and application (Masse et al., 2019). Activities may include operating equipment, assembling materials, or performing routine procedures under supervision. Immediate application of knowledge, combined with constructive feedback, supports skill development, vocational readiness, and professional confidence (Mayombe, 2024).

8.4.5 Peer modelling and collaborative learning: This represents another effective multi-modal strategy. In peer-supported learning environments, employees observe colleagues who demonstrate effective task performance and then practise similar procedures themselves. Collaborative learning can improve motivation and skill acquisition in professional training contexts (Rashwan et al., 2024). Experienced employees can serve as role models, while group-based training activities promote teamwork, communication, and shared problem-solving. These approaches support both learning and social inclusion within workplace settings (Fantozzi & Schiraldi, 2025).

8.4.6 Aligning instruction with cognitive processing strengths: Effective workplace training requires alignment between instructional methods and employees' cognitive processing strengths. Workers with intellectual disabilities may learn more effectively through visual, auditory, or experiential approaches. Visual learning tools, including infographics and structured guides, can simplify complex information and improve understanding (Kardgar et al., 2024). Similarly, immersive technologies such as augmented reality can provide personalised instructional support tailored to individual learning needs (Ajao et al., 2024). By combining visual supports, demonstrations, hands-on learning, and collaborative strategies, organisations can design multi-modal training systems that respond to diverse learning profiles while strengthening training effectiveness.

8.5 ASSISTIVE AND DIGITAL TECHNOLOGIES IN WORKPLACE TRAINING

Assistive and digital technologies increasingly shape contemporary approaches to workplace training and support for workers with intellectual disabilities. These technologies provide practical tools that help employees learn job tasks, manage responsibilities, communicate effectively, and navigate workplace environments. When organisations integrate such technologies thoughtfully into training systems, they can strengthen skill acquisition while reducing barriers associated with complex job routines. At the same time, effective implementation requires careful attention to the balance between technological assistance and human support. Workers with intellectual disabilities often benefit from structured guidance and interpersonal interaction alongside technological tools.

Role of Assistive Technology in Workplace Skill Development

Definition and Types

Assistive technology (AT) includes devices, tools, and digital systems that support individuals in performing tasks more independently. In workplace training, these technologies simplify job procedures, support memory, and provide structured prompts. Common examples include reminders, visual prompts, scheduling systems, and navigation aids that guide employees through task sequences and workplace responsibilities (Morash-Macneil et al., 2018). Some of the benefits of using AT include:

1. **Improving task accuracy and productivity:** Technological support provides step-by-step guidance during job activities, helping employees complete tasks more accurately and efficiently.
2. **Reducing cognitive demands during task performance:** Visual prompts and digital instructions reduce the cognitive load associated with remembering complex procedures.
3. **Supporting consistent work routines and learning:** Structured guidance during task performance reinforces learning and strengthens workplace routines.
4. **Promoting independence and autonomy:** Technology-supported learning systems enable workers with intellectual disabilities to perform tasks with increased independence (Gupta, 2019).
5. **Reducing the need for continuous supervision:** When employees rely on digital reminders or visual prompts, they can maintain task accuracy while requiring less direct supervision.

6. **Strengthening confidence and workplace participation:** Assistive technologies support independence and competence, which can enhance confidence among workers with intellectual disabilities.

Interactive Applications and Task-Prompting Systems

Interactive applications and task-prompting systems represent another important category of assistive technologies used in workplace training. Many digital tools now provide structured prompts that guide employees through complex tasks step by step. These systems often include visual cues, audio reminders, and automated feedback to help employees stay focused while completing their job responsibilities.

For workers with intellectual disabilities who experience challenges related to memory or sequencing, digital prompting systems can provide essential support during workplace training. These technologies allow employees to follow structured procedures without memorising every step of a task. Randall et al. (2025) note that assistive technologies supporting task completion and independence are increasingly used in both workplace and daily living environments for individuals with intellectual and developmental disabilities.

Consumer technologies such as smartphones, wearable devices, and mobile applications have also expanded opportunities for workplace support. These tools can deliver reminders, alarms, and visual prompts that guide employees through routine job activities. In vocational environments, such technologies may support workers with intellectual disabilities by offering real-time prompts during task completion and enabling workers to manage their responsibilities more independently (Paul et al., 2022).

Simulation and Digital Skill Rehearsal

Digital technologies can also support workplace learning through simulated practice environments. While traditional vocational training often relies on direct instruction and hands-on experience, digital platforms allow employees to practise job tasks in controlled settings before performing them in real workplaces.

Technology-supported rehearsal environments enable employees to develop familiarity with workplace procedures and build confidence during training. Morash-Macneil et al. (2018) emphasise that technology-based learning tools can improve productivity and skill acquisition when integrated into structured training programmes for individuals with intellectual disabilities. Through repeated practice, employees can refine their understanding of job routines without the pressure associated with immediate workplace performance.

Simulation technologies can therefore provide valuable opportunities for rehearsal and reinforcement. Workers may review instructions, repeat procedures, and gradually develop competence before applying these skills in actual work environments. This process supports gradual learning and reduces anxiety that may arise when employees encounter unfamiliar tasks.

Communication and Accessibility Technologies

Communication technologies also play a significant role in supporting workplace participation for workers with intellectual disabilities. Tools such as speech-to-text systems, text-to-speech software, and simplified communication platforms can assist employees who have difficulty reading, writing, or verbal expression.

Accessible communication tools enable workers to understand written instructions, communicate with supervisors, and receive feedback more effectively. Heinz-Jakobs et al. (2025) emphasise that intelligent assistive technologies can improve workplace inclusion by strengthening accessibility and communication across organisational environments. When workers have access to appropriate communication tools, they are better positioned to participate in workplace discussions, training activities, and collaborative tasks.

Communication technologies can also enhance social interaction within the workplace. By supporting clearer communication, these tools allow workers with intellectual disabilities to interact more confidently with colleagues and supervisors. Improved communication can therefore strengthen teamwork, workplace relationships, and participation in organisational activities.

Ethical Considerations in Technology Use

Although assistive technologies provide important benefits, organisations must consider ethical issues when implementing digital tools in workplace training. Technology should enhance autonomy and participation rather than create dependency or replace human interaction.

Staff perspectives highlight the importance of maintaining a balanced approach to technology use. Rasouli et al. (2023) report that professionals working with individuals with intellectual disabilities often express concerns about the potential over-reliance on assistive technologies. When digital tools replace meaningful interpersonal engagement, workers may experience reduced opportunities for social learning and workplace integration.

Ethical implementation, therefore, requires thoughtful planning and monitoring. Organisations should introduce assistive technologies as supportive tools that complement existing training practices rather than replacing supervision, mentorship, and collaborative learning opportunities.

Barriers to Technology Adoption

Despite their potential benefits, several factors can limit the adoption of assistive technologies in workplace environments. Financial constraints often represent a major barrier. Some specialised assistive devices require substantial investment, which may discourage organisations from implementing them widely.

Infrastructure and accessibility considerations also influence technology adoption. Workplace environments may lack the technological infrastructure necessary to support certain digital systems effectively. Organisational systems sometimes require adaptation to ensure compatibility with assistive technologies.

Limited knowledge and training can further restrict effective implementation. Employees and supervisors may require instruction on how assistive technologies function and how they can be integrated into workplace routines. Without appropriate training, technological tools may remain underutilised (Jääskeläinen & Nevala, 2012).

Integrating Technology with Human Support

Successful use of assistive technologies depends on integrating digital tools with human support systems. Technological solutions should function as complementary resources within broader workplace training programmes rather than operating independently.

Supported employment research demonstrates that workers with intellectual disabilities benefit most when technological tools are combined with coaching, mentoring, and structured supervision. Heman et al. (2022) emphasise that such integrated support systems improve employment outcomes and strengthen workplace participation.

Organisations should therefore prioritise balanced support systems that combine technological resources with interpersonal guidance. When digital tools operate alongside mentorship and collaborative training environments, workers with intellectual disabilities can benefit from both technological efficiency and human support.

Toward Inclusive Technological Work Environments

Assistive and digital technologies provide significant opportunities to strengthen workplace training and participation for workers with intellectual disabilities. These tools can support task completion, communication, and skill development while promoting greater independence in employment settings.

However, effective implementation requires inclusive design and organisational commitment. Employers must consider ethical implications, ensure accessibility, and provide adequate training for both staff and employees. Reinersmann et al. (2025) demonstrate that the successful implementation of digital assistive technologies depends on workplace infrastructure, usability, and organisational support.

When organisations integrate assistive technologies thoughtfully into workplace training systems, they can create more inclusive employment environments. Such systems allow workers with intellectual disabilities to participate meaningfully in professional roles while continuing to develop their skills, confidence, and independence.

8.6 CREATING PSYCHOLOGICALLY SAFE LEARNING ENVIRONMENTS

Workplace training environments significantly impact not only skill acquisition but also the emotional experiences of employees, particularly those with intellectual disabilities. A positive psychological climate enhances participation, confidence, and perseverance in learning tasks. Psychologically safe settings encourage employees to ask questions, practice, make mistakes, and seek help without fear of judgment. By fostering such environments, organisations promote inclusive training that values time, repetition, and supportive feedback, boosting the engagement and confidence of workers with intellectual disabilities.

Reducing Training Anxiety and Fear of Failure

Workers with intellectual disabilities may experience anxiety when learning unfamiliar workplace tasks, particularly in environments where mistakes are interpreted as failures rather than opportunities for learning. Training programmes that emphasise supportive guidance and predictable routines can reduce this anxiety and create a sense of security during skill development. Structured learning environments allow employees to concentrate on mastering tasks rather than worrying about potential errors.

Supportive and predictable learning structures contribute to confidence and independence among individuals with intellectual disabilities. Edwards et al. (2025) show that structured transition programmes for autistic youth with intellectual disabilities create psychologically safe environments where participants feel supported while developing new competencies. Similar principles can guide workplace training environments, where predictable routines and clear expectations help employees approach tasks with greater confidence.

Mentorship also helps reduce training anxiety. Joyce et al. (2025) report that mentoring relationships and flexible workplace roles improve well-being and job satisfaction among employees with intellectual disabilities. Mentors provide reassurance, model effective work practices, and guide employees through challenging tasks, thereby supporting gradual competence development in workplace settings.

Encouraging Repetition Without Stigma

Skill development in workplace training frequently requires repeated practice. Workers with intellectual disabilities may need additional opportunities to rehearse tasks before achieving mastery. For this reason, training systems must present repetition as a natural and accepted part of learning rather than as a sign of failure.

Accessible training approaches help normalise repetition within workplace learning environments. Training materials designed for individuals with intellectual disabilities often incorporate simplified language, visual supports, and structured formats that support comprehension and engagement. Gomez-Borges et al. 2025) demonstrate that accessible learning strategies, including Easy Read formats and simplified instructional materials, reduce barriers to participation for employees with intellectual disabilities.

When organisations adopt accessible training practices, repetition becomes a constructive element of the learning process. Trainers can encourage employees to practise tasks at their own pace while emphasising gradual progress. Such approaches create learning environments where workers feel comfortable refining their skills, gaining confidence and competence.

Positive Reinforcement and Encouragement

Positive reinforcement represents a powerful strategy for promoting learning and skill development among workers with intellectual disabilities. Encouraging feedback, recognition of effort, and acknowledgement of successful performance can motivate employees to continue practising new skills.

Behavioural skills training provides one example of how reinforcement supports learning. Miltenberger and Novotny (2022) demonstrate that behavioural training approaches incorporating modelling, practice, and reinforcement effectively teach safety and vocational skills to individuals with developmental disabilities. In workplace training contexts, reinforcement strategies may include verbal praise, recognition of improvement, or structured reward systems that acknowledge successful task completion.

Positive reinforcement also strengthens confidence and resilience. When employees receive supportive feedback after attempting new tasks, they are more likely to perceive challenges as manageable learning opportunities. This perspective encourages persistence and supports long-term skill development.

Feedback Systems That Promote Growth

Constructive feedback is another essential component of psychologically safe learning environments. Effective feedback systems focus on guiding improvement rather than emphasising mistakes. Workers with intellectual disabilities benefit from clear, specific feedback delivered respectfully.

Growth-oriented feedback enables employees to understand how their performance can improve while maintaining confidence in their abilities. Ben Amram and Shapira-Lishchinsky (2021) show that mentoring strategies that emphasise reflection and supportive dialogue strengthen self-efficacy among professionals supporting individuals with intellectual disabilities. Similar feedback approaches can be applied in workplace training contexts.

Trainers can provide constructive feedback through demonstrations, guided practice, or collaborative problem-solving. When employees receive feedback in a supportive manner, they are more likely to remain engaged in learning and continue refining their skills.

Trauma-Informed and Dignity-Centred Practices

Psychologically safe learning environments also require attention to emotional well-being and dignity. Some workers with intellectual disabilities may have previously experienced educational or employment environments where mistakes were criticised or where their abilities were underestimated. Trauma-informed approaches recognise the importance of creating environments that prioritise respect, trust, and emotional safety.

Trauma-informed training emphasises calm communication, supportive relationships, and consistent guidance. Graham et al. (2016) highlight the value of attachment-informed models that focus on building trusting relationships and fostering a sense of belonging among individuals with intellectual disabilities. These approaches recognise that effective learning occurs in environments where individuals feel respected and valued.

Person-centred practices further support psychological safety by recognising individual strengths, preferences, and goals. In the opinion of Edwards et al. (2025) person-centred approaches promote autonomy and emotional well-being by ensuring that individuals with intellectual disabilities participate in decisions related to their learning and development.

Building Supportive Workplace Learning Cultures

Creating psychologically safe learning environments ultimately requires organisational commitment. Employers, supervisors, and trainers play essential roles in establishing workplace cultures that value patience, inclusion, and respect. When organisations promote supportive training practices, workers with intellectual disabilities can develop skills without fear of judgment or exclusion.

Inclusive workplace cultures encourage employees to ask questions, practise tasks repeatedly, and seek assistance when needed. These practices reinforce the understanding that learning is a gradual process rather than a test of immediate competence.

Psychologically safe learning environments, therefore, form a foundation for effective workplace training. By reducing anxiety, encouraging repetition, reinforcing progress, and promoting dignity-centred practices, organisations can develop training systems that enable workers with intellectual disabilities to build confidence, strengthen skills, and participate meaningfully in the workforce.

8.7 TRAINING THE TRAINERS: BUILDING CAPACITY AMONG SUPERVISORS AND HR TEAMS

Effective workplace inclusion for workers with intellectual disabilities depends not only on accessible training systems but also on the competencies of supervisors and human resource (HR) professionals responsible for implementing them. These professionals shape workplace learning environments, monitor progress, and influence organisational attitudes toward disability inclusion. Targeted training equips supervisors and HR teams with the skills required to provide inclusive coaching, apply appropriate monitoring strategies, and foster supportive workplace cultures. Strengthening trainer capacity, therefore, represents a critical component of sustainable inclusive employment.

Disability Awareness and Attitudinal Training

Disability awareness training is a foundational component of capacity-building for supervisors and HR teams. Many barriers experienced by workers with intellectual disabilities arise from misconceptions about disability and a limited understanding of inclusive practices. Training programmes that address attitudes, stereotypes, and ethical considerations can improve supervisors' knowledge of disability inclusion and strengthen their ability to support diverse employees.

Employer training interventions that incorporate video case studies, role-play scenarios, and simulated workplace situations have demonstrated positive effects on attitudes toward hiring and supporting workers with intellectual disabilities. Ben-Amram and Shapira-Lishchinsky (2025) show that experiential training methods encourage reflection on workplace challenges and enhance psychological empowerment among employers and supervisors. These approaches allow participants to examine real workplace scenarios while developing confidence in inclusive decision-making.

Such awareness training also helps supervisors recognise the strengths and capabilities of workers with intellectual disabilities. When managers develop a deeper understanding of inclusive practices, they are more likely to implement supportive training strategies and create respectful workplace environments that encourage participation and professional growth.

Coaching Skills for Inclusive Instruction

Supervisors and HR teams must also develop coaching skills to deliver inclusive workplace instruction. Workers with intellectual disabilities often benefit from structured guidance, demonstrations, and supportive feedback during training activities. Effective trainers, therefore, require practical skills in modelling tasks, adapting instruction, and supporting diverse learning needs.

Train-the-trainer models offer an effective framework for developing these competencies. Riches et al. (2011) demonstrate that active support training programmes can transform staff practices by equipping trainers with strategies that promote meaningful participation among individuals with intellectual disabilities. Interactive workshops, reflective discussions, and practical exercises allow supervisors to practise inclusive coaching techniques and strengthen their instructional abilities.

Coaching effectiveness increases when theoretical training is combined with practical workplace experience. Rhodes and Hamilton (2006) emphasise the value of integrating conceptual learning with vivo training, where supervisors practise coaching strategies in real-world settings. Person-centred planning approaches further strengthen inclusive instruction by encouraging trainers to focus on workers with intellectual disabilities' strengths, preferences, and learning styles.

Monitoring Progress Without Micromanagement

Supervisors must also learn to monitor employee progress without creating environments characterised by excessive control or micromanagement. While workers with intellectual disabilities benefit from structured guidance, overly intrusive supervision can reduce autonomy and undermine confidence.

Effective monitoring strategies emphasise independence while maintaining appropriate support. Becerra et al. (2018) demonstrate that natural supports such as graphic prompts and visual aids can enable workers with intellectual disabilities to complete office tasks successfully without constant supervision. These supports allow supervisors to monitor outcomes while giving employees greater autonomy in completing tasks.

Training programmes that promote self-management strategies can also reduce the need for intensive oversight. Sandjojo et al. (2018) is of the opinion that teaching individuals with intellectual disabilities self-management skills strengthens independence and reduces reliance on continuous supervision. Supervisors who understand these approaches can better balance support with autonomy in workplace training environments.

Cultural Competence and Communication Strategies

Inclusive workplace training also requires cultural competence and effective communication. Supervisors and HR professionals must recognise that workers with intellectual disabilities bring diverse experiences, abilities, and communication preferences to the workplace.

Human resource practices that prioritise diversity and inclusion can significantly improve employees' workplace experiences with intellectual disabilities. Bartram et al. (2021) emphasise the importance of aligning HR policies with inclusive values to ensure that recruitment, training, and supervision practices support equitable participation.

Effective communication strategies also play a central role in inclusive supervision. Balasuriya et al, (2022) emphasise the importance of collaborative approaches in which supervisors and employees jointly engage in workplace tasks and problem-solving processes. Such interactions encourage shared understanding and strengthen communication between supervisors and workers with intellectual disabilities.

Accountability Mechanisms for Inclusive Training

Sustaining inclusive training practices requires accountability mechanisms that encourage supervisors to consistently apply inclusive strategies. Train-the-trainer programmes often include structured workshops, follow-up sessions, and monitoring processes that reinforce learning outcomes and promote continued application of inclusive principles.

Structured training initiatives illustrate how organisations can strengthen accountability within training systems. Marks et al. (2019) demonstrate that train-the-trainer programmes can improve staff knowledge and workplace practices when supported by ongoing workshops and reinforcement activities. Earlier evaluations of similar models emphasise the importance of structured training cycles and organisational commitment in sustaining inclusive practices (Marks et al., 2013).

Organisations can also strengthen accountability by identifying workplace champions who lead inclusion initiatives. (Wilson et al. (2023) show that staff-led champion programmes promote sustained improvements in organisational practices by encouraging peer leadership and shared responsibility. In workplace training contexts, such champions help reinforce inclusive learning practices among supervisors and HR teams.

Strengthening Organisational Capacity for Inclusive Training

Building capacity among supervisors and HR professionals ultimately strengthens organisational readiness for inclusive employment. Trainers who understand disability awareness, inclusive coaching strategies, and effective monitoring practices are better equipped to support workers with intellectual disabilities in developing workplace skills.

Training the trainers, therefore, represents a strategic investment in inclusive workplace development. By equipping supervisors and HR teams with the knowledge, attitudes, and practical skills required for inclusive training delivery, organisations can create learning environments that empower workers with intellectual disabilities while strengthening overall workforce capability.

8.8 MEASURING TRAINING EFFECTIVENESS AND WORKPLACE SKILL TRANSFER

Training evaluation ensures that workplace learning initiatives produce meaningful outcomes for workers with intellectual disabilities. Organisations must determine whether training improves job performance and whether employees can apply learned competencies within everyday work environments. Evaluation, therefore, focuses on observable workplace behaviour, practical competence, and functional performance rather than theoretical knowledge or written examinations.

- **Performance-based evaluation methods:** One effective approach to training evaluation is to observe workers as they perform real-world tasks. Supervisors can assess task accuracy, sequencing, and independence during routine work activities. Structured observation tools, such as task analyses and performance checklists, help trainers document how employees perform their responsibilities and identify areas that require additional support. These tools also allow organisations to track performance improvements while maintaining consistent evaluation standards across training programmes.
- **Use of digital and simulated training environments:** Technological learning environments have expanded opportunities for evaluating workplace learning. Virtual or immersive training systems allow individuals with intellectual disabilities to practise tasks in simulated contexts that replicate real workplace conditions. Michalski et al. (2023) describe how virtual training environments enable trainers to observe task performance while employees repeat activities and refine their skills. Blended training programmes that combine digital instruction with practical application may also strengthen vocational competence and improve task performance (Lo et al., 2024).
- **Competency demonstration in practical contexts**: Demonstration-based assessment offers a more inclusive way of evaluating workplace learning. Instead of relying on written examinations, workers demonstrate their abilities by performing job tasks while supervisors observe their actions. Trainers can assess how employees interpret instructions, operate equipment, and respond to routine workplace demands. Digital learning platforms that include video instructions, pictograms, and simplified guidance also support skill development and enable workers to practise tasks independently (Benda et al., 2019).
- **Monitoring the stability of learned skills:** Training evaluation must also determine whether employees retain their skills after training is complete. Skill stability refers to the ability to perform tasks consistently over time. Supervisors may conduct follow-up observations during routine work activities to determine whether workers continue to apply the competencies they have learned. Periodic refresher sessions and structured prompts can reinforce previously learned skills, particularly when tasks involve multiple steps or complex procedures (Smith et al., 2025).
- **Connecting training outcomes with workplace participation**: Effective evaluation extends beyond technical competence to include broader aspects of workplace participation. Successful employment often requires communication, collaboration, and adaptation to workplace expectations. Training programmes that include communication and interpersonal skills can strengthen

workplace interaction and improve employees' ability to engage with colleagues and supervisors (Liu et al., 2024).

Enhancing Inclusive Employment Through Training Evaluation

This can be achieved through the following:

- **Aligning training content with workplace responsibilities**: Training is most effective when it reflects the actual demands of the workplace. Support professionals, or labour mediators, often assist organisations in matching job tasks to workers' competencies. These professionals help ensure that training programmes reflect real workplace expectations and support communication between employers and employees (Izuzquiza Gasset & Rodríguez Herrero, 2016).
- **Continuous improvement through evaluation feedback: Evaluation** findings contribute to the ongoing refinement of workplace training initiatives. Organisations can analyse performance outcomes to improve instructional strategies and ensure that training programmes remain accessible and relevant for workers with intellectual disabilities. Emerging assessment technologies increasingly allow evaluation processes to adapt to individual learning profiles and cognitive abilities (Poonkuzhali et al., 2025).
- **Using evaluation to strengthen inclusive employment systems:** Effective evaluation combines performance observation, competency demonstrations, and ongoing monitoring of workplace behaviour. These approaches help organisations identify successful training strategies and ensure that workers can apply skills consistently in their jobs. By prioritising practical competence and workplace participation, evaluation systems support sustained skill development and stronger employment opportunities for workers with intellectual disabilities.

8.9 CONCLUSION

Workplace training extends beyond the acquisition of immediate job skills. It provides a foundation for long-term employment stability and professional development for workers with intellectual disabilities. Effective training systems should connect learning opportunities with broader career pathways within organisations. Access to structured progression routes allows training to function as a pathway for growth rather than a short-term intervention. Linking skill development to advancement opportunities enables employees with intellectual disabilities to envision sustained participation in the workforce. Sustainable workplace growth also depends on continuous skill development and lifelong learning opportunities. As workplace technologies, processes, and organisational expectations evolve, workers require ongoing learning experiences to adapt and expand their competencies.

Organisations that prioritise continuous learning create environments in which employees strengthen existing skills while gradually acquiring new capabilities. The integration of Universal Design for Learning (UDL) principles within organisational culture further strengthens inclusive workplace training. UDL promotes flexible instructional strategies, multiple forms of communication, and accessible learning resources that address diverse learning needs. When organisations embed these principles in everyday training practices, learning opportunities become more inclusive and responsive to individual differences.

Training initiatives should also align with inclusive leadership practices and organisational policy frameworks. Leadership commitment to inclusion ensures that workplace training receives institutional support through clear policies, accessible resources, and equitable participation opportunities. Such alignment strengthens the sustainability of inclusive employment practices. This chapter emphasised the value of structured training systems that support skill acquisition, workplace participation, and long-term professional growth. The discussion now turns to Chapter 9, which examines career development, advancement, and workplace belonging for workers with intellectual disabilities.

REFERENCES

Ahmad, W., Shokeen, R., Raj, R., Ramkumar, B. V., Singh, R. R., & Mohammad, S. (2026). Transition of Persons With Intellectual and Developmental Disabilities From School to Work: Evidence- Based Practices. In *Vocational Rehabilitation for Students with Developmental Disabilities* (pp. 79–132). Transition from Education to Employment., DOI: 10.4018/979-8-3693-9541-7.ch003

Ajao, S. O., Aworinde, H. O., Falola, P. B., Adeniyi, A. E., & Sakpere, A. B. (2024). Augmented Reality in Experiential Learning: An Overview. *IEEE International Conference on Emerging and Sustainable Technologies for Power and ICT in a Developing Society, NIGERCON*, (2024). DOI: 10.1109/NIGERCON62786.2024.10927359

Alexander, J., Ford, J., Raghavendra, P., & Clark, J. (2018). Nature and extent of on-the-job training for employees with an intellectual disability: A pilot study. *Research and Practice in Intellectual and Developmental Disabilities*, *5*(2), 138–148. DOI: 10.1080/23297018.2017.1359661

Alstete, J. W., Meyer, J. P., & Beutell, N. J. (2024). Empowering neurodivergent students in management education with gradual release of responsibility. *International Journal of Management Education*, *22*(1), 100941. Advance online publication. DOI: 10.1016/j.ijme.2024.100941

Amalarethinam, D. I. G., & Muthulakshmi, P. (2012). DAGITIZER - A tool to generate a directed acyclic graph through a randomiser to model scheduling in grid computing. *Advances in Intelligent and Soft Computing, 167 AISC*(VOL. 2), 969–978. DOI: 10.1007/978-3-642-30111-7_93

Balasuriya, S. S., Sitbon, L., & Brereton, M. (2022). A Support Worker Perspective on Use of New Technologies by People with Intellectual Disabilities. *ACM Transactions on Accessible Computing*, *15*(3), 1–21. Advance online publication. DOI: 10.1145/3523058

Becerra, M.-T., Montanero, M., & Lucero, M. (2018). Graphic support resources for workers with intellectual disability engaged in office tasks: A comparison with verbal instructions from a workmate. *Disability and Rehabilitation*, *40*(4), 435–443. DOI: 10.1080/09638288.2016.1258739 PMID: 27973913

Beckman, P. (2009). Universal design for learning: A field experiment comparing specific classroom actions. *15th Americas Conference on Information Systems 2009, AMCIS 2009, 1*, 514–523. https://www.scopus.com/inward/record.uri?eid=2-s2.0-84870264980&partnerID=40&md5=7ca9608d47d0a918db27d4bf3f50434a

Ben Amram, M., & Shapira-Lishchinsky, O. (2021). Mentoring strategies and their impact on social workers' attitudes. *Journal of Social Work : JSW, 21*(3), 374–393. DOI: 10.1177/1468017320911506

Ben-Amram, M., & Shapira-Lishchinsky, O. (2025). Employer Training Interventions in Supported Employment Workplaces and Their Impact on Hiring Attitudes. *International Journal of Training and Development*. Advance online publication. DOI: 10.1111/ijtd.70015

Benda, P., Pavlík, J., & Masner, J. (2019). Practical education of adults with intellectual disabilities using a web course. *Problems of Education in the 21st Century, 77*(4), 463–477. DOI: 10.33225/pec/19.77.463

Bryant, B. R., Rao, K., & Ok, M. W. (2015). Universal Design for Learning and Assistive Technology: Promising Developments. In *Human-Computer Interaction: Concepts, Methodologies, Tools, and Applications: Volume 1-4* (Vols. 1–4, pp. 567–582). DOI: 10.4018/978-1-4666-8789-9.ch025

Bryant, L., & Hemsley, B. (2024). Augmented reality: A view to future visual supports for people with disability. *Disability and Rehabilitation. Assistive Technology, 19*(3), 800–813. DOI: 10.1080/17483107.2022.2125090 PMID: 36149835

Burgin, H., Hooper, J., Forbes-Nicholson, A., & Koutoukidis, G. (2026). Evaluating the Impact of Integrated Practical Placement Programmes on Students With Intellectual Disabilities. *Journal of Applied Research in Intellectual Disabilities, 39*(1), e70184. Advance online publication. DOI: 10.1111/jar.70184 PMID: 41607296

Can, M., & Cengiz, M. I. (2026). The Impact of Instructional Approaches on Scaling and Root Planning Skill Learning in Preclinical Periodontal Education. *Journal of Dental Education, 90*(2), 196–203. DOI: 10.1002/jdd.13934 PMID: 40346747

Carlson, S. R., Morningstar, M. E., & Munandar, V. (2020). Workplace supports for employees with intellectual disability: A systematic review of the intervention literature. *Journal of Vocational Rehabilitation, 52*(3), 251–265. DOI: 10.3233/JVR-201075

Chattopadhyay, R. (2025). Inclusive digital training systems and learning equity in the workplace: Evidence from a neurodiverse workforce. *Journal of Workplace Learning*, •••, 1–17. DOI: 10.1108/JWL-06-2025-0178

Cohen, N. R., & Sekuler, R. (2010). Chunking and compound cueing of movement sequences: Learning, retention, and transfer. *Perceptual and Motor Skills, 110*(3), 736–750. DOI: 10.2466/pms.110.3.736-750 PMID: 20681328

Collett-Schmitt, K., McKendree, A., Rubey, K., & McManus Warnell, J. (2025). Beyond the Backlash: Integrating DEI in business education to develop responsible leaders. *International Journal of Management Education*, *23*(3), 101212. Advance online publication. DOI: 10.1016/j.ijme.2025.101212

Courtad, C. A. (2019). Making your classroom smart: Universal design for learning and technology. *Smart Innovation. Systems and Technologies*, *144*, 501–510. DOI: 10.1007/978-981-13-8260-4_44

Doussard, C., Garbe, E., Morales, J., & Billion, J. (2024). Universal Design for the Workplace: Ethical Considerations Regarding the Inclusion of Workers with Disabilities. *Journal of Business Ethics*, *194*(2), 285–296. DOI: 10.1007/s10551-023-05582-y

Edwards, C., Cai, R. Y., Love, A., White, L. M., Harris, K., Brooker, K., Kendall, E., & Gibbs, V. (2025). Beyond the "service cliff": Experiences of an inclusive postschool transition program for autistic youth with intellectual disability. *Advances in Autism*, *11*(4), 385–399. Advance online publication. DOI: 10.1108/AIA-06-2025-0053

Fantozzi, I. C., & Schiraldi, M. M. (2025). Bridging education and industry: University challenges and serious games for professional skill development. *The TQM Journal*. Advance online publication. DOI: 10.1108/TQM-12-2024-0511

Faulkner, A. (2018). Lucidchart for Easy Workflow Mapping. *Serials Review*, *44*(2), 157–162. DOI: 10.1080/00987913.2018.1472468

Foster-Cohen, S., & Mirfin-Veitch, B. (2017). Evidence for the effectiveness of visual supports in helping children with disabilities access the mainstream primary school curriculum. *Journal of Research in Special Educational Needs*, *17*(2), 79–86. DOI: 10.1111/1471-3802.12105

Frolli, A., Cerciello, F., Esposito, C., & Sica, L. S. (2022). Universal Design for Learning: A new educational approach. *CEUR Workshop Proceedings*, *3371*, •••. https://www.scopus.com/inward/record.uri?eid=2-s2.0-85154043738&partnerID=40&md5=1cb3dddc557a5ea6284bcf5e99a11670

Fry, R. (2018). Information reduction and studio project frameworks. *Proceedings of the 20th International Conference on Engineering and Product Design Education, E and PDE 2018*. https://www.scopus.com/inward/record.uri?eid=2-s2.0-85057729051&partnerID=40&md5=8ad8dcbe5e1e848ad751b703133470d0

Gomez-Borges, A., Martínez, I. M., & Salanova, M. (2025). Adapting a Positive Psychological Intervention for Employees with and Without Intellectual Disabilities. *Healthcare (Basel), 13*(17), 2096. Advance online publication. DOI: 10.3390/healthcare13172096 PMID: 40941448

Graham, A., Harbottle, C., & King, D. (2016). Resolve: A community-based forensic learning disability service specialising in supporting male sex offenders – our model, approach and evidence base for effective intervention. *Journal of Intellectual Disabilities and Offending Behaviour, 7*(4), 186–194. DOI: 10.1108/JIDOB-10-2014-0014

Hall, C., Dahl-Leonard, K., Denton, C. A., Stevens, E. A., & Capin, P. (2021). Fostering Independence While Teaching Students With or at Risk for Reading Disabilities. *Teaching Exceptional Children, 54*(2), 124–133. DOI: 10.1177/0040059921994596

Heinz-Jakobs, M., Görmez, S., Johnson, H. L., Gerken, J., Pascher, M., Barbareschi, G., Balasuriya, S. S., Sitbon, L., & Röcker, C. (2025). AT@Work: Intelligent Assistive Technologies for Enabling Workplace Inclusion. *ASSETS 2025 - Proceedings of the 27th International ACM SIGACCESS Conference on Computers and Accessibility.* DOI: 10.1145/3663547.3748637

Heman, P., Rhodes, D., & Cox, C. (2022). Electronic assistive technology use and supported employment. *Journal of Applied Research in Intellectual Disabilities, 35*(5), 1244–1249. DOI: 10.1111/jar.13005 PMID: 35596577

Ho, S.-B., & Liausvia, F. (2013). Incremental rule chunking for problem solving. *Proceedings - 1st BRICS Countries Congress on Computational Intelligence, BRICS-CCI 2013*, 323–328. DOI: 10.1109/BRICS-CCI-CBIC.2013.61

Izuzquiza Gasset, D., & Rodríguez Herrero, P. (2016). Evaluación de la metodología Empleo con Apoyo (ECA) en el Programa Promentor (UAM-PRODIS). El ajuste competencial. *Siglo Cero. Revista Española Sobre Discapacidad Intelectual, 47*(1), 37. DOI: 10.14201/scero201613754

Jääskeläinen, K., & Nevala, N. (2012). Use of assistive technology in workplaces of employees with physical and cognitive disabilities. *Lecture Notes in Computer Science (Including Subseries Lecture Notes in Artificial Intelligence and Lecture Notes in Bioinformatics), 7382 LNCS*(PART 1), 223–226. DOI: 10.1007/978-3-642-31522-0_33

Joyce, A., Campbell, P., Crosbie, J., & Wilson, E. (2024). Workplace Structures and Culture That Support the Wellbeing of People with an Intellectual Disability. *International Journal of Environmental Research and Public Health, 21*(11), 1453. Advance online publication. DOI: 10.3390/ijerph21111453 PMID: 39595719

Joyce, A., Campbell, P., Crosbie, J., & Wilson, E. (2025). Wellbeing and job satisfaction among employees with intellectual disability. *Frontiers in Public Health, 13*, 1503932. Advance online publication. DOI: 10.3389/fpubh.2025.1503932 PMID: 40124410

Kardgar, A., Lucietto, A. M., & Winikus, J. (2024). Board 178: Educational Infographics, A Review Paper. *ASEE Annual Conference and Exposition, Conference Proceedings*. https://www.scopus.com/inward/record.uri?eid=2-s2.0-85202070452&partnerID=40&md5=e724710f1302467cff3f687ce2604f83

Kearney, K. B., Miller, B., Downey, A., & Carey, G. (2026). Using the Extended Job Coaching Model in a Postsecondary Education Program for Gaining and Maintaining Employment. In *Implementing Inclusive Postsecondary Programs for Students With Intellectual Disabilities* (pp. 239–267). DOI: 10.4018/979-8-3373-2767-9.ch009

Leung, A., Moldovan, L., & Ata, M. (2023). Teaching economics in higher education with universal design for learning. *International Review of Economics Education, 44*, 100273. Advance online publication. DOI: 10.1016/j.iree.2023.100273

Lin, N. C., & Cheng, H.-F. (2010). Effects of gradual release of responsibility model on language learning. *Procedia: Social and Behavioral Sciences, 2*(2), 1866–1870. DOI: 10.1016/j.sbspro.2010.03.1000

Lin, S.-C., & Lehto, M. R. (2008). A Bayesian Based Machine Learning Application to Task Analysis. In *Encyclopedia of Data Warehousing and Mining: Second Edition* (pp. 133–139). DOI: 10.4018/978-1-60566-010-3.ch022

Liu, Y., Fang, Y., Hu, L., Chen, N., Li, X., & Cai, Y. (2024). Inclusive leadership and employee workplace well-being: The role of vigor and supervisor developmental feedback. *BMC Psychology, 12*(1), 540. Advance online publication. DOI: 10.1186/s40359-024-02029-5 PMID: 39375786

Lo, H. S., Sher, Y. J., Hong, J. C., Chang, H. K., & Wu, T. F. (2024). The effects of blended learning on the car detailing skills of students with intellectual disabilities. *Journal of Educational Technology & Society, 27*(3), 46–60. DOI: 10.30191/ETS.202407_27(3).RP03

Maqbool, F., Ansari, S., Aslam, T., & Ansari, A. (2021). Experiential Versus Traditional Education System: A Comparative Study of Engineering Education Methodologies in Higher Education. In *Lecture Notes on Data Engineering and Communications Technologies* (Vol. 78, pp. 724–736). DOI: 10.1007/978-3-030-79203-9_55

Marchiori, R. S., & Song, S. (2024). A Game-Based Learning Method to Promote Soft Skills in Construction Education. *ASEE Annual Conference and Exposition, Conference Proceedings*. https://www.scopus.com/inward/record.uri?eid=2-s2.0-85202015507&partnerID=40&md5=009d6d4619265e26cb25f6c92c024c73

Marks, B., Sisirak, J., & Chang, Y.-C. (2013). Efficacy of the HealthMatters Program Train-the-Trainer Model. *Journal of Applied Research in Intellectual Disabilities*, *26*(4), 319–334. DOI: 10.1111/jar.12045 PMID: 23589506

Marks, B., Sisirak, J., Chang, Y.-C., & Murphy, R. (2019). Impact of the HealthMatters Train-the-Trainer Program on the Health and Health Behaviors of Staff Supporting Adults With Intellectual and Developmental Disabilities. *Workplace Health & Safety*, *67*(8), 423–435. DOI: 10.1177/2165079919828739 PMID: 31007138

Masse, C., Martinez, P., Mertiny, P., & Ahmad, R. (2019). A Hybrid Method Based on Systems Approach to Enhance Experiential Learning in Mechatronic Education. *2019 IEEE 7th International Conference on Control, Mechatronics and Automation, ICCMA 2019*, 403–407. DOI: 10.1109/ICCMA46720.2019.8988746

Mayombe, C. (2024). Promoting youths' skills acquisition through experiential learning theory in vocational education and training in South Africa. *Higher Education. Skills and Work-Based Learning*, *14*(1), 130–145. DOI: 10.1108/HESWBL-10-2022-0216

McCabe, D. (2023). Managing Inclusion and Diversity in Organizations: A Strategic Approach to Human Capital. In *Inclusive Territories 1: Role of Enterprises and Organizations: Volume 1* (Vol. 1, pp. 91–104). DOI: 10.1002/9781394255535.ch5

Michalski, S. C., Gallomarino, N. C., Szpak, A., May, K. W., Lee, G., Ellison, C., & Loetscher, T. (2023). Improving real-world skills in people with intellectual disabilities: An immersive virtual reality intervention. *Virtual Reality (Waltham Cross)*, *27*(4), 3521–3532. DOI: 10.1007/s10055-023-00759-2 PMID: 37360807

Miltenberger, R. G., & Novotny, M. A. (2022). Teaching Safety Skills to Individuals with Developmental Disabilities. *Advances in Neurodevelopmental Disorders*, *6*(3), 270–279. DOI: 10.1007/s41252-022-00248-8

Mohamad, G., & Pozzi, E. (2023). STUDENTS' INFORMATIONAL NEEDS: Applying the Principles of Universal Design to Address Inequity in High-Needs Schools During Virtual Learning. In *Digital Learning in High-Needs Schools: A Critical Approach to Technology Access and Equity in PreK-12* (pp. 83–96). DOI: 10.4324/9781003274537-9

Morash-Macneil, V., Johnson, F., & Ryan, J. B. (2018). A Systematic Review of Assistive Technology for Individuals With Intellectual Disability in the Workplace. *Journal of Special Education Technology, 33*(1), 15–26. DOI: 10.1177/0162643417729166

Munyofu, M., Swain, W. J., Ausman, B. D., Lin, H., Kidwai, K., & Dwyer, F. (2007). The effect of different chunking strategies in complementing animated instruction. *Learning, Media and Technology, 32*(4), 407–419. DOI: 10.1080/17439880701690109

Novembli, M. S., Hasanah, N., & Fitriani, D. (2024). Investigating the Impact of Universal Design for Learning: Empowering Students with Disabilities in Higher Education. *E3S Web of Conferences, 593*. DOI: 10.1051/e3sconf/202459304004

O'Shea, G., & Clegg, B. A. (2006). Stimulus and response chunking in the Hebb Digits task. *Psychological Research, 70*(3), 180–192. DOI: 10.1007/s00426-004-0198-1 PMID: 15818496

Ortlieb, E., & Schatz, S. (2019). Passing the pen: A gradual release model of the recursive writing process. In *Literacy Research* (Vol. 10, pp. 205–215). Practice and Evaluation., DOI: 10.1108/S2048-045820190000010013

Panda, R. K., Raut, D. K., & Biswal, P. (2018). Inclusive training using technology at workplace: A critical review for an infrastructure company. *International Journal of Civil Engineering and Technology, 9*(4), 602–607. https://www.scopus.com/inward/record.uri?eid=2-s2.0-85046361996&partnerID=40&md5=dffbd9c97dd1f24f7f530cfd6adfebbf

Paul, C. D., Thomas, E. V., Marelle, C., Hussain, S. Z., Doulin, A. M., & Jimenez, E. (2022). Using wireless technology to support individuals with intellectual and developmental disabilities in vocational settings: A focus group study. *Journal of Vocational Rehabilitation, 56*(3), 303–312. DOI: 10.3233/JVR-221193

Perrotta, P., Novis, D. A., Nelson, S., Blond, B., Stankovic, A., & Talbert, M. (2020). Workflow mapping - A Q-probes study of preanalytic testing processes: A college of american pathologists q-probes study of 35 clinical laboratories. *Archives of Pathology & Laboratory Medicine, 144*(12), 1517–1524. DOI: 10.5858/arpa.2020-0043-CP PMID: 32579404

Poonkuzhali, S., Sangeetha Archana, J., Naresh, A., & Naidhruv Raj, R. (2025). GenAI-Powered Adaptive Assessments for Livelihood Skills in Individuals with Intellectual Disabilities. *Lecture Notes in Networks and Systems, 1383 LNNS*, 127–136. DOI: 10.1007/978-981-96-5754-4_12

Precin, P. (2010). The use of visual imagery to enhance sequencing of work tasks. *Work (Reading, Mass.), 36*(4), 373–379. DOI: 10.3233/WOR-2010-1040 PMID: 20714092

Ramkumar, P., Acuna, D. E., Berniker, M., Grafton, S. T., Turner, R. S., & Kording, K. P. (2016). Chunking as the result of an efficiency computation trade-off. *Nature Communications, 7*(1), 12176. Advance online publication. DOI: 10.1038/ncomms12176 PMID: 27397420

Randall, K., Drew, H., Gilman, E., & Dixon, E. (2025). Assistive Technology Uses and Barriers in the Home and Workplace for Adults With Intellectual and Developmental Disabilities. *Journal of Applied Research in Intellectual Disabilities, 38*(1), e13306. Advance online publication. DOI: 10.1111/jar.13306 PMID: 39462768

Rashwan, Z. I., Narayanan, G., Khonji, L. M., Stalin, G. K., Gangadurai, N., & Bayoumi, M. M. (2024). Integrating peer instruction and peer assessment with competency-based four-step approach: Effectiveness on wound dressing skill acquisition and motivation among nursing students. *Teaching and Learning in Nursing, 19*(1), e150–e159. DOI: 10.1016/j.teln.2023.10.005

Rasouli, O., Kvam, L., Husby, V. S., Røstad, M., & Witsø, A. E. (2023). Understanding the possibilities and limitations of assistive technology in health and welfare services for people with intellectual disabilities, staff perspectives. *Disability and Rehabilitation. Assistive Technology, 18*(7), 989–997. DOI: 10.1080/17483107.2021.1963856 PMID: 34403623

Read, E. K., & Baillie, S. (2013). Using cognitive task analysis to create a teaching protocol for Bovine Dystocia. *Journal of Veterinary Medical Education, 40*(4), 397–402. DOI: 10.3138/jvme.0213-033R PMID: 24077313

Reinersmann, A., Heinz-Jakobs, M., Bicker, E., & Röcker, C. (2025). How Technology Systems on the Labour Market for Persons With Disability. In *Applied Human Factors and Ergonomics International* (Vol. 169, pp. 38–47). DOI: 10.54941/ahfe1006152

Rhodes, J., & Hamilton, D. (2006). An Insight into Implementing Person-Centred Active Support. *Tizard Learning Disability Review, 11*(3), 31–36. DOI: 10.1108/13595474200600025

Riches, V. C., Harman, A. D., Keen, D., Pennell, D., Harley, J. H., & Walker, M. (2011). Transforming staff practice through active support. *Journal of Intellectual & Developmental Disability, 36*(3), 156–166. DOI: 10.3109/13668250.2011.598499 PMID: 21843030

Rutherford, M., Baxter, J., Grayson, Z., Johnston, L., & O'Hare, A. (2020). Visual supports at home and in the community for individuals with autism spectrum disorders: A scoping review. *Autism, 24*(2), 447–469. DOI: 10.1177/1362361319871756 PMID: 31451016

Salehomoum, M. (2019). Scaffolding development of self-regulated and strategic literacy skills in deaf or hard-of-hearing students: A review of the literature through the lens of the gradual release of responsibility model. In *Literacy Research* (Vol. 10, pp. 153–168). Practice and Evaluation., DOI: 10.1108/S2048-045820190000010010

Sandjojo, J., Zedlitz, A. M. E. E., Gebhardt, W. A., Hoekman, J., Dusseldorp, E., den Haan, J. A., & Evers, A. W. M. (2018). Training staff to promote self-management in people with intellectual disabilities. *Journal of Applied Research in Intellectual Disabilities, 31*(5), 840–850. DOI: 10.1111/jar.12440 PMID: 29479785

Satpathy, I., Patnaik, B. C. M., & Raut, D. K. (2018). Inclusive training in manufacturing industry: A review. *International Journal of Mechanical Engineering and Technology, 9*(9), 63–70. https://www.scopus.com/inward/record.uri?eid=2-s2.0-85054015812&partnerID=40&md5=84a2ee28ddcf6af8fada969cc1bf75e7

Smith, R. P., Ma, F., & Roe, S. J. (2025). Diversity, equity, inclusion, and belonging (DEIB): A snapshot in hospitality and tourism academia job openings. *Journal of Teaching in Travel & Tourism, 25*(2), 127–146. DOI: 10.1080/15313220.2025.2495833

Taylor, A. J., Slocum, V., & Rhodes, A. L. (2026). Assistive Technology and Universal Design for Learning. In *An Evidence-Based Guide to Assistive Technology* (pp. 28–41). Meeting the Needs of All Students with Disabilities., DOI: 10.4324/9781003524090-4

Wilson, N. J., Lin, Z., Pithouse, M., Morrison, B., Sumar, B., & George, A. (2023). Qualitative Insights from A Novel Staff-Led Oral Health Champions Program Within a Residential Service For People With Intellectual and Developmental Disability. *Journal of Intellectual Disabilities, 27*(3), 728–745. DOI: 10.1177/17446295221095654 PMID: 35549753

Wu, S., Élteto, N., Dasgupta, I., & Schulz, E. (2022). Learning Structure from the Ground up-Hierarchical Representation Learning by Chunking. *Advances in Neural Information Processing Systems, 35*. https://www.scopus.com/inward/record.uri?eid=2-s2.0-85162641991&partnerID=40&md5=bbb6c979822010fa90a2185771e63ab8

Yang, H.-Y., Yeh, S.-C., Wu, E. H.-K., & Hong, W. (2021). The effectiveness of virtual reality technology applying in vocational training on occupational competency among the students with intellectual disability in senior high school. *2021 IEEE International Conference on Social Sciences and Intelligent Management, SSIM 2021*. DOI: 10.1109/SSIM49526.2021.9555179

Yasak, Z., & Alias, M. (2016). Developing a learning hierarchy for identifying pre-requisites to training goals in vocational education. *2015 IEEE Conference on E-Learning, e-Management and e-Services, IC3e 2015*, 49–51. DOI: 10.1109/IC3e.2015.7403485

Yuan, Q., Kazemi, M., Xu, X., Noble, I., Imbrasaite, V., & Ramachandran, D. (2024). TaskLAMA: Probing the Complex Task Understanding of Language Models. *Proceedings of the AAAI Conference on Artificial Intelligence*, *38*(17), 19468–19476. DOI: 10.1609/aaai.v38i17.29918

Chapter 9
Natural Supports and the Role of Co-Workers as Allies

ABSTRACT

This chapter examines the role of natural support and co-workers as allies in fostering inclusive workplaces for workers with intellectual disabilities. It discusses how peer relationships, mentoring, and collaborative work practices strengthen participation, learning, and workplace belonging. Attention is given to preparing co-workers as peer mentors, developing inclusive communication practices, and integrating natural supports with formal job coaching systems. The chapter also explores organisational practices and leadership approaches that cultivate collaborative cultures where employees support one another through everyday workplace interactions. By strengthening peer networks and shared responsibility, organisations can build sustainable support systems that enhance job satisfaction, workplace inclusion, and long-term employment participation for workers with intellectual disabilities.

9.1 INTRODUCTION

Inclusive employment for workers with intellectual disabilities increasingly emphasises not only formal workplace support but also the everyday relationships that sustain participation and belonging. While structured training, job coaching, and organisational accommodation remain important, long-term workplace success often depends on informal interactions among colleagues. These interactions form what is commonly referred to as *natural supports*—the unpaid, relationship-based assistance provided by co-workers, supervisors, and members of the workplace community. Natural supports help individuals with intellectual disabilities navigate

DOI: 10.4018/979-8-3373-9185-4.ch009

workplace routines, understand organisational culture, and develop meaningful professional relationships (Athamanah et al. 2024; Friedman, 2021).

Natural supports differ fundamentally from formal support systems. Formal supports are typically delivered through structured programmes, such as job coaching, disability accommodations, and specialised training designed to address specific employment outcomes (Boselie et al., 2025). These supports are essential during the initial employment phases, when workers need structured guidance to learn tasks and understand workplace expectations. In contrast, natural support emerges organically within the workplace through everyday collaboration, mentorship, and shared problem-solving among colleagues. Co-workers who offer guidance during tasks, explain workplace norms, or provide encouragement during challenging moments contribute to the development of inclusive social environments that strengthen employee engagement (Voorhees, 2022); (Friedman, 2021).

The presence of natural support significantly enhances workplace participation for workers with intellectual disabilities. Everyday interactions with colleagues create opportunities for informal learning that extend beyond formal training sessions. Workplace routines often involve collaborative activities where employees observe one another, exchange feedback, and develop practical skills through shared experiences. Such interactions serve as powerful learning opportunities by integrating skill development with social participation. Informal mentoring relationships, for instance, allow workers with intellectual disabilities to gain both vocational knowledge and social confidence, strengthening their capacity to function effectively within workplace teams Billett & Noble (2020), (Riera Claret et al., 2020).

Natural support also contributes to several positive employment outcomes. Workers who experience supportive peer relationships are more likely to develop independence in their roles and rely less heavily on external assistance. These relationships promote social integration by encouraging participation in workplace communities and fostering a sense of belonging among employees. Research examining natural support networks has shown that individuals with intellectual and developmental disabilities often demonstrate stronger workplace engagement, longer job tenure, and improved job satisfaction when they are connected to supportive peer networks Athamanah et al. (2024); (Weiner & Zivolich, 2003).

Another important advantage of natural supports lies in their sustainability. Because these supports are embedded within everyday workplace interactions, they often continue long after formal job coaching has ended. Organisations that cultivate peer mentoring and collaborative workplace cultures therefore create environments in which employees naturally support one another. Such environments reduce dependence on specialised external services while strengthening workplace cohesion and productivity Rezai et al., (2023).

Developing effective natural support systems, however, requires intentional organisational strategies. Co-workers must be prepared to act as allies who encourage inclusion, respect diversity, and support colleagues in ways that promote dignity and independence. Training programmes that raise disability awareness and equip employees with mentoring skills can help create supportive peer networks within organisations. When co-workers understand their role in fostering inclusive workplaces, everyday interactions become powerful mechanisms for learning, collaboration, and mutual support Enehaug & Spjelkavik, 2025).

This chapter explores how natural supports operate within workplace environments and how co-workers can function as allies who contribute to inclusive employment. It examines the distinctions between formal and informal support systems, highlights the value of peer relationships in workplace learning, and discusses strategies for cultivating inclusive organisational cultures. Through these discussions, the chapter emphasises that sustainable inclusion emerges not only from policies and programmes but also from the relationships that develop within everyday work experiences.

9.2 THE ROLE OF CO-WORKERS AS WORKPLACE ALLIES

Inclusive employment depends not only on organisational policies and formal training structures but also on the attitudes and behaviours demonstrated by employees during everyday workplace interactions. In team-based work environments, co-workers often influence how inclusion is experienced in practice. Their willingness to collaborate, communicate respectfully, and provide informal assistance can determine whether workers with intellectual disabilities experience the workplace as supportive and equitable. When colleagues intentionally promote participation and respect within teams, they contribute to inclusive organisational cultures.

Key aspects of the role of co-workers as workplace allies include the following:

- **Understanding allyship in inclusive workplaces:** Allyship refers to the conscious effort by individuals to support colleagues from marginalised groups and challenge practices that limit participation (Ashburn-Nardo, 2015). In workplaces that include workers with intellectual disabilities, allyship involves recognising the importance of equitable participation and ensuring that colleagues are included in work discussions, team activities, and decision-making processes.
- **Promoting inclusive everyday workplace interactions:** Workplace inclusion is strengthened through daily interactions among colleagues. Positive peer relationships improve communication and teamwork within organisations (Bourke, 2025). When employees demonstrate patience, openness, and

cooperation, workplace environments become more supportive for individuals with diverse learning and communication styles. In contrast, exclusionary attitudes can create barriers to participation and weaken team cohesion (Frøyland, 2025).

- **Providing practical workplace assistance:** Co-workers frequently support colleagues with intellectual disabilities through routine collaboration, task clarification, and supportive communication. These interactions often occur naturally during work activities, allowing employees to learn tasks within authentic workplace contexts (Meacham et al., 2017). Practical assistance may involve demonstrating procedures, explaining task sequences, or offering reminders about workplace responsibilities.
- **Supporting skill development through peer interaction:** Workplace support that emerges through peer collaboration contributes to both skill development and social participation (Carlson et al., 2020). When employees work together, learning becomes embedded in daily work routines rather than limited to formal training sessions.
- **Encouraging respectful attitudes and shared responsibility:** Workplace attitudes strongly influence the quality of support provided by colleagues. Co-workers who recognise the reliability and contributions of employees with intellectual disabilities tend to foster more supportive work environments (Kumar et al, 2019). Respectful perceptions encourage teamwork and promote a shared sense of responsibility for inclusive practice.
- **Strengthening communication within teams:** Effective communication plays an important role in supporting inclusion. Clear communication strategies help ensure that workplace expectations remain understandable for all employees. Communication tools and inclusive practices can strengthen collaboration and improve task performance for workers with intellectual disabilities (Pouliot et al., 2017).
- **Building respectful workplace relationships and mentoring:** Inclusive workplaces depend on respectful relationships among employees. Interpersonal interactions strongly influence how individuals with intellectual disabilities perceive fairness and belonging within organisations (Li, 2004). Peer mentoring can strengthen these relationships by providing guidance, encouragement, and knowledge sharing during workplace activities (Meacham et al., 2017; .Sartore et al., 2021)
- **Encouraging collaboration and shared problem-solving:** Peer encouragement and informal guidance can significantly influence the confidence and motivation of workers with intellectual disabilities. Colleagues may explain procedures, provide feedback, or demonstrate alternative approaches to completing tasks during routine work activities (Lindsay & Cagliostro, 2020:

Travers, 2017). Teams that engage in collaborative problem-solving also strengthen communication and cooperation within the workplace(Pietrantoni et al., 2024). Such collaborative environments allow employees with intellectual disabilities to participate actively in decision-making processes while developing interpersonal and workplace skills (Tsirkas (2025).

Co-workers who adopt an allyship mindset, therefore, play an important role in strengthening inclusive employment environments. Through everyday collaboration, respectful communication, and shared problem-solving, they support both individual learning and collective workplace success. In such environments, routine interactions become opportunities for workers with intellectual disabilities to develop skills, collaborate, and grow professionally.

9.3 PREPARING CO-WORKERS TO SERVE AS PEER MENTORS

Workplaces that seek to strengthen inclusion for workers with intellectual disabilities must prepare co-workers to function as effective peer mentors. Structured preparation enables colleagues to offer practical guidance, emotional support, and collaborative assistance while maintaining respect for independence and dignity.

Training Co-Workers to Support Inclusive Workplace Practices

Inclusive workplaces often begin with deliberate efforts to prepare employees to work effectively within diverse teams. According to Ashuro & Kant (2025), diversity and inclusion training initiatives can shape how employees understand their responsibilities toward colleagues with different abilities. Such programmes help co-workers recognise the value of inclusive practices while developing skills that support collaboration and mutual respect. Training that emphasises cultural competence, communication strategies, and disability awareness encourages employees to view inclusion as a normal component of everyday workplace interaction rather than a specialised obligation.

Workplace mentoring also serves as an effective mechanism for strengthening natural support systems. Mentoring relationships create opportunities for experienced employees to guide colleagues through everyday work activities while building professional confidence. Through mentoring, employees with intellectual disabilities receive encouragement and practical advice that help them adapt to workplace expectations (Enehaug & Spjelkavik 2025). Peer mentoring, therefore, complements formal workplace supports and creates opportunities for learning that occur naturally within daily work routines.

Developing Mentoring Skills

Effective peer mentors require interpersonal and instructional skills to support colleagues constructively. Mentors frequently demonstrate workplace tasks, explain procedures, and provide feedback that helps colleagues improve their performance. De La Calle-Duran & Garcia (2024) highlight mentoring skills such as modelling appropriate work behaviours, offering constructive feedback, and guiding colleagues through complex tasks. These practices enable mentees to develop both technical competence and workplace confidence.

Structured preparation programmes can strengthen these mentoring capabilities. Organisations may organise peer leadership seminars, workshops, or scenario-based training sessions that allow employees to practise mentoring roles. These programmes often include role-playing exercises and guided discussions that help participants consider how to respond to workplace challenges (Pon-Barry et al., 2017). Scenario-based instruction allows mentors to explore realistic workplace situations and practise communication and problem-solving strategies before applying them in daily work activities (Chine et al., 2023).

Mentoring responsibilities also require organisational support. Mentors often invest considerable time and energy in assisting colleagues, and these responsibilities may become demanding when combined with regular work duties. Billett (2003) notes that organisations that recognise mentoring as an important workplace role typically provide resources and management support that help mentors balance these responsibilities. Such support ensures that mentoring remains a constructive and sustainable component of workplace inclusion.

Addressing Misconceptions About Disability

Disability awareness programmes can help address misconceptions that may influence workplace interactions. (Schuhl et al., 2020) describe how structured awareness initiatives encourage employees to reflect on assumptions about disability and recognise the capabilities of colleagues with disabilities. These initiatives often include educational sessions, guided discussions, and perspective-taking activities that help participants understand the experiences of individuals with disabilities in workplace environments.

Awareness programmes also encourage more positive workplace attitudes. Training that highlights the strengths, contributions, and professional capabilities of workers with intellectual disabilities can challenge stereotypes and promote inclusive behaviour. Thaver et al. (2025) explain that attitudinal change often occurs when individuals engage in reflection and dialogue about inclusion. As employees develop a deeper understanding of disability-related issues, they are more likely to demonstrate empathy and cooperation in their interactions with colleagues.

Educational resources that explain disability concepts and inclusive practices can further support this process. González et al. (2024) note that disability education programmes often combine knowledge development with practical strategies for supporting colleagues. These initiatives encourage employees to approach workplace relationships with openness and respect, thereby contributing to more inclusive organisational cultures.

Balancing Assistance with Respect for Independence

Peer mentors must learn to provide support while respecting the independence of colleagues with intellectual disabilities. Effective mentoring focuses on empowering employees to develop their own capabilities rather than creating dependency. Westerlund et al. (2006) emphasise mentoring approaches that encourage guidance and encouragement while allowing individuals to practise tasks independently.

Mentors can maintain this balance by offering assistance when necessary and encouraging colleagues to attempt tasks independently before intervening. Supportive feedback reinforces confidence and helps individuals reflect on their progress. Cassiani et al. (2020) explain that mentoring relationships that promote autonomy help mentees develop self-confidence and decision-making skills.

Reflection also contributes to effective mentoring. Opportunities for mentors to discuss their experiences and receive feedback from supervisors or training coordinators can help them refine their approach when supporting colleagues. These reflective practices help mentors maintain a balance between guidance and independence while strengthening their capacity to support inclusive workplaces.

Preparing co-workers to serve as peer mentors therefore strengthens natural support systems within organisations. When employees develop mentoring skills, disability awareness, and inclusive communication strategies, they become better equipped to support colleagues in constructive and respectful ways. The following section examines how organisational cultures can further strengthen these natural support networks by fostering workplace environments that encourage collaboration and shared responsibility for inclusion.

9.4 CREATING WORKPLACE CULTURES THAT ENCOURAGE NATURAL SUPPORT SYSTEMS

Workplace cultures that encourage natural assistance among employees do not emerge spontaneously; they develop through deliberate organisational practices and consistent leadership commitment. When organisations promote collaboration, respectful communication, and shared responsibility, they create environments in which natural support systems can flourish and sustain inclusive employment.

Organisational Practices that Promote Collaboration and Peer Support

Collaborative workplace cultures often develop when organisations intentionally encourage cooperation and peer engagement among employees. Ganapathy (2025) notes that collaborative environments strengthen relationships across diverse teams and promote collective responsibility for workplace outcomes. Organisational practices that emphasise teamwork, shared problem-solving, and peer interaction enable employees to support one another in ways that extend beyond formal job roles. When such practices become embedded in everyday operations, collaboration becomes a routine feature of organisational culture.

Leadership plays a central role in shaping these collaborative environments. Inclusive leadership fosters psychological safety, open communication, and mutual respect among employees, creating conditions in which individuals feel comfortable offering support to colleagues Kakada & Bisen (2025). Leadership approaches that acknowledge diverse perspectives and encourage teamwork reinforce these behaviours across the organisation. Morgan et al. (2025) further explain that inclusive leadership strengthens cooperation by recognising contributions from all employees and promoting shared responsibility in achieving workplace goals.

Peer support initiatives can further reinforce collaborative cultures. Programmes designed to encourage employees to assist one another often strengthen workplace relationships while supporting employee well-being. For instance, peer-based initiatives such as the *Sustaining Resilience at Work* programme encourage employees to support colleagues while developing their own coping strategies Agarwal et al. (2020). These initiatives help employees build trust and empathy while strengthening supportive workplace interactions. Similar programmes have also been associated with stronger organisational cultures in which employees actively contribute to the well-being of their colleagues (Quinn et al.,2025).

Organisations that prioritise peer support frequently provide training and resources that enable employees to engage in supportive practices. Organisational guidance can help employees understand how to assist colleagues constructively while maintaining professional boundaries Levandowski et al. (2025). Supportive organisational environments also allow informal peer relationships to develop naturally, strengthening collaboration and workplace cohesion over time (Gray et al., 2017).

Integrating Natural Supports into Team-Based Work Structures

Natural support systems become particularly effective when integrated into team-based work structures. Athamanah et al. (2024) describe mentoring, peer guidance, and collaborative assistance as important mechanisms that strengthen inclusive employment environments. When employees work within team-based structures, they naturally exchange knowledge, offer assistance, and support one another during routine work activities.

Organisations can reinforce natural support systems by embedding them within workplace processes. Mentoring relationships and peer-led supervision practices enable employees to guide colleagues during work tasks while strengthening professional relationships. Evidence from inclusive employment initiatives indicates that combining formal workplace supports with natural peer assistance can strengthen workplace participation and engagement Piccone et al. (2024).

Mentorship programmes also create structured opportunities for employees to support one another. Through mentoring relationships, experienced workers share knowledge, demonstrate tasks, and provide encouragement to colleagues who may require additional support. These relationships contribute to greater workplace inclusion and increased confidence among employees with intellectual disabilities Enehaug & Spjelkavik (2025).

Trust-based workplace relationships further strengthen the integration of natural supports. Collaborative employment environments often develop when organisations encourage cooperation and mutual trust among employees. Trust strengthens teamwork and allows employees to offer assistance without hesitation (Mank et al., 2003). Flexible work structures can also contribute to these relationships, as collaborative work environments that encourage knowledge sharing and joint problem-solving often enhance peer interaction and support (Xiao & Seagull., 2007).

Encouraging Inclusive Communication and Mutual Respect

Communication practices significantly influence whether workplace cultures encourage natural support systems. Inclusive communication requires employees to interact in ways that reflect respect, openness, and recognition of diversity. Communication approaches that use respectful language and acknowledge differences in experience help create environments in which employees feel valued and included (Odunayo & Ng., 2026).

Organisations can strengthen inclusive communication through training initiatives and leadership modelling. Strategic internal communication practices help employees understand their roles in supporting workplace diversity and inclusion while reinforcing shared organisational values (Lee & Lee., 2025). Clear communication also promotes collaboration by ensuring that employees understand workplace expectations and feel confident participating in discussions.

Dialogic communication further strengthens workplace relationships. Communication processes that encourage open discussion, feedback, and reflection allow employees to engage constructively with colleagues (Phan., 2025). These practices enable employees to exchange ideas and collaborate on workplace challenges while strengthening mutual understanding.

Psychological safety also contributes to inclusive communication environments. Employees who feel safe expressing their perspectives are more likely to participate in team discussions and collaborative decision-making (Wilson & Adderley., 2025). Environments characterised by psychological safety therefore support open dialogue and reinforce mutual respect among employees.

Leadership Strategies that Reinforce Inclusive Workplace Norms

Leadership approaches strongly influence whether inclusive practices become embedded in organisational culture. Leaders who demonstrate empathy, humility, and cultural awareness create environments in which employees feel valued and respected. Ferdman (2020) notes that inclusive leadership strengthens collaboration and recognises the importance of diverse experiences in shaping organisational success.

Several leadership strategies can reinforce inclusive workplace norms. Cross-generational collaboration initiatives encourage employees from different backgrounds to share knowledge and support one another in professional development (Ganapathy., 2025). Such initiatives strengthen cooperation and enhance team cohesion.

Mentorship programmes also support inclusive leadership practices. Organisational models that integrate peer mentorship and collaborative learning provide opportunities for employees to develop leadership skills while assisting colleagues (Byrne et al., 2022). These initiatives strengthen both professional development and workplace relationships.

Accountability mechanisms ensure that inclusive practices remain embedded within organisational structures. Leadership frameworks that incorporate monitoring and evaluation processes encourage organisations to maintain their commitment to inclusion King et al.2024). Evidence-informed decision-making further supports organisational efforts to address bias and strengthen equitable workplace practices Oberai (2025).

Workplace cultures that encourage natural support systems therefore develop through coordinated organisational practices, leadership strategies, and everyday interactions among employees. When organisations prioritise collaboration, inclusive communication, and supportive leadership, natural support networks become integrated into workplace routines. These environments strengthen inclusion, cooperation, and a sense of belonging for workers with intellectual disabilities.

9.5 INTEGRATING NATURAL SUPPORTS WITH FORMAL JOB COACHING SYSTEMS FOR WORKERS WITH INTELLECTUAL DISABILITIES

Inclusive employment initiatives often rely on a combination of structured professional support and the everyday assistance provided by colleagues within the workplace. Integrating natural supports with formal job coaching systems creates a balanced approach that promotes both skill development and long-term workplace participation for workers with intellectual disabilities. Rather than treating formal coaching and peer assistance as separate mechanisms, organisations can combine these approaches to establish support structures that strengthen independence while ensuring that guidance remains accessible when necessary.

Complementary Roles of Job Coaches, Supervisors, and Peer Mentors

Formal job coaching typically represents the initial stage of workplace integration for workers with intellectual disabilities. Job coaches provide structured instruction during the early phases of employment, guiding employees through job tasks, workplace routines, and organisational expectations. This type of structured support helps workers develop the foundational competencies required to participate confidently in workplace activities. Athamanah et al. (2024) explain that job coaches frequently monitor workplace performance and assist employees in developing strategies for managing responsibilities effectively.

Supervisors and co-workers contribute to this support structure in different yet complementary ways. Their daily interactions with workers with intellectual disabilities create opportunities for learning through observation, collaboration, and shared experience. Aldersey et al. (2025) describe natural workplace relationships as an important source of social connection and informal guidance that complements technical instruction from job coaches. Supervisors often clarify workplace expectations, while peer mentors provide assistance during routine work tasks and offer encouragement when challenges arise.

Effective workplace inclusion frequently depends on collaboration among these different support roles. According to Piccone et al. (2024), employment programmes that coordinate the efforts of job coaches, supervisors, and co-workers create stronger support networks within organisations. In such settings, job coaches initially guide training while gradually encouraging colleagues within the workplace to participate in supportive roles. Through this collaborative approach, workers with intellectual disabilities develop both practical job skills and meaningful workplace relationships.

Gradual Transition from External Coaching to Natural Workplace Supports

Sustainable workplace inclusion often requires a gradual transition from intensive professional support to natural workplace assistance. During the initial phase of employment, job coaches typically provide direct guidance to help employees understand job expectations and workplace procedures. As employees gain confidence and experience, however, these external supports can gradually decrease.

Many employment programmes adopt phased transition models that allow workers to develop independence over time. Nuri et al. (2025) describe a step-down approach in which job coaches reduce their involvement as natural workplace supports become stronger. As this transition occurs, supervisors and co-workers increasingly provide day-to-day assistance, while job coaches shift toward a consultative or monitoring role.

Trust plays an important role in facilitating this transition. Workers with intellectual disabilities often become more comfortable seeking assistance from colleagues when supportive relationships have developed within the workplace. Reynolds et al. (2018) discuss integrated support frameworks that combine personal strengths, workplace relationships, and community resources to support long-term independence. These frameworks encourage individuals to rely on multiple support sources rather than depending exclusively on professional services.

Integrated support models, therefore, enable organisations to move from reliance on external coaching toward sustainable workplace relationships. As employees gain experience and confidence, the role of coaches shifts from continuous supervision to occasional consultation.

Strengthening the Sustainability of Support through Team-Based Assistance

Team-based support systems play an important role in sustaining workplace inclusion for workers with intellectual disabilities. Rather than relying on a single individual for assistance, team-based models distribute supportive responsibilities among supervisors, co-workers, and organisational leaders. This collaborative approach ensures that support remains available even when workplace conditions change.

Piccone et al. (2024) describe organisational practices in which workplace teams collectively support employees with intellectual disabilities. In these environments, co-workers assist with routine tasks, supervisors monitor progress, and job coaches remain available when specialised guidance is required. Such arrangements help maintain stability within support systems while reducing dependence on a single source of assistance.

Flexible organisational policies further strengthen these integrated support structures. Support systems that adapt to workplace changes, evolving job responsibilities, or individual needs are more likely to remain effective over time. According to Nuri et al., 2025)Flexible support arrangements allow organisations to combine formal and natural assistance in ways that respond to specific workplace contexts.

Training also contributes to the sustainability of these systems. When co-workers and supervisors receive guidance on how to support colleagues with intellectual disabilities, natural support networks become more reliable. (Becerra Traver et al., 2014) describe workplace orientation and employment as support programmes that prepare employees to participate effectively in inclusive work environments. Such preparation ensures that support systems remain stable and effective as organisational conditions evolve.

Monitoring and Maintaining Effective Peer Support Relationships

Even well-established natural support systems benefit from ongoing monitoring and reflection. Organisations must ensure that peer relationships remain constructive and that workers with intellectual disabilities continue to receive appropriate support. Carlson et al. (2020) note that regular evaluation of workplace support arrangements helps identify areas where additional assistance may be required.

Evaluation processes may include observing workplace interactions, collecting employee feedback, or reviewing performance outcomes. These approaches allow organisations to assess whether support relationships remain effective and whether employees continue to experience positive workplace outcomes.

Workplace culture also plays an important role in maintaining effective support networks. Aldersey et al. (2025) observe that organisations characterised by collaboration and mutual respect are more likely to sustain strong peer support systems. In such environments, employees perceive assisting colleagues as a natural aspect of teamwork rather than an additional responsibility.

Organisational policies and resources further influence the success of integrated support systems. Piccone et al. (2024) highlight the importance of addressing systemic barriers that may limit inclusive employment initiatives, such as restrictive funding structures and limited workplace resources. When organisations align policies, training programmes, and leadership practices with inclusive objectives, integrated support systems become more effective.

Integrating natural supports with formal job-coaching systems, therefore, provides a comprehensive approach to workplace inclusion for workers with intellectual disabilities. By combining structured professional guidance with everyday peer assistance, organisations establish support structures that promote independence, strengthen workplace relationships, and support long-term employment participation.

9.6 STRENGTHENING WORKPLACE BELONGING THROUGH PEER NETWORKS

Workplace belonging is an important dimension of inclusive employment for workers with intellectual disabilities. Peer networks play a central role in shaping how employees experience acceptance, participation, and recognition within organisational environments. When colleagues provide encouragement, guidance, and everyday assistance, workers with intellectual disabilities are more likely to feel valued as members of their teams. Supportive peer relationships help individuals navigate workplace expectations, develop confidence, and participate more actively in daily work routines.

Peer networks also create opportunities for social inclusion through shared activities and team engagement. Collaborative tasks, group discussions, and informal workplace interactions allow employees to build relationships that extend beyond formal job responsibilities. Participation in team meetings, joint problem-solving, and workplace celebrations can strengthen interpersonal connections and encourage workers with intellectual disabilities to contribute their perspectives. These shared experiences foster trust and mutual respect among colleagues and reinforce a sense of collective identity in the workplace.

Supportive peer relationships also influence job satisfaction and employment stability. Employees who experience positive workplace relationships often report higher levels of motivation and commitment to their roles. When colleagues provide encouragement and recognise each other's contributions, workers are more likely to remain engaged and confident in their abilities. Strong peer networks, therefore, contribute to improved job retention and long-term participation in inclusive employment settings.

Strengthening workplace belonging through peer networks creates a foundation for further professional development. As workers with intellectual disabilities build confidence and social connections within their organisations, opportunities for career growth become more accessible. The next chapter builds on this discussion by examining how inclusive workplaces can support career advancement and leadership opportunities for workers with intellectual disabilities.

REFERENCES

Agarwal, B., Brooks, S. K., & Greenberg, N. (2020). The role of peer support in managing occupational stress: A qualitative study of the sustaining resilience at work intervention. *Workplace Health & Safety*, *68*(2), 57–64. DOI: 10.1177/2165079919873934 PMID: 31538851

Aldersey, H. M., Xu, X., Piccone, C., Nelson, M., Thomson, D., Pauls, R., & Perry, L. (2025). Formal and natural supports: Perspectives from adults with intellectual and developmental disabilities, family members, and support workers. *Journal of Policy and Practice in Intellectual Disabilities*, *22*(2), e70011. Advance online publication. DOI: 10.1111/jppi.70011

Ashburn-Nardo, L. (2015). What can allies do? In Colella, A. J., & King, E. B. (Eds.), *The Oxford handbook of workplace discrimination* (pp. 373–386). Oxford University Press., DOI: 10.1093/oxfordhb/9780199363643.013.27

Ashuro, T., & Kant, S. (2025). The impact of cross-cultural perspectives on labor practices by mediating role of inclusive strategies in Ethiopia. In *Advanced labor studies research and modern practice* (pp. 169–193). IGI Global., DOI: 10.4018/979-8-3373-1962-9.ch006

Athamanah, L. S., Cushing, L. S., Fastzkie, E. M., & Brown, E. R. (2024). Natural supports in competitive integrated employment: A scoping review. *Journal of Vocational Rehabilitation*, *60*(3), 327–339. DOI: 10.3233/JVR-240017

Billett, S. (2003). Workplace mentors: Demands and benefits. *Journal of Workplace Learning*, *15*(3), 105–113. DOI: 10.1108/13665620310468441

Billett, S., & Noble, C. (2020). Utilizing pedagogically rich work activities to promote professional learning. *Education et Didactique*, *14*(3), 137–150. DOI: 10.4000/educationdidactique.7943

Boselie, P., van Harten, J., & van Os, L. (2025). Human resource management. In *Shaping inclusive workplaces for persons with disabilities: A management and HRM practitioner perspective* (pp. 29–41). Springer., DOI: 10.1007/978-3-031-96315-5_3

Bourke, J. (2025). Time to delve into the weeds: Illuminating the diversity to performance black box by exploring co-worker relationships. In *Research handbook on global diversity management* (pp. 108–122). Edward Elgar Publishing., DOI: 10.4337/9781035311170.00015

Byrne, L., Roennfeldt, H., Wolf, J., Linfoot, A., Foglesong, D., Davidson, L., & Bellamy, C. (2022). Effective peer employment within multidisciplinary organizations: Model for best practice. *Administration and Policy in Mental Health*, *49*(2), 283–297. DOI: 10.1007/s10488-021-01162-2 PMID: 34478040

Carlson, S. R., Morningstar, M. E., & Munandar, V. (2020). Workplace supports for employees with intellectual disability: A systematic review of the intervention literature. *Journal of Vocational Rehabilitation*, *52*(3), 251–265. DOI: 10.3233/JVR-201075

Cassiani, C., Stinson, J., & Lindsay, S. (2020). E-mentoring for youth with physical disabilities preparing for employment: A content analysis of support exchanged between participants of a mentored and non-mentored group. *Disability and Rehabilitation*, *42*(14), 1963–1970. DOI: 10.1080/09638288.2018.1543360 PMID: 30641025

Chine, D. R., Chhabra, P., Adeniran, A., Kopko, J., Tipper, C., Gupta, S., & Koedinger, K. R. (2023). Scenario-based training and on-the-job support for equitable mentoring. In *Lecture Notes in Networks and Systems* (Vol. 581, pp. 581–592). Springer., DOI: 10.1007/978-3-031-21569-8_54

De La Calle-Duran, M.-C., & Garcia, I. C. (2024). Mentoring and empowering employees: How to develop management skills through mentoring. In *Developing managerial skills for global business success* (pp. 121–131). IGI Global., DOI: 10.4018/979-8-3693-3057-9.ch008

Enehaug, H., & Spjelkavik, Ø. (2025). Mentorship. In *Shaping inclusive workplaces for persons with disabilities: A management and HRM practitioner perspective* (pp. 57–69). Springer., DOI: 10.1007/978-3-031-96315-5_5

Ferdman, B. M. (2020). Inclusive leadership: The fulcrum of inclusion. In *Inclusive leadership: Transforming diverse lives, workplaces, and societies* (pp. 3–24). Routledge., DOI: 10.4324/9780429449673-1

Friedman, C. (2021). Natural supports: The impact on people with intellectual and developmental disabilities' quality of life and service expenditures. *Journal of Family Social Work*, *24*(2), 118–135. DOI: 10.1080/10522158.2020.1861158

Frøyland, K. (2025). Co-worker support and resistance. In *Shaping inclusive workplaces for persons with disabilities: A management and HRM practitioner perspective* (pp. 97–109). Springer., DOI: 10.1007/978-3-031-96315-5_8

Ganapathy, V. (2025). Building collaboration in a multigenerational workforce. In *Enhancing workplace productivity through gender equity and intergenerational communication* (pp. 167–194). IGI Global., DOI: 10.4018/979-8-3373-2903-1.ch007

González, C. C., Vasquez, R. C., & Reed, B. J. (2024). Disability awareness and inclusion. In *Innovative approaches in counselor education for students with disabilities* (pp. 1–32). IGI Global., DOI: 10.4018/979-8-3693-3342-6.ch001

Gray, M., Davies, K., & Butcher, L. (2017). Finding the right connections: Peer support within a community-based mental health service. *International Journal of Social Welfare*, *26*(2), 188–196. DOI: 10.1111/ijsw.12222

Kakada, P., & Bisen, S. (2025). Empowering change: The role of inclusive leadership in organisational evolution. In *Managing change: Sustainable practices, inclusive leadership, and gender equality in the digital industrial revolution* (pp. 149–167). Emerald Publishing., DOI: 10.1108/978-1-83608-650-520251008

King, S., Roberts-Turner, R., & Floyd, T. T. (2024). Inclusive leadership: A framework to advance diversity, equity, inclusion, and cultivate belonging. *Nurse Leader*, *22*(2), 132–139. DOI: 10.1016/j.mnl.2023.11.006

Kumar, A., Srivastava, S. K., & Singh, K. K. (2019). Study on attitude of co-workers towards employees with intellectual disabilities. *Indian Journal of Public Health Research & Development*, *10*(12), 720–724. DOI: 10.37506/v10/i12/2019/ijphrd/192049

Lee, Y., Tao, W., Li, J.-Y., & Yoon, D. (2025). Drivers of employee engagement with organizational diversity: The power of strategic internal communication. *Public Relations Review*, *51*(3), 102583. Advance online publication. DOI: 10.1016/j.pubrev.2025.102583

Li, E. P. Y. (2004). Self-perceived equal opportunities for people with intellectual disability. *International Journal of Rehabilitation Research. Internationale Zeitschrift fur Rehabilitationsforschung. Revue Internationale de Recherches de Readaptation*, *27*(3), 241–245. DOI: 10.1097/00004356-200409000-00011 PMID: 15319696

Lindsay, S., & Cagliostro, E. (2020). A web-based intervention for youth with physical disabilities: Comparing the role of mentors in 12- and 4-week formats. *JMIR Pediatrics and Parenting*, *3*(1), e15813. Advance online publication. DOI: 10.2196/15813 PMID: 31913132

Mank, D., Cioffi, A., & Yovanoff, P. (2003). Supported employment outcomes across a decade: Is there evidence of improvement in the quality of implementation? *Mental Retardation*, *41*(3), 188–197. DOI: 10.1352/0047-6765(2003)41<188:SEO-AAD>2.0.CO;2 PMID: 12737612

Meacham, H., Cavanagh, J., Shaw, A., & Bartram, T. (2017). HRM practices that support the employment and social inclusion of workers with an intellectual disability. *Personnel Review*, *46*(8), 1475–1492. DOI: 10.1108/PR-05-2016-0105

Morgan, J., Silver, M., & Degbey, W. Y. (2025). Inclusive leadership. In *Elgar encyclopedia of leadership* (pp. 109–111). Edward Elgar Publishing., DOI: 10.4337/9781035307074.00052

Nuri, R. P., Piccone, C., Gaurav, N., Thomson, D., Pauls, R., Perry, L., & Aldersey, H. M. (2025). The limits and contributions of formal support: Service providers' perspectives on balancing formal and natural support for people with disabilities and their families in Canada. *Journal of Developmental and Physical Disabilities*, *37*(1), 129–156. DOI: 10.1007/s10882-023-09944-2 PMID: 39867962

Oberai, H. (2025). Embracing inclusive leadership to bias reduction in HRM. In *Navigating bias in human resource management* (pp. 101–129). IGI Global., DOI: 10.4018/979-8-3693-7132-9.ch004

Odunayo, A., & Ng, Z. (2026). Navigating inclusive language in veterinary medicine: A step toward a more equitable workplace. *Veterinary Ophthalmology*, *29*(1), e70025. Advance online publication. DOI: 10.1111/vop.70025 PMID: 40356033

Phan, N. (2025). Transforming internal communication: Strategies for engagement and organizational success. *Business and Professional Communication Quarterly*, 23294906251378735. Advance online publication. DOI: 10.1177/23294906251378735

Piccone, C., Xu, X., Thomson, D., Gaurav, N., & Aldersey, H. M. (2024). Enabling formal and natural supports for adults with developmental disabilities in British Columbia, Canada: Experiences of three organizations. *Disabilities*, *4*(4), 1076–1092. DOI: 10.3390/disabilities4040067

Pietrantoni, L., Mazzetti, G., San Román Niaves, M., Kubik, R., Giusino, D., & De Angelis, M. (2024). Enhancing team dynamics through digital coaching: The role of managerial and peer support. *European Journal of Training and Development*, *48*(10), 16–36. DOI: 10.1108/EJTD-12-2023-0193

Pon-Barry, H., Packard, B. W.-L., & St. John, A. (2017). Expanding capacity and promoting inclusion in introductory computer science: A focus on near-peer mentor preparation and code review. *Computer Science Education, 27*(1), 54–77. DOI: 10.1080/08993408.2017.1333270

Pouliot, D. M., Müller, E., Frasché, N. F., Kern, A. S., & Resti, I. H. (2017). A tool for supporting communication in the workplace for individuals with intellectual disabilities and/or autism. *Career Development and Transition for Exceptional Individuals, 40*(4), 244–249. DOI: 10.1177/2165143416683927

Quinn, M. A., Chaudhari, A., Brazeau, C., Lawrence, E., & Olson, K. (2025). How peer support helps heal the culture of medicine from within. *NEJM Catalyst Innovations in Care Delivery, 6*(1). Advance online publication. DOI: 10.1056/CAT.23.0373

Reynolds, M. C., Palmer, S. B., & Gotto, G. S. (2018). Reconceptualizing natural supports for people with disabilities and their families. *International Review of Research in Developmental Disabilities, 54*, 177–209. DOI: 10.1016/bs.irrdd.2018.07.006

Rezai, M., Lindsay, S., Ahmed, H., & Vijayakumar, A. (2023). Workplace inclusion: A scoping review of the qualitative literature. *Work (Reading, Mass.), 75*(1), 59–73. DOI: 10.3233/WOR-211343 PMID: 36591672

Riera Claret, C., Sahagún, M. Á., & Selva, C. (2020). Peer and informal learning among hospital doctors: An ethnographic study focused on routines, practices and relationships. *Journal of Workplace Learning, 32*(4), 285–301. DOI: 10.1108/JWL-11-2018-0141

Sartore, G.-M., Pourliakas, A., & Lagioia, V. (2021). Peer support interventions for parents and carers of children with complex needs. *Cochrane Database of Systematic Reviews, 2021*(12), CD010618. Advance online publication. DOI: 10.1002/14651858.CD010618.pub2 PMID: 34923624

Schuhl, J., Chatard, A., & Lambert, É. (2020). Reducing stigmatisation of employees with disability: Example of a brief intervention in a company [RÉDUIRE LA STIGMATISATION DES SALARIÉS RECONNUS HANDICAPÉS: EXEMPLE D'UNE ACTION DE SENSIBILISATION EN ENTREPRISE]. *Le Travail Humain, 83*(2), 91–114. DOI: 10.3917/th.832.0091

Thaver, T., Lim, L., & Liau, A. K. (2025). Social inclusion through attitudinal change in Singaporean teachers. *International Journal of Developmental Disabilities, 71*(6), 879–895. DOI: 10.1080/20473869.2025.2494040 PMID: 40959443

Traver, M. T. B., Fustes, M. L., & Fernández, M. M. (2017). How do employees help co-workers with intellectual disabilities? A work coaching experience in supported employment [¿cómo ayudan los compañeros de trabajo a los empleados con discapacidad intelectual? Una experiencia de coaching laboral en empleo con apoyo]. *Revista Española de Orientación y Psicopedagogía, 28*(1), 51–71. DOI: 10.5944/reop.vol.28.num.1.2017.19358

Tsirkas, K. (2025). Understanding and using soft skills for autistic people. In *Empowering innovations in advanced autism research and management* (pp. 333–348). IGI Global., DOI: 10.4018/979-8-3693-8176-2.ch014

Voorhees, H. L. (2022). Informal and formal networks. In *The international encyclopedia of health communication* (pp. 1–6). Wiley., DOI: 10.1002/9781119678816.iehc0584

Weiner, J. S., & Zivolich, S. (2003). A longitudinal report for three employees in a training consultant model of natural support. *Journal of Vocational Rehabilitation, 18*(3), 199–202. DOI: 10.3233/JVR-2003-00196

Westerlund, D., Granucci, E. A., Gamache, P., & Clark, H. B. (2006). Effects of peer mentors on work-related performance of adolescents with behavioral and/or learning disabilities. *Journal of Positive Behavior Interventions, 8*(4), 244–251. DOI: 10.1177/10983007060080040601

Wilson, P. M., & Adderley, S. C. (2025). Enhancing workplace well-being: Inclusive leadership in the Bahamas. In *Leading inclusive workplaces through digital transformation and organizational change* (pp. 189–223). IGI Global., DOI: 10.4018/979-8-3373-5127-8.ch007

Xiao, Y., & Seagull, F. J. (2007). Emergent CSCW systems: The resolution and bandwidth of workplaces. *International Journal of Medical Informatics, 76*(Suppl. 1), 261–266. DOI: 10.1016/j.ijmedinf.2006.05.037 PMID: 16822715

Chapter 10
Supervision Reimagined: Communication, Feedback, and Growth

ABSTRACT

This chapter examines how supportive supervision can strengthen motivation, learning, and workplace participation for employees with intellectual disabilities. It explores supervisory practices that promote clear communication, constructive feedback, goal-setting, and accessible performance reviews in inclusive workplaces. Emphasis is placed on creating psychologically safe environments where employees feel respected, supported, and encouraged to develop their skills. The chapter also highlights the role of coaching, reflective learning, and collaborative supervision in reinforcing continuous professional growth. By recognising employee strengths and encouraging gradual independence, supervisors can foster confidence, engagement, and sustained workplace participation. These practices contribute to organisational cultures that value inclusion while preparing employees for long-term career development and meaningful employment opportunities.

10.1 INTRODUCTION

Supervision plays a central role in shaping how inclusive employment experiences are for workers with intellectual disabilities. In contemporary workplaces, supervisors no longer function solely as task monitors or administrative overseers. Effective supervision now involves guiding employees through clear communication, constructive feedback, and developmental support that strengthens both competence and confidence in the workplace. When supervisory practices align with inclusive organisational values, they create environments where workers with intellectual

DOI: 10.4018/979-8-3373-9185-4.ch010

disabilities can participate meaningfully, develop their abilities, and experience a sense of belonging within workplace communities.

Estreder et al. (2024) note that autonomy-supportive supervision can enhance the well-being and satisfaction of workers with intellectual disabilities. Supervisory approaches that recognise employee strengths and encourage participation in workplace activities allow individuals to feel valued within their teams. Inclusive supervision, therefore, requires supervisors to understand how communication practices, feedback processes, and leadership behaviours influence daily workplace experiences.

Traditional models of supervision have often prioritised compliance, productivity monitoring, and rule enforcement. Although such approaches may support organisational efficiency, they do not always create conditions that enable workers with intellectual disabilities to learn, grow, and contribute confidently within workplace teams. Meacham et al. (2017) indicate that inclusive employment improves when workplace practices simultaneously support task competence and social participation. Supervisory practices must therefore adapt in order to provide guidance that supports both performance and workplace inclusion.

Growth-oriented leadership is an approach that prioritises employee development, collaboration, and continuous learning (Franken et al., 2025). Supervisors who adopt this perspective move beyond controlling work processes and instead focus on helping employees develop skills and confidence over time. Within inclusive workplaces, growth-oriented supervision encourages employees with intellectual disabilities to strengthen their capabilities while receiving guidance that recognises progress and effort.

According to Liu & Tuntinakhongul (2024), developmental feedback from supervisors can strengthen employee engagement and workplace vitality. Constructive feedback helps employees understand expectations and provides encouragement that supports skill development. Supportive supervisory practices, therefore, contribute to environments in which employees feel motivated to develop their abilities and participate actively in workplace tasks. Cavanagh et al. (2021) opined that subtle forms of misunderstanding or exclusion may limit the participation of workers with intellectual disabilities within organisational settings. Supervisors play an important role in addressing these challenges by promoting respectful communication and equitable workplace interactions. Clear instructions, accessible feedback, and respectful engagement contribute to workplace climates where employees feel supported rather than marginalised.

Dalton & Sweeney (2013) highlight the importance of communication supports that help individuals with intellectual disabilities understand workplace expectations and express their perspectives effectively. Supervisors who adopt clear, structured communication strategies enable employees to navigate work tasks with greater confidence and reduce uncertainty.

Inclusive workplace environments develop when interpersonal relationships are built on mutual respect and constructive interaction Novak et al. (2011). Supervisors influence these relationships by modelling inclusive attitudes and encouraging collaborative engagement among team members. In the view of Zhong et al. (2022), leadership behaviours characterised by fairness and openness often influence organisational culture and employee attitudes. Wilson & Adderley (2025) describe inclusive supervision as a relational process that combines professional guidance with empathy and respect. Supervisors who cultivate supportive relationships with employees create opportunities for dialogue, learning, and collaboration. Such relationships enable workers with intellectual disabilities to participate as valued members of workplace teams.

This chapter explores how supervision can be reimagined to support communication, feedback, and professional growth for workers with intellectual disabilities. The following sections examine approaches to inclusive communication, constructive feedback, accessible performance evaluation, and supportive coaching practices that strengthen workplace participation and development.

10.2 ACCESSIBLE COMMUNICATION STRATEGIES FOR EFFECTIVE SUPERVISION

Inclusive supervision requires communication practices that enable workers with intellectual disabilities to understand expectations, participate confidently in workplace activities, and engage productively with colleagues. Communication functions as a central mechanism through which supervisors guide task performance, clarify responsibilities, and support employee participation within teams.

10.2.1 Clear and Consistent Expectations

Effective supervision begins with clear explanations of job responsibilities and workplace expectations. Workers with intellectual disabilities often perform more effectively when supervisors present instructions in straightforward and predictable ways. Ambiguous instructions or inconsistent guidance may create uncertainty, affecting task completion and workplace confidence (Tuffrey-Wijne & McEnhill, 2008). Supervisors who articulate expectations carefully help employees understand what is required and how tasks should be completed.

Consistency further improves understanding. Reinforcing instructions, confirming comprehension, and maintaining stable communication routines allow employees to interpret workplace expectations with greater clarity. Communication tools designed for individuals with intellectual disabilities help structure workplace interactions and clarify expectations among team members (Pouliot et al., 2017). Such approaches ensure that guidance remains understandable and reliable across different work situations.

Truong et al. (2021) describe training programmes that help supervisors examine their communication approaches and develop greater awareness of inclusive practices. Professional preparation of this kind equips supervisors with practical strategies for presenting workplace expectations in ways employees can easily understand.

10.2.2 Plain Language and Visual Guidance

Plain language is essential for effective supervisory communication. Instructions that use simple vocabulary and direct phrasing enable employees with intellectual disabilities to understand tasks without unnecessary complexity. Communication barriers often arise when supervisors rely on technical terms or abstract explanations that may be difficult to interpret (Chew et al., 2009). Supervisors who communicate in clear, concise language help employees engage more confidently with their workplace responsibilities.

Visual support strengthens this process by presenting information in concrete and recognisable forms. Photographs, diagrams, symbols, and demonstrations can clarify instructions that may otherwise be difficult to interpret through verbal explanation alone. Communication tools that outline personal interaction preferences and workplace routines help colleagues understand how best to communicate with employees with intellectual disabilities (Pouliot et al., 2017).

Embley (2024) describes task analysis as a practical strategy that divides complex work activities into sequential steps. Supervisors who organise instructions in this way allow employees to approach tasks gradually, reducing confusion and supporting consistent performance.

10.2.3 Adapting Communication to Individual Needs

Supervisors must recognise that employees interpret and express information differently. Some individuals rely primarily on spoken communication, while others respond more effectively to visual guidance, demonstration, or alternative communication tools. Individuals with intellectual disabilities may communicate through gestures, assistive devices, or symbolic systems, which requires supervisors to adjust their communication practices accordingly (Chew et al., 2009).

Primeau & Talley (2019) describe specialised communication training programmes that prepare professionals to respond to diverse cognitive and learning needs. Supervisors who develop these competencies are better prepared to ensure that workplace instructions remain understandable and accessible.

Adaptability also involves allowing employees sufficient time to process information and respond to instructions. Rushed communication may limit understanding, whereas patient interaction enables employees to clarify information and confirm expectations. Flexible supervisory approaches, therefore, help create communication environments that accommodate varied learning styles and abilities.

10.2.4 Two-Way Communication and Active Listening

Effective supervision requires more than simply issuing instructions; it also involves listening to employees and creating opportunities for dialogue. Two-way communication allows workers with intellectual disabilities to seek clarification, express ideas, and contribute to workplace discussions. Person-centred communication approaches encourage individuals to participate actively in conversations about their responsibilities and experiences (Martínez-Carrascal et al., 2023).

Active listening strengthens these interactions. Supervisors who listen attentively acknowledge employee perspectives and encourage collaborative problem-solving within teams. Such interactions promote trust and mutual understanding, which are essential for inclusive workplace relationships.

(Choe et al., 2019) describe collaborative communication practices that encourage empathy and shared understanding among colleagues. Supervisors who promote open dialogue foster environments where employees feel comfortable asking questions and discussing workplace challenges.

Communication environments must also support respectful expression of personal perspectives. Employees are more likely to communicate openly when they feel that their views will be received without criticism or dismissal (Tuffrey-Wijne & Rose, 2017). Supervisors who encourage respectful discussion therefore strengthen workplace cultures that value participation and mutual respect.

10.3 DELIVERING CONSTRUCTIVE FEEDBACK THAT BUILDS CONFIDENCE

Supervisors influence how employees interpret their performance through the tone, timing, and clarity of feedback interactions. When feedback is delivered respectfully and clearly, employees can better understand expectations and refine the skills required for effective workplace participation. Communication practices that support understanding and engagement, therefore, remain fundamental to inclusive supervision (Dalton & Sweeney, 2013).

10.3.1 Principles of Respectful and Constructive Feedback

Effective feedback provides clear information about performance and behaviour. Employees benefit when supervisors describe observable actions rather than offering vague or general comments. Specific feedback enables workers to recognise successful practices and identify areas that require improvement. Ambiguous comments may create uncertainty and limit opportunities for learning (Uetz et al., 2024). Supervisors, therefore, strengthen workplace learning when they describe performance in precise, understandable terms.

According to Duffy (2013), feedback is most effective when it is timely, specific, and directed toward improvement. Providing guidance soon after task completion helps employees connect supervisory comments to their recent actions. This approach supports continuous learning rather than delayed evaluation.

Respectful communication also shapes how employees receive feedback. Supervisors who use clear explanations and supportive language help employees interpret guidance without confusion or discomfort. Accessible communication strategies allow workers with intellectual disabilities to understand workplace expectations more easily (Chew et al., 2009). Tools designed to clarify communication preferences and workplace routines further support understanding among employees and colleagues (Pouliot et al., 2017).

10.3.2 Encouragement and Corrective Guidance

Balanced feedback helps sustain motivation and confidence. Supervisors who recognise effective performance before addressing areas requiring improvement create an environment that supports learning. Positive reinforcement encourages employees to continue developing their abilities while remaining receptive to corrective guidance (Varia & Middleton, 2012).

However, Lipinska (2021) notes that feedback combining encouragement with corrective suggestions supports engagement and motivation. Employees are more willing to reflect on performance when supervisors acknowledge progress and effort. This balanced approach allows feedback to function as developmental guidance rather than criticism.

Recognition of strengths also contributes to a stronger sense of competence. Workers who receive acknowledgement for well-executed tasks often demonstrate greater confidence and commitment to their roles. Encouraging feedback therefore supports both learning and participation in workplace tasks (Porter et al., 2024). Supervisory recognition of employee capabilities can also enhance workplace satisfaction and well-being among workers with intellectual disabilities (Estreder et al., 2024).

10.3.3 Real-Time Feedback for Learning

Immediate feedback strengthens learning by allowing employees to adjust their actions in real time. Supervisors who provide guidance during or shortly after task completion enable workers to correct errors and refine their skills without delay. Continuous feedback, therefore, contributes to improved performance and skill development (Rivera et al., 2021).

Regan & Weiss (2020) describe coaching approaches in which supervisors provide brief guidance during work activities. These interactions allow employees to modify their behaviour in real time while maintaining productivity. Real-time feedback may also involve demonstration or guided practice. Supervisors who model correct procedures while explaining task steps provide employees with opportunities to observe and apply appropriate techniques. Clear communication during such interactions is particularly important for workers with intellectual disabilities because accessible explanations strengthen task understanding (Dalton & Sweeney, 2013).

Technological developments have also introduced new methods for delivering immediate feedback. Digital coaching tools and immersive training systems can support learning by providing instant guidance during skill development activities (Geisen & Klatt, 2022). Although such technologies may not always be necessary in everyday workplaces, they illustrate the benefits of timely feedback during learning processes.

10.3.4 Feedback Practices that Protect Confidence

Constructive supervision requires attention to the emotional impact of feedback. Feedback delivered in ways that threaten self-esteem may reduce motivation and discourage participation in workplace tasks. Employees who receive criticism without guidance may feel uncertain about their abilities or hesitant to attempt new responsibilities (Kluger & Van Dijk, 2010).

Murtagh (2014) notes that feedback practices based primarily on external judgement can weaken intrinsic motivation. Supervisors, therefore, need to ensure that feedback supports learning and independence rather than reliance on constant approval. Constructive feedback should guide employees toward improvement while reinforcing their sense of competence.

Feedback should also extend beyond routine administrative evaluation. Conversations about performance should encourage reflection, development, and skill improvement rather than measuring outcomes. When supervisors frame feedback as an opportunity for learning, employees are more likely to interpret guidance as supportive (Armengol et al., 2023). Inclusive leadership approaches that promote respectful dialogue further strengthen constructive supervisory relationships within workplace teams (Zhong et al., 2022).

10.4 SETTING ATTAINABLE GOALS AND SUPPORTING SKILL DEVELOPMENT FOR WORKERS WITH INTELLECTUAL DISABILITIES

Supervisors who guide employees through structured goal-setting processes help workers understand expectations, track progress, and develop confidence in their abilities. Inclusive supervision, therefore, connects everyday work tasks with broader developmental objectives that support competence and professional growth (Meacham et al., 2017; Estreder et al., 2024).

10.4.1 Establishing Clear and Achievable Workplace Goals: Workplace goals must be realistic, meaningful, and aligned with employees' abilities and aspirations. Person-centred planning provides an effective framework for this purpose by enabling workers with intellectual disabilities to identify their strengths, preferences, and career interests. This approach encourages collaborative decision-making in which supervisors and employees jointly determine appropriate objectives rather than imposing externally defined targets (Ozment & Patten, 2026; Ahmad et al., 2026).

Lawlor & York (2007) note that structured goal-attainment approaches help organisations evaluate progress while maintaining individualised expectations. When goals reflect both personal capabilities and workplace requirements, employees are more likely to experience success through gradual skill development.

The Self-Determined Career Development Model (SDCDM) illustrates how structured goal-setting approaches can strengthen job performance among workers with disabilities. Devlin (2008) reports that employees who engage in SDCDM-guided planning frequently meet or exceed the expectations of supervisors and job coaches. Through this model, employees identify objectives, develop action plans, and monitor their progress toward meaningful outcomes.

Clear goal definitions also support supervisory communication. When workplace expectations are expressed through specific objectives, employees can more easily understand the purpose of their tasks and the standards guiding performance. Accessible communication, therefore, plays a crucial role in helping workers interpret and pursue workplace goals effectively (Dalton & Sweeney, 2013; Chew et al., 2009).

10.4.2 Using Step-by-Step Goal Planning and Task Breakdowns: Structured planning translates broader objectives into practical workplace actions. Step-by-step planning models guide employees and supervisors through stages that promote gradual skill development. Ryan et al. (2024) describe the DECIDE model as a framework that supports systematic goal planning through stages that include identifying objectives, developing strategies, and evaluating outcomes.

Breaking complex tasks into manageable steps is particularly beneficial for workers with intellectual disabilities. Task analysis allows supervisors to present work activities in sequential stages that are easier to understand and perform. Embley (2024) explains that structured task breakdowns reduce confusion and support independent task completion.

Baer et al. (2021) indicate that step-by-step task guidance improves work performance while gradually reducing dependence on external assistance. As employees gain familiarity with workplace routines, supervisors can reduce direct supervision and encourage greater independence in task completion.

Structured task organisation also helps employees recognise incremental progress. Dividing tasks into smaller components allows workers to experience regular achievements that reinforce motivation and confidence. Supervisors can then monitor progress while offering targeted guidance at each stage of development (Devlin, 2008; Pouliot et al., 2017).

10.4.3 Encouraging Employee Participation in Goal-Setting: Employee participation is central to effective goal-setting processes. Workers who actively contribute to defining their goals often demonstrate stronger motivation and commitment to achieving them. Burke et al. (2021) observe that individuals with intellectual disabilities benefit from opportunities to identify personal objectives and participate in decisions related to their employment pathways.

Self-determination frameworks such as the Self-Determined Learning Model of Instruction (SDLMI) support this participatory approach. Through SDLMI, employees learn to define goals, develop action plans, and evaluate progress over time (Kuld et al., 2023). Such approaches strengthen autonomy and encourage individuals to take an active role in their professional development.

Supervisors play an important role in facilitating this participation. Creating environments where employees feel comfortable expressing their ideas and preferences supports collaborative planning. Dörfler & Kulnik (2020) note that person-centred goal setting depends on dialogue that respects individual perspectives and abilities. Trust between supervisors and employees therefore becomes essential for meaningful participation.

Active involvement in goal-setting conversations also strengthens employees' sense of ownership over their work. Understanding how tasks contribute to broader objectives encourages engagement and confidence in workplace activities (Martin & Jones, 2023; Truong et al., 2021).

10.4.4 Linking Short-Term Goals with Long-Term Development: Effective goal-setting strategies connect short-term objectives with long-term professional development. Immediate goals enable employees to master specific tasks, while long-term goals provide direction for career progression and skill advancement. Siperstein et al. (2014) highlight the importance of early employment experiences and community-based training programmes in supporting long-term employment outcomes for individuals with intellectual disabilities.

Baer et al. (2021) explain that structured workplace experiences help employees develop adaptive behaviours, communication skills, and work habits that support future career opportunities. Supervisors who link everyday tasks to broader developmental pathways help employees recognise the long-term value of their work experiences. Organisational environments also influence professional development. Fajardo-Castro et al. (2024) indicate that workplaces that support autonomy, competence, and social connection contribute to higher levels of well-being and development among workers with intellectual disabilities.

Supportive supervision further reinforces these pathways. Supervisors who provide encouragement, constructive feedback, and accessible communication enable employees to progress from basic task competence toward greater workplace responsibility (Estreder et al., 2024; Zhong et al., 2022).

10.5 CONDUCTING ACCESSIBLE AND INCLUSIVE PERFORMANCE REVIEWS

Performance reviews help employees understand their progress, recognise achievements, and identify areas for improvement. Evaluation systems must be understandable, supportive, and meaningful. When designed with accessibility in mind, reviews move beyond administrative assessment and become opportunities for dialogue, learning, and professional development. Supervisors need to structure evaluations to promote clarity, participation, and fairness.

Designing Understandable and Meaningful Evaluations: Effective performance reviews require careful preparation and a clear structure. Rather than concentrating feedback into a single annual meeting, supervisors should distribute evaluation discussions across several shorter sessions. This approach allows employees to process information gradually and reflect on their progress more effectively. O'Donovan (2005) explains that regular informal check-ins throughout the year help supervisors and employees track achievements, challenges, and developmental needs. These ongoing interactions make formal reviews more productive because key issues have already been discussed.

Clear evaluation criteria are equally important. When performance standards remain ambiguous, employees may struggle to understand how their work is assessed. Transparent criteria help employees interpret expectations and recognise how their contributions align with organisational objectives. Islam et al. (2025) observe that unclear or subjective evaluation systems can reinforce bias within workplaces. Establishing consistent and inclusive standards therefore strengthens fairness and improves employee understanding of the evaluation process.

Supervisors can further support comprehension by explaining criteria through accessible communication methods. Simple language, practical examples, and visual explanations help employees interpret feedback more confidently. These strategies ensure that performance reviews function as learning opportunities rather than sources of confusion or anxiety.

Using Multiple Methods for Assessing Performance: Inclusive evaluation systems benefit from multiple methods for assessing employee performance. Relying on a single measure may overlook important aspects of workplace contribution. Combining different forms of feedback provides supervisors with a more comprehensive understanding of how employees perform their roles.

Collaborative evaluation practices offer one useful strategy. DiCecco (2007) explains that jointly developed job descriptions and evaluation criteria clarify expectations and strengthen employee engagement. When employees participate in defining these standards, they gain a clearer understanding of their responsibilities and performance goals.

Multi-source feedback can further improve evaluation accuracy. Input from peers, supervisors, and other colleagues who regularly interact with the employee offers a broader perspective on performance. Islam et al. (2025) note that incorporating multiple viewpoints helps reduce subjectivity and produces more balanced assessments. For workers with intellectual disabilities, such approaches may also reveal strengths that traditional evaluation methods might overlook.

These varied assessment methods allow supervisors to recognise a wide range of contributions, including teamwork, reliability, communication, and collaboration. Such qualities are essential in inclusive workplaces and should be reflected in evaluation processes.

Involving Employees in Reflective Discussions: Performance reviews should encourage employees to participate actively in discussions about their work and development. Reflective dialogue enables workers to share their perspectives, identify challenges, and consider strategies for improvement. When employees contribute to these conversations, evaluations become collaborative rather than unilateral assessments.

"Performance Evaluations" (2025) describes reflective evaluation processes as opportunities for supervisors and employees to examine achievements and identify future development goals together. Such discussions help employees understand how their work contributes to organisational objectives while encouraging personal reflection.

Supervisors can strengthen participation by allowing employees to prepare before review meetings. Inviting employees to reflect on their accomplishments, challenges, and learning experiences beforehand helps them approach discussions with greater confidence.

Training initiatives can also improve participation. Henderson et al. (2024) note that workshops designed to explain evaluation procedures enable individuals with learning disabilities to engage more effectively in review discussions. When employees understand how evaluations operate, they can communicate their perspectives more clearly and participate more fully in decision-making.

Ensuring Fairness, Transparency, and Clarity: Fairness and transparency are central to inclusive performance evaluation. Employees must understand how ratings, development opportunities, and career decisions are determined. Consistent procedures and clear documentation help maintain trust in the review process. Addressing bias is particularly important. Islam et al. (2025) note that subjective judgment within evaluation systems may reinforce inequalities if accountability measures are absent.

Transparent criteria and structured procedures, therefore, ensure that employees are assessed consistently. Organisations can strengthen fairness further by aligning performance reviews with broader inclusion goals. Hung et al. (2025) explain that evaluation systems incorporating equity-focused practices encourage recognition of diverse contributions and support inclusive organisational cultures.

10.6 COACHING FOR GROWTH: SUPPORTING CONTINUOUS LEARNING IN THE WORKPLACE

Coaching-based supervision provides ongoing guidance that supports skill development, confidence building, and workplace participation. Unlike traditional supervision, which focuses primarily on monitoring performance, coaching prioritises learning, reflection, and collaboration. When supervisors adopt coaching practices, they create environments where employees gradually develop competence while receiving constructive guidance.

Integrating Coaching Practices into Everyday Supervision

Coaching practices can be embedded in everyday supervisory interactions to support continuous development. Coaching supervision creates opportunities for employees to reflect on their experiences, strengthen skills, and build professional confidence (Stock et al., 2025). In inclusive workplaces, these interactions help workers with intellectual disabilities interpret workplace expectations and develop strategies for performing tasks more effectively.

Perrault & Coleman (2006) describe coaching supervision as a developmental process that supports professional learning and ethical practice. Supervisors who incorporate coaching behaviours into daily interactions encourage employees to analyse their work experiences and identify areas for improvement. This approach shifts supervision from directive instruction to collaborative learning.

Managerial coaching behaviours also influence performance and engagement. Budhiraja, (2023) explains that facilitation-based coaching strengthens both task performance and contextual workplace behaviours. Supervisors who encourage discussion, collaborative problem-solving, and reflection help employees develop practical skills while strengthening confidence in their abilities.

Peer coaching models further support workplace learning. Alsaleh et al. (2017) note that peer coaching cycles often include planning discussions, observation of work practices, and reflective dialogue. These structured interactions allow employees to learn from one another while reinforcing professional competence.

Encouraging Reflective Learning and Skill Reinforcement

Reflective learning is central to coaching because it encourages employees to examine their experiences and identify strategies for improvement. Reflective practice allows individuals to analyse what they have learned, consider alternative approaches, and apply insights to future tasks (Matsuo, 2012). In inclusive workplaces, reflection helps workers with intellectual disabilities understand how their actions influence outcomes.

Structured reflective activities strengthen this learning process. Lockyer et al. (2004) highlight the value of reflective discussions, goal setting, and self-assessment in supporting professional development. When supervisors encourage employees to review their experiences and evaluate how tasks were completed, learning becomes more deliberate and purposeful.

Technological tools can also support reflective learning. Fessl et al. (2015) describe digital reflection applications that prompt employees to analyse workplace experiences and identify lessons from daily activities. These tools guide users through reflective questions that encourage thoughtful examination of decisions and behaviours.

Subsequent studies show that workplace reflection technologies can strengthen learning when integrated carefully into routine workflows (Fessl et al., 2017; Renner et al., 2020). Such tools prompt employees to consider how their experiences contribute to skill development. However, these technologies must be introduced thoughtfully so they enhance rather than interrupt workplace activities.

Peer coaching and mentorship further reinforce reflective learning. Boillat & Elizov (2014) explain that mentoring relationships allow employees to discuss challenges, exchange experiences, and gain new insights into workplace practices. These interactions help employees evaluate their performance and develop improved approaches to their work.

Supporting Employees During Workplace Challenges and Transitions

Workplace learning frequently occurs alongside challenges and transitions. Employees may need to adapt to new tasks, organisational changes, or evolving job responsibilities. Coaching supervision provides an important framework for supporting employees during these periods.

Turner & Holdsworth (2023) highlight resilience as an important factor in managing workplace challenges. Coaching interactions can strengthen resilience by helping employees clarify goals, identify coping strategies, and maintain focus during demanding situations. Supervisors who provide encouragement and constructive guidance enable employees to approach challenges with greater confidence.

Support during organisational entry is also essential. Birkle & Seifried (2024) observe that newcomers benefit from structured guidance, mentorship, and supportive relationships during their transition into new workplaces. Coaching-based supervision helps employees understand expectations while developing the skills needed to perform their roles effectively.

Organisational support further strengthens this transition. Morley (2024) notes that flexible work arrangements, mentoring programmes, and supportive management practices help employees adjust to new demands. These forms of assistance are particularly important for workers with intellectual disabilities who may require additional guidance during periods of adjustment.

Psychological safety also influences how employees navigate change. Clarke et al. (2024) indicate that workplaces characterised by trust and open communication enable employees to seek assistance without fear of criticism. Similarly, Lee (2021) reports that supportive organisational climates reduce stress during periods of change. Supervisors who cultivate such environments encourage employees to discuss challenges openly and request guidance when needed.

Strengthening Collaboration Between Supervisors, Job Coaches, and Peer Mentors

Continuous workplace learning often relies on collaboration among supervisors, job coaches, and peer mentors. Each participant contributes unique knowledge and support that strengthens employee development. Coordinated collaboration ensures that employees receive consistent guidance across different aspects of their work.

Arora & Parthasarathy (2025) explain that effective collaborative models depend on shared goals, open communication, and mutual learning among participants. When supervisors and mentors coordinate their efforts, they create coherent learning environments that reinforce workplace expectations and development.

Peer mentoring programmes also support workplace learning. Sears et al. (2017) note that mentoring relationships promote trust, shared learning, and ongoing support among colleagues. These relationships give employees opportunities to discuss workplace experiences and receive guidance from peers familiar with their roles.

Mentoring can also contribute to leadership development. Sunderman & Adebayo (2025) explain that peer mentoring strengthens communication skills, problem-solving abilities, and professional confidence for both mentors and mentees.

Group supervision approaches further support collaborative coaching systems. Wingrove et al. (2020) describe group supervision models grounded in self-determination theory as promoting competence, autonomy, and relatedness among participants. Through shared reflection and dialogue, supervisors, mentors, and coaches create supportive learning environments that reinforce employee development.

10.7 CONCLUSION: BUILDING MOTIVATING WORK ENVIRONMENTS THROUGH SUPPORTIVE SUPERVISION

Supportive supervision plays a central role in shaping workplace environments where employees with intellectual disabilities can develop confidence, strengthen skills, and participate meaningfully in organisational life. When supervisors adopt inclusive leadership practices that prioritise clear communication, constructive feedback, and collaborative learning, they create conditions that support both employee development and organisational effectiveness. Such environments encourage employees to view supervision not as control but as guidance that supports growth and professional advancement.

A key element of supportive supervision is the creation of psychologically safe environments. In workplaces characterised by respect, openness, and trust, employees feel comfortable asking questions, sharing ideas, and seeking assistance when challenges arise. Psychological safety encourages learning because employees are more willing to experiment with new approaches and develop their skills without fear of judgement. For workers with intellectual disabilities, such environments are particularly important, as they promote participation and confidence in workplace interactions.

Recognising achievements also strengthens motivation and engagement. Supervisors who acknowledge progress, effort, and accomplishments help employees recognise the value of their contributions. Positive recognition reinforces employee strengths and encourages continued development. This practice not only builds confidence but also supports a sense of belonging within workplace teams.

At the same time, effective supervision balances encouragement with independence. Employees benefit when supervisors provide guidance that gradually enables them to perform tasks with greater autonomy. By combining supportive coaching with opportunities for independent problem-solving, supervisors help employees develop competence while maintaining access to assistance when needed.

These supervisory practices contribute to workplaces that motivate employees to learn, participate, and grow. The next chapter builds on these foundations by examining how organisations can sustain inclusive cultures and create long-term employment opportunities that support the continued success of workers with intellectual disabilities.

REFERENCES

Ahmad, W., Shokeen, R., & Raj, R. Nazli, Ramkumar, B. V., Singh, R. R., & Mohammad, S. (2026). Transition of persons with intellectual and developmental disabilities from school to work: Evidence-based practices. In *Vocational rehabilitation for students with developmental disabilities: Transition from education to employment* (pp. 79–132). IGI Global. DOI: 10.4018/979-8-3693-9541-7.ch003

Alsaleh, A., Alabdulhadi, M., & Alrwaished, N. (2017). Impact of peer coaching strategy on pre-service teachers' professional development growth in Kuwait. *International Journal of Educational Research*, *86*, 36–49. DOI: 10.1016/j.ijer.2017.07.011

Armengol, J. V., Alcalde, I. H., Ibáñez, D. G., & Ferrer, S. E. (2023). Feed back as a teaching tool: Its impact on the motivation of higher education students [El Feed Back como Herramienta Docente: Su Impacto en la Motivación de los Estudiantes de Educación Superior]. *UCJC Business and Society Review*, *20*(76), 104–149. DOI: 10.3232/UBR.2023.V20.N1.03

Arora, P., & Parthasarathy, P. D. (2025). Collaboration model—Optimizing collaborative models in distance learning to enhance student learning through workplace and academic integration. *Lecture Notes in Networks and Systems*, *1206*, 881–894. DOI: 10.1007/978-981-96-0201-8_55

Baer, H., Welker, K., & Cox, C. (2021). Work performance and support needs analysis of students with intellectual disabilities. *Journal of Vocational Rehabilitation*, *55*(3), 251–270. DOI: 10.3233/JVR-211167

Birkle, S., & Seifried, J. (2024). Perceived challenges when changing employer: What newcomers experience as helpful during organizational entry. *Journal of Personnel Psychology*, *23*(3), 156–167. DOI: 10.1027/1866-5888/a000342

Boillat, M., & Elizov, M. (2014). Peer coaching and mentorship. In *Faculty development in the health professions: A focus on research and practice* (pp. 159–179). Springer., DOI: 10.1007/978-94-007-7612-8_8

Budhiraja, S. (2023). Continuous learning and employee performance: A moderated examination of managers' coaching behavior in India. *Personnel Review*, *52*(1), 200–217. DOI: 10.1108/PR-04-2020-0272

Burke, K. M., Shogren, K. A., & Carlson, S. (2021). Examining types of goals set by transition-age students with intellectual disability. *Career Development and Transition for Exceptional Individuals*, *44*(3), 135–147. DOI: 10.1177/2165143420959055

Cavanagh, J., Meacham, H., Pariona-Cabrera, P., & Bartram, T. (2021). Subtle workplace discrimination inhibiting workers with intellectual disability from thriving at the workplace. *Personnel Review, 50*(7–8), 1739–1756. DOI: 10.1108/PR-10-2021-0723

Chew, K. L., Iacono, T., & Tracy, J. (2009). Overcoming communication barriers: Working with patients with intellectual disabilities. *Australian Family Physician, 38*(1–2), 10–14. PMID: 19283229

Choe, A. Y., Unaka, N. I., Schondelmeyer, A. C., Bignall, W. J. R., Vilvens, H. L., & Thomson, J. E. (2019). Inpatient communication barriers and drivers when caring for limited English proficiency children. *Journal of Hospital Medicine, 14*(10), 607–613. DOI: 10.12788/jhm.3240 PMID: 31339836

Clarke, E., Näswall, K., Wong, J., Pawsey, F., & Malinen, S. (2024). Enabling successful change in a high-demand working environment: A case study in a health care organization. *Journal of Health Organization and Management, 38*(2), 248–263. DOI: 10.1108/JHOM-02-2023-0051 PMID: 38509014

Dalton, C., & Sweeney, J. (2013). Communication supports in residential services for people with an intellectual disability. *British Journal of Learning Disabilities, 41*(1), 22–30. DOI: 10.1111/j.1468-3156.2011.00717.x

Devlin, P. (2008). Enhancing the job performance of employees with disabilities using the Self-Determined Career Development Model. *Education and Training in Developmental Disabilities, 43*(4), 502–513. DOI: 10.1177/215416470804300409

DiCecco, V. (2007). Performance evaluations. *Printwear, 20*(6), 24–28.

Dörfler, E., & Kulnik, S. T. (2020). Despite communication and cognitive impairment—person-centred goal-setting after stroke: A qualitative study. *Disability and Rehabilitation, 42*(25), 3628–3637. DOI: 10.1080/09638288.2019.1604821 PMID: 31020863

Duffy, K. (2013). Providing constructive feedback to students during mentoring. *Nursing Standard, 27*(31), 50–56. DOI: 10.7748/ns2013.04.27.31.50.e7334 PMID: 23641638

Embley, C. (2024). Overcoming barriers in job coaching for adults with intellectual disability in supported employment. *Review of Disability Studies, 20*(1).

Estreder, Y., Martínez-Tur, V., Moliner, C., Gracia, E., & Lira, E. (2024). The voice of persons with intellectual disability: Why does autonomy support make them feel better? *Applied Psychology, 73*(3), 1055–1070. DOI: 10.1111/apps.12487

Fajardo-Castro, L. V., Martínez-Tur, V., Moliner, C., Plavsic, A., & Arbués, J. (2024). Organizational context and satisfaction of basic needs of workers with intellectual disability as sources of well-being. *Social Sciences (Basel, Switzerland), 13*(10), 523. Advance online publication. DOI: 10.3390/socsci13100523

Fessl, A., Wesiak, G., Rivera-Pelayo, V., Feyertag, S., & Pammer, V. (2015). In-app reflection guidance for workplace learning. *Lecture Notes in Computer Science, 9307*, 85–99. DOI: 10.1007/978-3-319-24258-3_7

Fessl, A., Wesiak, G., Rivera-Pelayo, V., Feyertag, S., & Pammer, V. (2017). In-app reflection guidance: Lessons learned across four field trials at the workplace. *IEEE Transactions on Learning Technologies, 10*(4), 488–501. DOI: 10.1109/TLT.2017.2708097

Franken, E., Plimmer, G., & Hussain, A. (2025). Growth-oriented leadership: Developing leadership capacity throughout the organisation. In *Leadership and leadership development: Critical perspectives and contemporary approaches* (pp. 12–33). Routledge., DOI: 10.4324/9781032624976-2

Geisen, M., & Klatt, S. (2022). Real-time feedback using extended reality: A current overview and further integration into sports. *International Journal of Sports Science & Coaching, 17*(5), 1178–1194. DOI: 10.1177/17479541211051006

Henderson, A., Cassidy, J., Croydon, A., & Nind, M. (2024). Inclusive peer review: Reflections on an adapted citizens' jury with people with learning disabilities. *British Journal of Learning Disabilities, 52*(4), 666–675. DOI: 10.1111/bld.12603

Hung, D. Y., Levy, L. C., Rundall, T. G., Reponen, E., Huen, W., & Shortell, S. M. (2025). Advancing equity: Lean leader practices and a path forward. *The Milbank Quarterly, 103*(3), 918–939. DOI: 10.1111/1468-0009.70037 PMID: 40772572

Islam, R., French, E., & Ali, M. (2025). Subjectivity in performance review systems: Unveiling the mechanisms of gender bias and leadership disparity in the information technology industry. *International Journal of Human Resource Management, 36*(22), 4039–4073. DOI: 10.1080/09585192.2026.2623102

Kluger, A. N., & Van Dijk, D. (2010). Feedback, the various tasks of the doctor, and the feedforward alternative. *Medical Education, 44*(12), 1166–1174. DOI: 10.1111/j.1365-2923.2010.03849.x PMID: 21091758

Kuld, P. B., Frielink, N., Zijlmans, M., Schuengel, C., & Embregts, P. J. C. M. (2023). Promoting self-determination of persons with severe or profound intellectual disabilities: A systematic review and meta-analysis. *Journal of Intellectual Disability Research, 67*(7), 589–629. DOI: 10.1111/jir.13036 PMID: 37165964

Lawlor, D., & York, M. (2007). Assessing goal attainment for quality improvement. *Journal of Intellectual Disabilities*, *11*(3), 241–255. DOI: 10.1177/1744629507080786 PMID: 17846047

Lee, H. (2021). Changes in workplace practices during the COVID-19 pandemic: The roles of emotion, psychological safety and organisation support. *Journal of Organizational Effectiveness*, *8*(1), 97–128. DOI: 10.1108/JOEPP-06-2020-0104

Lipinska, J. (2021). Is feedback always motivating? Attitudes of Polish-speaking high school students from bilingual classes towards corrective feedback in writing [Le feedback est-il toujours motivant? Les attitudes des bacheliers polonophones de classes bilingues envers la rétroaction corrective écrite]. *Neofilolog*, *1*(56), 39–54. DOI: 10.14746/n.2021.56.1.4

Liu, Y., Fang, Y., Hu, L., Chen, N., Li, X., & Cai, Y. (2024). Inclusive leadership and employee workplace well-being: The role of vigor and supervisor developmental feedback. *BMC Psychology*, *12*(1), 540. Advance online publication. DOI: 10.1186/s40359-024-02029-5 PMID: 39375786

Lockyer, J., Gondocz, S. T., & Thivierge, R. L. (2004). Knowledge translation: The role and place of practice reflection. *The Journal of Continuing Education in the Health Professions*, *24*(1), 50–56. DOI: 10.1002/chp.1340240108 PMID: 15069912

Martin, A.-M., & Jones, V. (2023). Communication as a basis for person-centred support. In *Intellectual disabilities: Health and social care across the lifespan* (pp. 15–24). Springer., DOI: 10.1007/978-3-031-27496-1_2

Martínez-Carrascal, J. A., Muñoz-Sánchez, R., & Sánchez-Rodríguez, M. T. (2023). Person-centred communication in intellectual disability services. [Note: This reference appears in the chapter text but was not found in the provided Scopus export; it is listed here as cited.]. *Journal of Intellectual Disabilities*.

Matsuo, M. (2012). Leadership of learning and reflective practice: An exploratory study of nursing managers. *Management Learning*, *43*(5), 609–623. DOI: 10.1177/1350507612440413

Meacham, H., Cavanagh, J., Shaw, A., & Bartram, T. (2017). HRM practices that support the employment and social inclusion of workers with an intellectual disability. *Personnel Review*, *46*(8), 1475–1492. DOI: 10.1108/PR-05-2016-0105

Morley, M. (2024). Returning to work. Part 2: What can be done from an employer's perspective? *In Practice*, *46*(10), 542–544. DOI: 10.1002/inpr.496

Murtagh, L. (2014). The motivational paradox of feedback: Teacher and student perceptions. *Curriculum Journal*, *25*(4), 516–541. DOI: 10.1080/09585176.2014.944197

Novak, J., Feyes, K. J., & Christensen, K. A. (2011). Application of intergroup contact theory to the integrated workplace: Setting the stage for inclusion. *Journal of Vocational Rehabilitation, 35*(3), 211–226. DOI: 10.3233/JVR-2011-0573

O'Donovan, J. (2005). Managing the performance review process. *Civil Engineers Australia, 77*(6), 69.

Ozment, L., & Patten, B. (2026). From campus to career: Strategies for inclusive employment success. In *Implementing inclusive postsecondary programs for students with intellectual disabilities* (pp. 211–238). IGI Global., DOI: 10.4018/979-8-3373-2767-9.ch008

Performance evaluations. (2025). *Human Resource Management International Digest, 33*(6), 6–8. DOI: 10.1108/HRMID-06-2025-0159

Perrault, E. L. J., & Coleman, H. D. J. (2006). Coaching within social work field education. *The Clinical Supervisor, 23*(2), 47–64. DOI: 10.1300/J001v23n02_04

Porter, J. M., Velten, J., Badami, R., Nezakatolhossaini, M., & Lotfinejad, M. (2024). Knowledge of results about more accurate versus less accurate trials: Differential effects on psychological variables and motor learning in adolescent females. *Polish Journal of Sport and Tourism, 31*(1), 12–16. DOI: 10.2478/pjst-2024-0002

Pouliot, D. M., Müller, E., Frasché, N. F., Kern, A. S., & Resti, I. H. (2017). A tool for supporting communication in the workplace for individuals with intellectual disabilities and/or autism. *Career Development and Transition for Exceptional Individuals, 40*(4), 244–249. DOI: 10.1177/2165143416683927

Primeau, M. S., & Talley, B. (2019). Intellectual disabilities and health care communication: A continuing education program for providers. *Journal of Continuing Education in Nursing, 50*(1), 20–25. DOI: 10.3928/00220124-20190102-06 PMID: 30645655

Regan, K., & Weiss, M. P. (2020). Bug-in-ear coaching for teacher candidates: What, why, and how to get started. *Intervention in School and Clinic, 55*(3), 178–184. DOI: 10.1177/1053451219842218

Renner, B., Wesiak, G., Pammer-Schindler, V., Prilla, M., Müller, L., Morosini, D., Mora, S., Faltin, N., & Cress, U. (2020). Computer-supported reflective learning: How apps can foster reflection at work. *Behaviour & Information Technology, 39*(2), 167–187. DOI: 10.1080/0144929X.2019.1595726

Rivera, M., Qiu, L., Kumar, S., & Petrucci, T. (2021). Are traditional performance reviews outdated? An empirical analysis on continuous, real-time feedback in the workplace. *Information Systems Research, 32*(2), 517–540. DOI: 10.1287/isre.2020.0979

Ryan, A. K., Miller, L., Rose, T. A., & Johnston, L. M. (2024). Child-led goal setting and evaluation tools for children with a disability: A scoping review. *Developmental Medicine and Child Neurology, 66*(12), 1558–1569. DOI: 10.1111/dmcn.15959 PMID: 38760984

Sears, J. S., Hall, M. T., Harris, L. M., Mount, S., Willauer, T., Posze, L., & Smead, E. (2017). "Like a marriage": Partnering with peer mentors in child welfare. *Children and Youth Services Review, 74*, 80–86. DOI: 10.1016/j.childyouth.2017.01.023

Siperstein, G. N., Heyman, M., & Stokes, J. E. (2014). Pathways to employment: A national survey of adults with intellectual disabilities. *Journal of Vocational Rehabilitation, 41*(3), 165–178. DOI: 10.3233/JVR-140711

Stock, J., Williams, H., & Peat, R. (2025). Coaching supervision: Supporting staff development and wellbeing. In *Coaching and mentoring students in higher education: A practitioner guide to developing independent learners* (pp. 268–293). Routledge., DOI: 10.4324/9781003486015-9

Sunderman, H. M., & Adebayo, B. (2025). Peer mentoring for leader development. In *Moving the needle: What we know (and don't know) about developing leaders* (pp. 283–296). Edward Elgar Publishing. DOI: 10.1108/978-1-83708-544-620251023

Truong, A., Alverbratt, C., Ekström-Bergström, A., & Antonsson, H. (2021). Caring for persons with intellectual disabilities and challenging behavior: Staff experiences with a web-based training program. *Frontiers in Psychiatry, 12*, 580923. Advance online publication. DOI: 10.3389/fpsyt.2021.580923 PMID: 33584380

Tuffrey-Wijne, I., & McEnhill, L. (2008). Communication difficulties and intellectual disability in end-of-life care. *International Journal of Palliative Nursing, 14*(4), 189–194. DOI: 10.12968/ijpn.2008.14.4.29133 PMID: 18681347

Tuffrey-Wijne, I., & Rose, T. (2017). Investigating the factors that affect the communication of death-related bad news to people with intellectual disabilities by staff in residential and supported living services: An interview study. *Journal of Intellectual Disability Research, 61*(8), 727–736. DOI: 10.1111/jir.12375 PMID: 28386983

Turner, M., & Holdsworth, S. (2023). Developing resilience: Examining the protective factors of early career construction professionals. *Construction Management and Economics, 41*(10), 805–819. DOI: 10.1080/01446193.2023.2208238

Uetz, M., Ananthakrishnan, S., Tulsky, A., Demers, L. B., & Noronha, C. (2024). More specific feedback: Why "confidence" in feedback is too ambiguous. *Postgraduate Medical Journal, 100*(1185), 521–522. DOI: 10.1093/postmj/qgad106 PMID: 37973406

Varia, S., & Middleton, H. (2012). How to make the most of feedback. *The Pharmaceutical Journal, 289*(7719–7720), 205–208.

Wilson, A. B., & Adderley, U. (2025). Inclusive supervision in practice. [Note: This reference appears in the chapter text but was not found in the provided Scopus export; it is listed here as cited.]. *Journal of Applied Research in Intellectual Disabilities.*

Wingrove, A., Lai, Y.-L., Palmer, S., & Williams, S. (2020). Self-determination theory: A theoretical framework for group supervision with internal coaches. *International Journal of Evidence Based Coaching and Mentoring, 18*(2), 183–196. DOI: 10.24384/jxxd-st61

Zhong, J., Li, Y., & Luo, J. (2022). The trickle-down effects of inclusive leadership on employees' innovative behavior: The joint moderating effects of vicarious learning and organizational inclusion climate. *Journal of Leadership & Organizational Studies, 29*(3), 342–358. DOI: 10.1177/15480518211059941

Chapter 11
Reasonable Accommodations and Assistive Technology in Action

ABSTRACT

This chapter examines reasonable accommodations and assistive technology (AT) as central pillars of inclusive employment for workers with intellectual disabilities (ID). It traces a conceptual shift from compliance-driven adjustments to strategic, equity-oriented interventions embedded within social-relational and strengths-based frameworks. The chapter categorizes accommodations across a low- to high-tech continuum, demonstrating that effectiveness depends on alignment with individual needs, task demands, and organizational context. Implementation is framed as an iterative process involving person-centered needs assessment, job analysis, co-design, and trial-based evaluation. A multi-layered funding ecosystem—integrating internal budgeting, government incentives, and vocational rehabilitation—is presented as essential for sustainability. Ultimately, the chapter positions accommodations not as isolated fixes but as catalysts for organizational learning, cultural transformation, and systemic inclusion.

11.1 INTRODUCTION

Reasonable accommodations constitute a central mechanism within policies and practices for supporting workers with intellectual disabilities (ID), as they directly address structural, social, and functional barriers that limit equitable participation in employment. Across the literature, accommodations are consistently defined as

DOI: 10.4018/979-8-3373-9185-4.ch011

modifications or adjustments that enable individuals with ID to perform job tasks effectively by aligning workplace demands with individual capabilities (Gold et al., 2012). These accommodations encompass a wide range of interventions, including assistive technologies, workplace personal assistance services (PAS), and task-related adjustments, all of which contribute to improved job retention, performance, and workplace integration. Importantly, accommodations are not merely compensatory mechanisms but transformative practices that reconfigure the relationship between individuals and their work environments, thereby enhancing productivity and supporting sustainable employment outcomes.

Beyond functional performance, reasonable accommodations play a critical role in fostering inclusive organisational environments. Inclusive workplace practices such as supportive supervision, equitable peer relationships, and access to meaningful job roles are essential for embedding workers with ID into the social fabric of organisations (Fajardo-Castro et al., 2024). Accommodations, in this sense, extend beyond individualised adjustments and operate as catalysts for broader organisational learning and cultural transformation. Interventions that involve training supervisors and coworkers have been shown to reduce stigma, improve interpersonal dynamics, and strengthen inclusive workplace climates (Carlson et al., 2020). As a result, accommodation contributes not only to task performance but also to relational belonging, which is fundamental for long-term inclusion.

A significant shift in literature has been the reconceptualisation of accommodations from compliance-driven obligations to productivity-enhancing and equity-oriented strategies. Traditionally, workplace accommodations have been framed within legal mandates, particularly under frameworks such as the Americans with Disabilities Act (ADA), which require employers to provide reasonable adjustments to ensure equal access to employment opportunities (Dong et al., 2022; Keays, 2025). These legal frameworks establish accommodations as essential components of non-discrimination and rights-based employment protections. However, compliance alone has proven insufficient for achieving meaningful inclusion, particularly in contexts where organisational knowledge, attitudes, and resources remain limited (Dong et al., 2022).

Emerging evidence demonstrates that accommodations generate substantial organizational and individual benefits that extend beyond legal compliance. Empirical studies indicate that accommodations—including assistive technologies, flexible work arrangements, and task restructuring—significantly enhance job performance, job tenure, and employee satisfaction (Dall & Madsen, 2025; Sundar, 2017). These benefits are not limited to functional outcomes but also include psychosocial gains, such as increased autonomy, self-efficacy, and workplace well-being (Dean et al., 2022; Pereira-Silva et al., 2018). Technological innovations, including context-aware prompting systems and AI-enabled tools, further illustrate how accommodations can improve productivity by reducing cognitive load and minimizing errors (Philips et al., 2024). From an organizational perspective, these improvements translate into reduced turnover costs, enhanced team performance, and stronger overall productivity (Solovieva & Walls, 2013). This body of evidence reinforces the understanding that accommodations should be positioned not as costs, but as strategic investments in human capital.

The relevance of reasonable accommodations has become increasingly pronounced in the context of modern workplaces characterized by technological advancement and evolving job demands. Assistive technology (AT), in particular, has emerged as a key enabler of inclusive employment, supporting productivity, independence, and workplace integration for individuals with ID. Technologies such as visual and auditory prompting systems, portable electronic devices, and task-analysis applications enable workers to complete tasks more independently and accurately, reducing reliance on continuous supervision (Morash-Macneil et al., 2018; Randall et al., 2020). Furthermore, AI-driven tools and speech recognition systems enhance communication and collaboration, facilitating more effective interaction with colleagues and supervisors (Babu et al., 2026; Peña et al., 2024a). These developments highlight the growing importance of integrating assistive technologies into workplace practices to ensure accessibility in increasingly digital and complex work environments.

At the same time, the effectiveness of accommodations is shaped by broader organizational and systemic factors, including policies, training, and legal frameworks. Employer awareness and training are critical for improving the implementation of accommodations, particularly in relation to assistive technologies and regulatory requirements (Rumrill et al., 2023; VanderMolen et al., 2025). However, persistent challenges such as employer misconceptions regarding costs, administrative complexity, and legal risks continue to limit the adoption of accommodations, despite evidence that many are low-cost and yield significant benefits (Shinall, 2020). These challenges underscore the need for a shift in organizational mindset toward recognizing accommodations as integral components of inclusive workplace systems.

Despite their demonstrated impact, reasonable accommodations remain underutilized in many organizational contexts due to attitudinal, structural, and resource-related barriers. Workers with ID frequently encounter limited access to competitive employment, insufficient post-placement support, and ongoing stigma related to perceived productivity and capability (Dearing, 2021). Addressing these barriers requires not only the provision of accommodations but also systemic changes in organizational culture, policy alignment, and capacity building. In this regard, accommodations must be understood as part of a broader ecosystem of inclusion that integrates individual support, organizational practices, and policy frameworks.

This chapter examines reasonable accommodations and assistive technology as central components of policies and practices for supporting workers with intellectual disabilities. It begins by outlining the conceptual foundations that inform inclusive accommodation practices, followed by a detailed exploration of the types of accommodations available across technological levels. The chapter then discusses practical strategies for implementation, including individualized assessment and co-design approaches, as well as funding mechanisms that support sustainable adoption. Key challenges and ethical tensions are analyzed to highlight complexities in practice, and a case illustration is provided to demonstrate real-world application. The chapter concludes by synthesizing these insights and situating accommodations within broader organizational systems, providing a foundation for the subsequent discussion on ecosystem-level support.

11.2 CONCEPTUAL FOUNDATION

The conceptual foundation of reasonable accommodations within policies and practices for supporting workers with intellectual disabilities (ID) is deeply shaped by evolving understandings of disability, inclusion, and organizational design. Central to this foundation is the distinction between the medical and social models of disability, which fundamentally influence how accommodations are defined, implemented, and evaluated in workplace contexts.

The medical model conceptualizes disability as an individual deficit requiring remediation, thereby positioning accommodations as corrective adjustments aimed at compensating for functional limitations. Within this framework, workplace accommodations tend to focus on discrete, task-specific modifications designed to improve individual performance capacity. In contrast, the social model reframes disability as a product of environmental, organizational, and relational barriers, shifting attention from the individual to the systems in which they operate. This distinction has significant implications for policies and practices for supporting workers with intellectual disabilities, as it expands the scope of accommodations from isolated adjustments to broader organizational and relational interventions (Garrels & Sigstad, 2021; Morris, Christianson-Barker, Stainton, Mills, Schroeder, et al., 2024).

Empirical evidence consistently demonstrates that workplace practices informed by the social-relational model are more effective in supporting workers with ID. These practices emphasize inclusive organizational climates, mentoring relationships, supervisor training, and opportunities for meaningful participation, all of which contribute to improved retention, engagement, and job satisfaction (Meacham et al., 2017; Tucker & Nash, 2023). Conversely, approaches grounded solely in the medical model risk underestimating the importance of social dynamics and organizational culture, thereby limiting the effectiveness of accommodations (Bialik & Mhiri, 2022). This suggests that accommodations are most impactful when embedded within systems that actively address environmental and relational barriers, rather than focusing exclusively on individual deficits.

The influence of disability models extends beyond conceptual framing to shape practical decision-making within organizations. Multi-stakeholder studies indicate that managerial attitudes, knowledge, and assumptions significantly affect whether accommodations are offered, accepted, or effectively implemented (Morris, Christianson-Barker, Stainton, Mills, Schroeder, et al., 2024; Taylor et al., 2022). In many cases, barriers to accommodation are not primarily technical but social, arising from stigma, lack of awareness, and limited organizational readiness. Inclusive leadership and relationship-building practices have been shown to mitigate these barriers, highlighting the importance of aligning organizational culture with inclusive principles (Meacham et al., 2017). This reinforces the notion that accommodations are not isolated interventions but components of a broader socio-organizational system.

Within this evolving conceptual landscape, increasing attention has been given to strengths-based and customized approaches to employment. These approaches emphasize aligning individual capabilities with job roles through co-designed accommodations, moving away from deficit-oriented perspectives toward asset-based frameworks (Carr-Kirby, 2025; Christianson-Barker et al., 2025). Co-design processes, which involve active participation of workers with ID in shaping their accommodations, have been identified as particularly effective in enhancing both performance and inclusion. This reflects a broader shift toward participatory and person-centered practices in policies and practices for supporting workers with intellectual disabilities.

Closely related to these developments is the relationship between universal design (UD) and individualized accommodations. Universal design is defined as the proactive creation of environments, processes, and systems that are accessible to the widest possible range of users without the need for specialized adaptations (Caldwell et al., 2024). In workplace contexts, UD may include accessible communication systems, flexible workflows, and inclusive recruitment practices that benefit all employees, including those with intellectual disabilities. By embedding accessibility into standard organizational practices, UD reduces the need for reactive, individualized adjustments and helps normalize inclusion.

However, the literature consistently emphasizes that universal design cannot fully replace individualized accommodations. While UD establishes an accessible baseline, individualized supports remain necessary to address specific functional, cognitive, or contextual needs (Alajmi et al., 2025; Caldwell et al., 2024). Rather than being mutually exclusive, UD and individualized accommodations are best understood as complementary approaches. When implemented together, they create a hybrid model in which universal design expands participation opportunities while individualized accommodations ensure equity at the level of individual experience

(Christianson-Barker et al., 2025; Asmuß & Thomsen, 2024). This integrated approach is particularly important in policies and practices for supporting workers with intellectual disabilities, given the diversity of needs and work contexts.

From a policy perspective, this hybrid model aligns with international frameworks that emphasize both inclusion and equity. Universal design supports inclusion by reducing systemic barriers, while individualized accommodations address specific needs to ensure equitable participation. Empirical evidence indicates that organizations adopting this dual approach—combining accessible environments with targeted supports—achieve better employment outcomes, including improved performance, retention, and inclusion (Gjertsen et al., 2021). This reinforces the importance of designing workplace systems that are both broadly accessible and individually responsive.

Another critical dimension of the conceptual foundation concerns the relationship between rights-based and needs-based approaches. Rights-based frameworks position accommodations as essential components of equal opportunity and non-discrimination, grounded in legal and ethical principles. Needs-based approaches, on the other hand, focus on the practical supports required for effective job performance. The literature suggests that these perspectives should not be treated as competing but as complementary, with effective policies and practices integrating both. Such integration allows organizations to move beyond compliance toward meaningful inclusion, ensuring that accommodations are both legally mandated and functionally effective.

Empirical evidence further underscores the impact of accommodations on workplace performance and inclusion. Across multiple studies, accommodations—including job coaching, task modification, and assistive technologies—are associated with improved task performance, productivity, and participation for workers with ID (Kerdar et al., 2025). These improvements are particularly pronounced when accommodations are aligned with job demands and supported by adequate training and organizational resources. Assistive technologies, in particular, have been shown to enhance independence, accuracy, and efficiency, especially when integrated into inclusive workplace systems (Buettgen & Klassen, 2020).

Beyond performance, accommodations contribute significantly to broader inclusion outcomes. Evidence indicates that accommodations, when combined with inclusive management practices and supportive workplace relationships, enhance social participation, job satisfaction, and overall well-being (Cavanagh et al., 2016). These outcomes highlight that inclusion is not solely a function of task performance but also of relational and psychosocial factors. In this sense, accommodations serve as both functional supports and social enablers, facilitating full participation in workplace life.

The effectiveness of accommodations, however, is influenced by a range of contextual factors. Organizational culture, managerial competence, availability of resources, and policy alignment all play critical roles in shaping outcomes. For example, organizations that foster disclosure-friendly environments and invest in manager training are more likely to achieve positive accommodation outcomes, including improved performance and retention (Gormley, 2015; Morris, Christianson-Barker, Stainton, Mills, Rowley, et al., 2024). Conversely, lack of awareness, fear of stigma, and limited resources can hinder both the uptake and effectiveness of accommodations. These findings underscore the importance of systemic approaches that address not only individual needs but also organizational and structural conditions.

In summary, the conceptual foundation of reasonable accommodations and assistive technology in policies and practices for supporting workers with intellectual disabilities is characterized by a shift toward integrated, systemic, and inclusive frameworks. The interplay between social and medical models highlights the need to address both individual and environmental factors, while the integration of universal design and individualized accommodations provides a comprehensive approach to accessibility and equity. Empirical evidence further demonstrates that accommodations enhance both performance and inclusion, particularly when implemented within supportive organizational systems. These insights provide a critical foundation for understanding the diverse types of accommodations available, which will be explored in the next section.

11.3 TYPES OF ACCOMMODATIONS

The range of accommodations available within policies and practices for supporting workers with intellectual disabilities (ID) spans a continuum from low-tech, highly accessible supports to advanced, technology-enabled systems. Across the literature, a consistent finding is that no single type of accommodation is universally effective; rather, the effectiveness of accommodations depends on the alignment between task demands, individual capabilities, and organizational context. This aligns with multi-level frameworks such as the Human Activity Assistive Technology (HAAT) perspective, which emphasizes the interaction between user, task, and environment in determining accommodation success (Kerdar et al., 2025; Marinaci et al., 2023).

Within this continuum, accommodations can be broadly categorized into low-tech, mid-tech, and high-tech solutions. While these categories differ in complexity and scalability, they are not hierarchical; instead, they function most effectively when integrated into multimodal strategies that combine simplicity, accessibility, and technological support. The literature consistently highlights that both low-tech and high-tech accommodations can enhance task performance, independence, and workplace participation, but their success is contingent on organizational practices, training, and inclusive workplace cultures (Marinaci et al., 2023; Shahin et al., 2020).

11.3.1. Low-Tech Solutions

Low-tech accommodations represent the most accessible and widely implemented forms of support for workers with intellectual disabilities. These solutions are typically low-cost, easy to deploy, and adaptable across diverse workplace contexts, making them foundational components of inclusive employment practices. Despite their simplicity, low-tech accommodations have demonstrated substantial effectiveness in supporting task performance and independence, particularly when integrated with supportive supervision and training (Heman et al., 2022; Randall et al., 2024).

Visual Checklists

Visual task supports, including pictorial checklists and step-by-step visual guides, are among the most commonly used low-tech accommodations. These tools function by externalizing task sequences, thereby reducing cognitive load and minimizing reliance on memory and complex verbal instructions. Evidence indicates that visual supports improve task clarity, promote consistency, and enhance independence in both structured and semi-structured work environments (Farzana et al., 2025; Marinaci et al., 2023).

In practice, visual checklists enable workers with ID to follow clearly defined steps, reducing ambiguity and increasing confidence in task execution. When aligned with actual job tasks and reinforced through coaching, these tools can significantly improve performance and reduce the need for continuous supervision (Randall et al., 2024). However, their effectiveness depends on careful customization to individual communication styles and workplace requirements, highlighting the importance of context-sensitive design.

Task Segmentation

Task segmentation, or the breakdown of complex activities into smaller, manageable steps, represents another critical low-tech strategy. By decomposing tasks into sequential components, this approach reduces cognitive and attentional demands, enabling workers with ID to engage more effectively with job requirements. This strategy is particularly effective for routine or repetitive tasks, where clear structure supports consistency and accuracy. The literature emphasizes that task segmentation is most effective when combined with other supports, such as visual cues or coaching, to reinforce learning and facilitate skill acquisition (Marinaci et al., 2023). Moreover, segmentation supports not only task completion but also skill development, as workers gradually build competence through repeated exposure to structured task sequences.

Color Coding

Color coding is a simple yet effective strategy for enhancing task organization and environmental navigation. By associating specific colors with tasks, tools, or work areas, this approach provides intuitive visual cues that support decision-making and reduce errors. Although less frequently discussed as a standalone intervention, color coding is often integrated into broader visual support systems, contributing to improved task clarity and workflow efficiency.

Collectively, low-tech accommodations demonstrate that effective support does not necessarily require complex technology. Instead, their strength lies in their accessibility, adaptability, and alignment with everyday workplace practices. However, their implementation is not without challenges, including inconsistent use, lack of training, and organizational barriers that can limit their effectiveness if not addressed (Randall et al., 2024; Shahin et al., 2020).

11.3.2. Mid-Tech Solutions

Mid-tech accommodations occupy an intermediate space between low-tech supports and advanced digital systems, offering enhanced functionality while remaining relatively accessible and cost-effective. These solutions often involve basic digital tools that support time management, task sequencing, and self-regulation, such as timers, mobile applications, and reminder systems. Timers and digital reminders are widely used to support time awareness, task initiation, and task completion. For workers with intellectual disabilities, managing time and maintaining task sequences can present significant challenges, particularly in dynamic or multi-tasking environments. Mid-tech solutions address these challenges by providing structured prompts that guide behavior and reinforce task routines. Mobile applications, in particular, have emerged as versatile tools for supporting workplace participation. These applications can deliver visual prompts, reminders, and step-by-step instructions, effectively extending the functionality of low-tech supports into digital formats. Evidence suggests that such tools can enhance task adherence, self-management, and independence, particularly when integrated with training and organizational support (Randall et al., 2024; Zhou et al., 2025).

Importantly, mid-tech solutions often serve as a bridge between low-tech and high-tech accommodations, combining simplicity with scalability. They allow for greater flexibility and customization while remaining accessible to a wide range of users. However, their effectiveness depends on user training, technological familiarity, and organizational policies that support the use of personal or workplace devices (Marelle et al., 2022).

11.3.3. High-Tech Assistive Technologies

High-tech accommodations encompass a diverse range of digital and technology-enabled supports designed to address complex task demands and enhance workplace accessibility. These include mobile devices, wearable technologies, immersive training systems, and AI-enabled tools, all of which offer significant potential for improving productivity, independence, and inclusion.

AI Tools

Artificial intelligence (AI)-enabled tools represent a rapidly evolving area of assistive technology with significant implications for workplace inclusion. AI-based systems, such as intelligent prompting tools and assistive agents, can provide real-time guidance, adaptive feedback, and task-specific instructions, enabling workers with ID to engage more independently with complex tasks (Randall et al., 2024). These systems function by analyzing user behavior and environmental context to deliver personalized support, thereby reducing cognitive load and enhancing task performance. For example, AI-enabled assistants can guide workers through multi-step processes, provide reminders, and offer encouragement, effectively complementing human support systems. While the evidence base for AI applications in workplace contexts remains emergent, early findings suggest that these tools hold promise for enhancing autonomy and reducing reliance on continuous supervision (Wuttke et al., 2025).

Speech-to-Text and Communication Technologies

Communication technologies, including speech-to-text systems and AI-assisted communication tools, play a critical role in supporting workplace interaction and collaboration. These tools enable workers with ID to communicate more effectively with colleagues and supervisors, facilitating participation in team-based activities and reducing barriers to social integration. Portable visual and communication technologies, such as video prompting systems and social-behavior supports, further enhance communication by providing structured guidance for social interactions. Evidence indicates that these tools can improve employment-related social behaviors and support integration into workplace environments (Peña et al., 2024b).

Cognitive Support Tools

High-tech cognitive support tools, including mobile applications, wearable devices, and immersive training systems (e.g., virtual and augmented reality), are designed to support memory, attention, and task execution. These tools are particularly valuable for complex or dynamic tasks that require sustained attention and adaptive problem-solving. Immersive technologies such as VR and AR have been used to simulate workplace environments, enabling workers with ID to develop skills and practice tasks in controlled settings. While evidence suggests potential benefits in terms of skill acquisition and motivation, the literature also highlights variability in outcomes and the need for more robust, real-world evaluations (Wuttke et al., 2025). Wearable and wireless technologies further extend these capabilities by providing continuous prompts, monitoring, and feedback, supporting both task performance and self-regulation. However, the adoption of these technologies is often constrained by barriers such as cost, complexity, and organizational resistance ((Heman et al., 2022; Marelle et al., 2022).

Across all categories, a key insight from the literature is that the effectiveness of accommodations is not determined solely by their technological sophistication but by their alignment with user needs, task requirements, and organizational context. Low-tech solutions offer accessibility and ease of implementation, while high-tech solutions provide scalability and support for complex tasks. Mid-tech solutions bridge these approaches, offering flexible and adaptable supports. Importantly, the literature consistently emphasizes the value of multimodal strategies that combine different types of accommodations. Such approaches enable organizations to address diverse needs while optimizing both efficiency and effectiveness (Marinaci et al., 2023). However, successful implementation requires addressing persistent barriers, including training gaps, organizational resistance, and policy constraints, which can limit the adoption of both low-tech and high-tech supports (Marelle et al., 2022). In this context, assistive technologies—including AI-enabled tools—should not be viewed as standalone solutions but as components of integrated support systems that include organizational practices, social supports, and policy frameworks. This integrated perspective is essential for ensuring that accommodations contribute not only to task performance but also to broader goals of inclusion, autonomy, and workplace participation.

11.4 IMPLEMENTATION STRATEGIES

The implementation of reasonable accommodations for workers with intellectual disabilities (ID/IDD) requires more than the selection of tools or adjustments;

it demands a systematic, evidence-based process that integrates individual needs, job demands, organizational context, and policy frameworks. Across the literature, effective implementation is consistently framed as a dynamic, iterative, and person-centered process, rather than a one-time intervention. Central to this process are five interrelated strategies: individualized needs assessment, job analysis, co-design with employees and stakeholders, trial and evaluation, and structured documentation.

These strategies are grounded in systems-oriented frameworks such as the Human Activity Assistive Technology (HAAT) model and rights-based approaches (e.g., CRPD), which emphasize alignment between the individual, the task, and the environment, as well as measurable improvements in quality of life and workplace participation (Gómez et al., 2020; Marinaci et al., 2023). Together, they form a coherent pathway for translating inclusive policies into sustainable workplace practices.

11.4.1. Needs Assessment (Individualized and Person-Centered)

A foundational step in implementing accommodations is conducting a comprehensive, individualized needs assessment grounded in person-centered planning and self-determination. The literature emphasizes that accommodations are most effective when they reflect the worker's goals, preferences, strengths, and lived experiences, rather than being imposed as standardized solutions (Sinclair et al., 2023). Person-centered approaches enable workers with ID/IDD to actively participate in identifying the supports they require, fostering agency and engagement in the accommodation process. Empirical evidence shows that when individuals are involved in decision-making, they are more likely to advocate for appropriate accommodations, align work tasks with personal interests, and sustain long-term employment outcomes (Sinclair et al., 2023). Furthermore, structured support around disclosure and decision-making enhances workers' ability to navigate workplace expectations and request accommodations effectively (Tomas et al., 2023).

From a policy perspective, aligning needs assessment with rights-based frameworks—such as CRPD-informed quality-of-life indicators—ensures that accommodations are not only functional but also meaningful in terms of autonomy, social inclusion, and overall wellbeing (Gómez et al., 2020). This expands the purpose of accommodations from task performance alone to broader life outcomes, reinforcing their role within inclusive employment systems.

Importantly, needs assessment is not a one-time activity. As workplace roles evolve and individuals develop new skills, ongoing reassessment is necessary to ensure that accommodations remain relevant and effective. This iterative approach reflects the dynamic nature of both work environments and individual development.

11.4.2 Job Analysis

Following needs assessment, job analysis serves as a critical mechanism for translating individual needs into concrete accommodation strategies. Job analysis involves systematically examining job tasks, workflows, and environmental conditions to identify where barriers exist and what supports are required to enable successful performance.

The HAAT framework provides a structured lens for this process by emphasizing the interaction between the individual (human), the activity (task), and the assistive technology (tool) within a specific context (Marinaci et al., 2023). Through this lens, job analysis moves beyond generic job descriptions to identify precise task demands, cognitive requirements, and environmental constraints that shape performance.

Evidence indicates that task-focused analysis enables more precise and effective accommodation design by identifying which elements of a job require modification or support. For example, breaking down tasks into components can reveal specific points where visual supports, prompting systems, or assistive technologies can enhance performance (Marelle et al., 2022). Additionally, job analysis supports the integration of natural supports, such as coworker assistance and team-based problem solving, which have been shown to improve productivity, engagement, and job retention (Athamanah et al., 2024). Crucially, job analysis also facilitates alignment between accommodations and organizational workflows, ensuring that supports are not disruptive but integrated into everyday work practices. This alignment is essential for sustainability, as accommodations that conflict with existing systems are less likely to be adopted or maintained.

11.4.3 Co-Design with Employee and Stakeholders

Co-design, or participatory design, represents a central strategy for ensuring that accommodations are usable, acceptable, and contextually relevant. This approach involves active collaboration among workers with ID/IDD, employers, supervisors, family members, and support professionals in the design and implementation of accommodations. The literature consistently highlights co-design as a best practice for bridging the gap between theoretical solutions and real-world application. By involving knowledge users in the design process, co-design ensures that accommodations reflect lived experiences, workplace realities, and organizational constraints (Palumbo et al., 2023). Empirical examples, such as the development of disability disclosure decision aids through participatory design, demonstrate how co-design improves usability, reduces decision conflict, and enhances the relevance of workplace tools (Tomas et al., 2023). Similarly, research on employment transitions emphasizes the importance of preparing accommodations collaboratively during pre-employment phases and continuing this collaboration after job placement (Sung & Nasamran, 2023). Co-design also strengthens organizational buy-in by engaging employers and coworkers in the accommodation process. This shared ownership reduces resistance, enhances understanding, and fosters a culture of inclusion. Moreover, co-design facilitates the integration of accommodations into organizational policies and practices, supporting long-term sustainability. Importantly, co-design is not limited to initial implementation. Ongoing collaboration is necessary to adapt accommodations as job roles, technologies, and organizational contexts evolve.

11.4.4 Trial and Evaluation

Implementation of accommodations requires a trial-and-evaluation approach that allows for iterative refinement based on real-world performance. The literature emphasizes that accommodations should be tested in practice, evaluated using multiple methods, and adjusted as needed to optimize effectiveness. Evaluation of accommodations typically involves a combination of quantitative and qualitative measures. Quantitative indicators include employment status, job tenure, hours worked, wages, and task performance metrics such as accuracy and efficiency (Vigna et al., 2024). These measures provide objective evidence of whether accommodations support sustained employment and productivity. Complementing these metrics, qualitative methods—such as interviews and observations—capture the lived experiences of workers, supervisors, and coworkers, providing insight into usability, satisfaction, and contextual factors that influence effectiveness (Tomas et al., 2023). This multi-method approach enables a more comprehensive understanding of how accommodations function in practice.

Mixed-method designs are particularly valuable, as they link measurable outcomes with explanatory insights, revealing not only whether accommodations work, but how and why they work (Sung et al., 2023). Additionally, rights-based evaluation frameworks, such as CRPD-aligned quality-of-life indicators, expand evaluation beyond productivity to include autonomy, social participation, and wellbeing (Gómez et al., 2020). Evaluation also extends to assistive technology adoption, where factors such as usage rates, training effectiveness, and organizational barriers are assessed. Evidence indicates that the success of assistive technologies depends heavily on training, onboarding, and workplace culture, rather than the technology itself (Marelle et al., 2022). Overall, trial and evaluation should be understood as continuous processes that inform ongoing improvement, rather than final stages of implementation.

11.4.5 Documentation and Institutionalization

The final component of implementation is systematic documentation, which plays a critical role in ensuring consistency, accountability, and scalability of accommodations. Documentation involves recording the rationale, design, implementation process, and outcomes of accommodations, as well as any adjustments made during evaluation. From a practical perspective, documentation supports communication among stakeholders, including employees, supervisors, HR professionals, and external support services. It provides a clear record of what accommodations are in place, how they are used, and how they contribute to performance and inclusion. At an organizational level, documentation enables the integration of accommodations into HR practices, policies, and training programs, transforming individual adjustments into institutional knowledge. This process is essential for scaling inclusive practices across teams and departments. Policy-oriented research further emphasizes the importance of documenting how accommodations align with broader frameworks, such as CRPD indicators and organizational inclusion goals (Gould, 2024). Such alignment ensures that accommodations contribute to systemic outcomes, rather than remaining isolated interventions. Moreover, documentation supports evaluation and accountability by providing data that can be used to assess effectiveness, inform decision-making, and justify resource allocation. It also facilitates knowledge transfer, enabling organizations to replicate successful practices and avoid repeating ineffective strategies.

Across these five strategies, a clear pattern emerges: effective implementation of accommodations is integrative, iterative, and context-sensitive. Needs assessment identifies individualized requirements; job analysis translates these into task-specific supports; co-design ensures usability and acceptance; trial and evaluation refine effectiveness; and documentation institutionalizes learning and sustainability. Critically, these components are interdependent rather than sequential. For example, evaluation may reveal the need for revised job analysis, while co-design may reshape initial needs assessments. This iterative dynamic reflects the complexity of workplace inclusion and underscores the importance of flexibility in implementation.

The literature consistently demonstrates that accommodations are most effective when embedded within broader organizational systems, including inclusive culture, training, and policy alignment (Palumbo et al., 2023; Gould, 2024). Without such integration, even well-designed accommodations risk being underutilized or unsustainable.

In this sense, implementation strategies are not merely operational steps but mechanisms for translating inclusive employment policies into lived workplace realities. By adopting a structured yet flexible approach grounded in evidence and collaboration, organizations can move beyond compliance toward meaningful, sustained inclusion of workers with intellectual disabilities.

11.5 FUNDING AND RESOURCE MECHANISMS

The successful implementation of reasonable accommodations and assistive technologies (AT) for workers with intellectual disabilities (ID) is fundamentally shaped by the availability, accessibility, and structure of funding mechanisms. Across policy and empirical literature, a consistent finding is that financial considerations—both real and perceived—remain one of the most significant determinants of whether accommodations are adopted, sustained, or scaled within organizations. However, contrary to common assumptions, the cost burden of accommodations is often mitigated through a combination of internal organizational strategies, public incentives, and external support systems, particularly vocational rehabilitation (VR) services. Rather than viewing funding as a constraint, the literature increasingly frames it as a multi-layered ecosystem that distributes costs across employers, governments, and support institutions. This distributed model reduces financial risk, aligns incentives, and enables accommodations to function as long-term investments in productivity, retention, and inclusion rather than short-term expenditures (Bonardi et al., 2024).

11.5.1. Internal Budgeting: From Cost Center to Strategic Investment

At the organizational level, internal budgeting represents the first layer of financing for workplace accommodations. Traditionally, accommodations have been perceived as additional costs imposed on employers, often leading to reluctance in hiring or supporting workers with disabilities. However, emerging evidence challenges this perception by demonstrating that accommodations can generate measurable economic benefits through improved retention, productivity, and reduced turnover costs (Jansen et al., 2021).

From a strategic perspective, internal budgeting for accommodations should be reframed as an investment in human capital and organizational performance. Studies indicate that when accommodations enable workers with ID to perform tasks more effectively, reduce errors, and maintain consistent engagement, organizations benefit from enhanced productivity and operational efficiency (Marinaci et al., 2023). Moreover, the cost of accommodations is often offset over time by reduced recruitment and training expenses, particularly in roles where stability and reliability are critical (Chandola & Rouxel, 2021).

Importantly, the literature highlights that the actual cost of many accommodations—especially low- and mid-tech solutions—is relatively modest. In some contexts, costs are described as negligible or manageable, particularly when integrated into existing workflows and supported by organizational practices (Cheausuwantavee & Keeratiphanthawong, 2021). This suggests that the primary barrier is not cost itself but perceived financial risk, which can be addressed through better information, planning, and alignment with broader organizational strategies. To operationalize internal budgeting effectively, organizations must integrate accommodation planning into HR policies, workforce development strategies, and operational planning. This includes allocating dedicated resources, embedding accommodations into standard onboarding and training processes, and recognizing their contribution to organizational goals such as diversity, equity, and inclusion (DEI).

11.5.2 Government Incentives: Reducing Barriers and Aligning Employer Behavior

Government incentives constitute a critical mechanism for reducing the financial barriers associated with workplace accommodations. Across multiple national contexts, public policies employ a combination of wage subsidies, tax incentives, and direct funding programs to encourage employers to hire and retain workers with intellectual disabilities.

Wage Subsidies and Salary Support

Wage subsidies are among the most widely used policy instruments, designed to offset the perceived or actual productivity gap and reduce the cost burden of employment. Evidence from countries such as Australia and Denmark demonstrates that wage-subvention schemes, flexi-job arrangements, and reimbursement frameworks can significantly lower employer costs while supporting sustainable employment outcomes (Hwang et al., 2024). Similarly, targeted co-financing programs—such as Poland's COVID-19 "Anti-crisis Shield"—illustrate how governments can provide direct financial support tied to employment retention, covering a substantial portion of wages for workers with disabilities (Stańczyk, 2020). These mechanisms not only reduce immediate financial pressure but also stabilize employment during periods of economic uncertainty.

Tax Incentives and Financial Benefits

Tax-based incentives represent another low-friction mechanism for encouraging accommodation investment. These include tax credits, deductions, and allowances for workplace modifications and accessibility improvements. Policy analyses indicate that such incentives effectively lower the cost of accommodations, making them more attractive to employers while aligning private incentives with public inclusion goals (Amstutz, 2022).

Direct Grants and Accessibility Funds

In addition to indirect incentives, many governments provide direct grants and dedicated funds to support workplace adaptations and assistive technologies. These programs are designed to cover upfront capital costs, which are often the most significant barrier to implementation. For example, accessibility funds and grant programs in North America and Europe provide financial support for assistive devices, workplace modifications, and related services, enabling employers to implement accommodations without bearing the full cost (Bonardi et al., 2024). In Australia, the National Disability Insurance Scheme (NDIS) exemplifies a comprehensive funding model that integrates health, rehabilitation, and employment supports, providing resources for assistive technologies and services that enable workplace participation (Schofield et al., 2024). Such integrated models highlight the importance of cross-sector coordination in financing accommodations.

Policy-Level Implications

Collectively, these incentives demonstrate that government policy plays a pivotal role in shaping employer behavior by reducing financial risk and creating enabling conditions for inclusion. However, the effectiveness of these mechanisms depends on their accessibility, awareness among employers, and alignment with organizational practices. Without adequate dissemination and support, even well-designed incentives may remain underutilized.

11.5.3 External Support: Vocational Rehabilitation (VR) Services as a Financing Backbone

Beyond internal and governmental mechanisms, vocational rehabilitation (VR) services represent a central pillar in the financing and coordination of workplace accommodations. VR systems operate at the intersection of employment, health, and social services, providing both financial resources and technical expertise to support inclusive employment.

Direct Funding and Resource Coordination

VR services typically fund or coordinate access to assistive technologies, workplace adaptations, training, and job support services as part of a person-centered employment strategy. This includes not only the acquisition of devices but also the provision of ongoing support, such as job coaching, training, and environmental modifications (Bonardi et al., 2024). Importantly, VR funding extends beyond one-time interventions to support longitudinal employment trajectories, ensuring that accommodations evolve alongside workers' needs and career development. This continuity is particularly critical for sustaining employment outcomes for workers with ID.

Integration with Public Policy and Health Systems

In many contexts, VR services are integrated with broader disability funding systems, such as the NDIS in Australia or Medicaid-related programs in the United States. This integration enables coordinated financing across sectors, ensuring that accommodations are supported not only as workplace interventions but also as components of broader health and social care systems (Schofield et al., 2024). Such integrated models are increasingly associated with value-based approaches to funding, where investments in accommodations are justified by improvements in employment outcomes, health, and quality of life (Ervin, 2024). This shifts the focus from short-term cost containment to long-term value creation.

Employer Partnerships and Transition Support

VR services also play a critical role in facilitating partnerships between employers and support systems, particularly during transitions into employment. Studies on transition-to-work programs highlight the importance of VR funding in providing accommodations, training, and ongoing support during early employment stages, where risks of job loss are highest (Cubillos et al., 2020). Through these partnerships, VR services act as intermediaries that reduce complexity for employers, provide technical expertise, and ensure that accommodations are effectively implemented and sustained.

Across these three domains—internal budgeting, government incentives, and VR services—a clear pattern emerges: effective financing of workplace accommodations is distributed, coordinated, and context-dependent. No single funding mechanism is sufficient on its own; rather, successful implementation relies on the interaction of multiple funding streams that collectively reduce barriers and enable sustained investment. From an organizational perspective, internal budgeting establishes the foundation for accommodation practices. Government incentives then reduce financial risk and align employer behavior with inclusion goals, while VR services provide specialized support and long-term coordination. Together, these mechanisms create a comprehensive financing ecosystem that supports both initial implementation and ongoing sustainability. However, the literature also highlights significant variability across countries and systems, with differences in funding availability, policy design, and institutional capacity influencing outcomes (Niedziółka, 2024). This variability underscores the importance of contextualizing funding strategies within specific policy environments. Ultimately, financing should not be viewed as a barrier but as a strategic enabler of inclusion, capable of transforming accommodations from isolated interventions into integrated components of organizational and societal systems. By leveraging multiple funding mechanisms and aligning them with organizational practices and policy frameworks, stakeholders can create sustainable pathways for supporting workers with intellectual disabilities in the workplace.

REFERENCES

Alajmi, M., Persch, A., Taylor, A., Dean, B., Rosenberg, C. R., & Graham, J. E. (2025). Supported Employment for People With Developmental Disabilities During COVID: A Scoping Review. *Journal of Vocational Rehabilitation*, *62*(3), 244–257. DOI: 10.1177/10522263251326408

Amstutz, J. M. (2022). Reclaiming America as the Land of Opportunity: How International Law Can Help the United States Increase Employment for Persons With Intellectual Disabilities. *Indiana International & Comparative Law Review*, *32*(4), 563–599. DOI: 10.18060/26853

Athamanah, L. S., Cushing, L. S., Fastzkie, E. M., & Brown, E. R. (2024). Natural Supports in Competitive Integrated Employment: A Scoping Review. *Journal of Vocational Rehabilitation*, *60*(3), 327–339. DOI: 10.3233/JVR-240017

Babu, C. V. S., Logambigai, R., & Akshaya, A. S. (2026). Leveraging AI and Speech Recognition Tools for Vocational Rehabilitation of Students With Developmental Disabilities From Education to Employment. In *Vocational Rehabilitation for Students with Developmental Disabilities* (pp. 237–272). Transition from Education to Employment., DOI: 10.4018/979-8-3693-9541-7.ch008

Bialik, K., & Mhiri, M. (2022). Barriers to Employment for People With Intellectual Disabilities in Low- and Middle-income Countries: Self-advocate and Family Perspectives. *Journal of International Development*, *34*(5), 988–1001. DOI: 10.1002/jid.3659

Bonardi, A., Abend, S. L., & Ne'eman, A. (2024). Healthcare Access and Delivery for People With Intellectual and Developmental Disability in the United States: Policy, Payment, and Practice Considerations. *Journal of Policy and Practice in Intellectual Disabilities*, *21*(2), e12487. Advance online publication. DOI: 10.1111/jppi.12487

Buettgen, A., & Klassen, T. (2020). The Role of the Nonprofit Sector as a Site for Inclusive Employment. *Canadian Journal of Nonprofit and Social Economy Research*, *11*(2), 15. DOI: 10.29173/cjnser.2020v11n2a367

Caldwell, N., Holyfield, C., Lorah, E. R., & Rackensperger, T. (2024). Reducing Linguistic Profiling of Individuals With Communication Disabilities to Enhance Careers: Avoiding Assumptions Based on Speech, Language and Communication Mode. *Career Development International*, *29*(3), 367–380. DOI: 10.1108/CDI-07-2023-0230

Carlson, S. R., Morningstar, M. E., & Munandar, V. (2020). Workplace supports for employees with intellectual disability: A systematic review of the intervention literature. *Journal of Vocational Rehabilitation, 52*(3), 251–265. DOI: 10.3233/JVR-201075

Carr-Kirby, K., Horton, S., Sutherland, C. A., Paraschak, V., & Weir, P. (2025). 'I Don't Think They've Ever Seen People Like Me Do Jobs Like This': Exploring Hope Within Strengths-Based Employment Services for People With Disability. *Journal of Applied Research in Intellectual Disabilities, 38*(6), e70147. Advance online publication. DOI: 10.1111/jar.70147 PMID: 41177549

Cavanagh, J., Bartram, T., Meacham, H., Bigby, C., Oakman, J., & Fossey, E. (2016). Supporting Workers With Disabilities: A Scoping Review of the Role of Human Resource Management in Contemporary Organisations. *Asia Pacific Journal of Human Resources, 55*(1), 6–43. DOI: 10.1111/1744-7941.12111

Chandola, T., & Rouxel, P. (2021). The Role of Workplace Accommodations in Explaining the Disability Employment Gap in the UK. *Social Science & Medicine, 285*, 114313. DOI: 10.1016/j.socscimed.2021.114313 PMID: 34399292

Cheausuwantavee, T., & Keeratiphanthawong, S. (2021). Employment for Persons With Disabilities in Thailand: Opportunities and Challenges in the Labor Market. *Journal of Population and Social Studies, 29*, 384–400. DOI: 10.25133/JPSSv292021.024

Christianson-Barker, J., Franzius, A., Mills, R. A., Lomness, A., & Hole, R. (2025). Employing Strength: A Scoping Review of Customized Employment Practices to Support Inclusive Employment for People With Intellectual Disabilities. *Journal of Vocational Rehabilitation, 63*(2), 119–140. DOI: 10.1177/10522263251356445

Cubillos, L., Muñoz, J., Caballero, J., Mendoza, M. C., Pulido, A., Carpio, K., Udutha, A. K., Botero, C., Borrero, E., Rodríguez, D., Cutipé, Y., Emeny, R. T., Schifferdecker, K. E., & Torrey, W. C. (2020). Addressing Severe Mental Illness Rehabilitation in Colombia, Costa Rica, and Peru. *Psychiatric Services (Washington, D.C.), 71*(4), 378–384. DOI: 10.1176/appi.ps.201900306 PMID: 31896339

Dall, T., & Madsen, M. B. (2025). Workplace Accommodations. In *Shaping Inclusive Workplaces for Persons with Disabilities: A Management and HRM Practitioner Perspective* (pp. 71–84). DOI: 10.1007/978-3-031-96315-5_6

Dean, E. E., Garrels, V., Sigstad, H. M. H., & Wendelborg, C. (2022). Employer willingness to hire people with intellectual disability: The influence of employer experience, perception of work, and social responsibility. *Journal of Vocational Rehabilitation, 57*(1), 85–95. DOI: 10.3233/JVR-221201

Dearing, K. (2021). Exploring a non-universal understanding of waged work and its consequences: Sketching out employment activation for people with an intellectual disability. *Evidence & Policy*, *17*(2), 261–277. DOI: 10.1332/174426421X16140992285741

Dong, D., Butler, R., & Herbert, J. (2022). Evaluation of the effectiveness of developing real-world software projects as a motivational device for bridging theory and practice. *Journal of Further and Higher Education*, *46*(9), 1275–1289. DOI: 10.1080/0309877X.2022.2070727

Ervin, D. A. (2024). The State of Medical Care for Adults With Intellectual and/or Developmental Disabilities. *Medical Care*, *63*(1S), S1–S7. DOI: 10.1097/MLR.0000000000001977 PMID: 39642008

Fajardo-Castro, L. V., Martínez-Tur, V., Moliner, C., Plavsic, A., & Arbués, J. (2024). Organizational Context and Satisfaction of Basic Needs of Workers with Intellectual Disability as Sources of Well-Being. *Social Sciences (Basel, Switzerland)*, *13*(10), 523. Advance online publication. DOI: 10.3390/socsci13100523

Farzana, W., Sarker, F., Chau, T., & Mamun, K. A. (2025). Technological Evolvement in AAC Modalities to Foster Communications of Verbally Challenged ASD Children: A Systematic Review. *IEEE Access : Practical Innovations, Open Solutions*, *13*, 122943–122959. DOI: 10.1109/ACCESS.2021.3055195

Garrels, V., & Sigstad, H. M. H. (2021). Employment for Persons With Intellectual Disability in the Nordic Countries: A Scoping Review. *Journal of Applied Research in Intellectual Disabilities*, *34*(4), 993–1007. DOI: 10.1111/jar.12880 PMID: 33709541

Gjertsen, H., Hardonk, S., & Ineland, J. (2021). Work Inclusion for People With Intellectual Disabilities in Three Nordic Countries: The Current Policy and Challenges. *Scandinavian Journal of Disability Research*, *23*(1), 360–370. DOI: 10.16993/sjdr.821

Gold, P. B., Oire, S. N., Fabian, E. S., & Wewiorski, N. J. (2012). Negotiating reasonable workplace accommodations: Perspectives of employers, employees with disabilities, and rehabilitation service providers. *Journal of Vocational Rehabilitation*, *37*(1), 25–37. DOI: 10.3233/JVR-2012-0597

Gómez, L. E., Monsalve, A., Morán, L., Alcedo, M. Á., Lombardi, M., & Schalock, R. L. (2020). Measurable Indicators of CRPD for People With Intellectual and Developmental Disabilities Within the Quality of Life Framework. *International Journal of Environmental Research and Public Health*, *17*(14), 5123. DOI: 10.3390/ijerph17145123 PMID: 32679924

Gormley, M. E. (2015). Workplace Stigma Toward Employees With intellectual Disability: A Descriptive Study1. *Journal of Vocational Rehabilitation*, *43*(3), 249–258. DOI: 10.3233/JVR-150773

Gould, J. B. (2024). From Policy to Practice: Socio-Ecological Challenges in Implementing the Home and Community Based Settings Rule. *Journal of Disability Policy Studies*, *36*(1), 29–39. DOI: 10.1177/10442073241289081

Heman, P., Rhodes, D., & Cox, C. (2022). Electronic Assistive Technology Use and Supported Employment. *Journal of Applied Research in Intellectual Disabilities*, *35*(5), 1244–1249. DOI: 10.1111/jar.13005 PMID: 35596577

Hwang, G., Jensen, N. K., & Wadiwel, D. J. (2024). Disability, Employment and Welfare Reform: A Comparative Analysis of Australia and Denmark. *The Australian Journal of Social Issues*, *59*(4), 1013–1030. DOI: 10.1002/ajs4.327

Jansen, J., Ooijen, R., Koning, P., Boot, C. R. L., & Brouwer, S. (2021). The Role of the Employer in Supporting Work Participation of Workers With Disabilities: A Systematic Literature Review Using an Interdisciplinary Approach. *Journal of Occupational Rehabilitation*, *31*(4), 916–949. DOI: 10.1007/s10926-021-09978-3 PMID: 33978875

Keays, D. (2025). Institutional forces and disability: How external pressures shape workplace accommodation within organizations. *The International Journal of Organizational Analysis*, •••, 1–14. DOI: 10.1108/IJOA-06-2025-5611

Kerdar, S. H., Kirchhoff, B. M., Adolph, L., & Bächler, L. (2025). Technological Interventions for Vocational Inclusion of Individuals With Disabilities: A Scoping Review. *Journal of Vocational Rehabilitation*, *63*(3), 325–341. DOI: 10.1177/10522263251376943

Marelle, C., Thomas, E. V., & Paul, C. D. (2022). A Survey of Wireless Technology Supporting Individuals With Intellectual and Developmental Disabilities in the Workplace. *Journal of Special Education Technology*, *38*(4), 434–444. DOI: 10.1177/01626434221131463

Marinaci, T., Russo, C., Savarese, G., Stornaiuolo, G., Faiella, F., Carpinelli, L., Navarra, M., Marsico, G., & Mollo, M. (2023). An Inclusive Workplace Approach to Disability Through Assistive Technologies: A Systematic Review and Thematic Analysis of the Literature. *Societies (Basel, Switzerland)*, *13*(11), 231. DOI: 10.3390/soc13110231

Meacham, H., Cavanagh, J., Shaw, A., & Bartram, T. (2017). HRM practices that support the employment and social inclusion of workers with an intellectual disability. *Personnel Review*, *46*(8), 1475–1492. DOI: 10.1108/PR-05-2016-0105

Morash-Macneil, V., Johnson, F., & Ryan, J. B. (2018). A Systematic Review of Assistive Technology for Individuals With Intellectual Disability in the Workplace. *Journal of Special Education Technology*, *33*(1), 15–26. DOI: 10.1177/0162643417729166

Morris, R., Christianson-Barker, J., Stainton, T., Mills, R. A., Rowley, C., Cox, J. B., Schroeder, M., & Hole, R. (2024). 'They Don't Think I Can Do It': Experiences of <scp>self-advocates</Scp>, Employment Specialists, and Employers on Employment of Adults With Intellectual Disability. *Journal of Applied Research in Intellectual Disabilities*, *37*(3), e13231. Advance online publication. DOI: 10.1111/jar.13231 PMID: 38561915

Morris, R., Christianson-Barker, J., Stainton, T., Mills, R. A., Schroeder, M., Cox, J. B., Rowley, C., & Hole, R. (2024). Employment Practices as Experienced by Persons With Intellectual Disability, Employers, and Employment Specialists Across Canada. *Journal of Vocational Rehabilitation*, *61*(1), 55–66. DOI: 10.3233/JVR-240019

Niedziółka, M. (2024). Legal, Institutional and Financial Forms of State Aid for Disabled Students. *Zeszyty Naukowe Uniwersytetu Przyrodniczo-Humanistycznego W Siedlcach Seria Administracja I Zarządzanie*, *61*(134). DOI: 10.34739/zn.2023.61.20

Palumbo, R., Hinna, A., & Manesh, M. F. (2023). Aiming at Inclusive Workplaces: A Bibliometric and Interpretive Review at the Crossroads of Disability Management and Human Resource Management. *Journal of Management & Organization*, *31*(4), 1664–1687. DOI: 10.1017/jmo.2023.4

Peña, H.Jr, Gilson, C. B., Morissette, L., Rogers, A., Kesavalu, A., & Sabella, M. (2024b). A review of visually supported portable technology to support employment-related social behaviors for young adults with autism and developmental disorders. *Journal of Vocational Rehabilitation*, *61*(3), 331–347. Advance online publication. DOI: 10.1177/10522263241285217

Peña, H.Jr, Gilson, C. B., Morissette, L., Rogers, A. B., Kesavalu, A., & Sabella, M. (2024a). A Review of Visually Supported Portable Technology to Support Employment-Related Social Behaviors for Young Adults With Autism and Developmental Disorders. *Journal of Vocational Rehabilitation*, *61*(3), 331–347. DOI: 10.1177/10522263241285217

Pereira-Silva, N. L., Furtado, A. V., & Andrade, J. F. C. D. M. (2018). Workplace inclusion from the standpoint of individuals with intellectual disabilities. *Temas em Psicologia*, *26*(2), 1017–1030. DOI: 10.9788/TP2018.2-17En

Philips, G. R., Huang, M., & Bodine, C. (2024). Helping or Hindering: Inclusive Design of Automated Task Prompting for Workers with Cognitive Disabilities. *ACM Transactions on Accessible Computing*, *16*(4), 1–23. Advance online publication. DOI: 10.1145/3628447

Randall, K. N., Drew, H., Gilman, E., & Dixon, E. (2024). Assistive Technology Uses and Barriers in the Home and Workplace for Adults With Intellectual and Developmental Disabilities. *Journal of Applied Research in Intellectual Disabilities*, *38*(1), e13306. Advance online publication. DOI: 10.1111/jar.13306 PMID: 39462768

Randall, K. N., Johnson, F., Adams, S. E., Kiss, C. W., & Ryan, J. B. (2020). Use of a iPhone Task Analysis Application to Increase Employment-Related Chores for Individuals With Intellectual Disabilities. *Journal of Special Education Technology*, *35*(1), 26–36. DOI: 10.1177/0162643419836410

Rumrill, P. D., Rumrill, S. P., Wickert, K., Sheppard-Jones, K., Baumunk, M., & Roessler, R. T. (2023). A "win-win" perspective on workplace accommodations: RETAIN Kentucky's self-advocacy guide to promote successful return to work and stay at work outcomes for workers with disabilities. *Work (Reading, Mass.)*, *74*(1), 3–10. DOI: 10.3233/WOR-223651 PMID: 36463483

Schofield, D., Shrestha, R., Tan, O., Lim, K. K., Rajkumar, R., West, S., Boyle, J., Murray, L., Leffler, M., Christie, L., Rice, M. W., Hart, N., Li, J., Tanton, R., Roscioli, T., & Field, M. (2024). The Healthcare and Societal Costs of Familial Intellectual Disability. *International Journal of Environmental Research and Public Health*, *21*(3), 299. DOI: 10.3390/ijerph21030299 PMID: 38541298

Shahin, S., Reitzel, M., Rezze, B. D., Ahmed, S., & Anaby, D. (2020). Environmental Factors That Impact the Workplace Participation of Transition-Aged Young Adults With Brain-Based Disabilities: A Scoping Review. *International Journal of Environmental Research and Public Health*, *17*(7), 2378. DOI: 10.3390/ijerph17072378 PMID: 32244476

Shinall, J. B. (2020). Anticipating accommodation. *Iowa Law Review*, *105*(2), 621–686. https://www.scopus.com/inward/record.uri?eid=2-s2.0-85088559194&partnerID=40&md5=d391a81a39b49bda5649527cfca39c16

Sinclair, J., Gilson, C. B., & Dulas, H. M. (2023). "I'm Going to Be a Working Person": Self-Determination in Employment Settings for Adults With Intellectual and Developmental Disabilities. *Career Development and Transition for Exceptional Individuals*, *47*(3), 159–171. DOI: 10.1177/21651434231186136

Solovieva, T. I., & Walls, R. T. (2013). Implications of Workplace Accommodations for Persons With Disabilities. *Journal of Workplace Behavioral Health, 28*(3), 192–211. DOI: 10.1080/15555240.2013.808079

Stańczyk, K. (2020). "Anti-Crisis Shield" as an Example of State Interventionism During the Crisis Caused by the Covid-19 Virus Pandemic in Poland. *European Research Studies Journal, XXIII*(Special Issue 3), 116–136. DOI: 10.35808/ersj/1857

Sundar, V. (2017). Operationalizing workplace accommodations for individuals with disabilities: A scoping review. *Work (Reading, Mass.), 56*(1), 135–155. DOI: 10.3233/WOR-162472 PMID: 28128784

Sung, C., Fisher, M. H., Okyere, C., Park, J., & Choi, H. (2023). Employment Outcomes and Support Needs of Michigan Project SEARCH Graduates With Intellectual and Developmental Disabilities: A Mixed-Method Study. *Journal of Vocational Rehabilitation, 59*(3), 233–249. DOI: 10.3233/JVR-230042

Sung, C., & Nasamran, A. (2023). *Work Disability*. 553–575. DOI: 10.1037/0000339-026

Taylor, J. P., Avellone, L., Brooke, V., Wehman, P., Inge, K. J., Schall, C., & Iwanaga, K. (2022). The Impact of Competitive Integrated Employment on Economic, Psychological, and Physical Health Outcomes for Individuals With Intellectual and Developmental Disabilities. *Journal of Applied Research in Intellectual Disabilities, 35*(2), 448–459. DOI: 10.1111/jar.12974 PMID: 34994035

Tomas, V., Hsu, S., Kingsnorth, S., Anagnostou, E., Kirsh, B., & Lindsay, S. (2023). Development and Usability Testing of a Web-Based Workplace Disability Disclosure Decision Aid Tool for Autistic Youth and Young Adults: Qualitative Co-Design Study. *JMIR Formative Research, 7*, e44354. DOI: 10.2196/44354 PMID: 37104002

Tucker, B. P., & Nash, E. (2023). Good for Business: Towards A management Control Research agenda Relating To the employment of Workers With intellectual Disability. *Journal of Accounting Literature, 47*(1), 129–149. DOI: 10.1108/JAL-01-2023-0013

VanderMolen, J., Ward-Sutton, C., & Dudick, B. (2025). Human Resources Management Professionals Familiarity and Comfort of Assistive Technology and Workplace Accommodations. *Journal of Vocational Rehabilitation, 62*(3), 258–267. DOI: 10.1177/10522263251326411

Vigna, E., Meek, A., & Beyer, S. (2024). Supported Employment, Quality of Jobs and Employment Typicalness: The Experience of the Engage to Change Project. *Journal of Applied Research in Intellectual Disabilities, 37*(3), e13226. Advance online publication. DOI: 10.1111/jar.13226 PMID: 38520180

Wuttke, L., Dirks, S., & Bühler, C. (2025). How Can the New Technologies of Augmented Reality, Mixed Reality, and Virtual Reality Support People With Neurodevelopmental Disorders in the Workplace? *Technology and Disability*, *37*(3), 212–220. DOI: 10.1177/10554181251355423

Zhou, K., Richard, C., & Kim, J. (2025). Employment-Related Assistive Technologies for Autistic Individuals: A Scoping Review. *Journal of Vocational Rehabilitation*, *62*(2), 191–206. DOI: 10.1177/10522263241312742

Chapter 12
The Vital Role of Vocational Rehabilitation and Employment Services

ABSTRACT

This chapter examines vocational rehabilitation (VR) and employment services as critical components of an ecosystem supporting inclusive employment for workers with intellectual disabilities (ID). Moving beyond organizational practices, it conceptualizes employment outcomes as co-produced through multi-level interactions among VR agencies, community providers, job coaches, employers, and government actors. Grounded in supported employment, ecosystem theory, and inter-organizational collaboration, the chapter analyzes core practices—talent pipeline development, job matching, skill development, and on-the-job support—that operationalize inclusive employment. It further explores partnership strategies essential for system coordination, including formal governance structures, communication systems, role clarity, and sustainability mechanisms. The chapter concludes that sustainable inclusion requires intentional alignment of actors, resources, and policies within an integrated, collaborative ecosystem.

12.1 INTRODUCTION

The implementation of inclusive employment for workers with intellectual disabilities (ID) cannot be fully understood through an organizational lens alone. While Chapter 11 has demonstrated the importance of workplace accommodations and assistive technologies within organizational systems, a growing body of evidence emphasizes that these efforts are inherently embedded within a broader ecosystem of support. This ecosystem includes vocational rehabilitation (VR) systems, employment

DOI: 10.4018/979-8-3373-9185-4.ch012

service providers, policy frameworks, and cross-sector partnerships that collectively shape access to, participation in, and sustainability of employment for workers with ID (Taylor et al., 2022; Wehman et al., 2021). From this ecosystem perspective, inclusion is not the sole responsibility of individual organizations but rather the outcome of interconnected systems working in coordination. VR and employment services function as critical intermediaries that bridge the gap between workers, employers, and policy environments. They do not merely support individuals in finding jobs; they actively shape the conditions under which inclusive employment becomes possible, scalable, and sustainable (Novak, 2015; Wehman et al., 2018).

A central contribution of VR systems lies in their role as catalysts for system-level change. Across multiple studies, VR agencies are shown to promote competitive integrated employment (CIE) as the preferred outcome, aligning practice with policy frameworks such as Workforce Innovation and Opportunity Act (WIOA) and Employment First initiatives. These policy-driven shifts have redirected attention away from segregated employment models toward integrated, community-based work, fundamentally reshaping how employment pathways for workers with ID are designed and implemented (Friedman & Rizzolo, 2017; Wehman et al., 2021). This shift is not merely ideological but operational. VR professionals play a key role in coordinating services, facilitating employer engagement, and ensuring that individuals with ID are placed in open labor market settings with appropriate supports. In doing so, they translate policy commitments into actionable practices, bridging the persistent gap between formal inclusion mandates and real-world employment outcomes (Wehman et al., 2018). At the same time, the literature clearly demonstrates that organizations cannot achieve inclusive employment independently. Even when organizations are committed to inclusion and equipped with internal accommodation strategies, they often face limitations in expertise, resources, and systemic coordination. VR and employment services address these limitations by providing specialized knowledge, funding pathways, job coaching, and long-term support mechanisms that extend beyond what most organizations can sustain internally (Nevala et al., 2019). For example, access to employment is often contingent on coordinated efforts across multiple systems, including education, transportation, and disability services. VR agencies play a central role in aligning these systems, ensuring that individuals can transition into employment with the necessary supports in place. Without such coordination, even well-designed organizational initiatives may fail to produce sustainable outcomes due to fragmented services or unmet support needs (Kudla et al., 2024). Furthermore, VR systems contribute significantly to employment retention and workplace functioning. Evidence consistently shows that ongoing supports—such as job coaching, workplace accommodations, and tailored training—are critical for sustaining employment among workers with ID. These supports are often coordinated and funded through VR systems, highlighting their role not only in facilitating entry into employment but also in ensuring long-term success (Ellenkamp et al., 2015)

From an outcomes perspective, the ecosystem approach is strongly associated with improved economic and psychosocial outcomes. Workers with ID who participate in integrated employment models supported by VR systems tend to experience higher earnings, greater job stability, and enhanced quality of life compared to those in segregated settings (Betz, 2023). These findings reinforce the argument that inclusive employment is most effective when supported by coordinated, system-level interventions rather than isolated organizational efforts. However, the literature also highlights important challenges and nuances within this ecosystem. Barriers such as employer stigma, limited access to VR services in certain regions, and variability in policy implementation continue to affect outcomes. Additionally, debates persist regarding the scalability and cost-effectiveness of different service models, such as supported employment (SE) versus customized employment (CE). These complexities underscore the need for ongoing coordination, policy refinement, and organizational engagement to fully realize the potential of VR systems (Christianson-Barker et al., 2025). Taken together, these insights point to a fundamental conclusion: inclusive employment for workers with intellectual disabilities is co-produced across organizational and systemic levels. Organizations provide the immediate context for work, but VR and employment services create the enabling conditions that make inclusion feasible, effective, and sustainable. This interdependence challenges the notion of organizational self-sufficiency and instead positions inclusion as a shared responsibility across multiple stakeholders. Accordingly, this chapter examines the vital role of vocational rehabilitation and employment services within this ecosystem. It explores how these systems contribute to access, retention, and workplace outcomes, how they interact with organizational practices, and how effective partnerships can be developed to support inclusive employment. By shifting the focus from internal organizational processes to broader systemic dynamics, this chapter extends the discussion of inclusion from "what organizations do" to "how systems work together" to support workers with intellectual disabilities.

12.2 CONCEPTUAL FOUNDATION

12.2.1 Supported Employment as a Systems-Level Framework

Supported employment (SE) has evolved from a service model focused on individual job placement into a comprehensive systems-level framework that integrates policy, practice, and cross-sector coordination to support workers with intellectual disabilities (ID). Rather than operating as a discrete intervention, SE is increasingly conceptualized as a policy-practice architecture that aligns multiple stakeholders—including education systems, vocational rehabilitation (VR), employers, families, and community services—toward the shared goal of competitive integrated employment (CIE) (Carter et al., 2017; Roux et al., 2019). This expanded conceptualization reflects a shift from fragmented service delivery toward coordinated, ecosystem-based employment pathways. For example, state-level initiatives such as TennesseeWorks demonstrate how SE can function as a systems-change mechanism, supported by backbone organizations, multi-stakeholder governance structures, and shared accountability frameworks (Carter et al., 2017). In this model, SE is not merely about placing individuals into jobs but about aligning systems to sustain employment outcomes over time.

Policy frameworks further reinforce this systems-level perspective. The Employment First paradigm positions integrated employment as the default outcome for individuals with ID, driving alignment across funding mechanisms, service delivery models, and employer engagement strategies (Roux et al., 2019). Similarly, global frameworks such as the Disability Inclusion and Accountability Framework emphasize embedding disability inclusion within organizational and policy systems, highlighting the need for institutionalized accountability and continuous evaluation (Weltbank, 2022). Importantly, SE also reflects a dual-customer approach, recognizing both the worker and the employer as central stakeholders. This perspective shifts the focus from supply-driven models—where individuals are prepared for employment in isolation—to demand-driven approaches that involve employers as active partners in job design, accommodation, and support processes (Roux et al., 2019). As such, SE provides a conceptual bridge between individual-level supports and organizational inclusion practices.

12.2.2 Employment Ecosystem Theory

The effectiveness of supported employment is best understood through the lens of ecosystem theory, which conceptualizes employment as the product of interactions among multiple interdependent actors, systems, and environments. In this perspective, employment outcomes for workers with ID are not determined solely by individual capabilities or organizational practices but emerge from dynamic interactions across policy, service, and labor market systems (Andreassen et al., 2020). Ecosystem theory highlights the importance of multi-level coordination, where actors such as VR agencies, employers, education systems, and community organizations operate within interconnected networks. These networks facilitate access to resources, information, and support, enabling individuals with ID to navigate complex employment pathways. The literature on networked employment services identifies multiple traditions—rehabilitation, disability, welfare, and governance—

that collectively contribute to these ecosystems, emphasizing that no single system is sufficient in isolation (Andreassen et al., 2020).

A key feature of employment ecosystems is the presence of governance structures and coordination mechanisms that align actors toward shared goals. Concepts such as backbone organizations, shared measurement systems, and collective impact frameworks illustrate how coordination can be structured to sustain collaboration over time (Flippo & Butterworth, 2018; Guerrero et al., 2018). These mechanisms are essential for overcoming fragmentation and ensuring continuity of support across different stages of employment. Ecosystem theory also incorporates insights from institutional logics, which explain how different value systems—such as market efficiency, professional standards, state regulation, and community norms—shape the organization and delivery of employment services (Fuertes et al., 2020). These logics influence how collaboration is structured, how resources are allocated, and how success is defined, leading to variations in implementation across contexts. From this perspective, employment systems are inherently context-sensitive and adaptive. Effective ecosystems require the ability to navigate competing logics, align incentives across stakeholders, and respond to local conditions. This reinforces the need for flexible, collaborative approaches that can accommodate diversity in policy environments, organizational capacities, and labor market conditions.

12.2.3 Inter-Organizational Collaboration

At the core of both supported employment and ecosystem theory is the principle of inter-organizational collaboration, which serves as the primary mechanism through which inclusive employment systems are operationalized. Collaboration across organizations—spanning public, private, and nonprofit sectors—enables the coordination of resources, expertise, and services necessary to support workers with ID throughout the employment lifecycle (Andreassen et al., 2020). The literature conceptualizes collaboration not merely as structural coordination but as a relational process grounded in trust, reciprocity, and shared goals. Drawing on social exchange theory, relational perspectives emphasize that effective partnerships depend on ongoing interaction, mutual commitment, and the development of collaborative routines that sustain cooperation over time (Asmuß & Thomsen, 2024). These relational dynamics are critical for translating formal agreements into meaningful outcomes in workplace settings.

A complementary perspective is provided by boundary-spanning theory, which focuses on the role of individuals and roles that connect different organizational domains. Boundary spanners—such as VR counselors, job coaches, and case managers—facilitate communication, coordinate services, and bridge gaps between systems, enabling individuals with ID to access integrated supports (Lindsay & Dutton,

2011). This highlights that collaboration is not only institutional but also enacted through professional practices and interpersonal interactions. Inter-organizational collaboration is also shaped by power dynamics and interdependencies among actors. Research on employer–nonprofit partnerships shows that collaboration often involves negotiation, strategic alignment, and the management of asymmetries in resources and influence (Katz & Sasson, 2017). Recognizing and addressing these dynamics is essential for ensuring equitable participation and effective partnership outcomes. Furthermore, collaboration is embedded within broader governance frameworks, which define roles, responsibilities, and accountability mechanisms. Multi-stakeholder partnerships (MSPs) and cross-sector collaborations provide formal structures for coordination, enabling actors to align strategies, share resources, and jointly address complex challenges. These governance arrangements are particularly important for scaling inclusive employment practices and ensuring sustainability over time.

Bringing these perspectives together, the conceptual foundation of this chapter positions vocational rehabilitation and employment services within an integrated employment ecosystem characterized by three interrelated components:

1. Supported employment as a policy-practice framework that aligns stakeholders, funding, and service delivery toward competitive integrated employment
2. Ecosystem dynamics that emphasize multi-level interactions, governance structures, and contextual adaptation
3. Inter-organizational collaboration as the mechanism through which coordination, resource sharing, and service integration are achieved

This integrated framework highlights that inclusive employment is not the result of isolated interventions but emerges from the alignment of systems, relationships, and institutional structures. It also underscores the importance of viewing VR services not as standalone providers but as embedded actors within a broader network of collaboration and governance. At the same time, the literature identifies important nuances and tensions within this framework. These include the balance between centralized coordination and local autonomy, the management of power asymmetries within partnerships, and the resource-intensive nature of integrated support models (Fuertes et al., 2020; Katz & Sasson, 2017). Addressing these challenges requires ongoing adaptation, stakeholder engagement, and investment in collaborative capacity. The conceptual foundation presented here provides a theoretical lens for understanding how vocational rehabilitation and employment services contribute to inclusive employment systems. It establishes the basis for the subsequent sections of this chapter, which examine how these concepts are operationalized in practice to support access, retention, and workplace outcomes for workers with intellectual disabilities.

12.3. KEY ACTORS IN THE ECOSYSTEM

Inclusive employment for workers with intellectual disabilities (ID) is operationalized through the coordinated efforts of multiple actors within the employment ecosystem. This section identifies the key actors who enact, mediate, and sustain inclusive employment in practice. The literature consistently highlights vocational rehabilitation (VR) agencies, community-based providers, job coaches, and government agencies as central actors whose roles are interconnected and mutually reinforcing (Grossi et al., 2019; Taylor & Whittenburg, 2024). These actors do not function independently; rather, they operate within interdependent networks characterized by shared responsibilities, braided funding, and collaborative governance structures. Their effectiveness depends on coordination, alignment of goals, and the ability to bridge institutional boundaries across education, employment, and social service systems (Butterworth et al., 2017).

12.3.1 Vocational Rehabilitation (VR) Agencies

Vocational rehabilitation agencies occupy a central position within the employment ecosystem, functioning as both service providers and system coordinators. Their role is shaped by policy mandates—particularly under frameworks such as the Workforce Innovation and Opportunity Act (WIOA)—which emphasize competitive integrated employment (CIE), Pre-Employment Transition Services (Pre-ETS), and supported or customized employment approaches (Roux et al., 2019; Taylor, Whittenburg, et al., 2021). At the operational level, VR agencies provide a comprehensive range of services, including career counseling, job placement, on-the-job supports, and funding for training and assistive technologies. These services are critical for enabling access to employment and supporting individuals with ID throughout the employment lifecycle (Huber et al., 2017). In particular, customized employment (CE) has emerged as a key VR-supported strategy, designed to align individual strengths with employer needs, thereby improving job matching and employment outcomes (Smith et al., 2016). Beyond direct service provision, VR agencies play a crucial role in facilitating interagency collaboration and aligning systems. They coordinate with education systems, community providers, and employers to support school-to-work transitions and to ensure continuity of services. Policy requirements—such as allocating a portion of VR funding to Pre-ETS—reflect a shift toward earlier and more proactive engagement with individuals with ID, reinforcing VR's role as a gateway to the employment ecosystem (Taylor et al., 2024). However, the literature also highlights variability in VR service delivery across regions, influenced by differences in policy implementation, funding structures, and organizational capacity. These variations affect access to services, quality of support, and employment outcomes, underscoring the importance of standardization combined with contextual adaptation (Taylor et al., 2021; (Leahy et al., 2018; Taylor, Avellone, et al., 2021).

12.3.2 NGOs and Community Providers (CRPs)

Community-based providers, often referred to as Community Rehabilitation Programs (CRPs), play a pivotal role as bridging actors between systems and everyday employment contexts. They are responsible for delivering community-based services, facilitating work-based learning experiences, and supporting individuals in navigating transitions from school to employment (Jones-Parkin et al., 2021). A key function of community providers is the development of individualized employment pathways, including discovery processes, job development, and coordination with employers. These providers work closely with VR agencies and other stakeholders to braid funding and align services, ensuring that supports are continuous and responsive to individual needs (Swarbrick et al., 2017). Evidence shows that embedding community providers—such as Career Coaches—within school settings significantly improves employment outcomes. This approach increases access to work-based experiences, strengthens connections to adult services, and facilitates smoother transitions into competitive employment (Grossi et al., 2019). In this sense, community providers function as boundary-spanning actors, linking educational environments with labor market opportunities. Despite their central role, community providers often face challenges related to workforce turnover, resource constraints, and fragmented funding streams. These challenges can disrupt service continuity and limit the effectiveness of employment supports. The literature therefore emphasizes the importance of interagency collaboration and stable funding mechanisms to sustain the contributions of community providers within the ecosystem (Jones-Parkin et al., 2021).

12.3.3 Job Coaches and Employment Specialists

Job coaches and employment specialists represent the frontline implementers of supported and customized employment practices. They play a critical role in translating policy frameworks and organizational strategies into day-to-day workplace support for individuals with ID (Grossi et al., 2019). Their responsibilities include conducting discovery processes, supporting job development, providing on-the-job training, and facilitating communication between employees, employers, and other stakeholders. In many cases, job coaches serve as the primary point of contact for individuals with ID, ensuring that supports are tailored, responsive, and sustained over time (Taylor et al., 2024). Importantly, job coaches function as boundary spanners within the ecosystem, connecting multiple systems and actors. They coordinate with VR agencies, schools, community providers, and employers, enabling the integration of services and supports across contexts. Research indicates that embedding job coaches within educational settings enhances alignment between school-based preparation and post-school employment, leading to improved transition outcomes (Grossi et al., 2019). The effectiveness of job coaching is closely linked to broader system conditions, including funding structures, interagency coordination, and workforce stability. High turnover among job coaches and limited resources can undermine continuity of support, highlighting the need for investment in workforce development and sustainable funding models (Jones-Parkin et al., 2021). Additionally, the adoption of a dual-customer approach—which treats both employers and job seekers as key stakeholders—has strengthened the role of job coaches in fostering employer engagement and sustaining employment relationships (Chun et al., 2024; Haines et al., 2018).

12.3.4 Government Agencies and Policy Actors

Government agencies provide the policy, regulatory, and funding infrastructure that shapes the functioning of the employment ecosystem. Their role extends beyond program administration to include the design of policies, allocation of resources, and establishment of accountability mechanisms that influence how services are delivered and coordinated (Roux et al., 2019). A key contribution of government actors is the promotion of Employment First and competitive integrated employment (CIE) as policy priorities. Through legislation, funding requirements, and performance metrics, governments incentivize the adoption of inclusive employment practices and the reduction of segregated employment models (Taylor, Whittenburg, et al., 2021). Government agencies also play a central role in facilitating interagency collaboration. Initiatives such as Partnerships in Employment (PIE) demonstrate how state-level governance structures can align multiple stakeholders—including VR agencies, education systems, community providers, and employers—around shared goals. These initiatives often involve backbone organizations, shared data systems, and formal agreements that enable coordination and accountability (J. Christensen et al., 2017). Furthermore, government agencies are responsible for braiding funding across systems, integrating resources from VR, education, Medicaid, and other programs to support comprehensive employment services. This funding integration is essential for sustaining long-term supports and preventing service fragmentation (Jones-Parkin et al., 2021). However, the literature also highlights challenges related to policy implementation, including variability across regions, gaps in addressing specific populations (such as individuals with ID), and limitations in data sharing and evaluation. These challenges underscore the need for ongoing policy refinement, targeted interventions, and robust evaluation frameworks (Hartman et al., 2025; Scheef et al., 2023).

Taken together, these actors form a multi-layered ecosystem of support, in which each plays a distinct yet interconnected role:

- VR agencies provide coordination, funding, and core services
- Community providers deliver localized, individualized supports
- Job coaches operationalize inclusion at the workplace level
- Government agencies establish policy frameworks and funding structures

The effectiveness of this ecosystem depends on inter-organizational collaboration, shared goals, and aligned incentives. Evidence consistently shows that multi-stakeholder approaches—characterized by collective impact frameworks, embedded roles, and braided funding—are associated with improved employment outcomes, including higher rates of competitive integrated employment and stronger transitions from school to work (Grossi et al., 2019). At the same time, the literature highlights the importance of addressing systemic challenges such as workforce instability, funding fragmentation, and regional disparities. These issues require coordinated solutions that strengthen governance structures, enhance collaboration, and ensure equitable access to services across contexts. The employment ecosystem for workers with intellectual disabilities is sustained through the interdependence of actors and the quality of their collaboration. Understanding these roles provides a foundation for examining how these actors collectively contribute to employment access, retention, and outcomes, which is the focus of the next section.

12.4. CORE PRACTICES

The effectiveness of vocational rehabilitation (VR) and employment services in supporting workers with intellectual disabilities (ID) is ultimately realized through a set of core practices that translate policy and collaboration into tangible employment outcomes. Across the literature, four interrelated practices consistently emerge as central: talent pipeline development, job matching, skill development, and on-the-job support. These practices are grounded in supported employment (SE) and customized employment (CE) frameworks, which emphasize individualized, integrated, and sustained approaches to employment (Riesen et al., 2015; Wehman et al., 2021). Importantly, these practices are not sequential but iterative and interconnected, forming a continuous cycle that supports recruitment, placement, and long-term retention. Their effectiveness depends on fidelity to evidence-based models, employer engagement, and alignment with organizational and ecosystem-level supports (Brinchmann et al., 2019).

12.4.1 Talent Pipeline Development

Talent pipeline development refers to the processes through which individuals with ID are prepared, identified, and connected to employment opportunities. The literature emphasizes that effective pipelines are not supply-driven but are built through active collaboration between VR services, employers, and education systems (Iwanaga et al., 2018). A key component of pipeline development is the implementation of disability-inclusive recruitment practices, including accessible hiring processes, formal inclusion policies, and proactive employer engagement. Evidence shows that organizations with strong disability inclusion climates—characterized by supportive leadership, inclusive HR practices, and reduced stigma—are significantly more likely to recruit and hire individuals with disabilities (Iwanaga et al., 2018). VR professionals play a critical role in shaping these pipelines by assessing organizational readiness, engaging employers, and facilitating inclusive recruitment strategies. Tools such as disability inclusion climate assessments enable VR practitioners to identify barriers within organizations and to design targeted interventions that enhance recruitment outcomes (Chan et al., 2024). Furthermore, talent pipeline development increasingly involves early and structured work-based learning experiences, particularly through transition programs such as Project SEARCH. These programs integrate education, VR services, and employer partnerships to prepare individuals with ID for competitive employment, demonstrating promising outcomes in terms of job placement and skill acquisition (Wehman et al., 2021). Overall, effective talent pipelines are characterized by proactive employer engagement, inclusive organizational practices, and early exposure to work environments, ensuring that individuals with ID are not only prepared for employment but also connected to meaningful opportunities.

12.4.2 Job Matching

Job matching is a critical process that determines the alignment between an individual's strengths, preferences, and support needs and the requirements of a specific job role. The literature consistently identifies job matching as a collaborative, data-driven, and multi-stakeholder process, involving VR professionals, job coaches, employers, and the individuals themselves (Persch et al., 2015). Effective job matching requires the integration of multiple data sources, including individual preferences, functional abilities, transportation considerations, and workplace supports. However, studies reveal that job matching practices are often heterogeneous and lack standardization, highlighting the need for structured, evidence-based frameworks to guide decision-making (Persch et al., 2015). Customized employment (CE) represents a key advancement in job matching practices. CE involves tailoring job roles to align with both the individual's strengths and the employer's needs, often through job carving and negotiation processes. Evidence suggests that CE contributes to improved placement quality, longer job tenure, and greater satisfaction for both employees and employers when implemented with fidelity (Brinchmann et al., 2019). Supported employment (SE) models further reinforce the importance of job matching by emphasizing place-then-train approaches, where individuals are placed in real work settings and provided with ongoing supports to succeed. This contrasts with traditional models that focus on pre-employment training without direct engagement with the labor market (Wehman et al., 2021). Programs such as Project SEARCH illustrate how structured, employer-partnered approaches to job matching can enhance outcomes, although the literature notes the need for continued support and evaluation to sustain long-term employment (J. J. Christensen et al., 2015). Effective job matching is characterized by individualization, collaboration, and alignment with real workplace contexts, supported by structured processes and ongoing evaluation.

12.4.3 Skill Development

Skill development within VR and employment services extends beyond traditional training to encompass contextualized, workplace-based learning that is directly linked to job demands. The literature emphasizes that skill development is most effective when integrated within supported employment frameworks, where learning occurs in real work environments rather than in isolated training settings (Wehman et al., 2021). A central principle of skill development is the alignment between training and actual job tasks, ensuring that individuals acquire relevant competencies that support job performance and retention. This includes both technical skills and soft skills, such as communication, problem-solving, and workplace social interaction (Ellenkamp et al., 2015). Supported employment models incorporate structured approaches to skill development, including on-the-job training, task analysis, and individualized instruction, delivered by job coaches and employment specialists. These approaches enable workers with ID to develop skills in context, enhancing both learning and transferability (Riesen et al., 2015). The literature also highlights the importance of career development and progression, noting that opportunities for advancement and skill growth are associated with higher retention and job satisfaction. Conversely, limited opportunities for development can negatively impact long-term employment outcomes (Kudla et al., 2024). Additionally, skill development is influenced by the work environment and organizational culture. Inclusive workplaces that provide ongoing training, supportive supervision, and opportunities for learning contribute to more effective skill acquisition and sustained employment (Iwanaga et al., 2018). Thus, skill development is best understood as a continuous, context-dependent process that integrates training, workplace experience, and organizational support.

12.4.4 On-the-Job Support

On-the-job support represents one of the most critical components of successful employment for workers with ID, particularly in sustaining long-term outcomes. The literature consistently identifies job coaching, workplace accommodations, natural supports, and employer collaboration as key elements of effective on-the-job support (Müller et al., 2018). Job coaching is central to this process, providing individualized support during initial placement and throughout employment. Job coaches assist with task acquisition, social integration, and communication with employers, acting as facilitators of both performance and inclusion (Vigna et al., 2024). A key feature of effective on-the-job support is the use of structured support and fading strategies, where intensive support is gradually reduced as the individual gains independence. This approach promotes autonomy while ensuring that support remains available when needed (Vigna et al., 2023). Workplace accommodations and universal design further enhance on-the-job support by aligning job demands with individual capabilities. Evidence shows that accommodations improve performance, job satisfaction, and retention, particularly when implemented collaboratively and integrated into workplace practices (Randall et al., 2024). Natural supports—such as coworkers, supervisors, and workplace routines—also play a significant role in sustaining employment. When combined with formal supports, natural supports contribute to social integration, reduce reliance on external assistance, and enhance long-term stability (Athamanah et al., 2024). Employer engagement is another critical factor, with inclusive workplace cultures, supportive management, and ongoing communication contributing to better employment outcomes. Employers who actively participate in accommodation and support processes are more likely to sustain inclusive employment practices (Brinchmann et al., 2019). Finally, emerging evidence highlights the role of technology-enabled supports, such as assistive tools and digital applications, in enhancing task performance and communication. However, their effectiveness depends on integration with existing support systems and organizational readiness (Cura & Kızılkum, 2024). Taken together, these core practices form an integrated model of vocational rehabilitation and employment support, characterized by:

- Proactive pipeline development through inclusive recruitment and employer engagement
- Individualized job matching based on strengths, preferences, and workplace needs
- Contextualized skill development embedded within real work environments
- Sustained on-the-job support through coaching, accommodations, and collaboration

The literature consistently shows that these practices are most effective when implemented with high fidelity to supported employment and customized employment models, supported by strong employer partnerships and aligned with broader ecosystem structures (Wehman et al., 2021). At the same time, outcomes are influenced by contextual factors such as policy environments, funding, and organizational capacity, highlighting the need for adaptive and context-sensitive implementation. Core practices serve as the operational bridge between ecosystem structures and employment outcomes, translating policy, collaboration, and theory into meaningful and sustainable employment opportunities for workers with intellectual disabilities.

12.5. PARTNERSHIP STRATEGIES

Sustaining inclusive employment for workers with intellectual disabilities (ID) requires more than the presence of multiple actors; it depends on the quality, structure, and durability of partnerships among vocational rehabilitation (VR) services, employers, community providers, and government agencies. The literature consistently demonstrates that effective partnerships are not ad hoc collaborations but are intentionally designed systems of coordination, supported by governance structures, shared goals, and aligned resources (Tucker et al., 2017). This section examines four critical dimensions of partnership strategies: formal versus informal collaboration, communication systems, role clarity, and long-term partnership sustainability. Together, these dimensions define how collaboration is operationalized and sustained within the employment ecosystem.

12.5.1 Formal vs. Informal Collaboration

Partnerships in inclusive employment systems operate along a continuum from informal coordination to formalized, institutionalized collaboration. While informal relationships—such as personal networks between VR counselors and employers—can facilitate flexibility and responsiveness, the literature emphasizes that formal collaboration mechanisms are essential for scalability, consistency, and sustainability (Freeze et al., 2017). Formal collaboration is typically structured through memoranda of agreement (MoAs), interagency contracts, and governance frameworks that define shared goals, responsibilities, and funding arrangements. State-level initiatives such as Partnerships in Employment (PIE) demonstrate that formalized cross-agency collaboration—supported by backbone organizations and Employment First policies—enables alignment across VR, education, developmental disability (DD) services, and labor systems (Butterworth et al., 2017). These formal structures also facilitate braided funding, allowing resources from multiple systems (e.g., VR, Medicaid, education) to be integrated into a cohesive service delivery model. Evidence shows that such funding integration reduces fragmentation and supports the continuity of services necessary for long-term employment outcomes (Jones-Parkin et al., 2021). However, informal collaboration remains important, particularly at the local level, where relationships between practitioners and employers can enhance responsiveness and innovation. The literature suggests that effective systems balance formal governance with informal relational dynamics, ensuring both structure and adaptability (Shogren, Wehmeyer, et al., 2017).

12.5.2 Communication Systems

Continuous and structured communication is a defining feature of effective partnerships. The literature highlights that communication systems must be institutionalized rather than incidental, enabling stakeholders to coordinate activities, share information, and monitor progress (Tucker et al., 2017). One widely adopted framework is the Collective Impact model, which emphasizes continuous communication as one of its core components. Within this model, regular cross-agency meetings, shared data systems, and joint planning processes are used to align stakeholders and sustain collaboration over time (Butterworth et al., 2017). Shared data infrastructure is particularly critical. Cross-agency data dashboards—tracking indicators such as employment rates, wages, and service utilization—enable data-driven decision-making and accountability. Evidence shows that partnerships with robust data systems are better able to maintain fidelity to evidence-based practices and demonstrate outcomes to stakeholders (Jones-Parkin et al., 2021). Communication systems also extend to employer engagement mechanisms, such as employer councils and advisory groups. These platforms facilitate ongoing dialogue between employers and service providers, ensuring that employment strategies remain aligned with labor market needs and organizational realities (Shogren, Dean, et al., 2017). At the operational level, communication must be multi-directional, involving not only agencies and employers but also individuals with ID and their support networks. This inclusive approach enhances transparency, trust, and responsiveness, contributing to more effective service delivery and employment outcomes (Khoronzhevych et al., 2021).

12.5.3 Role Clarity

Role clarity is a critical determinant of partnership effectiveness, particularly in complex, multi-actor systems. The literature consistently identifies ambiguity in roles and responsibilities as a barrier to effective collaboration, leading to duplication of efforts, service gaps, and inefficiencies (Butterworth et al., 2017). Effective partnerships address this challenge through explicit definition of roles within formal agreements and governance structures. Memoranda of agreement, contracts, and interagency frameworks specify responsibilities related to service provision, funding, data sharing, and accountability, ensuring that each actor understands their function within the system (Jones-Parkin et al., 2021). Role clarity is particularly important in the coordination between VR agencies, community providers, and employers. For example:

- VR agencies typically lead assessment, funding, and coordination
- Community providers deliver direct services and supports
- Employers provide workplace opportunities and integration

Clearly defined roles enable these actors to operate in a complementary rather than competitive manner, enhancing system efficiency and effectiveness. In addition to formal role definitions, the literature emphasizes the importance of professional capacity-building and training to support role clarity. Cross-agency training initiatives and professional development programs help align understanding of evidence-based practices, expectations, and collaborative processes (Hall et al., 2018). Furthermore, role clarity must be accompanied by shared accountability mechanisms, ensuring that all actors are responsible for achieving common outcomes, particularly competitive integrated employment (CIE) (Butterworth et al., 2017).

12.5.4 Long-Term Partnership Sustainability

Sustaining partnerships over time is one of the most significant challenges in inclusive employment systems. (Butterworth et al., 2017). A central element is the presence of a backbone organization, which provides leadership, coordination, and accountability for cross-agency collaboration. Backbone organizations facilitate governance processes, maintain stakeholder engagement, and ensure continuity of efforts beyond individual programs or funding cycles (Tucker et al., 2017). Another key factor is braided and sustainable funding, which integrates resources from multiple systems and ensures continuity of services. Evidence shows that partnerships supported by stable, multi-source funding are more likely to achieve and sustain positive employment outcomes (Canady, 2020). Capacity-building is also essential, particularly in developing the skills of VR professionals, job coaches, and community providers. Training in evidence-based practices, such as customized employment and discovery, enhances the quality of services and supports the long-term effectiveness of partnerships (Shogren, Dean, et al., 2017). Early and continuous employer engagement further contributes to sustainability. Partnerships that involve employers in planning, implementation, and evaluation are more likely to maintain alignment with labor market needs and to sustain employment opportunities for individuals with ID (Riesen et al., 2022). Finally, data-driven evaluation and continuous improvement are critical for sustaining partnerships. Regular monitoring of outcomes, combined with feedback mechanisms, enables stakeholders to identify challenges, refine strategies, and demonstrate impact to funders and policymakers (Butterworth et al., 2017).

The literature converges on a clear conclusion: effective partnerships in inclusive employment systems are intentional, structured, and continuously maintained. They are characterized by:

- Formal governance structures complemented by informal relational networks
- Institutionalized communication systems supported by shared data and continuous dialogue
- Clear roles and responsibilities aligned with shared goals and accountability
- Sustainable funding and capacity-building mechanisms that support long-term collaboration

At the same time, successful partnerships must remain adaptive and context-sensitive, balancing fidelity to evidence-based models with responsiveness to local conditions. Variability in capacity, funding, and stakeholder engagement requires tailored approaches that preserve core elements—such as backbone leadership, shared metrics, and employer engagement—while allowing flexibility in implementation (Shogren et al., 2017; Tucker et al., 2017). Partnership strategies serve as the connective tissue of the employment ecosystem, enabling coordination across actors, alignment of resources, and sustained delivery of inclusive employment practices. They transform fragmented systems into integrated, collaborative networks capable of supporting meaningful and lasting employment outcomes for workers with intellectual disabilities.

REFERENCES

Andreassen, T. A., Breit, E., & Saltkjel, T. (2020). Research Approaches to Networked Employment Services: A Systematic Review. *Social Policy and Administration, 54*(7), 1179–1197. DOI: 10.1111/spol.12597

Asmuß, B., & Thomsen, C. (2024). Workplace Inclusion Through Social Partnerships: A Relational Perspective. *Group & Organization Management, 50*(4), 1385–1418. DOI: 10.1177/10596011241288117

Athamanah, L. S., Cushing, L. S., Fastzkie, E. M., & Brown, E. R. (2024). Natural Supports in Competitive Integrated Employment: A Scoping Review. *Journal of Vocational Rehabilitation, 60*(3), 327–339. DOI: 10.3233/JVR-240017

Betz, C. L. (2023). Health Care Transition Planning for Adolescents and Emerging Adults With Intellectual Disabilities and Developmental Disabilities: Distinctions and Challenges. *Journal for Specialists in Pediatric Nursing, 28*(3), e12415. Advance online publication. DOI: 10.1111/jspn.12415 PMID: 37380603

Brinchmann, B., Widding-Havneraas, T., Modini, M., Rinaldi, M., Moe, C. F., McDaid, D., Park, A., Killackey, E., Harvey, S. B., & Mykletun, A. (2019). A Meta-regression of the Impact of Policy on the Efficacy of Individual Placement and Support. *Acta Psychiatrica Scandinavica, 141*(3), 206–220. DOI: 10.1111/acps.13129 PMID: 31733146

Butterworth, J., Christensen, J., & Flippo, K. (2017). Partnerships in Employment: Building Strong Coalitions to Facilitate Systems Change for Youth and Young Adults. *Journal of Vocational Rehabilitation, 47*(3), 265–276. DOI: 10.3233/JVR-170901

Canady, V. A. (2020). Illinois Employment Model Serves as an Example for Others. *Mental Health Weekly, 30*(44), 6–7. DOI: 10.1002/mhw.32588

Carter, E. W., McMillan, E. D., & Willis, W. (2017). The TennesseeWorks Partnership: Elevating Employment Outcomes for People With Intellectual and Developmental Disabilities. *Journal of Vocational Rehabilitation, 47*(3), 365–378. DOI: 10.3233/JVR-170909

Chan, F., Iwanaga, K., Tansey, T. N., Ditchman, N., Wehman, P., Wu, J. R., & Chen, X. (2024). Assessing Evidence-Based Disability Inclusion Policy and Practices to Promote Employment of People With Disabilities in the Workplace: Scale Development and Validation. *Rehabilitation Counseling Bulletin*. Advance online publication. DOI: 10.1177/00343552241268757

Christensen, J., Richardson, K., & Hetherington, S. (2017). New York State Partnerships in Employment. *Journal of Vocational Rehabilitation, 47*(3), 351–363. DOI: 10.3233/JVR-170908

Christensen, J. J., Hetherington, S., Daston, M. M., & Riehle, E. (2015). Longitudinal Outcomes of Project SEARCH in Upstate New York. *Journal of Vocational Rehabilitation, 42*(3), 247–255. DOI: 10.3233/JVR-150746

Christianson-Barker, J., Franzius, A., Mills, R. A., Lomness, A., & Hole, R. (2025). Employing Strength: A Scoping Review of Customized Employment Practices to Support Inclusive Employment for People With Intellectual Disabilities. *Journal of Vocational Rehabilitation, 63*(2), 119–140. DOI: 10.1177/10522263251356445

Chun, J., Anderson, C., Rumrill, S., Richard, C., Zhou, K., Fry, H., & Froehlich, R. J. (2024). Promoting Quality Career Pathways for Individuals With Disabilities Through the Public Vocational Rehabilitation Program. *Journal of Vocational Rehabilitation, 60*(3), 299–310. DOI: 10.3233/JVR-240014

Cura, G., & Kızılkum, Ş. (2024). *Recruitment and Job Coaching for and With Intellectual Disability*. 103–109. DOI: 10.24140/nobarriers.v1.p02.04

Ellenkamp, J. J. H., Brouwers, E., Embregts, P. J. C. M., Joosen, M., & Weeghel, J. (2015). Work Environment-Related Factors in Obtaining and Maintaining Work in a Competitive Employment Setting for Employees With Intellectual Disabilities: A Systematic Review. *Journal of Occupational Rehabilitation, 26*(1), 56–69. DOI: 10.1007/s10926-015-9586-1 PMID: 26112400

Flippo, K., & Butterworth, J. (2018). Community Conversations and Transition Systems Change. *Journal of Disability Policy Studies, 29*(1), 7–11. DOI: 10.1177/1044207317739404

Freeze, S., Hall, A. C., Collins, S., Shumate, D., Thomas, C., & Brent, B. (2017). Different States, Common Issues: Moving mountains One Service at a Time. *Journal of Vocational Rehabilitation, 46*(3), 265–271. DOI: 10.3233/JVR-170861

Friedman, C., & Rizzolo, M. C. (2017). "Get Us Real Jobs:" Supported Employment Services for People With Intellectual and Developmental Disabilities In Medicaid Home and Community Based Services Waivers. *Journal of Vocational Rehabilitation, 46*(1), 107–116. DOI: 10.3233/JVR-160847

Fuertes, V., McQuaid, R., & Heidenreich, M. (2020). Institutional Logics of Service Provision: The National and Urban Governance of Activation Policies in Three European Countries. *Journal of European Social Policy, 31*(1), 92–107. DOI: 10.1177/0958928720974178

Grossi, T., Thomas, F., & Held, M. (2019). Making a Collective Impact: A School-to-Work Collaborative Model. *Journal of Vocational Rehabilitation*, *51*(3), 395–407. DOI: 10.3233/JVR-191054

Guerrero, A. M., Bennett, N. J., Wilson, K. A., Carter, N., Gill, D., Mills, M., Ives, C. D., Selinske, M. J., Larrosa, C., Bekessy, S., Januchowski-Hartley, F. A., Travers, H., Wyborn, C. A., & Nuno, A. (2018). Achieving the promise of integration in social-ecological research: A review and prospectus. *Ecology and Society*, *23*(3), art38. DOI: 10.5751/ES-10232-230338

Haines, K., Soldner, J. L., Zhang, L., Laurent, M.-L. S., Knabe, B., West-Evans, K., Mock, L., & Foley, S. (2018). Vocational Rehabilitation and Business Relations: Preliminary Indicators of State VR Agency Capacity. *Journal of Vocational Rehabilitation*, *48*(1), 133–145. DOI: 10.3233/JVR-170921

Hall, A. C., Butterworth, J., Winsor, J., Kramer, J. C., Nye-Lengerman, K., & Timmons, J. C. (2018). Building an Evidence-Based, Holistic Approach to Advancing Integrated Employment. *Research and Practice for Persons with Severe Disabilities : the Journal of TASH*, *43*(3), 207–218. DOI: 10.1177/1540796918787503

Hartman, E., Brinck, E. A., Anderson, C. A., & Hergenrather, K. C. (2025). Education and Pre-Employment Transition Service Predictors of Wages for Transition Age Youth With Disabilities. *Journal of Vocational Rehabilitation*, *63*(2), 147–159. DOI: 10.1177/10522263251356241

Huber, M. J., Oswald, G., Chan, F., Shaw, L. R., & Wilson, J. F. (2017). A Call for a National Evidence-Based Programs and Practices Registry in Vocational Rehabilitation. *Journal of Vocational Rehabilitation*, *46*(1), 11–18. DOI: 10.3233/JVR-160838

Iwanaga, K., Chen, X., Wu, J.-R., Lee, B., Chan, F., Bezyak, J., Grenawalt, T. A., & Tansey, T. N. (2018). Assessing Disability Inclusion Climate in the Workplace: A Brief Report. *Journal of Vocational Rehabilitation*, *49*(2), 265–271. DOI: 10.3233/JVR-180972

Jones-Parkin, T., Thomas, F., Hess, K., & Snyder, A. (2021). Employment First and Transition: Utah School-to-Work Initiative. *Journal of Vocational Rehabilitation*, *54*(3), 265–271. DOI: 10.3233/JVR-211135

Katz, H., & Sasson, U. (2017). Businesses, Nonprofits and Strategic Bridging: The Case of Workforce Integration in Israel. *Society and Business Review*, *12*(2), 121–135. DOI: 10.1108/SBR-05-2016-0034

Khoronzhevych, M., Maximova-Mentzoni, T., Gubrium, E., & Muller, A. E. (2021). Participant Engagement in Supported Employment: A Systematic Scoping Review. *Journal of Occupational Rehabilitation, 32*(3), 414–425. DOI: 10.1007/s10926-021-09987-2 PMID: 34086158

Kudla, A., Dinelli, E. J., Capraro, P., Crown, D., Sheth, M., Trierweiler, R., Munsell, E. G. S., Wong, J., & Heinemann, A. W. (2024). *Person-, Job-, and Environment-Related Factors Associated With Long-Term Job Retention of People With Physical Disabilities.* DOI: 10.21203/rs.3.rs-4797921/v1

Leahy, M. J., Valle, R. J. D., Landon, T. J., Iwanaga, K., Sherman, S. G., Reyes, A., & Chan, F. (2018). Promising and Evidence-Based Practices in Vocational Rehabilitation: Results of a National Delphi Study. *Journal of Vocational Rehabilitation, 48*(1), 37–48. DOI: 10.3233/JVR-170914

Lindsay, C., & Dutton, M. (2011). Promoting Healthy Routes Back to Work? Boundary Spanning Health Professionals and Employability Programmes in Great Britain. *Social Policy and Administration, 46*(5), 509–525. DOI: 10.1111/j.1467-9515.2011.00823.x

Müller, E., VanGilder, R., & Kiasi, D. (2018). Employer Satisfaction With Project SEARCH Interns, Hires, and Support Received From Project SEARCH Teams. *Journal of Vocational Rehabilitation, 49*(3), 339–350. DOI: 10.3233/JVR-180978

Nevala, N., Pehkonen, I., Teittinen, A., Vesala, H., Pörtfors, P., & Anttila, H. (2019). The Effectiveness of Rehabilitation Interventions on the Employment and Functioning of People With Intellectual Disabilities: A Systematic Review. *Journal of Occupational Rehabilitation, 29*(4), 773–802. DOI: 10.1007/s10926-019-09837-2 PMID: 31098847

Novak, J. A. (2015). Raising Expectations for U.S. Youth With Disabilities: Federal Disability Policy Advances Integrated Employment. *Center for Educational Policy Studies Journal, 5*(1), 91–110. DOI: 10.26529/cepsj.156

Persch, A., Cleary, D., Rutkowski, S., Malone, H. I., Darragh, A., & Case-Smith, J. (2015). Current Practices in Job Matching: A Project SEARCH Perspective on Transition. *Journal of Vocational Rehabilitation, 43*(3), 259–273. DOI: 10.3233/JVR-150774

Randall, K. N., Drew, H., Gilman, E., & Dixon, E. (2024). Assistive Technology Uses and Barriers in the Home and Workplace for Adults With Intellectual and Developmental Disabilities. *Journal of Applied Research in Intellectual Disabilities, 38*(1), e13306. Advance online publication. DOI: 10.1111/jar.13306 PMID: 39462768

Riesen, T., Morgan, R. L., & Griffin, C. (2015). Customized Employment: A Review Of the literature. *Journal of Vocational Rehabilitation*, *43*(3), 183–193. DOI: 10.3233/JVR-150768

Riesen, T., Snyder, A., Byers, R., Keeton, B., & Inge, K. J. (2022). An Updated Review of the Customized Employment Literature. *Journal of Vocational Rehabilitation*, *58*(1), 27–38. DOI: 10.3233/JVR-221222

Roux, A. M., Garfield, T., & Shattuck, P. (2019). Employment Policy and Autism: Analysis of State Workforce Innovation and Opportunity Act (WIOA) Implementation Plans. *Journal of Vocational Rehabilitation*, *51*(3), 285–298. DOI: 10.3233/JVR-191046

Scheef, A. R., Bruno, L., & Whittenburg, H. N. (2023). Supporting Positive Post-School Outcomes for Students With Disabilities in Rural Locations. *Rural Special Education Quarterly*, *43*(1), 36–43. DOI: 10.1177/87568705231214809

Shogren, K. A., Dean, E., Griffin, C., Steveley, J., Sickles, R., Wehmeyer, M. L., & Palmer, S. B. (2017). Promoting Change in Employment Supports: Impacts of a Community-Based Change Model. *Journal of Vocational Rehabilitation*, *47*(1), 19–24. DOI: 10.3233/JVR-170880

Shogren, K. A., Wehmeyer, M. L., Seo, H., Thompson, J. R., Schalock, R. L., Hughes, C., Little, T. D., & Palmer, S. B. (2017). Examining the Reliability and Validity of the Supports Intensity Scale–Children's Version in Children With Autism and Intellectual Disability. *Focus on Autism and Other Developmental Disabilities*, *32*(4), 293–304. DOI: 10.1177/1088357615625060

Smith, T. J., Dillahunt-Aspillaga, C., & Kenney, R. M. (2016). Implementation of Customized Employment Provisions of the Workforce Innovation and Opportunity Act Within Vocational Rehabilitation Systems. *Journal of Disability Policy Studies*, *27*(4), 195–202. DOI: 10.1177/1044207316644412

Swarbrick, M., Wilson, L., Becker, D., Swanson, S. J., Reese, S., & Bond, G. R. (2017). The Role of the Family Advocacy Team in Sustaining Supported Employment. *Journal of Vocational Rehabilitation*, *47*(1), 13–17. DOI: 10.3233/JVR-170879

Taylor, J. P., Avellone, L., Brooke, V., Wehman, P., Inge, K. J., Schall, C., & Iwanaga, K. (2022). The Impact of Competitive Integrated Employment on Economic, Psychological, and Physical Health Outcomes for Individuals With Intellectual and Developmental Disabilities. *Journal of Applied Research in Intellectual Disabilities*, *35*(2), 448–459. DOI: 10.1111/jar.12974 PMID: 34994035

Taylor, J. P., Avellone, L., Cimera, R. E., Brooke, V., Lambert, A., & Iwanaga, K. (2021). Cost-Benefit Analyses of Employment Services for Individuals With Intellectual and Developmental Disabilities: A Scoping Review. *Journal of Vocational Rehabilitation*, *54*(2), 193–206. DOI: 10.3233/JVR-201130

Taylor, J. P., & Whittenburg, H. (2024). The Promise and the Challenge of Pre-Employment Transition Services: The Workforce Innovation and Opportunity Act After Ten Years. *Journal of Vocational Rehabilitation*, *60*(2), 157–161. DOI: 10.3233/JVR-240002

Taylor, J. P., Whittenburg, H., Avellone, L., Rios, Y. C., Park, S., Poppen, M., & Tansey, T. (2024). The Impact of Pre-Employment Transition and Individualized Vocational Rehabilitation Services on Employment Outcomes for Youth With Disabilities. *Career Development and Transition for Exceptional Individuals*, *48*(2), 128–139. DOI: 10.1177/21651434241239967

Taylor, J. P., Whittenburg, H. N., Rooney-Kron, M., Gokita, T., Lau, S., Thoma, C. A., & Scott, L. A. (2021). Implementation of Pre–Employment Transition Services: A Content Analysis of Workforce Innovation and Opportunity Act State Plans. *Career Development and Transition for Exceptional Individuals*, *45*(2), 60–70. DOI: 10.1177/2165143421993027

Tucker, K., Feng, H., Gruman, C., & Crossen, L. (2017). Improving Competitive Integrated Employment for Youth and Young Adults With Disabilities: Findings From an Evaluation of Eight Partnerships in Employment Systems Change Projects. *Journal of Vocational Rehabilitation*, *47*(3), 277–294. DOI: 10.3233/JVR-170902

Vigna, E., Beyer, S., & Meek, A. (2023). A Demographic and Qualitative Analysis of the Determinants of Success in a National Supported Employment Project. *Journal of Applied Research in Intellectual Disabilities*, *36*(4), 787–795. DOI: 10.1111/jar.13094 PMID: 36919902

Vigna, E., Meek, A., & Beyer, S. (2024). Supported Employment, Quality of Jobs and Employment Typicalness: The Experience of the Engage to Change Project. *Journal of Applied Research in Intellectual Disabilities*, *37*(3), e13226. Advance online publication. DOI: 10.1111/jar.13226 PMID: 38520180

Wehman, P., Schall, C., Avellone, L., Brooke, A., Brooke, V., McDonough, J., & Whittenburg, H. N. (2021). *Achieving Competitive Integrated Employment for Individuals With Intellectual and Developmental Disabilities*. 333–355. DOI: 10.1037/0000195-013

Wehman, P., Taylor, J. P., Brooke, V., Avellone, L., Whittenburg, H. N., Ham, W., Brooke, A., & Carr, S. (2018). Toward Competitive Employment for Persons With Intellectual and Developmental Disabilities: What Progress Have We Made and Where Do We Need to Go. *Research and Practice for Persons with Severe Disabilities : the Journal of TASH*, *43*(3), 131–144. DOI: 10.1177/1540796918777730

Weltbank. (2022). Disability inclusion and accountability framework.

Chapter 13
Families, Guardians, and Self-Advocates: Partners in Employment

ABSTRACT

This chapter positions families, guardians, and self-advocates as essential partners within inclusive employment ecosystems for workers with intellectual disabilities (ID). Drawing on social capital, self-determination, and self-advocacy frameworks, it examines the multifaceted roles families play—providing emotional support, shaping employment trajectories, and navigating fragmented systems—while also addressing risks such as overprotection and constrained autonomy. Self-advocates are reframed as active agents whose voice and decision-making participation operationalize the principle of "nothing about us without us." Effective collaboration is achieved through structured communication, clear boundary setting, and co-produced planning that balances family involvement with worker autonomy. The chapter argues that sustainable inclusion requires relational ecosystems where families and self-advocates are recognized as integral stakeholders, not peripheral actors.

13.1 INTRODUCTION

Employment outcomes for workers with intellectual disabilities (ID) are increasingly understood not as the product of individual capacity or organizational practice alone, but as the result of complex, multi-layered social ecosystems in which families, guardians, and broader support networks play a central role. Across policy and practice frameworks, families are no longer viewed as peripheral actors but as core partners in shaping employment trajectories, influencing transitions to work, access to opportunities, and long-term employment sustainability (Garrels & Sigstad, 2023; Spencer et al., 2021). At the transition stage—from school to employment—

DOI: 10.4018/979-8-3373-9185-4.ch013

family involvement is particularly pronounced. Caregivers frequently assume lead roles in navigating fragmented systems, coordinating between education providers, vocational rehabilitation (VR) services, and employers. Qualitative evidence shows that families actively advocate for inclusive employment opportunities, seek out resources, and negotiate pathways that align with their aspirations for meaningful participation in the labor market (Garrels & Sigstad, 2023). However, this involvement often emerges not from structured system design but from necessity, as transitions are frequently described as inconsistent or "random" in the absence of coordinated policy frameworks (Garrels & Sigstad, 2023; Spencer et al., 2021).

This centrality of family involvement has led to a growing recognition within policy discourse that employment trajectories are co-constructed, shaped through ongoing interactions between individuals with ID, their families, and institutional systems. Policy frameworks increasingly emphasize family-inclusive transition planning, positioning caregivers as partners in goal-setting, decision-making, and service coordination (Spencer et al., 2021). Such approaches reflect a broader shift toward ecosystem-based models of employment, where outcomes depend on alignment across multiple actors rather than isolated interventions. Beyond transition, family influence extends across the lifespan, shaping employment decisions, access to supports, and workplace participation. Research indicates that even after individuals with ID enter postsecondary education or employment programs, families often remain involved in decisions related to job selection, working hours, benefits, and accommodations (Spencer et al., 2021). This sustained involvement reflects both the complexity of navigating employment systems and the enduring role of families as sources of support, advocacy, and stability. However, the influence of families is not uniform and is deeply shaped by policy environments and institutional contexts. Comparative studies demonstrate that in systems where inclusive employment is actively promoted—through supported employment programs and clear transition pathways—families are better positioned to advocate for and sustain participation in open labor markets (Peña-Quintana & Vega, 2022). Conversely, in contexts where policies favor segregated or sheltered employment, family efforts may be constrained by limited opportunities and systemic barriers, regardless of their aspirations for inclusion (Peña-Quintana & Vega, 2022). In addition to structural factors, family influence is also mediated by expectations, resources, and socio-economic conditions. Parental expectations regarding employment and independence have been shown to shape young people's aspirations and postsecondary plans, influencing their trajectories toward or away from competitive employment (Tucker et al., 2019). Families with greater access to information, education, and resources are often better equipped to navigate systems and advocate effectively, highlighting the role of social capital in shaping employment outcomes.

At the same time, the literature identifies important tensions within family involvement, particularly in relation to self-determination and autonomy. While families provide critical support and advocacy, their involvement can sometimes limit opportunities for independent decision-making if they assume primary control over employment choices (Spencer et al., 2021). This dual role—both enabling and constraining—underscores the need for balanced approaches that integrate family support with person-centered planning and supported decision-making frameworks. The emotional and practical demands placed on families further complicate their role. Caregivers frequently experience stress and uncertainty, particularly in navigating transitions, securing employment opportunities, and ensuring long-term stability for their family members with ID (Garrels & Sigstad, 2023). Policy analyses highlight the need for systems that not only engage families as partners but also support their well-being, recognizing that caregiver capacity directly influences employment outcomes (Majnemer et al., 2021). Beyond the immediate family, broader social support networks—including peers, coworkers, job coaches, and community organizations—also contribute to shaping employment trajectories. These networks provide practical assistance, emotional support, and access to opportunities, reinforcing the idea that employment outcomes are embedded within relational and social contexts (Shahin et al., 2020). Importantly, these networks interact with family involvement, either reinforcing or reshaping the role of families in employment processes.

The quality of employment outcomes is similarly influenced by the interaction between family involvement and workplace environments. Inclusive organizational cultures, supportive management practices, and accessible accommodations can enhance the effectiveness of family support by creating conditions where individuals with ID can thrive (Meacham et al., 2017). Conversely, unsupportive environments may place additional burdens on families, requiring them to compensate for gaps in workplace inclusion. Taken together, the evidence positions families as multifunctional actors within employment ecosystems, serving as advocates, coordinators, information brokers, and ongoing support providers. Their influence spans multiple stages of the employment trajectory, from early transition planning to long-term job retention and career development. However, this influence is not inherently positive or negative; rather, it is shaped by the interaction between family dynamics, policy frameworks, and organizational contexts.

This chapter builds on this understanding by examining how families, guardians, and self-advocates function as partners in employment, exploring both their contributions and the challenges associated with their involvement. It also considers how policy and practice can better integrate family engagement while safeguarding the autonomy and self-determination of individuals with ID. In doing so, the chapter advances a central argument: inclusive employment systems must move beyond individual- and organization-focused models to embrace relational and ecosystem-based approaches, in which families and social networks are recognized as integral components of sustainable employment outcomes for workers with intellectual disabilities.

13.2. CONCEPTUAL FOUNDATION

Understanding the role of families, guardians, and self-advocates in employment for workers with intellectual disabilities (ID) requires a robust theoretical grounding that moves beyond descriptive accounts toward integrated conceptual explanations. Three interrelated theoretical lenses—social capital theory, autonomy and self-determination frameworks, and self-advocacy models—provide a comprehensive foundation for explaining how relational dynamics, individual agency, and structural supports interact to shape employment outcomes. Together, these frameworks illuminate a central insight: employment inclusion is not solely an economic or organizational process but a relational and agentic phenomenon, mediated by networks, power dynamics, and the capacity of individuals with ID to exercise voice and choice within supported environments.

13.2.1 Social Capital and the Relational Foundations of Employment

Social capital theory offers a powerful lens for understanding how families and support networks influence employment inclusion. Broadly defined, social capital refers to the networks, relationships, and norms that enable access to resources and opportunities, including employment (Ellenkamp et al., 2015; Meacham et al., 2017). Within the context of intellectual disability, families function as key holders and mobilizers of social capital, acting as connectors, advocates, and mediators between individuals with ID and employment systems. Empirical evidence demonstrates that families often create bridging social capital, linking individuals with ID to employers, vocational rehabilitation (VR) services, job coaches, and community organizations. These connections are critical for accessing job opportunities, navigating recruitment processes, and sustaining employment over time (Voermans et al., 2023). In this sense, employment outcomes are not simply determined by individual qualifications but are significantly shaped by the density and quality of relational networks surrounding the individual. At the workplace level, social capital operates through interpersonal relationships and organizational climate. Interactions with coworkers, supervisors, and support staff contribute to a social environment that can either facilitate or hinder inclusion. Studies show that supportive workplace relationships—often reinforced by family engagement—are associated with improved job satisfaction, better performance, and increased retention among workers with ID (Flores et al., 2021). Importantly, social capital is not inherently positive; it is ambivalent and context-dependent. While family involvement can create pathways to employment, it can also reinforce dependency or limit exposure to broader opportunities, particularly when families favor sheltered or protected environments due to concerns about safety or discrimination (Voermans et al., 2023). This duality highlights that social capital can function both as a bridge to inclusion and a mechanism of constraint, depending on how it is mobilized within specific policy and cultural contexts. Furthermore, social capital operates across multiple levels:

- **Individual level**: enhancing motivation, confidence, and access to information
- **Organizational level**: shaping workplace climate and inclusion practices
- **Community level**: connecting individuals to broader employment ecosystems

This multi-level perspective underscores that inclusive employment is fundamentally a networked process, requiring alignment between personal relationships, organizational practices, and systemic supports (Voermans et al., 2023).

13.2.2 Autonomy, Self-Determination, and Supported Decision-Making

While social capital explains relational dynamics, autonomy and self-determination theories provide a framework for understanding individual agency within these relationships. Central to this perspective is Self-Determination Theory (SDT), which posits that human well-being and motivation are driven by the fulfillment of three basic psychological needs: autonomy, competence, and relatedness (C. B. Gilson et al., 2022). In employment contexts for workers with ID, these needs are particularly salient. Autonomy refers to the ability to make meaningful choices about work; competence involves the capacity to perform tasks effectively; and relatedness reflects the quality of social connections in the workplace. Research shows that when these needs are met, individuals with ID are more likely to experience higher job satisfaction, stronger engagement, and more sustainable employment outcomes (C. B. Gilson et al., 2022). The Psychology of Working Theory (PWT) complements SDT by emphasizing the role of work as a source of dignity, social connection, and economic participation. Within this framework, access to meaningful work is not only a matter of employment but also a fundamental component of social inclusion and human development (C. B. Gilson et al., 2022). A critical extension of these theories in the context of intellectual disability is the concept of supported decision-making (SDM), which aligns with the principles of the United Nations Convention on the Rights of Persons with Disabilities (CRPD). SDM recognizes that individuals with ID may require support in decision-making but asserts that such support should enhance, rather than replace, their autonomy. Within employment contexts, SDM involves practices such as:

- Facilitating informed choices about job roles and tasks
- Supporting communication of preferences and needs
- Ensuring that decisions reflect the individual's will and consent

This framework directly addresses the tension between family involvement and autonomy. While families often play a crucial role in supporting decision-making, SDM emphasizes that their involvement must be structured in ways that preserve the agency of the individual, avoiding substitution of preferences. Transition-to-work literature further reinforces the importance of autonomy-supportive environments. Programs that integrate person-centered planning, family engagement, and workplace supports are more effective in fostering self-determination and successful employment outcomes (Zidan et al., 2025). These findings highlight that autonomy is not achieved in isolation but is co-constructed through supportive relationships and inclusive environments. Additionally, frameworks such as the Job Demands–Resources (JD-R) model and social exchange theory provide insights into how workplace conditions influence autonomy and well-being. Supportive job resources—including training, accommodations, and positive relationships—enhance motivation and job satisfaction, while inclusive social exchanges foster trust and engagement (Flores et al., 2021).

13.2.3 Self-Advocacy as Agency in Practice

While autonomy theory provides a conceptual foundation, self-advocacy represents its practical expression in real-world contexts. Self-advocacy is defined as the ability of individuals with ID to understand their strengths and needs, articulate their preferences, and actively participate in decisions affecting their lives, including employment (Miller et al., 2022). Importantly, self-advocacy is not an individual trait alone but a relational and contextual process, shaped by opportunities, supports, and organizational practices. It is operationalized through four key domains:

- Knowledge of self (strengths, preferences, needs)
- Knowledge of rights
- Communication skills
- Leadership and participation in decision-making

Within employment policies and practices, self-advocacy is increasingly recognized as a core competency and outcome, particularly in transition programs and supported employment models. Programs emphasize the development of self-advocacy skills through person-centered planning, discovery processes, and real-world decision-making experiences (Reynders et al., 2024). A central mechanism for operationalizing self-advocacy is person-centered discovery, where individuals with ID actively define their interests, goals, and support needs. This process ensures that employment pathways are aligned with the individual's preferences rather than externally imposed expectations (Christianson-Barker et al., 2025). Self-advocacy is also closely linked to customized employment (CE) practices, where individuals play an active role in shaping job design and negotiating roles with employers. Evidence suggests that CE enhances both autonomy and employment outcomes by aligning job tasks with individual strengths while maintaining worker agency (Wehman et al., 2021). In recent years, self-advocacy has expanded into digital and multimedia domains, with technologies enabling individuals to express preferences, access information, and engage in decision-making processes more effectively (Watts et al., 2023). These developments highlight the evolving nature of self-advocacy as both a skill and a system-supported process. However, the literature also identifies tensions in the operationalization of self-advocacy. Family and support networks can either facilitate or constrain self-advocacy, depending on how decision-making power is distributed. When families dominate decisions, self-advocacy may be limited; when they act as facilitators, it can be strengthened (Voermans et al., 2023).

Bringing these frameworks together reveals a complex but coherent conceptual model. Social capital theory explains how relationships and networks shape access to employment opportunities. Autonomy and self-determination theories illuminate the importance of individual agency and psychological needs. Self-advocacy frameworks operationalize these concepts into actionable practices within employment contexts. The central insight emerging from this integration is that employment inclusion for workers with ID depends on a dynamic balance between relational support and individual agency. Families and networks provide essential resources and support, but these must be aligned with practices that center the voice, preferences, and autonomy of the individual. This balance is not static but must be continuously negotiated within policy, organizational, and interpersonal contexts. Effective systems are those that:

- Leverage social capital to expand opportunities
- Create autonomy-supportive environments
- Embed self-advocacy within everyday practices

At the same time, the literature highlights ongoing tensions, including:

- The risk of family overreach or gatekeeping

- Variability in policy and cultural contexts
- Limited operational models for supported decision-making at scale

Addressing these challenges requires intentional design of policies and practices that integrate family involvement while safeguarding autonomy, supported by training, governance structures, and accountability mechanisms. In sum, this conceptual foundation positions families, guardians, and self-advocates not as separate actors but as interdependent components of an inclusive employment system, where relationships and agency are mutually constitutive. This perspective provides the theoretical grounding for subsequent sections of the chapter, which examine how these dynamics are enacted in practice and how they can be optimized to support meaningful and sustainable employment outcomes.

13.3. ROLES OF FAMILIES AND GUARDIANS

Families and guardians occupy a central, multifaceted position in shaping the employment experiences of workers with intellectual disabilities (ID). Their roles extend beyond emotional support into domains of advocacy, decision-making, and practical facilitation, positioning them as both enablers and, at times, constraints within inclusive employment systems. The literature consistently highlights that family involvement operates through complex mechanisms that influence job access, workplace integration, performance, and long-term career trajectories (Shahin et al., 2020). This section examines three interrelated dimensions of family roles: emotional support, decision-making influence, and potential barriers such as overprotection, emphasizing the nuanced and context-dependent nature of their involvement.

13.3.1 Emotional Support as a Foundation for Employment Participation

Emotional support provided by families constitutes a foundational mechanism through which individuals with ID engage with employment opportunities. Across studies, families are identified as primary sources of encouragement, confidence-building, and psychological stability, which are essential for navigating the uncertainties of entering and sustaining employment (Meacham et al., 2017). This support is particularly critical during transitions from education to work, where individuals often face unfamiliar environments, new expectations, and potential social barriers. Families provide reassurance and continuity, helping individuals to develop self-confidence and resilience, which in turn enhances their readiness to participate in the workforce (Meacham et al., 2017). Emotional backing also reinforces motivation, enabling individuals to persist through challenges such as workplace adaptation, task learning, and social integration. Beyond individual-level effects, emotional support contributes to shaping workplace relationships and social climate. When families actively engage with employers and support services, they often legitimize the presence of workers with ID in the workplace, fostering acceptance and positive attitudes among coworkers and supervisors (Meacham et al., 2017). This relational dynamic enhances inclusion by creating an environment in which workers feel valued and supported. Moreover, emotional support is closely linked to job satisfaction and well-being. Workers with ID who experience strong support networks—including family involvement—report higher levels of satisfaction, greater sense of belonging, and improved socio-emotional outcomes. These factors are critical for long-term retention, as emotional well-being is strongly associated with sustained engagement in employment. However, emotional support is not merely passive encouragement; it is often intertwined with active involvement in problem-solving and adaptation. Families frequently assist in addressing workplace challenges, facilitating communication, and coordinating with job coaches or employers to ensure that support needs are met (Wehman et al., 2021). In this sense, emotional support operates as both a psychological and practical resource, bridging personal resilience with systemic navigation.

13.3.2 Decision-Making Influence and Shaping Employment Trajectories

Families and guardians exert significant influence over employment trajectories through their involvement in decision-making processes, including career planning, job selection, and transitions into employment. This influence is particularly pronounced in contexts where individuals with ID rely on support for navigating complex systems or where guardians hold formal decision-making authority. One of the most consistent findings across the literature is the role of parental expectations in shaping employment outcomes. Higher expectations for competitive, integrated employment are strongly associated with increased likelihood of individuals securing and maintaining such positions (K.-M. Gilson et al., 2018). Families who actively advocate for inclusive employment pathways often facilitate access to opportunities that might otherwise remain inaccessible. Decision-making influence is also evident in job matching and career planning. Families contribute valuable knowledge about the individual's strengths, preferences, and support needs, which can enhance the alignment between the worker and the job environment (Yon-Hernández et al., 2025). This collaborative approach is particularly effective when integrated into structured processes such as supported employment and transition planning, where families, job coaches, and employers work together to identify suitable roles.

Furthermore, families play a critical role in navigating systems and coordinating supports. Employment systems for individuals with ID are often fragmented, requiring coordination across multiple agencies and services. Families frequently act as intermediaries, ensuring continuity of support, accessing resources, and advocating for necessary accommodations (Peña-Quintana & Vega, 2022). This coordination function is essential for both initial job access and ongoing employment stability. In addition, families contribute to practical decision-making related to logistics, such as transportation, scheduling, and workplace adjustments. These factors are often decisive in determining whether individuals can access and sustain employment, particularly in contexts where infrastructure or services are limited (Shahin et al., 2020). However, decision-making influence is not without complexity. The literature highlights that effective decision-making requires alignment between family perspectives, worker preferences, and organizational realities. When these elements are aligned, employment outcomes are more likely to be positive and sustainable. Conversely, misalignment can lead to inappropriate job placements, reduced satisfaction, and challenges in retention. Importantly, the role of families in decision-making must be understood within the broader framework of supported decision-making and autonomy, as discussed in the previous section. While families provide essential support, their involvement should ideally function as a facilitator of the individual's voice rather than a substitute for it.

13.3.3 Barriers and Risks: Overprotection and Constrained Opportunities

While family involvement is often beneficial, the literature also identifies significant barriers and risks associated with certain forms of family engagement, particularly overprotection and low expectations. These dynamics can inadvertently constrain opportunities and limit the development of independence for individuals with ID. Overprotection is frequently cited as a key barrier. Families, motivated by concerns about safety, discrimination, or workplace demands, may discourage participation in competitive employment or favor more controlled environments such as sheltered workshops (Shahin et al., 2020). While these concerns are often valid, they can result in restricted exposure to opportunities and reduced likelihood of transitioning into integrated employment. Low expectations represent another critical constraint. When families do not believe that individuals with ID are capable of participating in competitive employment, they may not pursue or support opportunities that align with inclusive employment goals (Gilson et al., 2018). This can lead to self-fulfilling outcomes, where limited expectations translate into limited opportunities and outcomes.

The literature also highlights the risk of decision-making dominance, where families assume primary control over employment-related decisions, potentially undermining the autonomy and self-determination of the individual. In such cases, the worker's preferences may be overshadowed by family priorities, leading to mismatches between job roles and individual aspirations. Additionally, practical constraints such as transportation dependence can reinforce reliance on family support, limiting independence and flexibility in employment participation (Shahin et al., 2020). While families often provide essential logistical support, reliance on such support can create vulnerabilities, particularly if family circumstances change. Importantly, these barriers are not inherent to family involvement but are shaped by contextual factors, including policy environments, availability of supports, and cultural attitudes toward disability. In systems where inclusive employment is well-supported and resources are accessible, families are more likely to adopt enabling roles. Conversely, in contexts with limited support, families may adopt more protective strategies as a response to systemic constraints (Peña-Quintana & Vega, 2022). The evidence across studies converges on a nuanced understanding of family roles as both enabling and constraining, depending on how support is structured and enacted. Families provide essential emotional, practical, and advocacy support that enhances employment access, retention, and performance. At the same time, certain dynamics—such as overprotection or misaligned expectations—can limit opportunities and autonomy.

This duality underscores the need for balanced approaches that:

- Recognize families as critical partners in employment systems
- Support their involvement through structured collaboration
- Safeguard the autonomy and preferences of individuals with ID

Effective policies and practices therefore require mechanisms that align family involvement with person-centered and autonomy-supportive frameworks, ensuring that support enhances rather than constrains participation. In this sense, families and guardians should be understood not as external influences but as integral components of inclusive employment ecosystems, whose roles must be carefully integrated, supported, and guided within broader policy and organizational frameworks.

13.4. SELF-ADVOCATES

Self-advocates—individuals with intellectual disabilities (ID) who actively express their preferences, rights, and aspirations—are increasingly recognized as central agents in shaping their own employment trajectories. Contemporary policy and practice frameworks emphasize that inclusive employment cannot be achieved without meaningful participation of workers themselves, captured in the principle "nothing about us without us." This principle reframes individuals with ID not as passive recipients of support but as active decision-makers and contributors within employment systems (Balcázar & Suarez-Balcazar, 2017). This section examines three core dimensions of self-advocacy in employment contexts: agency and voice, participation in decision-making, and empowerment, highlighting how these elements interact with policy, organizational practices, and support systems to influence employment outcomes.

13.4.1 Agency and Voice: From Passive Recipients to Active Participants

At the core of self-advocacy is the concept of agency, defined as the capacity of individuals to make choices and act upon them in ways that shape their lives. In employment contexts, agency is expressed through the ability to articulate preferences, identify support needs, and engage in workplace interactions that reflect personal goals and values (Iwanaga et al., 2021). The literature consistently demonstrates that stronger self-advocacy skills are associated with improved employment outcomes, including higher job satisfaction, better alignment between job roles and individual strengths, and increased employment stability (Iwanaga et al., 2021). These outcomes arise because self-advocacy enables individuals to actively shape their work environments rather than passively adapting to them. Agency is also closely linked to voice, which refers to the ability to communicate needs, preferences, and concerns within workplace and policy contexts. Effective voice requires not only individual skills—such as communication and self-awareness—but also responsive environments that recognize and value the contributions of workers with ID (Sousa et al., 2024). Importantly, agency and voice are not solely individual attributes; they are relationally constructed. Opportunities to exercise voice depend on interactions with employers, coworkers, families, and service providers. When these actors create inclusive and supportive environments, individuals with ID are more likely to express themselves and participate actively in workplace processes (Ellenkamp et al., 2015). However, the literature also highlights that agency can be constrained by structural and cultural barriers, including limited access to information, lack of accommodations, and organizational practices that exclude workers from decision-making processes. These barriers underscore the need for systemic approaches that enable, rather than restrict, the expression of agency.

13.4.2 Decision-Making Participation: Operationalizing "Nothing About Us Without Us"

Participation in decision-making is the practical realization of self-advocacy. It involves the active involvement of individuals with ID in decisions related to employment pathways, job design, accommodations, and career development. This participation is central to the principle of "nothing about us without us," which calls for direct inclusion of individuals in processes that affect their lives (Phillips, 2011). Evidence indicates that when individuals with ID are involved in decision-making, employment outcomes improve across multiple dimensions. Participation enables better alignment between job roles and individual capabilities, enhances motivation, and fosters a sense of ownership over employment trajectories (Iwanaga et al., 2021). In practice, decision-making participation is operationalized through several mechanisms:

- Person-centered planning, where individuals define their goals and preferences
- Supported decision-making frameworks, which provide assistance without removing agency
- Collaborative workplace practices, such as involving workers in accommodation planning and performance reviews

These approaches ensure that decisions are informed by the lived experiences and perspectives of workers with ID, rather than imposed by external actors. Policy environments play a critical role in enabling decision-making participation. Frameworks such as Employment First initiatives and CRPD-aligned policies explicitly promote the inclusion of individuals with ID in planning, evaluation, and governance processes (Rogan & Rinne, 2021). These policies institutionalize participation, transforming it from an optional practice into a systemic requirement. At the organizational level, participatory practices include:

- Involving workers in job design and task allocation
- Including them in accommodation discussions
- Engaging them in feedback and performance evaluation processes

Such practices not only enhance individual outcomes but also contribute to more inclusive workplace cultures. However, the literature identifies ongoing challenges in fully realizing participatory decision-making. Organizational hierarchies, time constraints, and lack of training can limit the extent to which workers with ID are genuinely included in decision processes (Betz, 2023). In some cases, participation may be symbolic rather than substantive, highlighting the need for accountability mechanisms to ensure meaningful engagement.

13.4.3 Empowerment: Building Capacity and Transforming Systems

Empowerment represents the broader outcome of self-advocacy, encompassing the development of skills, confidence, and opportunities necessary for individuals with ID to exercise control over their employment and life choices. It is both an individual and systemic process, requiring the alignment of personal capacities with supportive environments. Research shows that empowerment is strongly linked to self-advocacy training and real-world practice opportunities. Programs that teach individuals how to request accommodations, communicate effectively, and participate in decision-making processes lead to significant improvements in autonomy and workplace participation (Grenwelge & Zhang, 2012). Effective empowerment strategies include:

- Structured self-advocacy training programs
- Work-based learning and transition supports
- Individualized employment planning
- Peer mentoring and leadership development initiatives

These approaches emphasize experiential learning, allowing individuals to practice self-advocacy in real-world contexts and develop confidence in their abilities (Zidan et al., 2025).

Empowerment is further supported by tools and technologies that facilitate communication and information sharing. Digital tools, such as electronic transition platforms and multimedia advocacy resources, enable individuals to express their preferences, document their needs, and engage with employers more effectively (Watts et al., 2023). At the policy level, empowerment is reinforced through frameworks that recognize self-advocacy as a measurable outcome of employment programs. Employment First policies, for example, promote the inclusion of self-advocates in governance structures, ensuring that their perspectives inform policy development and evaluation (Rogan & Rinne, 2021). However, empowerment cannot be achieved through individual capacity-building alone. The literature emphasizes that empowerment requires organizational readiness and systemic support, including:

- Employer awareness and training

- Accessible workplace environments
- Availability of accommodations and supports

Without these conditions, self-advocacy efforts may not translate into meaningful outcomes, placing undue responsibility on individuals rather than addressing structural barriers (Gross et al., 2020). The synthesis of evidence highlights that self-advocacy is not merely about expression but about power—specifically, the ability to influence decisions and shape outcomes. Agency, participation, and empowerment are interconnected dimensions that collectively enable individuals with ID to move from passive recipients of support to active agents within employment systems. At the same time, the literature underscores that self-advocacy must be understood within a relational and systemic context. Effective self-advocacy depends on:

- Supportive relationships with families, employers, and service providers
- Inclusive organizational cultures
- Enabling policy environments

This perspective reinforces that responsibility for inclusion does not rest solely with individuals with ID. Instead, it requires shared accountability across systems, ensuring that environments are designed to support agency and participation. A key tension emerges in balancing self-advocacy with support structures, particularly family involvement. While families can enhance self-advocacy by facilitating communication and access to resources, they can also constrain it if they dominate decision-making processes. This tension highlights the importance of supported decision-making frameworks that preserve the individual's voice while leveraging relational support. Ultimately, the principle of "nothing about us without us" provides a guiding framework for integrating self-advocacy into employment policies and practices. It calls for a shift from tokenistic inclusion to meaningful participation and shared decision-making, where individuals with ID are recognized as legitimate stakeholders in all aspects of employment. The literature converges on a clear conclusion: self-advocacy is a critical driver of inclusive employment outcomes, influencing job access, satisfaction, retention, and long-term career development. However, its effectiveness depends on the interaction between individual skills and systemic conditions. To fully realize the potential of self-advocacy, policies and practices must:

- Embed participatory decision-making at all levels
- Provide structured training and real-world opportunities
- Ensure organizational and environmental readiness
- Align family and stakeholder involvement with worker autonomy

In this sense, self-advocacy represents both a personal capability and a systemic principle, requiring coordinated efforts across individuals, organizations, and policy frameworks. This section completes the conceptual and practical balance of the chapter: while families and guardians provide essential support, self-advocates bring agency, voice, and direction, ensuring that employment systems are not only inclusive but also responsive to the aspirations and rights of workers with intellectual disabilities.

13.5. CORE PRACTICES

Effective collaboration among families, guardians, self-advocates, and professionals in inclusive employment does not occur organically; it requires intentional design of practices, communication systems, and governance structures. The literature consistently emphasizes that successful inclusion depends on how relationships are managed, particularly in terms of communication, boundary-setting, and collaborative planning (Khayatzadeh-Mahani et al., 2020). This section outlines three core practices that operationalize inclusive partnership models: communication strategies, boundary setting, and collaborative planning, highlighting how these elements interact to create coherent and sustainable employment systems for workers with intellectual disabilities (ID).

13.5.1 Communication Strategies: Building Shared Understanding and Alignment

Communication is the foundational mechanism through which stakeholders align expectations, coordinate actions, and sustain inclusive employment practices. The literature consistently demonstrates that proactive, structured, and ongoing communication is essential for effective collaboration between families, self-advocates, and professionals (Schutz et al., 2021). A key principle is the need for early and continuous information sharing, particularly during transition phases from education to employment. Families benefit from timely access to information about employment pathways, available supports, and organizational expectations, which reduces uncertainty and enables more informed participation in planning processes (Schutz et al., 2021). Regular communication channels—such as scheduled meetings, progress updates, and shared documentation—help maintain alignment across stakeholders and prevent fragmentation of support. Beyond frequency, the quality and framing of communication are equally important. Evidence suggests that communication should adopt a strengths-based perspective, emphasizing capabilities and potential rather than deficits. This approach not only shapes expectations but also reinforces a shared vision of employment as a normative and achievable outcome for individuals with ID (Garrels & Sigstad, 2021). Participatory communication models further enhance effectiveness by involving families and self-advocates in co-design processes. Co-produced strategies—such as jointly developed transition plans, workplace tools, and support mechanisms—are more likely to be relevant, accepted, and successfully implemented (Baine et al., 2024). Similarly, stakeholder engagement approaches, including workshops, consultations, and policy dialogues, strengthen legitimacy and uptake of inclusive practices (Khayatzadeh-Mahani et al., 2020). Importantly, communication must also address sensitive domains, such as personal boundaries, autonomy, and workplace relationships. The literature highlights the need for rights-based, consent-centered communication, particularly when navigating issues that involve dignity and personal agency. Practitioners must balance family involvement with the individual's right to privacy and self-determination, ensuring that communication practices do not inadvertently reinforce dependency or infantilization (Belluzzo et al., 2025). Finally, effective communication systems recognize the need for multi-channel engagement. Providing parallel but connected communication streams—for example, worker-centered planning meetings alongside family-focused updates—ensures that all stakeholders remain informed while maintaining a clear focus on the individual's voice (Schutz et al., 2021).

13.5.2 Boundary Setting: Balancing Collaboration and Autonomy

While collaboration is essential, it must be accompanied by clear boundaries to prevent role confusion, overreach, and unintended constraints on autonomy. The literature identifies boundary setting as a critical practice for maintaining ethical, effective, and sustainable partnerships (Hanson et al., 2023). A central element of boundary setting is the explicit delineation of roles and responsibilities among families, professionals, and self-advocates. Organizational policies and practice guidelines should clearly define:

- The scope of family involvement
- The responsibilities of professionals (e.g., job coaches, supervisors)
- The decision-making authority of the individual with ID

Such clarity reduces ambiguity and ensures that each stakeholder contributes in a complementary rather than conflicting manner (Hanson et al., 2023). Ecological frameworks further support boundary setting by situating roles within multiple system levels—from the immediate workplace (microsystem) to broader policy environments (macrosystem). This perspective helps organizations understand where family input is appropriate and where professional responsibilities should remain distinct (Hanson et al., 2023). A key practice within boundary setting is the implementation of shared decision-making with safeguards. While families and professionals provide valuable input, decision-making processes must prioritize the preferences and autonomy of the individual, aligning with self-determination principles discussed earlier (C. B. Gilson et al., 2022). This requires mechanisms to ensure that the individual's voice is not overshadowed by other stakeholders. Training plays a crucial role in supporting boundary management. Staff, supervisors, and job coaches need guidance on:

- Managing family involvement appropriately
- Maintaining confidentiality and consent
- Navigating ethical dilemmas and role conflicts

Such training ensures that boundary setting is not only a policy requirement but also a practiced competency within organizations (Joseph & Wilson, 2024). The literature also highlights the importance of addressing potential conflicts of interest, particularly when family expectations differ from workplace realities. Mechanisms such as neutral facilitators, independent coordinators, or structured mediation processes can help resolve conflicts while protecting the interests and autonomy of the worker (Schwartzman et al., 2023). Importantly, boundary setting should not be interpreted as limiting collaboration. Rather, it creates the conditions for effective and respectful partnership, where roles are clear, expectations are aligned, and the individual remains at the center of decision-making.

13.5.3 Collaborative Planning: Co-Producing Inclusive Employment Pathways

Collaborative planning represents the integration of communication and boundary-setting into coordinated, action-oriented processes. It involves the joint development of employment pathways, support strategies, and workplace practices by families, self-advocates, and professionals. The literature identifies co-production and participatory planning as central to effective inclusive employment practices. When stakeholders collaboratively design programs, policies, and workplace supports, outcomes are more likely to reflect the real needs and preferences of individuals with ID (Khayatzadeh-Mahani et al., 2020). One prominent model is the use of integrated transition and postsecondary programs, where families, educators, employers, and self-advocates work together to support movement into employment. These programs emphasize ongoing collaboration, social network development, and self-determination, resulting in more sustainable employment outcomes (Baine et al., 2024). Similarly, stakeholder-engaged frameworks, such as integrated knowledge translation (IKT), demonstrate how structured collaboration can produce shared understanding and coordinated action. Through consensus-building processes—such as workshops and policy dialogues—stakeholders collectively identify challenges and develop solutions, enhancing both relevance and implementation success (Khayatzadeh-Mahani et al., 2020). Participatory action research (PAR) extends this approach by involving self-advocates as co-researchers and co-designers, ensuring that lived experience informs both practice and policy. This model exemplifies how collaboration can move beyond consultation toward shared ownership and accountability (Perez-y-Perez et al., 2024). Another practical framework is the UNITE model (Understand, Navigate, Invest, Train, Elevate), which provides structured guidance for engaging families, self-advocates, and employers across the employment lifecycle. This model emphasizes continuous collaboration, targeted support, and capacity-building as key elements of sustainable inclusion (Baine et al., 2024).

Across these models, several common elements emerge:

- Shared goals and vision for inclusive employment
- Clear roles and responsibilities supported by boundary-setting practices
- Ongoing communication and feedback loops
- Mechanisms for accountability and evaluation

Importantly, collaborative planning must remain adaptive and context-sensitive. Different organizational, cultural, and policy contexts require tailored approaches that preserve core principles—such as participation, autonomy, and shared responsibility—while allowing flexibility in implementation (Hanson et al., 2023). The integration of communication strategies, boundary setting, and collaborative planning reveals a broader shift from traditional service delivery models toward co-governance in inclusive employment systems. In this model, families, self-advocates, and professionals are not merely participants but partners in designing, implementing, and evaluating employment practices. Effective systems are characterized by:

- Transparent and structured communication that aligns stakeholders
- Clear and ethical boundaries that protect autonomy and clarify roles
- Collaborative planning processes that co-produce inclusive solutions

At the same time, the literature underscores that collaboration must be carefully managed to avoid unintended consequences, such as role confusion or diminished autonomy. The most effective approaches are those that balance inclusivity with structure, ensuring that all voices are heard while maintaining clarity and accountability. Ultimately, core practices in inclusive employment are not isolated techniques but part of an integrated relational infrastructure that supports sustainable outcomes. By embedding these practices within organizational systems, policymakers and practitioners can move beyond fragmented efforts toward coherent, inclusive, and person-centered employment ecosystems.

REFERENCES

Baine, C., Gilson, C. B., & Hashemi, H. (2024). The Bridge to Somewhere: How Practitioners Can UNITE to Support Adults With Extensive Support Needs in Inclusive Employment Opportunities. *In Practice*, *4*(1–2), 17–26. DOI: 10.1177/27324745241295727

Balcázar, F. E., & Suarez-Balcazar, Y. (2017). *Promoting Empowerment Among Individuals With Disabilities.* 571–585. DOI: 10.1037/14954-034

Belluzzo, M., Giaquinto, V., Volpe, D., Esposito, C., Alfieri, E., & Amodeo, A. L. (2025). Navigating Body Perception, Affectivity, Intimacy, Gender Identity, and Sexuality: An Exploratory Qualitative Study in Young Adults With SMI, IDs, and ASD in a Community Setting. *International Journal of Environmental Research and Public Health*, *22*(5), 722. DOI: 10.3390/ijerph22050722 PMID: 40427837

Betz, C. L. (2023). Health Care Transition Planning for Adolescents and Emerging Adults With Intellectual Disabilities and Developmental Disabilities: Distinctions and Challenges. *Journal for Specialists in Pediatric Nursing*, *28*(3), e12415. Advance online publication. DOI: 10.1111/jspn.12415 PMID: 37380603

Christianson-Barker, J., Franzius, A., Mills, R. A., Lomness, A., & Hole, R. (2025). Employing Strength: A Scoping Review of Customized Employment Practices to Support Inclusive Employment for People With Intellectual Disabilities. *Journal of Vocational Rehabilitation*, *63*(2), 119–140. DOI: 10.1177/10522263251356445

Ellenkamp, J. J. H., Brouwers, E., Embregts, P. J. C. M., Joosen, M., & Weeghel, J. (2015). Work Environment-Related Factors in Obtaining and Maintaining Work in a Competitive Employment Setting for Employees With Intellectual Disabilities: A Systematic Review. *Journal of Occupational Rehabilitation*, *26*(1), 56–69. DOI: 10.1007/s10926-015-9586-1 PMID: 26112400

Flores, N., Moret-Tatay, C., Gutiérrez-Bermejo, B., Vázquez-Martínez, A., & Río, C. J. (2021). Assessment of Occupational Health and Job Satisfaction in Workers With Intellectual Disability: A Job Demands–Resources Perspective. *International Journal of Environmental Research and Public Health*, *18*(4), 2072. DOI: 10.3390/ijerph18042072 PMID: 33672616

Garrels, V., & Sigstad, H. M. H. (2021). Employment for Persons With Intellectual Disability in the Nordic Countries: A Scoping Review. *Journal of Applied Research in Intellectual Disabilities*, *34*(4), 993–1007. DOI: 10.1111/jar.12880 PMID: 33709541

Garrels, V., & Sigstad, H. M. H. (2023). Caregivers' Experiences With School–Work Transitions for Their Children With Disorders of Intellectual Development. *International Journal of Environmental Research and Public Health, 20*(3), 1892. DOI: 10.3390/ijerph20031892 PMID: 36767259

Gilson, C. B., Sinclair, J., Whirley, M. L., Li, Y., & Blustein, D. L. (2022). "More Than a Job, It's a Purpose": A Psychology of Working Perspective of the Working Experiences for Individuals With Intellectual and Developmental Disabilities. *Journal of Career Assessment, 30*(2), 367–386. DOI: 10.1177/10690727211048898

Gilson, K.-M., Johnson, S., Davis, E., Brunton, S., Swift, E., Reddihough, D., & Williams, K. (2018). Supporting the mental health of mothers of children with a disability: Health professional perceptions of need, role, and challenges. *Child: Care, Health and Development, 44*(5), 721–729. DOI: 10.1111/cch.12589 PMID: 30133770

Grenwelge, C., & Zhang, D. (2012). The Effects of the Texas Youth Leadership Forum Summer Training on the Self-Advocacy Abilities of High School Students With Disabilities. *Journal of Disability Policy Studies, 24*(3), 158–169. DOI: 10.1177/1044207312457415

Gross, J. M. S., Monroe-Gulick, A., Nye, C., Davidson-Gibbs, D., & Dedrick, D. (2020). Multifaceted Interventions for Supporting Community Participation Among Adults With Disabilities: A Systematic Review. *Campbell Systematic Reviews, 16*(2), e1092. Advance online publication. DOI: 10.1002/cl2.1092 PMID: 37131415

Hanson, S. L., Bruyère, S. M., Forber-Pratt, A. J., Reesman, J., & Sung, C. (2023). Guidelines for Assessment and Intervention With Persons With Disabilities: An Executive Summary. *The American Psychologist, 78*(8), 995–1009. DOI: 10.1037/amp0001150 PMID: 36931825

Iwanaga, K., Chan, F., Anderson, C., Ditchman, N., Kaya, C., Hartman, E., & Tansey, T. N. (2021). Demographic, Transition, and Vocational Rehabilitation Service Variables' Association With High School Completion Outcomes of Youth With Disabilities Receiving SSI. *Rehabilitation Counseling Bulletin, 65*(1), 23–36. DOI: 10.1177/0034355220970543

Joseph, J., & Wilson, R. (2024). Enhancing Disability Nursing Practice in Australia: Addressing Educational Preparedness. *International Journal of Mental Health Nursing, 33*(6), 1637–1665. DOI: 10.1111/inm.13373 PMID: 38873821

Khayatzadeh-Mahani, A., Wittevrongel, K., Nicholas, D. B., & Zwicker, J. D. (2020). Prioritizing barriers and solutions to improve employment for persons with developmental disabilities. *Disability and Rehabilitation, 42*(19), 2696–2706. DOI: 10.1080/09638288.2019.1570356 PMID: 30856355

Majnemer, A., McGrath, P. J., Baumbusch, J., Camden, C., Fallon, B., Lunsky, Y., Miller, S. P., Sansone, G., Stainton, T., Sumarah, J., Thomson, D., & Zwicker, J. (2021). Time to Be Counted: COVID-19 and Intellectual and Developmental Disabilities—an RSC Policy Briefing. *Facets*, *6*, 1337–1389. DOI: 10.1139/facets-2021-0038

Meacham, H., Cavanagh, J., Shaw, A., & Bartram, T. (2017). HRM practices that support the employment and social inclusion of workers with an intellectual disability. *Personnel Review*, *46*(8), 1475–1492. DOI: 10.1108/PR-05-2016-0105

Miller, A. L., Frye, D., Green, T., Mitchell, C., Garcia, G. A., Huereña, J., Moore, T. O., & Turnage, V. (2022). (Re)defining Their Place at the Table: Frank Discussions by Adults With Disabilities on Contemporary Self-advocacy. *Journal of Applied Research in Intellectual Disabilities*, *35*(3), 777–788. DOI: 10.1111/jar.12981 PMID: 35098612

Peña-Quintana, M. T., & Vega, L. E. S. (2022). The Transition to Employment in Wales and the Canary Islands for People With Intellectual Disabilities: Supported Employment. *Education Sciences*, *12*(11), 796. DOI: 10.3390/educsci12110796

Perez-y-Perez, M., Grant, J. A., & Cook, T. F. (2024). Stitching Together a PAR Project: "Work Active"—Supporting the Journey to Work for People With an Intellectual Disability. *Qualitative Inquiry*, *32*(1), 50–62. DOI: 10.1177/10778004241279180

Phillips, S. D. (2011). EU Disability Policy and Implications of EU Accession for Disability Rights in Education and Employment in Bulgaria, Romania, Croatia, and the Former Yugoslav Republic of Macedonia. *Journal of Disability Policy Studies*, *22*(4), 208–219. DOI: 10.1177/1044207311414710

Reynders, S. S., Lombardo, A., Davidson, E. J., Guan, J. L., Pawlowski, K. G., Simons, N. Z., & Baumer, N. (2024). 15 Years of Inclusive Employment in a Down Syndrome Clinic. *Work (Reading, Mass.)*, *79*(3), 1517–1523. DOI: 10.3233/WOR-240080 PMID: 39331058

Rogan, P. M., & Rinne, S. (2021). Launching a Statewide Employment First Initiative: Indiana's Work to Include Coalition. *Journal of Vocational Rehabilitation*, *54*(3), 255–260. DOI: 10.3233/JVR-211133

Schutz, M. A., Awsumb, J. M., Carter, E. W., & McMillan, E. D. (2021). Parent Perspectives on Pre-Employment Transition Services for Youth With Disabilities. *Rehabilitation Counseling Bulletin*, *65*(4), 266–278. DOI: 10.1177/0034355221993542

Schwartzman, B., Lanchak, E. R., Carter, E. W., Guest, L., McMillan, E. D., & Taylor, J. L. (2023). Family Perspectives on Promoting Paid Employment for Individuals With Intellectual and Developmental Disabilities. *Rehabilitation Counseling Bulletin, 68*(2), 79–91. DOI: 10.1177/00343552231213996

Shahin, S., Reitzel, M., Rezze, B. D., Ahmed, S., & Anaby, D. (2020). Environmental Factors That Impact the Workplace Participation of Transition-Aged Young Adults With Brain-Based Disabilities: A Scoping Review. *International Journal of Environmental Research and Public Health, 17*(7), 2378. DOI: 10.3390/ijerph17072378 PMID: 32244476

Sousa, C., Pereira, J., Tsvetkova, P., & Casimiro, C. (2024). *Perceptions of Inclusion Professionals on Employability of Individuals With Intellectual and Developmental Disabilities: A Transnational Study*. DOI: 10.36315/2024inpact036

Spencer, P., Haneghan, J. V., & Baxter, A. (2021). Exploring Social Networks, Employment and Self-Determination Outcomes of Graduates From a Postsecondary Program for Young Adults With an Intellectual Disability. *Journal of Vocational Rehabilitation, 55*(3), 251–270. DOI: 10.3233/JVR-211161

Tucker, M., Guillermo, M. S., & Corona, V. (2019). Career and Work-Based Learning Interventions for Young Recipients of Supplemental Security Income. *Journal of Vocational Rehabilitation, 51*(2), 145–157. DOI: 10.3233/JVR-191034

Voermans, M. A. C., Wilthagen, T., & Embregts, P. J. C. M. (2023). Informal Network Members' Perspectives and Experiences on Work for People With Intellectual Disabilities: A Thematic Synthesis. *Journal of Occupational Rehabilitation, 34*(1), 37–55. DOI: 10.1007/s10926-023-10128-0 PMID: 37421467

Watts, P., Kwiatkowska, G., & Minnion, A. (2023). Using Multimedia Technology to Enhance Self-advocacy of People With Intellectual Disabilities: Introducing a Theoretical Framework for 'Multimedia Advocacy.'. *Journal of Applied Research in Intellectual Disabilities, 36*(4), 739–749. DOI: 10.1111/jar.13107 PMID: 37062847

Wehman, P., Schall, C., Avellone, L., Brooke, A., Brooke, V., McDonough, J., & Whittenburg, H. N. (2021). *Achieving Competitive Integrated Employment for Individuals With Intellectual and Developmental Disabilities*. 333–355. DOI: 10.1037/0000195-013

Yon-Hernández, J. A., Gonzales, C. J. G., Bothra, S., Kecskemeti, K., Iosif, A., Takarae, Y., Ruder, S., McGurk, S. R., Mueser, K. T., & Solomon, M. (2025). Early Employment Outcomes in Autistic and Non-Autistic Youth: Challenges and Opportunities. *Journal of Autism and Developmental Disorders*. Advance online publication. DOI: 10.1007/s10803-025-07001-9 PMID: 40773082

Zidan, A., Gabay, D., Poirier, S.-È., Grandisson, M., Jacob, S., Ouimet, M., Julien-Gauthier, F., Martin-Roy, S., Lamontagne, M., Desmarais, C., & Dahan-Oliel, N. (2025). In What Contexts, How, and Why Do Transition to Adulthood Interventions Work for Adolescents Living With Disabilities: A Realist Review. *Journal of Vocational Rehabilitation*, *63*(2), 225–241. DOI: 10.1177/10522263251356223

Chapter 14
Financial Literacy and Benefits Navigation

ABSTRACT

This chapter examines financial literacy and benefits navigation as critical determinants of employment outcomes for workers with intellectual disabilities (ID). Drawing on welfare economics, incentive theory, and social protection frameworks, it analyzes how benefit structures—particularly work incentives and the "benefits cliff"—shape employment behavior through risk perception, decision-making, and sustainability. The chapter explores the multidimensional nature of financial literacy, encompassing budgeting, income management, and future planning, emphasizing the need for inclusive, contextualized education integrated with employment supports. It argues that sustainable inclusion requires aligning financial systems with employment goals, reducing uncertainty, and equipping individuals and families with the competencies to navigate complex policies. Ultimately, financial literacy is positioned not merely as an individual skill but as a systemic enabler of economic independence and long-term labor market participation.

14.1 INTRODUCTION

Employment participation among workers with intellectual disabilities (ID) is shaped not only by individual capabilities or workplace practices but also by the structure of financial systems, social protection policies, and economic incentives that govern access to work and income stability. Across policy contexts, financial barriers emerge as one of the most persistent and complex obstacles to inclusive employment, influencing both the decision to enter the labor market and the ability to sustain participation over time (Bergman et al., 2024). A central issue identified in the literature is the misalignment between disability benefits and employment incentives. Many social protection systems are designed to provide income security

DOI: 10.4018/979-8-3373-9185-4.ch014

and access to essential supports—such as healthcare, assistive technologies, and personal assistance—but these benefits are often contingent on limited or no employment. As a result, individuals with ID may face a situation in which entering paid work leads to a reduction or loss of critical supports, creating what is commonly referred to as a "benefit trap" or "benefits cliff" (Bergman et al., 2024). This structural tension generates significant disincentives for employment. Even when jobs are available, the net financial outcome of working may be uncertain or even negative once the loss of benefits and additional work-related costs are considered. Policy analyses consistently show that individuals with ID—and their families—must weigh the risks of losing stable support systems against the potential gains from employment, often resulting in cautious or delayed engagement with the labor market (McCaffrey et al., 2025).

Beyond direct disincentives, financial barriers also manifest through the costs associated with employment participation. These include transportation, workplace accommodations, assistive technologies, and ongoing support services such as job coaching. While some social protection systems provide funding for these supports, access is often inconsistent, fragmented, or administratively complex. Gaps in coverage or delays in service provision can disrupt employment trajectories, making it difficult for individuals to obtain or maintain jobs in competitive environments (Marinaci et al., 2023; McCaffrey et al., 2025). The complexity of navigating financial systems further compounds these challenges. Individuals with ID and their families frequently encounter difficulties in understanding eligibility criteria, benefit rules, and reporting requirements. Administrative burdens—such as paperwork, assessments, and compliance procedures—can act as barriers in themselves, limiting access to available supports and creating uncertainty about financial outcomes (Schofield et al., 2024). This complexity underscores the importance of financial literacy and benefits navigation as critical competencies within inclusive employment systems. Financial barriers are also deeply intertwined with household and family economic conditions. Families often bear significant direct and indirect costs associated with supporting individuals with ID, including caregiving responsibilities, reduced labor market participation, and out-of-pocket expenses for services and supports. These financial pressures can influence employment decisions, shaping both the opportunities available to individuals with ID and the capacity of families to support work transitions (Olney & Yates, 2025).

Importantly, financial insecurity does not only affect access to employment but also impacts job retention and long-term outcomes. Workers with ID who experience financial instability may face additional stress, reduced well-being, and limited capacity to manage workplace demands. Conversely, stable financial supports—when aligned with employment—can enhance participation, enabling individuals to engage more fully in work and pursue career development opportunities (Taylor et al., 2022). From a policy perspective, social protection systems can function as either enablers or barriers to inclusive employment, depending on their design and implementation. When benefits are structured to complement earnings—providing continued access to supports as individuals transition into work—they can facilitate entry into competitive integrated employment (CIE) and support long-term labor market attachment (Schofield et al., 2024). In contrast, systems that impose abrupt reductions in benefits or fail to integrate employment supports create conditions that discourage participation and reinforce dependency. The literature also highlights the importance of cross-sector coordination in addressing financial barriers. Employment outcomes for individuals with ID are influenced by the interaction of multiple systems, including social protection, labor markets, healthcare, and education. Fragmentation across these systems can lead to gaps in support, inconsistent incentives, and inefficiencies that undermine inclusion (Wendel et al., 2024). Integrated approaches that align policies and services across sectors are therefore essential for creating coherent and supportive financial environments. Another critical dimension is the role of employers and labor market dynamics. While financial incentives for employers—such as subsidies or tax benefits—can encourage hiring, the literature suggests that these measures alone are insufficient to overcome structural barriers. Effective inclusion requires a combination of financial supports, workplace accommodations, and organizational practices that enable individuals with ID to perform and progress in their roles (Dean et al., 2022). At a broader level, financial barriers reflect deeper structural inequalities related to poverty, unemployment, and social exclusion. Individuals with ID are disproportionately affected by these conditions, which limit access to education, training, and employment opportunities. Addressing financial barriers therefore requires not only targeted interventions but also systemic reforms that promote equity and inclusion across economic and social domains (Schofield et al., 2024).

Despite these challenges, the literature provides strong evidence that inclusive employment can yield significant economic and social benefits when supported by appropriate policies. Competitive integrated employment is associated with higher wages, improved well-being, and enhanced quality of life for individuals with ID. However, these outcomes are contingent on the presence of financial systems that support, rather than undermine, participation (Taylor et al., 2022). Taken together, the evidence underscores that financial barriers are not peripheral issues but are central determinants of employment outcomes for workers with intellectual disabilities. They shape incentives, access to opportunities, and the sustainability of employment, influencing decisions at both individual and systemic levels. This chapter builds on this foundation by examining how financial literacy and benefits navigation can address these barriers, enabling individuals with ID, their families, and employers to better understand and navigate complex financial systems. By aligning financial supports with employment goals, policymakers and practitioners can move toward more inclusive, equitable, and sustainable employment systems.

14.2 CONCEPTUAL FOUNDATION

Understanding financial barriers and employment outcomes for workers with intellectual disabilities (ID) requires a robust conceptual framework that integrates welfare economics, incentive theory, and social protection systems. These frameworks collectively explain how individuals make employment decisions, how policies shape those decisions, and why financial systems can either enable or constrain inclusive labor market participation. Rather than viewing employment as a purely individual choice, these perspectives position it as a structurally mediated decision, shaped by the interaction of financial incentives, behavioral responses, institutional design, and policy environments (Yosef et al., 2018).

14.2.1 Welfare Economics: The Logic of Work Versus Welfare

At its core, welfare economics provides a foundational lens for understanding employment decisions as a function of cost–benefit calculations between labor income and welfare support. Within this framework, individuals are conceptualized as making choices between "leisure" (non-employment supported by benefits) and "labor" (employment income), guided by the relative financial returns of each option. A central concept in this model is the replacement rate, defined as the ratio of welfare benefits to potential earnings from employment. When replacement rates are high—meaning welfare provides income comparable to or exceeding potential wages—the incentive to enter the labor market diminishes. Conversely, when employment yields significantly higher net returns, participation becomes more attractive (Yosef et al., 2018). However, applying this model to workers with ID reveals important complexities. Unlike the assumptions of standard economic models, individuals with ID face additional structural and non-monetary costs, including:

- The need for accommodations and support services
- Barriers in job matching and hiring practices
- Transportation and accessibility constraints
- Social stigma and workplace exclusion

These factors mean that the decision to work cannot be understood solely in terms of wage differentials. Instead, the net value of employment must account for both financial and non-financial costs, as well as the stability and predictability of income streams (Yosef et al., 2018). Moreover, welfare economics highlights the importance of adequacy and security in social protection systems. For individuals with ID, welfare benefits often provide not only income but also access to essential services and supports. As a result, the decision to leave welfare is not merely about income substitution but involves risking access to critical resources, making employment decisions inherently more complex and consequential. This perspective underscores a key policy implication: effective systems must balance income adequacy with incentives for participation, ensuring that individuals are not forced to choose between financial security and employment.

14.2.2 Incentive Theory and Behavioral Economics: Beyond Rational Choice

While welfare economics assumes rational decision-making, incentive theory—augmented by behavioral economics—recognizes that individuals often respond to incentives in non-linear and psychologically mediated ways. This is particularly relevant for workers with ID, whose employment decisions are shaped by uncertainty, perceived risks, and informational constraints. A central concept from behavioral economics is loss aversion, derived from prospect theory. Individuals tend to weigh potential losses more heavily than equivalent gains, meaning that the fear of losing benefits or financial stability can outweigh the perceived benefits of employment—even when employment is objectively more advantageous (Yosef et al., 2018). For workers with ID, loss aversion is amplified by several factors:

- Uncertainty about how earnings will affect benefits
- Limited access to clear and accessible financial information
- Dependence on stable supports (e.g., healthcare, assistive services)
- Past experiences of exclusion or instability in employment

These conditions create a risk-averse decision environment, where maintaining existing benefits may be perceived as safer than transitioning into employment. As a result, traditional policy approaches that rely solely on increasing financial incentives (e.g., higher wages or tax credits) may be insufficient to change behavior. Behavioral insights suggest that effective policy design must address not only objective incentives but also perceptions of risk and certainty. This includes:

- Providing clear, accessible information about earnings and benefits interactions
- Ensuring predictable and gradual transitions from welfare to work

- Reducing uncertainty through guaranteed supports during employment transitions

In addition, incentive theory highlights the role of institutional design in shaping behavior. Incentives must be aligned across stakeholders—including workers, employers, and service providers—to ensure that individual decisions are supported by broader system dynamics. Misaligned incentives can lead to unintended consequences, such as reduced employment participation or reliance on segregated work arrangements (Yosef et al., 2018). Importantly, this perspective shifts the focus from "motivating individuals" to designing systems that enable rational and confident decision-making, particularly for populations facing structural disadvantages.

14.2.3 Social Protection Systems: Structuring Opportunities and Constraints

Social protection systems represent the institutional context within which welfare economics and incentive theory operate. These systems encompass income supports, services, and policy frameworks that shape both the opportunities available to workers with ID and the constraints they face in accessing employment. A key insight from the literature is that social protection systems can function as either enablers or barriers, depending on their design. Systems that provide integrated supports—such as income assistance, job coaching, assistive technologies, and transportation—can reduce barriers to employment and support sustained participation. In contrast, fragmented or poorly coordinated systems can create gaps in support, limiting access and undermining outcomes (Yosef et al., 2018). From a theoretical perspective, social protection systems can be understood through multiple lenses:

1. Welfarist and Redistribution Frameworks

These frameworks examine how tax and transfer systems allocate resources and address inequalities. For workers with ID, optimal policy design must account for observable and non-observable dimensions of disability, ensuring that supports are targeted effectively while minimizing inefficiencies (Weisbach, 2007).

2. Rights-Based Frameworks

Grounded in legal and human rights principles, these frameworks emphasize the role of anti-discrimination laws and reasonable accommodations in enabling labor market participation. Policies aligned with rights-based approaches—such as those influenced by the UNCRPD—recognize employment as a fundamental right and emphasize the removal of structural barriers (Engstrom & Hausman, 2021).

3. Institutional and Governance Perspectives

These perspectives highlight the role of the state and institutional arrangements in shaping labor market outcomes. The interaction between welfare provision, labor market regulation, and employer behavior determines the extent to which inclusive employment is realized in practice (Jeong, 2010).

4. Innovation and Policy Evolution

Social protection systems are not static; they evolve in response to economic, social, and political pressures. Institutional innovation—such as new forms of social insurance or integrated employment programs—can reshape incentives and expand opportunities for workers with ID (Shiller, 2005). Across these frameworks, a common theme emerges: effective social protection systems must integrate financial supports with employment services, ensuring that individuals have both the resources and the opportunities to participate in the labor market.

14.2.4 Integrative Analysis: Aligning Incentives, Behavior, and Systems

The integration of welfare economics, incentive theory, and social protection systems reveals a comprehensive understanding of employment participation among workers with ID. These frameworks collectively demonstrate that employment outcomes are shaped by the interaction of financial incentives, behavioral responses, and institutional design.

Several key insights emerge from this integration:

1. **Incentives Alone Are Insufficient**

Monetary incentives must be complemented by supports that reduce non-financial barriers and address behavioral responses such as loss aversion.

2. **Predictability and Security Are Critical**

Individuals are more likely to engage in employment when financial outcomes are stable and predictable, and when transitions do not threaten access to essential supports.

3. **Systems Must Be Integrated and Coordinated**

Fragmented systems create gaps and inefficiencies, while coordinated approaches align incentives and supports across sectors.

4. **Policy Design Must Be Person-Centered and Context-Sensitive**

Effective systems account for the diverse needs, preferences, and constraints of workers with ID, rather than relying on one-size-fits-all approaches.

5. **Rights and Economics Must Be Balanced**

Inclusive employment requires both economic incentives and rights-based protections, ensuring that participation is both feasible and equitable.

Taken together, these conceptual frameworks support a shift from viewing financial systems as neutral background conditions to recognizing them as active determinants of inclusion or exclusion. Welfare economics explains the logic of decision-making, incentive theory reveals the behavioral complexities of those decisions, and social protection systems provide the institutional context that shapes outcomes. For workers with ID, this synthesis highlights the need for policies that:

- Align financial incentives with employment goals
- Reduce perceived and actual risks associated with work
- Provide stable and accessible supports
- Integrate economic, social, and rights-based considerations

In this sense, financial inclusion is not merely about income but about designing systems that enable participation, autonomy, and long-term stability in the labor market. This conceptual foundation provides the basis for the subsequent sections of the chapter, which will examine how financial literacy, benefits navigation, and policy design can translate these principles into practical strategies for supporting workers with intellectual disabilities.

14.3 THE BENEFITS SYSTEM

The structure of the benefits system—particularly social security programs, work incentives, and benefit withdrawal mechanisms—plays a ative role in shaping employment participation among workers with intellectual disabilities (ID). While these systems are designed to provide income security and access to essential supports, their interaction with earnings often creates complex and sometimes contradictory incentives, influencing decisions not only to enter employment but also to remain, progress, or withdraw from the labor market (Weber et al., 2022). This section examines three core components of the benefits system: social security frameworks, work incentives, and the phenomenon of the benefits cliff, highlighting how their design translates into real-world employment outcomes.

14.3.1 Social Security Systems: Foundations of Income Security and Risk

Social security systems constitute the primary institutional mechanism through which workers with ID access income support, healthcare, and disability-related services. These systems are foundational in reducing poverty and providing stability, particularly for individuals who face structural barriers to employment. However, social security systems are not neutral; their design directly shapes labor market behavior. A central mechanism is the way benefits interact with earnings, determining the net financial gain from employment. In many systems, benefits are means-tested or tied to income thresholds, meaning that as earnings increase, benefits are reduced or withdrawn (Krekó et al., 2023). This creates a trade-off between income security and employment participation. For workers with ID, who often rely on a combination of supports—including income assistance, housing subsidies, transportation, and vocational services—this trade-off is particularly significant. Employment decisions are therefore influenced not only by wages but by the broader configuration of supports embedded within social security systems (Maestas, 2019). Cross-national evidence demonstrates substantial variation in how social security systems manage this trade-off. Some systems emphasize strict thresholds and rapid withdrawal of benefits, while others implement gradual phase-outs or partial benefit retention, allowing individuals to maintain access to supports as they transition into employment (Weber et al., 2022). These differences produce markedly different employment outcomes, particularly in terms of job retention and wage progression. Importantly, social security systems also interact with broader employment policies, such as supported employment (SE) and competitive integrated employment (CIE). While these programs aim to promote inclusion in the labor market, their effectiveness is contingent on a benefits system that supports rather than penalizes participation (Taubner et al., 2021).

14.3.2 Work Incentives: Aligning Earnings and Participation

Work incentives are policy mechanisms designed to encourage employment by ensuring that individuals experience tangible financial gains from working. These incentives may take various forms, including earnings disregards, partial benefit offsets, tax credits, or transitional supports. The central objective of work incentives is to address the disincentives created by traditional benefit structures, particularly by ensuring that increases in earnings do not result in disproportionate losses of benefits. When effectively designed, work incentives can enhance both labor market entry and sustained participation, enabling workers with ID to pursue competitive employment and career progression (Maestas, 2019). Empirical evidence suggests that gradual benefit reduction mechanisms—such as partial offsets or earnings disregards—are more effective than abrupt withdrawal systems. These approaches allow individuals to retain a portion of their benefits as earnings increase, thereby smoothing the transition from welfare to work and reducing financial risk (Weber et al., 2022; Krekó et al., 2023). In contrast, systems that rely on all-or-nothing thresholds often create strong disincentives, as individuals may face sudden and significant losses of income or supports when crossing specific earnings limits. Such designs can discourage not only entry into employment but also wage progression and career advancement, as individuals may intentionally limit their hours or earnings to avoid triggering benefit reductions (Maestas, 2019). Work incentives also play a critical role in supporting supported employment (SE) and competitive integrated employment (CIE) pathways. When combined with employment supports—such as job coaching, training, and workplace accommodations—effective incentives can amplify the benefits of these programs, leading to improved retention, higher earnings, and better psychosocial outcomes (Taylor et al., 2022; Taubner et al., 2021). However, the effectiveness of work incentives is influenced by several factors:

- **Clarity and transparency of rules**, which affect understanding and decision-making
- **Administrative complexity**, which can limit access and uptake
- **Coordination across programs**, which determines the cumulative impact of multiple benefits

Without alignment across these dimensions, work incentives may fail to achieve their intended effects, highlighting the importance of integrated policy design.

14.3.3 The Benefits Cliff: A Structural Barrier to Employment Progression

Among the most significant challenges within benefits systems is the phenomenon known as the benefits cliff. This refers to situations where a small increase in earnings leads to a disproportionate and abrupt loss of benefits, resulting in little or no net financial gain—or even a net loss—despite increased work effort. The benefits cliff is typically associated with high effective marginal tax rates (EMTRs), where the combined loss of benefits and taxes can exceed the additional income earned. In extreme cases, EMTRs can exceed 100%, meaning that individuals are financially worse off by working more (Weber et al., 2022; Krekó et al., 2023). For workers with ID, the impact of benefits cliffs is particularly pronounced due to their reliance on multiple interconnected supports. As earnings increase, individuals may lose access not only to income benefits but also to:

- Healthcare coverage
- Housing subsidies
- Transportation support
- Employment services

This creates a situation in which the total resource package declines, undermining both financial stability and employment sustainability (Maestas, 2019). The consequences of benefits cliffs extend beyond initial employment decisions to affect long-term career trajectories. Evidence shows that individuals may:

- Limit working hours to remain below thresholds
- Decline promotions or wage increases
- Exit employment altogether to regain lost benefits

These behaviors reflect rational responses to system design, rather than lack of motivation, highlighting the structural nature of the problem.

14.3.4 Policy Innovations and Mitigation Strategies

Recognizing the limitations of traditional benefit structures, policymakers have introduced various strategies to mitigate the effects of benefits cliffs and enhance work incentives. One widely discussed approach is the implementation of gradual benefit phase-outs, where benefits are reduced incrementally as earnings increase. This approach lowers EMTRs and ensures that individuals experience consistent net gains from work (Weber et al., 2022; Krekó et al., 2023). Another strategy involves hold-harmless provisions, which temporarily protect individuals from losing benefits during transitions into employment. These mechanisms provide a safety net during critical adjustment periods, reducing perceived and actual risks associated with entering the workforce. Policy experiments—such as pilot programs that decouple earnings from benefit eligibility—demonstrate that reducing financial risk can improve both employment retention and income stability, although results vary depending on program design and implementation (Maestas, 2019). However, the literature also highlights challenges in implementing these reforms. Issues such as low program uptake, administrative complexity, and limited awareness can reduce effectiveness, underscoring the need for complementary strategies such as financial literacy training and benefits counseling.

14.3.5 Cross-National Variations and System Design Implications

Comparative analyses reveal significant differences in how countries structure their benefits systems and work incentives. For example:

- The United States has historically relied on **threshold-based systems**, creating pronounced cliff effects
- European systems often incorporate **gradual phase-outs**, though variations exist in generosity and thresholds
- Some countries combine high levels of support with strict eligibility rules, creating mixed effects on participation

These variations demonstrate that policy design matters, and that similar levels of support can produce different outcomes depending on how benefits are structured and integrated with employment systems (Weber et al., 2022; Krekó et al., 2023). A key lesson from cross-national evidence is the importance of alignment between benefits and employment supports. Systems that integrate financial incentives with services such as job coaching, training, and accommodations are more likely to achieve sustainable employment outcomes for workers with ID (Taylor et al., 2022).

The analysis of social security systems, work incentives, and benefits cliffs highlights a central conclusion: the design of benefits systems is a decisive factor in shaping employment outcomes for workers with intellectual disabilities. Effective systems are characterized by:

- **Gradual and predictable benefit transitions** that avoid abrupt cliffs
- **Integrated supports** that address both financial and non-financial barriers
- **Transparent and accessible rules** that reduce uncertainty and enable informed decision-making
- **Alignment across programs and sectors** to minimize cumulative disincentives

Conversely, poorly designed systems—particularly those with abrupt thresholds and fragmented supports—can undermine employment participation, limit career progression, and reinforce dependency. Ultimately, benefits systems must move beyond a narrow focus on income support toward a broader objective of enabling participation, progression, and economic inclusion. This requires a shift from static models of welfare provision to dynamic systems that support individuals throughout their employment journeys. This section sets the stage for the next part of the chapter, which will explore how financial literacy and benefits navigation can equip individuals, families, and practitioners with the tools needed to navigate these complex systems effectively and make informed employment decisions.

14.4 IMPACT ON EMPLOYMENT BEHAVIOR

Financial systems do not merely shape structural opportunities; they fundamentally influence how workers with intellectual disabilities (ID) perceive risk, make decisions, and sustain participation in employment over time. The interaction between benefit design, financial uncertainty, and policy environments produces behavioral responses that affect not only entry into employment but also job retention, progression, and long-term stability (Ravinskaya et al., 2022). This section examines three interconnected dimensions of employment behavior: risk perception, decision-making processes, and employment sustainability, highlighting how financial systems translate into lived experiences and behavioral outcomes for workers with ID.

14.4.1 Risk Perception: Financial Uncertainty as a Behavioral Driver

Risk perception is a central mechanism through which financial systems influence employment behavior. For workers with ID, employment decisions are rarely based on wages alone; instead, they involve complex evaluations of financial, health, and social risks, particularly those associated with losing benefits and support systems. A key concern identified across the literature is the risk of losing essential benefits, including income support, healthcare coverage, and access to services. These benefits are often tightly linked to eligibility criteria based on income or work status, creating uncertainty about what will happen if an individual increases earnings or work hours (Spreat, 2018). As a result, employment is frequently perceived not only as an opportunity but also as a potential threat to financial stability. This perception is reinforced by the complexity and opacity of benefit systems. Workers with ID and their families often lack clear, accessible information about how employment will affect their benefits, leading to uncertainty and cautious decision-making. Administrative processes—such as eligibility reassessments and reporting requirements—further contribute to perceptions of instability. Risk perception is also shaped by non-financial considerations, including:

- Continuity of healthcare and support services
- Job security and workplace accommodations
- Social inclusion and workplace relationships

These factors interact with financial concerns to create a multi-dimensional risk environment, where individuals weigh not only economic outcomes but also broader aspects of well-being and security. Importantly, risk perception extends beyond workers to include families and employers. Families may be hesitant to support employment transitions if they perceive a risk to financial stability or essential supports, while employers may evaluate the perceived costs and risks of hiring individuals with ID, including training, accommodations, and liability (Wedgwood et al., 2013). The literature consistently shows that when risk is perceived as high—particularly when benefits are unstable or uncertain—individuals are more likely to:

- Delay entering employment
- Prefer sheltered or subsidized work arrangements
- Limit working hours or earnings

These responses reflect rational adaptations to perceived system risks, underscoring the importance of reducing uncertainty and enhancing predictability in policy design.

14.4.2 Decision-Making: Navigating Complex and Uncertain Systems

Employment decision-making among workers with ID is shaped by the interaction of financial incentives, perceived risks, and institutional contexts. Unlike traditional economic models that assume rational optimization, real-world decision-making is influenced by uncertainty, incomplete information, and social context. A central finding across the literature is that individuals with ID—and their families—engage in risk-averse decision-making, prioritizing stability and continuity over potential gains. This is particularly evident in decisions about transitioning from benefits to employment, where the possibility of losing supports may outweigh the anticipated benefits of work (Ravinskaya et al., 2022). Decision-making is further influenced by the structure of policy environments and service systems. Integrated models—such as supported employment programs and Individual Placement and Support (IPS)—can reduce uncertainty by providing ongoing support, clear pathways, and coordinated services. These models distribute responsibility across stakeholders and ensure continuity of supports, thereby facilitating more confident decision-making (McDowell et al., 2021) Conversely, fragmented or inconsistent systems can exacerbate uncertainty, leading to suboptimal or constrained decisions. For example, activation policies that emphasize rapid entry into employment without addressing financial risks may push individuals toward precarious or unpaid work arrangements, rather than sustainable competitive employment (Dearing, 2021). Decision-making is also shaped by policy narratives and expectations, including the promotion of "Employment First" approaches. While these frameworks emphasize the value of competitive employment, their effectiveness depends on whether underlying financial systems support this goal. Without alignment between policy rhetoric and financial realities, individuals may experience a disconnect between expectations and feasible options (Spreat, 2018). Additionally, decision-making processes are often collective rather than individual, involving families, service providers, and employers. These actors influence decisions through:

- Providing information and guidance
- Shaping expectations and aspirations
- Mediating access to opportunities and supports

This collective dimension highlights the importance of shared understanding and coordinated decision-making, particularly in complex financial environments.

14.4.3 Employment Sustainability: From Entry to Long-Term Stability

While financial barriers influence initial entry into employment, their impact on long-term sustainability is equally significant. Employment sustainability refers to the ability of individuals to maintain, progress, and derive benefits from employment over time, rather than experiencing short-term or unstable participation. The literature identifies benefit-related disincentives as a major factor undermining sustainability. When benefits are tied to non-work status or limited earnings, individuals may face structural constraints on career progression, including:

- Limiting work hours to retain benefits
- Avoiding promotions or wage increases
- Cycling in and out of employment

These patterns reflect the presence of fiscal cliffs and eligibility thresholds, which disrupt employment trajectories and reduce long-term stability (Ravinskaya et al., 2022). Sustainability is also influenced by the continuity of supports. Employment is more likely to be sustained when individuals have access to:

- Ongoing financial supports (e.g., partial benefits, subsidies)
- Stable healthcare coverage
- Continuous job coaching and workplace accommodations

Integrated service models that combine these elements—such as supported employment frameworks—are associated with longer job tenure and improved employment outcomes (McDowell et al., 2021; Wehman et al., 2021). In contrast, time-limited or conditional supports can create instability, particularly when individuals lose access to services as they increase earnings or transition between programs. This can lead to premature withdrawal from employment or reliance on precarious job arrangements. Another critical factor in sustainability is the interaction between financial security and well-being. Workers with ID who experience stable income and support systems are more likely to:

- Remain engaged in employment
- Develop skills and pursue career advancement
- Experience improved psychological and social outcomes

Conversely, financial instability can lead to stress, reduced motivation, and increased risk of job loss, reinforcing cycles of exclusion.

14.4.4 Integrative Perspective: Behavioral Pathways and System Design

The interaction between risk perception, decision-making, and employment sustainability reveals a coherent set of behavioral pathways through which financial systems influence employment outcomes for workers with ID.

Three key mechanisms emerge:

1. **Perceived Risk Shapes Entry Decisions**

High perceived risk—particularly related to benefit loss—discourages entry into employment or leads to cautious engagement.

2. **Decision-Making Reflects System Complexity**

Uncertainty and fragmentation in policy systems lead to risk-averse and sometimes constrained decisions, often prioritizing stability over opportunity.

3. **Structural Disincentives Undermine Sustainability**

Benefits cliffs, eligibility thresholds, and discontinuous supports disrupt long-term employment trajectories, limiting progression and stability.

These mechanisms highlight that employment behavior is not solely determined by individual motivation but is deeply embedded in policy design and institutional context.

The evidence underscores the need for behaviorally informed policy design, which recognizes that individuals respond not only to objective incentives but also to perceptions of risk, uncertainty, and stability. Effective systems should:

- Reduce financial risk by ensuring continuity of benefits and supports
- Enhance predictability through clear and transparent rules
- Support informed decision-making through accessible information and guidance
- Promote sustainability by aligning benefits with long-term employment goals

In this sense, financial systems must move beyond static incentive structures toward dynamic, person-centered designs that support individuals throughout their employment journeys. This section provides a critical bridge to the next part of the chapter, which will examine how financial literacy and benefits navigation strategies can equip individuals, families, and practitioners to navigate these behavioral and structural challenges effectively, enabling more confident and sustainable participation in the labor market.

14.5 FINANCIAL LITERACY

Financial literacy is increasingly recognized as a foundational capability for economic independence, employment stability, and self-determination among workers with intellectual disabilities (ID). Within policy and practice, financial literacy extends beyond basic money-handling skills to encompass budgeting, income management, and forward planning, enabling individuals to navigate complex financial systems and make informed decisions about work and daily life (Dam et al., 2022; Kang et al., 2025; Melo et al., 2023). Importantly, financial literacy operates at the intersection of individual capability and systemic accessibility. While skills development is essential, its effectiveness depends on inclusive education approaches, supportive environments, and integration with broader employment and social protection systems. This section examines three core dimensions of financial literacy: budgeting, income management, and planning, highlighting their role in supporting sustainable employment outcomes.

14.5.1 Budgeting: Building Everyday Financial Competence

Budgeting represents the most immediate and practical dimension of financial literacy, enabling individuals to allocate resources, track expenses, and make informed spending decisions. For workers with ID, budgeting skills are essential for managing income derived from employment and balancing it with daily living costs. The literature consistently emphasizes that effective budgeting education must move beyond abstract instruction to incorporate contextualized, real-world learning experiences. Programs that include activities such as shopping simulations, price comparisons, and hands-on money handling are more effective in promoting understanding and skill transfer (Hopkins & O'Donovan, 2019). A key principle is the use of Universal Design for Learning (UDL), which ensures that financial education is accessible to individuals with diverse cognitive profiles. UDL-based approaches incorporate:

- Visual supports and simplified materials
- Hands-on and experiential learning
- Repetition and scaffolding of concepts

These strategies enable individuals to engage with budgeting concepts in ways that align with their learning needs and preferences (Melo et al., 2023; Kang et al., 2025). Budgeting also plays a critical role in supporting self-determination and autonomy. By developing the ability to manage their own finances, individuals with ID gain greater control over their daily lives and are better equipped to make independent decisions about spending and saving. This aligns with broader policy goals of promoting independent living and social inclusion (Dam et al., 2022). However, the effectiveness of budgeting skills depends on ongoing support and reinforcement. Families, caregivers, and professionals often play a crucial role in helping individuals apply budgeting skills in real-life contexts, highlighting the importance of an ecosystem approach to financial literacy (Melo et al., 2023).

5.2 Income Management: Linking Earnings to Stability and Work

Income management extends beyond budgeting to encompass the ability to manage earnings, understand financial flows, and make decisions about income use over time. For workers with ID, effective income management is closely linked to employment outcomes, as it influences both financial stability and the perceived benefits of work. A central aspect of income management is understanding the relationship between earnings, expenses, and financial obligations. Financial literacy programs that integrate income management skills help individuals:

- Monitor income from employment
- Understand deductions, taxes, and benefit interactions
- Balance spending with saving and future needs

These competencies are particularly important in the context of complex benefit systems, where individuals must navigate interactions between wages and social protection programs (Melo et al., 2023; Kang et al., 2025). The literature highlights that income management skills contribute to employment stability by enabling individuals to:

- Anticipate financial changes associated with work
- Manage fluctuations in income
- Avoid financial crises that could disrupt employment

In this sense, income management acts as a stabilizing mechanism, supporting sustained participation in the labor market. Effective income management education is characterized by multimodal and applied approaches, including:

- Simulated financial scenarios (e.g., managing a monthly paycheck)
- Community-based instruction (e.g., using banking services)
- Integration with digital tools and financial technologies

These approaches facilitate the transfer of learning to real-world contexts, ensuring that individuals can apply their skills in everyday financial situations (Melo et al., 2023; Kang et al., 2025). Importantly, income management is also linked to broader economic participation, including opportunities for entrepreneurship and income diversification. Studies on microenterprise initiatives suggest that financial literacy and business skills can enable individuals with ID to pursue alternative employment pathways, enhancing autonomy and economic independence (Hutchinson et al., 2020). However, income management skills must be supported by accessible financial systems, including inclusive banking services and simplified financial products. Without such supports, individuals may face barriers in applying their skills, limiting the impact of financial literacy interventions.

14.5.3 Planning: Future-Oriented Financial Decision-Making

Planning represents the most advanced dimension of financial literacy, involving the ability to anticipate future needs, set goals, and make strategic financial decisions. For workers with ID, planning is essential for navigating long-term employment trajectories, managing financial risks, and achieving economic independence. Financial planning includes several key components:

- Setting short- and long-term financial goals
- Saving for future expenses or emergencies
- Understanding the financial implications of employment decisions
- Preparing for life transitions (e.g., changes in benefits, career progression)

The literature emphasizes that planning skills are closely linked to self-determination and empowerment, as they enable individuals to take an active role in shaping their financial futures (Melo et al., 2023; Dam et al., 2022). Effective financial planning education requires integration of cognitive, practical, and contextual elements, including:

- Problem-based learning approaches
- Real-world scenarios and simulations
- Opportunities for decision-making and reflection

These approaches help individuals develop not only technical skills but also the ability to evaluate options and make informed choices (Heitplatz, 2020). Planning is also closely connected to employment sustainability, as it enables individuals to anticipate and manage changes in income, benefits, and work conditions. For example, understanding how increased earnings may affect benefits can help individuals make strategic decisions about work hours and career progression. However, the literature identifies significant challenges in developing planning skills among individuals with ID, including:

- Limited access to comprehensive financial education programs
- Variability in cognitive and adaptive abilities
- Lack of integration between financial education and employment services

These challenges highlight the need for systematic and sustained interventions, as well as the integration of financial planning within broader policy and practice frameworks.

14.5.4 Integrative Perspective: Financial Literacy as a Capability System

The integration of budgeting, income management, and planning reveals financial literacy as a multidimensional capability system, rather than a set of isolated skills. These dimensions are interdependent and collectively support economic independence, employment stability, and social inclusion. Several key insights emerge from the literature:

1. **Financial Literacy Enables Employment Participation**

By improving understanding of financial systems and outcomes, financial literacy reduces uncertainty and supports informed decision-making.

2. **Skills Must Be Contextualized and Applied**

Effective programs emphasize real-world application, ensuring that learning translates into everyday financial behavior.

3. **Support Systems Are Essential**

Families, educators, and service providers play a critical role in reinforcing skills and facilitating application.

4. **Integration with Employment Systems Is Critical**

Financial literacy must be embedded within supported employment and transition-to-work programs to maximize impact.

5. **Accessibility and Inclusion Are Key**

Programs must be designed using inclusive approaches, such as UDL, to accommodate diverse needs and abilities.

Financial literacy is not merely an educational objective but a strategic intervention for enabling inclusive employment systems. By equipping individuals with the skills to manage income, navigate financial systems, and plan for the future, financial literacy enhances both individual agency and systemic effectiveness. However, its impact depends on alignment with broader policy and practice frameworks. Financial literacy alone is insufficient without:

- Accessible and supportive financial systems
- Integrated employment and social protection policies
- Ongoing support and coaching

When these elements are aligned, financial literacy becomes a powerful tool for promoting economic independence, employment sustainability, and long-term inclusion for workers with intellectual disabilities. This section sets the stage for the next part of the chapter, which will explore how benefits navigation and policy interventions can further support individuals in managing complex financial systems and optimizing employment outcomes.

REFERENCES

Bergman, J., Ratcliffe, S. E., Harvey-Smith, L., & Williams, L. A. (2024). *Initiatives for Workplace Equity and Inclusion: A Series of Rapid Systematic Reviews of the Peer-Reviewed Literature*. DOI: 10.31219/osf.io/zmvjn

Dam, L. T., Heidler, P., & King, I. (2022). Access, Understanding, Promotion and Maintenance of Good Health: Evaluation of Knowledge Transfer of People With Intellectual Disabilities to Bridge the Health Information and Disease Prevention in Public Health. *Frontiers in Public Health*, *10*, 915970. Advance online publication. DOI: 10.3389/fpubh.2022.915970 PMID: 36238251

Dean, E. E., Garrels, V., Sigstad, H. M. H., & Wendelborg, C. (2022). Employer willingness to hire people with intellectual disability: The influence of employer experience, perception of work, and social responsibility. *Journal of Vocational Rehabilitation*, *57*(1), 85–95. DOI: 10.3233/JVR-221201

Dearing, K. (2021). Work Aspirations, Intellectual Disability and 'Cruelling Out' the Mark in the Job Club. *The Sociological Review*, *70*(3), 564–579. DOI: 10.1177/00380261211044619

Engstrom, D. F., & Hausman, D. (2021). Rights, Redistribution, and the Rise of the "Litigation State": The Case of Disability Discrimination Laws. *Law & Social Inquiry*, *46*(3), 788–825. DOI: 10.1017/lsi.2020.25

Heitplatz, V. N. (2020). Fostering Digital Participation for People With Intellectual Disabilities and Their Caregivers: Towards a Guideline for Designing Education Programs. *Social Inclusion (Lisboa)*, *8*(2), 201–212. DOI: 10.17645/si.v8i2.2578

Hopkins, S., & O'Donovan, R. (2019). Using Complex Learning Tasks to Build Procedural Fluency and Financial Literacy for Young People With Intellectual Disability. *Mathematics Education Research Journal*, *33*(1), 163–181. DOI: 10.1007/s13394-019-00279-w

Hutchinson, C., Lay, K., Alexander, J., & Ratcliffe, J. (2020). People With Intellectual Disabilities as Business Owners: A Systematic Review of Peer-reviewed Literature. *Journal of Applied Research in Intellectual Disabilities*, *34*(2), 459–470. DOI: 10.1111/jar.12836 PMID: 33280214

Jeong, D. Y. (2010). The Role of the State in Industrial Relations. *Seoul Journal of Business*, *16*(2), 95–126. DOI: 10.35152/snusjb.2010.16.2.004

Kang, S., Kastberg, S. E., & Mason, B. A. (2025). Financial Literacy for Individuals With Intellectual and Developmental Disabilities: Border Crossing Required. *School Science and Mathematics*, *125*(1), 18–32. DOI: 10.1111/ssm.18326

Krekó, J., Prinz, D., & Weber, A. (2023). *Take-Up and Labor Supply Responses to Disability Insurance Earnings Limits*. DOI: 10.1596/1813-9450-10325

Maestas, N. (2019). Identifying Work Capacity and Promoting Work: A Strategy for Modernizing the SSDI Program. *The Annals of the American Academy of Political and Social Science*, *686*(1), 93–120. DOI: 10.1177/0002716219882354 PMID: 32719569

Marinaci, T., Russo, C., Savarese, G., Stornaiuolo, G., Faiella, F., Carpinelli, L., Navarra, M., Marsico, G., & Mollo, M. (2023). An Inclusive Workplace Approach to Disability Through Assistive Technologies: A Systematic Review and Thematic Analysis of the Literature. *Societies (Basel, Switzerland)*, *13*(11), 231. DOI: 10.3390/soc13110231

McCaffrey, N., Dew, A., Philpott, C. J., Ingold, J., McVilly, K., Smith-Merry, J., Livingstone, A., & Hutchinson, C. (2025). Impact of Employment Support in Different Work Environments on Individuals With Intellectual Disability and Their Families From Their Own Perspectives: Protocol for a Systematic Review of Qualitative Evidence. *BMJ Open*, *15*(6), e098312. DOI: 10.1136/bmjopen-2024-098312 PMID: 40588391

McDowell, C., Ennals, P., & Fossey, E. (2021). Vocational Service Models and Approaches to Improve Job Tenure of People With Severe and Enduring Mental Illness: A Narrative Review. *Frontiers in Psychiatry*, *12*, 668716. Advance online publication. DOI: 10.3389/fpsyt.2021.668716 PMID: 34305676

Melo, B. B. V. de, Silveira-Maia, M., & RIBEIRO, S. B. (2023). Full Financial Education Programmes for People With Disabilities: A Scoping Review. *Revista Brasileira De Educação Especial, 29*. DOI: 10.1590/1980-54702023v29e0222

Olney, S., & Yates, S. (2025). The Costs of Living With Disability in Australia: Accounting for Variable Disability-Related Deprivation in Poverty Measures. *The Australian Economic Review*, *58*(S1). Advance online publication. DOI: 10.1111/1467-8462.70017

Ravinskaya, M., Verbeek, J., Langendam, M., Daams, J. G., Hulshof, C., Madan, I., Verstappen, S., Hagendijk, M., Kunz, R., & Hoving, J. L. (2022). Extensive Variability of Work Participation Outcomes Measured in Randomized Controlled Trials: A Systematic Review. *Journal of Clinical Epidemiology*, *142*, 60–99. DOI: 10.1016/j.jclinepi.2021.10.013 PMID: 34715311

Schofield, D., Shrestha, R., Tan, O., Lim, K. K., Rajkumar, R., West, S., Boyle, J., Murray, L., Leffler, M., Christie, L., Rice, M. W., Hart, N., Li, J., Tanton, R., Roscioli, T., & Field, M. (2024). The Healthcare and Societal Costs of Familial Intellectual Disability. *International Journal of Environmental Research and Public Health, 21*(3), 299. DOI: 10.3390/ijerph21030299 PMID: 38541298

Shiller, R. J. (2005). Behavioral Economics and Institutional Innovation. *Southern Economic Journal, 72*(2), 268. DOI: 10.2307/20062111

Spreat, S. (2018). Employment Incentives to Support "Employment First.". *Global Journal of Intellectual & Developmental Disabilities, 5*(3). Advance online publication. DOI: 10.19080/GJIDD.2018.05.555665

Taubner, H., Tideman, M., & Nyman, C. S. (2021). Employment Sustainability for People With Intellectual Disability: A Systematic Review. *Journal of Occupational Rehabilitation, 32*(3), 353–364. DOI: 10.1007/s10926-021-10020-9 PMID: 34958449

Taylor, J. P., Avellone, L., Brooke, V., Wehman, P., Inge, K. J., Schall, C., & Iwanaga, K. (2022). The Impact of Competitive Integrated Employment on Economic, Psychological, and Physical Health Outcomes for Individuals With Intellectual and Developmental Disabilities. *Journal of Applied Research in Intellectual Disabilities, 35*(2), 448–459. DOI: 10.1111/jar.12974 PMID: 34994035

Weber, A., Prinz, D., & Krekó, J. (2022). *Take-Up and Labour Supply Responses to Disability Insurance Earnings Limits*. DOI: 10.1920/wp.ifs.2022.2022

Wedgwood, N., Smith, L., Shuttleworth, R., & Llewellyn, G. (2013). An Eye Opening Experience: A Critical Turning Point in the Life of a Young Woman With a Severe Visual Impairment. *Journal of Social Inclusion, 4*(1), 5–23. DOI: 10.36251/josi60

Weisbach, D. A. (2007). A Welfarist Approach to Disabilities. SSRN *Electronic Journal*. DOI: 10.2139/ssrn.1008985

Wendel, C., Gray, R. C., Goddard, K. S., & Hall, J. P. (2024). Navigating New Normals: The Influence of COVID-19 Policies on Community Access and Well-Being of People With Mobility Disabilities in Everyday Life. *Frontiers in Public Health, 12*, 1401777. Advance online publication. DOI: 10.3389/fpubh.2024.1401777 PMID: 39026588

Yosef, L., Soffer, M., & Malul, M. (2018). From Welfare to Work and From Work to Welfare: A Comparison of People With and Without Disabilities. *Journal of Disability Policy Studies, 29*(4), 226–234. DOI: 10.1177/1044207318782674

Chapter 15
Implementing Inclusion:
A Step-by-Step Framework for Organizations

ABSTRACT

This chapter presents a step-by-step framework for organizations to bridge the persistent gap between policy intention and effective implementation of inclusive employment for workers with intellectual disabilities (ID). Grounded in organizational change theory and system transformation perspectives, the APIS framework comprises four iterative phases: Assess (organizational readiness, culture, and gap analysis), Plan (strategic integration, measurable KPIs, and resource allocation), Implement (policy execution, training, and leadership engagement), and Sustain (monitoring, continuous improvement, and scaling). The chapter argues that sustainable inclusion requires coordinated, multi-level change—embedding practices within HRM systems, fostering inclusive culture, and aligning governance with accountability. Moving beyond compliance, this framework equips organizations to translate inclusion from symbolic commitment into enduring, transformative practice.

15.1 INTRODUCTION

Over the past decades, organizations across sectors have increasingly adopted policies and public commitments to disability inclusion, including the employment of workers with intellectual disabilities (WWID). These commitments are often grounded in rights-based frameworks, corporate social responsibility (CSR), and the growing recognition of the business and social value of inclusive workplaces. However, despite this progress, a persistent and well-documented challenge remains: the gap between intention and implementation (Bell, 2019). This gap reflects a fundamental disconnect between what organizations say and what they do. While

DOI: 10.4018/979-8-3373-9185-4.ch015

many organizations articulate inclusive values and establish formal diversity policies, translating these commitments into consistent, measurable, and sustainable workplace practices remain uneven and often incomplete. As a result, workers with intellectual disabilities frequently experience limited access to meaningful inclusion, inconsistent accommodations, and barriers to long-term career development, even within organizations that publicly endorse inclusion (Man & Kangas, 2019; Morris et al., 2024). At its core, this implementation gap is not simply a matter of compliance failure but a reflection of systemic and organizational complexities. Inclusion requires coordinated action across multiple domains, including:

- Human resource management (HRM) systems
- Workplace culture and leadership practices
- Job design and accommodation processes
- Monitoring and evaluation mechanisms
- External support systems and policy alignment

The absence of alignment across these domains often results in fragmented or symbolic implementation, where policies exist but are not effectively operationalized in everyday workplace practices (Agius et al., 2024; Pereira et al., 2024).

One of the most critical insights from the literature is that formal policy adoption does not guarantee meaningful inclusion. Organizations may meet regulatory requirements or adopt diversity policies without fundamentally changing workplace practices or cultures. This creates what can be described as an "illusion of inclusion", where compliance is achieved on paper but not experienced in practice by workers with intellectual disabilities. For example, organizations may provide nominal accommodations or conduct one-time training sessions without embedding these practices into core operational systems, such as recruitment, onboarding, performance management, and career progression. As a result, inclusion remains peripheral rather than integrated, limiting its impact on both employee outcomes and organizational performance (Cavanagh et al., 2016). This disconnect is further exacerbated by weak enforcement mechanisms and limited accountability structures. Even in contexts where legal frameworks mandate inclusion, inconsistent enforcement and lack of monitoring can reduce the effectiveness of policies, allowing organizations to maintain compliance without achieving substantive change (Bell, 2019).

Implementing inclusion is inherently complex because it requires organizations to reconfigure multiple interconnected systems simultaneously. Unlike discrete interventions, inclusion is a systemic transformation, involving changes in processes, behaviors, and institutional norms. One major challenge lies in the heterogeneity of needs among workers with intellectual disabilities. Effective inclusion requires individualized accommodations and supports, tailored to each worker's cognitive, adaptive, and social profile. This necessitates ongoing assessment, resource allocation, and cross-functional collaboration, which can strain organizational capacity if not systematically structured (Agius et al., 2024; Marinaci et al., 2023). Additionally, organizational culture plays a decisive role. Research consistently highlights that attitudes of managers and coworkers significantly influence the success of inclusion efforts. Negative perceptions, low expectations, or lack of awareness can undermine even well-designed policies, leading to exclusionary practices and limited opportunities for advancement (Shahin et al., 2020). Another layer of complexity arises from the need to integrate assistive technologies (AT) and accommodations into workplace processes. While AT has demonstrated significant benefits for productivity, independence, and job satisfaction, its effectiveness depends on proper selection, training, and ongoing evaluation. Without these elements, technological solutions may fail to achieve their intended impact (Bergman et al., 2024).

A further barrier to effective implementation is the difficulty of measuring inclusion outcomes. Traditional organizational metrics—such as hiring rates or retention figures—capture only a limited aspect of inclusion. They often fail to reflect critical dimensions such as:

- Job satisfaction and well-being
- Sense of belonging and social integration
- Opportunities for growth and advancement
- Quality of accommodations and supports

This measurement gap creates challenges in evaluating the effectiveness of inclusion strategies and identifying areas for improvement. Without comprehensive and person-centered metrics, organizations may overestimate their success while overlooking the lived experiences of workers with intellectual disabilities (Jacob & Pillay, 2023). Moreover, the absence of robust monitoring systems limits the ability to create feedback loops, which are essential for continuous improvement. When organizations do not systematically collect and analyze data on inclusion outcomes, they are less able to refine policies, address barriers, and scale successful practices. The gap between policy and practice has significant implications for both individuals and organizations. For workers with intellectual disabilities, this misalignment often results in:

- Reduced job satisfaction and engagement
- Limited social inclusion and workplace participation
- Restricted opportunities for career advancement
- Increased risk of job instability or turnover

For organizations, the consequences include missed opportunities to realize the full benefits of inclusion, such as enhanced innovation, improved team dynamics, and stronger organizational culture. Without effective implementation, the business case for inclusion remains underutilized (Agius et al., 2024). At a broader level, policy–practice gaps contribute to systemic inequities, as the quality of inclusion varies across organizations, sectors, and regions. Workers with intellectual disabilities in resource-rich or highly committed organizations may experience meaningful inclusion, while others face persistent barriers, leading to uneven outcomes and disparities (Bell, 2019; Marinaci et al., 2023). Addressing the gap between intention and implementation requires a shift from viewing inclusion as a policy objective to understanding it as a system design challenge. Effective inclusion depends on the integration of multiple elements, including:

- Leadership commitment and accountability
- Inclusive HRM practices and organizational culture
- Individualized accommodations and assistive technologies
- Continuous training and awareness
- Robust monitoring and evaluation systems
- Alignment with external supports and policy frameworks

The literature consistently emphasizes that no single intervention is sufficient. Instead, sustainable inclusion emerges from the alignment of these components within a coherent organizational framework (Man & Kangas, 2019; Pereira et al., 2024). This perspective reframes inclusion as an ongoing, iterative process, requiring continuous adaptation, learning, and improvement. Organizations must move beyond one-time initiatives or compliance-driven approaches toward systematic and integrated strategies that embed inclusion into the core of their operations. Building on this understanding, this chapter proposes a step-by-step framework for implementing inclusion within organizations. The framework is designed to guide organizations through a structured process of:

1. Assessing current practices and identifying gaps
2. Planning and designing inclusive systems and policies
3. Implementing interventions across organizational domains
4. Sustaining and scaling inclusion through monitoring and continuous improvement

By translating theoretical insights and empirical evidence into actionable steps, the chapter aims to bridge the gap between policy commitment and practical implementation, enabling organizations to create inclusive workplaces that are not only compliant but also effective, sustainable, and transformative. Ultimately, the central argument of this chapter is that inclusion is not achieved through isolated actions or symbolic commitments, but through systematic, coordinated, and evidence-based implementation strategies. Only by addressing the structural and organizational dynamics that shape practice can organizations move from intention to impact in supporting workers with intellectual disabilities.

15.2 CONCEPTUAL FOUNDATION

The implementation of inclusive employment for workers with intellectual disabilities (WWID) cannot be adequately understood through isolated interventions or compliance-based approaches. Instead, the literature consistently positions disability inclusion as a form of organizational change, requiring systemic transformation across structures, processes, and culture. This perspective reframes inclusion from a static policy objective into a dynamic, multi-level change process embedded within organizational systems (Alonso et al., 2023; Suresh & Dyaram, 2020). This section develops the conceptual foundation for implementing inclusion by integrating two central ideas: organizational change theory and inclusion as system transformation. Together, these perspectives provide a comprehensive framework for understanding how organizations can move from policy commitment to sustained, effective inclusion.

15.2.1 Organizational Change Theory: Inclusion as Strategic Transformation

Organizational change theory provides a foundational lens for understanding how inclusive employment practices are implemented and sustained. Across the literature, disability inclusion is conceptualized not as an isolated initiative but as a strategic, organization-wide transformation, requiring coordinated interventions at multiple levels (Suresh & Dyaram, 2020).

15.2.1.1 Change Management and Organization Development (OD)

From a change management and organization development (OD) perspective, inclusion is framed as a planned and deliberate transformation process. This involves:

- Diagnosing organizational barriers and readiness
- Designing interventions aligned with organizational goals
- Implementing changes across systems and processes
- Sustaining change through monitoring and adaptation

Suresh and Dyaram (2020) emphasize that disability inclusion must be integrated into broader OD frameworks, aligning organizational strategy, HR practices, and disability management approaches. This perspective highlights that inclusion is not achieved through ad hoc accommodations but through systematic redesign of organizational practices. Empirical examples reinforce this view. HRM innovations such as buddy systems, structured onboarding, and socialization programs demonstrate how inclusion can be embedded into organizational processes, shaping how workers with ID are integrated into workplace culture and workflows (Meacham et al., 2017). These practices illustrate that change occurs not only through policy but through institutionalized routines and practices.

15.2.1.2 Management Control and Governance Systems

Organizational change is also influenced by management control systems (MCS), which shape how inclusion is governed, monitored, and evaluated. Tucker and Nash (2023) distinguish between compliance-oriented and performance-oriented control systems, showing that different governance approaches produce different inclusion outcomes.

- **Compliance-oriented systems** focus on meeting legal requirements but may result in minimal or symbolic implementation
- **Performance-oriented systems** integrate inclusion into organizational objectives, linking it to productivity, retention, and organizational performance

This distinction highlights the importance of aligning inclusion with organizational performance systems, ensuring that it is treated as a strategic priority rather than a peripheral obligation.

15.2.2 Institutional and Legitimacy Perspectives: External Drivers of Change

While internal organizational processes are critical, change is also shaped by external pressures and institutional environments. Institutional and neo-institutional theories explain how organizations adopt inclusion practices in response to:

- Legal and regulatory requirements
- Social expectations and norms
- Industry standards and competitive pressures

Organizations often engage in inclusion practices as a means of seeking legitimacy, adopting policies and initiatives that align with societal expectations (Jurado-Caraballo et al., 2020). However, this can lead to variations in implementation:

- Some organizations internalize inclusion as a core value and integrate it into practice
- Others adopt symbolic measures to maintain legitimacy without substantive change

This perspective helps explain the policy–practice gap identified in the introduction. External pressures may drive policy adoption, but without internal alignment and commitment, implementation remains limited. Importantly, institutional theory also highlights the need for alignment across macro, meso, and micro levels. Policies and regulations (macro) must be translated into organizational systems (meso) and everyday practices (micro) to achieve meaningful inclusion (Alonso et al., 2023).

15.2.3 Social and Relational Theories: Inclusion as Lived Practice

While structural and institutional factors shape inclusion, its success ultimately depends on social and relational dynamics within the workplace. Social exchange theory and relational frameworks emphasize that inclusion is enacted through interactions, relationships, and workplace climate.

Research highlights the importance of:

- Supervisor support and leadership behavior
- Peer relationships and mentoring
- Trust, communication, and social integration

These relational factors influence not only job performance but also sense of belonging, engagement, and well-being among workers with ID (Meacham et al., 2017). From this perspective, inclusion is not simply a structural condition but a social process, requiring changes in attitudes, behaviors, and norms. Organizational change must therefore address both formal systems and informal dynamics, ensuring that inclusive practices are supported by an inclusive culture.

15.2.4 Leadership and Organizational Culture as Change Drivers

Leadership and organizational culture are consistently identified as central levers of change in implementing inclusion. Diversity management frameworks emphasize that inclusion requires a shift from compliance-based approaches to learning- and effectiveness-oriented models, where diversity is valued as a source of organizational strength (Bartram et al., 2019). Leadership plays a critical role in:

- Setting strategic priorities and allocating resources
- Modeling inclusive behaviors and expectations
- Embedding inclusion into organizational values and norms

Barroso et al. (2023) highlight the gap between corporate sustainability narratives and lived experiences, emphasizing that leadership commitment must translate into concrete practices to achieve meaningful inclusion. Organizational culture, in turn, shapes how policies are interpreted and enacted. A culture that values inclusion supports:

- Acceptance and normalization of accommodations
- Positive attitudes toward workers with ID
- Collaborative and supportive work environments

Without cultural alignment, even well-designed policies may fail to produce desired outcomes.

15.2.5 Inclusion as System Transformation: A Multi-Level Perspective

Building on organizational change theory, the literature conceptualizes disability inclusion as a system-level transformation, spanning multiple interconnected levels.

15.2.5.1 Macro–Meso–Micro Alignment

A key framework for understanding this transformation is the alignment of:

- **Macro level**: Policies, regulations, and societal norms
- **Meso level**: Organizational systems, HR practices, and culture
- **Micro level**: Individual experiences, interactions, and outcomes

Alonso et al. (2023) emphasize that sustainable inclusion requires coordination across these levels, ensuring that policy goals are translated into organizational practices and ultimately experienced by individuals. This ecological perspective highlights that inclusion is not achieved through isolated interventions but through coordinated, system-wide strategies.

15.2.5.2 Ecological and Systems Approaches

Ecological systems theory provides a useful lens for understanding how different levels interact. Organizational practices are influenced by:

- External policy environments
- Internal structures and processes
- Individual characteristics and experiences

Effective inclusion strategies must therefore address interdependencies across systems, ensuring that changes at one level are supported by changes at others (Alonso et al., 2023; Bergman et al., 2024).

2.5.3 Policy–Practice Integration

A central challenge in system transformation is achieving policy–practice integration. This involves embedding inclusive principles into:

- Organizational policies and procedures
- HRM practices and workflows
- Training and development programs
- Monitoring and evaluation systems

The literature emphasizes that inclusion must be institutionalized, becoming part of everyday organizational operations rather than remaining a separate initiative (Bartram et al., 2019; Meacham et al., 2017).

15.2.6 Theoretical Frameworks for Integration

The integration of inclusive practices into organizational systems is supported by a combination of theoretical frameworks:

1. **Social Model and Rights-Based Frameworks**

These provide the normative foundation, framing inclusion as a matter of rights and equity rather than charity ("No Barriers", 2024).

2. **Change Management and OD Theories**

These guide the design and implementation of systemic transformation, emphasizing planning, leadership, and sustained change (Suresh & Dyaram, 2020).

3. **Institutional Theory**

This explains how external pressures shape organizational behavior and highlights the importance of legitimacy and policy alignment (Jurado-Caraballo et al., 2020).

4. **HRM and Diversity Management Frameworks**

These focus on integrating inclusion into organizational practices, emphasizing culture, leadership, and employee experience (Bartram et al., 2019).

5. **Relational and Social Exchange Theories**

These explain how inclusion is enacted through relationships and social dynamics within the workplace (Meacham et al., 2017).

6. **Systems and Ecosystem Approaches**

These emphasize coordination across multiple levels and stakeholders, ensuring sustainability and scalability (Alonso et al., 2023; Bergman et al., 2024).

Together, these frameworks provide a comprehensive toolkit for understanding and implementing inclusion as a system-level transformation. The integration of organizational change theory and system transformation perspectives leads to a central conclusion: inclusive employment for workers with intellectual disabilities requires coordinated, multi-level organizational change. Key principles emerging from this synthesis include:

- Inclusion must be embedded in organizational strategy and governance
- Change must address both structures and social dynamics
- Implementation requires alignment across macro, meso, and micro levels
- Sustained inclusion depends on continuous monitoring and adaptation
- Multiple theoretical frameworks must be integrated to guide practice

These principles provide the conceptual foundation for the step-by-step framework presented in the next section of this chapter. By translating theory into actionable strategies, the framework aims to support organizations in moving from intention to implementation, achieving inclusion that is not only compliant but also effective, sustainable, and transformative.

15.4 PHASE 1: ASSESS

The Assess phase represents the critical starting point of the APIS framework, providing the diagnostic foundation upon which all subsequent inclusion efforts are built. Without a rigorous and multidimensional assessment, organizations risk implementing fragmented or ineffective initiatives that fail to address underlying barriers. The literature consistently emphasizes that successful inclusion for workers with intellectual disabilities (WWID) depends on a comprehensive understanding of organizational readiness, culture, and capacity for change. This phase moves beyond superficial evaluation to examine the deep structures and dynamics that shape inclusion outcomes, including organizational climate, leadership commitment, resource availability, and stakeholder engagement. It integrates three core components: organizational readiness assessment, culture audit, and gap analysis, each of which contributes to a holistic understanding of the organization's starting point.

15.4.1 Organizational Readiness: Capacity and Willingness for Change

Organizational readiness refers to the extent to which an organization is prepared, willing, and capable of implementing inclusive employment practices. It is a multidimensional construct encompassing both psychological and structural elements, including:

- Commitment to change
- Confidence in the ability to implement change (change efficacy)
- Availability of resources and infrastructure
- Alignment of policies and processes

Weiner's conceptualization of organizational readiness—operationalized through tools such as the Organizational Readiness for Implementing Change (ORIC)—distinguishes between change commitment (the shared resolve to pursue inclusion) and change efficacy (the shared belief in the ability to do so effectively). Empirical evidence demonstrates that higher levels of readiness are associated with faster adoption and more successful implementation of new practices. In addition, multidimensional readiness frameworks identify four key domains:

1. Organizational climate for change
2. Attitudes toward innovation and inclusion
3. Commitment to change
4. Capacity to implement change

These domains provide a structured lens for assessing readiness in inclusive employment contexts (Castañeda et al., 2012; Houtven et al., 2023). Importantly, readiness is not a static condition but a malleable and evolving state. Organizations may exhibit high commitment but low capacity, or vice versa, requiring targeted capacity-building interventions. This underscores the importance of assessing readiness not only before implementation but also throughout the change process, enabling continuous adjustment and improvement (Wippold et al., 2024).

15.4.2 Tools and Methods for Readiness Assessment

Effective readiness assessment requires the use of structured, evidence-based tools combined with qualitative insights. Several instruments are highlighted in the literature:

- **ORIC (Organizational Readiness for Implementing Change)**

Measures change commitment and efficacy, providing predictive insights into adoption and implementation trajectories (Houtven et al., 2023).

- **ODQ (Organizational Diagnostic Questionnaire)**

Based on Weisbord's Six-Box Model, assesses key organizational dimensions including purpose, structure, relationships, rewards, leadership, and supporting mechanisms (Khan et al., 2023).

- **Community and Organizational Readiness Surveys**

Evaluate climate, capacity, and stakeholder engagement, enabling benchmarking and targeted interventions (Castañeda et al., 2012).

Beyond quantitative tools, the literature emphasizes the importance of mixed-method approaches, combining:

- Surveys and diagnostic instruments
- Stakeholder interviews and focus groups
- Document analysis (policies, HR procedures)

This approach provides a richer and more nuanced understanding of readiness, capturing both measurable indicators and contextual dynamics (Bendixen et al., 2022).

15.4.3 Culture Audit: Understanding Norms, Attitudes, and Inclusion Climate

While readiness focuses on capacity and intention, a culture audit examines the deeper social and normative environment within which inclusion initiatives are implemented. Organizational culture shapes how policies are interpreted, how employees interact, and whether inclusion is experienced as meaningful or symbolic.

Key dimensions of culture relevant to inclusion include:

- Attitudes toward disability and diversity
- Perceptions of fairness and equity
- Openness to change and innovation
- Psychological safety and trust

Research indicates that even well-designed policies can fail if organizational culture does not support inclusion. Negative attitudes, low expectations, or stigma can undermine accommodations and limit opportunities for workers with ID, highlighting the need to assess and address cultural barriers (Smith & Parmenter, 2023). A culture audit should therefore examine:

- Employee perceptions of inclusion and belonging
- Supervisor attitudes and behaviors
- Communication practices and accessibility
- Informal norms and workplace dynamics

Importantly, culture audits must include multiple perspectives, particularly those of workers with ID, their families, and support professionals. This ensures that assessments reflect lived experiences rather than solely managerial viewpoints.

15.4.4 Stakeholder Engagement: Capturing Multi-Level Perspectives

A defining feature of effective assessment processes is stakeholder inclusivity. Inclusion initiatives operate within complex ecosystems involving multiple actors, including:

- Organizational leadership and HR professionals
- Supervisors and coworkers
- Workers with intellectual disabilities
- Families, job coaches, and vocational specialists

- External partners such as service providers and educators

Engaging these stakeholders in the assessment process provides several benefits:

- Enhances the accuracy and relevance of findings
- Builds buy-in and shared ownership of change initiatives
- Identifies champions who can drive implementation

Bendixen et al. (2022) emphasize that stakeholder engagement is not merely consultative but should be collaborative, involving stakeholders in co-designing solutions and defining success metrics.

15.4.5 Gap Analysis: Identifying Discrepancies Between Current and Desired States

The final component of the Assess phase is gap analysis, which involves comparing the organization's current state with its desired inclusion outcomes. This process translates assessment findings into actionable insights by identifying:

- Structural gaps (e.g., absence of inclusive HR policies)
- Capacity gaps (e.g., lack of trained staff or resources)
- Cultural gaps (e.g., stigma or lack of awareness)
- Process gaps (e.g., ineffective onboarding or performance management systems)

Gap analysis is most effective when linked to a logic model, which connects inputs, activities, outputs, and outcomes. This approach enables organizations to:

- Identify which capacities are required to achieve desired outcomes
- Align resources and interventions with strategic goals
- Establish clear evaluation metrics (Isaacs et al., 2009)

For example, if the desired outcome is increased retention of workers with ID, gap analysis may reveal deficiencies in:

- Job coaching and support systems
- Workplace accommodations
- Supervisor training and communication

These insights provide a clear basis for targeted intervention design in the subsequent planning phase.

15.4.6 Readiness as a Predictor of Implementation Success

A critical insight from the literature is that organizational readiness is a strong predictor of implementation success. Organizations with higher levels of readiness—particularly in terms of commitment and efficacy—are more likely to:

- Adopt inclusive practices more quickly
- Implement interventions with greater fidelity
- Sustain inclusion over time (Houtven et al., 2023)

However, readiness alone is not sufficient. Its impact depends on interaction with:

- Organizational culture
- Leadership and governance structures
- External policy and funding environments

This reinforces the importance of a comprehensive assessment approach, which captures both readiness and contextual factors.

15.4.7 Iterative Assessment and Continuous Improvement

The Assess phase should not be viewed as a one-time activity but as an ongoing process integrated throughout the implementation lifecycle. Periodic reassessment enables organizations to:

- Monitor changes in readiness and capacity
- Identify emerging barriers or challenges
- Adjust strategies to maintain momentum

This iterative approach aligns with implementation science principles, emphasizing that readiness is dynamic and requires continuous monitoring and adaptation (Wippold et al., 2024). The Assess phase establishes the strategic foundation for inclusive organizational transformation, providing the data, insights, and shared understanding necessary to guide subsequent action. Key principles emerging from this phase include:

- Inclusion requires multidimensional readiness assessment

- Organizational culture must be explicitly examined and addressed
- Stakeholder engagement is essential for accuracy and buy-in
- Gap analysis translates diagnosis into actionable priorities
- Assessment must be iterative and integrated into ongoing processes

By grounding inclusion efforts in rigorous assessment, organizations can move beyond assumptions and develop targeted, evidence-based strategies that address real barriers and leverage existing strengths. This phase directly informs the next stage of the framework—Plan—where assessment findings are translated into structured strategies, interventions, and measurable goals for implementing inclusive employment.

15.5 PHASE 2: PLAN

Following a comprehensive assessment of organizational readiness, culture, and capacity, the Plan phase translates diagnostic insights into a coherent, strategic roadmap for inclusion. This phase is critical in ensuring that inclusion initiatives are not fragmented or reactive but instead aligned with organizational strategy, operational systems, and long-term goals. The literature consistently emphasizes that effective planning for the inclusion of workers with intellectual disabilities (WWID) requires three interrelated components: strategic integration, measurable performance frameworks, and resource alignment. Together, these elements ensure that inclusion is embedded within organizational systems and supported by clear accountability mechanisms (Eshete & Birbirssa, 2024).

15.5.1 Strategy Development: Embedding Inclusion into Organizational Systems

At the core of the Plan phase is the development of a comprehensive inclusion strategy that integrates disability inclusion into the organization's broader mission, governance, and operational practices. Rather than treating inclusion as a standalone initiative, the literature strongly advocates positioning it as a transformative, organization-wide strategy, aligned with diversity and inclusion (D&I) goals and organizational development (OD) frameworks (Gould et al., 2021).

15.5.1.1 Inclusion as Strategic Organizational Change

Strategic planning must conceptualize inclusion as a systemic transformation, requiring alignment across:

- Recruitment and hiring processes
- Onboarding and training systems
- Job design and accommodations
- Performance management and career pathways
- Organizational culture and communication

This integrative approach is supported by Strategic Human Resource Management (SHRM) frameworks, which emphasize the alignment of three core domains:

1. **Knowledge and skills** (training, competencies, awareness)
2. **Motivation and effort** (engagement, incentives, leadership support)
3. **Opportunities to contribute** (inclusive job design, accommodations, participation)

By coordinating these domains, organizations can create an inclusive climate that supports both individual performance and organizational outcomes (Eshete & Amentie, 2024).

15.5.1.2 Dual Framing: Business Case and Moral Imperative

Effective strategies are often grounded in a dual framing of inclusion:

- A business case, highlighting benefits such as innovation, productivity, retention, and organizational performance
- A moral and rights-based case, emphasizing equity, dignity, and social responsibility

This dual framing helps secure leadership commitment and sustain long-term engagement, particularly when supported by internal champions who advocate for inclusion across organizational levels (Gould et al., 2021).

15.5.1.3 Leadership and Governance in Strategy Development

Leadership plays a central role in shaping and legitimizing the inclusion strategy. Senior leaders are responsible for:

- Articulating a clear vision for inclusion
- Embedding inclusion into organizational values and policies
- Establishing governance structures and accountability mechanisms

Importantly, line managers serve as critical operational actors, translating strategic goals into day-to-day practices, including supervision, feedback, and accommodation processes (Wesley et al., 2024).

15.5.2 KPI and Metrics: Measuring Inclusion Across the Employee Lifecycle

A defining feature of effective planning is the development of robust, multidimensional Key Performance Indicators (KPIs) that translate inclusion goals into measurable outcomes. The literature emphasizes that measurement systems must go beyond compliance metrics to capture the full scope of inclusion, including both quantitative and qualitative dimensions (Aksnes & Ulstein, 2024; Tu n, 2018).

15.5.2.1 Inclusion Scorecard Framework

Organizations are encouraged to develop an inclusion scorecard, encompassing indicators across three levels:

- **Organizational level** (policy, governance, culture)
- **Workgroup level** (team dynamics, supervisor support)
- **Individual level** (employee outcomes and experiences)

This multi-level approach ensures that inclusion is measured holistically, reflecting both structural and experiential dimensions.

15.5.2.2 Core KPI Domains

The literature identifies several key domains for KPI development:

1. **Hiring and Representation**
    - o Percentage of employees with ID
    - o Recruitment and hiring rates
    - o Time-to-hire for inclusive roles
2. **Development and Advancement**
    - o Participation in training and development programs
    - o Promotion rates and career progression
    - o Accessibility of advancement pathways
3. **Accommodation and Accessibility**
    - o Time to implement accommodations
    - o Accessibility audit scores

- o Availability and effectiveness of assistive technologies

4. **Engagement and Retention**
   - o Employee retention and turnover rates
   - o Job tenure
   - o Engagement and satisfaction scores
5. **Leadership and Culture**
   - o Inclusion climate index
   - o Supervisor support ratings
   - o Leadership inclusivity behaviors
6. **Business and Organizational Outcomes**
   - o Productivity and quality metrics
   - o Safety and performance indicators
   - o Return on investment (ROI) for inclusion initiatives

These indicators enable organizations to link inclusion efforts to both employee outcomes and organizational performance, reinforcing the strategic value of inclusion (Eshete & Birbirssa, 2024; Wesley et al., 2024).

15.5.2.3 Qualitative and Experiential Metrics

In addition to quantitative KPIs, the literature highlights the importance of qualitative measures, including:

- Sense of belonging and inclusion
- Psychological safety
- Organizational identification
- Perceived fairness and equity

These measures capture the lived experiences of workers with ID, providing critical insights into the effectiveness of inclusion strategies (Alfalih & Ragmoun, 2025).

15.5.2.4 Accountability and Governance

KPIs must be accompanied by clear accountability structures, including:

- Assignment of ownership to leaders and managers
- Integration into performance evaluations
- Alignment with incentives and rewards

This ensures that inclusion is not optional but embedded within organizational accountability systems.

15.5.3 Resource Allocation: Enabling Implementation and Sustainability

Strategic planning must be supported by adequate and well-aligned resources, ensuring that inclusion initiatives are feasible, scalable, and sustainable. Resource allocation encompasses financial, human, and organizational resources, each of which plays a critical role in implementation.

15.5.3.1 Financial Resources and Budgeting

Organizations must allocate dedicated budgets for:

- Workplace accommodations and assistive technologies
- Training and capacity-building programs
- Job coaching and support services
- Monitoring and evaluation systems

The literature emphasizes that insufficient or inconsistent funding is a major barrier to implementation, highlighting the need for strategic and sustained investment.

15.5.3.2 Human Resources and Capability Development

Effective inclusion requires investment in human capital, including:

- Training for managers and employees on inclusive practices
- Development of internal expertise in disability inclusion
- Designation of inclusion champions and coordinators

These investments enhance organizational capacity and support the translation of strategy into practice.

15.5.3.3 Structural and Process Resources

Resource allocation must also address organizational structures and processes, including:

- Integration of inclusion into HR systems

- Development of accessible communication and workflows
- Establishment of coordination mechanisms across departments

These structural elements ensure that inclusion is embedded within organizational infrastructure, rather than dependent on individual initiatives.

15.5.3.4 External Partnerships and Ecosystem Resources

Organizations are encouraged to leverage external resources, including:

- Vocational rehabilitation services
- Disability employment agencies
- Educational institutions and training providers

Such partnerships enhance capacity, provide specialized expertise, and support the development of sustainable inclusion ecosystems (Kalargyrou & Costen, 2017).

15.5.4 Integrative Dynamics: Aligning Strategy, Metrics, and Resources

The effectiveness of the Plan phase depends on the alignment of strategy, metrics, and resources. These elements must function as an integrated system:

- Strategy defines the direction and priorities
- KPIs translate goals into measurable outcomes
- Resources enable implementation and sustainability

Misalignment among these components can undermine inclusion efforts. For example:

- Strong strategies without resources lead to implementation failure
- Metrics without strategy create fragmented efforts
- Resources without accountability reduce effectiveness

Therefore, planning must ensure coherence and integration, linking all elements within a unified framework. The Plan phase serves as the architectural design stage of inclusive transformation, translating assessment insights into structured, actionable strategies. It establishes the foundation for effective implementation by aligning organizational systems, defining measurable goals, and allocating necessary resources. Key principles emerging from this phase include:

- Inclusion must be embedded in organizational strategy and SHRM systems
- Measurement systems must be multidimensional and outcome-oriented
- Leadership and governance are critical for accountability and alignment
- Resource allocation must be strategic, sustained, and integrated
- Planning must balance global frameworks with local adaptation

By operationalizing these principles, organizations can move beyond intention and create a clear, actionable roadmap for inclusive employment. This phase directly informs the next stage of the framework—Implement—where strategies are translated into concrete practices, interventions, and organizational routines that support workers with intellectual disabilities in the workplace.

15.6 PHASE 3: IMPLEMENT

The Implement phase represents the transition from strategic planning to real-world execution, where inclusion is enacted through everyday practices, behaviors, and organizational routines. While earlier phases establish direction and structure, this phase determines whether inclusion initiatives are effectively translated into lived workplace realities for workers with intellectual disabilities (WWID). The literature consistently highlights that implementation success depends on the alignment of three critical elements: (1) effective policy execution through HRM systems, (2) comprehensive and continuous training, and (3) strong, authentic leadership engagement. These elements function interdependently, shaping how inclusion policies are interpreted, operationalized, and sustained within organizational contexts (Cavanagh et al., 2016; Bartram et al., 2019; Suresh & Dyaram, 2020).

15.6.1 Policy Execution: Translating Strategy into Practice

A central challenge in inclusive employment is the policy–practice gap, where organizations adopt inclusive policies but fail to translate them into consistent workplace practices. Effective implementation requires that policies are not only formally articulated but also embedded within organizational systems and routines.

15.6.1.1 Embedding Inclusion in HRM Systems

Inclusive policies must be operationalized across the entire employee lifecycle, including:

- Recruitment and selection

- Onboarding and socialization
- Training and development
- Performance management
- Retention and career progression

Research demonstrates that when inclusion is integrated into HRM systems, it becomes part of organizational infrastructure, rather than an isolated initiative. This systemic embedding ensures consistency and sustainability in practice (Suresh & Dyaram, 2020; Bartram et al., 2019).

15.6.1.2 Adaptability and Individualization

While policies provide structure, they must remain flexible and responsive to individual needs. Disability-inclusive HR practices are most effective when they balance:

- Standardization (for organizational coherence)
- Personalization (to address diverse support needs)

This balance enables organizations to maintain consistency while delivering tailored accommodations and supports that enhance employee performance and engagement (Aksnes & Ulstein, 2024).

15.6.1.3 Integrative Implementation Models

The literature identifies practical pathways for translating policy into action, such as:

- Recruitment → Development → Supervision models, which emphasize continuity across employment stages
- Organizational development (OD) approaches, which link inclusion to broader change processes

These models highlight that implementation is not a single event but a continuous, lifecycle-based process (Khan et al., 2022).

15.6.2 Training: Building Capability and Reducing Barriers

Training is consistently identified as a core mechanism for successful implementation, enabling employees, managers, and leaders to translate inclusion policies into effective practices.

15.6.2.1 Types of Training

Effective training programs typically include:

- Disability awareness training, addressing stigma, bias, and misconceptions
- Practical skills training, focusing on accommodations, communication, and support strategies
- Managerial training, equipping supervisors with tools for inclusive leadership and performance management

These programs enhance both knowledge and behavioral competence, enabling staff to support WWID effectively (Bartram et al., 2019).

15.6.2.2 Embedding Training in Organizational Systems

Training must be:

- Ongoing, rather than one-off
- Integrated into HR processes (onboarding, leadership development)
- Linked to performance expectations and accountability

Organizations that embed training within their systems are more likely to achieve consistent and sustainable implementation outcomes (Bergman et al., 2024).

15.6.2.3 Training as Culture Change Mechanism

Beyond skill development, training plays a critical role in shaping organizational culture by:

- Reducing stigma and bias
- Promoting empathy and understanding
- Encouraging inclusive behaviors

This cultural impact is essential for creating environments where WWID can fully participate and thrive.

15.6.3 Leadership Role: Driving and Sustaining Implementation

Leadership is widely recognized as the most critical factor in successful implementation. Leaders influence not only strategic direction but also the day-to-day enactment of inclusion practices.

15.6.3.1 Strategic Leadership

Senior leaders are responsible for:

- Demonstrating visible commitment to inclusion
- Allocating resources and removing barriers
- Embedding inclusion into organizational priorities

Their actions signal the importance of inclusion and legitimize efforts across the organization (Wehman et al., 2021; Suresh & Dyaram, 2020).

15.6.3.2 Frontline Leadership and Practice Leadership

Frontline managers play a pivotal role in implementation, as they are directly responsible for:

- Supervising employees with ID
- Providing feedback and support
- Implementing accommodations and adjustments

Research shows that effective frontline leadership is associated with:

- Improved job performance
- Higher engagement and satisfaction
- Greater inclusion and participation among WWID (Fajardo-Castro et al., 2025)

This highlights the importance of practice leadership, where managers actively support inclusion through daily interactions and decisions.

15.6.3.3 Leadership and Training Synergy

The interaction between leadership and training is critical. Training initiatives are most effective when:

- Supported by leadership commitment
- Reinforced through managerial behaviors
- Integrated into organizational culture

This synergy creates a reinforcing loop, where leadership and training jointly enhance inclusion outcomes (Cavanagh et al., 2016).

15.6.4 Organizational Practices Supporting Integration

Effective implementation requires a set of coordinated organizational practices that support the integration of WWID into mainstream work environments.

15.6.4.1 Inclusive HRM Practices

Key practices include:

- Accessible recruitment and onboarding processes
- Performance management systems that incorporate accommodations
- Career development opportunities tailored to individual needs

These practices ensure that inclusion is embedded across organizational processes, supporting both entry and long-term participation (Bartram et al., 2019).

15.6.4.2 Workplace Culture and Environment

A supportive organizational culture is essential for implementation. Key elements include:

- Barrier-free communication
- Positive attitudes toward diversity
- Inclusive team dynamics

Such environments reduce stigma and enable WWID to engage fully in workplace activities (Suresh & Dyaram, 2020).

15.6.4.3 Structured Support Systems

Structured supports, such as:

- Job coaching
- Mentoring programs
- Tailored job design

play a critical role in facilitating integration and retention. These supports ensure that employees receive the assistance needed to succeed in their roles (Wehman et al., 2021).

15.6.5 Contextual and Systemic Influences

Implementation is shaped by organizational context, including:

- Resource availability
- Organizational culture
- External policy and regulatory environments

These factors influence the extent to which policies are effectively translated into practice. For example, limited resources or weak leadership commitment may result in partial or inconsistent implementation (Kersten et al., 2022). Additionally, knowledge management and communication systems play a crucial role in ensuring that policies are understood and applied consistently across the organization.

15.6.6 Challenges and Tensions in Implementation

Despite strong frameworks, implementation often faces challenges, including:

- Gaps between policy and practice, particularly when managers lack training
- Variability across contexts, requiring adaptation of strategies
- Inconsistent leadership commitment, leading to uneven outcomes

These challenges highlight the need for continuous monitoring, support, and adaptation to ensure effective implementation. The Implement phase transforms inclusion from strategy into organizational practice, embedding it within everyday routines, interactions, and systems. Key principles emerging from this phase include:

- Policies must be translated into concrete HRM practices

- Training is essential for building capability and cultural change
- Leadership is the primary driver of implementation success
- Inclusion requires alignment between formal systems and informal practices
- Implementation must be adaptive and context-sensitive

By operationalizing these principles, organizations can ensure that inclusion is not merely aspirational but becomes a lived reality for workers with intellectual disabilities. This phase leads directly to the final stage of the framework—Sustain—which focuses on embedding, scaling, and continuously improving inclusive practices over time.

15.7 PHASE 4: SUSTAIN

The Sustain phase represents the culmination of the APIS framework, where inclusive employment practices for workers with intellectual disabilities (WWID) are embedded, stabilized, and continuously enhanced over time. While earlier phases focus on planning and execution, sustainability determines whether inclusion becomes part of the organization's core operations or remains a temporary initiative. The literature consistently identifies three interdependent pillars of sustainability:

(1) robust monitoring and evaluation (M&E) systems, (2) continuous improvement mechanisms, and (3) scaling strategies supported by governance and culture. Together, these elements ensure that inclusion is not only maintained but also adapted, expanded, and strengthened in response to evolving organizational and environmental conditions (Ristevski et al., 2024).

15.7.1 Monitoring and Evaluation: Measuring Long-Term Inclusion Outcomes

Sustaining inclusive employment requires moving beyond short-term metrics toward longitudinal, multidimensional evaluation frameworks. The literature emphasizes that organizations must systematically track not only whether workers with ID are employed, but also whether inclusion is meaningful, stable, and beneficial over time.

15.7.1.1 Multi-Dimensional M&E Frameworks

Effective M&E systems integrate indicators across three levels:

- **Process indicators** (e.g., policy implementation, training completion, availability of supports)
- **Proximal outcomes** (e.g., job satisfaction, engagement, autonomy, perceived inclusion)
- **Long-term outcomes** (e.g., employment stability, wage progression, well-being, social integration)

Frameworks such as the Disability and Wellbeing Monitoring Framework highlight the importance of capturing both organizational processes and individual outcomes, ensuring that evaluation reflects the full scope of inclusion (Bergman et al., 2024).

15.7.1.2 Longitudinal and Outcome-Oriented Evaluation

A key insight from the literature is the necessity of longitudinal data collection, which allows organizations to assess whether initial gains are sustained over time. Indicators commonly used include:

- Duration of employment and job retention
- Career progression and income growth
- Psychological well-being and job satisfaction
- Social participation and workplace relationships

Longitudinal approaches are essential for identifying patterns of success and failure, enabling organizations to understand the sustainability of inclusion practices (Taylor et al., 2022; Jacob & Pillay, 2023).

15.7.1.3 Mixed-Methods Evaluation

The literature strongly supports combining:

- Quantitative data (e.g., retention rates, productivity, wages)
- Qualitative insights (e.g., employee experiences, sense of belonging, perceived inclusion)

This mixed-method approach provides a comprehensive understanding of inclusion, capturing both measurable outcomes and lived experiences (O'Donovan et al., 2025).

15.7.1.4 Participatory Monitoring and Governance

A distinctive feature of sustainable inclusion is the use of participatory evaluation, where workers with ID are actively involved in:

- Defining evaluation criteria
- Monitoring outcomes
- Co-designing improvements

The establishment of advisory boards or governance structures that include people with ID strengthens accountability, legitimacy, and responsiveness, ensuring that evaluation processes remain aligned with stakeholder needs (Robinson et al., 2022).

15.7.2 Continuous Improvement: Embedding Adaptive Learning Systems

Monitoring alone is insufficient without mechanisms for translating data into action. The Sustain phase therefore emphasizes continuous quality improvement (CQI) as a core organizational capability.

15.7.2.1 CQI as an Organizational Routine

Continuous improvement involves embedding feedback loops into organizational processes, where:

- Evaluation data is regularly reviewed
- Insights are translated into policy and practice adjustments
- Outcomes are re-evaluated to assess effectiveness

This iterative cycle ensures that inclusion remains dynamic and responsive, rather than static (Ristevski et al., 2024).

15.7.2.2 Data-Driven Adaptation of Supports

Evidence highlights the importance of using data to refine:

- Job design and task allocation
- Workplace accommodations
- Training and support systems
- Job coaching and supervision strategies

For example, adjustments to job roles or support structures based on performance and well-being data can enhance both productivity and employee satisfaction, contributing to sustained employment outcomes (Flores et al., 2021; Nevala et al., 2019).

15.7.2.3 Organizational Learning and Policy Evolution

Sustainable inclusion requires organizations to function as learning systems, where:

- Policies are regularly updated based on evidence
- Training programs are revised to reflect new insights
- Resources are reallocated to address emerging needs

This process transforms inclusion from a fixed program into a continuously evolving practice, aligned with organizational learning principles (Watfern & Carnemolla, 2025).

7.2.4 Co-Production and Stakeholder Engagement

Continuous improvement is strengthened through co-production, where workers with ID and other stakeholders actively participate in:

- Evaluating outcomes
- Identifying challenges
- Designing solutions

This approach enhances relevance, reduces policy–practice gaps, and increases the sustainability of inclusion initiatives (Robinson et al., 2022).

15.7.3 Scaling: Expanding and Institutionalizing Inclusive Practices

Beyond maintaining existing practices, the Sustain phase focuses on scaling inclusion across organizational and systemic levels.

15.7.3.1 Institutionalization within Organizational Systems

Scaling begins with embedding inclusion into:

- Organizational policies and governance frameworks
- HRM systems and workflows
- Budgeting and resource allocation processes

When inclusion becomes part of "core business", it is less vulnerable to changes in leadership, funding, or priorities (Ristevski et al., 2024).

15.7.3.2 Expansion Across Organizational Units

Organizations can scale inclusion by:

- Replicating successful practices across departments
- Standardizing effective models while allowing local adaptation
- Sharing best practices internally

This approach enables organizations to move from pilot programs to organization-wide implementation.

15.7.3.3 Cross-Sector and Ecosystem Scaling

Sustainability is further enhanced through cross-sector collaboration, including partnerships with:

- Vocational rehabilitation services
- Education and training institutions
- Health and social services
- Community organizations

Such collaborations create integrated support ecosystems, enabling inclusion to extend beyond organizational boundaries.

15.7.3.4 Policy Alignment and External Support

Scaling also depends on alignment with:

- National and regional policy frameworks
- Funding mechanisms and incentives
- Regulatory environments

Organizations that align with broader policy systems are better positioned to sustain and expand inclusion initiatives over time.

15.7.4 Challenges and Tensions in Sustaining Inclusion

Despite strong frameworks, sustaining inclusion presents several challenges:

- **Limited longitudinal data**, making it difficult to assess long-term impact
- **Variability across contexts**, requiring adaptation of practices
- **Balancing competing priorities**, such as productivity, safety, and inclusion
- Risk of symbolic compliance, where inclusion is maintained in policy but not in practice

These challenges highlight the need for adaptive, evidence-based approaches that can respond to changing conditions and emerging insights. The Sustain phase transforms inclusion into a self-reinforcing organizational capability, ensuring that practices are maintained, improved, and expanded over time. Key principles emerging from this phase include:

- Sustainability requires robust, multidimensional M&E systems
- Continuous improvement must be embedded through CQI processes
- Inclusion must be institutionalized within governance and culture
- Scaling depends on organizational integration and cross-sector collaboration
- Stakeholder participation is essential for legitimacy and adaptability

Ultimately, sustaining inclusion means moving beyond implementation toward system integration and evolution, where inclusion becomes an enduring feature of organizational identity and practice. This completes the APIS framework, providing organizations with a comprehensive model for moving from intention to sustained, scalable inclusion for workers with intellectual disabilities.

REFERENCES

Agius, M., Heiman, T., Sula, G., Tsvetkova, P., Nanchen, B., Tkaczyk, A. H., & Sousa, C. (2024). *Supporting Workplace Inclusion: Reasonable Accommodations and Assistive Technologies for Individuals With Intellectual Disability*. 111–127. DOI: 10.24140/nobarriers.v1.p02.05

Aksnes, S. Y., & Ulstein, J. (2024). Sustainable Employment for People With Disabilities: A Scoping Review on Workplace Practices and Positive Employment Outcomes. *Scandinavian Journal of Disability Research*, *26*(1). Advance online publication. DOI: 10.16993/sjdr.1089

Alfalih, A., & Ragmoun, W. (2025). The Impact of Transformational Leadership on the Workplace Well-Being of Employees With Disabilities: Series Mediation and Moderation Process. *Frontiers in Public Health*, *13*, 1506257. Advance online publication. DOI: 10.3389/fpubh.2025.1506257 PMID: 40443931

Alonso, M. Á. V., Schalock, R. L., Gómez, L. E., & Navas, P. (2023). A Systematic Approach to Implementing, Evaluating, and Sustaining the Shared Citizenship Paradigm in the Disability Field. *Behavioral Sciences (Basel, Switzerland)*, *13*(12), 970. DOI: 10.3390/bs13120970 PMID: 38131825

Barroso, C. L., Mañas-Viniegra, L., Sánchez, J. S., & García, F. G. (2023). Disability and Employability in the Audio-Visual Sector: The (Dis)connection Between Corporate Social Sustainability Goals and the Employment Experiences of People With Disabilities. *El Profesional de la Información*, e320604. Advance online publication. DOI: 10.3145/epi.2023.nov.04

Bartram, T., Cavanagh, J., Meacham, H., & Pariona-Cabrera, P. (2019). Re-calibrating HRM to Improve the Work Experiences for Workers With Intellectual Disability. *Asia Pacific Journal of Human Resources*, *59*(1), 63–83. DOI: 10.1111/1744-7941.12230

Bell, M. (2019). People With Intellectual Disabilities and Labour Market Inclusion: What Role for EU Labour Law? *European Labour Law Journal*, *11*(1), 3–25. DOI: 10.1177/2031952519882953

Bendixen, R., Benevides, T., Ideishi, R., Smythe, R. T., Taylor, J. P., Umeda, C., Kerfeld, C. A., & Jirikowic, T. (2022). Community Conversations: Stakeholder-Identified Research Priorities to Foster Community Participation for Individuals With Intellectual and Developmental Disability. *Frontiers in Rehabilitation Sciences*, *3*, 873415. Advance online publication. DOI: 10.3389/fresc.2022.873415 PMID: 36188970

Bergman, J., Ratcliffe, S. E., Harvey-Smith, L., & Williams, L. A. (2024). *Initiatives for Workplace Equity and Inclusion: A Series of Rapid Systematic Reviews of the Peer-Reviewed Literature*. DOI: 10.31219/osf.io/zmvjn

Castañeda, S. F., Holscher, J. T., Mumman, M. K., Salgado, H., Keir, K. B., Foster-Fishman, P. G., & Talavera, G. A. (2012). Dimensions of Community and Organizational Readiness for Change. *Progress in Community Health Partnerships*, *6*(2), 119. DOI: 10.1353/cpr.2012.0021 PMID: 22820232

Cavanagh, J., Bartram, T., Meacham, H., Bigby, C., Oakman, J., & Fossey, E. (2016). Supporting Workers With Disabilities: A Scoping Review of the Role of Human Resource Management in Contemporary Organisations. *Asia Pacific Journal of Human Resources*, *55*(1), 6–43. DOI: 10.1111/1744-7941.12111

Eshete, S. K., & Amentie, C. (2024). *Strategic Human Resource Management (SHRM) and Inclusion for Promoting Workplace Creativity and Innovation: Systematic Review*. DOI: 10.21203/rs.3.rs-3850810/v1

Eshete, S. K., & Birbirssa, Z. A. (2024). Strategic Human Resource Management (SHRM) in Creating Inclusive Workplace: Systematic Review. *SAGE Open*, *14*(4), 21582440241287667. Advance online publication. DOI: 10.1177/21582440241287667

Flores, N., Moret-Tatay, C., Gutiérrez-Bermejo, B., Vázquez-Martínez, A., & Río, C. J. (2021). Assessment of Occupational Health and Job Satisfaction in Workers With Intellectual Disability: A Job Demands–Resources Perspective. *International Journal of Environmental Research and Public Health*, *18*(4), 2072. DOI: 10.3390/ijerph18042072 PMID: 33672616

Gould, R., Mullin, C., Harris, S. P., & Jones, R. (2021). Building, Sustaining and Growing: Disability Inclusion in Business. *Equality, Diversity and Inclusion*, *41*(3), 418–434. DOI: 10.1108/EDI-06-2020-0156

Houtven, C. H. V., Drake, C., Malo, T. L., Decosimo, K., Tucker, M., Sullivan, C., D'Adolf, J., Hughes, J. M., Christensen, L., Grubber, J. M., Coffman, C. J., Sperber, N., Wang, V., Allen, K. D., Hastings, S. N., Shea, C. M., & Zullig, L. L. (2023). Ready, Set, Go! The Role of Organizational Readiness to Predict Adoption of a Family Caregiver Training Program Using the Rogers' Diffusion of Innovation Theory. *Implementation Science Communications*, *4*(1), 69. Advance online publication. DOI: 10.1186/s43058-023-00447-x PMID: 37337208

Isaacs, B., Clark, C., Correia, S., & Flannery, J. (2009). Utility of Logic Models to Plan Quality of Life Outcome Evaluations. *Journal of Policy and Practice in Intellectual Disabilities*, *6*(1), 52–61. DOI: 10.1111/j.1741-1130.2008.00197.x

Jacob, U. S., & Pillay, J. (2023). Studies Related to Employment of Persons With Intellectual Disability: A Systematic Review. *Journal of Vocational Rehabilitation, 59*(2), 169–181. DOI: 10.3233/JVR-230035

Jurado-Caraballo, M. Á., García, C. Q., & Rodríguez-Fernández, M. (2020). Trends and Opportunities in Research on Disability and Work: An Interdisciplinary Perspective. *Business Research Quarterly, 25*(4), 366–388. DOI: 10.1177/2340944420972715

Kalargyrou, V., & Costen, W. M. (2017). Diversity Management Research in Hospitality and Tourism: Past, Present and Future. *International Journal of Contemporary Hospitality Management, 29*(1), 68–114. DOI: 10.1108/IJCHM-09-2015-0470

Kersten, M. C. O., Taminiau, E. F., Weggeman, M., & Embregts, P. J. C. M. (2022). Contextual Factors Related to the Execution of Knowledge Strategies in Intellectual Disabilities Organizations. *Knowledge and Process Management, 29*(3), 242–254. DOI: 10.1002/kpm.1700

Khan, S. HASSAN, M. U., Parveen, I., Mutalib, R. A., & Khan, M. A. (2023). *An Organizational Diagnosis for Change Readiness: A Case of the Department of Special Education Government of Punjab*. DOI: 10.20944/preprints202305.0926.v1

Man, J., & Kangas, M. (2019). Best Practice Adherence and Workplace Facilitators and Hindrances for Psychologists Working With Individuals With Intellectual Disabilities and Co-Morbid Mental Health Concerns. *Journal of Policy and Practice in Intellectual Disabilities, 16*(3), 239–249. DOI: 10.1111/jppi.12288

Marinaci, T., Russo, C., Savarese, G., Stornaiuolo, G., Faiella, F., Carpinelli, L., Navarra, M., Marsico, G., & Mollo, M. (2023). An Inclusive Workplace Approach to Disability Through Assistive Technologies: A Systematic Review and Thematic Analysis of the Literature. *Societies (Basel, Switzerland), 13*(11), 231. DOI: 10.3390/soc13110231

Meacham, H., Cavanagh, J., Shaw, A., & Bartram, T. (2017). Innovation Programs at the Workplace for Workers With an Intellectual Disability. *Personnel Review, 46*(7), 1381–1396. DOI: 10.1108/PR-08-2016-0214

Morris, R., Christianson-Barker, J., Stainton, T., Mills, R. A., Schroeder, M., Cox, J. B., Rowley, C., & Hole, R. (2024). Employment Practices as Experienced by Persons With Intellectual Disability, Employers, and Employment Specialists Across Canada. *Journal of Vocational Rehabilitation, 61*(1), 55–66. DOI: 10.3233/JVR-240019

Nevala, N., Pehkonen, I., Teittinen, A., Vesala, H., Pörtfors, P., & Anttila, H. (2019). The Effectiveness of Rehabilitation Interventions on the Employment and Functioning of People With Intellectual Disabilities: A Systematic Review. *Journal of Occupational Rehabilitation*, *29*(4), 773–802. DOI: 10.1007/s10926-019-09837-2 PMID: 31098847

O'Donovan, M., Wedgwood, N., Westermann, G., Rillotta, F., & Aitken, T. (2025). Personal, Social and Vocational Outcomes of Inclusive University for People With Intellectual Disability. *Journal of Intellectual Disability Research*, *69*(12), 1448–1473. DOI: 10.1111/jir.70042 PMID: 41016861

Pereira, E., Nsair, S., Pereira, L. R., & Grant, K. (2024). Constructive alignment in a graduate-level project management course: An innovative framework using large language models. *International Journal of Educational Technology in Higher Education*, *21*(1), 25. Advance online publication. DOI: 10.1186/s41239-024-00457-2

Ristevski, E., McCook, F., Thompson, S., Duncan, Z., Lawler, B., & Broxham, C. (2024). Initiatives to Facilitate the Social Inclusion of People With Intellectual Disability in Physical Activities With Others in Community-based Sporting, Recreation and Leisure Activities: A Scoping Review. *Journal of Applied Research in Intellectual Disabilities*, *37*(3), e13238. Advance online publication. DOI: 10.1111/jar.13238 PMID: 38622495

Robinson, S., Carnemolla, P., Lay, K., & Kelly, J. (2022). Involving People With Intellectual Disability in Setting Priorities for Building Community Inclusion at a Local Government Level. *British Journal of Learning Disabilities*, *50*(3), 364–375. DOI: 10.1111/bld.12469

Shahin, S., Reitzel, M., Rezze, B. D., Ahmed, S., & Anaby, D. (2020). Environmental Factors That Impact the Workplace Participation of Transition-Aged Young Adults With Brain-Based Disabilities: A Scoping Review. *International Journal of Environmental Research and Public Health*, *17*(7), 2378. DOI: 10.3390/ijerph17072378 PMID: 32244476

Smith, P., & Parmenter, T. R. (2023). Measuring the Impact of Employment on Persons With a Disability as a Means of Improving the Quality of Employment Outcomes. *Journal of Health and Rehabilitation Sciences*, *2*(1), 1–15. DOI: 10.33700/jhrs.2.1.61

Suresh, V., & Dyaram, L. (2020). Towards a Confluence: Disability Inclusion and Organizational Change. *Journal of Indian Business Research*, *12*(4), 625–644. DOI: 10.1108/JIBR-03-2019-0068

Tu n, L. T. (2018). Engaging Employees With Disabilities in Vietnamese Business Context. *Employee Relations*, *40*(5), 822–847. DOI: 10.1108/ER-06-2017-0134

Tucker, B. P., & Nash, E. (2023). Good for Business: Towards a Management Control Research Agenda Relating to the Employment of Workers with Intellectual Disability. *Journal of Accounting Literature*, *47*(1), 129–149. DOI: 10.1108/JAL-01-2023-0013

Watfern, C., & Carnemolla, P. (2025). Inclusive Climate Action: A Scoping Review on the Representation and Inclusion of People With Intellectual Disability in Climate Change Research. *British Journal of Learning Disabilities*, *53*(3), 428–445. DOI: 10.1111/bld.12632

Wesley, S., Jackson, K. N., Ramos, D. M., Vanbeber, S., & Mujtaba, B. G. (2024). Marriott Hotel's Practices in Mitigating Discrimination Through Inclusionary Employee Resource Groups. *Journal of Business Diversity*, *24*(1). Advance online publication. DOI: 10.33423/jbd.v24i1.6897

Wippold, G. M., Crichlow, Z. R., Garcia, K. A., Domlyn, A. M., Sanchez, S. B., Frank, L., Mote, T., Frary, S. G., & Woods, T. O. (2024). Assessing Organizational Readiness for the Clean Cuts and Sharp Minds Collective: A Barbershop Health Promotion Network. *Implementation Science Communications*, *5*(1), 42. Advance online publication. DOI: 10.1186/s43058-024-00584-x PMID: 38627824

Compilation of References

Abravan, A., Correia, D., Gasnier, A., Shakhverdian, S., van der Stok, T., Bertholet, J., Dubois, L. J., Jereczek-Fossa, B. A., Eng, M. P., Spalek, M., Petit, S. F., Franco, P., & Petit-Steeghs, V. (2023). Qualitative study on diversity, equity, and inclusion within radiation oncology in Europe. *International Journal of Radiation Oncology, Biology, Physics, 116*(2), 246–256. DOI: 10.1016/j.ijrobp.2023.02.009 PMID: 36792016

Adjo, J., Maybank, A., & Prakash, V. (2021). Building inclusive work environments. *Pediatrics, 148*, Article e2021051440E. https://doi.org/DOI: 10.1542/peds.2021-051440E

Agarwal, B., Brooks, S. K., & Greenberg, N. (2020). The role of peer support in managing occupational stress: A qualitative study of the sustaining resilience at work intervention. *Workplace Health & Safety, 68*(2), 57–64. DOI: 10.1177/2165079919873934 PMID: 31538851

Agasti, N. R., Martha, S. S., & Mohanty, I. (2026). HR analytics & inclusive growth: Driving sustainable development for Generation Z and beyond. In *Navigating digital disruption: Strategies for sustainable business management* (pp. 326–332). Routledge., DOI: 10.4324/9781003716617-58

Agius, M., Heiman, T., Sula, G., Tsvetkova, P., Nanchen, B., Tkaczyk, A. H., & Sousa, C. (2024). *Supporting Workplace Inclusion: Reasonable Accommodations and Assistive Technologies for Individuals With Intellectual Disability*. 111–127. DOI: 10.24140/nobarriers.v1.p02.05

Agovino, M., Marchesano, K., & Garofalo, A. (2019). Policies based on mandatory employment quotas for disabled workers: The case of Italy. *Modern Italy, 24*(3), 295–315. DOI: 10.1017/mit.2019.14

Ahmad, M., Raziq, M. M., & Akhtar, M. N. (2026). Inclusive leadership and employee well-being: A study of the mediating role of psychological safety. *Leadership & Organisation Development Journal, 47*(1), 1–18.

Ahmad, W., Shokeen, R., Raj, R., Ramkumar, B. V., Singh, R. R., & Mohammad, S. (2026). Transition of Persons with Intellectual and Developmental Disabilities from School to Work: Evidence-Based Practices. In *Vocational Rehabilitation for Students with Developmental Disabilities: Transition from Education to Employment* (pp. 79-132). IGI Global Scientific Publishing. https://doi.org/DOI: 10.4018/979-8-3693-9541-7.ch003

Ajao, S. O., Aworinde, H. O., Falola, P. B., Adeniyi, A. E., & Sakpere, A. B. (2024). Augmented Reality in Experiential Learning: An Overview. *IEEE International Conference on Emerging and Sustainable Technologies for Power and ICT in a Developing Society, NIGERCON*, (2024). DOI: 10.1109/NIGERCON62786.2024.10927359

Akkerman, A., Janssen, C. G. C., Kef, S., & Meininger, H. P. (2016). Job satisfaction of people with intellectual disabilities in integrated and sheltered employment: An exploration of literature. *Journal of Policy and Practice in Intellectual Disabilities, 13*(3), 205–216. DOI: 10.1111/jppi.12168

Akkerman, A., Kef, S., & Meininger, H. P. (2018). Job satisfaction of people with intellectual disabilities: The role of basic psychological need fulfilment and workplace participation. *Disability and Rehabilitation, 40*(10), 1192–1199. DOI: 10.1080/09638288.2017.1294205 PMID: 28288522

Aksnes, S. Y., & Ulstein, J. (2024). Sustainable Employment for People With Disabilities: A Scoping Review on Workplace Practices and Positive Employment Outcomes. *Scandinavian Journal of Disability Research, 26*(1). Advance online publication. DOI: 10.16993/sjdr.1089

Akyeampong, G. B.-D., Ajonbadi, H. A., & Mordi, C. (2025). International laws and framework on disability and employment: The Ghanaian context. In *Careers in Africa: Trends, opportunities and challenges* (pp. 111–133). Springer., DOI: 10.1007/978-3-031-68214-8_6

Al Zmammi, R. A., & Ateeq, A. (2025). The Impact of an Ethical Onboarding Program on Employee Engagement. In *Studies in Systems* (Vol. 584, pp. 677–685). Decision and Control., DOI: 10.1007/978-3-031-85898-7_58

Alajmi, M., Persch, A., Taylor, A., Dean, B., Rosenberg, C. R., & Graham, J. E. (2025). Supported Employment for People With Developmental Disabilities During COVID: A Scoping Review. *Journal of Vocational Rehabilitation, 62*(3), 244–257. DOI: 10.1177/10522263251326408

Aldersey, H. M., Xu, X., Piccone, C., Nelson, M., Thomson, D., Pauls, R., & Perry, L. (2025). Formal and natural supports: Perspectives from adults with intellectual and developmental disabilities, family members, and support workers. *Journal of Policy and Practice in Intellectual Disabilities, 22*(2), e70011. Advance online publication. DOI: 10.1111/jppi.70011

Alexander, J., Ford, J., Raghavendra, P., & Clark, J. (2018). Nature and extent of on-the-job training for employees with an intellectual disability: A pilot study. *Research and Practice in Intellectual and Developmental Disabilities, 5*(2), 138–148. DOI: 10.1080/23297018.2017.1359661

Alfalih, A., & Ragmoun, W. (2025). The Impact of Transformational Leadership on the Workplace Well-Being of Employees With Disabilities: Series Mediation and Moderation Process. *Frontiers in Public Health, 13*, 1506257. Advance online publication. DOI: 10.3389/fpubh.2025.1506257 PMID: 40443931

Alonso, M. Á. V., Schalock, R. L., Gómez, L. E., & Navas, P. (2023). A Systematic Approach to Implementing, Evaluating, and Sustaining the Shared Citizenship Paradigm in the Disability Field. *Behavioral Sciences (Basel, Switzerland), 13*(12), 970. DOI: 10.3390/bs13120970 PMID: 38131825

Alsaleh, A., Alabdulhadi, M., & Alrwaished, N. (2017). Impact of peer coaching strategy on pre-service teachers' professional development growth in Kuwait. *International Journal of Educational Research, 86*, 36–49. DOI: 10.1016/j.ijer.2017.07.011

Alstete, J. W., Meyer, J. P., & Beutell, N. J. (2024). Empowering neurodivergent students in management education with gradual release of responsibility. *International Journal of Management Education, 22*(1), 100941. Advance online publication. DOI: 10.1016/j.ijme.2024.100941

Alves, A. P. R., & da Silva, N. R. (2020). What the people with intellectual disability think about their participation in the work from two case studies. *Revista Brasileira de Educação Especial, 26*(1), 109–124. DOI: 10.1590/s1413-65382620000100007

Amalarethinam, D. I. G., & Muthulakshmi, P. (2012). DAGITIZER - A tool to generate a directed acyclic graph through a randomiser to model scheduling in grid computing. *Advances in Intelligent and Soft Computing, 167 AISC*(VOL. 2), 969–978. DOI: 10.1007/978-3-642-30111-7_93

Ambrose, A. (2018). An introduction to transitional thinking. In *The transitional approach to change* (pp. 1–28). Routledge., DOI: 10.4324/9780429483523-1

Amstutz, J. M. (2022). Reclaiming America as the Land of Opportunity: How International Law Can Help the United States Increase Employment for Persons With Intellectual Disabilities. *Indiana International & Comparative Law Review*, *32*(4), 563–599. DOI: 10.18060/26853

Anand, P., & Sevak, P. (2017). The role of workplace accommodations in the employment of people with disabilities. *IZA Journal of Labor Policy*, *6*(1), 12. Advance online publication. DOI: 10.1186/s40173-017-0090-4

Andreassen, T. A., Breit, E., & Saltkjel, T. (2020). Research Approaches to Networked Employment Services: A Systematic Review. *Social Policy and Administration*, *54*(7), 1179–1197. DOI: 10.1111/spol.12597

Andre, T., Meyer, R., Chik, K., & Lofgren, E. (2015). Experience Map: A tool to help training managers develop learning experiences. *Procedia Manufacturing*, *3*, 1511–1518. DOI: 10.1016/j.promfg.2015.07.405

An, N. B. (2024). A global lens: Comparing international and Vietnamese laws on work for persons with disabilities. In *Sustainable Legacies: A Legal Inquiry into PwDs' Rights in Vietnam's Development* (pp. 19–45). Springer., DOI: 10.1007/978-981-97-9566-6_2

Antonopoulos, C. R., Sugden, N., & Saliba, A. (2023). Implicit bias toward people with disabilities: A systematic review and meta-analysis. *Rehabilitation Psychology*, *68*(2), 121–134. DOI: 10.1037/rep0000493 PMID: 37079819

Antonova, V. K., Aleksandrova, M. Y., Prisyazhniuk, D. I., & Ryabichenko, T. A. (2022). Inclusive organizational culture as an anomaly: The impact of company size on the manifestation of inclusive norms and practices [Инклюзивная организационная культура как аномалия: Взаимосвязь размера компании и проявления в ней инклюзивных норм и практик]. *Monitoring Obshchestvennogo Mneniya: Ekonomicheskie i Sotsial'nye Peremeny*, *4*, 172–198. DOI: 10.14515/monitoring.2022.4.2223

Antonova, V., Prisyazhniuk, D., & Ryabichenko, T. (2021). Investment and inclusion as a norm of life: Attitudes of Russian HR-managers to inclusive employment. *Zhurnal Issledovanii Sotsial'noi Politiki*, *19*(3), 373–388. DOI: 10.17323/727-0634-2021-19-3-373-388

Argüeso, M. S. (2025). Intellectual disability and borderline intellectual ability: Keys for a better labour market insertion. *Oñati Socio-Legal Series*, *15*(3), 790–817. DOI: 10.35295/osls.iisl.2170

Armengol, J. V., Alcalde, I. H., Ibáñez, D. G., & Ferrer, S. E. (2023). Feed back as a teaching tool: Its impact on the motivation of higher education students [El Feed Back como Herramienta Docente: Su Impacto en la Motivación de los Estudiantes de Educación Superior]. *UCJC Business and Society Review*, *20*(76), 104–149. DOI: 10.3232/UBR.2023.V20.N1.03

Arora, P., & Parthasarathy, P. D. (2025). Collaboration model—Optimizing collaborative models in distance learning to enhance student learning through workplace and academic integration. *Lecture Notes in Networks and Systems*, *1206*, 881–894. DOI: 10.1007/978-981-96-0201-8_55

Arpangi, S., Suwondo, D., Laksana, A. W., & Yassine, C. (2025). Integrating Australian employment law practice in support of people with disabilities in Indonesia. *Khazanah Hukum*, *7*(2), 236–254. DOI: 10.15575/kh.v7i2.44946

Arruda, C. T. (2016). What we can intend: Recognition and collective intentionality. *The Southern Journal of Philosophy*, *54*(1), 5–26. DOI: 10.1111/sjp.12162

Ashburn-Nardo, L. (2015). What can allies do? In Colella, A. J., & King, E. B. (Eds.), *The Oxford handbook of workplace discrimination* (pp. 373–386). Oxford University Press., DOI: 10.1093/oxfordhb/9780199363643.013.27

Ashuro, T., & Kant, S. (2025). The impact of cross-cultural perspectives on labor practices by mediating role of inclusive strategies in Ethiopia. In *Advanced labor studies research and modern practice* (pp. 169–193). IGI Global., DOI: 10.4018/979-8-3373-1962-9.ch006

Aslam, U., Coombs, C., & Doherty, N. F. (2012). Benefits realisation from ERP systems: The role of customisation. In ECIS 2012 - Proceedings of the 20th European Conference on Information Systems.

Asmuß, B., & Thomsen, C. (2024). Workplace Inclusion Through Social Partnerships: A Relational Perspective. *Group & Organization Management*, *50*(4), 1385–1418. DOI: 10.1177/10596011241288117

Asrifan, A., Sudirman, R., Supriadi, S., & Utiarahman, N. (2026). The intersection of political economy and workplace equity: Implications for talent acquisition. In *Developing diversity, equity, and inclusion policies for talent acquisition and retention* (pp. 59–90). IGI Global., DOI: 10.4018/979-8-3373-2312-1.ch003

Aswathy, S. A., & Jayalakshmi, G. (2024). Role of institutional support in enhancing faculty job satisfaction and performance. In *Public sector and workforce management in the digital age* (pp. 197–217). IGI Global., DOI: 10.4018/979-8-3373-1137-1.ch010

Athamanah, L. S., Cushing, L. S., Fastzkie, E. M., & Brown, E. R. (2024). Natural supports in competitive integrated employment: A scoping review. *Journal of Vocational Rehabilitation, 60*(3), 327–339. DOI: 10.3233/JVR-240017

Atiku, S. O., Soneye, F. A., & Anane-Simon, R. (2023). Fostering psychological safety for team effectiveness in family businesses: Insights from Royal Savoy Hotel. In *Cases on the Interplay Between Family* (pp. 84–121). Society, and Entrepreneurship., DOI: 10.4018/978-1-6684-8748-8.ch004

Auvinen, P., & Arminen, I. (2013). An airline checklist use as a sociomaterial practice. *Proceedings of the Annual Hawaii International Conference on System Sciences*, 1590–1599. DOI: 10.1109/HICSS.2013.80

Azambuja, M., Pereira, R., Breitman, K., & Endler, M. (2010). An architecture for public and open submission systems in the cloud. *Proceedings of the 2010 IEEE 3rd International Conference on Cloud Computing*, 513–517. https://doi.org/DOI: 10.1109/CLOUD.2010.77

Babikian, V. A., & Hamdani, Y. (2023). Social enterprises and transition to employment for people labelled with intellectual and developmental disabilities. *Current Developmental Disorders Reports, 10*(1), 40–46. DOI: 10.1007/s40474-023-00267-7

Baboolal, S. O., & Singaram, V. S. (2024). Implementation and Impact of an Adapted Digital Perioperative Competency-Building Tool to Enhance Teaching, Learning And Feedback in Postgraduate Competency-Based Medical Education. *Journal of Surgical Education, 81*(5), 722–740. DOI: 10.1016/j.jsurg.2024.01.015 PMID: 38492984

Babu, C. V. S., Logambigai, R., & Akshaya, A. S. (2026). Leveraging AI and Speech Recognition Tools for Vocational Rehabilitation of Students With Developmental Disabilities From Education to Employment. In *Vocational Rehabilitation for Students with Developmental Disabilities* (pp. 237–272). Transition from Education to Employment., DOI: 10.4018/979-8-3693-9541-7.ch008

Bacon, N., & Hoque, K. (2022). The treatment of disabled individuals in small, medium-sized, and large firms. *Human Resource Management, 61*(2), 137–156. DOI: 10.1002/hrm.22084

Baer, H., Welker, K., & Cox, C. (2021). Work performance and support needs analysis of students with intellectual disabilities. *Journal of Vocational Rehabilitation, 55*(3), 251–270. DOI: 10.3233/JVR-211167

Baine, C., Gilson, C. B., & Hashemi, H. (2024). The Bridge to Somewhere: How Practitioners Can UNITE to Support Adults With Extensive Support Needs in Inclusive Employment Opportunities. *In Practice*, *4*(1–2), 17–26. DOI: 10.1177/27324745241295727

Baker, P. M. A., & Moon, N. W.Baker Paul M.A.Moon Nathan W. (2008). Policy change and the accommodating workplace: Issues, barriers, and opportunities. *Assistive Technology Research Series*, *22*, 161–174. DOI: 10.3233/978-1-58603-902-8-161

Bakker, A. B., & Van Woerkom, M. (2018). Strengths used in organisations: A positive approach to occupational health. *Canadian Psychology*, *59*(1), 38–46. DOI: 10.1037/cap0000120

Balasuriya, S. S., Sitbon, L., & Brereton, M. (2022). A Support Worker Perspective on Use of New Technologies by People with Intellectual Disabilities. *ACM Transactions on Accessible Computing*, *15*(3), 1–21. Advance online publication. DOI: 10.1145/3523058

Balcázar, F. E., & Suarez-Balcazar, Y. (2017). *Promoting Empowerment Among Individuals With Disabilities*. 571–585. DOI: 10.1037/14954-034

Balint, B. (2020). To code or not to code: Obtaining value from the customisation of packaged application software. In *Research Anthology on Recent Trends, Tools, and Implications of Computer Programming* (pp. 1426–1445). IGI Global. DOI: 10.4018/978-1-7998-3016-0.ch065

Balint, B. (2015). Obtaining value from the customisation of packaged business software: A model and simulation. *International Journal of Enterprise Information Systems*, *11*(1), 33–49. DOI: 10.4018/ijeis.2015010103

Banihammad, B. A., Al Mirza, J. J., Ashraf, A. A., & Kumaresan, R. S. (2023). Creating an inclusive and skilled workforce. Society of Petroleum Engineers - ADIPEC. *ADIP*, *2023*. Advance online publication. DOI: 10.2118/215968-MS

Bano, M., Zowghi, D., Mourao, F., Kaur, S., & Zhang, T. (2025). Requirements for inclusive AI-driven recruitment: Lessons learned from an industry workshop. *Proceedings of the IEEE International Conference on Requirements Engineering*, 292–302. https://doi.org/DOI: 10.1109/RE63999.2025.00035

Barow, T. (2025). "Needed and valuable instead of just being employed": Vocational training, work and social usefulness regarding people with intellectual disability in Sweden, 1945–1989. *Nordic Journal of Educational History*, *12*(2), 63–87. DOI: 10.36368/njedh.v12i2.1314

Barroso, C. L., Mañas-Viniegra, L., Sánchez, J. S., & García, F. G. (2023). Disability and Employability in the Audio-Visual Sector: The (Dis)connection Between Corporate Social Sustainability Goals and the Employment Experiences of People With Disabilities. *El Profesional de la Información*, e320604. Advance online publication. DOI: 10.3145/epi.2023.nov.04

Bartels, L. K., Nordstrom, C. R., & Koski, J. A. (2006). A structured interview demonstration. *Teaching of Psychology*, *33*(1), 55–57. DOI: 10.1207/s15328023top3301_12

Bartram, T., Cavanagh, J., Meacham, H., & Pariona-Cabrera, P. (2019). Re-calibrating HRM to Improve the Work Experiences for Workers With Intellectual Disability. *Asia Pacific Journal of Human Resources*, *59*(1), 63–83. DOI: 10.1111/1744-7941.12230

Becerra, M.-T., Montanero, M., & Lucero, M. (2018). Graphic support resources for workers with intellectual disability engaged in office tasks: A comparison with verbal instructions from a workmate. *Disability and Rehabilitation*, *40*(4), 435–443. DOI: 10.1080/09638288.2016.1258739 PMID: 27973913

Beckman, P. (2009). Universal design for learning: A field experiment comparing specific classroom actions. *15th Americas Conference on Information Systems 2009, AMCIS 2009, 1*, 514–523. https://www.scopus.com/inward/record.uri?eid=2-s2.0-84870264980&partnerID=40&md5=7ca9608d47d0a918db27d4bf3f50434a

Belgasm, H., Alzubi, A., Iyiola, K., & Khadem, A. (2025). Interpersonal Conflict and Employee Behavior in the Public Sector: Investigating the Role of Workplace Ostracism and Supervisors' Active Empathic Listening. *Behavioral Sciences (Basel, Switzerland)*, *15*(2), 194. Advance online publication. DOI: 10.3390/bs15020194 PMID: 40001825

Bell, M. (2019). People With Intellectual Disabilities and Labour Market Inclusion: What Role for EU Labour Law? *European Labour Law Journal*, *11*(1), 3–25. DOI: 10.1177/2031952519882953

Belluzzo, M., Giaquinto, V., Volpe, D., Esposito, C., Alfieri, E., & Amodeo, A. L. (2025). Navigating Body Perception, Affectivity, Intimacy, Gender Identity, and Sexuality: An Exploratory Qualitative Study in Young Adults With SMI, IDs, and ASD in a Community Setting. *International Journal of Environmental Research and Public Health*, *22*(5), 722. DOI: 10.3390/ijerph22050722 PMID: 40427837

Ben Amram, M., & Shapira-Lishchinsky, O. (2021). Mentoring strategies and their impact on social workers' attitudes. *Journal of Social Work : JSW*, *21*(3), 374–393. DOI: 10.1177/1468017320911506

Ben-Amram, M., & Shapira-Lishchinsky, O. (2025). Employer training interventions in supported employment workplaces and their impact on hiring attitudes. *International Journal of Training and Development*. Advance online publication. DOI: 10.1111/ijtd.70015

Benda, P., Pavlík, J., & Masner, J. (2019). Practical education of adults with intellectual disabilities using a web course. *Problems of Education in the 21st Century, 77*(4), 463–477. DOI: 10.33225/pec/19.77.463

Bender, D. E., Overman, B., & Arnold, M. S. (2005). The Americans With Disabilities Act: Explaining legislative intent through experiential learning. *The Journal of Health Administration Education, 22*(4), 435–458.

Bendixen, R., Benevides, T., Ideishi, R., Smythe, R. T., Taylor, J. P., Umeda, C., Kerfeld, C. A., & Jirikowic, T. (2022). Community Conversations: Stakeholder-Identified Research Priorities to Foster Community Participation for Individuals With Intellectual and Developmental Disability. *Frontiers in Rehabilitation Sciences, 3*, 873415. Advance online publication. DOI: 10.3389/fresc.2022.873415 PMID: 36188970

Bennett, T., & Randolph, D. S. (2010). Employment and disability: The role of the Americans with Disabilities Act. *Journal of Employment Counseling, 47*(2), 50–58.

Bentley, T., & Clarke, J. (2005). Workplace accommodation for employees with disabilities: A review of the literature. *Journal of Occupational Rehabilitation, 15*(3), 329–342.

Bergman, J., Ratcliffe, S. E., Harvey-Smith, L., & Williams, L. A. (2024). *Initiatives for Workplace Equity and Inclusion: A Series of Rapid Systematic Reviews of the Peer-Reviewed Literature*. DOI: 10.31219/osf.io/zmvjn

Bernstein, P. S., Combs, C. A., Shields, L. E., Clark, S. L., & Eppes, C. S. (2017). The development and implementation of checklists in obstetrics. *American Journal of Obstetrics and Gynecology, 217*(2), B2–B6. DOI: 10.1016/j.ajog.2017.05.032 PMID: 28549984

Betz, C. L. (2023). Health Care Transition Planning for Adolescents and Emerging Adults With Intellectual Disabilities and Developmental Disabilities: Distinctions and Challenges. *Journal for Specialists in Pediatric Nursing, 28*(3), e12415. Advance online publication. DOI: 10.1111/jspn.12415 PMID: 37380603

Bezyak, J., Chan, F., Tansey, T. N., Wu, J.-R., Iwanaga, K., & Lee, D. (2024). Changing human resource professionals from gatekeepers to enablers of disability employment: Lessons learned from disability-employment research. *Journal of Vocational Rehabilitation. Article, 10522263241300813*. Advance online publication. DOI: 10.1177/10522263241300813

Bialik, K., & Mhiri, M. (2022). Barriers to employment for people with intellectual disabilities in low- and middle-income countries: Self-advocate and family perspectives. *Journal of International Development*, *34*(5), 988–1001. DOI: 10.1002/jid.3659

Bigby, C., Wilson, N. J., Balandin, S., & Stancliffe, R. J. (2011). Disconnected expectations: Staff, family, and supported employee perspectives about retirement. *Journal of Intellectual & Developmental Disability*, *36*(3), 167–174. DOI: 10.3109/13668250.2011.598852 PMID: 21843031

Billett, S. (2003). Workplace mentors: Demands and benefits. *Journal of Workplace Learning*, *15*(3), 105–113. DOI: 10.1108/13665620310468441

Billett, S., & Noble, C. (2020). Utilizing pedagogically rich work activities to promote professional learning. *Education et Didactique*, *14*(3), 137–150. DOI: 10.4000/educationdidactique.7943

Birkle, S., & Seifried, J. (2024). Perceived challenges when changing employer: What newcomers experience as helpful during organizational entry. *Journal of Personnel Psychology*, *23*(3), 156–167. DOI: 10.1027/1866-5888/a000342

Bleasby, C., Coffey, L.-A., Sweeney, H., & Thompson, J. (2025). Developing social worker student belonging, engagement and confidence through peer mentoring: a case study exploration. In *Building Student Belonging in Higher Education* (pp. 195–214). Perspectives on Driving and Developing Change., DOI: 10.1108/978-1-80592-242-120251025

Boillat, M., & Elizov, M. (2014). Peer coaching and mentorship. In *Faculty development in the health professions: A focus on research and practice* (pp. 159–179). Springer., DOI: 10.1007/978-94-007-7612-8_8

Bonardi, A., Abend, S. L., & Ne'eman, A. (2024). Healthcare Access and Delivery for People With Intellectual and Developmental Disability in the United States: Policy, Payment, and Practice Considerations. *Journal of Policy and Practice in Intellectual Disabilities*, *21*(2), e12487. Advance online publication. DOI: 10.1111/jppi.12487

Bourke, J. (2025). Time to delve into the weeds: Illuminating the diversity to performance black box by exploring co-worker relationships. In *Research handbook on global diversity management* (pp. 108–122). Edward Elgar Publishing., DOI: 10.4337/9781035311170.00015

Bozic, N. (2013). Developing a strength-based approach to educational psychology practice: A multiple case study. *Educational and Child Psychology, 30*(4), 18–29. DOI: 10.53841/bpsecp.2013.30.4.18

Bozic, N., Lawthom, R., & Murray, J. (2018). Exploring the context of strengths–A new approach to strength-based assessment. *Educational Psychology in Practice, 34*(1), 26–40. DOI: 10.1080/02667363.2017.1367917

Brannick, M. T., Cadle, A., & Levine, E. L. (2012). Job analysis for knowledge, skills, abilities, and other characteristics, predictor measures, and performance outcomes. In *The Oxford Handbook of Personnel Assessment and Selection*. Oxford University Press., DOI: 10.1093/oxfordhb/9780199732579.013.0007

Brecher, E., Bragger, J., & Kutcher, E. (2006). The structured interview: Reducing biases toward job applicants with physical disabilities. *Employee Responsibilities and Rights Journal, 18*(3), 155–170. DOI: 10.1007/s10672-006-9014-y

Bredgaard, T. (2025). Inclusive job design. In *Shaping inclusive workplaces for persons with disabilities: A management and HRM practitioner perspective* (pp. 85–95). Springer., DOI: 10.1007/978-3-031-96315-5_7

Breit, E., Bråthen, M., & Sadeghi, T. (2025). Distinctions between inclusive and non-inclusive companies for persons with disability: Exploring the impact of COM-B and HRM practices. *Work (Reading, Mass.), 81*(2), 2651–2661. DOI: 10.1177/10519815251320275 PMID: 40421555

Brinchmann, B., Widding-Havneraas, T., Modini, M., Rinaldi, M., Moe, C. F., McDaid, D., Park, A., Killackey, E., Harvey, S. B., & Mykletun, A. (2019). A Meta-regression of the Impact of Policy on the Efficacy of Individual Placement and Support. *Acta Psychiatrica Scandinavica, 141*(3), 206–220. DOI: 10.1111/acps.13129 PMID: 31733146

Brooke, A. M., Taylor, J. P., Inge, K., Wright, T., Wehman, P., McDonough, J., & Brooke, V. (2025). Employer perceptions of hiring and initial support of employees with disabilities. *Rehabilitation Counseling Bulletin, 68*(4), 249–261. DOI: 10.1177/00343552241265317

Bryant, B. R., Rao, K., & Ok, M. W. (2015). Universal Design for Learning and Assistive Technology: Promising Developments. In *Human-Computer Interaction: Concepts, Methodologies, Tools, and Applications: Volume 1-4* (Vols. 1–4, pp. 567–582). DOI: 10.4018/978-1-4666-8789-9.ch025

Bryant, B. R. (2012). Assistive technology and support provision for individuals with intellectual and developmental disabilities: Introduction to the topical issue. *Journal of Special Education Technology*, *27*(2), 1–2. DOI: 10.1177/016264341202700201

Bryant, L., & Hemsley, B. (2024). Augmented reality: A view to future visual supports for people with disability. *Disability and Rehabilitation. Assistive Technology*, *19*(3), 800–813. DOI: 10.1080/17483107.2022.2125090 PMID: 36149835

Budhiraja, S. (2023). Continuous learning and employee performance: A moderated examination of managers' coaching behavior in India. *Personnel Review*, *52*(1), 200–217. DOI: 10.1108/PR-04-2020-0272

Buettgen, A., & Klassen, T. (2020). The Role of the Nonprofit Sector as a Site for Inclusive Employment. *Canadian Journal of Nonprofit and Social Economy Research*, *11*(2), 15. DOI: 10.29173/cjnser.2020v11n2a367

Burge, P., Ouellette-Kuntz, H., & Lysaght, R. (2007). Public views on employment of people with intellectual disabilities. *Journal of Vocational Rehabilitation*, *26*(1), 29–37. DOI: 10.3233/JVR-2007-00360

Burgin, H., Hooper, J., Forbes-Nicholson, A., & Koutoukidis, G. (2026). Evaluating the Impact of Integrated Practical Placement Programmes on Students With Intellectual Disabilities. *Journal of Applied Research in Intellectual Disabilities*, *39*(1), e70184. Advance online publication. DOI: 10.1111/jar.70184 PMID: 41607296

Burke, J., Bezyak, J., Fraser, R. T., Pete, J., Ditchman, N., & Chan, F. (2013). Employers' attitudes towards hiring and retaining people with disabilities: A review of the literature. *Australian Journal of Rehabilitation Counselling*, *19*(1), 21–38. DOI: 10.1017/jrc.2013.2

Burke, K. M., Shogren, K. A., & Carlson, S. (2021). Examining types of goals set by transition-age students with intellectual disability. *Career Development and Transition for Exceptional Individuals*, *44*(3), 135–147. DOI: 10.1177/2165143420959055

Bushby, K., Chan, J., Druif, S., Ho, K., & Kinsella, E. A. (2015). Ethical tensions in occupational therapy practice: A scoping review. *British Journal of Occupational Therapy*, *78*(4), 212–221. DOI: 10.1177/0308022614564770

Butler, T., Falk, E., & Kleinbaum, A. M. (2025). Workplace inclusion: A social network perspective. *Research in Organizational Behavior*, *45*, 100221. Advance online publication. DOI: 10.1016/j.riob.2025.100221

Butterworth, J., Christensen, J., & Flippo, K. (2017). Partnerships in Employment: Building Strong Coalitions to Facilitate Systems Change for Youth and Young Adults. *Journal of Vocational Rehabilitation*, *47*(3), 265–276. DOI: 10.3233/JVR-170901

Butterworth, J., Winsor, J. E., Kamau, E., Migliore, A., & Mahoehney, D. (2024). The state of employment for people with IDD: Implications for practice, policy, and equity. *Intellectual and Developmental Disabilities*, *62*(3), 225–240. DOI: 10.1352/1934-9556-62.3.225 PMID: 38802097

Büttner, J. C., Degenbeck, V. K., Schütz, V. G., & Melchers, K. G. (2026). More than bias reduction? How applicants view anonymous application procedures. *International Journal of Selection and Assessment*, *34*(2), e70054. Advance online publication. DOI: 10.1111/ijsa.70054

Byrne, L., Roennfeldt, H., Wolf, J., Linfoot, A., Foglesong, D., Davidson, L., & Bellamy, C. (2022). Effective peer employment within multidisciplinary organizations: Model for best practice. *Administration and Policy in Mental Health*, *49*(2), 283–297. DOI: 10.1007/s10488-021-01162-2 PMID: 34478040

Caldwell, C., & Peters, R. (2018). New employee onboarding – psychological contracts and ethical perspectives. *Journal of Management Development*, *37*(1), 27–39. DOI: 10.1108/JMD-10-2016-0202

Caldwell, N., Holyfield, C., Lorah, E. R., & Rackensperger, T. (2024). Reducing Linguistic Profiling of Individuals With Communication Disabilities to Enhance Careers: Avoiding Assumptions Based on Speech, Language and Communication Mode. *Career Development International*, *29*(3), 367–380. DOI: 10.1108/CDI-07-2023-0230

Canady, V. A. (2020). Illinois Employment Model Serves as an Example for Others. *Mental Health Weekly*, *30*(44), 6–7. DOI: 10.1002/mhw.32588

Can, M., & Cengiz, M. I. (2026). The Impact of Instructional Approaches on Scaling and Root Planning Skill Learning in Preclinical Periodontal Education. *Journal of Dental Education*, *90*(2), 196–203. DOI: 10.1002/jdd.13934 PMID: 40346747

Carey, E. (2021). Aligning with the flow of control: A grounded theory study of choice and autonomy in decision-making practices of people with intellectual disabilities. *International Journal of Qualitative Studies on Health and Well-Being, 16*(1), Article 1857053. https://doi.org/DOI: 10.1080/17482631.2020.1857053

Carlson, S. R. (2022). Pre-employment transition services: What secondary special education teachers need to know. *Intervention in School and Clinic*, *57*(5), 338–342. DOI: 10.1177/10534512211032631

Carlson, S. R., Morningstar, M. E., & Munandar, V. (2020). Workplace supports for employees with intellectual disability: A systematic review of the intervention literature. *Journal of Vocational Rehabilitation*, *52*(3), 251–265. DOI: 10.3233/JVR-201075

Carr-Kirby, K., Horton, S., Sutherland, C. A., Paraschak, V., & Weir, P. (2025). 'I don't think they've ever seen people like me do jobs like this': Exploring hope within strengths-based employment services for people with disability. *Journal of Applied Research in Intellectual Disabilities*, *38*(6), e70147. DOI: 10.1111/jar.70147 PMID: 41177549

Carroll, R. A., Halbur, M., & Preas, E. J. (2025). Autism spectrum disorder and other developmental disabilities. In *Applied behavior analysis for clinical, educational, and training applications* (pp. 305–326). Elsevier., DOI: 10.1016/B978-0-443-22361-7.00011-3

Carter, E. W., McMillan, E. D., & Willis, W. (2017). The TennesseeWorks Partnership: Elevating Employment Outcomes for People With Intellectual and Developmental Disabilities. *Journal of Vocational Rehabilitation*, *47*(3), 365–378. DOI: 10.3233/JVR-170909

Carus, I., & Messina, M. (2025). Skills for life, skills for careers, skills for inclusion. *European Public and Social Innovation Review*, *10*. Advance online publication. DOI: 10.31637/epsir-2025-1721

Casadei, T. (2018). Disability and law. *Rivista di Filosofia del Diritto*, *7*(2), 273–279. DOI: 10.4477/91675

Casalino, N., Żuchowski, I., Veglianti, E., Borin, B., & Skrodzki, I. (2024). Improving managerial approaches and human resources strategies in the banking sector regarding inclusion, diversity, social equity and organisational intelligence. *Law and Economics Yearly Review*, *13*, 281–312.

Cassiani, C., Stinson, J., & Lindsay, S. (2020). E-mentoring for youth with physical disabilities preparing for employment: A content analysis of support exchanged between participants of a mentored and non-mentored group. *Disability and Rehabilitation*, *42*(14), 1963–1970. DOI: 10.1080/09638288.2018.1543360 PMID: 30641025

Castañeda, S. F., Holscher, J. T., Mumman, M. K., Salgado, H., Keir, K. B., Foster-Fishman, P. G., & Talavera, G. A. (2012). Dimensions of Community and Organizational Readiness for Change. *Progress in Community Health Partnerships*, *6*(2), 119. DOI: 10.1353/cpr.2012.0021 PMID: 22820232

Caughron, J. J., Peterson, D. K., & Mumford, T. V. (2013). Job analysis. In *The Encyclopedia of Human Resource Management*. Wiley.

Cavanagh, J., Bartram, T., Meacham, H., Bigby, C., Oakman, J., & Fossey, E. (2017). Supporting workers with disabilities: A scoping review of the role of human resource management in contemporary organisations. *Asia Pacific Journal of Human Resources*, *55*(1), 6–43. DOI: 10.1111/1744-7941.12111

Cavanagh, J., Meacham, H., Pariona-Cabrera, P., & Bartram, T. (2021). Subtle workplace discrimination inhibiting workers with intellectual disability from thriving at the workplace. *Personnel Review*, *50*(7/8), 1739–1756. DOI: 10.1108/PR-10-2021-0723

Chandola, T., & Rouxel, P. (2021). The Role of Workplace Accommodations in Explaining the Disability Employment Gap in the UK. *Social Science & Medicine*, *285*, 114313. DOI: 10.1016/j.socscimed.2021.114313 PMID: 34399292

Chandrasekaran, P., Thekkumkara, S. N., Jothibalan, A., Jagannathan, A., Jayarajan, D., & Reddy, S. K. (2022). Hybrid supported employment approach for persons with intellectual disabilities in India: Evidence based case studies. *Journal of Psychosocial Rehabilitation and Mental Health*, *9*(3), 317–323. DOI: 10.1007/s40737-021-00241-9 PMID: 34642615

Chan, F., Iwanaga, K., Tansey, T. N., Ditchman, N., Wehman, P., Wu, J. R., & Chen, X. (2024). Assessing Evidence-Based Disability Inclusion Policy and Practices to Promote Employment of People With Disabilities in the Workplace: Scale Development and Validation. *Rehabilitation Counseling Bulletin*. Advance online publication. DOI: 10.1177/00343552241268757

Chattopadhyay, R. (2025). Inclusive digital training systems and learning equity in the workplace: Evidence from a neurodiverse workforce. *Journal of Workplace Learning*, •••, 1–17. DOI: 10.1108/JWL-06-2025-0178

Cheausuwantavee, T., & Keeratiphanthawong, S. (2021). Employment for Persons With Disabilities in Thailand: Opportunities and Challenges in the Labor Market. *Journal of Population and Social Studies*, *29*, 384–400. DOI: 10.25133/JPSSv292021.024

Chen, A., O'Neill, J., Phillips, K. G., Houtenville, A. J., & Katz, E. (2023). Relationship of business practices and characteristics to supervisors' perceived effectiveness of disability recruitment. *Journal of Vocational Rehabilitation, 59*(3), 301–310. DOI: 10.3233/JVR-230047

Cheng, C., Oakman, J., & Bigby, C. (2015). Supported employment for people with intellectual disability: A systematic review. *Journal of Intellectual Disability Research, 59*(12), 1109–1122.

Chew, K. L., Iacono, T., & Tracy, J. (2009). Overcoming communication barriers: Working with patients with intellectual disabilities. *Australian Family Physician, 38*(1–2), 10–14. PMID: 19283229

Chicoine, B., & Kirschner, K. L. (2022). Considering dignity of risk in the care of people with intellectual disabilities: A clinical perspective. *Perspectives in Biology and Medicine, 65*(2), 189–198. DOI: 10.1353/pbm.2022.0014 PMID: 35938426

Chine, D. R., Chhabra, P., Adeniran, A., Kopko, J., Tipper, C., Gupta, S., & Koedinger, K. R. (2023). Scenario-based training and on-the-job support for equitable mentoring. In *Lecture Notes in Networks and Systems* (Vol. 581, pp. 581–592). Springer., DOI: 10.1007/978-3-031-21569-8_54

Choe, A. Y., Unaka, N. I., Schondelmeyer, A. C., Bignall, W. J. R., Vilvens, H. L., & Thomson, J. E. (2019). Inpatient communication barriers and drivers when caring for limited English proficiency children. *Journal of Hospital Medicine, 14*(10), 607–613. DOI: 10.12788/jhm.3240 PMID: 31339836

Chordiya, R. (2022). Organizational inclusion and turnover intentions of federal employees with disabilities. *Review of Public Personnel Administration, 42*(1), 60–87. DOI: 10.1177/0734371X20942305

Christensen, J. J., Hetherington, S., Daston, M. M., & Riehle, E. (2015). Longitudinal Outcomes of Project SEARCH in Upstate New York. *Journal of Vocational Rehabilitation, 42*(3), 247–255. DOI: 10.3233/JVR-150746

Christensen, J., Richardson, K., & Hetherington, S. (2017). New York State Partnerships in Employment. *Journal of Vocational Rehabilitation, 47*(3), 351–363. DOI: 10.3233/JVR-170908

Christianson-Barker, J., Franzius, A., Mills, R., Lomness, A., & Hole, R. (2025). Employing strength: A scoping review of customized employment practices to support inclusive employment for people with intellectual disabilities. *Journal of Vocational Rehabilitation, 63*(2), 119–140. DOI: 10.1177/10522263251356445

Christianson-Barker, J., Morris, R., Stainton, T., Cox, J., Rowley, C., Schroeder, M., Mills, R., & Hole, R. (2025). Addressing barriers to employment for workers with an intellectual disability in Canada: A focus group study. *Research and Practice in Intellectual and Developmental Disabilities*, *12*(2), 195–210. DOI: 10.1080/23297018.2025.2501261

Chun, J., Anderson, C., Rumrill, S., Richard, C., Zhou, K., Fry, H., & Froehlich, R. J. (2024). Promoting Quality Career Pathways for Individuals With Disabilities Through the Public Vocational Rehabilitation Program. *Journal of Vocational Rehabilitation*, *60*(3), 299–310. DOI: 10.3233/JVR-240014

Clark, E., Olympia, D. E., Jensen, J., Heathfield, L. T., & Jenson, W. R. (2004). Striving for autonomy in a contingency-governed world: Another challenge for individuals with developmental disabilities. *Psychology in the Schools*, *41*(1), 143–153. DOI: 10.1002/pits.10146

Clarke, E., Näswall, K., Wong, J., Pawsey, F., & Malinen, S. (2024). Enabling successful change in a high-demand working environment: A case study in a health care organization. *Journal of Health Organization and Management*, *38*(2), 248–263. DOI: 10.1108/JHOM-02-2023-0051 PMID: 38509014

Climie, E., & Henley, L. (2016). A renewed focus on strengths-based assessment in schools. *British Journal of Special Education*, *43*(2), 108–121. DOI: 10.1111/1467-8578.12131

Cohen, N. R., & Sekuler, R. (2010). Chunking and compound cueing of movement sequences: Learning, retention, and transfer. *Perceptual and Motor Skills*, *110*(3), 736–750. DOI: 10.2466/pms.110.3.736-750 PMID: 20681328

Collett-Schmitt, K., McKendree, A., Rubey, K., & McManus Warnell, J. (2025). Beyond the Backlash: Integrating DEI in business education to develop responsible leaders. *International Journal of Management Education*, *23*(3), 101212. Advance online publication. DOI: 10.1016/j.ijme.2025.101212

Copeland, S. R., Luckasson, R., & Shauger, R. (2014). Eliciting perceptions of satisfaction with services and supports from persons with intellectual disability and developmental disabilities: A review of the literature. *Journal of Intellectual Disability Research*, *58*(12), 1141–1155. DOI: 10.1111/jir.12114 PMID: 24433252

Cortéséro, R., Kerbourc'H, S., Mélo, D., & Poli, A. (2013). Recruiters under pressure. Discrimination and diversity through the prism of interwoven discursive registers [Recruteurs sous tensions. Discrimination et diversité au prisme de registres argumentaires enchevêtrés]. *Sociologie du Travail*, *55*(4). Advance online publication. DOI: 10.4000/sdt.6474

Costa, B., & Rodrigues, R. I. (2025). The Invisible Bond: Exploring the Sequential Mediation of Interpersonal Connections and Engagement in the Relationship Between the Onboarding Process and Talent Retention. *Administrative Sciences, 15*(7), 281. Advance online publication. DOI: 10.3390/admsci15070281

Courtad, C. A. (2019). Making your classroom smart: Universal design for learning and technology. *Smart Innovation. Systems and Technologies, 144*, 501–510. DOI: 10.1007/978-981-13-8260-4_44

Cox, J. S. (2009). Redefining disability. *Paper360, 4*(1), 32.

Craven-Staines, S., & Finch, J. (2025). Equality, diversity and inclusion at Teesside doctorate in clinical psychology: Working towards inclusive interview processes. *Clinical Psychology Forum, 1*(385), 22–27. DOI: 10.53841/bpscpf.2025.1.385.22

Crawford, R. H. (2005). Equity in testing deaf and hard of hearing individuals-legal considerations. In *Assessing deaf adults: Critical issues in testing and evaluation* (pp. 93–108). Gallaudet University Press.

Croes, R., Lee, S. H., Renduchintala, C., Badu-Baiden, F., & Tavares, K. (2025). Tourism, quality of life, and disability: An agency perspective. *Journal of Hospitality & Tourism Research (Washington, D.C.)*. Advance online publication. DOI: 10.1177/10963480251361952

Cubillos, L., Muñoz, J., Caballero, J., Mendoza, M. C., Pulido, A., Carpio, K., Udutha, A. K., Botero, C., Borrero, E., Rodríguez, D., Cutipé, Y., Emeny, R. T., Schifferdecker, K. E., & Torrey, W. C. (2020). Addressing Severe Mental Illness Rehabilitation in Colombia, Costa Rica, and Peru. *Psychiatric Services (Washington, D.C.), 71*(4), 378–384. DOI: 10.1176/appi.ps.201900306 PMID: 31896339

Cuervo-Botero, G.-R., Zuñiga-Bolívar, S.-M., Abella-León, C., & Betancur-Agudelo, J.-E. (2025). Reasonable accommodations for the social and productive inclusion of persons with disabilities in Colombia: Progress and implementation challenges. *Prisma Social*, (50), 189–219. DOI: 10.65598/rps.5859

Cura, G., & Kızılkum, Ş. (2024). *Recruitment and Job Coaching for and With Intellectual Disability*. 103–109. DOI: 10.24140/nobarriers.v1.p02.04

Dahooie, J. H., Habibollahi, H., & Qorbani, A. R. (2022). Identifying and prioritizing barriers of Industry 4.0 adoption, using fuzzy Delphi and group ZBWM: A case study in an emerging economy. In *Lecture Notes in Operations Research* (pp. 209–227). Springer., DOI: 10.1007/978-3-030-89795-6_15

Dall, M. (2026). Job matching for people with disabilities: A systematic review. *Journal of Vocational Rehabilitation, 64*(2), 145–160.

Dall, T., & Madsen, M. B. (2025). Workplace accommodations. In *Shaping Inclusive Workplaces for Persons with Disabilities: A Management and HRM Practitioner Perspective* (pp. 71–84). Springer., DOI: 10.1007/978-3-031-96315-5_6

Dalton, C., & Sweeney, J. (2013). Communication supports in residential services for people with an intellectual disability. *British Journal of Learning Disabilities, 41*(1), 22–30. DOI: 10.1111/j.1468-3156.2011.00717.x

Dam, L. T., Heidler, P., & King, I. (2022). Access, Understanding, Promotion and Maintenance of Good Health: Evaluation of Knowledge Transfer of People With Intellectual Disabilities to Bridge the Health Information and Disease Prevention in Public Health. *Frontiers in Public Health, 10*, 915970. Advance online publication. DOI: 10.3389/fpubh.2022.915970 PMID: 36238251

Dar, H., & Dar, M. A. (2024). Redefining Success of the Tourism Sector Through Technological Advancements. In *AI Technologies for Personalized and Sustainable Tourism* (pp. 201–214). DOI: 10.4018/979-8-3693-5678-4.ch008

De Feo, J. A., & Barnard, W. W. (2005). A roadmap for change. *Quality Progress, 38*(1), 24–30. https://www.scopus.com/inward/record.uri?eid=2-s2.0-12344312247&partnerID=40&md5=7ee1533c75c9a71de5c50ace75fd9102

De Gennaro, D. (2019). *Job crafting: The art of redesigning a job*. FrancoAngeli. DOI: 10.1108/9781838672195

de Jonge, D., & Gibson, L. (2009). Effective utilization of assistive devices in the workplace. In *Ergonomics for Rehabilitation Professionals* (pp. 477–506). CRC Press. DOI: 10.1201/9780849382697.ch14

De La Calle-Duran, M.-C., & Garcia, I. C. (2024). Mentoring and empowering employees: How to develop management skills through mentoring. In *Developing managerial skills for global business success* (pp. 121–131). IGI Global., DOI: 10.4018/979-8-3693-3057-9.ch008

Dean, E. E., Burke, K. M., Shogren, K. A., & Wehmeyer, M. L. (2017). Promoting self-determination and integrated employment through the self-determined career development model. *Advances in Neurodevelopmental Disorders, 1*(2), 55–62. DOI: 10.1007/s41252-017-0011-y

Dean, E. E., Garrels, V., Sigstad, H. M. H., & Wendelborg, C. (2022). Employer willingness to hire people with intellectual disability: The influence of employer experience, perception of work, and social responsibility. *Journal of Vocational Rehabilitation, 57*(1), 85–95. DOI: 10.3233/JVR-221201

Dearing, K. (2020). 'Not worth the minimum wage?' Unpacking the complexities of intellectual disability and its intersection with employment structures. *Scandinavian Journal of Disability Research, 22*(1), 360–370. DOI: 10.16993/sjdr.729

Dearing, K. (2021). Exploring a non-universal understanding of waged work and its consequences: Sketching out employment activation for people with an intellectual disability. *Evidence & Policy, 17*(2), 261–277. DOI: 10.1332/174426421X16140992285741

Dearing, K. (2021). Work Aspirations, Intellectual Disability and 'Cruelling Out' the Mark in the Job Club. *The Sociological Review, 70*(3), 564–579. DOI: 10.1177/00380261211044619

Dehuri, B. K., & Mukund, B. (2020). Recent trends and issues in vocational rehabilitation of people with ID. In *Research anthology on rehabilitation practices and therapy* (pp. 1202–1228). IGI Global., DOI: 10.4018/978-1-7998-3432-8.ch059

Delap, L. (2024). Slow workers: Labelling and labouring in Britain, c. 1909–1955. *Social History of Medicine, 37*(1), 160–182. DOI: 10.1093/shm/hkad043 PMID: 38947272

Demerouti, E., Peeters, M., & Van den Heuvel, M. (2025). Job crafting interventions. In *Transformative Work Design: Synthesis and New Directions* (pp. 439–464). Oxford University Press. DOI: 10.1093/oso/9780197692554.003.0017

Deredzai, M., Maupa, B., & Mashiri, W. (2024). Social inclusion tactics for people with intellectual and developmental disabilities: Support for families of people with intellectual and developmental disabilities in Zimbabwe. In *Social inclusion tactics for people with intellectual and developmental disabilities* (pp. 367–388). IGI Global., DOI: 10.4018/979-8-3693-3176-7.ch016

Devlin, P. (2008). Enhancing the job performance of employees with disabilities using the Self-Determined Career Development Model. *Education and Training in Developmental Disabilities, 43*(4), 502–513. DOI: 10.1177/215416470804300409

Dew, A., Collings, S., Dillon Savage, I., Gentle, E., & Dowse, L. (2019). "Living the life I want": A framework for planning engagement with people with intellectual disability and complex support needs. *Journal of Applied Research in Intellectual Disabilities, 32*(2), 401–412. DOI: 10.1111/jar.12538 PMID: 30358022

Di Maggio, I., Santilli, S., Nota, L., & Ginevra, M. C. (2019). The predictive role of self-determination and psychological empowerment on job satisfaction in persons with intellectual disability. *Advances in Neurodevelopmental Disorders, 3*(2), 197–203. DOI: 10.1007/s41252-019-00110-4

DiCecco, V. (2007). Performance evaluations. *Printwear, 20*(6), 24–28.

Donald, C. G., & Ralston, J. D. (2005). Supremacy or subordination? Is the issue of ADA and CBA conflicts resolved? *Employee Relations Law Journal, 31*(2), 55–78.

Dong, D., Butler, R., & Herbert, J. (2022). Evaluation of the effectiveness of developing real-world software projects as a motivational device for bridging theory and practice. *Journal of Further and Higher Education, 46*(9), 1275–1289. DOI: 10.1080/0309877X.2022.2070727

Dong, S., Eto, O., Liu, L., & Villaquiran, A. (2023). Examining psychosocial factors associated with receiving workplace accommodations among people with disabilities. *Work (Reading, Mass.), 75*(3), 799–811. DOI: 10.3233/WOR-220230

Dong, S., Hespe, P., & Monagas, K. (2022). Requesting workplace accommodation among individuals with mobility disabilities: A qualitative investigation on barriers and facilitators. *Journal of Applied Rehabilitation Counseling, 53*(3), 193–209. DOI: 10.1891/JARC-D-21-00005

Dörfler, E., & Kulnik, S. T. (2020). Despite communication and cognitive impairment—person-centred goal-setting after stroke: A qualitative study. *Disability and Rehabilitation, 42*(25), 3628–3637. DOI: 10.1080/09638288.2019.1604821 PMID: 31020863

Dos Santos Rodrigues, P., Luecking, R. G., Glat, R., & Daquera, A. F. C. (2013). Improving workforce outcomes among persons with disabilities in Brazil through youth apprenticeships and customized employment. *Journal of Vocational Rehabilitation, 38*(3), 185–194. DOI: 10.3233/JVR-130633

Doussard, C., Garbe, E., Morales, J., & Billion, J. (2024). Universal design for the workplace: Ethical considerations regarding the inclusion of workers with disabilities. *Journal of Business Ethics, 194*(2), 285–296. DOI: 10.1007/s10551-023-05582-y

Dreher, K., & Willerton, R. (2025). ETHICS AND PLAIN LANGUAGE. In *The Routledge Handbook of Ethics in Technical and Professional Communication* (pp. 282–297). DOI: 10.4324/9781003434375-33

DuBois, D. L.. (2025). Person-centered planning and employment outcomes for adults with intellectual disabilities. *Intellectual and Developmental Disabilities, 63*(1), 22–35.

Duffy, K. (2013). Providing constructive feedback to students during mentoring. *Nursing Standard, 27*(31), 50–56. DOI: 10.7748/ns2013.04.27.31.50.e7334 PMID: 23641638

Durocher, E., Kinsella, E. A., McCorquodale, L., & Phelan, S. (2016). Ethical tensions related to systemic constraints: Occupational alienation in occupational therapy practice. *OTJR (Thorofare, N.J.)*, *36*(4), 216–226. DOI: 10.1177/1539449216665117 PMID: 27591435

Duvdevany, I., Or-Chen, K., & Fine, M. (2016). Employers' willingness to hire a person with intellectual disability in light of the regulations for adjusted minimum wages. *Journal of Vocational Rehabilitation*, *44*(1), 33–41. DOI: 10.3233/JVR-150778

Dyer, J. L., Twillman, N., & Sequeira, N. (2006). Determining the barriers to employment of HIV+ clients. *Journal of Social Work in Disability & Rehabilitation*, *5*(1), 21–43. DOI: 10.1300/J198v05n01_02

Edwards, C., Cai, R. Y., Love, A., White, L. M., Harris, K., Brooker, K., Kendall, E., & Gibbs, V. (2025). Beyond the "service cliff": Experiences of an inclusive postschool transition program for autistic youth with intellectual disability. *Advances in Autism*, *11*(4), 385–399. Advance online publication. DOI: 10.1108/AIA-06-2025-0053

Efeoğlu, İ. E., & Kılınçarslan, Ö. (2024). How do individuals with autism participate in work life? A study on inclusive employability. *Equality, Diversity and Inclusion*, *43*(2), 173–187. DOI: 10.1108/EDI-09-2022-0254

Elahdi, A., & Alnahdi, G. H. (2022). Factors associated with workers' attitudes towards employment of persons with intellectual disabilities in Saudi Arabia. *Journal of Applied Research in Intellectual Disabilities*, *35*(3), 856–866. DOI: 10.1111/jar.12990 PMID: 35174588

Elemam, R. F., & Abdelaal, H. M. (2025). The impact of structured assessment attempts and instructor feedback on clinical competency development in dental assistant training. *BMC Medical Education*, *25*(1), 1412. Advance online publication. DOI: 10.1186/s12909-025-07842-z PMID: 41088169

Ellenkamp, J. J. H., Brouwers, E. P. M., Embregts, P. J. C. M., Joosen, M. C. W., & van Weeghel, J. (2016). Work environment-related factors in obtaining and maintaining work in a competitive employment setting for employees with intellectual disabilities: A systematic review. *Journal of Occupational Rehabilitation*, *26*(1), 56–69. DOI: 10.1007/s10926-015-9586-1 PMID: 26112400

Ellington, J. K., Rehwaldt, R., & Knapp, S. (2015). Job analysis in human resource management. *The Journal of Applied Psychology*, *100*(3), 789–802.

Elmezzi, K., & Deering, S. (2019). Checklists in emergencies. *Seminars in Perinatology*, *43*(1), 18–21. DOI: 10.1053/j.semperi.2018.11.004 PMID: 30473312

Embley, C. (2024). Overcoming barriers in job coaching for adults with intellectual disability in supported employment. *Review of Disability Studies, 20*(1).

Emens, E. F. (2008). Integrating accommodation. *University of Pennsylvania Law Review, 156*(4), 839–922.

Encalada, A. V. (2021). The potential of the legal capacity law reform in Peru to transform mental health provision. In *Mental health, legal capacity, and human rights* (pp. 124–139). Cambridge University Press., DOI: 10.1017/9781108979016.011

Engelbrecht, M., van Niekerk, L., & Shaw, L. (2023). Supported employment for youth with intellectual disability: Promoting occupational justice. *Journal of Occupational Science, 30*(3), 403–419. DOI: 10.1080/14427591.2022.2146159

Engstrom, D. F., & Hausman, D. (2021). Rights, Redistribution, and the Rise of the "Litigation State": The Case of Disability Discrimination Laws. *Law & Social Inquiry, 46*(3), 788–825. DOI: 10.1017/lsi.2020.25

Ertelt, A., Renkl, A., & Spada, H. (2006). Making a difference - Exploiting the full potential of instructionally designed on-screen videos. *ICLS 2006 - International Conference of the Learning Sciences, Proceedings, 1*, 154–160.

Ervin, D. A. (2024). The State of Medical Care for Adults With Intellectual and/or Developmental Disabilities. *Medical Care, 63*(1S), S1–S7. DOI: 10.1097/MLR.0000000000001977 PMID: 39642008

Eshete, S. K., & Amentie, C. (2024). *Strategic Human Resource Management (SHRM) and Inclusion for Promoting Workplace Creativity and Innovation: Systematic Review*. DOI: 10.21203/rs.3.rs-3850810/v1

Eshete, S. K., & Birbirssa, Z. A. (2024). Strategic Human Resource Management (SHRM) in Creating Inclusive Workplace: Systematic Review. *SAGE Open, 14*(4), 21582440241287667. Advance online publication. DOI: 10.1177/21582440241287667

Estreder, Y., Martínez-Tur, V., Moliner, C., Gracia, E., & Lira, E. (2024). The voice of persons with intellectual disability: Why does autonomy support make them feel better? *Applied Psychology, 73*(3), 1055–1070. DOI: 10.1111/apps.12487

Fajardo-Castro, L. V., Martínez-Tur, V., Moliner, C., Plavsic, A., & Arbués, J. (2024). Organizational context and satisfaction of basic needs of workers with intellectual disability as sources of well-being. *Social Sciences (Basel, Switzerland), 13*(10), 523. Advance online publication. DOI: 10.3390/socsci13100523

Fantozzi, I. C., & Schiraldi, M. M. (2025). Bridging education and industry: University challenges and serious games for professional skill development. *The TQM Journal*. Advance online publication. DOI: 10.1108/TQM-12-2024-0511

Farzana, W., Sarker, F., Chau, T., & Mamun, K. A. (2025). Technological Evolvement in AAC Modalities to Foster Communications of Verbally Challenged ASD Children: A Systematic Review. *IEEE Access : Practical Innovations, Open Solutions*, *13*, 122943–122959. DOI: 10.1109/ACCESS.2021.3055195

Fasciglione, M. (2015). Article 27 of the CRPD and the right of inclusive employment of people with autism. In *Protecting the rights of people with autism in the fields of education and employment: International, European and national perspectives* (pp. 145–170). Springer., DOI: 10.1007/978-3-319-13791-9_6

Faulkner, A. (2018). Lucidchart for Easy Workflow Mapping. *Serials Review*, *44*(2), 157–162. DOI: 10.1080/00987913.2018.1472468

Ferdman, B. M. (2013). The practice of inclusion in diverse organizations: Toward a systemic and inclusive framework. In *Diversity at work: The practice of inclusion* (pp. 3–54). Wiley., DOI: 10.1002/9781118764282.ch1

Ferdman, B. M. (2020). Inclusive leadership: The fulcrum of inclusion. In *Inclusive leadership: Transforming diverse lives, workplaces, and societies* (pp. 3–24). Routledge., DOI: 10.4324/9780429449673-1

Ferri, D., Broderick, A., & Leahy, A. (2025). The global governance of disability rights: Complexities, participatory trends and intersections. In *Research Handbook on Global Governance* (pp. 299–329). Edward Elgar Publishing., DOI: 10.4337/9781789906332.00025

Fessl, A., Wesiak, G., Rivera-Pelayo, V., Feyertag, S., & Pammer, V. (2015). In-app reflection guidance for workplace learning. *Lecture Notes in Computer Science*, *9307*, 85–99. DOI: 10.1007/978-3-319-24258-3_7

Fessl, A., Wesiak, G., Rivera-Pelayo, V., Feyertag, S., & Pammer, V. (2017). In-app reflection guidance: Lessons learned across four field trials at the workplace. *IEEE Transactions on Learning Technologies*, *10*(4), 488–501. DOI: 10.1109/TLT.2017.2708097

Fillary, R., & Pernice, R. (2006). Social inclusion in workplaces where people with intellectual disabilities are employed: Implications for supported employment professionals. *International Journal of Rehabilitation Research. Internationale Zeitschrift fur Rehabilitationsforschung. Revue Internationale de Recherches de Readaptation*, *29*(1), 31–36. DOI: 10.1097/01.mrr.0000185952.87304.63 PMID: 16432387

Finstad, G. L.. (2022). Barriers to employment for individuals with intellectual disabilities: A systematic review. *Journal of Vocational Rehabilitation, 56*(3), 245–260.

Flippo, K., & Butterworth, J. (2018). Community Conversations and Transition Systems Change. *Journal of Disability Policy Studies, 29*(1), 7–11. DOI: 10.1177/1044207317739404

Flores, N., Moret-Tatay, C., Gutiérrez-Bermejo, B., Vázquez-Martínez, A., & Río, C. J. (2021). Assessment of Occupational Health and Job Satisfaction in Workers With Intellectual Disability: A Job Demands–Resources Perspective. *International Journal of Environmental Research and Public Health, 18*(4), 2072. DOI: 10.3390/ijerph18042072 PMID: 33672616

Flynn, R., Brez, J., & Fritz, E. (2025). Standardizing Orientation Checklists. *Journal for Nurses in Professional Development.* Advance online publication. DOI: 10.1097/NND.0000000000001196 PMID: 40996164

Folguera Bellmunt, C. (2026). Supported internships: Vocational training and labor inclusion for students with intellectual and developmental disabilities. *Equality, Diversity and Inclusion, 45*(1), 86–100. DOI: 10.1108/EDI-05-2024-0218

Foster-Cohen, S., & Mirfin-Veitch, B. (2017). Evidence for the effectiveness of visual supports in helping children with disabilities access the mainstream primary school curriculum. *Journal of Research in Special Educational Needs, 17*(2), 79–86. DOI: 10.1111/1471-3802.12105

Francescutti, C., Diminutto, M., & Zorzi, S. (2022). Work and occupation. In *Textbook of psychiatry for intellectual disability and autism spectrum disorder* (pp. 941–968). Springer., DOI: 10.1007/978-3-319-95720-3_38

Franken, E., Plimmer, G., & Hussain, A. (2025). Growth-oriented leadership: Developing leadership capacity throughout the organisation. In *Leadership and leadership development: Critical perspectives and contemporary approaches* (pp. 12–33). Routledge., DOI: 10.4324/9781032624976-2

Freeze, S., Hall, A. C., Collins, S., Shumate, D., Thomas, C., & Brent, B. (2017). Different States, Common Issues: Moving mountains One Service at a Time. *Journal of Vocational Rehabilitation, 46*(3), 265–271. DOI: 10.3233/JVR-170861

Friedman, C. (2021). Natural supports: The impact on people with intellectual and developmental disabilities' quality of life and service expenditures. *Journal of Family Social Work, 24*(2), 118–135. DOI: 10.1080/10522158.2020.1861158

Friedman, C., & Rizzolo, M. C. (2017). "Get Us Real Jobs:" Supported Employment Services for People With Intellectual and Developmental Disabilities In Medicaid Home and Community Based Services Waivers. *Journal of Vocational Rehabilitation, 46*(1), 107–116. DOI: 10.3233/JVR-160847

Fried, Y., Slowik, L. H., Shperling, Z., Franz, C., Ben-David, H. A., Avital, N., & Yeverechyahu, U. (2003). The moderating effect of job security on the relation between role clarity and job performance: A longitudinal field study. *Human Relations, 56*(7), 787–805. DOI: 10.1177/00187267030567002

Frolli, A., Cerciello, F., Esposito, C., & Sica, L. S. (2022). Universal Design for Learning: A new educational approach. *CEUR Workshop Proceedings, 3371*, •••. https://www.scopus.com/inward/record.uri?eid=2-s2.0-85154043738&partnerID=40&md5=1cb3dddc557a5ea6284bcf5e99a11670

Fry, R. (2018). Information reduction and studio project frameworks. *Proceedings of the 20th International Conference on Engineering and Product Design Education, E and PDE 2018.* https://www.scopus.com/inward/record.uri?eid=2-s2.0-85057729051&partnerID=40&md5=8ad8dcbe5e1e848ad751b703133470d0

Fuentes, K., & Lindsay, S. (2022). Workplace accommodations during the COVID-19 pandemic: A scoping review of the impacts and implications for people with disabilities. *Work (Reading, Mass.), 74*(2), 381–406. DOI: 10.3233/WOR-220129

Fuertes, V., McQuaid, R., & Heidenreich, M. (2020). Institutional Logics of Service Provision: The National and Urban Governance of Activation Policies in Three European Countries. *Journal of European Social Policy, 31*(1), 92–107. DOI: 10.1177/0958928720974178

Fumasoli, T., & Goastellec, G. (2015). Global models, disciplinary and local patterns in academic recruitment processes. In *Academic work and careers in Europe: Trends, challenges, perspectives* (pp. 69–93). Springer., DOI: 10.1007/978-3-319-10720-2_4

Gahane, S., Khode, P., Kapse, A., Sharma, D., & Anawade, P. (2026). Techniques and best practices for creating accessible websites and applications. *Lecture Notes in Networks and Systems, 1457 LNNS*, 523–531. https://doi.org/DOI: 10.1007/978-981-96-7496-1_42

Gallo, I., & Melé, D. (2025). Work integration of people with mental disorders through social enterprise: A humanistic-personalist framework and case study. *Journal of Business Ethics, 199*(4), 693–713. DOI: 10.1007/s10551-024-05853-2

Ganapathy, V. (2025). Building collaboration in a multigenerational workforce. In *Enhancing workplace productivity through gender equity and intergenerational communication* (pp. 167–194). IGI Global., DOI: 10.4018/979-8-3373-2903-1.ch007

Gardner, A. K., Costa, P., & Willis, R. E. (2022). Getting on the same page: The impact of interviewer education and structured interviews on interrater agreement in residency interviews. *Journal of Surgical Education*, *79*(6), e12–e16. DOI: 10.1016/j.jsurg.2022.05.013 PMID: 35803882

Gardner, K. M. (2014). Developing a customized multiple interview for dental school admissions. *Journal of Dental Education*, *78*(4), 597–604. DOI: 10.1002/j.0022-0337.2014.78.4.tb05711.x PMID: 24706690

Garrels, V., & Sigstad, H. M. H. (2021). Employment for persons with intellectual disability in the Nordic countries: A scoping review. *Journal of Applied Research in Intellectual Disabilities*, *34*(4), 993–1007. DOI: 10.1111/jar.12880 PMID: 33709541

Garrels, V., & Sigstad, H. M. H. (2023). Caregivers' Experiences With School–Work Transitions for Their Children With Disorders of Intellectual Development. *International Journal of Environmental Research and Public Health*, *20*(3), 1892. DOI: 10.3390/ijerph20031892 PMID: 36767259

Gasset, D. I., & Ero, P. R. H. (2016). Evaluation of the methodology supported employment in promentor program (UAM-PRODIS). Competence setting [Evaluación de la metodología empleo con apoyo (ECA) en el programa promentor (UAM-PRODIS). El ajuste competencial]. *Siglo Cero*, *47*(1), 37–54. DOI: 10.14201/scero201613754

Geisen, M., & Klatt, S. (2022). Real-time feedback using extended reality: A current overview and further integration into sports. *International Journal of Sports Science & Coaching*, *17*(5), 1178–1194. DOI: 10.1177/17479541211051006

Gendera, S., Alexander, J., Burton, J., Fisher, K. R., & Robinson, S. (2025). People with disability influencing sustained improvements to employment. *Social Policy and Administration*. Advance online publication. DOI: 10.1111/spol.70022

General Comment No. 8 (2022) on the right of persons with disabilities to work and employment. (. (2022). International. *Human Rights Law Review*, *11*(2), 273–303. DOI: 10.1163/22131035-11020004

George, G., Kulkarni, M., & Varghese, B. (2025). AI in creating inclusive work environments for neurodiverse employees. *Advances in Autism*. Advance online publication. DOI: 10.1108/AIA-05-2025-0046

Gerritsen, C. (2022). Structured diagnostic interview schedules. In *Comprehensive clinical psychology* (2nd ed., Vol. 4, pp. 72–85). Elsevier., DOI: 10.1016/B978-0-12-818697-8.00112-6

Geyer, P. D. (2021). Acquiring workplace accommodations when management support is voluntary: Crafting jobs and accommodations. *Journal of Rehabilitation*, *87*(3), 31–35.

Ghanbari, Z., Abouee-Mehrizi, A., Rasoulzadeh, Y., & Hokmabadi, R. (2024). Psychometric properties of the Persian version of the Fleishman Job Analysis Survey (FJAS). *Work (Reading, Mass.)*, *77*(1), 113–121. DOI: 10.3233/WOR-220004 PMID: 37483042

Ghose, A., Kochher, H. S., & Ali, S. M. A. (2024). Towards equity and inclusion: Legal exploration for inclusive business practices integrating CSR and disability rights in India. In *Bridging Human Rights and Corporate Social Responsibility: Pathways to a Sustainable Global Society* (pp. 127–154). IGI Global. DOI: 10.4018/979-8-3693-2325-0.ch006

Gignac, M. A. M., Bowring, J., Navaratnerajah, L., Saunders, R., Jetha, A., Thompson, A., Shaw, W. S., Franche, R.-L., Van Eerd, D., Irvin, E., Tompa, E., Macdermid, J. C., & Smith, P. M. (2025). The Job Demands and Accommodation Planning Tool (JDAPT): A nine-month evaluation of use, changes in self-efficacy, presenteeism, and absenteeism in workers with chronic and episodic disabilities. *Journal of Occupational Rehabilitation*, *35*(3), 625–640. DOI: 10.1007/s10926-024-10231-w PMID: 39120861

Gilson, C. B., Sinclair, J., Whirley, M. L., Li, Y., & Blustein, D. L. (2022). "More Than a Job, It's a Purpose": A Psychology of Working Perspective of the Working Experiences for Individuals With Intellectual and Developmental Disabilities. *Journal of Career Assessment*, *30*(2), 367–386. DOI: 10.1177/10690727211048898

Gilson, K.-M., Johnson, S., Davis, E., Brunton, S., Swift, E., Reddihough, D., & Williams, K. (2018). Supporting the mental health of mothers of children with a disability: Health professional perceptions of need, role, and challenges. *Child: Care, Health and Development*, *44*(5), 721–729. DOI: 10.1111/cch.12589 PMID: 30133770

Gingerich, E. F. R. (2021). Working for inclusion: Addressing legal and ethical safeguards for LGBTQ employees. In *The Palgrave handbook of workplace well-being* (pp. 1379–1403). Palgrave Macmillan., DOI: 10.1007/978-3-030-30025-8_65

Girshausen, R., Graf, S., Holz, T., Lorenz, J., Masson, T., Wolff, J., & Azad, N. (2025). Einarbeitung in der Notfallmedizin. *Medizinische Klinik, Intensivmedizin und Notfallmedizin, 120*(6), 473–480. DOI: 10.1007/s00063-025-01281-w PMID: 40293484

Gjertsen, H., Hardonk, S., & Ineland, J. (2021). Work Inclusion for People With Intellectual Disabilities in Three Nordic Countries: The Current Policy and Challenges. *Scandinavian Journal of Disability Research, 23*(1), 360–370. DOI: 10.16993/sjdr.821

Glade, R., Koch, L. C., & Rumrill, P. D. (2020). Employer practices and the employment of people with disabilities: A review of the literature. *Journal of Vocational Rehabilitation, 52*(3), 221–234.

Glade, R., Koch, L. C., Zaandam, A., Simon, L. S., Manno, C. M., Rumril, P. D., & Rosen, C. C. (2020). Recommendations from employees with disabilities for creating inclusive workplaces: Results from a grounded theory investigation. *Journal of Vocational Rehabilitation, 53*(1), 77–88. DOI: 10.3233/JVR-201087

Godden, L., & Hoessler, C. (2024). (Re)designing for equity, access and inclusion in work-integrated learning. *. *International Journal of Work-Integrated Learning, 25*(1), 37–50.

Gold, P. B., Oire, S. N., Fabian, E. S., & Wewiorski, N. J. (2012). Negotiating reasonable workplace accommodations: Perspectives of employers, employees with disabilities, and rehabilitation service providers. *Journal of Vocational Rehabilitation, 37*(1), 25–37. DOI: 10.3233/JVR-2012-0597

Golovko, D., & Schumann, J. H. (2019). Influence of company Facebook activities on recruitment success. *Journal of Business Research, 104*, 161–169. DOI: 10.1016/j.jbusres.2019.06.029

Gomes-Machado, M. L., Santos, F. H., Schoen, T., & Chiari, B. (2016). Effects of vocational training on a group of people with intellectual disabilities. *Journal of Policy and Practice in Intellectual Disabilities, 13*(1), 33–40. DOI: 10.1111/jppi.12144

Gomez-Borges, A., Martínez, I. M., & Salanova, M. (2025). Adapting a Positive Psychological Intervention for Employees with and Without Intellectual Disabilities. *Healthcare (Basel), 13*(17), 2096. Advance online publication. DOI: 10.3390/healthcare13172096 PMID: 40941448

Gómez, L. E., Monsalve, A., Morán, L., Alcedo, M. Á., Lombardi, M., & Schalock, R. L. (2020). Measurable Indicators of CRPD for People With Intellectual and Developmental Disabilities Within the Quality of Life Framework. *International Journal of Environmental Research and Public Health*, *17*(14), 5123. DOI: 10.3390/ijerph17145123 PMID: 32679924

González, C. C., Vasquez, R. C., & Reed, B. J. (2024). Disability awareness and inclusion. In *Innovative approaches in counselor education for students with disabilities* (pp. 1–32). IGI Global., DOI: 10.4018/979-8-3693-3342-6.ch001

Gonzalez, K., Tillman, C. J., & Holmes, J. J. (2020). Coming home: Why veterans with disabilities withhold workplace accommodation requests. *Human Relations*, *73*(10), 1439–1466. DOI: 10.1177/0018726719875810

Gonzalez, P. A., & Karimy, P. (2025). Breaking barriers: Retention strategies for underrepresented groups in the IT workforce. *Americas Conference on Information Systems, AMCIS 2025, 7*, 4352–4356.

Goodman, N., Deane, S., Hyseni, F., Soffer, M., Shaheen, G., & Blanck, P. (2024). Perceptions and bias of small business leaders in employing people with different types of disabilities. *Journal of Occupational Rehabilitation*, *34*(2), 359–372. DOI: 10.1007/s10926-024-10201-2

Gormley, M. E. (2015). Workplace stigma toward employees with intellectual disability: A descriptive study. *Journal of Vocational Rehabilitation*, *43*(3), 249–258. DOI: 10.3233/JVR-150773

Gould, J. B. (2024). From Policy to Practice: Socio-Ecological Challenges in Implementing the Home and Community Based Settings Rule. *Journal of Disability Policy Studies*, *36*(1), 29–39. DOI: 10.1177/10442073241289081

Gould, R., Mullin, C., Harris, S. P., & Jones, R. (2021). Building, Sustaining and Growing: Disability Inclusion in Business. *Equality, Diversity and Inclusion*, *41*(3), 418–434. DOI: 10.1108/EDI-06-2020-0156

Graham, A., Harbottle, C., & King, D. (2016). Resolve: A community-based forensic learning disability service specialising in supporting male sex offenders – our model, approach and evidence base for effective intervention. *Journal of Intellectual Disabilities and Offending Behaviour*, *7*(4), 186–194. DOI: 10.1108/JIDOB-10-2014-0014

Grant, G., Ramcharan, P., & Goward, P. (2003). Resilience, family care, and people with intellectual disabilities. *International Review of Research in Mental Retardation*, *26*, 135–173. DOI: 10.1016/S0074-7750(03)01004-8

Gray, M., Davies, K., & Butcher, L. (2017). Finding the right connections: Peer support within a community-based mental health service. *International Journal of Social Welfare*, *26*(2), 188–196. DOI: 10.1111/ijsw.12222

Grenwelge, C., & Zhang, D. (2012). The Effects of the Texas Youth Leadership Forum Summer Training on the Self-Advocacy Abilities of High School Students With Disabilities. *Journal of Disability Policy Studies*, *24*(3), 158–169. DOI: 10.1177/1044207312457415

Grijseels, M., Zuiderent-Jerak, T., & Regeer, B. J. (2023). Technologies for inclusive employment: Beyond the prosthetic fix—social transformation axis. *Disability & Society*, *38*(9), 1534–1557. DOI: 10.1080/09687599.2021.1997720

Grossi, T., Thomas, F., & Held, M. (2019). Making a Collective Impact: A School-to-Work Collaborative Model. *Journal of Vocational Rehabilitation*, *51*(3), 395–407. DOI: 10.3233/JVR-191054

Gross, J. M. S., Monroe-Gulick, A., Nye, C., Davidson-Gibbs, D., & Dedrick, D. (2020). Multifaceted Interventions for Supporting Community Participation Among Adults With Disabilities: A Systematic Review. *Campbell Systematic Reviews*, *16*(2), e1092. Advance online publication. DOI: 10.1002/cl2.1092 PMID: 37131415

Guerrero, A. M., Bennett, N. J., Wilson, K. A., Carter, N., Gill, D., Mills, M., Ives, C. D., Selinske, M. J., Larrosa, C., Bekessy, S., Januchowski-Hartley, F. A., Travers, H., Wyborn, C. A., & Nuno, A. (2018). Achieving the promise of integration in social-ecological research: A review and prospectus. *Ecology and Society*, *23*(3), art38. DOI: 10.5751/ES-10232-230338

Gustafsson, J., Peralta, J., & Danermark, B. (2018). Supported employment and social inclusion - experiences of workers with disabilities in wage subsidised employment in Sweden. *Scandinavian Journal of Disability Research*, *20*(1), 26–36. DOI: 10.16993/sjdr.36

Gutierrez, B. D. (2025). Developing a performance management system for employees with hidden disabilities. In *New Horizons in Leadership: Inclusive Explorations in Health, Technology, and Education* (pp. 221–237). IGI Global. DOI: 10.4018/979-8-3693-6437-6.ch010

Haase, T., Termath, W., Berndt, D., & Dick, M. (2020). Assistive technologies: Companion or controller? Appropriation instead of instruction. *WMSCI 2020 - 24th World Multi-Conference on Systemics, Cybernetics and Informatics. Proceedings*, *3*, 150–155. https://www.scopus.com/inward/record.uri?eid=2-s2.0-85096598538&partnerID=40&md5=97269c23e7550175259327de80ca3adf

Hadush, G., & Mekonen, B. (2020). Exploring tax incentive mechanisms to strengthen the inclusion of persons with disabilities in the private workforce in Ethiopia. *International Studies in Human Rights, 131*, 241–260. DOI: 10.1163/9789004415966_012

Hafsteinsdóttir, Á., & Hardonk, S. C. (2023). Understanding work inclusion: Analysis of the perspectives of people with intellectual disabilities on employment in the Icelandic labor market. *Work (Reading, Mass.), 75*(2), 433–445. DOI: 10.3233/WOR-211219 PMID: 36641711

Haines, K., Soldner, J. L., Zhang, L., Laurent, M.-L. S., Knabe, B., West-Evans, K., Mock, L., & Foley, S. (2018). Vocational Rehabilitation and Business Relations: Preliminary Indicators of State VR Agency Capacity. *Journal of Vocational Rehabilitation, 48*(1), 133–145. DOI: 10.3233/JVR-170921

Hall, A. C., Butterworth, J., Winsor, J., Kramer, J. C., Nye-Lengerman, K., & Timmons, J. C. (2018). Building an Evidence-Based, Holistic Approach to Advancing Integrated Employment. *Research and Practice for Persons with Severe Disabilities : the Journal of TASH, 43*(3), 207–218. DOI: 10.1177/1540796918787503

Hall, C., Dahl-Leonard, K., Denton, C. A., Stevens, E. A., & Capin, P. (2021). Fostering Independence While Teaching Students With or at Risk for Reading Disabilities. *Teaching Exceptional Children, 54*(2), 124–133. DOI: 10.1177/0040059921994596

Hameed, S., Huq, L., Musendo, D. J. N., Banks, L. M., Olenja, J., & Shakespeare, T. (2024). "I don't know whether it's priority, or capacity, or both": Implementation gaps in employment policies targeting people with disabilities in Kenya and Bangladesh. *Disabilities, 4*(4), 781–800. DOI: 10.3390/disabilities4040048

Hamzah, N. R., Hanid, M. F. A., & Zakaria, M. I. (2025). The effect of segmented-interactive video demonstration on student performance in procedural skills among healthcare students. *Advances in Health Sciences Education : Theory and Practice*. Advance online publication. DOI: 10.1007/s10459-025-10471-2 PMID: 40889025

Hanson, S. L., Bruyère, S. M., Forber-Pratt, A. J., Reesman, J., & Sung, C. (2023). Guidelines for Assessment and Intervention With Persons With Disabilities: An Executive Summary. *The American Psychologist, 78*(8), 995–1009. DOI: 10.1037/amp0001150 PMID: 36931825

Hanvey, C. (2018). Data collection methods. In *Wage and Hour Law: Guide to Methods and Analysis* (pp. 19–46). Springer. DOI: 10.1007/978-3-319-74612-8_2

Hao, Y., & Li, P. (2020). Employment legal framework for persons with disabilities in China: Effectiveness and reasons. *International Journal of Environmental Research and Public Health, 17*(14). *International Journal of Environmental Research and Public Health, 4976*(14), 1–20. DOI: 10.3390/ijerph17144976

Harju, L. K., Tims, M., Hakanen, J. J., & Khapova, S. N. (2023). Crafting for oneself while considering others: How the relational design of work shapes job crafting. *International Journal of Human Resource Management, 35*(1), 67–97. DOI: 10.1080/09585192.2023.2211711

Hartman, E., Brinck, E. A., Anderson, C. A., & Hergenrather, K. C. (2025). Education and Pre-Employment Transition Service Predictors of Wages for Transition Age Youth With Disabilities. *Journal of Vocational Rehabilitation, 63*(2), 147–159. DOI: 10.1177/10522263251356241

Hartnett, H. P., Stuart, H., Thurman, H., Loy, B., & Batiste, L. C. (2011). Employers' perceptions of the benefits of workplace accommodations: Reasons to hire, retain and promote people with disabilities. *Journal of Vocational Rehabilitation, 34*(1), 17–23. DOI: 10.3233/JVR-2010-0530

Hedenus, A., Backman, C., & Håkansson, P. (2021). Whom do you know? Recruiters' motives for assessing jobseekers' online networks. *International Journal of Human Resource Management, 32*(8), 1754–1777. DOI: 10.1080/09585192.2019.1579245

Heinz-Jakobs, M., Görmez, S., Johnson, H. L., Gerken, J., Pascher, M., Barbareschi, G., Balasuriya, S. S., Sitbon, L., & Röcker, C. (2025). AT@Work: Intelligent Assistive Technologies for Enabling Workplace Inclusion. *ASSETS 2025 - Proceedings of the 27th International ACM SIGACCESS Conference on Computers and Accessibility*. DOI: 10.1145/3663547.3748637

Heitplatz, V. N. (2020). Fostering Digital Participation for People With Intellectual Disabilities and Their Caregivers: Towards a Guideline for Designing Education Programs. *Social Inclusion (Lisboa), 8*(2), 201–212. DOI: 10.17645/si.v8i2.2578

Heman, P., Rhodes, D., & Cox, C. (2022). Electronic assistive technology use and supported employment. *Journal of Applied Research in Intellectual Disabilities, 35*(5), 1244–1249. DOI: 10.1111/jar.13005 PMID: 35596577

Henderson, A., Cassidy, J., Croydon, A., & Nind, M. (2024). Inclusive peer review: Reflections on an adapted citizens' jury with people with learning disabilities. *British Journal of Learning Disabilities, 52*(4), 666–675. DOI: 10.1111/bld.12603

Hennessy, T., McMahon, J., & Doody, O. (2026). Informing the design of inclusive post-secondary education: A qualitative exploration of the perspectives of individuals with intellectual disabilities. *British Journal of Learning Disabilities*, *54*(2), 263–275. Advance online publication. DOI: 10.1111/bld.70033

He, Y. (2021). Research on job crafting based on the theory of strength perspective. *IOP Conference Series. Earth and Environmental Science*, *632*(4), 042034. Advance online publication. DOI: 10.1088/1755-1315/632/4/042034

Ho, S.-B., & Liausvia, F. (2013). Incremental rule chunking for problem solving. *Proceedings - 1st BRICS Countries Congress on Computational Intelligence, BRICS-CCI 2013*, 323–328. DOI: 10.1109/BRICS-CCI-CBIC.2013.61

Hodges, T. D., & Asplund, J. (2009). Strengths development in the workplace. In *Oxford Handbook of Positive Psychology and Work*. Oxford University Press., DOI: 10.1093/oxfordhb/9780195335446.013.0017

Hoeh, E., & Bonat, M. L. (2020). Higher education faculty addressing the diverse learning needs of students with disabilities within the universal design for learning framework. In *Ethics in Higher Education* (pp. 97–126). https://www.scopus.com/inward/record.uri?eid=2-s2.0-85125611492&partnerID=40&md5=57caac83e681dad9f368e3efa153f866

Hopkins, S., & O'Donovan, R. (2019). Using Complex Learning Tasks to Build Procedural Fluency and Financial Literacy for Young People With Intellectual Disability. *Mathematics Education Research Journal*, *33*(1), 163–181. DOI: 10.1007/s13394-019-00279-w

Hoske, M. T. (2023a). How control-system integration advances competitiveness. *Control Engineering*, *70*(3), 29.

Hoske, M. T. (2023b). How to determine ROI and get buy-in for workforce digital transformation. *Control Engineering*, *70*(3), 27.

Houtven, C. H. V., Drake, C., Malo, T. L., Decosimo, K., Tucker, M., Sullivan, C., D'Adolf, J., Hughes, J. M., Christensen, L., Grubber, J. M., Coffman, C. J., Sperber, N., Wang, V., Allen, K. D., Hastings, S. N., Shea, C. M., & Zullig, L. L. (2023). Ready, Set, Go! The Role of Organizational Readiness to Predict Adoption of a Family Caregiver Training Program Using the Rogers' Diffusion of Innovation Theory. *Implementation Science Communications*, *4*(1), 69. Advance online publication. DOI: 10.1186/s43058-023-00447-x PMID: 37337208

Howlett, S., & Harvey, R. (2012). Rachel's story: A bridge to inclusion. *JANZSSA. Journal of the Australian and New Zealand Student Services Association*, (39), 42–48.

Huang, W.-T. (2024). Designing effective career websites: A study on user experience and job seeker engagement. *Communications in Computer and Information Science, 2314 CCIS*, 144–155. https://doi.org/DOI: 10.1007/978-981-97-9910-7_12

Huber, M. J., Oswald, G., Chan, F., Shaw, L. R., & Wilson, J. F. (2017). A Call for a National Evidence-Based Programs and Practices Registry in Vocational Rehabilitation. *Journal of Vocational Rehabilitation*, *46*(1), 11–18. DOI: 10.3233/JVR-160838

Huber, M., & Pochstein, F. (2025). Attitudes towards individuals with intellectual disabilities: Comparison between Special Olympic partners and non-partners during the Special Olympics World Summer Games 2023. *Journal of Intellectual & Developmental Disability*, *50*(2), 211–220. DOI: 10.3109/13668250.2024.2405972 PMID: 40390320

Hujerat, E. (2024). Managing employees with disabilities: The impact of employer behavior and workplace climate from an employee perspective in Israel. In *Springer Proceedings in Business and Economics* (pp. 817–839). Springer., DOI: 10.1007/978-981-97-0996-0_50

Hung, D. Y., Levy, L. C., Rundall, T. G., Reponen, E., Huen, W., & Shortell, S. M. (2025). Advancing equity: Lean leader practices and a path forward. *The Milbank Quarterly*, *103*(3), 918–939. DOI: 10.1111/1468-0009.70037 PMID: 40772572

Hutchinson, C., Lay, K., Alexander, J., & Ratcliffe, J. (2020). People With Intellectual Disabilities as Business Owners: A Systematic Review of Peer-reviewed Literature. *Journal of Applied Research in Intellectual Disabilities*, *34*(2), 459–470. DOI: 10.1111/jar.12836 PMID: 33280214

Hwang, G., Jensen, N. K., & Wadiwel, D. J. (2024). Disability, Employment and Welfare Reform: A Comparative Analysis of Australia and Denmark. *The Australian Journal of Social Issues*, *59*(4), 1013–1030. DOI: 10.1002/ajs4.327

Hyseni, F., Kruse, D., Schur, L., & Blanck, P. (2023). Disability, workplace inclusion and organizational citizenship behaviour: An exploratory study of the legal profession. *Journal of Participation and Employee Ownership*, *6*(1), 31–50. DOI: 10.1108/JPEO-10-2022-0017 PMID: 38528853

Iftikhar, A., Mohammad, S. I., Alqudah, M. N., Al-Adwan, A. S., Vasudevan, A., Ali, I., & Farhan, M. (2025). Evaluating inclusivity and fairness of AI recruitment tools for hiring people with disabilities in the United Arab Emirates (UAE) [Evaluación de la Inclusividad y la Equidad de las Herramientas de Reclutamiento de IA para la Contratación de Personas con Discapacidad en los Emiratos Árabes Unidos (EAU)]. *Data and Metadata*, *4*, 487. Advance online publication. DOI: 10.56294/dm2025487

Ilies, R., Liu, Y., Aw, S., Heras, M. L., & Rofcanin, Y. (2024). Why does using personal strengths at work increase employee engagement? Who makes the most out of it, and how? *Journal of Occupational Health Psychology*, *29*(2), 113–129. DOI: 10.1037/ocp0000374 PMID: 38647463

Inoue, M. (2019). Assessments and interventions to address challenging behavior in individuals with intellectual disability and autism spectrum disorder in Japan: A consolidated review. *Yonago Acta Medica*, *62*(2), 169–181. DOI: 10.33160/yam.2019.06.001 PMID: 31320821

Isaacs, B., Clark, C., Correia, S., & Flannery, J. (2009). Utility of Logic Models to Plan Quality of Life Outcome Evaluations. *Journal of Policy and Practice in Intellectual Disabilities*, *6*(1), 52–61. DOI: 10.1111/j.1741-1130.2008.00197.x

Isetti, D., & Eadie, T. (2016). The Americans with Disabilities Act and voice disorders: Practical guidelines for voice clinicians. *Journal of Voice*, *30*(3), 293–300. DOI: 10.1016/j.jvoice.2015.04.006

Islam, R., French, E., & Ali, M. (2025). Subjectivity in performance review systems: Unveiling the mechanisms of gender bias and leadership disparity in the information technology industry. *International Journal of Human Resource Management*, *36*(22), 4039–4073. DOI: 10.1080/09585192.2026.2623102

Iwanaga, K., Chan, F., Anderson, C., Ditchman, N., Kaya, C., Hartman, E., & Tansey, T. N. (2021). Demographic, Transition, and Vocational Rehabilitation Service Variables' Association With High School Completion Outcomes of Youth With Disabilities Receiving SSI. *Rehabilitation Counseling Bulletin*, *65*(1), 23–36. DOI: 10.1177/0034355220970543

Iwanaga, K., Chan, F., Bezyak, J., Wu, J. R., Lee, D., Rumrill, P., West, A. E., Zapata, P., Ho, H., Tansey, T. N., & Wehman, P. (2024). Fortune 500 companies and employment of people with disabilities: The intermediary role of disability inclusion policies and practices. *Journal of Vocational Rehabilitation*, *61*(1), 17–24. DOI: 10.3233/JVR-240026

Iwanaga, K., Chen, X., Wu, J.-R., Lee, B., Chan, F., Bezyak, J., Grenawalt, T. A., & Tansey, T. N. (2018). Assessing Disability Inclusion Climate in the Workplace: A Brief Report. *Journal of Vocational Rehabilitation*, *49*(2), 265–271. DOI: 10.3233/JVR-180972

Jääskeläinen, K., & Nevala, N. (2012). Use of assistive technology in workplaces of employees with physical and cognitive disabilities. *Lecture Notes in Computer Science (Including Subseries Lecture Notes in Artificial Intelligence and Lecture Notes in Bioinformatics), 7382 LNCS*(PART 1), 223–226. DOI: 10.1007/978-3-642-31522-0_33

Jacob, U. S., & Pillay, J. (2023). Studies related to employment of persons with intellectual disability: A systematic review. *Journal of Vocational Rehabilitation, 59*(2), 169–181. DOI: 10.3233/JVR-230035

Jaffrès, F., & Guével, M.-R. (2017). Quota and non-discrimination approach on employment of persons with disabilities in the French public service: What are the employers' practices? [L'emploi des personnes handicapées dans la fonction publique: Entre quota et non-discrimination, quelles pratiques des employeurs?]. *Travail et Emploi*, (152), 33–57. DOI: 10.4000/travailemploi.7759

Jahoda, A., Banks, P., Dagnan, D., Kemp, J., Kerr, W., & Williams, V. (2009). Starting a new job: The social and emotional experience of people with intellectual disabilities. *Journal of Applied Research in Intellectual Disabilities, 22*(5), 421–425. DOI: 10.1111/j.1468-3148.2009.00497.x

Jaiswal, A., Gangwani, A., Rakesh, N., Oberoi, M., Chauhan, P., & Dewangan, B. K. (2025). Interview assistance system for deaf and mute candidates using real-time sign language translation and speech recognition. *2025 4th OPJU International Technology Conference on Smart Computing for Innovation and Advancement in Industry 5.0*. https://doi.org/DOI: 10.1109/OTCON65728.2025.11070383

Jakobsen, K. (2009). The right to work: Experiences of employees with rheumatism. *Journal of Occupational Science, 16*(2), 120–127. DOI: 10.1080/14427591.2009.9686651

James, M. (2018). Strategic readiness. In *The international encyclopedia of strategic communication* (pp. 1–5). Wiley., DOI: 10.1002/9781119010722.iesc0178

Jansen, J., Ooijen, R., Koning, P., Boot, C. R. L., & Brouwer, S. (2021). The Role of the Employer in Supporting Work Participation of Workers With Disabilities: A Systematic Literature Review Using an Interdisciplinary Approach. *Journal of Occupational Rehabilitation, 31*(4), 916–949. DOI: 10.1007/s10926-021-09978-3 PMID: 33978875

Javahery, H., Gower, M., Sinnig, D., & Forbrig, P. (2011). Patterns for usable accessible design. *Lecture Notes in Computer Science, 6761*(Part 1), 248–257. DOI: 10.1007/978-3-642-21602-2_28

Jayasekara, C., Senarathne, I., Wickramasinghe, A., Jayathilaka, N., Thelijjagoda, S., De Silva, H., Giguruwa, N., & Abeysinghe, N. (2023). Artificial intelligence agent to identify the correct human resources. *ICAC 2023 - 5th International Conference on Advancements in Computing*, 424–429. https://doi.org/DOI: 10.1109/ICAC60630.2023.10417197

Jenson, C. M., Hutchins, A. J., & Rowlands, G. (2006). Is small-group education the key to retention of sessional GPs? *Education for Primary Care*, *17*(3), 218–226. DOI: 10.1080/14739879.2006.11864065 PMID: 28240104

Jeong, D. Y. (2010). The Role of the State in Industrial Relations. *Seoul Journal of Business*, *16*(2), 95–126. DOI: 10.35152/snusjb.2010.16.2.004

Johnsen, T. L., Fyhn, T., Jordbru, A., Torp, S., Tveito, T. H., & Øyeflaten, I. (2022). Workplace inclusion of people with health issues, immigrants, and unemployed youths—A qualitative study of Norwegian leaders' experiences. *Frontiers in Psychology*, *13*, 687384. DOI: 10.3389/fpsyg.2022.687384 PMID: 35783778

Jones-Parkin, T., Thomas, F., Hess, K., & Snyder, A. (2021). Employment First and Transition: Utah School-to-Work Initiative. *Journal of Vocational Rehabilitation*, *54*(3), 265–271. DOI: 10.3233/JVR-211135

Jordán de Urríes, F. B., & Verdugo, M. Á. (2012). Sheltered employment versus supported employment: A review of the literature. *Journal of Vocational Rehabilitation*, *37*(2), 85–95.

Joseph, J., & Wilson, R. (2024). Enhancing Disability Nursing Practice in Australia: Addressing Educational Preparedness. *International Journal of Mental Health Nursing*, *33*(6), 1637–1665. DOI: 10.1111/inm.13373 PMID: 38873821

Joyce, A., Campbell, P., Crosbie, J., & Wilson, E. (2024). Workplace structures and culture that support the wellbeing of people with an intellectual disability. *International Journal of Environmental Research and Public Health*, *21*(11), 1453. Advance online publication. DOI: 10.3390/ijerph21111453 PMID: 39595719

Joyce, A., Campbell, P., Crosbie, J., & Wilson, E. (2025). Wellbeing and job satisfaction among employees with intellectual disability. *Frontiers in Public Health*, *13*, 1503932. Advance online publication. DOI: 10.3389/fpubh.2025.1503932 PMID: 40124410

Jupille, J., Deloffre, S., Leguay, D., & Chirio-Espitalier, M. (2025). Disability, recruitment and job retention: Identifying barriers and facilitators from the employers' point of view. *Work (Reading, Mass.)*, *80*(1), 202–211. DOI: 10.3233/WOR-230444 PMID: 39121145

Jurado-Caraballo, M. Á., García, C. Q., & Rodríguez-Fernández, M. (2020). Trends and Opportunities in Research on Disability and Work: An Interdisciplinary Perspective. *Business Research Quarterly, 25*(4), 366–388. DOI: 10.1177/2340944420972715

Juujärvi, S., Nummela, O., & Sinervo, T. (2023). Aspects of ethical conflicts and their implications for work-related well-being: A cross-sectional study among health and social care professionals. *Scandinavian Journal of Work and Organisational Psychology, 8*(1). *Article, 1*(1), 1–15. DOI: 10.16993/sjwop.176

Kåhlin, I., & Haglund, L. (2009). Psychosocial strengths and challenges related to work among persons with intellectual disabilities. *Occupational Therapy in Mental Health, 25*(2), 151–163. DOI: 10.1080/01642120902859055

Kakada, P., & Bisen, S. (2025). Empowering change: The role of inclusive leadership in organisational evolution. In *Managing change: Sustainable practices, inclusive leadership, and gender equality in the digital industrial revolution* (pp. 149–167). Emerald Publishing., DOI: 10.1108/978-1-83608-650-520251008

Kalargyrou, V. (2014). Gaining a competitive advantage with disability inclusion initiatives. *Journal of Human Resources in Hospitality & Tourism, 13*(2), 120–145. DOI: 10.1080/15332845.2014.847300

Kalargyrou, V., & Costen, W. M. (2017). Diversity Management Research in Hospitality and Tourism: Past, Present and Future. *International Journal of Contemporary Hospitality Management, 29*(1), 68–114. DOI: 10.1108/IJCHM-09-2015-0470

Kang, S., Kastberg, S. E., & Mason, B. A. (2025). Financial Literacy for Individuals With Intellectual and Developmental Disabilities: Border Crossing Required. *School Science and Mathematics, 125*(1), 18–32. DOI: 10.1111/ssm.18326

Karanikolas, P., & Qian-Khoo, J. X. (2025). Enablers and barriers to youth employment: An employment ecosystem approach. *Encyclopedia, 5*(2), 73. Advance online publication. DOI: 10.3390/encyclopedia5020073

Kardgar, A., Lucietto, A. M., & Winikus, J. (2024). Board 178: Educational Infographics, A Review Paper. *ASEE Annual Conference and Exposition, Conference Proceedings*. https://www.scopus.com/inward/record.uri?eid=2-s2.0-85202070452&partnerID=40&md5=e724710f1302467cff3f687ce2604f83

Katz, H., & Sasson, U. (2017). Businesses, Nonprofits and Strategic Bridging: The Case of Workforce Integration in Israel. *Society and Business Review, 12*(2), 121–135. DOI: 10.1108/SBR-05-2016-0034

Kauppila, O.-P. (2014). So, What am i supposed to do? A multilevel examination of role clarity. *Journal of Management Studies, 51*(5), 737–763. DOI: 10.1111/joms.12042

Kaye, H. S., Jans, L. H., & Jones, E. C. (2011). Why don't employers hire and retain workers with disabilities? *Journal of Occupational Rehabilitation*, *21*(4), 526–536. DOI: 10.1007/s10926-011-9302-8

Kearney, K. B., Miller, B., Downey, A., & Carey, G. (2026). Using the Extended Job Coaching Model in a Postsecondary Education Program for Gaining and Maintaining Employment. In *Implementing Inclusive Postsecondary Programs for Students With Intellectual Disabilities* (pp. 239–267). DOI: 10.4018/979-8-3373-2767-9.ch009

Keays, D. (2025). Institutional forces and disability: How external pressures shape workplace accommodation within organizations. *The International Journal of Organizational Analysis*, •••, 1–14. DOI: 10.1108/IJOA-06-2025-5611

Kerdar, S. H., Kirchhoff, B. M., Adolph, L., & Bächler, L. (2025). Technological Interventions for Vocational Inclusion of Individuals With Disabilities: A Scoping Review. *Journal of Vocational Rehabilitation*, *63*(3), 325–341. DOI: 10.1177/10522263251376943

Kersten, M. C. O., Taminiau, E. F., Weggeman, M., & Embregts, P. J. C. M. (2022). Contextual Factors Related to the Execution of Knowledge Strategies in Intellectual Disabilities Organizations. *Knowledge and Process Management*, *29*(3), 242–254. DOI: 10.1002/kpm.1700

Khan, S. HASSAN, M. U., Parveen, I., Mutalib, R. A., & Khan, M. A. (2023). *An Organizational Diagnosis for Change Readiness: A Case of the Department of Special Education Government of Punjab*. DOI: 10.20944/preprints202305.0926.v1

Khayatzadeh-Mahani, A., Wittevrongel, K., Nicholas, D. B., & Zwicker, J. D. (2020). Prioritizing barriers and solutions to improve employment for persons with developmental disabilities. *Disability and Rehabilitation*, *42*(19), 2696–2706. DOI: 10.1080/09638288.2019.1570356 PMID: 30856355

Khoronzhevych, M., Maximova-Mentzoni, T., Gubrium, E., & Muller, A. E. (2021). Participant Engagement in Supported Employment: A Systematic Scoping Review. *Journal of Occupational Rehabilitation*, *32*(3), 414–425. DOI: 10.1007/s10926-021-09987-2 PMID: 34086158

Kiettikunwong, N., Narot, P., & Deeod, P. (2025). Advancing disability inclusion in Thailand through AI for sustainable development. *International Journal of Developmental Disabilities*, *71*(6), 919–928. DOI: 10.1080/20473869.2025.2521666

Kim, Y., & Uysal, N. (2025). Transparent Communication and Employee Outcomes: The Mediating Role of Workplace Sense of Community in Enhancing Voice, Loyalty, and Positive Work Behaviors. *International Journal of Business Communication*, 23294884251349496. Advance online publication. DOI: 10.1177/23294884251349496

King, S., Roberts-Turner, R., & Floyd, T. T. (2024). Inclusive leadership: A framework to advance diversity, equity, inclusion, and cultivate belonging. *Nurse Leader*, *22*(2), 132–139. DOI: 10.1016/j.mnl.2023.11.006

Kinnear, B., Santen, S. A., Kelleher, M., Martini, A., Ferris, S., Edje, L., Warm, E. J., & Schumacher, D. J. (2023). How Does TIMELESS Training Impact Resident Motivation for Learning, Assessment, and Feedback? Evaluating a Competency-Based Time-Variable Training Pilot. *Academic Medicine*, *98*(7), 828–835. DOI: 10.1097/ACM.0000000000005147 PMID: 36656286

Kittinger, R., & Bender, J. (2015). Methods for determining the role of fatigue and cognitive load on behaviour detection officers' (BDOs) performance in the field. *Lecture Notes in Computer Science*, *9183*, 36–43. DOI: 10.1007/978-3-319-20816-9_4

Kluger, A. N., & Van Dijk, D. (2010). Feedback, the various tasks of the doctor, and the feedforward alternative. *Medical Education*, *44*(12), 1166–1174. DOI: 10.1111/j.1365-2923.2010.03849.x PMID: 21091758

Kohli, J., & Vedeler, J. S. (2023). Social exclusion and disability: Exploring the role of ingroup/outgroup dynamics in employment. In *Citizenship and social exclusion at the margins of the welfare state* (pp. 78–91). Routledge., DOI: 10.4324/9781003347279-7

Krekó, J., Prinz, D., & Weber, A. (2023). *Take-Up and Labor Supply Responses to Disability Insurance Earnings Limits*. DOI: 10.1596/1813-9450-10325

Kudla, A., Dinelli, E. J., Capraro, P., Crown, D., Sheth, M., Trierweiler, R., Munsell, E. G. S., Wong, J., & Heinemann, A. W. (2024). *Person-, Job-, and Environment-Related Factors Associated With Long-Term Job Retention of People With Physical Disabilities*. DOI: 10.21203/rs.3.rs-4797921/v1

Kukla, M., & Bond, G. (2012). Job match and job tenure in persons with severe mental illness. *Journal of Rehabilitation*, *78*(1), 11–15.

Kuld, P. B., Frielink, N., Zijlmans, M., Schuengel, C., & Embregts, P. J. C. M. (2023). Promoting self-determination of persons with severe or profound intellectual disabilities: A systematic review and meta-analysis. *Journal of Intellectual Disability Research*, *67*(7), 589–629. DOI: 10.1111/jir.13036 PMID: 37165964

Kulik, C. T., & Roberson, L. (2008). Diversity initiative effectiveness: What organisations can (and cannot) expect from diversity recruitment, diversity training, and formal mentoring programs. In *Diversity at Work* (pp. 265–317). Cambridge University Press., DOI: 10.1017/CBO9780511753725.010

Kumar, A., Srivastava, S. K., & Singh, K. K. (2019). Study on attitude of co-workers towards employees with intellectual disabilities. *Indian Journal of Public Health Research & Development, 10*(12), 720–724. DOI: 10.37506/v10/i12/2019/ijphrd/192049

Lacroux, A., & Martin-Lacroux, C. (2020). Anonymous résumés: An effective preselection method? *International Journal of Selection and Assessment, 28*(1), 98–111. DOI: 10.1111/ijsa.12275

Laflamme, A.-M. (2017). Mental disorders and reasonable accommodation at work: The potential of Quebec law. *Sante Mentale au Quebec, 42*(2), 39–56. DOI: 10.7202/1041913ar PMID: 29267412

Lamontagne, R. M. (2015). Ethical dilemmas in the workplace: HR managers' perceptions of behavioural influences with implications for building an ethical culture in organisations. *International Journal of Knowledge. Culture and Change Management, 15*, 1–21.

Lawlor, D., & York, M. (2007). Assessing goal attainment for quality improvement. *Journal of Intellectual Disabilities, 11*(3), 241–255. DOI: 10.1177/1744629507080786 PMID: 17846047

Lawrence, K., Mellifont, D., & Bulkeley, K. (2026). Disability employment policy in Australia: Barriers and facilitators to workforce participation. *Social Policy and Administration, 60*(1), 112–123. DOI: 10.1111/spol.13147

Lazauskaite-Zabielske, J., Ziedelis, A., & Urbanaviciute, I. (2021). Who benefits from time-spatial job crafting? The role of boundary characteristics in the relationship between time-spatial job crafting, engagement and performance. *Baltic Journal of Management, 16*(1), 1–19. DOI: 10.1108/BJM-07-2020-0236

Leahy, M. J., Valle, R. J. D., Landon, T. J., Iwanaga, K., Sherman, S. G., Reyes, A., & Chan, F. (2018). Promising and Evidence-Based Practices in Vocational Rehabilitation: Results of a National Delphi Study. *Journal of Vocational Rehabilitation, 48*(1), 37–48. DOI: 10.3233/JVR-170914

Leasher, M. K., Miller, C. E., & Gooden, M. P. (2009). Rater effects and attitudinal barriers affecting people with disabilities in personnel selection. *Journal of Applied Social Psychology, 39*(9), 2236–2274. DOI: 10.1111/j.1559-1816.2009.00523.x

Lecours, A., Laribi, S., Laliberté, M., & Kiki, G. M. (2025). Mapping transversal competences for vocational education learners in response to transformations in the world of work: A scoping review. *Education + Training*, •••, 1–18. Advance online publication. DOI: 10.1108/ET-08-2025-0678

Lee, C. E., Koo, J., & Li, C. (2026). Application of machine learning to predict employment attainment among individuals with intellectual and developmental disabilities. *Research in Developmental Disabilities*, *168*, 105181. DOI: 10.1016/j.ridd.2025.105181 PMID: 41386177

Lee, H. (2021). Changes in workplace practices during the COVID-19 pandemic: The roles of emotion, psychological safety and organisation support. *Journal of Organizational Effectiveness*, *8*(1), 97–128. DOI: 10.1108/JOEPP-06-2020-0104

Lee, W.-J., & Lee, J.-K. (2017). Role clarity and organizational commitment in food manufacturing and distribution firms: The mediating role of creativity. *Journal of Distribution Science*, *15*(1), 115–121. DOI: 10.15722/jds.15.1.201701.115

Lee, Y., Tao, W., Li, J.-Y., & Yoon, D. (2025). Drivers of employee engagement with organizational diversity: The power of strategic internal communication. *Public Relations Review*, *51*(3), 102583. Advance online publication. DOI: 10.1016/j.pubrev.2025.102583

Lefera, M., & Swart, A. J. (2020). Reflecting on the success of a Peer Mentorship Programme - A scholarly personal narrative. *2020 IFEES World Engineering Education Forum - Global Engineering Deans Council, WEEF-GEDC 2020*. DOI: 10.1109/WEEF-GEDC49885.2020.9293640

Legarreta, R. E. (2025). The reform of termination of contract of employment due to permanent invalidity and its connection to the implementation of reasonable accommodations [La reforma de la extinción del contrato de trabajo por incapacidad permanente y su vinculación con la implementación de adaptaciones razonables]. *Trabajo y Derecho*, *129*, 1–26. DOI: 10.32029/2386-8112.02.129.2025

Leggat, S. G. (2009). A guide to performance management for the health information manager. *The HIM Journal*, *38*(3), 11–17. DOI: 10.1177/183335830903800303 PMID: 19875850

Leung, A., Moldovan, L., & Ata, M. (2023). Teaching economics in higher education with universal design for learning. *International Review of Economics Education*, *44*, 100273. Advance online publication. DOI: 10.1016/j.iree.2023.100273

Leung, K., Clement, L., Lewis, J., & Saul, N. (2024). A tool for clarifying expectations in undergraduate research experiences. *Journal of Microbiology & Biology Education*, *25*(2), e00204-23. Advance online publication. DOI: 10.1128/jmbe.00204-23 PMID: 38842314

Liang, Z. (2025). CHECK Visual Schedules to Support Individuals on the Autism Spectrum. *Intervention in School and Clinic*, *60*(4), 228–235. DOI: 10.1177/10534512241300157

Liao, C. L. (2007). Collaboration and dialogue: Video as an agent in extending and enriching learning and writing. *ACM SIGGRAPH 2007: Educators Program. Article*, *5*, 5. Advance online publication. DOI: 10.1145/1282040.1282046

Li, E. P. Y. (2004). Self-perceived equal opportunities for people with intellectual disability. *International Journal of Rehabilitation Research. Internationale Zeitschrift fur Rehabilitationsforschung. Revue Internationale de Recherches de Readaptation*, *27*(3), 241–245. DOI: 10.1097/00004356-200409000-00011 PMID: 15319696

Lin, S.-C., & Lehto, M. R. (2008). A Bayesian Based Machine Learning Application to Task Analysis. In *Encyclopedia of Data Warehousing and Mining: Second Edition* (pp. 133–139). DOI: 10.4018/978-1-60566-010-3.ch022

Lindsay, C., & Dutton, M. (2011). Promoting Healthy Routes Back to Work? Boundary Spanning Health Professionals and Employability Programmes in Great Britain. *Social Policy and Administration*, *46*(5), 509–525. DOI: 10.1111/j.1467-9515.2011.00823.x

Lindsay, S., & Cagliostro, E. (2020). A web-based intervention for youth with physical disabilities: Comparing the role of mentors in 12- and 4-week formats. *JMIR Pediatrics and Parenting*, *3*(1), e15813. Advance online publication. DOI: 10.2196/15813 PMID: 31913132

Lindsay, S., Dain, N., & Hsu, S. (2024). Exploring the employment experiences of young adults with multiple minoritised identities: A qualitative study focusing on race and non-apparent disabilities. *PLoS One*, *19*(11), e0313295. Advance online publication. DOI: 10.1371/journal.pone.0313295 PMID: 39485781

Lindsay, S., Goodfellow, A., Stergiou-Kita, M., Kirsh, B., & Lero, D. (2017). Inclusionary business practices for recruiting and retaining people with disabilities: A scoping review. In *Physical disabilities: Perspectives, risk factors and quality of life* (pp. 17–45). Nova Science Publishers.

Lin, N. C., & Cheng, H.-F. (2010). Effects of gradual release of responsibility model on language learning. *Procedia: Social and Behavioral Sciences*, *2*(2), 1866–1870. DOI: 10.1016/j.sbspro.2010.03.1000

Lin, Q., Sun, R., & Zhu, Q. (2026). Adaptive job recrafting of gig workers: Concept, measurement, and validation of its impact on job satisfaction. *Acta Psychologica*, *262*, 106034. Advance online publication. DOI: 10.1016/j.actpsy.2025.106034 PMID: 41351970

Lin, S.-C., & Lehto, M. R. (2007). A Bayesian methodology for semi-automated task analysis. *Lecture Notes in Computer Science*, *4557*(1), 697–704. DOI: 10.1007/978-3-540-73345-4_79

Lipinska, J. (2021). Is feedback always motivating? Attitudes of Polish-speaking high school students from bilingual classes towards corrective feedback in writing [Le feedback est-il toujours motivant? Les attitudes des bacheliers polonophones de classes bilingues envers la rétroaction corrective écrite]. *Neofilolog*, *1*(56), 39–54. DOI: 10.14746/n.2021.56.1.4

Liu, Y., Fang, Y., Hu, L., Chen, N., Li, X., & Cai, Y. (2024). Inclusive leadership and employee workplace well-being: The role of vigor and supervisor developmental feedback. *BMC Psychology*, *12*(1), 540. Advance online publication. DOI: 10.1186/s40359-024-02029-5 PMID: 39375786

Lockyer, J., Gondocz, S. T., & Thivierge, R. L. (2004). Knowledge translation: The role and place of practice reflection. *The Journal of Continuing Education in the Health Professions*, *24*(1), 50–56. DOI: 10.1002/chp.1340240108 PMID: 15069912

Lo, H. S., Sher, Y. J., Hong, J. C., Chang, H. K., & Wu, T. F. (2024). The effects of blended learning on the car detailing skills of students with intellectual disabilities. *Journal of Educational Technology & Society*, *27*(3), 46–60. DOI: 10.30191/ETS.202407_27(3).RP03

Lord, J. E., Raja, D. S., & Blanck, P. (2015). Law and people with disabilities. In *International Encyclopedia of the Social & Behavioral Sciences* (2nd ed., pp. 497–503). Elsevier., DOI: 10.1016/B978-0-08-097086-8.86053-5

Lourenço, B., & Rodrigues, R. (2025). Organisational onboarding and talent retention: The mediating role of workplace attachment and supervisor support. *Social Sciences & Humanities Open*, *12*, 101909. Advance online publication. DOI: 10.1016/j.ssaho.2025.101909

Lovegrove, E., Bertilone, D., Brown, J., & Beaumont-Bilsby, E. (2025). Harnessing lived experience to promote accessible employment journeys. In W4A 2025 - Proceedings of the 22nd International Web for All Conference (pp. 18–21). ACM. DOI: 10.1145/3744257.3744264

Lysaght, R., Krupa, T., & Packalen, K. (2024). From exclusion to inclusion. In *The Routledge companion to disability and work* (pp. 67–83). Routledge., DOI: 10.4324/9781003350781-7

Lysaght, R., Ouellette-Kuntz, H., & Lin, C.-J. (2012). Untapped potential: Perspectives on the employment of people with intellectual disability. *Work (Reading, Mass.)*, *41*(4), 409–422. DOI: 10.3233/WOR-2012-1318 PMID: 22495411

Maclean, N., Geiger, M., & Ned, L. (2024). Employment equity targets: How a state-owned enterprise recruits people with disabilities. *SA Journal of Human Resource Management*, *22*(0), a2355. Advance online publication. DOI: 10.4102/SAJHRM.v22i0.2355

Macurová, P., Ludvík, L., & Žwaková, M. (2017). The driving factors, risks and barriers of the Industry 4.0 concept. *Journal of Applied Economic Sciences*, *12*(7), 2003–2011.

Maestas, N. (2019). Identifying Work Capacity and Promoting Work: A Strategy for Modernizing the SSDI Program. *The Annals of the American Academy of Political and Social Science*, *686*(1), 93–120. DOI: 10.1177/0002716219882354 PMID: 32719569

Mahmoudi-Dehaki, M., Nasr-Esfahani, N., & Vasan, S. (2025). The Transformative Role of Assistive Technology in Enhancing Quality of Life for Individuals With Disabilities. In *Assistive Technology Solutions for Aging Adults and Individuals with Disabilities* (pp. 45–72). https://doi.org/DOI: 10.4018/9798369363089.ch003

Majnemer, A., McGrath, P. J., Baumbusch, J., Camden, C., Fallon, B., Lunsky, Y., Miller, S. P., Sansone, G., Stainton, T., Sumarah, J., Thomson, D., & Zwicker, J. (2021). Time to Be Counted: COVID-19 and Intellectual and Developmental Disabilities—an RSC Policy Briefing. *Facets*, *6*, 1337–1389. DOI: 10.1139/facets-2021-0038

Major, D. A., & Morganson, V. L. (2008). An inclusive IS&T work climate. In *Encyclopedia of information science and technology* (2nd ed., pp. 1899–1905). IGI Global., DOI: 10.4018/978-1-60566-026-4.ch299

Making it work: Employment of people with disabilities. (2011). Recruitment and retention of people with disabilities employment issue brief #1. In *Making it work: Employment of people with disabilities* (pp. 49–58). Disability and Business Technical Assistance Centers.

Malekinezhad, F., & Courtney, P. (2026). Framing the shift to supported employment: Exploring the impacts of a person-centred programme evaluation approach through peer led participatory research. *Evaluation and Program Planning, 114*, 102723. Advance online publication. DOI: 10.1016/j.evalprogplan.2025.102723 PMID: 41151422

Man, J., & Kangas, M. (2019). Best Practice Adherence and Workplace Facilitators and Hindrances for Psychologists Working With Individuals With Intellectual Disabilities and Co-Morbid Mental Health Concerns. *Journal of Policy and Practice in Intellectual Disabilities, 16*(3), 239–249. DOI: 10.1111/jppi.12288

Mank, D., Cioffi, A., & Yovanoff, P. (2003). Supported employment outcomes across a decade: Is there evidence of improvement in the quality of implementation? *Mental Retardation, 41*(3), 188–197. DOI: 10.1352/0047-6765(2003)41<188:SEO-AAD>2.0.CO;2 PMID: 12737612

Mansour, S., & Mohanna, D. (2024). How does organisational support for innovation influence job crafting and knowledge sharing behaviours? A comparison between teleworkers and office workers. *International Journal of Manpower, 45*(9), 1673–1700. DOI: 10.1108/IJM-02-2024-0106

Maqbool, F., Ansari, S., Aslam, T., & Ansari, A. (2021). Experiential Versus Traditional Education System: A Comparative Study of Engineering Education Methodologies in Higher Education. In *Lecture Notes on Data Engineering and Communications Technologies* (Vol. 78, pp. 724–736). DOI: 10.1007/978-3-030-79203-9_55

Marbin, J., Hutchinson, Y.-V., & Schaeffer, S. (2021). Avoiding the virtual pitfall: Identifying and mitigating biases in graduate medical education videoconference interviews. *Academic Medicine, 96*(8), 1120–1124. DOI: 10.1097/ACM.0000000000003914 PMID: 33464743

Marchiori, R. S., & Song, S. (2024). A Game-Based Learning Method to Promote Soft Skills in Construction Education. *ASEE Annual Conference and Exposition, Conference Proceedings*. https://www.scopus.com/inward/record.uri?eid=2-s2.0-85202015507&partnerID=40&md5=009d6d4619265e26cb25f6c92c024c73

Marelle, C., Vinoski Thomas, E., & Donehower Paul, C. (2023). A survey of wireless technology supporting individuals with intellectual and developmental disabilities in the workplace. *Journal of Special Education Technology, 38*(4), 434–444. DOI: 10.1177/01626434221131463

Maria Szulc, J., Davies, J., Tomczak, M. T., & McGregor, F.-L. (2021). AMO perspectives on the well-being of neurodivergent human capital. *Employee Relations, 43*(4), 858–872. DOI: 10.1108/ER-09-2020-0446

Marinaci, T., Russo, C., Savarese, G., Stornaiuolo, G., Faiella, F., Carpinelli, L., Navarra, M., Marsico, G., & Mollo, M. (2023). An Inclusive Workplace Approach to Disability Through Assistive Technologies: A Systematic Review and Thematic Analysis of the Literature. *Societies (Basel, Switzerland), 13*(11), 231. DOI: 10.3390/soc13110231

Marks, B., Sisirak, J., & Chang, Y.-C. (2013). Efficacy of the HealthMatters Program Train-the-Trainer Model. *Journal of Applied Research in Intellectual Disabilities, 26*(4), 319–334. DOI: 10.1111/jar.12045 PMID: 23589506

Marks, B., Sisirak, J., Chang, Y.-C., & Murphy, R. (2019). Impact of the HealthMatters Train-the-Trainer Program on the Health and Health Behaviors of Staff Supporting Adults With Intellectual and Developmental Disabilities. *Workplace Health & Safety, 67*(8), 423–435. DOI: 10.1177/2165079919828739 PMID: 31007138

Martin, A.-M., & Jones, V. (2023). Communication as a basis for person-centred support. In *Intellectual disabilities: Health and social care across the lifespan* (pp. 15–24). Springer., DOI: 10.1007/978-3-031-27496-1_2

Martínez-Carrascal, J. A., Muñoz-Sánchez, R., & Sánchez-Rodríguez, M. T. (2023). Person-centred communication in intellectual disability services. [Note: This reference appears in the chapter text but was not found in the provided Scopus export; it is listed here as cited.]. *Journal of Intellectual Disabilities.*

Masse, C., Martinez, P., Mertiny, P., & Ahmad, R. (2019). A Hybrid Method Based on Systems Approach to Enhance Experiential Learning in Mechatronic Education. *2019 IEEE 7th International Conference on Control, Mechatronics and Automation, ICCMA 2019*, 403–407. DOI: 10.1109/ICCMA46720.2019.8988746

Matsuo, M. (2012). Leadership of learning and reflective practice: An exploratory study of nursing managers. *Management Learning, 43*(5), 609–623. DOI: 10.1177/1350507612440413

Mayfield, M., & Mayfield, J. (2011). Effective performance feedback for learning in organizations and organizational learning. *Development and Learning in Organizations, 26*(1), 15–18. DOI: 10.1108/14777281211189128

Mayombe, C. (2024). Promoting youths' skills acquisition through experiential learning theory in vocational education and training in South Africa. *Higher Education. Skills and Work-Based Learning, 14*(1), 130–145. DOI: 10.1108/HESWBL-10-2022-0216

May-Simera, C. (2018). Is the Irish (Republic of) Comprehensive Employment Strategy fit for purpose in promoting the employment of people with intellectual disabilities in the open labor market? *Journal of Policy and Practice in Intellectual Disabilities, 15*(4), 284–294. DOI: 10.1111/jppi.12259

McAuliffe, D., & Greenslade, L. (2025). Turn it and turn it again: The updated inclusive model of ethical decision making. *Ethics & Social Welfare, 19*(2), 161–173. DOI: 10.1080/17496535.2025.2483668

McCabe, D. (2023). Managing Inclusion and Diversity in Organizations: A Strategic Approach to Human Capital. In *Inclusive Territories 1: Role of Enterprises and Organizations: Volume 1* (Vol. 1, pp. 91–104). DOI: 10.1002/9781394255535.ch5

McCaffrey, N., Dew, A., Philpott, C. J., Ingold, J., McVilly, K., Smith-Merry, J., Livingstone, A., & Hutchinson, C. (2025). Impact of Employment Support in Different Work Environments on Individuals With Intellectual Disability and Their Families From Their Own Perspectives: Protocol for a Systematic Review of Qualitative Evidence. *BMJ Open, 15*(6), e098312. DOI: 10.1136/bmjopen-2024-098312 PMID: 40588391

McCollin, M. J., & Obiakor, F. E. (2009). Transition from school to adult life. In *International Encyclopedia of Education* (3rd ed., pp. 876–879). Elsevier., DOI: 10.1016/B978-0-08-044894-7.01121-0

McDowell, C., Ennals, P., & Fossey, E. (2021). Vocational Service Models and Approaches to Improve Job Tenure of People With Severe and Enduring Mental Illness: A Narrative Review. *Frontiers in Psychiatry, 12*, 668716. Advance online publication. DOI: 10.3389/fpsyt.2021.668716 PMID: 34305676

McDowell, C., & Fossey, E. (2015). Workplace accommodations for people with mental illness: A scoping review. *Journal of Occupational Rehabilitation, 25*(1), 197–206. DOI: 10.1007/s10926-014-9512-y PMID: 24841728

McEwin, A. (2017). Working together: Technology as the foundation for better employment outcomes for people with disability. In *Proceedings of the 14th Web for All Conference, W4A 2017*, Article a1. https://doi.org/DOI: 10.1145/3058555.3058556

McKinney, E. L., & Swartz, L. (2021). Employment integration barriers: Experiences of people with disabilities. *International Journal of Human Resource Management, 32*(10), 2298–2320. DOI: 10.1080/09585192.2019.1579749

Meacham, H., Bartram, T., & Cavanagh, J. (2020). Career management: The transition process for workers with disabilities. In *The Palgrave Handbook of Disability at Work* (pp. 99–114). Palgrave Macmillan., DOI: 10.1007/978-3-030-42966-9_6

Meacham, H., Cavanagh, J., Shaw, A., & Bartram, T. (2017). HRM practices that support the employment and social inclusion of workers with an intellectual disability. *Personnel Review, 46*(8), 1475–1492. DOI: 10.1108/PR-05-2016-0105

Meacham, H., Cavanagh, J., Shaw, A., & Bartram, T. (2017). Innovation Programs at the Workplace for Workers With an Intellectual Disability. *Personnel Review, 46*(7), 1381–1396. DOI: 10.1108/PR-08-2016-0214

Mégret, F., & Msipa, D. (2014). Global reasonable accommodation: How the convention on the rights of persons with disabilities changes the way we think about equality. *South African Journal on Human Rights, 30*(2), 252–274. DOI: 10.1080/19962126.2014.11865109

Melo, B. B. V. de, Silveira-Maia, M., & RIBEIRO, S. B. (2023). Full Financial Education Programmes for People With Disabilities: A Scoping Review. *Revista Brasileira De Educação Especial, 29*. DOI: 10.1590/1980-54702023v29e0222

Meltzer, A., Robinson, S., & Fisher, K. R. (2020). Barriers to finding and maintaining open employment for people with intellectual disability in Australia. *Social Policy and Administration, 54*(1), 88–101. DOI: 10.1111/spol.12523

Menachery, T. J. (2018). Employees shaping their own jobs: How to enable job crafting? *Human Resource Management International Digest, 26*(5), 27–29. DOI: 10.1108/HRMID-05-2018-0106

Meneley, T., Crawford, L., & Huddleston, G. (2021). Sherry: "Inclusion" interpreted through a life-story lens. *International Journal of Developmental Disabilities, 67*(1), 67–78. DOI: 10.1080/20473869.2019.1613849 PMID: 34141400

Menke, C. (2025). Equality, interpellation, liberation: Three vectors of recognition. In *Recognition: Historical and philosophical perspectives* (pp. 422–436). Routledge., DOI: 10.4324/9781003686521-33

Men, L. R., & Stacks, D. (2014). The Effects of Authentic Leadership on Strategic Internal Communication and Employee-Organization Relationships. *Journal of Public Relations Research, 26*(4), 301–324. DOI: 10.1080/1062726X.2014.908720

Michalski, S. C., Gallomarino, N. C., Szpak, A., May, K. W., Lee, G., Ellison, C., & Loetscher, T. (2023). Improving real-world skills in people with intellectual disabilities: An immersive virtual reality intervention. *Virtual Reality (Waltham Cross), 27*(4), 3521–3532. DOI: 10.1007/s10055-023-00759-2 PMID: 37360807

Migliore, A., Grossi, T., Mank, D., & Rogan, P. (2008). Why do adults with intellectual disabilities work in sheltered workshops? *Journal of Vocational Rehabilitation, 28*(1), 29–40. DOI: 10.3233/JVR-2008-00402

Migliore, A., Mank, D., Grossi, T., & Rogan, P. (2008). Integrated employment or sheltered workshops: Preferences of adults with intellectual disabilities. *Journal of Vocational Rehabilitation, 29*(1), 23–32.

Mihić, S. S., & Kiš-Glavaš, L. (2010). Work and social competence of people with intellectual disabilities: Barriers for employers in their employment. *Revija za Socijalnu Politiku, 17*(3), 387–399. DOI: 10.3935/rsp.v17i3.912

Mikołajczyk-Lerman, G., & Potoczna, M. (2019). Enhancing autonomy through the occupational engagement of adults with intellectual disabilities: Supported employment model applied by the Polish Association for Persons with Intellectual Disabilities (Branch in Zgierz). *Przegląd Socjologii Jakościowej, 15*(4), 184–203. DOI: 10.18778/1733-8069.15.4.09

Milanović-Dobrota, B. (2018). Barriers to employing persons with intellectual disability - Employers' perception. *Specijalna Edukacija i Rehabilitacija, 17*(3), 189–212. DOI: 10.5937/specedreh17-16987

Milanović-Dobrota, B., Jelić, S., Buha, N., & Japundža-Milisavljević, M. (2025). Employer perspectives on hiring individuals with intellectual disabilities: A case study from Serbia. *Journal of Applied Research in Intellectual Disabilities, 38*(2), e70045. Advance online publication. DOI: 10.1111/jar.70045 PMID: 40156224

Miller, A. L., Frye, D., Green, T., Mitchell, C., Garcia, G. A., Huereña, J., Moore, T. O., & Turnage, V. (2022). (Re)defining Their Place at the Table: Frank Discussions by Adults With Disabilities on Contemporary Self-advocacy. *Journal of Applied Research in Intellectual Disabilities, 35*(3), 777–788. DOI: 10.1111/jar.12981 PMID: 35098612

Miltenberger, R. G., & Novotny, M. A. (2022). Teaching Safety Skills to Individuals with Developmental Disabilities. *Advances in Neurodevelopmental Disorders*, *6*(3), 270–279. DOI: 10.1007/s41252-022-00248-8

Mishra, A., & Ray, A. K. (2024). Ethical decision-making, diversity, and inclusion: Building the foundation for sustainable business success through shared values. In *Organization, purpose and values: Integrating diversity, equity and inclusion* (pp. 3–20). Routledge., DOI: 10.4324/9781003501374-2

Mittal, S., Kanwal, P., & Dang, T. T. (2025). Impact of Workplace Social Connections on Employee Wellbeing and Happiness. In *Insights on Wellbeing and Happiness in the Workplace* (pp. 109–129). DOI: 10.4018/979-8-3693-2939-9.ch006

Modise, J. R., Olivier, M. P., & Miruka, O. (2014). Reasonable accommodation for people with disabilities in the labour market. *Mediterranean Journal of Social Sciences*, *5*(4), 578–588. DOI: 10.5901/mjss.2014.v5n4p578

Mohamad, G., & Pozzi, E. (2023). STUDENTS' INFORMATIONAL NEEDS: Applying the Principles of Universal Design to Address Inequity in High-Needs Schools During Virtual Learning. In *Digital Learning in High-Needs Schools: A Critical Approach to Technology Access and Equity in PreK-12* (pp. 83–96). DOI: 10.4324/9781003274537-9

Moore, C., & Friedman, M. (2017). Informed choice in employment for people with intellectual disabilities. *Journal of Policy and Practice in Intellectual Disabilities*, *14*(2), 123–130.

Moore, K., McDonald, P., & Bartlett, J. (2018). Emerging trends affecting future employment opportunities for people with intellectual disability: The case of a large retail organisation. *Journal of Intellectual & Developmental Disability*, *43*(3), 328–338. DOI: 10.3109/13668250.2017.1379250

Moore, M. E., & Huberty, L. L. (2020). Strategic planning for the inclusion of people with disabilities into work organizations. In *The Palgrave handbook of disability at work* (pp. 187–202). Palgrave Macmillan., DOI: 10.1007/978-3-030-42966-9_11

Moore, R., & Friedman, M. (2017). The role of informed choice in advancing competitive integrated employment. *Journal of Vocational Rehabilitation*, *46*(2), 245–264. DOI: 10.3233/JVR-160860

Morales-Sánchez, R., & Cabello-Medina, C. (2013). The role of four universal moral competencies in ethical decision-making. *Journal of Business Ethics*, *116*(4), 717–734. DOI: 10.1007/s10551-013-1817-9

Morash-Macneil, V., Johnson, F., & Ryan, J. B. (2018). A systematic review of assistive technology for individuals with intellectual disability in the workplace. *Journal of Special Education Technology*, *33*(1), 15–26. DOI: 10.1177/0162643417729166

Moreno, J. V., Marshall, D. R., Girard, A., Mitchell, N. M. B., Minissian, M. B., & Coleman, B. (2024). An organizational commitment to diversity, equity, inclusion, and justice. *Nursing Administration Quarterly*, *48*(1), 33–48. DOI: 10.1097/NAQ.0000000000000611 PMID: 38051208

Morgan, C. L., & Keys, B. (2026). Dignity of risk in inclusive postsecondary education programs. In *Implementing inclusive postsecondary programs for students with intellectual disabilities* (pp. 413–460). IGI Global., DOI: 10.4018/979-8-3373-2767-9.ch015

Morgan, J., Silver, M., & Degbey, W. Y. (2025). Inclusive leadership. In *Elgar encyclopedia of leadership* (pp. 109–111). Edward Elgar Publishing., DOI: 10.4337/9781035307074.00052

Morgan, R. L. (2008). Job matching: Development and evaluation of a web-based instrument to assess degree of match among employment preferences. *Journal of Vocational Rehabilitation*, *29*(1), 29–38. DOI: 10.3233/JVR-2008-00424

Morley, M. (2024). Returning to work. Part 2: What can be done from an employer's perspective? *In Practice*, *46*(10), 542–544. DOI: 10.1002/inpr.496

Morris, R., Christianson-Barker, J., Stainton, T., Mills, R., Rowley, C., Cox, J., Schroeder, M., & Hole, R. (2024). 'They don't think I can do it': Experiences of self-advocates, employment specialists, and employers on employment of adults with intellectual disability. *Journal of Applied Research in Intellectual Disabilities*, *37*(3), e13231. DOI: 10.1111/jar.13231 PMID: 38561915

Morris, R., Christianson-Barker, J., Stainton, T., Mills, R., Schroeder, M., Cox, J., Rowley, C., & Hole, R. (2024). Employment practices as experienced by persons with intellectual disability, employers, and employment specialists across Canada. *Journal of Vocational Rehabilitation*, *61*(1), 55–66. DOI: 10.3233/JVR-240019

Morrissey, F. (2012). The United Nations Convention on the Rights of Persons with Disabilities: A new approach to decision-making in mental health law. *European Journal of Health Law*, *19*(5), 423–440. DOI: 10.1163/15718093-12341237 PMID: 23198484

Mosquera, P., & Soares, M. E. (2025). Onboarding: A key to employee retention and workplace well-being. *Review of Managerial Science*, *19*(12), 3687–3711. DOI: 10.1007/s11846-025-00864-3

Mostafa, A., & Wang, W. (2023). Competitive integrated employment for people with disabilities: A systematic review of policy and practice. *Disability and Rehabilitation, 45*(12), 1945–1958.

Mudiayi, D., Shariff, F., Bridgland, L., Mathura, P., & Ringrose, J. (2024). Elevating equity: Advancing diversity and inclusivity through trialing bias reduction tools in the general internal medicine program resident application process. *BMC Medical Education, 24*(1), 1265. Advance online publication. DOI: 10.1186/s12909-024-06244-x PMID: 39501300

Müller, E., VanGilder, R., & Kiasi, D. (2018). Employer Satisfaction With Project SEARCH Interns, Hires, and Support Received From Project SEARCH Teams. *Journal of Vocational Rehabilitation, 49*(3), 339–350. DOI: 10.3233/JVR-180978

Muñoz, P. M., Cardinal-Fernández, P., Morales Rodríguez, Á., Ruiz-Zaldibar, C., & de la Cuerda López, A. (2025). The Impact of an Onboarding Plan for Newly Hired Nurses and Nursing Assistants: Results of a Quasi-Experimental Study. *Nursing Reports, 15*(11), 398. Advance online publication. DOI: 10.3390/nursrep15110398 PMID: 41295822

Munyofu, M., Swain, W. J., Ausman, B. D., Lin, H., Kidwai, K., & Dwyer, F. (2007). The effect of different chunking strategies in complementing animated instruction. *Learning, Media and Technology, 32*(4), 407–419. DOI: 10.1080/17439880701690109

Murtagh, L. (2014). The motivational paradox of feedback: Teacher and student perceptions. *Curriculum Journal, 25*(4), 516–541. DOI: 10.1080/09585176.2014.944197

Nagtegaal, R., de Boer, N., van Berkel, R., & Tummers, L. (2025). Unlocking inclusive hiring: Understanding employers' decisions about hiring people with disabilities. *International Journal of Human Resource Management, 36*(20), 3717–3756. DOI: 10.1080/09585192.2025.2607539

Najm, N. A., & Ali, W. W. (2024). Organizational readiness and innovation in the Jordanian telecommunication companies. *International Journal of Productivity and Performance Management, 73*(1), 242–269. DOI: 10.1108/IJPPM-01-2022-0051

Napier, T. R., Howell, K. H., Scheid, C. R., & Miller-Graff, L. E. (2023). Empirically derived patterns of adverse childhood experiences and associations with prenatal social networks. *Psychology of Violence, 13*(3), 219–228. DOI: 10.1037/vio0000453

Nardodkar, R., Pathare, S., Ventriglio, A., Castaldelli-Maia, J., Javate, K. R., Torales, J., & Bhugra, D. (2016). Legal protection of the right to work and employment for persons with mental health problems: A review of legislation across the world. *International Review of Psychiatry (Abingdon, England)*, *28*(4), 375–384. DOI: 10.1080/09540261.2016.1210575 PMID: 27499197

Nevala, N., Pehkonen, I., Teittinen, A., Vesala, H., Pörtfors, P., & Anttila, H. (2019). The Effectiveness of Rehabilitation Interventions on the Employment and Functioning of People With Intellectual Disabilities: A Systematic Review. *Journal of Occupational Rehabilitation*, *29*(4), 773–802. DOI: 10.1007/s10926-019-09837-2 PMID: 31098847

Niccolini, R. R., & Basu, N. (2009). Disability and accommodation in the healthcare workplace. *Journal of Health & Life Sciences Law*, *2*(3), 93–120.

Nickerson, A. B., & Fishman, C. E. (2013). Promoting mental health and resilience through strength-based assessment in US schools. *Educational and Child Psychology*, *30*(4), 7–17. DOI: 10.53841/bpsecp.2013.30.4.7

Niederfranke, A., & Drewes, M. (2017). Non-standard forms of employment in a globalised world: Risk of undermining labour standards and social security provisions? *Sozialer Fortschritt*, *66*(12), 919–934. DOI: 10.3790/sfo.66.12.919

Niedziółka, M. (2024). Legal, Institutional and Financial Forms of State Aid for Disabled Students. *Zeszyty Naukowe Uniwersytetu Przyrodniczo-Humanistycznego W Siedlcach Seria Administracja I Zarządzanie*, *61*(134). DOI: 10.34739/zn.2023.61.20

Nigam, A., Kellam, J. F., Ambrose, C. G., & Tai, B. L. (2025). Impact of Quantitative Feedback on Motor Skill Acquisition in Bone Drilling: A Pilot Study Using Radar Plots. *Journal of Orthopaedic Trauma*, *39*(10S), S21–S26. DOI: 10.1097/BOT.0000000000003033

Nijhof, K., Boot, F. H., Naaldenberg, J., Leusink, G. L., & Bevelander, K. E. (2024). Health support of people with intellectual disability and the crucial role of support workers. *BMC Health Services Research*, *24*(1), 4. DOI: 10.1186/s12913-023-10206-2 PMID: 38167137

Norzin, T., Mehta, D., Sarwat, E., Basha, M. J., Dhrupadha, D. L., & Ramesh, S. (2025). Adaptive job portal for specially abled students. *2025 World Skills Conference on Universal Data Analytics and Sciences*. https://doi.org/DOI: 10.1109/WorldSUAS66815.2025.11199216

Nota, L., Santilli, S., Ginevra, M. C., & Soresi, S. (2014). Employer attitudes towards the work inclusion of people with disability. *Journal of Applied Research in Intellectual Disabilities, 27*(6), 511–520. DOI: 10.1111/jar.12081 PMID: 24288164

Novak, J. (2015). Social inclusion and employment for people with intellectual disabilities. *Journal of Intellectual Disability Research, 59*(8), 765–774.

Novak, J. (2017). Making the cut when applying for jobs online. *Journal of Vocational Rehabilitation, 46*(3), 293–299. DOI: 10.3233/JVR-170864

Novak, J. A. (2015). Raising Expectations for U.S. Youth With Disabilities: Federal Disability Policy Advances Integrated Employment. *Center for Educational Policy Studies Journal, 5*(1), 91–110. DOI: 10.26529/cepsj.156

Novak, J., Feyes, K. J., & Christensen, K. A. (2011). Application of intergroup contact theory to the integrated workplace: Setting the stage for inclusion. *Journal of Vocational Rehabilitation, 35*(3), 211–226. DOI: 10.3233/JVR-2011-0573

Novembli, M. S., Hasanah, N., & Fitriani, D. (2024). Investigating the Impact of Universal Design for Learning: Empowering Students with Disabilities in Higher Education. *E3S Web of Conferences, 593*. DOI: 10.1051/e3sconf/202459304004

Novikov, I. (2025). Beyond inclusion: How people with disabilities are involved in business [ЗА ПРЕДЕЛАМИ ИНКЛЮЗИИ: КАК ВОВЛЕКАЕТСЯ ТРУД ЛЮДЕЙ С ИНВАЛИДНОСТЬЮ В БИЗНЕС]. *Zhurnal Issledovanii Sotsial'noi Politiki, 23*(2), 289–308. DOI: 10.17323/727-0634-2025-23-2-289-308

Nuri, R. P., Piccone, C., Gaurav, N., Thomson, D., Pauls, R., Perry, L., & Aldersey, H. M. (2025). The limits and contributions of formal support: Service providers' perspectives on balancing formal and natural support for people with disabilities and their families in Canada. *Journal of Developmental and Physical Disabilities, 37*(1), 129–156. DOI: 10.1007/s10882-023-09944-2 PMID: 39867962

O'Donovan, J. (2005). Managing the performance review process. *Civil Engineers Australia, 77*(6), 69.

O'Donovan, M., Wedgwood, N., Westermann, G., Rillotta, F., & Aitken, T. (2025). Personal, Social and Vocational Outcomes of Inclusive University for People With Intellectual Disability. *Journal of Intellectual Disability Research, 69*(12), 1448–1473. DOI: 10.1111/jir.70042 PMID: 41016861

O'Shea, G., & Clegg, B. A. (2006). Stimulus and response chunking in the Hebb Digits task. *Psychological Research, 70*(3), 180–192. DOI: 10.1007/s00426-004-0198-1 PMID: 15818496

Oberai, H. (2025). Embracing inclusive leadership to bias reduction in HRM. In *Navigating bias in human resource management* (pp. 101–129). IGI Global., DOI: 10.4018/979-8-3693-7132-9.ch004

Ochrach, C., Thomas, K., Phillips, B., Mpofu, N., Tansey, T., & Castillo, S. (2022). Case study on the effects of a disability inclusive mindset in a large biotechnology company. *Journal of Work-Applied Management, 14*(1), 113–125. DOI: 10.1108/JWAM-06-2021-0045

Odunayo, A., & Ng, Z. (2026). Navigating inclusive language in veterinary medicine: A step toward a more equitable workplace. *Veterinary Ophthalmology*, *29*(1), e70025. Advance online publication. DOI: 10.1111/vop.70025 PMID: 40356033

Oliveira, R., De Castro Salgado, L. C., Seixas, F., & Cappelli, C. (2026). How Is Plain Language Applied in Interactive Systems Design? A Systematic Mapping Study. *Lecture Notes in Computer Science, 16111 LNCS*, 260–264. DOI: 10.1007/978-3-032-05008-3_49

Ollington, N., Gibb, J., & Harcourt, M. (2013). Online social networks: An emergent recruiter tool for attracting and screening. *Personnel Review*, *42*(3), 248–265. DOI: 10.1108/00483481311320390

Olney, S., & Yates, S. (2025). The Costs of Living With Disability in Australia: Accounting for Variable Disability-Related Deprivation in Poverty Measures. *The Australian Economic Review*, *58*(S1). Advance online publication. DOI: 10.1111/1467-8462.70017

Olsson, S., & Gustafsson, C. (2020). Employees' experiences of education and knowledge in intellectual disability practice. *Journal of Policy and Practice in Intellectual Disabilities*, *17*(3), 219–231. DOI: 10.1111/jppi.12338

Ortiz-Marcos, J. M., Invernón-Gómez, A. I., Medina-García, M., & Higueras-Rodríguez, L. (2024). Workplace inclusion of people with disabilities: Legislative challenges and practical solutions. *Revista Espanola de Orientacion y Psicopedagogia*, *35*(3), 105–122. DOI: 10.5944/reop.vol.35.num.3.2024.40820

Ortlieb, E., & Schatz, S. (2019). Passing the pen: A gradual release model of the recursive writing process. In *Literacy Research* (Vol. 10, pp. 205–215). Practice and Evaluation., DOI: 10.1108/S2048-045820190000010013

Osorio, M. L., & del Castillo, E. (2025). Customers' attitudes toward frontline employees with intellectual disabilities: Scale development and validation. *Journal of Service Research*. Advance online publication. DOI: 10.1177/10946705251391145

Palumbo, R., Hinna, A., & Manesh, M. F. (2023). Aiming at Inclusive Workplaces: A Bibliometric and Interpretive Review at the Crossroads of Disability Management and Human Resource Management. *Journal of Management & Organization*, *31*(4), 1664–1687. DOI: 10.1017/jmo.2023.4

Paluszkiewicz, M. (2025). A few comments on the employer's obligations towards an employee unable to perform his current job or position in the light of the latest international standards of equal treatment regardless of disability in employment *Acta Universitatis Lodziensis. Folia Iuridica*, *112*, 137–156. DOI: 10.18778/0208-6069.112.09

Panda, R. K., Raut, D. K., & Biswal, P. (2018). Inclusive training using technology at workplace: A critical review for an infrastructure company. *International Journal of Civil Engineering and Technology*, *9*(4), 602–607. https://www.scopus.com/inward/record.uri?eid=2-s2.0-85046361996&partnerID=40&md5=dffbd9c97dd1f24f7f530cfd6adfebbf

Pathirana, G. (2024). Beyond metrics: Crafting a dynamic performance evaluation system. In *Employee Performance Management for Improved Workplace Motivation* (pp. 145–171). DOI: 10.4018/979-8-3693-4387-6.ch006

Patil, R., Raheja, D. K., Nair, L., Deshpande, A., & Mittal, A. (2023). The Power of Psychological Safety: Investigating its Impact on Team Learning, Team Efficacy, and Team Productivity. *The Open Psychology Journal*, *16*(1), e187435012307090. Advance online publication. DOI: 10.2174/18743501-v16-230727-2023-36

Paul, C. D., Thomas, E. V., Marelle, C., Hussain, S. Z., Doulin, A. M., & Jimenez, E. (2022). Using wireless technology to support individuals with intellectual and developmental disabilities in vocational settings: A focus group study. *Journal of Vocational Rehabilitation*, *56*(3), 303–312. DOI: 10.3233/JVR-221193

Peña, H.Jr, Gilson, C. B., Morissette, L., Rogers, A., Kesavalu, A., & Sabella, M. (2024b). A review of visually supported portable technology to support employment-related social behaviors for young adults with autism and developmental disorders. *Journal of Vocational Rehabilitation*, *61*(3), 331–347. Advance online publication. DOI: 10.1177/10522263241285217

Peña-Quintana, M. T., & Vega, L. E. S. (2022). The Transition to Employment in Wales and the Canary Islands for People With Intellectual Disabilities: Supported Employment. *Education Sciences*, *12*(11), 796. DOI: 10.3390/educsci12110796

Pereira, E., Nsair, S., Pereira, L. R., & Grant, K. (2024). Constructive alignment in a graduate-level project management course: An innovative framework using large language models. *International Journal of Educational Technology in Higher Education, 21*(1), 25. Advance online publication. DOI: 10.1186/s41239-024-00457-2

Pereira-Silva, N. L., Furtado, A. V., & Andrade, J. F. C. D. M. (2018). Workplace inclusion from the standpoint of individuals with intellectual disabilities. *Temas em Psicologia, 26*(2), 1017–1030. DOI: 10.9788/TP2018.2-17En

Perez-Uribe, R. I., Ocampo-Guzman, D., & Moreno-Monsalve, N. (2022). *Handbook of research on promoting an inclusive organizational culture for entrepreneurial sustainability*. IGI Global., DOI: 10.4018/978-1-6684-5216-5

Perez-y-Perez, M., Grant, J. A., & Cook, T. F. (2024). Stitching Together a PAR Project: "Work Active"—Supporting the Journey to Work for People With an Intellectual Disability. *Qualitative Inquiry, 32*(1), 50–62. DOI: 10.1177/10778004241279180

Performance evaluations. (2025). *Human Resource Management International Digest, 33*(6), 6–8. DOI: 10.1108/HRMID-06-2025-0159

Perrault, E. L. J., & Coleman, H. D. J. (2006). Coaching within social work field education. *The Clinical Supervisor, 23*(2), 47–64. DOI: 10.1300/J001v23n02_04

Perrotta, P., Novis, D. A., Nelson, S., Blond, B., Stankovic, A., & Talbert, M. (2020). Workflow mapping - A Q-probes study of preanalytic testing processes: A college of american pathologists q-probes study of 35 clinical laboratories. *Archives of Pathology & Laboratory Medicine, 144*(12), 1517–1524. DOI: 10.5858/arpa.2020-0043-CP PMID: 32579404

Persch, A. C., Cleary, D. S., Rutkowski, S., Malone, H. I., Darragh, A. R., & Case-Smith, J. D. (2015). Current practices in job matching: A Project SEARCH perspective on transition. *Journal of Vocational Rehabilitation, 43*(3), 259–273. DOI: 10.3233/JVR-150774

Persson, H., Åhman, H., Yngling, A. A., & Gulliksen, J. (2015). Universal design, inclusive design, accessible design, design for all: Different concepts—one goal? On the concept of accessibility—historical, methodological and philosophical aspects. *Universal Access in the Information Society, 14*(4), 505–526. DOI: 10.1007/s10209-014-0358-z

Petrov, S., Oprea, B., & Opariuc-Dan, C. (2023). Psychological Safety and Job Performance: The Mediating Role of Work Engagement and Job Crafting. *Psihologia Resurselor Umane, 21*(2), 89–99. DOI: 10.24837/pru.v21i2.536

Phan, N. (2025). Transforming internal communication: Strategies for engagement and organizational success. *Business and Professional Communication Quarterly*, 23294906251378735. Advance online publication. DOI: 10.1177/23294906251378735

Philips, G. R., Huang, M., & Bodine, C. (2024). Helping or Hindering: Inclusive Design of Automated Task Prompting for Workers with Cognitive Disabilities. *ACM Transactions on Accessible Computing*, *16*(4), 1–23. Advance online publication. DOI: 10.1145/3628447

Phillips, S. D. (2011). EU Disability Policy and Implications of EU Accession for Disability Rights in Education and Employment in Bulgaria, Romania, Croatia, and the Former Yugoslav Republic of Macedonia. *Journal of Disability Policy Studies*, *22*(4), 208–219. DOI: 10.1177/1044207311414710

Piccolo, L., Gruber, B. C., Knobel, M., & Stähler, L. (2023). A digital support for people with disabilities entering the labour market: Ideation process and design requirements. In *ACM International Conference Proceeding Series* (pp. 265–270). https://doi.org/DOI: 10.1145/3582515.3609543

Piccone, C., Xu, X., Thomson, D., Gaurav, N., & Aldersey, H. M. (2024). Enabling formal and natural supports for adults with developmental disabilities in British Columbia, Canada: Experiences of three organizations. *Disabilities*, *4*(4), 1076–1092. DOI: 10.3390/disabilities4040067

Pierson, K., Oshodi, R., & Borowsky, I. (2026). Applying accessibility theory by implementing gradual, sustainable change in daily practice. *Academic Pediatrics*, *26*(3), 103205. Advance online publication. DOI: 10.1016/j.acap.2025.103205 PMID: 41490875

Pietrantoni, L., Mazzetti, G., San Román Niaves, M., Kubik, R., Giusino, D., & De Angelis, M. (2024). Enhancing team dynamics through digital coaching: The role of managerial and peer support. *European Journal of Training and Development*, *48*(10), 16–36. DOI: 10.1108/EJTD-12-2023-0193

Plotner, A. J., & Oertle, K. M. (2021). Employment support facilitator (job coach). In *Collaboration: A multidisciplinary approach to educating students with disabilities* (pp. 339–351). Routledge., DOI: 10.4324/9781003233688-28

Pogrebtsova, E., Luta, D., & Hausdorf, P. A. (2020). Selection of gender-incongruent applicants: No gender bias with structured interviews. *International Journal of Selection and Assessment*, *28*(1), 117–121. DOI: 10.1111/ijsa.12270

Pohl, M., Potzmann, B., Stoiber, C., & Aigner, W. (2025). Inconspicuous Guides: A Qualitative Study to Understand the Degree of Intrusiveness in Visualization Onboarding. *Proceedings of the International Joint Conference on Computer Vision, Imaging and Computer Graphics Theory and Applications, 1*, 706–717. DOI: 10.5220/0013135900003912

Polishko, N., & Zelinskyi, D. (2025). Inclusive labour market: Normative barriers and opportunities for persons with disabilities in Europe [Інклюзивний ринок праці: нормативні бар'єри та можливості людей з інвалідністю в Європі]. *Law. Human. Environment, 16*(3), 92–112. DOI: 10.31548/law/3.2025.92

Pollifroni, M., Ioana, A., Canuta, I. L., & Pollifroni, F. (2025). AI-driven e-recruitment in education and science: Moving towards good governance, prevention of corruption, administrative transparency, and bias-free decision-making. *Business Ethics and Leadership, 9*(2), 225–237. DOI: 10.61093/bel.9(2).225-237.2025

Pon-Barry, H., Packard, B. W.-L., & St. John, A. (2017). Expanding capacity and promoting inclusion in introductory computer science: A focus on near-peer mentor preparation and code review. *Computer Science Education, 27*(1), 54–77. DOI: 10.1080/08993408.2017.1333270

Poonkuzhali, S., Sangeetha Archana, J., Naresh, A., & Naidhruv Raj, R. (2025). GenAI-Powered Adaptive Assessments for Livelihood Skills in Individuals with Intellectual Disabilities. *Lecture Notes in Networks and Systems, 1383 LNNS*, 127–136. DOI: 10.1007/978-981-96-5754-4_12

Porter, J. M., Velten, J., Badami, R., Nezakatolhossaini, M., & Lotfinejad, M. (2024). Knowledge of results about more accurate versus less accurate trials: Differential effects on psychological variables and motor learning in adolescent females. *Polish Journal of Sport and Tourism, 31*(1), 12–16. DOI: 10.2478/pjst-2024-0002

Pouliot, D. M., Müller, E., Frasché, N. F., Kern, A. S., & Resti, I. H. (2017). A tool for supporting communication in the workplace for individuals with intellectual disabilities and/or autism. *Career Development and Transition for Exceptional Individuals, 40*(4), 244–249. DOI: 10.1177/2165143416683927

Precin, P. (2010). The use of visual imagery to enhance sequencing of work tasks. *Work (Reading, Mass.), 36*(4), 373–379. DOI: 10.3233/WOR-2010-1040 PMID: 20714092

Primeau, M. S., & Talley, B. (2019). Intellectual disabilities and health care communication: A continuing education program for providers. *Journal of Continuing Education in Nursing, 50*(1), 20–25. DOI: 10.3928/00220124-20190102-06 PMID: 30645655

Quinn, G. (2007). Disability discrimination law in the European Union. In *Equality Law in an Enlarged European Union: Understanding the Article 13 Directives* (pp. 231–277). Cambridge University Press. DOI: 10.1017/CBO9780511493898.009

Quinn, M. A., Chaudhari, A., Brazeau, C., Lawrence, E., & Olson, K. (2025). How peer support helps heal the culture of medicine from within. *NEJM Catalyst Innovations in Care Delivery*, *6*(1). Advance online publication. DOI: 10.1056/CAT.23.0373

Quintana, M.. (2022). Job coaching and supported employment for individuals with intellectual disabilities: A meta-analysis. *Journal of Applied Research in Intellectual Disabilities*, *35*(3), 631–644.

Rabenu, E., & Tziner, A. (2016). The role of the law in the employment of people with disabilities. *Journal of Organisational Behaviour, 37*(4), 537–553.

Rachanioti, E., Giaouri, S., Laskaraki, E., & Alevriadou, A. (2021). "Can I work here?": Employment barriers for individuals with intellectual disabilities in Greece. Journal of Intellectual Disability - Diagnosis and Treatment, 9(4), 354–362. DOI: 10.6000/2292-2598.2021.09.04.1

Rachanioti, E.. (2021). Barriers to employment for people with intellectual disabilities: A systematic review. *Journal of Vocational Rehabilitation*, *54*(2), 117–130.

Raju, U. S. N., Kadambari, K. V., & Venkata Subba Reddy, P. (2015). A new method of assessing the students using video assignments. *IEEE Global Engineering Education Conference*, 771–773. https://doi.org/DOI: 10.1109/EDUCON.2015.7096058

Ramkumar, P., Acuna, D. E., Berniker, M., Grafton, S. T., Turner, R. S., & Kording, K. P. (2016). Chunking as the result of an efficiency computation trade-off. *Nature Communications*, *7*(1), 12176. Advance online publication. DOI: 10.1038/ncomms12176 PMID: 27397420

Randall, K. N., Johnson, F., Adams, S. E., Kiss, C. W., & Ryan, J. B. (2020). Use of a iPhone Task Analysis Application to Increase Employment-Related Chores for Individuals With Intellectual Disabilities. *Journal of Special Education Technology*, *35*(1), 26–36. DOI: 10.1177/0162643419836410

Randall, K., Drew, H., Gilman, E., & Dixon, E. (2025). Assistive Technology Uses and Barriers in the Home and Workplace for Adults With Intellectual and Developmental Disabilities. *Journal of Applied Research in Intellectual Disabilities*, *38*(1), e13306. Advance online publication. DOI: 10.1111/jar.13306 PMID: 39462768

Rashid, M., Thompson-Hodgetts, S., & Nicholas, D. (2020). Tensions experienced by employment support professionals when seeking meaningful employment for persons with developmental disabilities. *Research in Developmental Disabilities*, *99*, 103603. Advance online publication. DOI: 10.1016/j.ridd.2020.103603

Rashid, T. (2015). Strength-based assessment. In *Positive psychology in practice: Promoting human flourishing in work, health, education, and everyday life* (2nd ed., pp. 519–542). Wiley., DOI: 10.1002/9781118996874.ch31

Rashwan, Z. I., Narayanan, G., Khonji, L. M., Stalin, G. K., Gangadurai, N., & Bayoumi, M. M. (2024). Integrating peer instruction and peer assessment with competency-based four-step approach: Effectiveness on wound dressing skill acquisition and motivation among nursing students. *Teaching and Learning in Nursing*, *19*(1), e150–e159. DOI: 10.1016/j.teln.2023.10.005

Rasouli, O., Kvam, L., Husby, V. S., Røstad, M., & Witsø, A. E. (2023). Understanding the possibilities and limitations of assistive technology in health and welfare services for people with intellectual disabilities, staff perspectives. *Disability and Rehabilitation. Assistive Technology*, *18*(7), 989–997. DOI: 10.1080/17483107.2021.1963856 PMID: 34403623

Ravindranathan, R., Usha, S., Tommy, R., & George, S. R. (2024). Interest and skill correlation model for career aligning of young persons with disabilities. Journal of Intellectual Disability - Diagnosis and Treatment, 12(4), 228–239. DOI: 10.6000/2292-2598.2024.12.04.5

Ravinskaya, M., Verbeek, J., Langendam, M., Daams, J. G., Hulshof, C., Madan, I., Verstappen, S., Hagendijk, M., Kunz, R., & Hoving, J. L. (2022). Extensive Variability of Work Participation Outcomes Measured in Randomized Controlled Trials: A Systematic Review. *Journal of Clinical Epidemiology*, *142*, 60–99. DOI: 10.1016/j.jclinepi.2021.10.013 PMID: 34715311

Read, E. K., & Baillie, S. (2013). Using cognitive task analysis to create a teaching protocol for Bovine Dystocia. *Journal of Veterinary Medical Education*, *40*(4), 397–402. DOI: 10.3138/jvme.0213-033R PMID: 24077313

Readhead, A., & Owen, F. (2020). Employment supports and outcomes for persons with intellectual and/or developmental disabilities: A review of recent findings. *Current Developmental Disorders Reports*, *7*(3), 155–162. DOI: 10.1007/s40474-020-00202-0

Regan, K., & Weiss, M. P. (2020). Bug-in-ear coaching for teacher candidates: What, why, and how to get started. *Intervention in School and Clinic*, *55*(3), 178–184. DOI: 10.1177/1053451219842218

Reinersmann, A., Heinz-Jakobs, M., Bicker, E., & Röcker, C. (2025). How Technology Systems on the Labour Market for Persons With Disability. In *Applied Human Factors and Ergonomics International* (Vol. 169, pp. 38–47). DOI: 10.54941/ahfe1006152

Reinersmann, A., Heinz-Jakobs, M., Bicker, E., & Röcker, C. (2025). Examples of implementing digital assistive technologies in the open labor market. *Communications in Computer and Information Science, 2524*, 161–171. DOI: 10.1007/978-3-031-94156-6_17

Renner, B., Wesiak, G., Pammer-Schindler, V., Prilla, M., Müller, L., Morosini, D., Mora, S., Faltin, N., & Cress, U. (2020). Computer-supported reflective learning: How apps can foster reflection at work. *Behaviour & Information Technology, 39*(2), 167–187. DOI: 10.1080/0144929X.2019.1595726

Reynders, S. S., Lombardo, A., Davidson, E. J., Guan, J. L., Pawlowski, K. G., Simons, N. Z., & Baumer, N. (2024). 15 Years of Inclusive Employment in a Down Syndrome Clinic. *Work (Reading, Mass.), 79*(3), 1517–1523. DOI: 10.3233/WOR-240080 PMID: 39331058

Reynolds, M. C., Palmer, S. B., & Gotto, G. S. (2018). Reconceptualizing natural supports for people with disabilities and their families. *International Review of Research in Developmental Disabilities, 54*, 177–209. DOI: 10.1016/bs.irrdd.2018.07.006

Rezai, M., Lindsay, S., Ahmed, H., & Vijayakumar, A. (2023). Workplace inclusion: A scoping review of the qualitative literature. *Work (Reading, Mass.), 75*(1), 59–73. DOI: 10.3233/WOR-211343 PMID: 36591672

Rhodes, J., & Hamilton, D. (2006). An Insight into Implementing Person-Centred Active Support. *Tizard Learning Disability Review, 11*(3), 31–36. DOI: 10.1108/13595474200600025

Riches, V. C. (2023). Employment and intellectual disability: A review of the literature. *Journal of Intellectual & Developmental Disability, 48*(2), 123–136.

Riches, V. C. (2023). The importance of economic participation for quality of life. In *Disability practice: Safeguarding quality service delivery* (pp. 79–99). Springer., DOI: 10.1007/978-981-99-6143-6_5

Riches, V. C., Harman, A. D., Keen, D., Pennell, D., Harley, J. H., & Walker, M. (2011). Transforming staff practice through active support. *Journal of Intellectual & Developmental Disability, 36*(3), 156–166. DOI: 10.3109/13668250.2011.598499 PMID: 21843030

Riera Claret, C., Sahagún, M. Á., & Selva, C. (2020). Peer and informal learning among hospital doctors: An ethnographic study focused on routines, practices and relationships. *Journal of Workplace Learning, 32*(4), 285–301. DOI: 10.1108/JWL-11-2018-0141

Riesen, T., Morgan, R. L., & Griffin, C. (2015). Customized Employment: A Review Of the literature. *Journal of Vocational Rehabilitation, 43*(3), 183–193. DOI: 10.3233/JVR-150768

Riesen, T., Snyder, A., Byers, R., Keeton, B., & Inge, K. J. (2022). An Updated Review of the Customized Employment Literature. *Journal of Vocational Rehabilitation, 58*(1), 27–38. DOI: 10.3233/JVR-221222

Rigotti, C., & Fosch-Villaronga, E. (2024). Fairness, AI & recruitment. *Computer Law & Security Review, 53*, 105966. Advance online publication. DOI: 10.1016/j.clsr.2024.105966

Risavy, S. D., Robie, C., Fisher, P. A., & Rasheed, S. (2022). Resumes vs. application forms: Why the stubborn reliance on resumes? *Frontiers in Psychology, 13*, 884205. Advance online publication. DOI: 10.3389/fpsyg.2022.884205 PMID: 35967708

Ristevski, E., McCook, F., Thompson, S., Duncan, Z., Lawler, B., & Broxham, C. (2024). Initiatives to Facilitate the Social Inclusion of People With Intellectual Disability in Physical Activities With Others in Community-based Sporting, Recreation and Leisure Activities: A Scoping Review. *Journal of Applied Research in Intellectual Disabilities, 37*(3), e13238. Advance online publication. DOI: 10.1111/jar.13238 PMID: 38622495

Rivera, M., Qiu, L., Kumar, S., & Petrucci, T. (2021). Are traditional performance reviews outdated? An empirical analysis on continuous, real-time feedback in the workplace. *Information Systems Research, 32*(2), 517–540. DOI: 10.1287/isre.2020.0979

Riviez, D. A. (2019). Employee learning disabilities and workforce learning. In *The Wiley handbook of global workplace learning* (pp. 215–240). Wiley., DOI: 10.1002/9781119227793.ch13

Roberts, R. C., & Flin, R. (2016). Behavioural rating of drillers' cognitive skills. In *SPE International Conference and Exhibition on Health, Safety, Security, Environment, and Social Responsibility*. Society of Petroleum Engineers. DOI: 10.2118/179270-MS

Robinson, M. A. (2010). Work sampling: Methodological advances and new applications. *Human Factors and Ergonomics in Manufacturing*, *20*(1), 42–60. DOI: 10.1002/hfm.20186

Robinson, S., Carnemolla, P., Lay, K., & Kelly, J. (2022). Involving People With Intellectual Disability in Setting Priorities for Building Community Inclusion at a Local Government Level. *British Journal of Learning Disabilities*, *50*(3), 364–375. DOI: 10.1111/bld.12469

Roczniewska, M., Rogala, A., Marszałek, M., Hasson, H., Bakker, A. B., & von Thiele Schwarz, U. (2023). Job crafting interventions: What works, for whom, why, and in which contexts? Research protocol for a systematic review with coincidence analysis. *Systematic Reviews*, *12*(1), 10. Advance online publication. DOI: 10.1186/s13643-023-02170-z PMID: 36670492

Rogan, P. M., & Rinne, S. (2021). Launching a Statewide Employment First Initiative: Indiana's Work to Include Coalition. *Journal of Vocational Rehabilitation*, *54*(3), 255–260. DOI: 10.3233/JVR-211133

Rogers, A. M. (2020). Avoiding the issue: A critique of organizational socialization research from feminist and minority perspectives. *Organization Development Journal*, *38*(1), 75–88. https://www.scopus.com/inward/record.uri?eid=2-s2.0-85089549634&partnerID=40&md5=e23e06cd3b99f40fc7c7a4e834fcc86e

Rogito, J., & Makabe, M. (2023). The Art and Act of Providing Feedback at the Workplace: Effective Feedback for Positive Results. *Pan-African Journal of Education and Social Sciences*, *4*(1), 49–56. https://www.scopus.com/inward/record.uri?eid=2-s2.0-105004581237&partnerID=40&md5=2142362703ec1934c29f9596f6f01b3f

Rössler, B. (2007). Work, recognition, emancipation. In *Recognition and power: Axel Honneth and the tradition of critical social theory* (pp. 135–163). Cambridge University Press., DOI: 10.1017/CBO9780511498732.006

Ross, W. E., Huang, K. H. C., & Jones, G. H. (2014). Executive onboarding: Ensuring the success of the newly hired department chair. *Academic Medicine*, *89*(5), 728–733. DOI: 10.1097/ACM.0000000000000214 PMID: 24667516

Roux, A. M., Garfield, T., & Shattuck, P. (2019). Employment Policy and Autism: Analysis of State Workforce Innovation and Opportunity Act (WIOA) Implementation Plans. *Journal of Vocational Rehabilitation*, *51*(3), 285–298. DOI: 10.3233/JVR-191046

Rumrill, P. D., Rumrill, S. P., Wickert, K., Sheppard-Jones, K., Baumunk, M., & Roessler, R. T. (2023). A 'win-win' perspective on workplace accommodations: RETAIN Kentucky's self-advocacy guide to promote successful return to work and stay at work outcomes for workers with disabilities. *Work (Reading, Mass.)*, *74*(1), 3–10. DOI: 10.3233/WOR-223651 PMID: 36463483

Ruppel, E. H. (2025). The making of a reserve army of labor: Paradoxes of American disability policy. *Critical Sociology*, *51*(3), 451–469. DOI: 10.1177/08969205241246446

Rusilowati, U., Muti, R. N., Mudrika, F., Kamil, M. F., Lutfiani, N., & Immanuel, A. J. (2025). Data-driven inclusive HR and leadership strategies for enhancing innovation and employee engagement. Proceeding - 2025 4th International Conference on Creative Communication and Innovative Technology. https://doi.org/DOI: 10.1109/ICCIT65724.2025.11167031

Rutherford, M., Baxter, J., Grayson, Z., Johnston, L., & O'Hare, A. (2020). Visual supports at home and in the community for individuals with autism spectrum disorders: A scoping review. *Autism*, *24*(2), 447–469. DOI: 10.1177/1362361319871756 PMID: 31451016

Ryan, A. K., Miller, L., Rose, T. A., & Johnston, L. M. (2024). Child-led goal setting and evaluation tools for children with a disability: A scoping review. *Developmental Medicine and Child Neurology*, *66*(12), 1558–1569. DOI: 10.1111/dmcn.15959 PMID: 38760984

Ryan, J., Brown, H. M., Borden, A., Devlin, C., Kedmy, A., Lee, A., Nicholas, D. B., & Thompson-Hodgetts, S. (2025). "It's really who they are and what they want": Staff perspectives on supporting autonomy for autistic adults with intellectual disabilities. *Journal of Applied Research in Intellectual Disabilities*, *38*(4), e70106. Advance online publication. DOI: 10.1111/jar.70106 PMID: 40731376

Sachse, M., & Melzer, J. (2025). Breaking barriers: Gamification in recruiting to overcome communication challenges - Psychological, social and cultural differences in perception and participation. *Proceedings of the International Conferences on Interfaces and Human Computer Interaction 2025; Game and Entertainment Technologies 2025; and Computer Graphics, Visualization, Computer Vision and Image Processing 2025*, 172–176.

Saleh, M. C., & Bruyère, S. M. (2018). Leveraging employer practices in global regulatory frameworks to improve employment outcomes for people with disabilities. *Social Inclusion (Lisboa)*, *6*(1), 18–28. DOI: 10.17645/si.v6i1.1201

Samuel, H. S., Etim, E. E., Nweke-Maraizu, U., & Shinggu, J. P. (2024). Promoting diversity, equity, and inclusion: Strategies for building capacity and fostering belonging. In *Building organizational capacity and strategic management in academia* (pp. 445–462). IGI Global., DOI: 10.4018/979-8-3693-6967-8.ch016

Sandjojo, J., Zedlitz, A. M. E. E., Gebhardt, W. A., Hoekman, J., Dusseldorp, E., den Haan, J. A., & Evers, A. W. M. (2018). Training staff to promote self-management in people with intellectual disabilities. *Journal of Applied Research in Intellectual Disabilities*, *31*(5), 840–850. DOI: 10.1111/jar.12440 PMID: 29479785

Sanrey, C., Conguista, T., Beyer, H., & Rohmer, O. (2026). Determinants of legal disclosure intentions in academia. *Disability & Society*, *41*(6), 1445–1469. Advance online publication. DOI: 10.1080/09687599.2026.2640939

Sarto, P. A., Lorzano, E. R., Artes, A., Bobis, H. M., Intal, G. L., Moreno, D. E., & Tan, M. E. (2026). A strategic approach to developing AbiliNet: Leveraging the business model canvas for an inclusive AI-driven job-matching platform. ICBIM 2025 - The 9th International Conference on Business and Information Management, 28–35. https://doi.org/DOI: 10.1145/3785171.3785188

Sartore, G.-M., Pourliakas, A., & Lagioia, V. (2021). Peer support interventions for parents and carers of children with complex needs. *Cochrane Database of Systematic Reviews*, *2021*(12), CD010618. Advance online publication. DOI: 10.1002/14651858.CD010618.pub2 PMID: 34923624

Satpathy, I., Patnaik, B. C. M., & Raut, D. K. (2018). Inclusive training in manufacturing industry: A review. *International Journal of Mechanical Engineering and Technology*, *9*(9), 63–70. https://www.scopus.com/inward/record.uri?eid=2-s2.0-85054015812&partnerID=40&md5=84a2ee28ddcf6af8fada969cc1bf75e7

Saxena, P., Agrawal, V., & Pradhan, I. P. (2025). AI-powered talent acquisition and recruitment. In *Human resource management and artificial intelligence: Automating and optimizing processes* (pp. 25–43). Routledge., DOI: 10.4324/9781003474265-2

Sayers, D. (2017). Rights not needs: Changing the legal model for special educational needs (SEN). In *The Palgrave Handbook of Disabled Children's Childhood Studies* (pp. 617–642). Palgrave Macmillan. DOI: 10.1057/978-1-137-54446-9_37

Scanlon, G., & Doyle, A. (2021). Transition stories: Voices of school leavers with intellectual disabilities. *British Journal of Learning Disabilities*, *49*(4), 456–466. DOI: 10.1111/bld.12433

Scheef, A. R., Bruno, L., & Whittenburg, H. N. (2023). Supporting Positive Post-School Outcomes for Students With Disabilities in Rural Locations. *Rural Special Education Quarterly*, *43*(1), 36–43. DOI: 10.1177/87568705231214809

Schofield, D., Shrestha, R., Tan, O., Lim, K. K., Rajkumar, R., West, S., Boyle, J., Murray, L., Leffler, M., Christie, L., Rice, M. W., Hart, N., Li, J., Tanton, R., Roscioli, T., & Field, M. (2024). The Healthcare and Societal Costs of Familial Intellectual Disability. *International Journal of Environmental Research and Public Health*, *21*(3), 299. DOI: 10.3390/ijerph21030299 PMID: 38541298

Schuhl, J., Chatard, A., & Lambert, É. (2020). Reducing stigmatisation of employees with disability: Example of a brief intervention in a company [RÉDUIRE LA STIGMATISATION DES SALARIÉS RECONNUS HANDICAPÉS: EXEMPLE D'UNE ACTION DE SENSIBILISATION EN ENTREPRISE]. *Le Travail Humain*, *83*(2), 91–114. DOI: 10.3917/th.832.0091

Schutz, M. A., Awsumb, J. M., Carter, E. W., & McMillan, E. D. (2021). Parent Perspectives on Pre-Employment Transition Services for Youth With Disabilities. *Rehabilitation Counseling Bulletin*, *65*(4), 266–278. DOI: 10.1177/0034355221993542

Schwartzman, B., Lanchak, E. R., Carter, E. W., Guest, L., McMillan, E. D., & Taylor, J. L. (2023). Family Perspectives on Promoting Paid Employment for Individuals With Intellectual and Developmental Disabilities. *Rehabilitation Counseling Bulletin*, *68*(2), 79–91. DOI: 10.1177/00343552231213996

Sears, J. S., Hall, M. T., Harris, L. M., Mount, S., Willauer, T., Posze, L., & Smead, E. (2017). "Like a marriage": Partnering with peer mentors in child welfare. *Children and Youth Services Review*, *74*, 80–86. DOI: 10.1016/j.childyouth.2017.01.023

Seewooruttun, L., & Scior, K. (2014). Interventions aimed at increasing knowledge and improving attitudes towards people with intellectual disabilities among lay people. *Research in Developmental Disabilities*, *35*(12), 3482–3495. DOI: 10.1016/j.ridd.2014.07.028 PMID: 25213473

Seotsanyana, M. B. (2025). Transforming Potential into Proficiency: Mentorship as a Catalyst for Professional Advancement in the Workplace. In *Fostering Lifelong Learning Through Mentoring in Adult Education* (pp. 283–320). DOI: 10.4018/979-8-3373-3516-2.ch011

Shabani, M., Heidarimoghadam, R., Faradmal, J., & Babamiri, M. (2025). Identify the cognitive, psychomotor and sensory-perceptual abilities required for the role of pre-hospital emergency medical personnel. *Work (Reading, Mass.)*, *80*(4), 1607–1616. DOI: 10.1177/10519815241295907 PMID: 40337819

Shahhosseini, A. M., Moayed, F. A., & McLeod, A. (2020). Strategies for increasing enrollment, retention, and graduation in two baccalaureate degree STEM programs: Mechanical Engineering Technology (MET) and Safety Management (SM). *ASEE Annual Conference and Exposition, Conference Proceedings*, Article 1253. DOI: 10.18260/1-2--35209

Shahin, S., Reitzel, M., Rezze, B. D., Ahmed, S., & Anaby, D. (2020). Environmental Factors That Impact the Workplace Participation of Transition-Aged Young Adults With Brain-Based Disabilities: A Scoping Review. *International Journal of Environmental Research and Public Health, 17*(7), 2378. DOI: 10.3390/ijerph17072378 PMID: 32244476

Shamshiri-Petersen, D., & Krogh, C. (2020). Disability disqualifies: A vignette experiment on Danish employers' intentions to hire applicants with physical disabilities. *Scandinavian Journal of Disability Research, 22*(1), 198–209. DOI: 10.16993/sjdr.661

Sharma, V., Rani, S., & Chauhan, D. (2024). Enhancing New Hire Onboarding Through Immersive Augmented Reality Training: A Comparative Study. *Proceedings of International Conference on Communication, Computer Sciences and Engineering, IC3SE 2024*, 1737–1740. DOI: 10.1109/IC3SE62002.2024.10593605

Shatil, T., Carew, M. T., Chowdhury, S., Biswas, D., Adiba, A., Banks, L. M., Shakespeare, T., & Das, N. (2024). Process evaluation of a disability-inclusive employment programme: Examining the design and implementation of STAR+. *Oxford Development Studies, 52*(2), 146–159. DOI: 10.1080/13600818.2024.2371125

Shaw, J., Wickenden, M., Thompson, S., & Mader, P. (2022). Achieving disability inclusive employment – Are the current approaches deep enough? *Journal of International Development, 34*(5), 942–963. DOI: 10.1002/jid.3692

Shiller, R. J. (2005). Behavioral Economics and Institutional Innovation. *Southern Economic Journal, 72*(2), 268. DOI: 10.2307/20062111

Shinall, J. B. (2020). Anticipating accommodation. *Iowa Law Review, 105*(2), 621–686.

Shinall, J. B. (2022). Without accommodation. *Industrial Law Journal, 97*(4), 1147–1201.

Shogren, K. A., Dean, E., Griffin, C., Steveley, J., Sickles, R., Wehmeyer, M. L., & Palmer, S. B. (2017). Promoting Change in Employment Supports: Impacts of a Community-Based Change Model. *Journal of Vocational Rehabilitation, 47*(1), 19–24. DOI: 10.3233/JVR-170880

Shogren, K. A., Wehmeyer, M. L., Seo, H., Thompson, J. R., Schalock, R. L., Hughes, C., Little, T. D., & Palmer, S. B. (2017). Examining the Reliability and Validity of the Supports Intensity Scale–Children's Version in Children With Autism and Intellectual Disability. *Focus on Autism and Other Developmental Disabilities*, *32*(4), 293–304. DOI: 10.1177/1088357615625060

Shurack, N. Y., & Roling, C. (2014). Incorporating the concept of quality of life in individual support plans. In *Quality of Life and Intellectual Disability: Knowledge Application to Other Social and Educational Challenges* (pp. 265–283). Nova Science Publishers.

Sigle, N., & Hertweck, D. (2026). Identification of barriers that lead to problems in the further training of employees. *Communications in Computer and Information Science*, *2787*, 265–276. DOI: 10.1007/978-3-032-15463-7_22

Sigstad, H. M. H., Garrels, V., Dean, E. E., & Wendelborg, C. (2025). Characteristics of workplaces and employers that embrace cognitive diversity on the work floor. *Intellectual and Developmental Disabilities*, *63*(2), 105–119. DOI: 10.1352/1934-9556-63.2.105 PMID: 40139232

Simmons, S. V., & Yawson, R. M. (2022). Developing leaders for disruptive change: An inclusive leadership approach. *Advances in Developing Human Resources*, *24*(4), 242–262. DOI: 10.1177/15234223221114359

Sinclair, J., Gilson, C. B., & Dulas, H. M. (2023). "I'm Going to Be a Working Person": Self-Determination in Employment Settings for Adults With Intellectual and Developmental Disabilities. *Career Development and Transition for Exceptional Individuals*, *47*(3), 159–171. DOI: 10.1177/21651434231186136

Siperstein, G. N., Heyman, M., & Stokes, J. E. (2014). Pathways to employment: A national survey of adults with intellectual disabilities. *Journal of Vocational Rehabilitation*, *41*(3), 165–178. DOI: 10.3233/JVR-140711

Smith, P. (2026). Families as system actors in discovery embedding co-production within the equilibrium systems model of employment. *Journal of Health and Rehabilitation Sciences*, *5*(1), 1–8. DOI: 10.33700/jhrs.5.1.202

Smith, P., McVilly, K. R., McGillivray, J., & Chan, J. (2018). Developing open employment outcomes for people with an intellectual disability utilising a social enterprise framework. *Journal of Vocational Rehabilitation*, *48*(1), 59–77. DOI: 10.3233/JVR-170916

Smith, P., & Parmenter, T. R. (2023). Measuring the Impact of Employment on Persons With a Disability as a Means of Improving the Quality of Employment Outcomes. *Journal of Health and Rehabilitation Sciences*, *2*(1), 1–15. DOI: 10.33700/jhrs.2.1.61

Smith, R. P., Ma, F., & Roe, S. J. (2025). Diversity, equity, inclusion, and belonging (DEIB): A snapshot in hospitality and tourism academia job openings. *Journal of Teaching in Travel & Tourism*, *25*(2), 127–146. DOI: 10.1080/15313220.2025.2495833

Smith, T. J., Dillahunt-Aspillaga, C., & Kenney, R. M. (2016). Implementation of Customized Employment Provisions of the Workforce Innovation and Opportunity Act Within Vocational Rehabilitation Systems. *Journal of Disability Policy Studies*, *27*(4), 195–202. DOI: 10.1177/1044207316644412

Soeker, S.. (2021). Employer attitudes towards hiring people with intellectual disabilities: A systematic review. *Journal of Vocational Rehabilitation*, *55*(1), 45–58.

Solovieva, T. I., & Walls, R. T. (2013). Implications of Workplace Accommodations for Persons With Disabilities. *Journal of Workplace Behavioral Health*, *28*(3), 192–211. DOI: 10.1080/15555240.2013.808079

Sourbati, M. (2012). Disabling communications? A capabilities perspective on media access, social inclusion and communication policy. *Media Culture & Society*, *34*(5), 571–587. DOI: 10.1177/0163443712442702

Sousa, C., Pereira, J., Tsvetkova, P., & Casimiro, C. (2024). *Perceptions of Inclusion Professionals on Employability of Individuals With Intellectual and Developmental Disabilities: A Transnational Study*. DOI: 10.36315/2024inpact036

Spencer, P., Haneghan, J. V., & Baxter, A. (2021). Exploring Social Networks, Employment and Self-Determination Outcomes of Graduates From a Postsecondary Program for Young Adults With an Intellectual Disability. *Journal of Vocational Rehabilitation*, *55*(3), 251–270. DOI: 10.3233/JVR-211161

Spreat, S. (2018). Employment Incentives to Support "Employment First.". *Global Journal of Intellectual & Developmental Disabilities*, *5*(3). Advance online publication. DOI: 10.19080/GJIDD.2018.05.555665

Srour, C., & Py, J. (2023). Making job candidates more honest with a theory-based form: A field study. *Journal of Personnel Psychology*, *22*(2), 89–98. DOI: 10.1027/1866-5888/a000313

Stańczyk, K. (2020). "Anti-Crisis Shield" as an Example of State Interventionism During the Crisis Caused by the Covid-19 Virus Pandemic in Poland. *European Research Studies Journal*, *XXIII*(Special Issue 3), 116–136. DOI: 10.35808/ersj/1857

Steele, Y. (2024). *Impactful inclusion toolkit: 52 activities to help you learn and practice inclusion every day in the workplace*. Wiley.

Steur, J., & Wittek, R. (2005). The governance of transition processes in an organization: A cognitive mapping approach. *Academy of Management Annual Meeting Proceedings*. https://doi.org/DOI: 10.5465/ambpp.2005.18781706

Stock, J., Williams, H., & Peat, R. (2025). Coaching supervision: Supporting staff development and wellbeing. In *Coaching and mentoring students in higher education: A practitioner guide to developing independent learners* (pp. 268–293). Routledge., DOI: 10.4324/9781003486015-9

Stoddard, S., & Kraus, L. (2006). Arranging for personal assistance services and assistive technology at work. A report of the rehabilitation research and training centre on personal assistance services. *Disability and Rehabilitation. Assistive Technology*, *1*(1–2), 89–95. DOI: 10.1080/09638280500167365 PMID: 19256171

Stoiber, C., Moitzi, D., Stitz, H., Grassinger, F., Prakash, A. S. G., Girardi, D., Streit, M., & Aigner, W. (2024). VisAhoi: Towards a library to generate and integrate visualisation onboarding using high-level visualisation grammars. *Visual Informatics*, *8*(3), 1–17. DOI: 10.1016/j.visinf.2024.06.001

Stoiber, C., Walchshofer, C., Grassinger, F., Stitz, H., Streit, M., & Aigner, W. (2021). Design and Comparative Evaluation of Visualisation Onboarding Methods. *ACM International Conference Proceeding Series*. DOI: 10.1145/3481549.3481558

Strah, N., & Rupp, D. E. (2022). The role of job analysis in promoting workplace inclusion. *Journal of Business and Psychology*, *37*(4), 789–805.

Straub, C., Vinkenburg, C. J., & van Kleef, M. (2020). Career customisation: Putting an organisational practice to facilitate sustainable careers to the test. *Journal of Vocational Behavior*, *117*, 103320. Advance online publication. DOI: 10.1016/j.jvb.2019.103320

Strauser, D. G., Price, R. A., Brehmer, C. E., & Strauser, D. R. (2026). Exploring employer's successful hiring and retention practices of individuals with disabilities. *Rehabilitation Counseling Bulletin*, *69*(2), 109–119. DOI: 10.1177/00343552241265319

Struchen, M. A., Davis, L. C., Bogaards, J. A., Hudler-Hull, T., Clark, A. N., Mazzei, D. M., Sander, A. M., & Caroselli, J. S. (2011). Making connections after brain injury: Development and evaluation of a social peer-mentoring program for persons with traumatic brain injury. *The Journal of Head Trauma Rehabilitation*, *26*(1), 4–19. DOI: 10.1097/HTR.0b013e3182048e98 PMID: 21209559

Sulewski, J. S.. (2017). From sheltered workshops to integrated employment: A review of the literature. *Journal of Vocational Rehabilitation*, *46*(3), 273–284.

Sullivan, D. W., & Swider, B. W. (2025). The influence of friends' person-organization fit during recruitment. *The Journal of Applied Psychology*, *110*(2), 238–255. DOI: 10.1037/apl0001226 PMID: 39115896

Sundar, V. (2017). Operationalizing workplace accommodations for individuals with disabilities: A scoping review. *Work (Reading, Mass.)*, *56*(1), 135–155. DOI: 10.3233/WOR-162472

Sunderman, H. M., & Adebayo, B. (2025). Peer mentoring for leader development. In *Moving the Needle: What We Know (and Don't Know) About Developing Leaders* (pp. 283–296). https://www.scopus.com/inward/record.uri?eid=2-s2.0-105012207489&partnerID=40&md5=26baa48055850f4c2b2c51d90aa24b93

Sunderman, H. M., & Adebayo, B. (2025). Peer mentoring for leader development. In *Moving the needle: What we know (and don't know) about developing leaders* (pp. 283–296). Edward Elgar Publishing. DOI: 10.1108/978-1-83708-544-620251023

Sung, C., & Nasamran, A. (2023). *Work Disability*. 553–575. DOI: 10.1037/0000339-026

Sung, C., Fisher, M. H., Okyere, C., Park, J., & Choi, H. (2023). Employment Outcomes and Support Needs of Michigan Project SEARCH Graduates With Intellectual and Developmental Disabilities: A Mixed-Method Study. *Journal of Vocational Rehabilitation*, *59*(3), 233–249. DOI: 10.3233/JVR-230042

Suresh, V., & Dyaram, L. (2020). Towards a Confluence: Disability Inclusion and Organizational Change. *Journal of Indian Business Research*, *12*(4), 625–644. DOI: 10.1108/JIBR-03-2019-0068

Suresh, V., & Dyaram, L. (2020). Workplace disability inclusion in India: Review and directions. *Management Research Review*, *43*(12), 1545–1562. DOI: 10.1108/MRR-11-2019-0479

Suresh, V., & Dyaram, L. (2022). Diversity in disability: Leaders' accounts on inclusive employment in the Indian context. *Equality, Diversity and Inclusion*, *41*(3), 454–473. DOI: 10.1108/EDI-05-2020-0133

Suresh, V., & Dyaram, L. (2023). Job matching for persons with disabilities: An exploratory study. *Employee Responsibilities and Rights Journal*, *35*(4), 475–492. DOI: 10.1007/s10672-022-09421-6

Swarbrick, M., Wilson, L., Becker, D., Swanson, S. J., Reese, S., & Bond, G. R. (2017). The Role of the Family Advocacy Team in Sustaining Supported Employment. *Journal of Vocational Rehabilitation, 47*(1), 13–17. DOI: 10.3233/JVR-170879

Szeluga-Romańska, M. (2025). Barriers to Knowledge Sharing During the Onboarding Process. *Proceedings of the European Conference on Knowledge Management, ECKM, 2*, 981–986. DOI: 10.34190/eckm.26.2.4092

Taubner, H., Tideman, M., & Nyman, C. S. (2021). Employment Sustainability for People With Intellectual Disability: A Systematic Review. *Journal of Occupational Rehabilitation, 32*(3), 353–364. DOI: 10.1007/s10926-021-10020-9 PMID: 34958449

Taylor, A. J., Slocum, V., & Rhodes, A. L. (2026). Assistive Technology and Universal Design for Learning. In *An Evidence-Based Guide to Assistive Technology* (pp. 28–41). Meeting the Needs of All Students with Disabilities., DOI: 10.4324/9781003524090-4

Taylor, J. P., Avellone, L., Brooke, V., Wehman, P., Inge, K. J., Schall, C., & Iwanaga, K. (2022). The Impact of Competitive Integrated Employment on Economic, Psychological, and Physical Health Outcomes for Individuals With Intellectual and Developmental Disabilities. *Journal of Applied Research in Intellectual Disabilities, 35*(2), 448–459. DOI: 10.1111/jar.12974 PMID: 34994035

Taylor, J. P., Avellone, L., Cimera, R. E., Brooke, V., Lambert, A., & Iwanaga, K. (2021). Cost-Benefit Analyses of Employment Services for Individuals With Intellectual and Developmental Disabilities: A Scoping Review. *Journal of Vocational Rehabilitation, 54*(2), 193–206. DOI: 10.3233/JVR-201130

Taylor, J. P., & Whittenburg, H. (2024). The Promise and the Challenge of Pre-Employment Transition Services: The Workforce Innovation and Opportunity Act After Ten Years. *Journal of Vocational Rehabilitation, 60*(2), 157–161. DOI: 10.3233/JVR-240002

Taylor, J. P., Whittenburg, H. N., Rooney-Kron, M., Gokita, T., Lau, S. J., Thoma, C. A., & Scott, L. A. (2022). Implementation of pre-employment transition services: A content analysis of Workforce Innovation and Opportunity Act state plans. *Career Development and Transition for Exceptional Individuals, 45*(2), 60–70. DOI: 10.1177/2165143421993027

Taylor, J. P., Whittenburg, H., Avellone, L., Rios, Y. C., Park, S., Poppen, M., & Tansey, T. (2024). The Impact of Pre-Employment Transition and Individualized Vocational Rehabilitation Services on Employment Outcomes for Youth With Disabilities. *Career Development and Transition for Exceptional Individuals, 48*(2), 128–139. DOI: 10.1177/21651434241239967

Taylor, M. A., & Wituk, E. (2025). Reasonable accommodation for neurodiversity: Legal, organizational and managerial considerations. *Employee Responsibilities and Rights Journal*. Advance online publication. DOI: 10.1007/s10672-025-09546-4

Taylor, M.. (2022). Competitive integrated employment for individuals with intellectual and developmental disabilities: A systematic review of outcomes. *Journal of Vocational Rehabilitation*, *56*(2), 123–140.

Terras, M. M., Jarrett, D., & McGregor, S. A. (2021). The importance of accessible information in promoting the inclusion of people with an intellectual disability. *Disabilities*, *1*(3), 132–150. DOI: 10.3390/disabilities1030011

Thaver, T., Lim, L., & Liau, A. K. (2025). Social inclusion through attitudinal change in Singaporean teachers. *International Journal of Developmental Disabilities*, *71*(6), 879–895. DOI: 10.1080/20473869.2025.2494040 PMID: 40959443

Thomson, A. E., Van Mulligen, L., Winsor Murray, J., Adair, J., Schira, H. R., Ramage, M., & Torres-Salbach, S. (2026). Workplace accommodations for nurses who experience disabilities: A scoping review. *Canadian Journal of Nursing Research*, 08445621261430964. Advance online publication. DOI: 10.1177/08445621261430964 PMID: 41787870

Tims, M., & Twemlow, M. (2024). A contemporary view on job crafting. In *Elgar Encyclopedia of Occupational Health Psychology* (pp. 4–6). Edward Elgar Publishing., DOI: 10.4337/9781035313389.ch02

Tjimuku, M., Atiku, S. O., & Villet, H. J. (2025). Inclusive leadership: A catalyst for ethical work climate and enhanced employee performance in diverse workforce. In *Advances in ethical work climate and employee well-being* (pp. 331–354). IGI Global., DOI: 10.4018/979-8-3693-8819-8.ch016

Tomás, J., & Fluixá, C. (2020). Workplace accommodations for people with intellectual disabilities: A systematic review. *Journal of Intellectual Disability Research*, *64*(10), 789–802.

Tomas, V., Hsu, S., Kingsnorth, S., Anagnostou, E., Kirsh, B., & Lindsay, S. (2023). Development and Usability Testing of a Web-Based Workplace Disability Disclosure Decision Aid Tool for Autistic Youth and Young Adults: Qualitative Co-Design Study. *JMIR Formative Research*, *7*, e44354. DOI: 10.2196/44354 PMID: 37104002

Tomaszewski, B.. (2024). Employment outcomes for adults with intellectual and developmental disabilities: A 20-year review. *Intellectual and Developmental Disabilities*, *62*(1), 12–25.

Tompa, J., Buchmeister, B., & Vujica Herzog, N. (2025). Inclusive workplace design using MOCAP technology. *International Journal of Simulation Modelling*, *24*(4), 577–588. DOI: 10.2507/IJSIMM24-4-737

Towns, D. M., & Moore, J. E. (2005). Who is running the asylum? A practical approach to managing mental disabilities under the ADA. *Employee Relations Law Journal*, *30*(4), 27–41.

Traver, M. T. B., Fustes, M. L., & Fernández, M. M. (2017). How do employees help co-workers with intellectual disabilities? A work coaching experience in supported employment [¿cómo ayudan los compañeros de trabajo a los empleados con discapacidad intelectual? Una experiencia de coaching laboral en empleo con apoyo]. *Revista Española de Orientación y Psicopedagogía*, *28*(1), 51–71. DOI: 10.5944/reop.vol.28.num.1.2017.19358

Troger, H. (2022). Strength-based deployment. In *Management for Professionals* (pp. 85–98). Springer., DOI: 10.1007/978-3-031-06166-0_4

Truong, A., Alverbratt, C., Ekström-Bergström, A., & Antonsson, H. (2021). Caring for persons with intellectual disabilities and challenging behavior: Staff experiences with a web-based training program. *Frontiers in Psychiatry*, *12*, 580923. Advance online publication. DOI: 10.3389/fpsyt.2021.580923 PMID: 33584380

Tsirkas, K. (2025). Understanding and using soft skills for autistic people. In *Empowering innovations in advanced autism research and management* (pp. 333–348). IGI Global., DOI: 10.4018/979-8-3693-8176-2.ch014

Tu n, L. T. (2018). Engaging Employees With Disabilities in Vietnamese Business Context. *Employee Relations*, *40*(5), 822–847. DOI: 10.1108/ER-06-2017-0134

Tucker, B. P., & Nash, E. (2023). Good for Business: Towards A management Control Research agenda Relating To the employment of Workers With intellectual Disability. *Journal of Accounting Literature*, *47*(1), 129–149. DOI: 10.1108/JAL-01-2023-0013

Tucker, K., Feng, H., Gruman, C., & Crossen, L. (2017). Improving Competitive Integrated Employment for Youth and Young Adults With Disabilities: Findings From an Evaluation of Eight Partnerships in Employment Systems Change Projects. *Journal of Vocational Rehabilitation*, *47*(3), 277–294. DOI: 10.3233/JVR-170902

Tucker, M.. (2017). Interagency collaboration for employment of people with disabilities: A systematic review. *Journal of Vocational Rehabilitation*, *47*(1), 1–14.

Tucker, M., Guillermo, M. S., & Corona, V. (2019). Career and Work-Based Learning Interventions for Young Recipients of Supplemental Security Income. *Journal of Vocational Rehabilitation*, *51*(2), 145–157. DOI: 10.3233/JVR-191034

Tueme, N. (2021). All in the family: The role of family networks, collective action frames, and identity in Latino movement participation. *Sociology Compass*, *15*(4), e12866. Advance online publication. DOI: 10.1111/soc4.12866

Tuffrey-Wijne, I., & McEnhill, L. (2008). Communication difficulties and intellectual disability in end-of-life care. *International Journal of Palliative Nursing*, *14*(4), 189–194. DOI: 10.12968/ijpn.2008.14.4.29133 PMID: 18681347

Tuffrey-Wijne, I., & Rose, T. (2017). Investigating the factors that affect the communication of death-related bad news to people with intellectual disabilities by staff in residential and supported living services: An interview study. *Journal of Intellectual Disability Research*, *61*(8), 727–736. DOI: 10.1111/jir.12375 PMID: 28386983

Turner, M., & Holdsworth, S. (2023). Developing resilience: Examining the protective factors of early career construction professionals. *Construction Management and Economics*, *41*(10), 805–819. DOI: 10.1080/01446193.2023.2208238

Uetz, M., Ananthakrishnan, S., Tulsky, A., Demers, L. B., & Noronha, C. (2024). More specific feedback: Why "confidence" in feedback is too ambiguous. *Postgraduate Medical Journal*, *100*(1185), 521–522. DOI: 10.1093/postmj/qgad106 PMID: 37973406

Ulrich, T. A., Boring, R. L., McJunkin, T., & Rege, A. (2019). A visualisation approach to performing task analysis of time series event log data from a microworld simulation. *Proceedings of the Human Factors and Ergonomics Society Annual Meeting*, *63*(1), 1867–1871. DOI: 10.1177/1071181319631534

Urrejola-Contreras, G. P., Pérez, M. A., Herrera-Miranda, F., López, B., Gary Zambra, B., & Hernández Pérez, K. (2025). Adaptations in the workplace as a labour inclusion strategy for people with physical disabilities: An integrative review. *Work (Reading, Mass.)*, *80*(3), 962–973. DOI: 10.1177/10519815241289677 PMID: 40297889

Uslu, B. (2017). The influence of organisational features in high-ranked universities: The case of Australia. *Journal of Higher Education Policy and Management*, *39*(5), 471–486. DOI: 10.1080/1360080X.2017.1354755

Valentine, S. R., Hanson, S. K., & Fleischman, G. M. (2019). The presence of ethics codes and employees' internal locus of control, social aversion/malevolence, and ethical judgment of incivility: A study of smaller organizations. *Journal of Business Ethics*, *160*(3), 657–674. DOI: 10.1007/s10551-018-3880-8

Van der Ploeg, R. (2018). Role of employers in transforming disability into ability: Learning from Dutch mistakes. In *Transforming Disability Welfare Policies: Towards Work and Equal Opportunities* (pp. 341–347). Routledge. DOI: 10.4324/9781315235769-41

Van Laar, C., Meeussen, L., Veldman, J., Van Grootel, S., Sterk, N., & Jacobs, C. (2019). Coping with stigma in the workplace: Understanding the role of threat regulation, supportive factors, and potential hidden costs. *Frontiers in Psychology*, *10*, 1879. Advance online publication. DOI: 10.3389/fpsyg.2019.01879 PMID: 31507478

VanderMolen, J., Ward-Sutton, C., & Dudick, B. (2025). Human Resources Management Professionals Familiarity and Comfort of Assistive Technology and Workplace Accommodations. *Journal of Vocational Rehabilitation*, *62*(3), 258–267. DOI: 10.1177/10522263251326411

Varga, A. (2025). Equality of opportunity, sustainable development, and the role of civil society in higher education ethical and socio-philosophical approaches in international and Hungarian contexts [Esélyegyenlőség, fenntartható fejlődés és a civil társadalom szerepe a felsőoktatásban: Etikai és társadalomfilozófiai megközelítés nemzetközi és magyarországi kontextusban]. *Civil Szemle*, *9*(Special Issue), 41–55. DOI: 10.62560/CSZ.2025.05.3

Varia, S., & Middleton, H. (2012). How to make the most of feedback. *The Pharmaceutical Journal*, *289*(7719–7720), 205–208.

Vaucher, C., Cudré-Mauroux, A., & Piérart, G. (2021). Perceptions and understandings of self-determination in the context of relationships between people with intellectual disabilities and social care professionals. *International Journal of Developmental Disabilities*, *67*(2), 121–130. DOI: 10.1080/20473869.2019.1623595 PMID: 34141405

Vedeler, J. S., & Anvik, C. H. (2023). What's the 'problem' with workplace accommodation? A disability policy journey over time. *Scandinavian Journal of Disability Research*, *25*(1), 119–131. DOI: 10.16993/sjdr.918

Verma, A., & Singh, S. (2024). Job analysis and job evaluation. In *Clinical Laboratory Management* (pp. 23–28). Springer., DOI: 10.1007/978-3-031-46420-1_5

Vigna, E., Beyer, S., & Meek, A. (2023). A Demographic and Qualitative Analysis of the Determinants of Success in a National Supported Employment Project. *Journal of Applied Research in Intellectual Disabilities*, *36*(4), 787–795. DOI: 10.1111/jar.13094 PMID: 36919902

Vigna, E., Meek, A., & Beyer, S. (2024). Supported Employment, Quality of Jobs and Employment Typicalness: The Experience of the Engage to Change Project. *Journal of Applied Research in Intellectual Disabilities, 37*(3), e13226. Advance online publication. DOI: 10.1111/jar.13226 PMID: 38520180

Vijayakumar, P.. (2023). Employer attitudes toward hiring people with disabilities: A systematic review. *Journal of Vocational Rehabilitation, 58*(2), 145–160.

Vlachos, E. (2024). The transition from school to adult life and independent living for individuals with disabilities: Development tools and programs. In *Tools for Promoting Independent Living Skills in Individuals with Disabilities* (pp. 235–260). IGI Global., DOI: 10.4018/979-8-3693-6026-2.ch011

Vlachou, A., Roka, O., & Stavroussi, P. (2021). Experiences of workers with disabilities receiving supported employment services in Greece. *Journal of Intellectual Disabilities, 25*(2), 151–167. DOI: 10.1177/1744629519871172 PMID: 31476953

Voermans, M. A. C., Taminiau, E. F., Giesbers, S. A. H., & Embregts, P. J. C. M. (2021). The value of competitive employment: In-depth accounts of people with intellectual disabilities. *Journal of Applied Research in Intellectual Disabilities, 34*(1), 239–249. DOI: 10.1111/jar.12802 PMID: 32945056

Voermans, M. A. C., Wilthagen, T., & Embregts, P. J. C. M. (2023). Informal Network Members' Perspectives and Experiences on Work for People With Intellectual Disabilities: A Thematic Synthesis. *Journal of Occupational Rehabilitation, 34*(1), 37–55. DOI: 10.1007/s10926-023-10128-0 PMID: 37421467

Von Schrader, S., Malzer, V., & Bruyère, S. M. (2014). Perspectives on disability disclosure: The importance of employer practices and workplace climate. *Employee Responsibilities and Rights Journal, 26*(4), 251–269.

Voorhees, H. L. (2022). Informal and formal networks. In *The international encyclopedia of health communication* (pp. 1–6). Wiley., DOI: 10.1002/9781119678816.iehc0584

Wagner, J. A.III. (2024). Inter-team coordination in multiteam systems: Mechanisms, transitions, and precipitants. *Organizational Psychology Review, 14*(3), 425–448. DOI: 10.1177/20413866231153537

Wang, Y., Luo, J., Guo, L., & Zhao, H. (2025). Seeing opportunities from conflicts: Exploring third parties' mixed reactions to ethical conflict in the workplace. *Journal of Business Ethics*. Advance online publication. DOI: 10.1007/s10551-025-06213-4

Watfern, C., & Carnemolla, P. (2025). Inclusive Climate Action: A Scoping Review on the Representation and Inclusion of People With Intellectual Disability in Climate Change Research. *British Journal of Learning Disabilities, 53*(3), 428–445. DOI: 10.1111/bld.12632

Watts, P., Kwiatkowska, G., & Minnion, A. (2023). Using Multimedia Technology to Enhance Self-advocacy of People With Intellectual Disabilities: Introducing a Theoretical Framework for 'Multimedia Advocacy.'. *Journal of Applied Research in Intellectual Disabilities, 36*(4), 739–749. DOI: 10.1111/jar.13107 PMID: 37062847

Weber, A., Prinz, D., & Krekó, J. (2022). *Take-Up and Labour Supply Responses to Disability Insurance Earnings Limits*. DOI: 10.1920/wp.ifs.2022.2022

Wedgwood, N., Smith, L., Shuttleworth, R., & Llewellyn, G. (2013). An Eye Opening Experience: A Critical Turning Point in the Life of a Young Woman With a Severe Visual Impairment. *Journal of Social Inclusion, 4*(1), 5–23. DOI: 10.36251/josi60

Wehman, P., Schall, C., Avellone, L., Brooke, A., Brooke, V., McDonough, J., & Whittenburg, H. N. (2021). *Achieving Competitive Integrated Employment for Individuals With Intellectual and Developmental Disabilities*. 333–355. DOI: 10.1037/0000195-013

Wehman, P.. (2018). Competitive integrated employment for people with disabilities: The role of policy and practice. *Journal of Vocational Rehabilitation, 49*(1), 1–12.

Wehman, P., Taylor, J. P., Brooke, V., Avellone, L., Whittenburg, H. N., Ham, W., Brooke, A., & Carr, S. (2018). Toward Competitive Employment for Persons With Intellectual and Developmental Disabilities: What Progress Have We Made and Where Do We Need to Go. *Research and Practice for Persons with Severe Disabilities : the Journal of TASH, 43*(3), 131–144. DOI: 10.1177/1540796918777730

Wehmeyer, M. L., Parent, W., Lattimore, J., Obremski, S., Poston, D., & Rousso, H. (2009). Promoting self-determination and self-directed employment planning for young women with disabilities. *Journal of Social Work in Disability & Rehabilitation, 8*(3–4), 117–131. DOI: 10.1080/15367100903200429 PMID: 20183627

Weiner, J. S., & Zivolich, S. (2003). A longitudinal report for three employees in a training consultant model of natural support. *Journal of Vocational Rehabilitation, 18*(3), 199–202. DOI: 10.3233/JVR-2003-00196

Weisbach, D. A. (2007). A Welfarist Approach to Disabilities. SSRN *Electronic Journal*. DOI: 10.2139/ssrn.1008985

Wells, M. M., Thelen, L., & Ruark, J. (2007). Workspace personalization and organizational culture: Does your workspace reflect you or your company? *Environment and Behavior*, *39*(5), 616–634. DOI: 10.1177/0013916506295602

Weltbank. (2022). Disability inclusion and accountability framework.

Welti, F. (2018). Work disability policy in Germany: Experiences of collective and individual participation and cooperation. In *The science and politics of work disability prevention* (pp. 171–188). Routledge., DOI: 10.4324/9780429443398-11

Welti, F. (2025). People with disabilities. In *The Elgar companion to decent work and the sustainable development goals* (pp. 236–246). Edward Elgar Publishing., DOI: 10.4337/9781035300907.00026

Wendel, C., Gray, R. C., Goddard, K. S., & Hall, J. P. (2024). Navigating New Normals: The Influence of COVID-19 Policies on Community Access and Well-Being of People With Mobility Disabilities in Everyday Life. *Frontiers in Public Health*, *12*, 1401777. Advance online publication. DOI: 10.3389/fpubh.2024.1401777 PMID: 39026588

Wesley, S., Jackson, K. N., Ramos, D. M., Vanbeber, S., & Mujtaba, B. G. (2024). Marriott Hotel's Practices in Mitigating Discrimination Through Inclusionary Employee Resource Groups. *Journal of Business Diversity*, *24*(1). Advance online publication. DOI: 10.33423/jbd.v24i1.6897

Westerlund, D., Granucci, E. A., Gamache, P., & Clark, H. B. (2006). Effects of peer mentors on work-related performance of adolescents with behavioral and/or learning disabilities. *Journal of Positive Behavior Interventions*, *8*(4), 244–251. DOI: 10.1177/10983007060080040601

Whitaker, T. R. (2019). Banging on a locked door: The persistent role of racial discrimination in the workplace. *Social Work in Public Health*, *34*(1), 22–27. DOI: 10.1080/19371918.2019.1572564 PMID: 30700222

Whittenburg, H. N., Rooney-Kron, M., Carlson, S. R., Malouf, E. T., & Taylor, J. P. (2024). Use of research-based transition recommendations for youth with disabilities in Workforce Innovation and Opportunity Act plans. *Rehabilitation Counseling Bulletin*, *67*(4), 283–294. DOI: 10.1177/00343552231155218

Wichinsky, L., Thomlison, B., & Pennell, J. (2012). Exploring organizational culture and climate in community coalitions. *Community Development (Columbus, Ohio)*, *43*(2), 133–146. DOI: 10.1080/15575330.2011.567418

Wided, R., & Abdulaziz, A. (2024). Facilitating sustainable employment for people with physical disabilities: A pathway to inclusion: An ISM-MICMAC approach. *Journal of Disability Research*, *3*(6), e20240070. Advance online publication. DOI: 10.57197/JDR-2024-0070

Wiesel, I., Bigby, C., van Holstein, E., & Gleeson, B. (2024). Three modes of inclusion of people with intellectual disability in mainstream services: Mainstreaming, differentiation and individualisation. *Disability & Society*, *39*(1), 40–61. DOI: 10.1080/09687599.2022.2060803

Wilson, A. B., & Adderley, U. (2025). Inclusive supervision in practice. [Note: This reference appears in the chapter text but was not found in the provided Scopus export; it is listed here as cited.]. *Journal of Applied Research in Intellectual Disabilities*.

Wilson, M. G. (2012). Essential job functions and reasonable accommodation. *Journal of Applied Rehabilitation Counseling*, *43*(4), 3–10.

Wilson, N. J., Lin, Z., Pithouse, M., Morrison, B., Sumar, B., & George, A. (2023). Qualitative Insights from A Novel Staff-Led Oral Health Champions Program Within a Residential Service For People With Intellectual and Developmental Disability. *Journal of Intellectual Disabilities*, *27*(3), 728–745. DOI: 10.1177/17446295221095654 PMID: 35549753

Wilson, P. M., & Adderley, S. C. (2025). Enhancing workplace well-being: Inclusive leadership in the Bahamas. In *Leading inclusive workplaces through digital transformation and organizational change* (pp. 189–223). IGI Global., DOI: 10.4018/979-8-3373-5127-8.ch007

Wingrove, A., Lai, Y.-L., Palmer, S., & Williams, S. (2020). Self-determination theory: A theoretical framework for group supervision with internal coaches. *International Journal of Evidence Based Coaching and Mentoring*, *18*(2), 183–196. DOI: 10.24384/jxxd-st61

Wippold, G. M., Crichlow, Z. R., Garcia, K. A., Domlyn, A. M., Sanchez, S. B., Frank, L., Mote, T., Frary, S. G., & Woods, T. O. (2024). Assessing Organizational Readiness for the Clean Cuts and Sharp Minds Collective: A Barbershop Health Promotion Network. *Implementation Science Communications*, *5*(1), 42. Advance online publication. DOI: 10.1186/s43058-024-00584-x PMID: 38627824

Wittenburg, D. C., & Loprest, P. J. (2007). Early transition experiences of transition-age child SSI recipients: New evidence from the national survey of children and families. *Journal of Disability Policy Studies*, *18*(3), 176–187. DOI: 10.1177/10442073070180030601

Wu, S., Élteto, N., Dasgupta, I., & Schulz, E. (2022). Learning Structure from the Ground up-Hierarchical Representation Learning by Chunking. *Advances in Neural Information Processing Systems, 35*. https://www.scopus.com/inward/record.uri?eid=2-s2.0-85162641991&partnerID=40&md5=bbb6c979822010fa90a2185771e63ab8

Wuttke, L., Dirks, S., & Bühler, C. (2025). How Can the New Technologies of Augmented Reality, Mixed Reality, and Virtual Reality Support People With Neurodevelopmental Disorders in the Workplace? *Technology and Disability*, *37*(3), 212–220. DOI: 10.1177/10554181251355423

Xiao, Y., & Seagull, F. J. (2007). Emergent CSCW systems: The resolution and bandwidth of workplaces. *International Journal of Medical Informatics*, *76*(Suppl. 1), 261–266. DOI: 10.1016/j.ijmedinf.2006.05.037 PMID: 16822715

Yaeda, J. (2009). Transition from secondary school to employment in Japan for students with disabilities. In *Educational Transitions: Moving Stories from Around the World* (pp. 205–220). Routledge. DOI: 10.4324/9780203859124-22

Yan, C. O. (2026). Redesigning employment systems for neurodivergent inclusion: A structural, intersectional, and theoretical inquiry. In *Vocational rehabilitation for students with developmental disabilities: Transition from education to employment* (pp. 339–376). IGI Global., DOI: 10.4018/979-8-3693-9541-7.ch011

Yang, H.-Y., Yeh, S.-C., Wu, E. H.-K., & Hong, W. (2021). The effectiveness of virtual reality technology applying in vocational training on occupational competency among the students with intellectual disability in senior high school. *2021 IEEE International Conference on Social Sciences and Intelligent Management, SSIM 2021*. DOI: 10.1109/SSIM49526.2021.9555179

Yang, M. M. (2026). Mitigating disability bias in hiring: The role of inclusion-focused generative AI in complex HR decisions. *Human Resource Management Journal*, *36*(3), 553–565. Advance online publication. DOI: 10.1111/1748-8583.70044

Yang, X., & Zhao, Q. (2025). Making crowdsourcing contests better: The power of task clarity. *Management Decision*. Advance online publication. DOI: 10.1108/MD-09-2024-2153

Yasak, Z., & Alias, M. (2016). Developing a learning hierarchy for identifying pre-requisites to training goals in vocational education. *2015 IEEE Conference on E-Learning, e-Management and e-Services, IC3e 2015*, 49–51. DOI: 10.1109/IC3e.2015.7403485

Yatheesha, V. H., Reddy, S. K., Angothu, H., Vranda, M. N., Raju, K. T., & Pallerla, S. (2024). Caregivers' perspectives on reasonable accommodation for persons with severe mental disorders at the workplace. *Indian Journal of Occupational and Environmental Medicine*, *28*(3), 177–181. DOI: 10.4103/ijoem.ijoem_195_23 PMID: 39618901

Yeung, C., Kohno, T., & Roesner, F. (2024). Analyzing the (in)accessibility of online advertisements. *Proceedings of the ACM SIGCOMM Internet Measurement Conference*, 92–106. https://doi.org/DOI: 10.1145/3646547.3688427

Yon-Hernández, J. A., Gonzales, C. J. G., Bothra, S., Kecskemeti, K., Iosif, A., Takarae, Y., Ruder, S., McGurk, S. R., Mueser, K. T., & Solomon, M. (2025). Early Employment Outcomes in Autistic and Non-Autistic Youth: Challenges and Opportunities. *Journal of Autism and Developmental Disorders*. Advance online publication. DOI: 10.1007/s10803-025-07001-9 PMID: 40773082

Yosef, L., Soffer, M., & Malul, M. (2018). From Welfare to Work and From Work to Welfare: A Comparison of People With and Without Disabilities. *Journal of Disability Policy Studies*, *29*(4), 226–234. DOI: 10.1177/1044207318782674

Yuan, Q., Kazemi, M., Xu, X., Noble, I., Imbrasaite, V., & Ramachandran, D. (2024). TaskLAMA: Probing the Complex Task Understanding of Language Models. *Proceedings of the AAAI Conference on Artificial Intelligence*, *38*(17), 19468–19476. DOI: 10.1609/aaai.v38i17.29918

Zeshan, M., Khalid, H., Rasool, S., Centobelli, P., Cerchione, R., & Morelli, M. (2025). Digitalisation for sustainable working environments: The role of job crafting and job resources on employee engagement. *Business Strategy and the Environment*, *34*(8), 10296–10312. DOI: 10.1002/bse.70103

Zhang, C., Zhang, J., Zhan, X., Zheng, Y., & Yang, G. (2025). Strengths use in the workplace and its effects on individual work outcomes: A meta-analysis. *Applied Psychology*, *74*(5), e70036. Advance online publication. DOI: 10.1111/apps.70036

Zhong, J., Li, Y., & Luo, J. (2022). The trickle-down effects of inclusive leadership on employees' innovative behavior: The joint moderating effects of vicarious learning and organizational inclusion climate. *Journal of Leadership & Organizational Studies*, *29*(3), 342–358. DOI: 10.1177/15480518211059941

Zhou, K., Richard, C., & Kim, J. (2025). Employment-Related Assistive Technologies for Autistic Individuals: A Scoping Review. *Journal of Vocational Rehabilitation*, *62*(2), 191–206. DOI: 10.1177/10522263241312742

Zidan, A., Gabay, D., Poirier, S.-È., Grandisson, M., Jacob, S., Ouimet, M., Julien-Gauthier, F., Martin-Roy, S., Lamontagne, M., Desmarais, C., & Dahan-Oliel, N. (2025). In What Contexts, How, and Why Do Transition to Adulthood Interventions Work for Adolescents Living With Disabilities: A Realist Review. *Journal of Vocational Rehabilitation*, *63*(2), 225–241. DOI: 10.1177/10522263251356223

Zink, D., Lee, B., & Allen, D. (2014). Structured and semistructured clinical interviews available for use among African American clients: Cultural considerations in the diagnostic interview process. In *Guide to psychological assessment with African Americans* (pp. 19–42). Springer., DOI: 10.1007/978-1-4939-1004-5_3

Zinnah, C. A., Xue, X. F., & Ali, A. (2025). It's The Details That Matter: Role Clarity and Creative Service Performance; The Moderation Role of Supervisor Bottom-Line Mentality. *Basic and Applied Social Psychology*, *47*(6), 361–376. DOI: 10.1080/01973533.2025.2528837

Zsifkovits, H., Woschank, M., & Pacher, C. (2021). A case study: Industry 4.0 and human factors in SMEs. In *Implementing Industry 4.0 in SMEs: Concepts, Examples and Applications* (pp. 233–261). Springer. DOI: 10.1007/978-3-030-70516-9_8

About the Authors

Udeme Samuel Jacob is an accomplished educator with qualifications including NCE, B. Ed in Teacher Education/Agricultural Science, an M. Ed, and a PhD in Special Education. His research focuses on inclusive education, particularly enhancing reading and social skills for individuals with intellectual disabilities. He also studies the management of aggressive behavior and interventions that improve attention spans. As a passionate advocate for education equity, Udeme believes that no child should be left behind in the learning process.

Mbulaheni Maguvhe is a distinguished academic specializing in inclusive education, currently serving as a full professor at the University of South Africa. With a career spanning over two decades, he has made significant contributions to the field, particularly for visually impaired learners. His expertise is underscored by a PhD focused on inclusive education policy and numerous leadership roles, including the UNESCO/UNISA Chair of Inclusive Education in Higher Education.

Sri Nurhayati is a prominent figure in the field of medicine, known for her extensive research and contributions to public health. With a strong focus on preventive care, she has dedicated her career to improving healthcare access and education in underserved communities. Her work encompasses various aspects of health policy, epidemiology, and community health programs. Dr. Nurhayati is also an advocate for women's health issues, often engaging in outreach initiatives. Through her leadership and expertise, she has inspired many young professionals in the medical field to pursue a career dedicated to service and innovation.

Index

A

B

C

D

E

I

M

P

S

T

W

www.ingramcontent.com/pod-product-compliance
Lightning Source LLC
LaVergne TN
LVHW061529290926
849162LV00004B/716